WITHDRAWN

D1457778

THE CORRESPONDENCE OF
EDMUND BURKE

EDITOR

THOMAS W. COPELAND
Professor of English, University of Massachusetts

EDITORIAL COMMITTEE

ALFRED COBBAN, *Professor of French History, University College, London*

HOLDEN FURBER, *Professor of History, University of Pennsylvania*

GEORGE H. GUTTRIDGE, *Professor of English History, University of California*

R. B. McDOWELL, *Lecturer in History and Fellow of Trinity College, Dublin*

ROBERT A. SMITH, *Research Associate, Yale University Library*

MISS L. S. SUTHERLAND, *Principal, Lady Margaret Hall, Oxford*

J. STEVEN WATSON, *Student of Christ Church, Oxford*

ADVISORY COMMITTEE

JULIAN F. BOYD, *Editor, The Papers of Thomas Jefferson*

RONALD S. CRANE, *Professor of English, Emeritus, University of Chicago*

THE EARL FITZWILLIAM, *Milton, Peterborough*

ALLEN T. HAZEN, *Professor of English, Columbia University*

CHARLES L. MOWAT, *Associate Professor of History, University of Chicago*

SIR LEWIS NAMIER, *Professor of Modern History, Emeritus, University of Manchester*

MICHAEL OAKESHOTT, *University Professor of Political Science, London School of Economics*

RICHARD PARES, *Fellow of All Souls, Oxford*

STANLEY PARGELLIS, *Librarian, Newberry Library, Chicago*

G. R. POTTER, *Professor of Modern History, University of Sheffield*

FREDERICK A. POTTLE, *Sterling Professor of English, Yale University*

L. F. POWELL, *Sometime Librarian of the Taylor Institution, Oxford*

GEORGE SHERBURN, *Professor of English, Emeritus, Harvard University*

ALAN SIMPSON, *Associate Professor of History, University of Chicago*

LEO STRAUSS, *Professor of Political Science, University of Chicago*

JACOB VINER, *Professor of Economics, Princeton University*

EDMUND BURKE

THE CORRESPONDENCE OF EDMUND BURKE

VOLUME I

APRIL 1744—JUNE 1768

EDITED BY
THOMAS W. COPELAND

DA
506
B9
A18
V.1

CAMBRIDGE
AT THE UNIVERSITY PRESS

THE UNIVERSITY OF CHICAGO PRESS
CHICAGO, ILLINOIS
1958

PUBLISHED BY
THE SYNDICS OF THE CAMBRIDGE UNIVERSITY PRESS
Bentley House, 200 Euston Road, London, N.W.1

AND

THE UNIVERSITY OF CHICAGO PRESS
Chicago 37

AGENTS

For Canada: The University of Toronto Press
For Australia: Georgian House Pty Limited
For Pakistan: J. B. Jeffery

Library of Congress Catalog Number: 58-5615

All rights reserved
Published 1958

Printed in Great Britain at the University Press, Cambridge
(Brooke Crutchley, University Printer)

CONTENTS

The portrait facing p. xv *is reproduced by kind permission of Dr Brendan O'Brien of Dublin, whose father, Mr William Dermod O'Brien, President of the Royal Hibernian Academy, purchased the original from descendants of Burke's family. The painter is not known; this is perhaps the early portrait by Thomas Worlidge* (1700–66) *which Burke mentions in a letter of* 13 *July* 1774.

PREFACE

In the summer of 1948 the 9th Earl Fitzwilliam agreed to the moving of a large body of manuscripts from Wentworth Woodhouse, the Yorkshire seat of his family, to the Central Library of the City of Sheffield. The largest collection of the private papers of Burke was among these manuscripts, and by the move became available to the general use of scholars for the first time since Burke's death in 1797. Slightly before the 9th Earl's decision another member of the Fitzwilliam family, Captain Thomas W. Fitzwilliam, who has since become the 10th Earl, made a similar decision, by which the second-largest body of Burke's papers, long preserved at Milton near Peterborough, was also opened to public use, being deposited with the Northamptonshire Record Society, first in Northampton, later at Lamport Hall.

These decisions, besides releasing Burke's own papers, make available the papers of his two principal patrons, the 2nd Marquess of Rockingham and the 4th Earl Fitzwilliam, whose manuscripts are of course indispensable to the study of Burke, since they supply the background of party correspondence against which many of Burke's letters must be studied. It is now possible for the first time to plan a complete and properly annotated edition of Burke's letters. The Earl Fitzwilliam has kindly agreed to allow all material in his collections to be used in preparing such an edition. Letters scattered in many other manuscript collections, some unpublished, some printed unsystematically in scores of separate books and periodicals, need to be re-examined in relation to the Fitzwilliam letters. The whole problem of Burke's correspondence can now be attacked with new advantages.

Burke himself placed little value upon his letters. He lacked that passion for exact records which infected many of his contemporaries, and rather inclined to the old-fashioned view that the *minutiae* of daily life ought not to be exposed to the public. Probably he would have saved very few of the letters written to him if his son Richard had not insisted upon it. At Richard's death he 'destroyed a cart load of them', according to his own statement. He also disposed of most of the Burke family correspondence—certainly extensive—except for letters to and from Richard, which he felt had some historic interest. Merely social notes—invitations, acceptances and the like—have almost entirely disappeared. The whole bulk of Burke's known surviving correspondence extends to about 1700 of his own letters and perhaps twice that number of letters written to him. A few hundred additional letters by and to the members of his family cannot be ignored, when they were written wholly or partly on his behalf.

Burke appointed as his literary executors two of his most devoted disciples, Dr French Laurence and Dr Walker King. They began work on his papers at least five years before his death, and almost thirty years after his death succeeded in completing the edition of his *Works* which is still on our shelves; the final volume came out in 1827. Laurence and King both intended that the *Works* should end with a biography, illustrated with letters. They therefore made an attempt to call in such letters as they could find in the hands of Burke's surviving correspondents, and held on to the whole body of the letters as the materials of the biography. As the biography was never written, the chief effect of their plan was to keep the main collection of Burke's letters from being printed or made accessible to other scholars for a period of thirty years. At King's death, in 1827, the collection passed to the 4th Earl Fitzwilliam, whom Mrs Burke had named as an additional literary executor after her husband's death. Lord Fitzwilliam was in his eightieth year when the papers came into his hands, so that it is not surprising that he was unable to make up the time Laurence and King had lost. Another sixteen years were to pass before his son, the 5th Earl Fitzwilliam, in collaboration with Sir Richard Bourke, brought out the four-volume work which they entitled *The Correspondence of Edmund Burke*.

This is the most comprehensive collection of Burke's letters yet made, and it is on the whole an accurate and creditable work. It did not, however, even at its appearance fully live up to the claim of its title. It was neither a complete nor a properly representative Correspondence. It was based almost solely upon the Fitzwilliam collection, ignoring Burke letters to be found elsewhere. By 1844 when it appeared—nearly fifty years after Burke's death—many single letters or small bodies of letters which Laurence and King had not succeeded in recovering had found their way into print. These were neglected. But so were important bodies of letters in the Fitzwilliam collection itself, such as all those Burke wrote to the General Assembly of New York in the period when he was their Agent in London, or all those he wrote to the 4th Earl Fitzwilliam.

There has been much miscellaneous publication of Burke letters since 1844. Substantial works like Gilson's *Correspondence of Edmund Burke and William Windham*, Samuels's *Early Life, Correspondence and Writings of Edmund Burke* and Hoffman's *Edmund Burke, New York Agent* are valuable supplements to the four-volume set. Many letters can be found in reports of the Historical Manuscripts Commission. The Commission was not able to examine Burke's own papers, but letters of his are scattered through the reports on other collections, and hence are reasonably accessible. Other letters are dispersed by ones and twos through biographies of Burke's friends, or appear in odd volumes with titles like *A Grammar of the Irish Language*, or *Gleanings from an Old Portfolio*. One very important correspondence—that of Burke with his Bristol friend Richard Champion—has to be picked out of a book called *Two Centuries of Ceramic Art in Bristol*. To find the Burke letters which are now in print, it is necessary to consult nearly 200 sources in books, magazines and newspapers.

The manuscript originals are nearly as widely scattered. Between 100 and 150 public and private collections contain Burke correspondence, ranging from single letters, often unpublished, to complete series such as Burke's eighty-three letters to Charles O'Hara. Many other manuscripts now lost to sight can be traced through the catalogues of dealers in autographs.

A volume already published gives a comprehensive survey of the entire Burke correspondence,[1] listing all manuscripts known to survive, with their present location, length, date, and condition, as well as the references to printed works in which they have been published wholly or in part. In this list-volume it seemed useful to record every Burke letter of which there is any trace, even when known only by references in other letters; it also seemed useful to treat fully the correspondence of the other members of Burke's immediate family. The total number of letters listed is just short of 7000, recording Burke's contacts with 1200 separate correspondents.

Burke certainly deserves a fuller *Correspondence* than the four-volume work issued in 1844, which printed only 305 of his letters. It is not practicable, and surely not desirable either, to print every letter recorded in the list-volume, merely because a text of it can be found. The family letters are not always relevant to Edmund's affairs. The letters to Edmund are frequently prolix and of no great importance.

The present edition aims at completeness in only one respect. It will include all of Edmund Burke's own letters which survive wholly or in part, omitting only 'public letters'—pamphlets given the form of letters —if they were printed in Burke's lifetime or clearly intended to be printed. It will also preserve abstracts of missing letters when they are full enough to be useful records of Burke's life or opinions. Mere mentions of letters known to be missing will not be included; a record

[1] *A Checklist of the Correspondence of Edmund Burke*, ed. Thomas W. Copeland and Milton Shumway Smith. Printed for the Index Society at the University Press, Cambridge, 1955.

of them is to be found in the *Checklist*. Letters written *to* Burke will be printed wholly or in part when in the opinion of the editors they are important themselves or necessary to the understanding of Burke's letters. Nearly all of Rockingham's letters to Burke, for example, will be included, but begging letters by office-seekers or the outpourings of voluble cranks are better ignored. Many in-letters of minor but genuine importance will be extracted or summarized. Letters written *for* Burke—most often by the members of his family—will be printed; but in the case where a family letter deals only partly with Burke's concerns, the editors may choose to omit or excerpt.

Some scholars will naturally regret any exclusions the editors make. But they are not wholly without remedies. The *Checklist* gives the location of manuscripts, and names the printed works in which they have been published. There will also be eventually a permanent Burke collection at Sheffield in which students may find the answers to further questions. Since the Sheffield Central Library already contains the largest single body of Burke MSS, it has seemed the proper place to collect reproductions of all Burke letters of which the originals are elsewhere. When the present edition has been completed, all photostats, microfilms, photo-copies and transcripts which have been used in preparing it will remain in the Library for the use of future scholars.

It is expected that the edition will come out at the rate of one volume a year. Eight editors have agreed to share the work; each will take responsibility for one chronological section of Burke's career which he will treat in a volume of his own. An index volume will complete the series. As the early volumes will be in the hands of readers for several years before the final index, each will be supplied with its own index—which however is merely temporary: an index of persons mentioned in the text and notes of that volume.

It is not yet possible to give an exact total of the letters to be included in the entire edition. For one thing, it is hoped that some discoveries will be made as our work progresses. Volume I, however, shows an advance over the four-volume *Correspondence* of 1844. We are printing 191 complete and six partially-preserved letters of Burke; the earlier work printed twenty-seven letters for the same period. Of our total of 197, 176 letters are here printed from manuscript. Twenty-four are printed for the first time, of which twelve belong to the most obscure period of Burke's career.

RULES OF TRANSCRIPTION

Where the original of any letter survives, its spelling, capitalization, punctuation and paragraphing will be followed exactly in this edition. There are three exceptions to this rule.

(1) Where the writer of the letter has used an abbreviation which would be familiar to his eighteenth-century reader but might strike a modern reader as strange or quaint (e.g. *ye* for *the*, *wch* for *which*, *obedt* for *obedient*), we will normally expand. In date-lines, addresses and proper names, however, such expansions can be misleading, and might deprive a reader of useful evidence, so that we will normally *not* expand abbreviations in these cases.

(2) Where the writer has begun a parenthesis or quotation with the proper mark but has failed to complete it—or has completed it but failed to begin it—we will supply the missing mark. We will follow a similar principle in the more important case of the breaks between sentences. It is common in letters of any period to find dashes or flourishes doing duty for proper stops at the ends of sentences; in old letters the griming or wearing away of the paper has often lost us stops which the writer himself did not omit. A missing stop, or—what is also common in the eighteenth century—a sentence begun without a capital letter, may needlessly confuse the reader who is not expecting a sentence break. We will therefore make it a rule (when we feel sure that a sentence break was intended), if a stop is clearly visible but no capital, to supply the capital; or conversely if a capital is visible but no stop, to supply the stop. This has not been necessary more than a few dozen times in Volume I, and most of these cases are in Burke's earliest letters.

(3) Where the writer is not Burke, we will occasionally normalize eccentricities of spelling, capitalization and the rest, but not without giving notice to the reader. In the present volume, quotations in the notes are normalized for two manuscript sources only: the Rockingham and the Newcastle Papers.

Where transcription is made from a printed text, it will be followed exactly except in matters of typography, which are likely to be a printer's or editor's choice rather than the writer's. Of printed sources, only the *Journals of the House of Commons* have been normalized in this volume.

Angle brackets, ⟨...⟩, are used to indicate words or phrases which are illegible, or to enclose uncertain readings.

The date given to a letter, in its heading and wherever it is cited in the notes, will be free of brackets only when (*a*) the letter has been seen in manuscript and has a complete date upon it in the writer's hand; or (*b*) the letter is from a printed source and no reason has been found to challenge a full date there given. Where an editor has inferred all or part of a date from postmarks, endorsements or contents, he will give his reasons in the headnote if they are not obvious. Addresses and any postmarks clearly discernible will be preserved. Endorsements will be preserved only when they supply useful facts, such as date of receipt. Franks, seals and wafers will normally be ignored. Letters which are cut, badly torn or otherwise damaged will be described. Copies and drafts will be identified as such.

ACKNOWLEDGEMENTS

This edition of Edmund Burke's letters, like its predecessor of more than a century ago, has been made possible primarily by the generosity of the Fitzwilliam family, who have put their collections of manuscripts at the disposal of the editors. The largest collection, now deposited at the Central Library of Sheffield, has made Sheffield the centre of our editorial operations. A smaller collection of Burke papers on deposit with the Northamptonshire Record Society, now in Lamport Hall, has also been made fully accessible, as have letters still in the private possession of Earl Fitzwilliam.

Other owners of Burke letters have been extremely generous. All who are named in our list of Manuscript Sources have kindly agreed to the publication of their letters, and deserve our fullest thanks. Of those who have been more than usually helpful we cannot resist naming at least a few: Dr Otto O. Fisher of Detroit, Michigan, who allowed us to check the Burke–Shackleton letters in his collection; Mr Donal F. O'Hara of Annaghmore, County Sligo, who gave us access to the letters of Burke to his ancestor, Charles O'Hara; and Mr James M. Osborn of New Haven, Connecticut, who both offered the full use of his Burke collections, and assisted us at every point with encouragement and advice.

Letters reprinted in this volume from Reginald Blunt's *Mrs Montagu, Her Letters and Friendships* are protected by copyright. We are indebted to Reginald Blunt's Executors and Messrs Constable and Company for permission to reprint. We are also indebted to Sotheby and Company for their permission to reprint portions of several letters known to us only by extracts in their catalogues.

Many individual scholars have made contributions to the present volume. The first of them, without whom the volume could not have been completed at all, is Mr John Brooke, now engaged upon the eighteenth-century section of the History of Parliament. Mr Brooke himself wrote many of the political notes in this volume, and gave its editor (not a professional historian) invaluable counsel; he has agreed to serve as historical consultant to all the volumes of the edition. Dr John Woods, also a permanent consultant, has had a very large share in the work of this volume; it is hard to imagine a scholar who would be either keener or more patient in the hunt for the buried facts of Burke's career. Dr Robert A. Smith of Yale University, a member of our Editorial Committee, has also assisted greatly, both in research and in the editorial labour.

Much of the work of the volume has been in identifying persons with whom Burke was connected. In this early period of his life, some of the problems are extremely difficult. The remoter members of the Burke and Nagle families would certainly have eluded us but for the assistance of Mr Basil O'Connell of the Genealogical Office in Dublin, whose knowledge of Burke genealogy is unequalled; we have relied upon him constantly. For those of Burke's early acquaintances who were Quakers we have found admirable records in the libraries of the Friends in Dublin and London. If it is proper to acknowledge here our obligations to the author of a printed work, we should like to express our obligations to Mr Gerrit P. Judd of Hofstra College, whose *Members of Parliament* (New Haven, 1955) does a great service to scholars by its full and accurate identifications. Mr Judd is not cited in our notes as an authority, but we have relied upon him for dates of birth and death of many scores of M.P.s.

We have called frequently for help from members of our Editorial and Advisory Committees, to all of whom we owe thanks for both suggestions and acts of assistance. Those to whom we are perhaps most indebted are Sir Lewis Namier, whose advice determined the main features of our editorial plan, and Professor G. R. Potter who gave counsel on innumerable problems, from the earliest period of the edition. Dr L. F. Powell helped us with many suggestions out of his long editorial experience. Of scholars not directly connected with the edition, Dr Edmond de Beer of London, Professor Ross Hoffman of Fordham University, Dr R. J. Hayes of the National Library of Ireland, Dr Peter Underdown of Worcester Training College and Dr John Weston of the University of Virginia have been most helpful. Professor Milton Smith, besides collaborating in the preparation of the *Checklist of the Correspondence of Burke*, assisted, along with Mrs Smith, in making transcriptions and in organizing the 'Burke Factory' in Sheffield. The greatest responsibility for carrying on the 'factory' has been with Mrs Valerie Jobling. On her all editors have joined in making the most unreasonable demands—and have never been disappointed.

Our chief debt to any institution is to the Sheffield City Libraries. From the beginning of our project nine years ago we have been constantly assisted by the former City Librarian, Mr J. P. Lamb, the present Librarian, Mr John Bebbington, the Chief Bibliographical Assistant, Miss Mary Walton, the Archivist, Miss Rosamond Meredith, and the staffs of the Local History and Reference Departments. We are also indebted to the other largest repository of Burke manuscripts, the Northamptonshire Record Society, now in Lamport Hall, Northampton; Miss Joan Wake, Mr P. I. King and their staff have been infinitely courteous and useful to us at all times.

The University of Sheffield has given us every encouragement and assistance in their power; as has the University of Chicago, both through their Press and by acting as the official sponsor of our project. Finally, none of the activities of our edition would have been possible without the generous financial aid that has been granted by the Trustees of the Carnegie Corporation of New York.

T. W. C.

SHEFFIELD
September 1957

INTRODUCTION

The letters in this volume are scattered over a period of nearly a quarter of a century, from Burke's sixteenth to his fortieth year. They are not scattered evenly. The first sixty letters, all written while Burke was an undergraduate at Trinity College, Dublin, record in considerable detail a period of not quite four years. These form a group by themselves. They are followed by sixty-five letters covering the entire period from Burke's graduation from Trinity at the age of nineteen to his appearance in the British House of Commons at the age of thirty-seven. These form a second, less coherent group. The eighteen years they span deserve the name Professor Wecter once proposed, 'the missing years in Edmund Burke's biography'. The 'missing years' come to an end when Burke's success as a parliamentary speaker brings him out of obscurity and on to the great stage of British politics. The last group of letters in this volume begins with the maiden speech in January of 1766 and extends to the close of the parliamentary session in June of 1768. There are seventy-two of Burke's letters preserved for these two-and-a-half years. That is about the number we should find in a similar period at any time from the 1760's to the end of Burke's career.

For some readers the first group of Burke's letters—those written in his college years—will be disappointing. They are not all that one might expect. Burke became in his maturity a writer of astonishing power. Hazlitt, Matthew Arnold and Leslie Stephen agreed in calling him the greatest master of English prose. Macaulay thought him the greatest man since Milton, and James Mackintosh and John Morley put him in a class with Shakespeare as 'above mere talent'. If his gifts were so extraordinary, it is natural to think that they would reveal themselves in almost any large body of his writing, even the writing of his early adolescence. Critics often speak of their eagerness to witness the trial flights of genius. Burke's sixty undergraduate letters, thirty-five of them written before his seventeenth birthday, are the rare case of the critics being given their hearts' desire. Alas for romantic hopes! The undergraduate letters are an entirely creditable series, but they are not much more vivid or interesting than other people's undergraduate letters. They do not record much of their writer's experience, perhaps because he had had very little. They do not give proof of a precocious sensitivity to language, being in fact rather carelessly written. What is most remarkable in them, a ranging energy of mind that was always a characteristic of Burke, is not in its adolescent phase an unusually winning virtue.

There is of course something impressive in mere naked ambition. The early letters give ample evidence of Burke's desire to excel, long before most types of excellence were within his power. He was determined to be a writer—at any cost of his own effort. That meant, as it usually does, that he often sat down to write when he had very little to say. A correspondence must be *kept up*. It also meant that friendly letters were always in some danger of turning into exercises. The young writer would see a chance of trying himself out in one of the accepted forms of composition. He seldom passed by such chances. There are, of course, letters in verse—of an unusually discouraging quality. There are imitations of various styles of prose. In the midst of more normal matters the reader suddenly realizes that he is being carried off into a passage of pulpit eloquence, or of genteel sentiment, or of popular philosophy. Burke will not keep his own character as a young boy of fifteen or sixteen; he is forever deciding to be an urbane controversialist, an expositor of the sciences or a teller of oriental tales. He is not equipped to succeed in most of his roles. Indeed he usually fails. But persistence is to be admired—not least when it endures many defeats.

The undergraduate letters were all addressed to a single correspondent, Burke's school friend Richard Shackleton. Burke had gone at the age of twelve to a school in the small village of Ballitore, about thirty miles south-west of Dublin. The Master of the school, Abraham Shackleton, an able and very serious Quaker, made a strong and lasting impression upon his most famous pupil. The Master's son, though three years Burke's senior, soon became his closest friend. The correspondence of the two boys began when Burke at the age of fifteen left school and returned to live in his father's house in Dublin, where he entered Trinity College. Richard Shackleton, being a Quaker, could not have entered Trinity even if he had been financially able; he remained in Ballitore, where he began assisting his father in the running of the school. He eventually became Master himself, as did his son after him.

Although only Burke's side of this early correspondence has survived, some of the qualities of Shackleton's letters are not hard to infer, and of course they had an influence on the character of Burke's letters. Shackleton was an unusually intelligent and serious boy, steadier and more settled than Burke was ever to become. He was also deeply religious. When his daughter, Mrs Mary Leadbeater, wrote an account of his life, she described how at five years old 'his heart experienced the touches of Divine love; and he sometimes withdrew to a retired spot, where he poured out his soul in prayer...and this tenderness continued, with very little interruption, to operate on his mind till the sixteenth year of his age'. He later thought of the years of his youth (the years when he had known Burke best) as a time of regrettable laxity.

Burke was not otherworldly like Shackleton, but he too was precociously serious. We catch an undertone of strangely mature anxiety in many of the early letters, even when they are outwardly most lighthearted. Burke is never quite sure that his older friend is treating him as an equal, and sometimes pleads piteously to be allowed to share his secrets. He is uncertain of the proper tone for describing his own activities; and affects more humility, or wit, or learning, even than one expects in adolescent letters. Occasionally there are signs of the unhappiness he is experiencing at home. The Burke household was divided on the religious issue: the father and sons were Protestant, the mother and daughter Catholic; both parents were nervous and irritable. One feels in many passages of Burke's letters to Shackleton that he is clinging to his friend as part of a more peaceful world than he knew in his own home.

It is a question, no doubt, how much one should allow oneself to read between the lines for hidden subtleties. The best reason for making every effort to sift the evidence of the early letters is that the evidence runs out so soon. The well-recorded period of Burke's youth ends when he takes his B.A. at Trinity in January of 1748. There is a single short letter written in the following month, and after that Burke's whole surviving correspondence for the two last years he remained in Ireland consists of two sentences and part of a third which biographers have quoted from letters now lost. In the spring of 1750, at the age of twenty-one, Burke crossed to London to study law at the Middle Temple. We have six letters—two of them highly uninformative poetic epistles—to tell us of his activities in his first two-and-a-half years in England. Then between the autumn of 1752 and the summer of 1757 comes the darkest period of all. To illuminate those five years there remains a single letter, which happens to be torn and incomplete.

These are the missing years indeed. We know little more of them from other sources than we do from the correspondence. Yet obviously they were years in which crucial decisions were made. When Burke began his studies in the Temple, he almost certainly expected on completing them to return to practise law in Dublin like his father and elder brother; the single letter of the darkest period mentions this expectation. By 1757 he had changed his mind. He gave up the law, and he decided against returning to Ireland. His father was deeply offended, and remained on bad terms with him for several years.

Burke's marriage in the spring of 1757 may have seemed to his father a further grievance. Jane Nugent brought her husband no fortune, and she was the daughter of a Roman Catholic. It is typical of our ignorance of this period that we do not know whether she was herself a Roman Catholic at the time, and we do not know where the marriage took place. We do know from abundant evidence that the match was a happy one. Burke was passionately devoted to his own home, which had all the unity and harmony his father's home had lacked. Jane was quiet and unassertive, with the patience and steadiness of temper her husband's nature needed. Her father, Dr Christopher Nugent, was equally tranquil; he seems to have been universally liked. The young couple shared his house in the early years of their marriage. Indeed Burke's younger brother Richard, who came over from Dublin at about the time of the marriage, also shared it, as did William Burke, Edmund's closest friend, who, being more prosperous than the rest, probably also shared the expenses.

It is not until 1759 that the obscurity of the missing years begins to clear. After ten years for which there are not ten complete letters, we at last regain the relative fulness of half-a-dozen letters in one year. Burke's life is not yet free from shadows, but he is no longer entirely invisible. We find him struggling to make his way as a writer. There are even signs that he is succeeding in the struggle. Dodsley, the most respectable of publishers, is backing him strongly—has already by 1759 published two books for him, the *Vindication of Natural Society* and the *Sublime and Beautiful*, besides engaging him as editor of the *Annual Register* and contracting to pay him £300 for a *History of England*. There is other patronage in sight. Mrs Montagu, 'Queen of the Blues', is his enthusiastic admirer; he seems to have a place in the circle of authors and artists cultivated by her and Lord Lyttelton. He is friendly with David Hume. We know, though not from his own correspondence, that in this period he impressed Johnson, met Garrick and Reynolds, and revived an early acquaintance with Goldsmith, his contemporary at Trinity College Dublin. We cannot of course judge the promise of a young man's career merely from half-a-dozen letters, even if supplemented by a few facts from other sources, but what we know of Burke's circumstances in the late 1750's might make us wonder why a career in literature so creditably begun was ultimately abandoned.

This is a question of great interest in Burke's life; it is illuminated only very obliquely by his letters. We never see him willingly resign his literary ambitions. Against his most stubborn intentions, they merely fail. The *Vindication* and the *Sublime and Beautiful* had both won him reputation, yet neither set him on the road to any further achievement. The *Annual Register* was completely successful as a periodical of its class; unfortunately, writing for periodicals was not a highly-regarded activity in the mid-eighteenth century, and Burke never chose to admit that he was editor of the *Register*. The *History of England* commissioned by Dodsley was perhaps his best chance of fortune; that really might have established the fame of a young writer. Burke clung to it for years, but was never able to complete it. Two lesser projects—the *Hints for an Essay on the Drama* and the more ambitious *Tract on the Popery Laws in Ireland*—were also begun and abandoned in the 1760's. How so many separate efforts by a man of Burke's abilities could end in failure, or in fruitless success, is genuinely puzzling. It does not seem to be accident. In some way Burke was not ready for the career as a writer on which he was so firmly resolved.

Letters tell us at least one aspect of the story. Burke was to make his final escape from frustration in the literary field only when another set of interests had become strong enough in his life to offer him an alternative. This happened very slowly. It is odd that we should be able to say of Edmund Burke that he was in his early thirties before there were really convincing signs that politics were to be his main concern. He was in his late thirties before he fully committed himself to a political career. The letters which show us the movement of his mind toward its ultimate goal are among the most essential documents of his biography.

The fullest group of these letters is to be found in a single correspondence: that of Burke with his Irish friend Charles O'Hara. This began in the late 1750's and was to continue until O'Hara's death in 1776. It has a claim to be considered Burke's most revealing correspondence. It is nearly his largest—including in all over 200 letters. It is also the one which most completely preserves one of his social relationships. It is not one-sided, like the early Shackleton correspondence; we have as many letters of O'Hara as of Burke, and dozens of letters back and forth between O'Hara and the other members of Burke's family, with all of whom he was on affectionate terms. The tone of intercourse is familiar, if not exactly the tone of equals. O'Hara was about fifteen years Burke's senior, but also wealthy, well-connected, at ease in the world, and much else that Burke was not. He had always the privilege of giving counsel out of his greater experience—was always a little in the role of a father-confessor. Burke did not resent a junior role. As Coleridge once said of him, 'Burke was a great courtier'. He welcomed relations with those who were wiser or stronger than he.

O'Hara knew men and affairs, in Ireland and in England. He visited London when he could, but when he was in Dublin or at his seat in County Sligo he had a vast curiosity for news of London. Burke strove to satisfy him, filling long and frequent letters with the day-to-day gossip of politics: anecdotes of the public figures, reports of speeches heard from the Visitors' Gallery of the House of Commons, judgments passed by others or by himself on the most recent happenings. In the first letters it is obvious enough that he writes as an outsider, with limited sources of information and no great range of experience or reflexion. But as the correspondence continues, both his knowledge and his interest increase. He begins to take sides, to blame and praise the actors and discuss events and trends in terms of principles. Before the last letters of the correspondence—well beyond the period of this volume—he is writing as a complete professional, at the centre of the affairs he describes.

It is astonishing, however, to see how slowly Burke himself accepted his destiny. He withheld himself from politics, clinging stubbornly to his literary hopes. We know very little of a connexion he made in the late 1750's with William Gerard Hamilton, a minor politician whom he served as some kind of secretary for six years. But we do know that when they made their agreement Burke insisted it was not to rule out his prior literary commitments, for which time had to be reserved. When the two men had been associated for about two years, Hamilton was appointed Chief Secretary to the Lord Lieutenant of Ireland. This took him to Dublin in the winters of 1761 and 1763. Service there must have had many attractions for Burke, but it did not alter his main purpose. When in the spring of 1763 Hamilton secured him a pension of £300 as a reward for his labours, he again took special pains to assert his literary aims, protesting in a long and earnest letter that he would rather refuse the pension outright than let the duties it required of him infringe upon that portion of time reserved for his own writing.

Burke's connexion with Hamilton ended in a serious quarrel in the early months of 1765. The letters, having told us little about the two men's six-year friendship, are very full about their final rupture, or at least about the feelings it aroused in Burke. The quarrel was undoubtedly one of the crucial events of his life. He had been serving Hamilton as a kind of political lieutenant. Apparently he had given satisfaction, for Hamilton, planning a career of his own in the House of Commons, wanted him to go on indefinitely in his subordinate role. The proposal of a long-term commitment infuriated Burke, who indignantly refused to enter into such 'slavery'. Hamilton, more attentive to his own needs than to Burke's pride, persisted in his offers. In a desperation of anger, Burke renounced their whole connexion, resigned the pension Hamilton had procured him (his main source of income), and broke off their relations forever.

It was an act of wild courage. Burke freed himself from Hamilton, but only by completely destroying the only financial security he had. In the spring of 1765, at the age of thirty-six, with a wife and child to support, he was left with no visible income beyond the £100 a year paid him by Dodsley for his anonymous labours on the *Annual Register*.

There is still no clear sign that Burke had relinquished his ambitions as a writer, but his efforts to regain some security again led him into politics. His services with Hamilton had ended in failure, but they had given him a kind of a profession. He could be useful as a Man of Business to some more satisfactory political patron. In the late spring of 1765 the letters show him attempting to attach himself to that brilliant if not very reliable figure, Charles Townshend. Perhaps the two men had even reached an agreement, before another and superior opportunity presented itself. In July of 1765 a new administration was being formed, in which the young Marquess of Rockingham was to be First Lord of the Treasury. Rockingham was in need of a private secretary, and though he had no previous acquaintance with Burke, offered him the post. If Burke could have seen into the future, he would have realized how fateful a decision he was making when he accepted. As it was, he regretted being unable to find a better opening, and took the offer with little enthusiasm. His friend William Burke, who secured an appointment as under-Secretary of State at the same time, was thought to be more fortunate than he.

In fact, the attachment to Rockingham finally settled the problem of Edmund Burke's career. In itself, perhaps, it need not have been even yet an absolute commitment to politics: Burke could have insisted, as he had with Hamilton, on reserving some part of his leisure for a prior undertaking. But—besides the fact that time had withered the literary hopes—Rockingham could offer much more than Hamilton ever had. He was one of the richest noblemen in England, had inherited with his estates a considerable political interest of his own, and was backed by some of the most prominent political leaders, including the Duke of Cumberland and the Duke of Newcastle. His personal qualities were those Burke valued most. He was loyal to his friends, ambitious, honourable, and for his years remarkably steady. And he needed an able lieutenant. For all his social and political advantages, Rockingham lacked confidence in himself. Burke's talents, his industry, and not least the experience he had gained in his six years with Hamilton, all equipped him to be extremely useful to such a patron.

One final step had to be taken before Burke was completely launched. He had to have a seat in Parliament. It was not Rockingham who supplied it. In effect it was William Burke. 'Cousin Will' was devoted to Edmund's interests to the point of putting them before his own. He had himself been promised a seat in Parliament by his close friend Earl Verney; when it became available, he proposed that it be given not to him but to Edmund. Earl Verney agreed, and in December of 1765 Edmund was elected by Verney's influence for the borough of Wendover in Buckinghamshire. In the following month, at the age of thirty-seven, he entered the House of Commons.

It had taken Burke more than half his life to decide that he belonged in politics. Once in, he made an end of hesitation. He hurled himself headlong into the *mêlée*—with immediate and astonishing success. His early speeches were praised by Pitt, and won him vast respect for his range and readiness of information. He was effective in debate, and soon stood in the highest rank of the speakers for Administration. By the end of his first session, in the spring of 1766, he had established a reputation as one of the leading orators in the House. Few men in the history of Parliament have risen more rapidly from obscurity to national fame.

The final group of letters in this volume show us Burke past the period of his apprenticeship. He is at last the public figure familiar to posterity: full of activity, full of zeal, confident of his purposes. His success in the House of Commons was all he had needed to make him indispensable to Rockingham, who remained his patron for nearly seventeen years. In his new security, or what appeared to be such, he decided to 'cast a little root' in England, his adopted country. With help from Will Burke and other friends, he bought an estate at Beaconsfield for something over £20,000. The years of hesitation and failure seemed to be entirely behind him. When an unfriendly sceptic, Sir John Hawkins, expressed wonder at his sudden rise, Dr Johnson rebuked him sharply: 'Now we who know Burke, know, that he will be one of the first men in this country.'

Burke himself was not quite so confident. Less than two years after his initial triumphs, he commented upon them in a letter to Charles O'Hara—one of the last letters in this volume:

> Every body congratulated me on coming into the House of Commons, as being in the certain Road of a great and speedy fortune; and when I began to be heard with some little attention, every one of my friends was sanguine. But in truth I was never so myself. I came into Parliament not at all as a place of preferment, but of refuge; I was pushed into it; and I must have been a Member, and that too with some Eclat, or be a little worse than nothing....

It was an odd comment to make on the brilliant opening of a great parliamentary career.

LIST OF SHORT TITLES

When letters by or to Burke are cited in this Volume without a particular reference, they will be from the main series of Burke letters, chronologically arranged (Bk 1), in the Sheffield Central Library. In this series there are some letters of which the originals are deposited with the Northamptonshire Record Society in Lamport Hall, Northampton; but in all cases photo-copies are at Sheffield. Letters and documents from other manuscript collections are cited by the following short titles:

Dr A. J. A. Alexander
: Dr A. J. A. Alexander, Woodford County, Kentucky.

Ballitore MSS
: A collection formerly owned by Mrs M. R. Backhouse, Chapel House, Lansdown, Bath. The letters were microfilmed while in Mrs Backhouse's possession. A film of the entire body of the MSS is in the National Library of Ireland; one reel covering Burke letters is in the Central Library, Sheffield.

Bristol Archives
: City Archives Department, The New Council House, College Green, Bristol 1.

British Museum
: British Museum, Great Russell Street, London, W.C. 1.

The Duke of Buccleuch
: His Grace the Duke of Buccleuch, Dalkeith House, Dalkeith, Midlothian, Scotland.

Dartmouth MSS
: MSS belonging to the Earl of Dartmouth, Patshull House, Woverhampton; now on deposit with the William Salt Library, Stafford.

Dr O. Fisher
: Dr Otto O. Fisher, 2475 Iroquois, Detroit, Michigan.

Fitzwilliam MSS (Milton)
: MSS in the possession of the Earl Fitzwilliam, Milton, Peterborough, Northamptonshire.

Fitzwilliam MSS (N.R.S.)
: A portion—roughly a fifth—of the main collection of Burke's papers, which came into the possession of the 4th Earl Fitzwilliam as the last survivor among Burke's literary executors, and which have been in the possession of the Fitzwilliam family ever since. This portion was formerly kept at Milton, near Peterborough, hence is sometimes cited by scholars under the name 'Milton MSS'. It is owned by the Earl Fitzwilliam, who has placed it on deposit with the Northamptonshire Record Society, now at Lamport Hall, Northamptonshire.

Fitzwilliam MSS (Sheffield)
: The larger portion of the Fitzwilliam Burke collection. It was formerly kept at Wentworth Woodhouse in Yorkshire, hence is sometimes cited by scholars under the name 'Wentworth Woodhouse MSS'. Owned by the Earl Fitzwilliam and placed on deposit with the Sheffield City Libraries, Sheffield.

Foljambe MSS
MSS in the possession of Captain E. W. S. Foljambe, Osberton, Worksop, Nottinghamshire.

Harvard Library
Harvard University, Cambridge 38, Massachusetts.

F. W. Hilles
Professor Frederick W. Hilles, Department of English, Yale University, New Haven, Connecticut.

Sir Edward Hoare, Bart.
Sir Edward Hoare, Bart., Woodside, Compton, near Guildford, Surrey.

Huntington Library
The Henry E. Huntington Library and Art Gallery, San Marino 15, California.

Hyde Collection
Mr and Mrs Donald Hyde, Four Oaks Farm, Somerville, New Jersey.

N. Loftus
N. Loftus, Esq., Bulcamp House, Halesworth, Suffolk.

Morgan Library
The Pierpont Morgan Library, 33 East 36th Street, New York 16, New York.

National Library of Ireland
Kildare Street, Dublin.

O'Hara MSS
MSS in the possession of Donal F. O'Hara, Esq., Annaghmore, Collooney, Sligo, Eire.

Osborn Collection
James M. Osborn, Yale University, New Haven, Connecticut.

Pennsylvania Historical Society
Historical Society of Pennsylvania, 1300 Locust Street, Philadelphia 7, Pennsylvania.

Portland MSS (Nottingham)
MSS belonging to the Duke of Portland; now on deposit with the Library of the University of Nottingham.

Public Record Office
Chancery Lane, London, W.C. 2.

Rockingham MSS
Letters and papers of the 2nd Marquess of Rockingham; among the Wentworth Woodhouse MSS owned by the Earl Fitzwilliam and now on deposit with the Sheffield City Libraries, Sheffield.

Victoria and Albert Museum
Cromwell Road, South Kensington, London, S.W. 7.

The following printed works are cited in this volume by short titles:

Adam Catalogue
Catalogue of the R. B. Adam Library, 3 vols. London, 1929; vol. IV, Buffalo, New York, 1930. Citations are all from vol. I, the portion separately paged and entitled 'Letters of Edmund Burke'.

LIST OF SHORT TITLES

Albemarle, *Memoirs of Rockingham*
George Thomas, Earl of Albemarle, *Memoirs of the Marquis of Rockingham*, 2 vols. London, 1852.

Barry, *Works*
James Barry, *Works*, 2 vols. London, 1809.

Beauties of Burke
Beauties of Burke, 2 vols. London, 1798.

Bisset (2nd ed.)
Robert Bisset, *Life of Edmund Burke*, 2nd ed., 2 vols. London, 1800.

Blunt, *Mrs Montagu*
Reginald Blunt, *Mrs Montagu, Her Letters and Friendships*, 2 vols. London, [1923].

Brooke, *Chatham Administration 1766–1768*
John Brooke, *The Chatham Administration 1766–1768*, London, 1956.

Chatham Correspondence
Correspondence of William Pitt, Earl of Chatham, ed. W. S. Taylor and J. H. Pringle, 4 vols. London, 1838–40.

Climenson, *Mrs Montagu*
Emily J. Climenson, *Elizabeth Montagu, the Queen of the Bluestockings: Her Correspondence from 1720 to 1761*, 2 vols. London, 1906.

Corr. (1844)
Edmund Burke, *Correspondence between 1744 and 1797*, ed. Charles William, Earl Fitzwilliam, and Richard Bourke, 4 vols. London, 1844.

Emin, *Autobiography*
Life and Adventures of Joseph Emin, London, 1792.

Fortescue
Correspondence of King George the Third, 1760–83, ed. Sir John Fortescue, 6 vols. London, 1927–8.

Garrick, *Corr.*
David Garrick, *Private Correspondence*, 2 vols. London, 1831.

Grafton, *Autobiography*
Autobiography and Correspondence of Augustus Henry, Third Duke of Grafton, ed. Sir W. R. Anson, London, 1898.

Grenville Papers
The Grenville Papers, ed. W. J. Smith, 4 vols. London, 1852–3.

Hist. MSS Comm. (*Dartmouth MSS*)
Historical Manuscripts Commission, Fifteenth Report, Appendix 1, London, 1896.

Hist. MSS Comm. (*Donoughmore MSS*)
Historical Manuscripts Commission, Twelfth Report, Appendix 9, London, 1891.

Hist. MSS Comm. (*Foljambe MSS*)
Historical Manuscripts Commission, Fifteenth Report, Appendix 5, London 1897.

Hoffman
Ross J. S. Hoffman, *Edmund Burke, New York Agent, With his letters to the New York Assembly and intimate correspondence with Charles O'Hara 1761–1776*, Philadelphia, 1956.

Leadbeater Papers
Mary Leadbeater, *Leadbeater Papers*, 2 vols. London, 1862.

Magnus
Sir Philip Magnus, *Edmund Burke*, London, 1939.

National Magazine
The National Magazine [*and Dublin Literary Gazette*], Dublin, 1830–1.

New Monthly Magazine
The New Monthly Magazine and Literary Journal (2nd series), London, 1821–71.

A Note-Book of Edmund Burke
A Note-Book of Edmund Burke, ed. H. V. F. Somerset, Cambridge, 1957.

Original Letters to Henry Flood
Original Letters to Henry Flood, London, 1820.

Philological Quarterly
Philological Quarterly, Iowa City, [Iowa], 1922– .

Prior (2nd ed.)
James Prior, *Memoir of the Life of Edmund Burke*, 2nd ed., 2 vols. London, 1826.

Prior (5th ed.)
Sir James Prior, *Life of Edmund Burke*, 5th ed. rev. London, 1891.

Prior, *Life of Goldsmith*
Sir James Prior, *Life of Goldsmith*, 2 vols. London, 1837.

Samuels
A. P. I. Samuels, *Early Life, Correspondence and Writings of Edmund Burke*, Cambridge, 1923.

Sotheby Catalogue
Sotheby and Company, 34 and 35 New Bond Street, London, W. 1.

Walpole, *Memoirs*
Horace Walpole, *Memoirs of the Reign of King George the Third*, ed. G. F. Russell Barker, 4 vols. London, 1894.

Wecter
Dixon Wecter, *Edmund Burke and His Kinsmen* (University of Colorado Studies, Series B, vol. 1, no. 1), Boulder, 1939.

Works (Bohn)
The Works of Edmund Burke, 8 vols. [Bohn's British Classics], London, 1854–89. References to Burke's *Works* will regularly cite this edition, as that most generally accessible to British scholars.

Works (Little, Brown)
The Works of Edmund Burke, rev. ed., 12 vols. [Little, Brown], Boston, 1865–7. References to Burke's *Works* will also regularly cite this edition, as most generally accessible to American scholars. The references, therefore, will be double (e.g. *Works* [Bohn], II, 354; [Little, Brown], II, 143).

THE CORRESPONDENCE

To Richard Shackleton—[*post* 14] *April* 1744

Source: MS Dr O. Fisher. Printed *Leadbeater Papers,* II, 3–6; Samuels, pp. 21–3.
Addressed: Mr Richd Shackleton | Wth Mr A. Shackleton's | in Ballitore
Franked: Free Wm Harward.
MS repaired with tape; about forty words are covered, but have been carefully copied (probably traced) on to the tape. This letter was written after Burke's admission to Trinity College, which was on 14 April 1744; what is said of 'expiration of Priviledge', and of Burke's encounter with Newcomen Herbert, and the timing of Richard Shackleton's visit to Dublin all suggest a date as much as ten days later.

When Burke left Ballitore School for the University at the age of 15 he returned to live in his father's house on Arran Quay, Dublin. Richard Shackleton (1726–92) remained at Ballitore, so that henceforth the two friends were about 30 miles apart. They began an active correspondence.

Dubn April 1744.

Dear Dicky

Since I am deprived of your company that was so agreeable to me, and the sweet hours that I spent in Ballitore in your Conversation and condemnd to noise smoak and Dublin town all I can do is to alleviate the pains of Absence by an Epistolary Correspondence but I here am stop'd by the expiration of Priviledge[1] which tho' a bar to us, yet it may be remedied in some measure by the Carman &c.[2] Without farther Prologue, I shall accquaint you with my adventures since I Left you which tho' perhaps not so entertaining nor so full of surprising Events as those of Don Quixot. Josy &c.[3] may serve to let you know that Dick Chidley[4] and I arrived pretty safe at this City rather of the Latest, for the Ρασκαλλει watch-man had the impudence to inform the Town how bad Travellers we were by crying, past twelve o'Clock. I was however Let in; went to bed, slept, and was sent in Company with Jack Baily[5] immediately after

[1] A Royal Warrant of 1693 provided that letters franked by members of Parliament could be passed free through the posts for fifty days before and after a parliamentary session (R. Alcock and F. Holland, *Postmarks of Great Britain and Ireland*, Cheltenham, 1940, p. 185). One such period expired on 25 April 1744 (*Pue's Occurrences*, 21–4 April 1744).

[2] 'The carman, the driver of a primitive two wheeled vehicle, drawn by one horse, was the common carrier of goods, small parcels, and frequently of letters throughout Ireland, previous to the introduction of railways' (*Leadbeater Papers*, II, 3 n.).

[3] Samuels suggests (p. 22 n.) that the reference is to Josey Delany (Joseph Delany, b. 1717). See below, letter of 11 June (p. 16), in which Burke recounts some of Delany's 'adventures'.

[4] Not identified.

[5] Probably John Bayly who entered Ballitore School 4 March 1736. See Ballitore School List, an appendix to vol. I of *Leadbeater Papers*; citations of dates from this list will translate the Quaker forms into the normal present forms—e.g. Eleventh Month and Twelfth Month into January and February—remembering that in Quaker usage before the change in the calendar March was still the first month of the year (Arnold Lloyd, *Quaker Social History*, London, 1950, p. 183).

Breakfast next morning (i.e.) monday morning, To Dr Pellasier[1] Fellow of Trinity Colledge near Dublin, a gentleman (since it falls in my way to give his conjectural Character) accounted one of the most Learned in the University. An exceeding good humour'd cleanly civil Fellow. N.B I judge by outward appearances. We were admitted into his Room and he has three very grand ones, he and Jack baily had a good Deal of Chat, and a Couple of men were setting up a Barometer in his Room so he could not for a while examine me: at Last he brought out France's Horace,[2] Dauphin's Virgil and Homer[3] with I dont know whos notes, He made me construe (Scriberis Vario &c and Eheu! Postume)[4] and in Virgil I began the 103 Line of the 6th Æn. and in Homer with the 227th Line of the 3d Iliad. and the 406th of the sixth and he was pleas'd to say (what I would not say after him unless to a particular friend) that I was a good Scholar understood the authors very well and seem'd to take pleasure in them, (yet by the by I dont know how he could tell that) and that I was more fit for the Colledge than three parts of my Class, but he told me I must be examined again by the Senior Lecturer, he was sent for but was not at home therefore Mr Pallasier told me I must have the trouble of calling again, he was going out and introduc'd me according to Custom I beleive to the Provost[5] who is an old sickly looking man. To be short this morning I was examined very strictly with another young Lad by Mr Aubins or Robbins (I dont know which) the Senior Lecturer[6] in the Odes Sermons and Epistles of Horace and am admitted.—I cannot express nor have I the knack of doing it how much I am oblig'd to your Father[7] for the extraordinary pains and care he has taken with me so as to merit the commendation of my Tutor and all I can do is to behave myself so as not to bring a scandal upon him or his School. Ive nout more to say but that yesterday I w⟨ent⟩ to J. Fletchers[8]

[1] The Rev. Dr John Pellissier (Pelishiere), *c.* 1703–81, who became Burke's tutor. Prior says he was 'represented by high college authority as a man of very ordinary acquirements, who when vice-provost in 1753, quitted the university for the living of Ardstraw, in the north of Ireland. To him Mr Burke owed few obligations, except, as it is said, having recommended to him the acquisition of multiform knowledge, rather than to devote his attention to any particular branch...' (2nd ed. I, 20).

[2] Philip Francis's edition of the *Odes, Epodes, and Carmen Seculare of Horace*, 2 vols. London, 1743. The editor was the father of Sir Philip Francis, Burke's friend and correspondent.

[3] Volumes in the so-called Delphin edition of the classics, originally prepared for the instruction of the son of Louis XIV. The title-page of each volume bore the inscription *Ad usum serenissimi Delphini*: hence the title of the series. Charles Butler (*Reminiscences*, London, 1822, II, 97–8) quoted Burke as saying while he held in his hand a ragged Delphin Virgil, that 'it was a book he always had within his reach'.

[4] Horace, *Odes*, I, vi, and II, xiv.

[5] The Rev. Dr Richard Baldwin (*c.* 1668–1758).

[6] The Rev. Dr John Obins (*c.* 1703–75), Fellow of Trinity College 1728.

[7] Abraham Shackleton (1696–1771).

[8] Jonathan Fletcher (d. 1746), a Quaker living in Meath Street.

to invite your Mother[1] she was not at home. I Left the Letters for her. Pray remember my Love to all my School fellows, and to Mr Burn[2] in particular. Tell Mastr Pearce[3] for his Comfort that I was examin'd in As in Pras.[4] And give Service to all the Girls[5] and inform Nanny Morris[6] that I have thought of her once or twice, and that if she has a mind for a Coach and six Let her tell what colour'd horses she will have and it shall be sent her by the first opportunity. But in the mean time give her a BOX and place it to account and this shall be sufficient Warrant for so doing.—It is almost Night and I must write to the Master[7] so I must conclude without more ado, all a one now.[8]

NED BURKE

I saw your friend Herbert at his Shop Door[9] as I went to the Colledge to Day and stood a while to speak to him. I went to see M: Brugh[10] but he was gone out of Town.

The Microcosm[11] will Leave Town the 28 so consider what to Do.

Send to me the next Carman that goes and Ill send you something; Or send Harry Bawn.[12]

Richard Shackleton paid a visit to Dublin and satisfied his curiosity about the Microcosm. He wrote his father 26 April (Ballitore MSS) that he had 'seen (this day) Ned Burke in his Gown, he has been examind by Dr Obbins two several times with great strictness and is enter'd with Approbation and Applause'.

[1] *Née* Margaret Wilkinson (*c.* 1688–1768).
[2] John Byrne, an usher at Ballitore School.
[3] Thomas Pearce entered Ballitore School 19 August 1738.
[4] The opening phrase of a *memoria technica* for the principal parts of Latin verbs, in *King Edward VI's First Latin Book:*

As in praesenti perfectum format in avi
Ut no, nos, navi....

[5] There were girls as well as boys among the younger pupils at Ballitore. One of Richard Shackleton's early duties in his father's school was teaching writing to the girls. See below, letter of 29 May, p. 11.
[6] Probably Anne Morris (b. 1719) of a Quaker family in Ballitore.
[7] Abraham Shackleton.
[8] The cry of the watchman on his rounds (Samuels, p. 23 n.).
[9] Newcomen Herbert, who entered Ballitore School 6 June 1735, had later moved to Dublin where he lived with his uncle, Cornelius Cox, a merchant on Essex Bridge (letter of Herbert to Shackleton 11 February 1743 in Ballitore MSS). He wrote Shackleton 24 April 1744: 'Mr Burke called to see me this day' (Ballitore MSS).
[10] Richard Brough or Bruff (b. *c.* 1724) was admitted to Trinity College 17 May 1743.
[11] An elaborate mechanical contraption exhibited at the 'Raven' on College Green throughout the winter and spring of 1744. It was described in repeated advertisements in the *Dublin Journal* as '*The Microcosm, or The World in Miniature, lately made* (*in Form of a Roman Temple*) *by Mr. Henry Bridges*, at a very great Expence, and 12 Years close Study and Application....Its height is 10 Feet, and Breadth in Basis 6 feet—The whole is most beautifully composed of Architecture, Sculpture, Painting, Musick and Astronomy, according to the best Rules and Principles, with vast Variety and Justice of moving Figures, and is allowed to be the honestest Piece of Mechanism that ever appeared in Europe'. Advertisements in the newspapers warned that it was to leave Dublin 28 April (*Pue's Occurrences* and *Dublin Journal* for 17–21 April).
[12] A servant of the Shackletons who frequently carried messages between Ballitore and Dublin.

To Richard Shackleton—10 *May* 1744

Source: MS Dr O. Fisher. Printed *Leadbeater Papers*, II, 6–7; Samuels, pp. 27–8.
Addressed: To | Mr Richd Shackleton | in Ballitore | Per | Killcullen Bridge.
Postmarked: MA|12.
MS torn at a fold; the lower part of the single sheet is missing.

Dubn May 10th 1744.

Dear Dicky

I thought to have had the pleasure of your conversation Longer in Town and to that end call'd at Mr Kearneys[1] the morning that you went off—but without saying any more you very well know the consequence without my telling it, such as usually happens, on such occasions, but perhaps you're now thinking that the next word that comes out will be, With all the marks of Wild despair, I tore my flowing Robes and rent my hair, bid woods and rocks be Witness of my Grief, and gods and men implor'd to my releif &c, &c, &c, and such Like stuff which people are apt to father upon Apollo and the Muses tho', God knows, that several children are calld by the Names of those that never got 'em, nor did I faint but very calmly said as usual that I was surpriz'd at the suddenness of your Departure, was sorry for it got my Wig and went to the College.

You said if I dont forget that you would read the same Authors that I do here which in my opinion is as usefull a thing as you c⟨ould⟩ do. Consult the Master about it and see how he approves of ⟨it. If⟩ he does you are better take it in hand immediately, it is ⟨as fol⟩lows, the 9 first Chapters of Burgersdiscius,[2] the 6 Last Æneids of Virgil, the Enchiridion of Epictetus with the Tabula Cebetis,[3] which my Tutor recommended to me as a very fine picture of human Life, it is the work of one Cebes an antient Theban Philosopher written in the allegorical way. I have no more to say because to tell the Truth, I have scarcely any Subject to talk upon

[1] On his visit to Dublin Richard Shackleton had stayed in the house of Michael Kearney, a barber-surgeon in Crow Street, father of Michael Kearney (1733–1814) who entered Ballitore School 13 September 1743.

[2] The *Institutionum Logicarum Libri Duo* of Franco Burgersdijck (1590–1635), a Dutch philosopher of the Rhamist school, was first published in Leyden in 1626 and became an influential textbook (see Samuels, pp. 28–9, and below, Burke's letter of 24 May, p. 7).

[3] A work once attributed to Cebes of Thebes, a friend and disciple of Socrates; it is now generally thought to have been written as late as the first century A.D. It develops the Platonic theory of pre-existence, and maintains that education consists in the formation of character.

To RICHARD SHACKLETON—[*ante* 24 *May* 1744]

Source: Ballitore MSS. Printed Samuels, pp. 31–3.
Addressed: To | Mr Richd Shackleton | in | Ballitore | Per Richd Burke.
MS undated, but this is probably the 'verse nonsense' to which Burke refers in his letter of 24 May.

I

What tho' the Distance of the Way
Divides my Friend and me,
And rules severe this Body Stay
My soul is all with thee

II

Or shall I stay or shall I go
And join my Breast with thine
And ev'ry mean restraint forego
For Pleasures half Divine.

III

This bold Design I well have weigh'd
In reasons nicest Scale
But, Oh! can Reason ever sway
When friendship must prevail.

IV

If Fate from thee, retards me here
Oh! How can I express,
The fatal cause of all my fear
The Loss of such a happiness.

V

Just as the Turtle in the Grove
Foresaken by her Mate
The once companion of her Love
In mournfull Coos Laments her fate.

VI

Thus O, my Friend debard from thee
The City and the waste
Are Desert Equally to me
No Pleasures can I taste.

VII

Not Thus if, (Oh! Transporting thought)
I could as once Possess
That Pleasure, rich with pleasure fraught
Which once I prized Less.

VIII

To walk with thee the Groves among
Or rove in flowry Meads
Where birds attune their early Song
Or where the Genius Leads.

IX

Harmonious Songsters of the Sky,
Who tune to Notes the Western breeze
Or you who mount on high
Or you who warble on the Trees

X

Witness ye Groves, ye Hills, ye woods,
How grief did rend my heart
Witness O, Griece[1] your Silver floods
When I my friend must part.

XI

Where will I Leave this Pleasing Dream
This soft Delusion of Ideal bliss
Yes I could Dwell for ever on the Theme
For ever on that subject Dwell.

XII

But I must wake to Scenes of Grief
And Leave the fancy'd Joy
And Patience call to my releif
For Pleasures not to Cloy.

[1] The Greese, a small river flowing through Ballitore.

XIII

The Trav'ler thus who half his Journey gone
Rests his faint Limbs beneath a shady Tree
And Dreams of Gilded Roofs and splendid Treats
When suddenly awak'd by rattling Storms
And the Loud clamours of the Thundring Sky
He Stirs affrighted, and around him sees
Black Dreary Desarts and Dire hail and Rain
And not a friendly Star to guide him in his way.

XIV

Too sure that pleasure ne'er will Cloy
But ever will abide,
That friendship's wholly made of Joy,
Which harbours Virtue for its guide
'For Love of Soul doth Love of Body pass
As much as purest gold Surmounts the meanest Brass.'

Spencer[1]

I send the Letter by my Brothers Hand[2]
Receive the Bearer for the Senders sake

E.B —

P.S. I am surprizd that you answerd not a Letter I sent you if you received it.—as for the Versification of the foregoing you must Pardon the frequent Changes of it for I designed in some things neither to be crampd with Rhime or a set measure of Verse. I send you it in this Dress to incite you to answer me in the Like. I am remembred to all. Your Father and Mother particularly.

To Richard Shackleton—24 *May* 1744

Source: MS Dr O. Fisher. Printed Samuels, pp. 29–31.
Addressed: To | Mr Richd Shackleton | att | ⟨Killcullen Br⟩idge
Postmarked: MA|24. MS badly torn.

Dubn May 24th 1744

Dear Dick,

I am now (and think in that posture thou beholdst me write) sitting at my own Bureau with Oh! hideous, Burgersdiscius, on one hand, and

[1] *Faerie Queene*, IV, ix, ii, 8–9.

[2] Burke's younger brother Richard (1733–94), who was still attending Ballitore School. It is convenient, and now a regular practice among Burke scholars and biographers, to call him 'Richard Burke, Sr' to distinguish him from 'Richard Burke, Jr' (1758–94), Edmund's son.

your two Letters[1] not to say agreable Favours on the other, and to follow the old Proverb, first come first serv'd, I shall first take into Consideration yours of the 15th Date, where after Diligently following you thro' each Paragraph till I come to the Conclusion I shall fall foul on your other and give it just the Same treatment, therefore, to begin.

I understand by your favour which with the highest reverence I received Last h[oly]day by the hands of the Nuncio of her μως σταρν'δ Μασυ[2] that the Theme I proposed to you being of the complex kind to use Burgy's Language, has therefore slipd your outward intellects which you allegorically call your Pocket which if I was ⟨minded⟩ I could prove by Logical instruments. And You for that reason ⟨adv⟩ise me to get Printed in Mr Faulkner's Paper[3] an advertisement of yours bidding a reward I confess far too Great for the Loss, for the said complex Theme, and I would follow your Direction but that The paper is already Burden'd with too many Triffles. Sir you mistake me in saying that I was not shock'd at your Departure, 'tis True I told you that I did not faint &c. but certainly I must have died, did I not fortifie myself with Such a Stock of Stoick Philosopha which The reverend Epictetus has arm'd me with for he has fairly convincd me that if I get a Thrashing its nothing to me it only afflicts my σομαδιον. If my friend Departs its nought to me, for no one can hurt me but myself. Such is the Character of Epictetus to whom you owe the Life of your friend. As to the Lectures as soon as I received your commands I went to M. Herbert who assures me that that course is not yet finished. But I am determind not to take him at his wor'd and would have waited on Mr Booth[4] to Day for I was at the College but that the Organs of my internal intellects were so replete with Divers Ideas both simple and complex that I entirely forgot it, yet Dear Dick may assure himself that I will not neglect by any means his Directions which give both to receive and perform such great pleasure. I will go before I seal this to Anglesea Street if I have the Least time and make Diligent enquiry Concerning the Course of the Lectures and hope to satisfie you for my neglect.

Well done, O brave, a noble resolution, worthy th'affair, and worthy

[1] No letters of Shackleton to Burke survive earlier than one dated 21 October 1766.

[2] A puzzling phrase; Burke was probably given the letter by a servant or pupil (female). 'Most starv'd Master' could mean Shackleton, whom Burke describes (letter of 11 June) as sickly-looking.

[3] The *Dublin Journal*, a bi-weekly published by George Faulkner (*c.* 1699–1775), Dublin's foremost bookseller. A squib in the issue for 18–21 August 1744 sounds as if it had been inspired by this passage of Burke's letter. It refers to 'Neddy-Booby of Trin. Col. Dub. remarkable for carrying his Ideas in his Pocket'.

[4] John Booth, a popular lecturer in Natural Philosophy. Shackleton attended his lectures in Dublin the following spring.

the Great resolver, Never Look Burgy in the face! By Jove th'thoughts divine, The Blackγυαρδ stuff, the hoard of exploded nonsense, the Scum of Pedantry, and the refuse of the Boghouse school-Philosophy, I assure you I stink of that Crabbed stuff as much as any vile fresh in the Uni. and I believe it will ruin me in my next Exanimation, Cujus animus meminisse horret, tactuque refugit.[1]

Well, now for the next, you desire me to shew my father The Barbers note[2] which Dirty bit of Paper cost me 2 pence, and will when he comes home, for he is abroad now, so I can return you no answer as to that, but I would have you if you think convenient stay till he comes that way which will be about the middle of next month and agree with him there in person. As to the next part be fully assur'd that no Labour of mine (for such is no Labour but a pleasure) shall be wanting to gain you the Desir'd intelligence. The affairs of your State I find are still moving in the Same orbit constant, Dirimis Ædificat's and such Like Crotchets running in his μασυ'ς Brain tho' I am fully persuaded that the Dining Room Tables will become retrograde.[3] I wonder that the French Count[4] and you have been so peaceble of Late, not that I doubt but you hate with all your hearts, for since the Great Quarrell in which he utter'd this Haughty Declaration, Py Chath, or Chath Tham me Bloeth. I vil Broke your Nhose you saunh of whoor. The ambitious views of this Potentate are very Plain, but I am not very Sollicitous about the Peace because I find he and his Great Ally Josy Deane[5] were Like to come to Broken noses on it, as for master Deane no one will impute it to want of Courage that He Did not fight but being very conscientious, and much afraid of the Vαισκοατ resolv'd Like a good Christian to take the Law of him. Its I protest a sad thing that a man cant give his own Little πεγγυ α ιερκινγ but telltale Brats must come into the world to say hi he, Dady was[6] Playing with mammy the other Day, its a D— of a thing—what does he pay his πεγγυ wages for if he καντ πεγγ 'ερ when he pleases.[7] However since I cant have the Pleasure of being there to tap the groaning ale and drink a safe uprising to the Woman in the Straw I hope you'l do it

[1] Which to remember, the mind shudders and draws back; see *Aeneid*, II, 12.

[2] Richard Burke (d. 1761) practised law in the Exchequer Court in Dublin. He is mentioned in the Ballitore MSS as giving legal advice to Shackleton's father. The 'Barber' whose note he was to see may be William Dillon, mentioned in Ballitore MSS as a local barber.

[3] The passage is mysterious. Shackleton's interest in astronomy, touched upon in several of the letters, was evidently a subject for raillery.

[4] MS: Court. Samuels's emendation of Count is plausible, as Burke seems to be speaking of a single student. Samuels (p. 30 n.) guesses the student to be Lewis Aimée, who entered Ballitore 20 January 1743/44. See below, letter of 14 July (p. 31).

[5] Joseph Deane entered Ballitore School 30 October 1742.

[6] MS: was was

[7] Burke is referring to a Ballitore scandal more fully discussed in his letter of 26 June.

for me. D'observe⟨ ⟩e Friend, never use that black-guard way of saying a⟨...⟩ the bottom of your F⟨...⟩

that I'm wi'd with read
always use for I tell
'em too short so I cer
I can tell you that
P.S. My Brother is w'you
verse nonsence with him
Bawn to me if he is goin
misd which will rot if they'l
Left behind him.

Blank for the Lectures.

When I had wrote thus far I went to th
but Mr Booth was not at home so I dep
wrote o'Monday till Thursdays Post. Tho'
day when I was informd that the Last Cour
ther began the night before, and that the sa
perform'd in this Course as were in the form
ones to be added. ⟨ ⟩day. I am ut

To RICHARD SHACKLETON—29 *May* 1744

Source: MS Dr O. Fisher. Printed *Leadbeater Papers*, II, 7–9; Samuels, pp. 33–4.
Addressed: To Mr Richd Shackleton at | Ballytore | Per Killcullen Bridge.

I can impute your Letter but to two Causes, the one want of a Subject to write on, and the other bad humour or the Spleen, which begot, as I suppose the scolding or jarring that runs thro' your Disagreeable favour or rather is the Very essence of it, and I assure you that if I had the Least Time to spare I would search your favours and would certainly find something which I would take δαμναβλυ ιλλ and afford me a subject Very proper to shew how excellent I was in the Thersitical way. Enough for this, proceed we now to take notice of the ⟨rem⟩aining Part of your favour. I find that the all con⟨quer⟩ing Power of Death is continuing to manifest itself among you, and that you have accompany'd to their Last Habitation a couple of your Neighbours, and the Next we shall hear of is alas! how can I say it Poor Mr B—[1] ah! how uncertain is human glory! how unstable the Greatness of mortals! to Day they are exalted high surrounded with Pomp and glory, to morrow they fall by

[1] A dog. One gathers from the last sentence of this letter that Shackleton had asked Burke to send him poison with which to dispose of the animal.

the hands of unrelenting Death (oh what a victim) Low, Low, into the cold and melancholly grave! Poor B— who could equal thee in the Chase, thou wert the faithful Servant indeed, thou wert the only Solace of thy Master in all his afflictions. When he sees thee dead how will he tear his hair, curse the Day of his Birth and wish to die. I must too, I think, sign the Death warrant, but seriously I would not have you kill the Poor Beast for the fault of his brutal Popish-Hugenot Master. I will however send the Thing if you will. Indeed I'm heartily Sorry for poor Mr Noel,[1] because I wish'd him well on the score of his innocence, and that nothing hinders but that we may be so, or worse ourselves one time or another; and I wonder that he should so entirely give himself over to Despair for a thing that is no ways out of the Common road of Life. To morrow, my Dear Dick, when you are performing that agreeable Task, of forming the hands of the fair to express in an pleasing manner by the pen the soft Ideas of their Breast, think, I say think (and forget your pleasures a while as you let loose one friendly sigh) that I stand examination before a Parcel of old Fellows whose business is to examine and cross examine me, then pity, and let your Pity draw one Sigh a Tribute to your Friend, which will cheer and animate my heart. I will the Next Post after the receipt of your answer to this, give you a full account of my Manner of spending my Life because I have small time Now—so conclude your

sincere friend

E B

May 29th 1744

When you send the Carman do not tell him what it is for nor send any Letter by him, for I shall take care of every thing.

To RICHARD SHACKLETON—9 *June* 1744

Source: Ballitore MSS. Printed *Corr.* (1844) I, 1–7; Samuels, pp. 34–7.
Addressed: To | Mr Richd Shackleton | at Ballitore. | per Killcullen-Bri⟨dge⟩.
Postmarked: IU|9. MS torn.

Dubn June 9th 1744 N B Dated.

Dear Dick

You find me as good as my Promise, in sending some more of my Rhimes to Trouble you, and what I said to you in a former favour that I am Like the rest of my Brother Pettifoggers, you find now to be true.

[1] Samuels suggests (p. 44 n.) that 'Mr Noel' was probably Felix O'Neil (*c.* 1713–*c.* 1787) who had been an usher at Ballitore School and who entered Trinity College 3 June 1733. See below, letters of 29 June [1744] (p. 23) and 5 April 1751 (p. 109).

What I send you here is a Day of my Life after the manner I usually spend it, I have put it in Verse for 2 Reasons, the Chief and principal of which is to engage you to answer it Like manner, and the other is that the Subject being in itself dry, and barren, and of course no pleasant reading, I have laid out what ornaments I could spare on it, (in the small time I have to do any thing) for your amusement, thus far by way of Proem or Preface. Proceed we now to the matter in hand.—And to begin —

Soon as Aurora from the blushing Skies
Bids the great Ruler of the Day to rise
No Longer Balmy Sleep my Limbs detains
I hate its Bondage, and detest its Chains;
'Fly Morpheus, fly, and Leave the foul embrace,
Let Nobler thoughts supply thy Loathsome place,
Let every Dream each fancy'd joy give way,
To the more solid comforts of the Day.'
See thro' the Lucid Substance of yon glass
Sols radiant Beams enlighten as they Pass,
Dispel each gloomy thought each care controul
And calm the rising tumults of the Soul!
See how its rays do ev'ry thought refine
And fire the Soul to raptures half Divine!
Led and inspir'd by such a guide I stray
Thro' fragrant Gardens, and the Pride of May,
Sweet Month! but oh! what daring Muse can give
Words worthy thee, and words Like to Live!
While each harmonious warbler of the Sky
Sends up his gratefull[1] notes to thank the high
The mighty ruler of the world below,
Parent of all, from whom our blessings flow:
Teach me O Lark, with thee to greatly rise,
T'exalt my Soul, and Lift it to the Skies,
To make each worldly joy as mean appear,
Unworthy care, when heavnly joys are near.
But O my Friend, the muse has swell'd her Song
From business has Detaind you quite too Long.
Avails my Morns Description ought to you
Who Morn and even in perfection view?
And now the Sun with a more piercing ray
Advises me I must no Longer Stay,

[1] MS: gratefulll

All dull with mournfull heavy Steps I go
The unwilling town receives me entring slow.
Returning home I natures wants appease,
Then to the College fate your friend conveys:
But here the Muse nor can nor will declare
What is my work and what my Studies there
'Tis not her theme, she still delights to sing
*The gently rising mount and bubbling Spring
But oft amid ⟨the⟩ Shady Parks I rove
Plung'd in the Deep ⟨rece⟩sses of the grove,
While Oh! embroild beneath the trees I Lye
Fann'd by the gales that voluntary fly!
O would some kinder genius me convey
To these fair banks where Grieces waters stray![1]
Where the tall firs oershade his Christall Floods
Or hide me in the thickest Gloom of Woods!
To bear me hence far from the City's noise
And give me all I ask the Country's Joys!
Now Sols bright beams grown fainter as he goes
Invites the whole Creation to repose,
Each bird gives oer her note; the Thrush alone
Fills the cool Groves when all the rest are gone.
Harmonious bird, daring till night to Stay!
And glean the Last remainders of the Day!
The slowly-moving hours bring on at Last
The pleasing time, (how tedious was the Past!)
Which shews me Herbert; he since thou art gone
My sole companion midst the Throngs of Town.
By the foul river's Side we take our way
Where Liffy rolls his dead dogs to the Sea,[2]
Arriv'd at Length at our appointed Stand
By waves enclosd, the Margin of the Land,[3]
Here once the Sea with a triumphing roar
Roll'd his huge billows to a distant Shore,
There swam the Dolphins hid in waves unseen
Where frisking Lambs now crop the verdant green,

* Helicon and Parnass [Burke's note].

[1] To Ballitore.

[2] See *Dunciad*, II, 259–60:

To where Fleet-ditch with disemboguing streams
Rolls the large tribute of dead dogs to Thames.

[3] Burke's evening walk was eastward along the Liffey to survey the harbour improvements Dublin had carried out a few years earlier.

Securd by mounds of everlas⟨ting stone,⟩
It stands for ever safe, unoverthrown
Firm while it bears upon its flinty ⟨breast⟩
The force of warring Storms, and swelling ⟨crest.⟩
Neptune indignant thus to be confin'd
Swells in the waves, and bellows in the win⟨d;⟩
Raising in heaps his pondrous watry Store
Hangs Like a mountain oer the trembling Shore,
Now, Now he bursts and with a hideous Sound
That shakes the Strong foundations of the Ground
Dreadful with complicated terrors falls
Discharging vengeance on the hated walls
The walls secur'd by well-compacted Stone
Repel the Monarch with a hollow groan.
Tis here we sit while in joint prospect rise
The Ocean, ships, and city to our eyes, [the North Wall [Burke's note]]
Enchanting Sight! when beauteous Sol half way
Merges his radiant body in the Sea,
And just withdrawing from our mortal Sight
Lengthens the Quivering Shadow of his Light.
But now inspir'd by what exalted Muse
What Lofty Song, what Numbers shall I chuse?
Or how adapt my verses to the theme
Great as the Subject, equal, and the Same?
Or how describe the horrors of the Deep,
Lull'd into peace and Loftiest waves asleep?
Not een a breath move oer the boundless flood
So calm, so peaceful, and so still it stood?
The Sun withdrawn, and the clear night oerspread
In all its starry glories 'bove our head.
While moon pale empress shines with borrow'd Light
Fills the alternate throne and rules the Night,
And other worlds descrying earth afar
Cry, 'see how Little Look's yon twinkling Star.'
It is not mine the glorious view to sing
These mighty wonders of th'almight King
But let my Soul in still amazement Lost
From thought to thought, and maze to maze be tost.
The adventrous task a Muse Like yours requires
That warms your Pen, and fills your breast with fires.
Thus far the muse has in a feeble Lay

Shew'd how I spend the various hours of Day
The Story placed in Order by the Sun
Shews where my Labours ended where begun.
this, What? Rhimes again! does
er me with his nonsense? this is
is, and mine among the rest, they wont
write, 'tis with a design to please, but they
n their views, they are odious to those t⟨...⟩
appear amiable, but does not this cure em
per, No, by no means, tho' the effect be taken away; the Cause still remains, Rhiming Like Love is, ⟨nullis⟩ medicabilis herbis,[1] nor perhaps the effect neither, for tho they please no one else they are sure however to please their own vanity. To this ascribe the foregoing which I insist that you will either answer in Verse by an account of your manner of spending your own Time, or that's true, you may Burlesque mine for Im sure it deserves it, either would be agreeable to your

s—e F—d
E BURKE

Here I send you a mottly Piece
of Verse and Prose mixtum gatherum.
To be taken after a walk
to the New road, to whet your stomach
⟨to⟩ be taken to digest what you got in Meeting
Like Sweetmeats after Solid food.
(Or Rather Pickles).

To RICHARD SHACKLETON—11 *June* 1744

Source: MS Dr O. Fisher. Printed *Leadbeater Papers*, II, 15–18; Samuels, pp. 37–9.
Addressed: To | Mr Richd Shackleton | at Ballitore | Per Killcullen-Bridge | 1st.

Dublin June 11th. 1744. 12. Clock with[out]
knowing any of your Astronomical
Devilments[2]

Returning yesterday from the College I met my fathers Clerk going to the Post office and thither with him I went, and with the utmost pleasure

[1] Curable by no herbs. Burke seems to be imitating two lines of Ovid:
Me miseram, quod amor non est medicabilis herbis.
Heroides, v, 149;
Ei mihi, quod nullis amor est sanabilis herbis.
Metamorphoses, I, 523.

[2] Presumably Shackleton made a display of his astronomical learning in dating the (missing) letter to which this is a reply.

received your 3 agreeable favours, so that without your Calculation I can[1] inform you that they blest my hands in due time, but unluckily (as such usually attends me) I opend your Last one first in which I perceiv'd—but now Let us omit it until its proper place where we will treat more fully of it. I am pleas'd to hear that your aunt[2] and Sister[3] arrived safe at your mansions I had not the ⟨satis⟩faction of seeing 'em before they went, tho' ⟨I can't⟩ attribute it to myself as I was at Fletchers to enquire for em, but the Birds were flown, I therefore left the Coushod[4] with Slater[5] but here since I mention him it wont I hope be amiss to give you an account of those I met the Day I went there, and by way of an Appendix the State of their affairs; but now I was just going to invoke some sacred muse who should in a pompous stile adapted to the greatness of the Subject describe the manner in which the State of their affairs lay: but I wisely considerd that you should think all I say spoke metaphoricaly and so not beleive a word of it; therefore I am resolved to confine myself to the Strict truth of the Narration.

As I came from fletchers: in Thomas Street by the Market house, who shou'd I meet? you woud not guess if you were thinking this Hour? guess if you can without Looking any farther—Josy! what Josy? why Josy Delany. Him I met in that juncture with no better cloathing than his Μαςυ'ς old waistcoat which he wore so long in Ballitore: exactly in the same cu[6] that he was there in all things about him, except a Basket full of some wooden things or other which he carried under his arm: veterem agnovit amicum,[7] we knew each other at first sight, after mutual salutations Questions about friends at Ballitore &c, &c. I asked him whether Dublin air agreed with him? (these were ⟨his⟩ words) Very indifferently repliys Josy, why so Josy? here he answerd nothing for a good while, at Las out it came—sure I'm marryd! to whom pray? to a Girl of this Town? where do you Live? in Dolphins Barne Lane. Thus we parted he look'd very thin and melancholy so it seems his affairs are but in a bad Situation the Waistcoat he ware was at Least 5 or 6 inches too wide. But now I come to what troubles me sincerely, and to him I think the most unfortunate of the 2 tho not in the poorest condition, I mean slater, poor Johnny! where now is that Liveliness sprightliness

[1] MS: I can I
[2] Mrs Daniel Barnard, *née* Mary Wilkinson (*c.* 1689–1767).
[3] Elizabeth Shackleton (1732–66).
[4] No meaning has been found for this word. Burke signs his letter of 21 June 'Coushod'.
[5] John Slater entered Ballitore School 3 June 1738.
[6] By 'cu' Burke seems to mean 'dress' or 'appearance'. The Oxford Dictionary gives 'Humour;...frame of mind' as one meaning for 'cue'.
[7] He recognized an old friend; see *Aeneid*, III, 82.

or even madness that was so agreeable in all your sportive actions, which render'd so diverting your every thought your every Word! O the Devil! no, no, not such a word to be got now from him, but a most dejected melancholy and sadness, I met him In the Street where indeed I think he could scarcely walk so pale of a yellowish paleness, I scarcely ever thought he could be. I went with him to the Shop, he spoke very little and that exceeding Low and faint. I ask'd him was he sick, he answerd, no, but he did not speak his mind. I beleive if his Condition does not be speedily mended he will not live a haff a year. For he is a mere Shackleton and has a very sickly Look. And this may be I think attributed to his Devil of an Aunt of whom I will give you when I see you next a full description of. I observ'd upon this that those who are most Lively and mad that way are usually quite sunk and dispirited in adversity as he is the most dispirited Lad I ever saw. But not ⟨to⟩ Detain you longer with a long digression equally disagreeable to us both for you cant but be grieved for poor Johnny as I am, I'm sure, if the first part concerning Josy was something Comic You have the Tragic in the Latter.—And to return to your favour

'Hills vales and Rocks with splitting Io's ring
Io Ricarde, Io Pean sing.'[1] So the 2 Boobies[2] have Left Ballitore, as they did Edenderry as it's probable will soon quit Portarlington. And then where the Devil will they go: their Travels are thus. The Boobies finding france too hot for 'em retird to Holland, from thence to London, thence to Dublin, thence to Edenderry, thence to Ballitore thence to Portarling— and where next.

To Richard Shackleton—[*circa* 14 *June* 1744]

Source: MS Dr O. Fisher. Printed *Leadbeater Papers*, II, 18–20; Samuels, pp. 39–41.
Addressed: To | Mr Richd Shackleton | at Ballitore | Per Killcullen-Bridge.
Postmarked: IU|14. *Endorsed:* June 14 | 1744.
MS repaired. Half a dozen words restored in another hand.

No malicious person, no sprite deceived you under the Borrowd name of your Friend, the Letter you say you got Under my Name was originally intended for my Brother so that will serve for an Apology for it, I have just made an Epigram on that for I think an excellent one may spring

[1] See Dryden and Lee, *Oedipus*, IV, i.

[2] Probably two of the French students at Ballitore; the rest of the passage suggests that they were Huguenot refugees. There had been a large colony of Huguenots at Portarlington since the end of the seventeenth century (see Grace Lee, *Huguenot Settlements in Ireland*, London, 1936, ch. VI).

from it but because I think the point which essentially constitutes the Beauty of writings of this kind was not justly plac'd I shewd the malice of my teeth to it. I am sorry I could not hit it for your amusement but It cant be help'd. It is a pity it was not the Hands of a better ⟨...⟩s. I perceive by the Date of your Letters that you ⟨are a⟩ great proficient in the Noble Science of Astronomy. I could hardly understand it for a while and indeed I think you're highly to be commended for your application to it. If I were to speak about it you are so well vers'd in all its Parts that you would perceive a thousand Errors in one Sentence, and as you are so well acquainted with all the Beauties of the Heavens I call em beauties, for beauty consists in Variety and uniformity and is that not abundantly shewn in the Motion and form of the Heavnly Bodies? What grander Idea can the mind of man form to itself than a prodigious, glorious, and firy globe hanging in the midst of an infinite and boundless space surrounded with bodies of whom our earth is scarcely any thing in comparison moving their rounds about its Body and held tight to their respective orbits by the attractive force inhærent to it while they are expended in the same space by the force of the Creators Almighty arm! And then Let us cast our eyes up to the spangled Canapy of heaven, where innumerable Luminaries at such an immense Distance from us cover the face of the Skies! All Suns as great as that which illumines us, surrounded with earths perhaps no way inferior to the Ball which we inhabit! and no part of the amazing whole unfilld! System running into System! and worlds bordering on worlds! Sun, earth, moon Stars be ye made, and they were made! the word of the Creator sufficient to create universe from Nothing; Pursue the Noble Task A nobler theme was never Sung.

'O may some heavnly Muse place you upon
The Lofty Tops of Tow'ring Helicon
Remove the mist that clouds your mortal eyes
Discover all the secrets of the Skies
Shew you these orbs that man has never seen
Of Longest Tubes assisted by the ken
While the great view in harmony Divine
You sing assisted by the tuneful 9.'

This shall be my form of Prayr till I hear from you again and receive these Strains with which the Divine Mantuan declares he was so enamourd.*

* Virg Georgick B II. 475 viz Poetry and astronomy. Me vero &c [Burke's note].

Herbert has desir'd me to beg of you to write to him and to keep up your old Correspondence and he says he would write 1st if he had any time for he goes to School every Day and attends at other Times a shop full of Business however if You will favour with a Hebdomadal Line he will contrive a way to answer it rather than be deprivd of your agreeable correspondence

Your sincerely affectionate
Friend E BURKE

What if you should send some 8 foot Rallery too!

To RICHARD SHACKLETON—21 *June* 1744

Source: MS Dr O. Fisher. Printed *Leadbeater Papers*, II, 20–2; Samuels, pp. 41–2.
Addressed: To | Richd Shackleton att | Ballitore | Per Killcullen-Bridge.
Postmarked: IU|⟨...⟩I.

The first part of this letter is elaborately ironical. Shackleton had addressed his last to Edmund Burke 'Esquire'. Burke replies as a man of station condescending to a social inferior.

Dublin June 21: 1744 Thursday twixt 2 and 3 from my own Bureau: you are hereby order'd to Date your Letters from the place you sit

Honest Dick

That Letter of yours came by post to my hands, and if I could spare time on such business I don't know but I might answer it particularly, but as I have affairs of much consequence to trouble me As you know being wholly taken up with attending one thing or other (which it is not material to tell you) since my Election, it were needless to inform you of more than that I am well as are all here, and that I desire you to be Diligent in ⟨your⟩ Business, take care not to let people lavish my substance, ⟨mind⟩ the Hay, and inform me how the Harvest goes on, w⟨hethe⟩r they will be well able to pay the Rents this year, and whether your wife spins better, for the Last I received was extraordinary ill. Take care once more, be diligent and you shall see the Effects of my munificence (an Old Coat or so) and on the contrary if you turn out idle or Dishonest be sure to feel the Marks of my highest Displeasure i.e. to be reducd once more to the wretched condition my extensive Charity has taken you out of. I wrote more than indeed I intended but because I find you careful and honest I grant you this favour extraordinary and hope that you will not grow conceited on it, nor assume airs that dont become men of your condition for this and all the numberless favours and kindnesses heaped on you by

your imperious and haughty
Master
EDMD BURKE Esqr

Answer this with humble Submis⟨sion⟩

Tell tom Lawless that if I dont hear a better account of him than heretofore he must no longer hope to have the honour of being my Servant.

The foregoing I wrote as I am an Esquire, but this I address to you as I am your sincere Friend plain N:B, and therefore I beg one favour of you, that is to Burn the Letter that I sent you about J:B.[1] and to inform me whether you shewd it to any one. I once more desire you to commit the Paper to the flames for Reasons I will tell you when I have next the pleasure of seeing you which I hope may be shortly.—The Error (about Dicks Letter) was insignificant and I thought at first the mistake was mine, supposing I had directed both to R:S: and on that foundation I built the Ep[igram] but was mistaken and If it were right (for not liking I tore it in Pieces) I cant remember a word on't. I met Mr Ramsay[2] twice walking about the College he lookd miserably and told me he had got no place. I saw Sands[3] when I went Last to receive your Letters and he got one from you and I was Luckily at hand to testifie the truth of Your asserting that the mice eat the Books in your own Bureau.

As to the Muse's being fled, I beleive it is a sham to deter me from compelling you by the Authority you have invested me with, to write such a Poem as you Order to do. I would not however have anything forc'd: write Burlesque if you will. I am sure you have an ample Subject, in so bad a piece as that I sent you. And if you have a mind for a Little more of the Muse's company you must not Study so hard, omit it for a few Days for she's a whore that hates hard Labour of any kind.

Now I have Stuffd my Devil I can write no more but that I am

Dear Sir
your Exceeding humble
Servant Coushod.[4]

[1] Burke's sister Juliana (1728–90). Shackleton paid some romantic attention to her at about this time. See below, letter of 5 July (p. 25).

[2] Possibly Robert Ramsay or Ramsey (b. *c.* 1695), a native of Dublin and graduate of Trinity College.

[3] Edward Sands entered Ballitore School 26 March 1742.

[4] See above, letter of 11 June (p. 16).

Excuse these Dashes for Garrett[1] is boxing, my ears and Desires to give his Respects to you.

* The Star was an asterism you thief![2]

Quid est Logica?[3]

To RICHARD SHACKLETON—26 *June* 1744

Source: MS Dr O. Fisher. Printed *Leadbeater Papers*, II, 9–10; Samuels, pp. 42–3.

Dear Dicks 2 agreeable favours of the 21st and 24th inst lie before me which I will endeavour to answer as well as I can.

Sir the cause of my sending you that high and mighty Epistle proceeded from your stiling me Esqr a title that I have not the Least right but as you the humblest of my humble Servants have been pleas'd to confer it on me I should think myself highly blaemable did I not make use of my just Prerogative. Yesterday about a couple of hours before I received your favour I had the honour of meeting the hon. Edwd Sands Esqr going to see the Militia of this City reviewed (who made a very handsome appearance and in my opinion could deal with an equal if not a superior Number of French)[4] so I saw Mr Sands a little too Late but you may assure yourself as I see him very often I will not fail to make all possible enquiry into the youth. I have considerd fully this affair of Peter and Peggy[5] and the more I consider it the more it surprizes me so that I dont wonder that it affords matter of Discourse to your Town, since it gives me sufficient Speculation unconcernd as I am in the matter and distant from the Scene of action. My opinion of the case I shall here give you: You know when first the rumour of Peters having a Correspondence with Peggy beyond that which subsists between Master and Servant flew about, I began to have a sort of suspicious beleif of the truth of the Story, but as Peter exerted himself strenuously in his own Vindication which joind to the winning behaviour of the man removed all suspicion of his Dishonesty, from me and I beleive most People, thus

[1] Burke's elder brother Garrett (*c.* 1725–65) was at this time living at home in Dublin. He was admitted to practice in the Exchequer Court June 1749 (*Dublin Courant*, 13–17 June 1749).

[2] Samuels suggests (p. 42 n.) that Burke may have used some astronomical figure in his (missing) previous letter to Shackleton; in his letter of [*circa* 14 June 1744] Burke's footnote is marked by an asterisk.

[3] Burke is quoting Burgersdijck.

[4] A review of militia on 25 June was described at length in *Pue's Occurrences* (23–6 June). Britain had been at war with France since the latter part of March.

[5] Peter Widdows, a tailor in Ballitore, and his maidservant. Burke referred cryptically to their scandalous relations in his letter of 24 May.

was the matter hushd for a time, till the wise and all powerfull providence of God thought fit to disclose it (who seldom suffers any wickedness to be long conceald) by the birth of a Child and now to consider truly the affair we shall find that Peter Widdows is really a very unfortunate man, most of the misfortunes which we dai⟨ly⟩ hear complaind of proceed either from our Pride, which suffers us to think nothing good enough for us, or from some imaginary Evils which our Discontedness never fails to shew us in the most glaring colours, but his misfortunes are of another Sort which cannot spring from the abovementioned Scource, he is now accus'd of 2 heinous Crimes, fornication and murder, of which he can not any ways get clear, he is forsaken be his friends and by his folly render'd perhaps too deservedly odious to the world, abandon'd to poverty, to the taunts and reproaches of an uncharitable world, a cripple with a couple of helpless children for whom or himself he can scarcely have the Least prospect of bread.[1] Human sufferings call for human compassion, we should rather Pity the wretched man than condemn him if we consider'd how easily we ourselves yield to vice, how strong temptation and how weak human nature! But I find that I am moralizing, a thing I am uncapable of, and so shall say no more but that the poor innocent Children of the unworthy father deserve greatly to be pitied and as I hear they have Relations in good Circumstances I think they should be so charitable as to take 'em from the hands of that whore who was Lately deliverd. I find Dear Dick is a great Proficient in Physick and has got no small insight into Midwifery, yet there is one thing which I cannot comprehend, you say she laid her hand on the Childs jugular vein before her delivery, how she could do that I cant comprehend. I beg of you as I am well assurd of your friendship I know you wont refuse to acquaint me of Dicks Behaviour[2] whether he is Chang'd for the better or the worse or whether he is as cross as usual, or whether he endeavours to please your father or those put over him &c impartially tell.

Night creeps on apace so that, tho I have abundance to say I must here break off ardently wishing for the happy time in which I shall see my friend with whom I may et novas audire et reddere voces.[3] I hope no longer time shall seperate us than[4] the middle of next

[1] Widdows had had children by his first wife, who died in 1737. Mrs Leadbeater (Shackleton's daughter) describes Widdows's sin, punishment and ultimate fate in terms less tragic than Burke's. She says he was disowned by the Friends 'for marrying his maid servant, who was not a member of the Society', but lived on very tranquilly in Ballitore; 'when bed-ridden he kept a little school' (*Leadbeater Papers*, I, 30).

[2] Richard Burke was nearly five years younger than Edmund.

[3] Again hear and exchange talk; see *Aeneid*, I, 408–9.

[4] MS: that

month and 'till then assure yourself that I will, and always will continue your

sincere friend E B.

Eight of the Clock Tuesday June 26th

1744 Pray send me a full account in your next of the Proceedings of your Court in the Case of P: W: &c. Leturae astronomicae sunt aeternae.[1] The inclosed deliver to Dick with my Love and his Mamas[2] Blessing desire him to write to me. I cant send any thing now.

To RICHARD SHACKLETON—29 *June* [1744]

Source: MS Dr O. Fisher. Printed *Leadbeater Papers*, II, 10–11; Samuels, pp. 43–4.
Addressed: To | Mr Richd Shackleton | at Ballitore | Per Killcullen-Bridge. *Postmarked:* IU|30. *Endorsed:* June 29 1744?

7 o Clock from my own Room just
returnd from the College June 29th —

Since I received Dear Dicks Last favour I happend to meet an old acquaintance of mine very unexpectedly and thus, after morning Lecture as its my Custom I walk with two or 3 of my acquaintance in the College Park, and sitting on the wall chatting about one thing or other I saw one I thought I knew, passing me along with the Park-keeper he stard at me, and I at him when we immediately knew one another to be honest Mr Noa⟨l⟩[3] and N: Burk, he told that he had lost his Testimonium[4] and was coming to get another if he could, told me that your Academy was in a flourishing conditon (in which may it long continue) and that he was in some haste ⟨and⟩ desired me to call on him that Evening, I Charged him not to disappoint me knowing what an odd Sort of a man he was, he did however notwithstanding my frequent admonitions and his as frequent Promises. I met him by chance next morning in Checquer Lane, after taxing him with breach of Promise, he informd me that ⟨he⟩ was going that Minute to[5] the Bishop to be ordaind and was to ⟨pass som⟩e Examination for which he told me he was but L⟨ittle⟩ prepard, but desired me to come to him this day and he would tell me all, I went and was once more disappointed, thus you see I cant give you any certain

[1] Astronomical [litterae—records?] are eternal.
[2] Burke's mother, *née* Mary Nagle (*c.* 1702–70).
[3] Samuels reads 'Noel' and argues convincingly that Mr Noel is Felix O'Neil, who was ordained 28 June (p. 44 n.; see above, letter of 29 May, p. 11). A 'Parson Noel' is mentioned in the Ballitore MSS.
[4] Candidates for ordination were required to produce the Testimonium of the Divinity School of Trinity College (Samuels, p. 44 n.).
[5] MS: to that Minute

account of him as yet but have I not been too prolix? and related trivial circumstances that I need not? I think I have, and been guilty of the same fault often before, but I wont transgress again and will endeavour to be a little more concise for the future. I cant however help telling you for my Life that I sometimes see M. Ramsay in the College but I shall say no more of him. I must by this send what I hope soon to say by word of mouth I desire to have my best respects to your father whose goodness and care to me was boundless, but I will omit here all I have to say because I shall better express to himself the remembrance I have of all his favours a remembrance which only Death will efface. No I mistake I will never be able to express myself, for when I would tell him the Dictates of a Sincere heart I am dashd: and look more like a Silly calf than a grateful Scholar But Let Dear Dick be assur'd that whatever my appearances may be that I am his sincere friend

E BURK

Desire my Brother to answer my Last Letter.

To RICHARD SHACKLETON—5 *July* 1744

Source: MS Dr O. Fisher. Printed *Leadbeater Papers*, II, 12–15; Samuels, pp. 48–50.
MS repaired with tape. Parts of about forty words restored in another hand.

Dublin July 5th 1744 From my own
Apartment Thursday 1/2 an hour after 12

Dear Dick I hope is convinced that I sit down to nothing with so great pleasure as to write to him, and that there is no enjoyment that I would not most willingly sacrifice unto it, and tho' I must confess my inability to entertain him with any thing which is not triffling I hope he will excuse me when he considers that I buy his correspondence at a dear rate evn at the Price of being ridiculous, which will shew how much I prize it. But this not to the purpose therefore I now proceed to answer your Letters (alias agreeable Faveurs) you hope I am genteel you say and impudent. As to the first I have not the least pretensions, but I really think I have Such a stock of the Latter that I may well say from more of it 'good Lord deliver us,' but I am very much afraid that I never shall be able to attain to that becoming confidence which renders a person so agreeable in all Companies he converses with another thing Dear Dick to tell my own imperfections is, I am quite dumb in mixt company[1] for

[1] In mixed, but not in all companies. Dr Johnson once said of him: 'So desirous is he to talk, that, if one is speaking at this end of the table, he'll speak to somebody at the other end' (*Boswell's Life of Johnson*, ed. G. B. Hill and L. F. Powell, Oxford, 1934–50, V, 34).

there the Discourse is more confind seldom extending farther than news, the weather and Dress which as Mr Addison justly remarks in the Spectator[1] is wonderful considering as ⟨the⟩re are a greater number of persons by, that more Ideas should not start up among em to furnish Topicks for conversation but this I am endeavouring to wean myself from. Never fear my losing your Letter in the College for it would be a terrible thing for me indeed if such a treasonable paper should be found after me besides I am too fond of Dear Dicks letters to expose after that manner by carrying em in my Pocket. I did not hear a word of that affair of Peters[2] at all and I dont beleive there is any such thing. I'll go however this Evening to Mr Gowan[3] and know the Truth of it from him. The things you order'd me to buy I will bring with me when I go towards your Regions. Your Criticism on your writing is both judicius and witty and since you give such hard names to such an excellent piece of Penmanship as yours pray what title will you give mine? And now to conclude the answer of your favour. My Sister alias your Dulcinea protests she will not have the Least compassion on your sufferings or favour you in any Sort unless you act the true Knight errant and obey these few commands[4] which she desires me to give you, and

1st That you immediately take horse attended only with one trusty Squire and go in search of adventures until you arrive at Scarecroania a great island in the Caspian sea where king Chrononhotonthologos[5] keeps his court and when you come there you must without delay march up to the castle the first gate of which is guarded by a Giant with a mighty Club calld Hurlothrumbo[6] him if you pass you go into an open court and thence to another gate which is Guarded by two dread Griffins who stand with open jaws ready to devour you, if you kill these you have free access into the next court in which stand five hundred valiant knights all casd in armour of shining steel and above them in a gallery 150 dire enchanters with invenomd spells all which you must conquer before you can come near the apartment of king Chrononhotonthologos. And even there you must penetrate through 50 thousand Brazen Doors lockd with inexorable Bolts, before you can touch the monarch of

[1] No. 68.

[2] Presumably of Peter Widdows; see above, letter of 26 June (p. 21).

[3] There were two Dublin printers named Gowan: Jonathan (H. R. Plomer *et al.*, *Dictionary of Printers and Booksellers in England, Scotland and Ireland from 1726 to 1775*, Bibliographical Society [London], 1932, p. 387); and George, married to a Quaker.

[4] Burke like a great many boys of his period was addicted to reading long romantic novels of the type ridiculed by Cervantes in *Don Quixote*. Samuels discusses this taste of Burke's in his introduction to this letter (pp. 45–8).

[5] The name of the King in Henry Carey's burlesque *Chrononhotonthologos* (1734).

[6] The name of a burlesque in five acts published in 1729 by Samuel Johnson (1691–1773), a Manchester dancing master.

Scarecroania him you must kill, take out his heart which is[1] hairy and in it you will find a little drop of Blood calld Cupido. This you must put in Phial which is on the summit of a tower in his castle 60 thousand yards high the walls of which are as smooth as Glass without Ladder or Step. You see the Danger undertake it if you will.

2d She desires you to take Ægypt in your way and you will find ranged among the Pyramids 800,000 Millions of valiant Soldiers and 60 millions of Enchanters headed by the Chief magician Kakistopoiomenos of the Square Cap these you cannot destroy for their Number any otherwise than by throwing down the Pyramids upon their heads. After this that your Mistress may see your conquest you must vanquish the giant Poluphlosboiomenos who is 70 thousand Cubits high and has 20,000 pair of Hands and make him carry to her all their heads.

So much for your fine flourish at the end of your favour now I proceed to your Last and inform you that I am perfectly easy on that Score and receive very few set downs. The Letter my father never saw it Lay in the Bureau which is now in my Custody so I soon got it into my hands and burnt it with the rest of my agreeable favours remember me kindly to my good friend Johnny Buckley and his father tell [him] I hope I shall soon have the pleasure of making the panasty with his wax[2] and I think let you and he say what you will it was an ingenious Device what? is there no affinity between wax and Tar? And I am sure Tar is the universal Medcine here notwithstanding the opposition of its Enemy's the Physicians. Does any one in your Villa, or Academy use it?[3] I wrote to Dick about cleanliness. Desire him to shew you the Letter and you will oblige me if you read it to him and take occasion from thence to recommend cleanliness to him. As you Chuse to represent yourself by a considerable man in the republick of Dullness I shall endeavour to exceed you by being king of it and stiling myself C: Cibber Esqr Laur.[4]

[1] MS: his

[2] No dictionary has been found to define 'panasty'. Mrs Leadbeater in describing the Shackleton household in the 1760's, offers a clue: 'There also lived in the family, at this time, an old man named John Buckley, son of Allan Buckley, a shoemaker, to whom Richard Shackleton and Edmund Burke resorted when they were boys, when Edmund used to amuse himself making mathematical figures out of Allan's wax' (*Leadbeater Papers*, I, 41).

[3] Bishop Berkeley's *Siris...Reflections and Inquiries Concerning the Virtues of Tar Water* had been published in April, and had launched a medical fashion in Dublin (see Samuels, p. 49 n.).

[4] In the previous year Pope had put Colly Cibber in place of Theobald as hero of the *Dunciad*.

To RICHARD SHACKLETON—7 *July* 1744

Source: MS Dr O. Fisher. Printed *Leadbeater Papers*, II, 23–5; Samuels, pp. 50–1.

Addressed: To | Mr Richd Shac⟨kleton⟩ | at Balli⟨tore⟩ | Per Killculle⟨n-Bridge⟩. *Postmarked:* IY|7.

Dublin July 7th 1744 from the Usual place past 6 o Clock.

Dear Dick

I receivd both your favours at the Same time i:e: Last wednesday and answered them, and since that am favourd with another which I have now before me and promise you not to forget bringing along with me (for I am pretty sure of going) the things you wrote for. I have your⟨s⟩ I shall never forgive you if you dont send me inclosed in your answer to this—here the Dancing Master interrupted me, how long he staid! how disagreeable were his tunes! because they Delayed me from conversing with Dear Dick. I am not very merry this evening my usual gaiety has forsook me for a while and left me in a serious mood, which naturally inclines my ⟨thoug⟩hts to something melancholly, and among others of the kind that entertaind me now, for I am wholly idle this afternoon, I shall (because I have nothing else to fill up this with at present) pen you down my reflections on a pretty Tragical accident that happend the other day, Mr Harding a Gentleman with whom my father is intimately acquainted,[1] had a Clerk a Lad untainted in his Character with any sort of crime and universally beloved by all that knew him, there livd in the Same house a Servant maid who took care of the Children to whom he had often proposed marriage and was as often refus'd, as he conducted the matter privately no one knew any thing of it, so it was hushd entirely for a while, when a french-man who used to teach his native Language to this Gentlemans Children and who it seems had a higher place in the Girls affections than the Clerk Lands from England; Generous minds would sooner die than gain their ends by a Dishonorable method, he saw that his rival was come to supplant him he scorn'd to manage matters with that low and mean Dexterity that it was in his power to have done a[s] he liv'd in the family, he saw that nothing was left to cure his unhappy passion but Death, to effect which in the greatest despair he went to an Apothecary's shop in Dames-street where he bought as

[1] Burke's father's will (printed in Samuels, pp. 405–7) mentions a debt of 'Six hundred pounds due to me from Ambrose Harding Esq.' Harding was called to the Dublin bar in 1728 (Wilson's *Dublin Directory*, 1766). The story Burke tells of his clerk's suicide is reported in *Pue's Occurrences* for 26–30 June: 'Tuesday Evening last a Young Man, Clerk to an eminent Lawer in Bride Street, Poisoned himself, because a Young Woman, with whom he was in Love, refused to Marry him.'

much white Arsenick as would send him to the other world. To shorten this melancholly Story, the effects of the Poison soon became visible and notwithstanding all the efforts of a family who Labourd heartily for his preservation he died after a great deal of struggling in unexpressible torments. This accident has alterd my Sentiments concerning Love, so that I am now not only convinced that there is such a thing as love, but that it may very probably be the scource of as many misfortunes as are usually ascribed to it this may I think be a sufficient example to shew to what Lengths an unrestrained Passion tho virtuous in itseff may carry a man and with how much craft and sutlety our great Enemy endeavours by all means to work our Destruction, how he lays a bait in every thing, and how much need we have to care Lest he make too sure of us, as is the case of that unfortunate youth.

Amidst this gloomy Prospect of unhappy Love Let me stile myself with a Pure and sincere affection Dear Dick's assured Friend

E B. Give the inclosed to my Brother.

To RICHARD SHACKLETON—10 *July* 1744

Source: MS Dr O. Fisher. Printed *Leadbeater Papers*, II, 25–7; Samuels, pp. 52–4.
Addressed: To | Mr Richd Shackleton | at Ballitore | per Killcullen-Bridge.
Postmarked: IY|14.

Tuesday past one oClock July 10 1744

Dear Dick

I assure you that I think your Treatise on selflove a very curious and judicious piece, which was entirely pleasing to me not only for the lively and natural Lines of poetry (which shone among your morality Like Diamonds set in Gold) but for the Curious remarks you made on that Passion which we vulgarly call love of women, tho' you have plainly provd it to be love of ourselves, but if you had read a little more of that Sprightly Dutch author Burgersdyck he would have taught you to have thrown your Syllogis⟨ms⟩ into a more concise method. Per test Mosvills ageable gai⟨...⟩[1] Miss what do you her there still? and do you teach her to ⟨...⟩? You desired me when I had nothing else to do to sit down and write a great big Panegyrick on Damer,[2] and what did I do? I immediately

[1] Portions of several words have been lost under a seal.

[2] John Damer (1674–1768), heir of Joseph Damer, a wealthy usurer. Burke later wrote some lines upon him, which Prior prints (5th ed. pp. 25–7), dated July 1747.

took Slate and Pencil fell to Scribling not any Panegyrick but a moral treatise forsooth, and I writ of that perhaps 10 or 12 lines but forseeing that I could not do it in Less than 200 lines at least and the muse being in a very bad humour, I left off; here take what I wrote

Almighty Selflove and her Power I sing
Of all we do first mover and first Spring
By her commands I undertake this Song
Be it her care its labours to prolong.
  Let me my friend arrest thine ear a while
Deign on this work propitiously to smile
As your Epistle and well write Essay
Serve as a torch to light me on my way
While I explore wild Selfloves mazy course
And trace the Passions to this common scource.[1]

I utterly detest all sort of Flattery and therefore you must not think that I would in any wise employ the Muse to any such mean ends; I am sorry I ever wrote any such to him,[2] but I am glad that they are now in the Lap of oblivion, I deny not but that the Gentleman has abundance of virtues sufficient to make him lovd and esteem'd by all that know him. Were he a Peer or one who posessd any eminent employment in the State I would think no crime in giving him a little spice of that flattery, but as he is a private Gentleman had he a million a year I should scorn for the sake of the finest presents he could possibly make me to send him a mean Scroll of Lying Verse; if he'd make me any other present, I would be ready to shew my gratitude in plain prose. This morning before I was out of my nest (having Lain longer than usual not being very well) I received your's by Harry Bawn, I have not bought the books as yet but will not fail to bring em with me when I shall have the pleasure of seeing you. Your treatise of Selflove puts me in mind of Popes Ethick Epistles[3] which I lately bought on Herberts recommendation, and I assure you they are very fine. Ill bring them with me too. Give my Love to Nephy[4] and tell him I long to see his sweet face. Who is your Chum?

[1] Between the verses and the right-hand margin of his page Burke wrote 'I intended to send it to you'.

[2] This may refer to an earlier version of the lines of 1747. Burke's father had been employed by Damer in the year 1741 in the sale of a considerable property (advertisement, *Dublin Journal*, 17–20 October 1741). The Burkes continued for several years to have financial relations with the Damer family (see letter at Sheffield, John Ridge to Burke 8 July [1766]).

[3] The *Moral Essays*.

[4] Daniel Barnard, nephew of Mrs Mary Barnard, entered Ballitore School 15 September 1743.

Desire Johnny Buckley to lay by all the scraps of wax he can spare for me to make panasty when I come to your parts.

1 AurengZeb[1]
2 Spanish fryar
3 Popes Ethick Epistles
4 Hammonds Miscella:
5 Gum Sandrick
6 Cottonstones

To RICHARD SHACKLETON—14 *July* 1744

Source: MS Dr O. Fisher. Printed *Leadbeater Papers*, II, 27–9; Samuels, pp. 54–5.
Addressed: To | ⟨Mr Richd⟩ Shackleton | ⟨at⟩ Ballitore | Per Killcullen.
Postmarked: IY|14.

Dubn July 14th 1744 from my usual place almost eleven o'Clock —

I don't in the least doubt but that before this time there has been a Court calld in Dear Dicks breast that I have therein been accus'd, found guilty, and condemn'd to the most rigorous punishments which the Law inflicts on Such crimes, but oh! how vain! and how little to be trusted are appearances! I that Ned burke that perfidious wretch, that criminal who was so deservedly found guilty of that most terrible breach of the Laws of friendship, even so far as to neglect answering his friends favour, and to have no excuse for it but his unpardonable Laziness, what neglect so fair an opportunity of cultivating so delightful and im⟨pro⟩ving Commerce? That ned burk I say that so seeming ⟨unpa⟩rdonable villian is entirely innocent of all the crimes Laid to his Charge he has answerd your Letters punctually and would not neglect doing it on any consideration, but accidents, unavoidable accidents which all the skill and cunning of man could not prevent or forsee, to be short I gave the Letter to my Brother to carry to the post office but he forgot to do it therefore I must send it along with this per to day's post, upon the whole I hope you will

[1] The six items numbered at the bottom of the MS were presumably to be taken to Shackleton when Burke next went to Ballitore. The first four are the books he apologized for not having yet bought: (1) and (2) Dryden's plays *Aurengzebe* and the *Spanish Friar*, (3) Pope's *Moral Essays* (at least a copy for Shackleton), and (4) (probably) Anthony Hammond's *New Miscellany of Original Poems* (2nd ed. 1740). (5) Gum Sandrick or 'sandarac' is a resin used in the preparation of spirit varnish. (6) 'Cottonstones' can only be guessed at. H. M. Matthews's *Dictionary of Americanisms* (Chicago and Oxford, 1951), quotes a late eighteenth-century description of 'what is called cotton stone': 'When it is washed and dried it looks white and fuzzy, and if laid in oil will burn like a candle for a long time, and fire will not consume it.'

be prevaild upon to repeal the Sentence, and your Petitioner as in Duty bound shall for ever pray.

I am glad to hear that you have parted with the noble Chevalier Aimè[1] whose good qualities, engaging behaviour and inimitable politeness has gained him the esteem and love of all those Who had the honour of his acquaintance, I am at a loss whether to prefer the noble sincerity, unaffected love, and noble greatness of soul and goodness of heart, qualities of which this charming youth was possesd of in so eminent a degree, or his agreeable and humble Politeness which gave a lustre and additional value to his virtues and which Render'd him so justly the darling of the people.

Go dear youth, be happy in what ever part of the world you shall range, let the angels who guard the just be your protectors among your Enemies. Let them guard you sleeping and attend you waking and spread their pinions for your Shield, let em convey you midst Nations inhabited by fiercest barbarians, that you may by the innate mildness and sweetness of your Disposition tame their uncultivated morals more sweetly than the Divine Orpheus tho' the woods followed and listned to his Song! Fly genrous Soul from the power of Envy, and you will subdue it, leave those who not knowing your noble qualities despise and hate you for 'em, go forth shew yourself to mankind nor hide from em that light which was destin'd to shine at once the Delight and wonder of the world!

Hah! I think I have pennd the Chevaliers Elogium which I hope will always be a good answer to the Satyrical farewell of my friend and herein I have proved the famous logical Thesis to be a lye i:e: Contraria non possunt simul esse vera sed possunt simul esse falsa. Negatur pars prior Satyra enim Elogio est contraria,[2] and here I fling away my Syllogisms and Devilments that, I was going to make for the Noise I just heard made me go down to know the Occasion and found that my Mother is just after all this Days sufferings brought to bed of a Girl.[3]

I am in haste but not in too much to assure Dear Dick that I am his

sincere Friend

E B

[1] See above, note to letter of 24 May (p. 9).

[2] Contraries cannot both be at the same time true but can be at the same time false. The first part is controverted since satire is contrary to eulogy.

[3] Ellen Burke was baptized in St Michan's church, Dublin, 19 July.

To RICHARD SHACKLETON—15 *October* 1744

Source: MS Dr O. Fisher. Printed *Leadbeater Papers*, II, 29–33; Samuels, pp. 56–8.
Addressed: To | Mr Richd Shackleton | Ballitore. MS repaired with tape; about sixty words restored in another hand.

Arran Quay October 15th 1744

The hurry of Examinations is at length over, and I sit down to write to Dear Dick with much greater pleasure since No business interrupts, or hinders me speaking my thoughts with the freedom of an undisturbed mind.

I am entirely of your opinion concerning being diligent. I know that it's the gate by which we must pass to knowledge and fortune, that without it we are both unserviceable to ourselves and our fellow-Creatures and a burthen to the Earth; Knowledge is Doubtless the greatest acquisition we can make because it is what Denominates us men and as you remark'd is the most essential difference between us and the brute-Beasts. I shall say no more about it, for fear I should be ask'd the question why I dont follow what I so much approve and be more Studious? Perhaps bona videoque proboque deteriora sequor,[1] is applicable to me. I know what is Good like the Athenians, but Dont practise like the Lacædemonians.[2] What would not I give to have my Spirits a little more settled? I am too giddy, this is the bane of my Life, it hurries me from my Studies to triffles and I am afraid it will hinder me from knowing any thing thoroughly. I have a Superficial knowlege of many things but Scarce the bottom of any, so that I have no manner of right to the preference you give me in the first.—As to the second I told you my opinion when I had last the pleasure of ⟨see⟩ing you, I have no relish at all for that sort of Life so[3] that I may say with Cowley If eer Ambition did my &c[4]

What made you stop short in the middle of your discourse? I am sure I should not be displeased at hearing all the praises you could possibly bestow on a belief which you profess and which you believe to be the true and pure Doctrine of Christ, we take different Roads tis true and since our intention is to please him who suffered the punishment of our sins to

[1] I see and approve the good; I follow the worse. See Ovid, *Metamorphoses*, VII, 20–1.
[2] Cicero, *De Senectute*, XVIII.
[3] MS: is
[4]
If e'er Ambition did my fancy cheat
With any wish so mean as to be great,
Continue Heaven still from me to remove
The humble blessings of the life I love.

Cowley, *Several Discourses by Way of Essays in Verse and Prose*, VI, 'Of Greatness'.

justifie us, He will I believe consider us accordingly, and receive us into that glory which was not merited by our own good Deeds but by his sufferings which attone for our Crimes. Far be it from me to exclude from Salvation such as beleive not as I do, but indeed it is a melancholy thing to consider the Diversities of Sects and opinions amongst us, Men should not for ⟨sm⟩all matters commit so great a Crime as breaking the unity of the Church, and I am Sure if the Spirit of humility the greatest of Christian virtues was our guide, our Sects and Religions would be much fewer. Give me leave to add also that since it is our misfortune to have so many different opinions we should not hide our Talent in the earth but exert it with all diligence in the great Affair for the Acomplishment of which we were sent into the world to wit Salvation. God all merciful, all good, has given us a guide, a Talent to direct us in the slippery paths of the world, let us then my Dear friend earnestly and heartily set to work praying the Divine being of his infinite mercy to help us in our Undertaking by the saving and enlightening assistance of his holy Spirit, while we seek what manner of Serving him will most please our great Creator, for it is impossible that all can be equally pleasing to him, who has declar'd that as there is but one God so there is but one faith, and one Baptism. O my friend what so⟨rt of⟩ an account will those have to give who as if they were asleep pass their lives without the least consideration of this, will it be a sufficient excuse for them to say that their intention was to serve God in that way no, no, it is the business of every one to search whether their way be good, and if any man who knows this to be his Duty as there is no Christian but does, if (I say) he willingly neglects this and be found in a wrong way he will not be held guiltless before God. Then, my Dear Dick let us take this into Consideration for indeed it is a Serious affair and worth the attention even of our whole lives and implore the assistance of the holy Spirit which leads into all Truth and endeavour to walk piously and Godlily in the path our great Redeemer has shew'd us confiding very little in our Strength but Casting ourselves upon him who died for us, and with great humility asking his assistance in knowing what manner of serving him will best please him that we may not be in the Number of those whose ignorance is justly imputed to themselves. If we do this I do not in the least doubt but that 'God of his great mercy will guide us in the right road.' I very m⟨uch⟩ approve of the method you laid down for our Correspondence I will as much as I can observe it. I must own that I cant with any freedom write better so you must excuse me in that part. And in point of Stile but I hope to improve in that by Degrees: I do not know to whom I can write with greater freedom and less regularity than to you for as the thoughts come Crouding into my head I cann⟨ot⟩ forbear putting 'em down be they in what order o⟨r disorder⟩ they will. You will excuse me for this and for what ⟨mistakes⟩ and incongruities you may find in my future ⟨letters⟩ because you will beleive that whether what I say ⟨be well or⟩ ill express'd it comes from a sincere heart and f⟨rom one⟩ who is sincerely your friend. God gives me good r⟨esolves⟩ sometimes and I lead a better life, they last for a ⟨time or⟩ so, sometimes more sometimes less and then thr⟨ough⟩ the fickleness of my temper and too great confiden⟨ce in my⟩self I fall into my old Courses, ay often far wo⟨rse. You⟩ see my weakness Dear Dick and my failings p⟨lead⟩ and pray for me, we will pray for one another rec⟨ipro⟩cally: Praise be to his holy name for all things, for every impulse of his Grace he gives me I praise him and trust that he will continue em to me, and make me persevere in 'em. Let us lead the best life we can and ma⟨ke⟩ it our Study to please him the best we can both in faith and works. I could write a great deal more with pleasure. I dare not say you would be tired with reading but that I find my Paper almost gone. —

P: S:'s I would have wrote to you last Sunday as you expected had not the boy being returning with the horses and I thought it a Convenient opportunity of answering your favour and sending a hat and a Couple of books to Mich Kearny[1] from his father. I went to visit him as you desired me and find him no way backward of the Character you gave me of him: I breakfasted with him this morning— Do not forget my Best respects to the Master all whose favours to me and all the advantages I received under his tuition I shall never forget—the same to Mrs Shackleton and Mrs Barnard[2] and my love to Dick tell him I am [in a] great hurry and will write next ⟨opportunity.⟩

To RICHARD SHACKLETON—I *November* 1744

Source: MS Dr O. Fisher. Printed *Corr.* (1844) I, 7–10; Samuels, pp. 59–60.
Addressed: To | Mr Richd Shackleton | at Ballitore | Per Killcullen-Bridge.
Postmarked: ⟨...⟩|I.

Arran Quay Nov: 1st 1744

My Dear Zelims kind Epistle had not been so long unanswer'd by his Mirza,[3] but for the hurry of business which has constantly attended me

[1] The younger Michael Kearney, later a friend and correspondent of Burke. See above, letter of 10 May 1744 (p. 4).

[2] Shackleton's aunt. See above, letter of 11 June (p. 16).

[3] Burke is trying his hand at a letter in the Oriental style. Lord Lyttelton had used the names Selim and Mirza in his *Letters from a Persian in England to his Friend at Ispahan*, London, 1735.

since I receivd it, so that the Post slip'd over unknown to me, but we dont stand on forms and Ceremonies like other correspondents, we know that tis not forgetfulness nor neglect of one another that can make a Gap in our intercourse. The joy of receiving a letter wipes away the impatience of waiting for it. It's so with me and I dare say with you too. I am in a Rhyming humour and I beleive I can express my sentiments to you better in verse than Prose on that head. And so take the best I can make in the time

As when some Cloud in the Æthereal way
Darkens the Sun and robs us of the Day,
Its hated Shadow grief projects around,
And spreads a gloomy horror on the Ground.
With universal Cry all nature mourns
No joys can taste until her light returns.
But when to humble Pray'rs indulgent heavn
A blast to Clear the Troubled Skies has givn,
Each bar removd—With a redoubled Blaze
The golden Sun pours forth his glorious Rays
With dazling Beams the wide horizon shines
Brighter than India covers in her mines:
Mankind confesses joy with new delight,
Drown'd in the Glorious ocean of the Light,
So Souls made one by friendships sacred Band
Possession must by absence understand,
The joys are doubled which we Miss a while
Lost Treasures found with greater Lustre smile—

I must my Dear Zelim beg pardon for having taken up so much of your time with triffles, and promise that in the rest of my Letter I shall treat of some thing of more importance, and first to answer yours. I am of your opinion that those poor Souls who never had the happiness of hearing that saving name shall in no wise be damn'd. But as you know my Dear Zelim there are several degrees of felicity, a lower one of which the mercy of God will suffer them to enjoy but not any thing to be compared to that of those who have liv'd and died in Christ. This is sincerely my Beleif of those, but I assure you that I dont think near so favourably of those Sectaries you mentioned, many of them breaking as they Confess themselves for matters of indifference and no way concernd in the onely affair that is necessary viz:, our Salvation and what a great Crime Schism is you cant be ignorant, this and the Reasons in my Last, (and if you consider) what will occur to yourself together with several texts will bring you to my way of thinking in that point. Let us endeavour to live according to the Rules of the Gospel and he that prescribed 'em I hope will consider our endeavours to please him and assist us in our designs. This my Friend is your advice and how hard is it for me to follow it! I am in the Enemies Country, the Townsman is beset on every side, it is here difficult to sit down to think seriously, O how happy are you that live in the Country. I assure you my Friend that without the Superior Grace of God I will find it very difficult to be even commonly virtuous. I dont like that part of your letter wherein you say you had the Testimonies of well doing in your Breast, whenever such motions rise again endeavour to suppress em, it is one of the Subtilest Stratagems that the Enemy of mankind uses to delude us, that by lulling us into a false peace his conquest may be the easier. We should always be in no other than the state of a pænitent because the most righteous of us is no better than a Sinner. Pray read the Parable of the Pharisee and Publican who prayed in the temple.

You see that I tell you what I think amiss in yours. Why dont you use the Same freedom with mine, do, I beg you because we shall be both of us improved by it.

I have a great deal to say but as this is a holiday and I am going to the College to evening prayr's I must write no more. But defer it till another time. I was going to say something of Natural Philosophy something of which I now read, and as you have lately been studying astronomy I beg you to communicate to me some of your observations and by which we may mutually improve.

To Richard Shackleton—24 *November* 1744

Source: MS Dr O. Fisher. Printed *Leadbeater Papers*, II, 34–6; Samuels, pp. 63–4.
Addressed: To | Mr Richd Shackleton | at Ballitore | Per Killcullen bridge. *Postmarked:* NO|27.
MS repaired with tape. Parts of four words restored in another hand.

Arran Quay Saturday Nov: 24th 1744

I dispatchd the business you were so kind as to favour me with and shall always think myself obliged by your Commands. Kerby[1] has the boots and Spurs safely lock'd up (as I saw,) and therefore thought it needless to remove em, but if you would have em sent to Mr Jacksons[2] or my

[1] (Kirby), keeper of The Churn in Thomas Court, Dublin (letter of Abraham to Richard Shackleton, 30 April 1744, in Ballitore MSS).

[2] Isaac Jackson (d. 1772), frequently mentioned in Ballitore MSS. He was a Dublin printer and bookseller (Plomer, *Dictionary of Printers*, p. 391).

lodgings they shall with the greatest pleasure. It but just this moment came into my head, that you desired me to go to Griersons[1] to enquire about the books, but before I seal this i'll go, and give you an account in the P:S:

My dear friend when last I had the inestimable Satisfaction of his Company, was pleased to appoint a Subject for our Correspondence (you Chose if I remember Astronomy) that might in some measure compensate for this tedious absence we are to endure, and make our Converse as well usefull as entertaining; tho I am sure nothing can come up to the sweet manner of passing our time we proposed but

frustrà Comprensa manus effugit imago,
Par levibus ventis volucrique simillima somno. Virg:[2]

So we have no remedy but Patience, and must endeavour to make it up by our Correspondence tho' I cant think that will answer near so well, for how might we, if we had the happiness of being once more together, mutually ⟨commu⟩nicate our thoughts, our difficulties and our pleasures ⟨in⟩ what we read, smoothing by that means the rugged path of knowledge, and deluding the tedious way by a friendly talk. For I know by my own experience that nothing gives one greater assistance in their Studies, than discoursing of them with a friend who they are sure will rather assist than deride the weakness of some notions they may have while employed in the dark and difficult Scenes of nature sca⟨nn⟩ing her ends and designs and tracing the almighty Wisdom thro' his works.

I have not seen such a flood in the Liffy as is now for some years, and our Cellars as well as all on the Quay are full of water and I like a good Child spent most of the morning sailing on it in a tub, and I beleive I should be at it till now, had not the water grown too deep and an accident befallen me which was this. After having made 2: or 3 pretty successfull voyages into the ocean of our Street kitchen I had a mind to try my fortune in the back sea, but to be short, as soon I enterd it I perceived at a distance 2 bottles in a terrible condition who making Signals of distress I made what sail I could to their relief but lo! my Ballast leaning Starboard sunk me to the bottom. So I was thrown ashore at a great distance from where I founderd, and having chang'd Cloaths my Courage as you may guess being pretty well coold I sat down to write to my Dear Dick. The Society[3] if you remember we had thoughts

[1] The shop of George Grierson (d. 1753), bookseller and publisher (*ibid.* p. 387).

[2] The form vainly clasped fled from my hands, even as light winds, and most like a winged dream; see *Aeneid*, II, 793–4; VI, 701–2.

[3] This is the first mention of the Society Burke and his friends later formed, a predecessor of the present Trinity College Historical Society; see below, letter of 28, 29 May 1747 (p. 90).

of erecting goes on but slowly for as Herbert informs me and I know myself members for our purpose are very scarce and tho we had the number we shall always think it imperfect while it wants you.

The Subjects of the Mod: Hist: 13th begins with Present State of Naples and ends with france: 14th france total: 15 france total.

HERBT[1]

To RICHARD SHACKLETON—25 *January* 1744/45

Source: MS Dr O. Fisher. Printed *Corr.* (1844), I, 11–13; Samuels, pp. 83–4.
Addressed: To | Mr Richd Shackleton | Schoolmaster at | Ballitore | Per Killcullen. MS repaired with tape; parts of about forty words restored by another hand. Some further deficiencies of MS have been supplied from a copy among the Ballitore MSS. Samuels places this and the following letter in the year 1745/6, but without giving adequate reason. Burke's date on this is clear; the following he dates 'thursday 31 Jan', and in 1744/5 31 January was a Thursday. The flood in the Liffey mentioned in both letters is described in the papers of 1744/5 (*Dublin Journal*, 22–6 January; *London Magazine and Monthly Chronologer*, sub 26 Jan., Dublin, 1745, v, pt I, 62).

Dublin Jan. 25th 1744–5

I received your favour the product of ill humour, yet will I endeavour to answer it in the best I can, tho' every thing around me conspires to excite in me a Contrary disposition, the melancholy gloom of the Day, the whistling winds, and the hoarse rumblings of the Swoln Liffy, with the flood which even where I write lays close siege to our whole Street not permitting any go in or out to supply us with the necessaries of Life; yet the joy of conversing with my friend, can dispel the cloudiness of the Day Lull the winds and stop the rapid passage of the flood! How happy was the time when we could mutually interchange our thoughts and pour the friendly Sentiments of our hearts without obstruction from our Lips unindebted to the pen and unimpeded by the post!

No one perhaps has seen such a flood here as we have now. The Quay wall which before our Door is I beleive about ⟨...⟩ foot high is scarce discernable seeming only as ⟨a mark⟩ to shew us where the bank once bounded the Liffey. All our Cellars are drownd not as before for that was but a triffle to this, for now the water comes up to the first floor of the House threatning us every minute with rising a great deal higher

[1] The last paragraph and signature were perhaps written for Herbert as a message to Shackleton. But Herbert's hand is similar enough to Burke's to make it possible too that he himself wrote both paragraph and signature at the end of Burke's letter. The reference is to the contents of volumes of Thomas Salmon's *Modern History or the Present State of All Nations*, a Dublin edition of which was published by George Grierson.

the Consequence of which would infallibly be the fall of the house and to add to our misfortune the inhabitants of the other Quay securd by their Situation deride the poor prisoners while from our Doors and windows we watch the rise and fall of the waters as Carefully as the Ægyptians Do the Nile but for different reasons.

It gives me pleasure to see nature in those great tho' terrible Scenes, it fills the mind with grand ideas, and turns the Soul in upon herself. This together with the sedentary Life I lead forc'd some reflections on me which perhaps otherwise would not have occurrd. I consider'd how little man is yet in is own mind how great! he is Lord and Master of all things yet Scarce can command any he is given a freedom of his will, but wherefore? was it but to torment and perplex him the more? How little avails this freedom if the objects he is to act upon be not as much disposd to obey as he to Command, what well Laid and what better executed Sheme of his is there but what a Small Change of nature is sufficient to defeat and entirely abolish! If but one element happens to encroach a Little on the other what confusion may it not Create in his affairs, what Havock, what destruction! The Servant Destined to his use confines, menaces, and frequently destroys this mighty this feeble Lord! I have a mind to go abroad to Day, my business and my Pleasures require it, but the River has overflown its banks, and I can't Stir without apparent Danger of my Life what then Shall I do, shall I rage fret and accuse Providence of injustice, no, Let ⟨me⟩ rather Lament that I do not what is always in ⟨reach⟩ what depends not on the fortuitous Changes of ⟨this⟩ world, nor the blind sport of fortune, but remains unalterably fixt in the mind, untouch'd tho this Shatter'd Globe should fall in pieces and bury us in the ruin that I do [not] lead a virtuous Life; Let it shew me how low I am, and of myself how weak how far from an independent being, given as a Sheep into the hands of the great Shepherd of all, on whom Let us Cast all our Care for he Careth for us!

My friend will excuse this long and perhaps impertinent discourse because I always Like that the Letter Should contain the thoughts that at that time employ me. If you dont like this method advertise me of it and I shall mend.

It is enough to say I sympathize with you in all your Griefs and really I think your Case Very hard for what more perplexing than to be thought Guilty and at the Same time unable to shew ones innocence. I received your per bawn which I will take notice of. The prayer book is not mine but Mr M[ichae]l Kearneys i'll send it per next opportunity. I think I shall bid my friend a good night and wait to know whether the water will permit me to send this to the post tomorrow.

To RICHARD SHACKLETON—31 *January* [1744/45]

Source: MS Dr O. Fisher. Printed Samuels, pp. 84–5.
Addressed: To | Mr Richd Shackleton | at Ballitore | Per Killcullen.
MS repaired with tape; five words restored in another hand.

My fathers office thursday 31 Jan:
1/2 hour after 12

Dear Dick

I expected to have had the pleasure of a Line or two from you in answer to mine of the great flood, but we who live in such a changeable climate must not be surpriz'd to meet frequent disappointments. Perhaps the Change of the weather has likewise Changed my friend who I hope is no Barometer, oh! I recant. I forgot that I am very much to be blamed on that Score myself but ⟨let⟩ my friend excuse the little sally of my Passion which I ⟨assu⟩re you was grounded on my affection for you. We have a Charming fine day here, (I hope you are blessd with the same) in recompence of all the bad we were troubled with for some time past which did inconceivable damage to those who had any goods in their Cellars, as for us we have receiv'd little or no Damage for as the water soon invaded us it as soon left us, but it is melancholy to see the poor people of the other parts of the town emptying their Cellars a labour not unlike that of some I dont know who in Hell for as fast as they teem out the water so fast does it through some subterraneous Channels return again—You have doubtless heard of Dr Taylor the famous occulist, who gives Lectures on the eye,[1] I have 1 of his tickets and was at his Lecture. Would you have my opinion of him? I think he is an arrant Quack, he is like a posture master in the Pulpit whereon he stands, and I often Lamented he had not the cups and balls his fingers were so nimble I beleive he would have done feats, in short his Lecture was more diverting than improving yet he has perform'd some Cures so that his practice is in my opinion contrary to his words.[2] I have a ticket to attend Doctor Baylie's Lectures on the Civil Law.[3] Take this in good part. Let it put you in a good humour and let it for my sake excuse any poor wretches for this whole day yours Eternally

E: BURKE.

[1] John Taylor (1703–72); he was a trained medical practitioner but discredited himself by pretending to more learning than he had, and by claiming extraordinary 'cures' which often turned out to be temporary. Dr Johnson called him 'an instance how far impudence could carry ignorance' (*Life of Johnson*, III, 390).

[2] Burke wrote a panegyric upon Dr Taylor (printed by Samuels, p. 87, from the Ballitore MSS; there is an additional copy among the MSS at Sheffield [Bk 27b]). Possibly it is intended to be ironical, though the intent could easily be missed.

[3] A course of lectures in law by Dr Hugh Baillie (d. 1776) was advertised in the *Dublin Journal* of 22–6 January.

Johnny McNemara[1] desires to gi' his respects to you and so does Garrett; Jack Baily will soon be in town w' us.

To RICHARD SHACKLETON—5 *February* 1744/45

Source: MS Dr O. Fisher.
Addressed: To | Mr Richd Shackleton | at Ballitore | Per Killcullen bridge.
Postmarked: FE|5.

From my Garrett on arran Quay Dubn
feb 5th 1744 past 12 noon

You have doubtless read of Semiramis, the Scriptures give us the history of Judith who beheaded Holoferness, in short without summing up all the heroines that we meet with in antient and modern history, it will be sufficient to say that I prefer miss Bess[2] to 'em all. How great, how truly noble is a publick Spirit and a generous Love of our Country! Its Scarce possible to conceive what havock that Stern and relentless Tyrant Death makes throughout the Globe, not to mention these multitudes that diseases sweep without noise and hurry to the Grave how many thousands of our brave countreymen fatten the belgick and american plains with their blood. Those breaches and damages that war and sickness make in nature could never be repaird had not that kind and indulgent Sex lent some assistance to help on the work, that noble heroine Elizabeth in particular laying aside all mean considerations of Self interest resolvd to sacrifice all for the good of her Country. I will not compare her to a virgin Queen of her name, tis true she bore infinite toils for the good of her people—Sed quis virtutem amplectitur ipsam, præmia si tollas[3]—she gaind by it immortal fame and reputation, but the most malicious tongues cannot report that of the generous Thornton on the contrary all she can expect is shame and infamy, I challenge all history to shew such an instance of heroism. I am sorry however that the girls of your Country are so much troubled with the dropsy all the remedy I can proscribe for em is to avoid the male⟨s who⟩ doubtless have a most malicious design of poisoning ⟨them⟩ with that disease and I dare wager

[1] Not identified.

[2] The behaviour of Elizabeth Thornton had scandalized the Quaker neighbourhood of Ballitore. A men's meeting at Carlow 6 February, concluding her 'with child by whoredom', asked the Ballitore Friends to 'draw up a few lines setting forth that we don't look upon her to be of our Society, and that we detest such Actions and to sign them and read 'em publicly' (records in Friends' Historical Library, 6 Eustace Street, Dublin). But the facts of the case were not completely established. Abraham Shackleton wrote to Mary Barnard in April (Ballitore MSS): 'A Consultation of midwives have declared that Betty Thornton neither is with, nor hath ever had a Child.'

[3] But who will embrace virtue herself if you remove the rewards? See Juvenal, *Satires*, x, 141–2.

that were they search'd ⟨the⟩ felonious instruments would be found about them.

You have so well described the folly of our Parson[1] that tho I have heard it before from a Gentleman in my Class one Harvey[2] yet is it entirely new to me nor do I wonder at all at his simplicity. I hope this accident will teach him more sense. I am sorry the Gentry of our nation are so depraved, jests upon religion are wicked jests, and in my opinion it was as great an affront on the Congregation (tho they not without reason Laugh'd) as on the Parson.—I long for the Continuation of your favour. Let me have it next post. Monsieur votre tres humble et tres obedient Serviteur.

E BURKE—

To RICHARD SHACKLETON—16 *February* 1744/45

Source: MS Dr O. Fisher. Printed Samuels, pp. 64–5.
Addressed: To | Mr Richd Shackleton | at Ballitore | Per Killcullen-bridge.
Postmarked: FE|1⟨...⟩. Upper left-hand corner of MS has been burnt away —probably by Shackleton to remove the name of the friend who was 'taking Physick'.

Cock Hill[3] Febr: 16th 1744–5
past 4 fine evening recd yours

has been taking Physick some time ago
not what ailment in his Leg or Clap or Pox;
time of his confinement I visited him and
me an elegant account of Mr Booths Lecture
Nature properties, gravity, &c of matter, together with very fine observations of his own on all, so that he is not one of those who go to those sort of places only to see and to be seen, and I am therefore the more apt to believe, the praises he bestows on Mr Booth (as indeed does all most every body that hears him) he informed me that you were to Come to Town, and desir'd me to make diligent enquiry for an Usher, which I have since done but I cannot find any who would engage for the wages the Master usually gives.[4] I have been ⟨to w⟩ait on

[1] The Anglican pupils at the Ballitore School attended church in the neighbouring town of Timolin (Samuels, p. 17); William Aishe (d. 1752) became vicar in 1735 (J. B. Leslie, *Glendalough Clergy Succession Lists* [typescript copy in the Church of Ireland Library, 52 St Stephen's Green, Dublin], p. 204).

[2] James Harvey (b. *c.* 1726) was admitted to Trinity College 5 April 1744.

[3] Burke's father had an office in Cock Hill, a narrow street adjoining the law courts (*Dublin Journal*, 17–20 October 1741).

[4] When proper candidates were ultimately found, Abraham Shackleton wrote Mary Barnard: 'the first has £16 and the other £10 per year' (letter of April 1745 in Ballitore MSS).

M[ichae]l Kearney. I gave him your best respects, ⟨and⟩ told him you were to come soon to Town, he answerd that he would be very glad to see you, and desird to return you the same Compliments. Come then my friend my genius Come along, Let us once more see you, dispel our fears. Let us have Certainty instead of hope, Come banish the night and bring on the Day, O my friend then shall I [be] compleatly happy, then (swift glide the hours and bring on the Glorious Day) shall we as formerly discuss together the Difficulties of our Studies, then—but Oh! how unable am I to express my Sentiments to you on that head, nor if I was wou'd these babes about me suffer me. Let it be sufficient to say that my Dear Dick is well acquainted if possible with the joy such an event gives me. Let me hear from you a monday in the mean time forgive this rascally Letter for it is not possible for me to write a better.

To RICHARD SHACKLETON—23 *February* 1744/45

Source: MS Dr O. Fisher. Printed *Leadbeater Papers*, II, 36–7; Samuels, p. 65.
Addressed: To | Mr Richd ⟨Shackleton⟩ Junr | Schoolemas⟨ter⟩.

Arran Quay Feb: 23 1744–5 past
4 o'Clock

Not guilty, this is my plea to the indictment which now lies before me, and I hope to have a fair tryal before Sentence passes on me, to enjoy at least that happy mark of our Liberty. I am indicted By the name of Edmd Burke &c of feloniously treacherously, and maliciously as not having the fear of God before my eyes, Carrying with me to a place Call'd ballitore ⟨a bo⟩ok the property of M: Kearney and that then ⟨and th⟩ere I the Said Edmd Burke like a false traiter did lend the said book to one of the Servants to the detriment of said M. Kearney his Majesties liege Subject &c. To all which except the Carrying the Book to Ballitore I answer as above.—I am really very much surpriz'd that any of your Girls should have the Confidence to assert such an abominable falsehood of me, the Book if you remember, lay in the room we slept in, and if I dont mistake you read some part of it as did your Sister, But I never lookd into to it after I left it with you much less did I presume to lend it to any one, pray tell me which of the girls says I did. I told M: Kearney that ⟨even⟩ing I brought him the book, to which he answered its very well. However if it be not found I am willing to pay for it. I sent the Belt to Paddy Byrne[1] per dick.

[1] Not identified.

Herbert informs me that booth will give another Course of Lectures before he leaves town and if the Senses conduce to fix any thing in our memory, if they strengthen and clear our ideas, if the Conversation of our friends can make our Studies agreeable, I am perswaded you'l receive the greatest benefit imaginable from his Lectures. I dare say that the Last is one of the motives that will bring you to Town, not to say the principal, if I may judge your breast by my own. You dont forget the Society we propos'd. I hope to see it once more flourish heighten'd and adornd by the presence of my friend, we have slept too long come and rouse us you see how essential you are to our happiness be not then cruel but since you have raisd our hopes to such a degree do not at once depress them.

The famous Dr Taylor still continues to Lecture on the eye and has a prodigious number of auditors, Last night he endeavourd to explode the opinions of the most famous among the ancients and moderns concerning the seat of vision and to set up in their Stead a new Hypthesis of his own, but what it is he has not as yet declared.—Herbert is angry you dont answer his Letters. I beleive I shall subscribe to Booths next Course.

To RICHARD SHACKLETON—[*circa* 5 *March*] 1744/45

Source: MS Dr O. Fisher. Printed *Leadbeater Papers*, II, 38–41; Samuels, pp. 66–8.
Addressed: To | Mr Richd Shackleton | at Ballitore | per Killcullen-bridge. *Postmarked:* MR|5.

Burke's date of 'Feb 30' is very likely a facetious reminder that he had received no letter at all.

Arran Quay Feb 30. 1744 recd yours

I cant say I have much to divert with this day, my Stock of ideas is almost spent with the constant and unthrifty use I make of them, but perhaps you'll say any thing from a friend is wellcome tho it were no more than that he's well not so neither, I should always give my friend the best in my power; and therefore that I may find some thing both to Divert you and employ myself, i'll cast my eyes back to the time when we could find matter enough for Conversation in the enjoyment of one another. I'll revive some of our old Discourses which will recall to our memory the time and place they passd in, and so render em more agreeable by the remembrance of the pleasures we then enjoyd. There is implanted in ⟨man⟩ (Doubtless for a good end) an insatiable Desire of truth ⟨we sp⟩are no pains in search of it, and when have found ⟨it (or)⟩

at least its appearance) we are again as uneasy to communicate the fruit of our Labours to others, there is no one more troubled with this failing than myself, it is against my Nature to see people in an opinion I think wrong without endeavouring to undeceive 'em, I'd willingly win the whole world to my own way of thinking, a failing it is, yet such a one, as with all my efforts I cant get rid of. Let this be a sufficient excuse for what I am just going to say.

We have often discoursed Concerning that part of the Creation calld Brutes, whom you not allow to have reason tis true most people of Late are of that opinion for all the Books I have read which touch on the Subject are on your Side of the Question, yet we are not blindly to follow the Common opinion of the world which is often the most false as is evident from a thousand examples, how justly do we admire at the Credulity and Sottishness of mankind who for many ages without further Examination swallowed down all the Errors and absurdities of Aristotle, and those not the mean and vulgar but even the greatest and Wisest men. I am perswaded that if you throw aside Prejudice the greatest obstacle we meet in search of truth you will upon hearing my reasons incline to think more favourably of your fellow Creatures, for I assure you it's no manner of Discredit to mans reason for others to share it with him, and lest you should misunderstand me I dont beleive that the Souls of Brutes are any way equal to that of man but that their reason is in an inferior or Subordinate degree nor Can it ever arrive at the lowest perfection of mans. Neither am I a Pythagorean to think it a Crime to kill and eat animals, no, they are a Link in Natures Chain and as we serve them so they serve us.

I shall begin with endeavouring to answer some objections which I beleive will take up all this paper and reserve the Proof to another opportunity having already almost transgress'd the bounds I prescribd myself at first. The first and most common objection is that those Creatures act all after the same manner in the Building of their nests, care of their young pursuit after their Prey &c in which they seem to be guided by something greater than reason else they would differ according to their different occasions. But this is impertinent because we build not upon it but freely own and allow it to be performed by instinct which is likewise to be found in men. This being Quite out of the Question Let us hear what is said against me in Chambers's Dictionary[1] under the Article Soul and really I am amaz'd that men of Sense should swallow such miserable reasoning now pray, hear it. 'As to the Souls of Brutes

[1] Ephraim Chambers, *Cyclopædia or Universal Dictionary of Arts and Sciences*, London, 1728.

the Cartesians deny its existence in the sense of the word stripping it of all its powers and faculties, the Peripateticks on the Contrary endow it with most of em.' Now pray attend 'the Cartesians argue that they have no perceptions or notices at all, or that they feel any Pain or Pleasure and that all they do is by the mechanism of their parts.' 'The maintainers of the contrary opinion assert that the appearance of sense caution and Love for their young &c argue that they have reason' 'and its true that all the actions of Beasts plainly express an understanding every thing that is regular expresses it even a machine or watch expresses it'—'all the motions of plants and brutes express it'—'but the intelligence Does not reside in the matter thereof, it is as distinct from the Beast or plant as that which made the wheels of a watch is different from the watch itself.' Now comes the best part if you be'nt already surfeited. 'Thus in Brutes there is neither understanding or soul they eat without pleasure and Cry without pain and grow without knowing it, they fear nothing know nothing, and if they act in such a manner as shews understanding it is because God to preserve them has formed their bodies to avoid whatever may hurt 'em, mechanically. Otherwise it might be said that the vilest insect or smallest grain may be said to have more understanding than the most knowing man. For it is evident that either of em contains more parts and produces more regular motions than we are capable of understanding. Thus does the great Malebranche argue against the Souls of Brutes.' Really these arguments scarce deserve a confutation yet you shall see an attempt towards one in my next. Send me some more objections.

To RICHARD SHACKLETON—12 *March* 1744/45

Source: MS Dr O. Fisher. Printed *Leadbeater Papers*, II, 41–2; Samuels, pp. 68–9.
Addressed: To | Mr Richd Shackleton | at Ballitore | Per Killcullen-Bridge.
Postmarked: MR|12.

Arran Quay March the 12th 1744–5 past five
my Last long unanswerd.

I can attribute your long Silence to nothing but the Dislike you have taken to my Letters in General, or to my last in particular; indeed I was afraid to undertake such a Subject, I could not had I my senses about me, but have remembred how disagreeable it was to you to hear the Defence of an opinion you thought absurd: and doubtless it was my duty to have submitted to your better judgement, instead of vindicating my errors, but if we beleive the Astrophilosophical Sons of Urania, there are times wherein we have not the least command of ourselves but are entirely at the will and pleasure of the Star that then has[1] the Ascendant over us, without control[2] its slaves and susceptible of any impression it is pleased to give us, in that condition I dont in the least question but I was at the time of my writing the last, ill fated, Billet: Leo, or some other of the Bestial Constellations highly affronted at the indignity offerd them of Late of stripping them of their rationality a priviledge ⟨they⟩ have been peaceably in possession time immemo⟨rial⟩ having the Ascendant over me while I held the pen ⟨in⟩ my hand not knowing what to write, they compelled me sore against my will to undertake a Defence of their prerogative against the most learned and judicious of their Enemies (but with what judgement you may Guess) therefore considering my Case, I hope you will pardon me a fault I committed by compulsion and since I am now free from their malign influence and have power of acting as I please I retract all has been said, as I am sensible it offends you, with a faithful promise never to trouble you more with the least mention of so disagreable a Subject. A few days or rather nights ago was demolishd a Convent of which the famous mother Price was Lady Abbess by some of our Scholars who had been ill us'd there,[3] one of em was taken and committed to the Black-Dog[4] but the rest happily escaped they were all the greatest part of this Day before the Provost and fellows on their Tryal which still continues the result of which will be I am afraid the Expulsion of a few and the admonition of most of em.[5] I am Dear Dick yours &c. I have something to say to you of D: Brugh[6] but I have no time.

To RICHARD SHACKLETON—15 [*March*] 1744/45

Source: MS Dr O. Fisher. Printed *Leadbeater Papers*, II, 43–4; Samuels, pp. 69–70.
Addressed: To | Mr Richd Shackleton | at Ballitore | Per Killcullen-Bridge.
Postmarked: MR|16. *Endorsed:* March 15th 1744.

Office, 15th 1744 six, o Clock
recd both yours. the Last just
this moment no sooner

As my father and Mother are to leave town tomorrow I beleive I shant have time to answer yours, and therefore sooner than leave one of your

[1] MS: as has [2] MS: controlll
[3] *Pue's Occurrences* under date of 9 March reports: 'Wednesday Night last a house of ill Fame in Liffey Street was almost demolished by the Mob.'
[4] The Marshalsea Prison of the Sheriff of the City of Dublin.
[5] Samuels (p. 69 n.) quotes from the College Register the sentence passed.
[6] See below, letter of 19 March (p. 49).

most agreeable favours a moment unanswerd i'll snatch this little opportunity from my other Business and have this ready to send by tomorrows post. I am pleasd that you can so readily excuse a fault I was afraid I had commited and, the more because you encourage me to go on by promising to give me your objections and not as some Perhaps would have done, pass me by with a malicious sneer on my ignorance, but you dont use me so you look on my Weakness with moderation, and endeavour to remove it by reason and mildness, you desire me to throw aside prejudice. I do freely and candidly and expect the same from you. Let us not Think that because an opinion is ours that therefore we are obliged to Defend it against all the reason and arguments that can be urged against us it is no shame to own we have been in the wrong, it only shews that we are wiser now than formerly, whereas to persist obstinately in opinion purely because it was ours betrays that we gain nothing by the Length of our lives or at least that we are unwilling to do it.

You tell me in the first of your favours that you beleive it is the Pride of being thought superior to you in understanding that inspires me with such a desire of Bringing you to my opinion. Perhaps its true, our Passions have springs that we are utterly unaccquainted with and tho it might not result from a Pride of being thought superior to you (as it did not) it might from the Pride of having such a one as you to back my opinion. [Do] not think that I take at all ill that you advise me for my good, just the Contrary you could not do me a greater pleasure, and I beg you to continue it from time as you see convenient. But not to digress to far from the Subject I beg you before we proceed any further casting aside all partiality carefully 1st to examine the actions of these creatures as the best rule we have to judge whether they have reason or not. 2d to observe what agreement theirs have with those of men and then to search their Causes. 3d to compare both observing this grand Maxim that like Effects spring from like Causes. I might here enumerate more methods but leave it to your better Judgement and maturer considerations only desiring you (contrary to the manner of most Disputants) not to be more intent on opposing me than finding out the Truth, therefore reason with yourself resolving neither to be guided in it by the general opinion either of the Learn'd or illiterate for I had much rather you should be brought to my way of thinking by your own reasoning than mine. Goodnight Dear Dick

yours E:B

To Richard Shackleton—19 *March* 1744/45

Source: Dr O. Fisher. Printed *Leadbeater Papers*, II, 45–7; Samuels, pp. 70–1.
Addressed: To | Mr Richd Shackleton | at Ballitore | Per Killcullen-Bridge.
Postmarked: MR|19.

March 19th 1744–5 from my Study,
make yourum nextum longerum

Dear Dick's favour of the 17th instant brought me the agreeable news, of his fathers having hired an assistant,[1] together with the Character of said assistant, who by your Account of him seems to be an agreeable Companion, and in my opinion a dangerous one too, (at Least to your friends in town whom probably his alluring Stories, and gilded Lies (as he is traveller) will make you forget, and entirely take away your desire of visiting this ⟨metr⟩opolis, to the Great Loss, and Grief of us who stile ourselves your friends, and promisd so much satisfaction to ourselves from your Company). But Jove avert the omen!

What I have to tell you concerning Brugh is this. Sometime ago (if you remember) you wrote to me that Annesly Hughes,[2] had told you that Dick Brugh, had been cautiond with a vix[3] to which I answered, I believ'd it was a groundless calumny, but th'other day I casually ask'd one in his Class, whether they knew such a man he answer'd, he did know such a Sizer, that he had Stood 2 Examinations, for which he receiv'd wretched Judgements, and that at the 3d he was Cautiond since when he never appeard at the College, this is the reason I suppose I could never see him.

I am of your mind concerning some of our discourses, whether God can sin, it looks a little presumptuous, but yet is useful, in Case a person should be attackd on that side. The Syllogism you made however is faulty, or is rather a Sophism, I will (I beg pardon for my presumption) shew you its faults, because I will a⟨fter⟩ make a few observations. God cannot Lye, to Lye is to sin therefore God cannot sin. The Sophistry is apparent, for Lying is not every Sin, tho all lies may be Sins, and tho a man may be a murtherer, yet it does not follow that he's a thief or that because he's no thief that therefore he's no murderer. The next piece of Sophistry in it, is a Quibble on the Word Sin, for in the minor proposi-

[1] Abraham Shackleton told Mary Barnard (Ballitore MSS, letter of April 1745) that he had hired 'James Mitchell (who has been twenty years in France) for Latin and French'.

[2] Annesley Hughes entered Ballitore School 5 November 1741; probably he is the Francis Annesley Hughes (*c.* 1727–*c.* 1775) who entered Trinity College 2 July 1743, though his schoolmaster is given as a Mr Noales, not Mr Shackleton.

[3] Presumably a warning that his work was barely (Lat. *vix*) satisfactory. The Trinity Examination Book records under the date of April 1744 a 'Vix med. for Greek' against the name of Richard Brough, Sizar; under 6 April 1745 'Bruffe' is cautioned for neglecting Greek Lectures, and under 8 July 1745 is put at the bottom of his class for the same fault.

tion its taken particularly, and in the conclusion universally, i:e its extension in the one is restraind by the Particular Lie, and in the other is quite undetermind. Neither is the conclusion the effect of the Premisses which is necessary to the Syllogism's being good. Pardon me Dear Dick for accusing you of Sophistry. We must Bear with one another when we tell our Errors, but perhaps you only made it to try me, did you?

There is nothing a man abhors more than being deceiv'd, and really nothing often may do him more prejudice, and therefore nothing he should endeavour more to avoid, what multitudes of things conspire to deceive, and Blindfold a Person in the pursuit of truth! He imbibes prejudice with his milk those he converses with impose on him, his Parents, and the very Books he reads, (which should be the repository of truth and reason when banishd from the rest of the world) all join to hoodwink his reason and make him see with eyes not his own, but above all himself hc has in that respect no greater Enemy than his own person, how fond are we of our own opinions of our own reasonings, purely because they are ours, the product the Children of our own Brain! How often do we invent false reasonings and Arguments to uphold em, and who to deceive but ourselves. I think its like the Story of the Miser, who is reported to have robbed himself when he could not use so any one else. You would hardly beleive this had you not experienc'd it in yourself just so it will be with me in our Controversy for if I should happen to fall in to any fallacys I will deceive myself as well as you; Conscious of the goodness of my Cause I long the Tryal Should come on and desire You to prepare your evidences and let it begin either next post or the one after how does my father and mother when did they arrive with you &c.

To RICHARD SHACKLETON—4 *July* 1745

Source: MS Dr O. Fisher. Printed *Leadbeater Papers*, II, 47–9; Samuels, pp. 75–7.

Dubn July 4th 1745 from my Bureau

Dear Dick

B: to S.

Your neglecting to answer our last letter has very much surprizd the whole Club, but as we are fully assured that you are incapable of forgetting your friends, we impute your silence to some laudable study that's too precious to be laid aside for answering our Nonsense, which like a noisy intruder breaks in upon that Charming Retirement, which seems to take up so much of Your thoughts, and which you have so finely described in a former favour—if that be the Case, Had I more than Captain Brazen's[1] Confidence, (which you will allow is pretty sufficient for one) I could not presume to Disturb you now, but come frankly and ingeniously (as a certain author has it) confess, that you have still some hankering ⟨som⟩e Desire for this smoaky Town, if not, I am sure you are a great ⟨co⟩nvert as ever I knew, true indeed, I never knew an admirer of the Town as you have formerly been, express himself in such raptures on purling streams, shady groves, and mossy banks, so that I am apt To suspect your last visit to this City has given you at once a surfeit of the Town, and a true relish for your rural pleasures—but where am I running from the matter in hand, in short we are a little angry, and take this as a reprimand, that we may have no more occasion to accuse you.

Another reason for troubling you with this (without the rest of the Club) is a report that John Dillon was lately killd in a Duel by Maurice Keating Junr[2] and that the provocation was given by Mr Dillon who would not be reconciled tho M. Keating endeavourd all that in him lay to pacifie him, representing to him his having a Wife and Children which himself had not, and the Value which himself and father[3] had for him yet nothing but by a Bullet to be sent out of the world would Satisfie the other which mr Keating very obligingly gave him, but as such Stories are usually told to the disadvantage of the Slain I wait to hear the account with all its Circumstances from you.

My third, Last, and principal reason, is to let you know, that your advice was taken, and has succeeded in effects as you foretold, for this day, judgements were given out for Last examinations, and I have got the præmium in my Division,[4] and perhaps would have answerd better than I did, had we not had—Wilder[5] for our Examiner, please to acquaint your father with this, for I am persuaded that as My improvement while under his care gave him pleasure, it will continue to do so tho' I am not immediately so at present, and that this account wont be disagreable.—

[1] A character in Farquhar's *Recruiting Officer*.

[2] Shackleton would have known more about this duel than Burke, since it took place at Ballitore 29 June (letter of Abraham Shackleton to Mary Barnard 30 June, Ballitore MSS). The John Dillon killed may have been the John Dillon who entered the School 13 August 1739; Maurice Keating Junior (d. 1777) was acquitted on a charge of murder and later became an M.P. for Harristown (T. U. Sadleir, 'County Kildare Members of Parliament', *Journal of County Kildare Archaeological Society*, VII (1912–14), 409–10).

[3] Maurice Keating (1690–1769), M.P. for County Kildare, 1727–60.

[4] 'Burke' is listed in the Trinity Examination Book under the date 4 July among 'Senior Freshmen...entitled to premiums for their good answering last Whitsuntide Examinations'.

[5] Theaker Wilder (*c.* 1717–77), a Fellow of Trinity famous for his eccentricity. He was Goldsmith's tutor and quarrelled violently with him. Prior says of him (*Life of Goldsmith*, I, 65): 'To such students as incurred his dislike, he proved a bitter persecutor at the public examinations....'

I'll either Chuse the Modern History, or the Spectator and Rollin,[1] what do you think?

Bosswell[2] has got the fellowship, and since there is in effect a fellowship vacant, for a living worth £670 per ann in the College gift has lately fallen so that your friend Macguire[3] may go in again this Living is worth the Acceptance of a Senior fellow so that I'm afraid Pellisier will resign.[4]

Jack bayly t'other day desired me to ask your Lowest price for a Couple of Boys that he says are intended for your School. I told him, twenty four pound a year two Guineas entrance and a Couple o' pieces of Plate but he was not Satisfied with that but desired me to desire you to Desire Mr Shackleton to acquaint me with your price. The Boys names is Ways,[5] and beleive me to be every *Way* and all*ways*

your friend
E. BURKE

Remember my love to Dick and tell ill write to him next post.

NEWCOMEN HERBERT *and* EDMUND BURKE *to* RICHARD SHACKLETON—16 *July* 1745

Source: MS Osborn Collection. Printed Samuels, pp. 72–3.
Addressed: To | Mr Richd Shackleton | at Ballitore | Near Killcullen Bridge.

Herbert writes his date in the Quaker manner. If he follows Quaker practice carefully he counts March the first month of the year; '5th month' is July (see above, letter of [*post* 14] April 1744, p. 1, n. 5).

Dub: 16th 5th mth 1745
In Councill behind Cox's Counter[6]
Present
Burke, and Herbert,
absent
Sisson[7]

[Herbert begins]

We the two former must first make excuse for the silence of the Latter whose diligent search after mamon prevented his attendance on this

[1] Probably one of the several forms taken by Charles Rollin's *Ancient History*, first published Paris, 1738–41. Prior (2nd ed. I, 22) claims to have seen a prize book Burke had been awarded 'by the college for proficiency in the classics in 1745'.

[2] John Boswell (*c.* 1722–50).

[3] Probably James McGuire (b. *c.* 1717) who had tried unsuccessfully for a fellowship the previous year (*Pue's Occurrences*, 15–19, 19–22 May 1744) and again in June 1745 (*Dublin Journal*, 4–8 June 1745).

[4] He did not. The livings of Rahy and Clondehonkey—those Burke refers to—were given to Dr John Obins in December (*London Magazine and Monthly Chronologer*, Dublin, 1745, V, pt I, 367; pt II, 646).

[5] No students of this name appear in the Ballitore School list.

[6] Newcomen Herbert lived with his uncle, Cornelius Cox, a merchant on Essex Bridge, Dublin. (See above, letter of [*post* 14] April 1744, p. 3.)

[7] Richard Sisson (d. 1767), in whose later career as a painter Burke took considerable interest. See Walter G. Strickland, *Dictionary of Irish Artists*, Dublin and London, 1913, II, 355–6. No evidence has been found for a statement of Strickland's that Burke and Sisson lived together in Paris 'for some months'.

occasion ⟨the⟩ necessity of which he humbly submits to your consideration and prays your absolution.

Secondly This might have gone sooner had it been wrote that it was not is owing entirely to the first mentioned Gent: who Nicky like here at my Elbow would persuade me to tell you it was not his fault, but I more conscientious am on the point of refusing this reasonable request, when he takes up a Glass and with an Emphatical Here's to ye, and at once staggers my resolution, so that I am now determined to speak as he dictates. What shall I say Burke—eh? Why tell him from me (Burke) that I think it entirely unnecessary to make any Compliment at all to a Friend and Member of the Club, for he will beleive his Friends uncapable of neglecting him, had not unavoidable necessity interposed, which was really the case.

So much by way of apology—or lies if you will—proceed we therefore to answer your Epistle. Why then we did receive it, but have not the least inclination to furnish matter for another pen by the imitation of so much Heroism as you therein relate.

[Burke begins]

All the news we have to entertain you with or our City affords is a most surprizing revolution which has lately happend in the Celestial regions over us, The glorious Luminary whom Mortals Call the Sun, the gods Apollo had for many revolutions of this our terrestrial Globe, shone with resplendent beams and gladend every heart with the hopes of approaching plenty and the reign of yellowbearded Ceres, each vocal bird in harmonious strains exceeding far the Labourd notes of Herbert's or Lafluys[1] flute which oft the obedient Logs and blocks to follow nod as if a ray of bright Apollos light unknown before had piercd the obdurate cover of the vast profound or Late beleived void there only found, and could your Soul such thought conceive with journey unfatigued, Laborious herbert, first was known to tire and grieve the tedious Longitude of Road, when lo the Saddend face of heavn lowerd, the cloud compelling hand of Jove had gatherd all his mighty store of grumbling thunder and loud piping Storms while in a fierce rage of hail fire and Rain he pours his rapid veangeance on this guilty Town, or in the more Laconick Stile of Rosicrusius The Weather is very Bad and the Streets dirty.

[Herbert begins]

Why indeed it needed explanation, or else I ⟨am⟩ affraid you would never have fathomed this vast abyss of profoundity, but from the whole

[1] Not identified.

you may easily colect the vast fertility of our Brains who disdain to write any thing intelligible but however this is only a flight of our Cogitative faculties and we may perhaps descend into the road of Common Sense the next time you hear from

HERBERT
and BURK[1]

To RICHARD SHACKLETON—16 *August* 1745

Source: MS Dr O. Fisher. Printed *Leadbeater Papers*, II, 50; Samuels, p. 78.

Ballidufe[2] Augst 16th 1745

I never had the name of a very punctual performer of my promises (to my shame I say it) but now I shall be quite outlawd; the very next post without any restrictions was the word, but I beleive I have mist a good many, and if I may be allowd to make any excuse I could tell you in my own Defence, that since I left you I had not time sufficient to write one Line, this may seem a Paradox to you but when I explain myself ⟨I⟩ am perswaded you will not only beleive what I say but pardon me for my seeming forgetfulness, .1°. Then, I did not come into this Country near so soon as I expected be⟨ing⟩ delayed by the Gentleman who traveld with us, who was sickly and after I arriv'd the races of Mallow took up 3 Days of my Time[3] after this the Assizes of Cork during which I had scarce a moments time on my hands call'd me from performing my promise to you in due time,—but, why do I trouble myself with making triffling excuses when I cant even now perform my promise as it is Just now supper time and the boy who is to Carry this to the post is teizing me to give it him. I therefore send you this as an excuse that I may use no preamble to what I will send next post without fail yours

E: BURKE

[1] Herbert has written Burke's name as well as his own.

[2] In County Cork; residence of some of Burke's maternal relations. (See below, letter of [17 April 1759], p. 125.)

[3] Races at Mallow were advertised to take place 29 July to 2 August (*Dublin Journal*, 16–20 July).

To RICHARD SHACKLETON—15 *October* [1745]

Source: MS Dr O. Fisher. Printed *Leadbeater Papers*, II, 51–2; Samuels, pp. 78–9.
Addressed: To | Mr Richd Shackleton | at Ballytore | Per Kill-Cullenbridge.
Endorsed: Oct: 15th 1745. *Postmarked:* OC|15. MS cut.

Dublin October 15th 1744

The hurry I have been In since I came to town prevented my performing the promise I made of writing to you at my arrival, and tho I am sensible that this is not the first excuse of the kind I have made yet As [it] is the most comprehensive one I could think of I hope you will accept of it and impute it not to my Neglect &c.

Your Letter I deliverd to sisson with whom I have not often been since I had the pleasure of seeing you, he seems very well inclind to begin a Correspondence with you and told me that he was thinking to write before he saw your favour which he promisd to answer per the next post so the triumvirate is again Compleat, and the place[1] vacant by the departure of our friend Herbert[2] is filled[3] up by a successor who I hope will make us some amends for all the good qualities we lost in our departed friend. Indeed in Herbert we have Lost every thing that could [make] a person agreeable for besides a sprightly Wit of which he was Master he had a particular evenness of Temper ⟨which⟩ made him appear Constantly the same and hinder'd us ⟨from⟩ those disgusts that a thorough Knowlege of those we have a regard for without it gives us—but we have lost him and must endeavour to fill the Chasm with new acquaintance new friendships. This is the way of the World and valuable a Treasure as a friend is, none is so soon forgotten none (at least in experience) so easily made up for—ιος φυλλως γενεη, τοιηδη ⟨και⟩ ανδρων.[4] Sisson continues still a Little melancholy as I told you I dare [say] you will find a spice of it in his Letters.—I am going to excuse my self for Leaving off[5] so soon, and beleive me I say the truth when I tell you that Downright necessity makes me[6] conclude hastily your friend.

Your Last frank did not pass—[7]

E BURK

[1] MS: the place the
[2] Herbert had left Ireland for the East Indies early in October.
[3] MS: fillled
[4] 'Even as are the generations of leaves, such are those also of men'; see *Iliad*, VI, 146.
[5] MS: of
[6] The four following words and the signature are cut off, but restored by another hand.
[7] In Burke's hand.

To Richard Shackleton—2 *November* 1745

Source: MS Dr O. Fisher. Printed *Leadbeater Papers*, II, 52–3; Samuels, p. 79.
Addressed: To | Mr Richd Shackleton | at Ballitore | Per Killcullen bridge.
Postmarked: NO|2. MS cut.

Novbr 2d 1745

I am at a very Great Loss to Account for your long Continued Silence, I did not Think my Dear Dick would so soon forget his freind in whose Company and whose Correspondence he used to express some pleasure in those happier times; Sickness could not have been the Occasion, I should have heard that from my Brother, what then should be the Occasion? I beleive I have discoverd it at length, palld with the long and insipid Converse of a person with all whose inmost thoughts you are acquainted, the Depth of whose notions you have tried, the fund of whose knowlege you have exhausted, with whom had you Corresponded any Longer you must have heard nothing but tedious repitions of the same treadbare stuff which has exercis'd your Patience so often before, you have resolved to make yourself Amends by entring into a Correspondence with some one who will have something new to divert you something solid to improve you in whom at once you may find an agreeable friend and wise instructor, and I beleive you are not deceivd in the person you have pitched on, you have had a part of his Character from me before, and I have not the Vanity to suppose myself any way his equal, far from Condemning your Conduct in this point I highly applaud it, and am glad you had resolution enough to shake off a troublesome Correspondent who might have been Some obstacle to your converse with a person in whom I am sure you will find all you have mist in me, as for myself I have not the confidence to expect you would often write to me all I shall desire will be a line once in a twelve month perhaps to let me see that tho I am unworthy your Correspondence that I still retain a place in your friendship this shall be enough for me who am still[1]

To Richard Shackleton—12 *November* 1745

Source: MS Dr O. Fisher. Printed *Leadbeater Papers*, II, 53–5; Samuels, p. 80. MS repaired with tape; parts of about twenty words restored by another hand.

Arran Quay Novbr 12th 1745

Silent, Solitary, and pensive, I sit down to answer your Letter, and tho I am not so much Master of my temper as to say I shall be quite

[1] Signature cut off.

Cheerfull, yet I hope the remembrance of the many gay tho innocent hours we have passd together which the present Occasion recalls will inspire me with Sentiments proper to keep me from being dull or tedious to you.

I am not at all Surpriz'd at what you tell me of———. I always thought his Character bore a near resemblance to Tigellius which Horace so finely and humourously describes in his 3d Satyr. Inconsistancy ⟨seem⟩s the Basis of it, as it gives rise to a Great many Friendships, so is it the Cause of their dissolution. In vain do we complain of ill offices, neglects, and Jealousies, whom we love for novelty, use will make us hate, and then excuses will easily be found. The very actions which were at first so very delightfull will now perhaps be the Very Cause of the misunderstanding. In vain do we endeavour to keep up such a friendship, all the endeavours or good Sense in our power will only Serve to heigten our Dislike.—This is the Case I beleive of ⟨...⟩ your cast of Friends. You are yourself (pardon the freedom of a friend) a little touch'd with this foible, as I have experienc'd, but C———[1] is nothing else: what variety of Characters have I known in him, when we were Schoolfellows tir'd of being diligent and Sober, long, with the Least provocation he fell into odd Courses, from which as little indulgence reclaim'd him, till he thought proper again to Change. He was in short, every thing by fits and nothing long[2]—when he left School, (at a time when the little follies which shew themselves there, if not worn out by goodsense, influence our Conduct and frequently much to our disadvantage). The Same inconstancy shewd itself at the University. The Letter he wrote your father was very inconsistent with the Account you had afterwards of him. When he had some years applied himself with a great expence to such Studies as qualifie a man for a Physician, he suddenly changes his mind and prepares for the Army and ten to one but he may turn himself another way yet. Thys far I have I beleive accounted for your falling out with your friends—but as I have said something concerning friendship and given one of the Causes of it perhaps I may some time else say something more of it for I have not time now. Pray if you have any hints on that or any other head let me be favourd with them in your next. You remember the preliminaries. Pray let me have a place in your affection, You never are out of mine.

EDMD BURKE

[1] Not identified.

[2] Dryden's *Absalom and Achitophel*, I, 548.

To RICHARD SHACKLETON—7 *December* 1745

Source: MS Dr O. Fisher. Printed *Leadbeater Papers,* II, 55–6; Samuels, p. 81.
Addressed: To | Mr Richd Shackleton | at Ballitore | per Killcullen Bridge.
Postmarked: DE|7.

Dublin Decbr 7th 1745

It would have given me the greatest Concern to have been depriv'd of the pleasure I flatter'd myself I should enjoy in your Company, were it not allayed by this reflection that I should only see you Constantly in the great grief you gave me a Specimen of and which was not in my power to dispell, and to tell you frankly my mind, much as I value that happiness I confess I would not buy it at so dear a rate, I would much rather not see you at all, than with a Disturbed mind.—I am surpriz'd at the malice of your Enemies which how you have made I confess I cannot understand, you must be strangely alter'd sure—but there are those who do mischief for mischief Sake, and are directly the reverse of those to who honour it is said, that they love Virtue purely for her beauty, these love malice for its deformity. Nor has their ill will ended in abusing you to your face there are some things reported here not much to your advantage, did I say not to your advantage? They are really so full of malice and folly as no one that has the Least acquaintance with you Can give any Sort [of] Credit to them. Why may not I be a partaker of your Sorrows? I am sure if you had any Secrets they are with none safer, I am very desirous of knowing a full account of your troubles, how they begun and how they ended, this will be a Satisfaction to me and perhaps an ease to your self, the accounts you gave me in town were very short and unsatisfactory, and really I did not beleive you would Leave us so soon. How did you rid your self of your Enemys? How does your father take all this? I am afraid but indifferently.—I beleive the way you fell into those troubles was by making too[1] free with such as Pope describes the Politick and wise,

> Men in their Loose unguarded hours they take—
> Not that themselves are wise but others weak.[2]

[1] MS: to

[2] *Essay on Man,* IV, 227–8.

To RICHARD SHACKLETON—28 *December* 1745

Source: MS Dr O. Fisher. Printed *Leadbeater Papers*, II, 57–9; Samuels, pp. 81–2.
Addressed: To | Mr Richd Shackleton | at Ballitore | per Killcullenbridge. *Postmarked:* DE|28.

Dublin Decbr 28. 1745

If to sympathize with you in all your afflictions and to bear a friendly part in your Sorrows could in any measure alleviate 'em I beleive I might claim the merit of being no indifferent Comforter but alas! we every day feell how little that avails and how much greater we will find the number of those that will insult us in our miseries than those will pity us.—I know how ill qualified I am for a Comforter and how disagreeable and unsuccessful an Office it is in itseff therefore I will say nothing on that head, nor will I send you to books or the Sayings of Philosophers, a mind at ease may improve, by them, and Seneca will infinitely please in Speculation but Experience will inform you better than I, that in time of affliction they are but Sorry Comforters, the tide of Passion is not to be stopp'd by such feeble dams, even the Thoughts of reasoning with it adds new flame to the fire and gives an additional vexation 'tis because most of these books are written in a reasoning and expostulatory manner, and Sorrow is a passion and a strong one and must not immediately be oppose'd by a direct Contrary which is reason the product of a Calm and undisturbed mind. Indulge your grief I am sure you have great occasion the malice of your Enemies has set every Engine at work to torment you and no one can so well see the Effect they have worked as yourself for you alone have felt 'em but at the Same time beleive me their power is not inexhaustible the Storm has been at the highest and must soon end, the time is come or is at hand when all will be over and your former peace be restored as fully or more so than ever,—when small missfortunes afflict us or when we receive them with intermission it is impossible to judge when they will end but when they fall upon your head at once and that in the Strongest manner and When there is nothing left to Compleat your misery Cheer up your heart hope the best for then it will surely end happily—There was a great man highly favourd by his prince and posses'd of all that is usually thought to Constitute the happiness of a man, but as all human affairs are full of instability, his Enemies plotted against him and made him suspected by the king as one who had bad designs against his person, by degrees he lost favour and fell Step by Step from his grandeur at Last his Enemies prevaild so far as to have him entirely disgrac'd—his Estate Confiscated and himself cast into a loathsome dungeon destitute of food and raiment other than the prison Commons bread and Water in this dismal Condition he was inform'd his Death was decreed. And while he lay under Sentence the keeper took Compassion on him and brought him a Vessell of some food he was very fond of. As it lay by him while he prepar'd to eat a rat ran by and fell into the Victuals a Creature to which he had a Violent Antipathy. Immediately he wiped his eyes bathd before in tears for his misfortunes and Cast away all Sorrow—now Says he my misfortunes are Compleated now they end next day the king sent for him convinced of his innocence restord him into favour and punishd his accusers —

To RICHARD SHACKLETON—16 *January* 1745/46

Source: MS Dr O. Fisher. Printed *Leadbeater Papers*, II, 59–60; Samuels, pp. 82–3.
Addressed: To | Mr Richd Shackleton | att Ballitore | per Killcullen Bridge.
Postmarked: IA|16.

Dublin January 16th 1746

Dear Dick

I am greatly afraid that my prediction has proved false—indeed I shall never trust again to any general observations if it has since I am taught by your example after having given you so much time to recover, that your troubles should still torment you—are you really still in sorrow? pray answer, pray keep me not any longer in this perplexing uncertainty. What Misfortune can be so strong, so lasting to make such an impression on you—it may be some Consolation to you, to impart them and their cause to a friend who tho' he could not remove might partake them—Solamen miseris socios habuisse doloris[1]—Would you take a sincere advice? pray indulge yourself in a little gaiety—I am afraid that by reflecting on your Crosses, other melancholy thoughts have come on you, and those have introduced others and have thus beyond measure lengthend out your Sorrows. The mind as the Spectator excellently observes communicates a tincture of its present disposition to every thing it Converses with as a man in the yellow Jaundice fancies every thing is yellow.[2] Thus when melancholy overspreads the mind we place every thing in a disagreeable view and indeed to Consider, and reflect on

[1] 'A solace to the unhappy to have had companions in grief.' There is a discussion of the source of this line in *Notes and Queries*, 6th ser., I, 132.

[2] Probably from Pope's *Essay on Criticism*, II, 358–9; the reference to jaundice is not in the *Spectator*.

things it needs not that Cast to make them appear disagreeable, Paschal tells us that nothing engages men to apply ⟨to⟩ business or diversion, but to drown thought to hinder us ⟨from sin⟩king into ourselves and seeing in what an unhappy and f⟨oolish⟩ condition we really are[1]—would it be amiss to use this remedy ⟨to⟩ dispell a little of that gloominess that Clouds you, and secured by a good Conscience say with the poet—Tristitiam et metus, Tradam protervis in mare Creticum portare Ventis[2]—the Cure is pleasant and I am sure unexceptionable—as I hope the Storm is now pretty well oe'rblown I wish you would in your answer give me a full account of the Rise[3] and progress of your Troubles, as there is no one wishes them a Conclusion more than your most sincere friend.

If the news is any amusement to you you shall have one every Thursday if the pacquet Comes in.

To RICHARD SHACKLETON—15 *February* 1745/46

Source: MS Dr O. Fisher. Printed *Leadbeater Papers*, II, 62–4; Samuels, p. 88.
Addressed: To | Mr Richd Shackleton | at Ballitore | per Killcullen L Bridge.
Postmarked: FE|15.

Dubn Feb. 15th 1745

I received your favour which I am much concerned to find in the usual Strain—alas how are our Letters Changd of Late? Instead of jests, merriment and Congratulations now they are filled with nothing but the narration of misfortunes and Condolements for them. Not that I am a bit displeas'd at your manner of writing I only lament the Cause of it, the Stile of the heart tho ever so melancholy is more agreeable to me than a forc'd Calmness, which only serves to aggravate your own affliction and keep me ignorant of it—indulge then your Sorrows I beg you in what you write, to me, but pardon me if I am so Curious and impertinent as not to be satisfied with what you have already acquainted me, I cannot thoroughly Sympathize with you, I cannot make your Case my own 'till I am inform'd of its Cause, and tho' the whole narration may be too long for the Compass of a Letter, I beg you'l abridge it omitting no material Circumstance in your next. Conceal not the Villians name who is the Cause of your afflictions that I may always hate the Idea of the wretch who dares betray the Secrets of his friend, is it

[1] Pascal's *Pensées*, ch. XXVI. There is some doubt among modern editors whether Pascal himself wrote the passage.

[2] Sadness and fear I will give to the wanton winds to carry away to the Cretan sea; see Horace, *Odes*, I, xxvi, 1–3.

[3] MS: their Rise

Tr—[1] is it—who is it? fear not to write the whole for no one sees your Letters but I: but Let us wave this—

I Was told t'other day by Rhames[2] that Our old friend Herbert was taken by the french. I was informd Since, that he was retaken and brought into Porsmouth.—I sometimes See Sisson, I told him that some misfortunes had befallen you without mentioning what they were—he seem's much concernd and allways speaks of you with the greatest affection—I beleive he's good natur'd, if So you have a friend more than you expected. There is no Evil I beleive but carries Some good along with it and if you make a proper use of the present, tho it does no more, will give you a little experience and teach you more Caution and reserve in trusting your acquaintance we live in a world where every one is on the Catch, and the only way to be Safe is to be Silent, Silent in any affair of Consequence, and I think it would not be a bad rule for every man to keep within what he thinks of others, of himself, and of his own Affairs. I wish the next account I hear from you may be a good one, no one more sincerely wishes it than he whom you may beleive your friend.

My love to brother. I hope he's a good boy.
My Respects to your father and Mother.

To RICHARD SHACKLETON—26 *April* [1746]

Source: MS Dr O. Fisher. Printed *Corr.* (1844) I, 16–18; Samuels, p. 91.
Addressed: To | Mr Richd Shackleton | at Ballitore | per Killcullenbridge.
Postmarked: A.P|26.
It is not clear why Burke wrote '1745' into his date-line. This letter was written after the defeat of the Young Pretender at Culloden, 16 April 1746. MS has been cut—probably for the signature.

April 26th (for fear I shd forget). 1745

Dear Dick

I received your English manuscript In answer to my Arabian[3] which I hope you have since been able to decypher. I protest when I wrote it I thought that tho' it was not as good yet it was as legible a hand as any in the world. You see how blind we are to our own imperfections. I shall however try to mend it and give you no just Cause of Complaint for the future.—This pretender who gave us so much disturbance for

[1] Perhaps James Trimble, engaged as an usher at Ballitore School the previous year (letter of Abraham Shackleton to Mary Barnard, April 1745, Ballitore MSS). See later reference to 'Tremble' in letter of [17 October 1747] (p. 96).

[2] Probably Joseph Rhames, Dublin printer and bookseller (Plomer, *Dictionary of Printers*, p. 400).

[3] Burke's letter has not survived; he may have imitated oriental script, or he may merely have written carelessly and been rebuked by Shackleton.

some time past is at length with his adherents entirely defeated and himself as some say taken prisoner, this is the most material or rather the only news here, tis Strange to see how the minds of people are in a few days changed, the very men who but awhile ago while they were alarmd by his progress so heartily cursed and hated those unfortunate creatures are now all pity and wish it could be terminated without bloodshed. I am sure I share in the general compassion, tis indeed melancholy to consider the state of those unhappy gentlemen who engag'd in this affair (as for the rest they lose but their lives) who have thrown away their lives and fortunes and destroy'd their families for ever in what I beleive they thought a just Cause.

My friend you put a wrong construction on what I calld indolence in my Letter, it was no more than a simple sloth which indeed hinderd me from doing much good but threw me into no ill action that I know of extraordinary, neither do I think I keep bad Company. I am however much obliged to you for your good advice and if you could without trouble I should be glad you'd continue it advice never comes so acceptably nor is it like to do so much good as from one who has our interest at heart, and which proceeds from a desire of improving not reproaching us. I hope I am Such

yours

To Richard Shackleton—[*circa* 15] *May* 1746

Source: MS Dr O. Fisher. Printed *Leadbeater Papers*, II, 76–8; Samuels, p. 92.
Addressed: To Mr Richd Shackleton | att Ballitore | per Killcullen Bridge.
Postmarked: M.A|15.

In the last I received from you, you complain of my neglecting to Continue our correspondence and I have now a thousand times more reason to reproach you with the same fault. I answerd your favour and apologizd for my neglect in the best manner I could and in as fair a hand, all this I thought was sufficient to induce you [to] forgive me, and favour me[1] with your Thoughts as usual—but I see you think me unworthy your notice—I am sorry for't—but to be serious I cant conceive what can be the reason that our Correspondence is become so slack of late—if our friendship was to be judged by it, I beleive very few would have any great opinion of it—I answer for myself—there is not the le⟨ast de⟩cay of it on my side—absence and time only r⟨ivet⟩ my affections more strongly. I could wish to see things establish'd on their former foundations. I shall not be backward in performing my part towards it, if I have

[1] MS: my

done nothing to make you averse to it. My father has put Dick to School in town:[1] you will send his trunk and whatever things he had to town, he tells me Houlden[2] has the key and some of his books. Desire him to put them into the trunk—and send the key—I saw this day your aunt and Sister for the first time tho I hear they have been Sometime in town. I hear too that the master has been in town but has not been so good as to call to see us—my father is very angry with him for it—I am very je ne scai quoi ish to day probably by staying within all this fine day if I am dull or too sententious attribute it to that—You will wonder when I tell you I have not left off poetical scribbling yet—I have done the other day the latter part of the 2d Georgick O fortunatos &c.[3] into English it was always a favourite part with us, maybe i'll send you it some other time—This is Very badly wrote, but for love of truth I would have excused myself by haste and made my apology accordingly—I shall however mend as I hear from you, but by the by I am in a little haste as Exam. for Scholarships come on next Thursday—all this is but triffling I know, however as they come from a friend and go to a friend I am sure they are excusable. I am with all sincerity

yours unalterably

May I dont know what day 1746—

To Richard Shackleton—[*circa* 24] *May* 1746

Source: MS Dr O. Fisher. Printed *Leadbeater Papers*, II, 78–9; Samuels, pp. 93–4.
Addressed: To | Mr Richd Shackleton | at Ballitore | per Killcullen Bridge.
Postmarked: M.A|24.

Dublin May 1746

Dear Dick

Your long silence gives me the greatest Concern, as I can attribute it to but one of these two accidents either of which would give me a very sensible affliction, namely that you are sick or have forgot me, if the former I heartily wish for your recovery and forgive your Silence, but methinks you might have imployed some friend to give me an account of it, if the latter which I can hardly beleive notwithstand[ing] appearances, I must acquiesce and trouble you no more. If it be not so, you will I hope satisfie me by writing the day you receive this third letter

[1] This move seems to have offended the Shackletons. Burke gives reasons for it in his letters of 1 June and 12 July (pp. 66, 67).
[2] Thomas Houlden entered Ballitore School 10 May 1743.
[3] Burke's translation of the second Georgic was later published anonymously in *Poems on Several Occasions* (see below, letter of [17 October 1747], p. 98); Prior reprinted it 2nd ed. I, 25–8, and there is a MS copy [Bk 27b] at Sheffield.

from me Since I was favourd with the like from you—There is another possible case which I have not mentiond that is you might not have got 'em, if so the Contents of the Last were to the best of my Knowledge, partly the same with this and partly to desire you to send my Brothers books as my father sends him here to School. Let me know in your answer whether your father would have a bank note sent him by post in payment of Dicks bill or whether he would appoint any one here to receive the mony as my father did not see Your aunt while in town.

I answerd the examination for Scholarships, whether I shall get any thing or not I cant say yet. Fellowships are over too. Mr Leland[1] gets one and I beleive Stokes, and Hasting[2] get the other two vacant. All answerd exceeding well—

Pray answer this, for till we renew our Correspondence on its former footing I have not Spirits to write any thing. I am your almost forgotten tho Sincere friend

To RICHARD SHACKLETON—1 *June* 1746

Source: MS Dr O. Fisher. *Printed Leadbeater Papers*, II, 79–81; Samuels, pp. 94–5.
Addressed: To | Mr Richd Shackleton at Ballitore | per Killcullen-bridge.
Postmarked: I.U|3.

Dublin June 1st 1746

Dear Dick

I should not have delayed one post to answer your most agreable and Long expected favour, had not the Scholarship (as I believe the news informd you I was elected) I got taken upon my whole attention these few days past for what with bargaining for a room in the Colledge and doubts whether I should accept the Scholarship and buying another Sort of gown I have had very little spare time. If I had you may be sure I should have dedicated it to our friendship.—You may perhaps be curious to know what advantages we have by a Scholarship. We have our Commons for nothing, 50 Shillings a year in the Cellar, are members and freemen of the University and have a Vote for a Member of Parliament, the ground rent of our Chamber, our Decrements[3] between 3 and

[1] The Rev. Dr Thomas Leland (1722–85), later a correspondent of Burke.

[2] The Rev. Dr John Stokes (*c.* 1721–81) received a fellowship in this year; John Hastings (d. 1757) not until 1748.

[3] In eighteenth-century Oxford decrements were 'Each Scholar's proportion for *Fuel*, *Candles*, *Salt*, and other *common* necessaries; originally *so* call'd as so much did, on these accounts, *decrescere*, or was *discounted* from a Scholar's Endowment' (*Reminiscences of Oxford by Oxford Men 1559–1850*, ed. Lilian Quiller Couch, Oxford Historical Society, 1892, p. 64 n.).

4 pound per annum forgiven and when we take our Degree have a good Chance for £15 per annum more. The manner of making and swearing a Scholar you may see in the University Statutes which you have. We were examin'd for 2 days in all the Roman and Greek authors of note. Dr Forster[1] who examined me [in] Catalines speech in Salust seem'd very well pleased at my answering and asked me from whose School I came (a Question I did not hear asked besides) and I told him.

I come now to your question about Dick and here laying my hand to my breast I declare without Circumlocution most sincerely that there was no sort of fault found with Dick's education nor Could, but on the Contrary I heard my father express the greatest Satisfaction at it (and really he could not do otherwise) for never were boys so carefully and well instructed so well both fed and taught as yours: but If I may guess at the reason of my father's bringing him to town (for you know I am not his privy-councellor)[2] was a desire of having Dick with him and My Mother in town for really he is fonder of him than he will own—I'll tell you a Story. T'other Day garrett met Eu: Stratford[3] and after some discourse says the Latter By G—d (I forget his name in Athy)[4] is ruining Mr Shackleton's School, he's destroying it by J–s–s—he's taking away all his Scholars—why there's Matt: Cullen[5]—and every body. Say's garrett What can be the reason? what fault do they find with Mr Shackleton to prefer Mr—. 'Its true by the L—d replies to'ther for look 'ye, d—mn me, he mends S—s faults, he gives abundance of play, not doing of which was t'others greatest fault, he gives abundance of play! This will bring him Shackletons Scholars by G—d, for we were with him like gally-slaves by heavns—book—book book &c &c. and a vast deal more of Stuff and all this seriously from another it might seem ironical—but a true genuine fool will always be one, you know Pray Lengthen Your future favours to your friend sincerely

[1] The Rev. Dr John Forster (*c.* 1707–88), a Fellow.

[2] Burke was on uneasy terms with his father. Prior quotes (5th ed., p. 32) a comment of Burke's friend Dennis in a letter of 1747: 'My dear friend Burke leads a very unhappy life from his father's temper, and what is worse, there is no prospect of bettering it. He must not stir out at night by any means, and if he stays at home there is some new subject for abuse. There is but one bright spirit in the family, and they'd willingly destroy it. All the little oddities which are found in men of genius and are below their care, are eternal matter for railing with them. Pity him, and wish a change, is all I can do.... Care, I believe, wears as many shapes as there are men, but that is the most intolerable which proceeds from want of liberty. This is my friend's case, who told me this morning he wants that jewel of life, "Peace of mind;" and his trouble was so great that he often forms desperate resolutions. Garret suffers equally, but is less sensible of it; for the purest spirits feel best.'

[3] Euseby Stratford entered Ballitore School 24 October 1742.

[4] George Baldrick, schoolmaster in Athy. Francis Stratford, Euseby's brother, attended his school. See Ethel Richardson, *Long Forgotten Days*, London, 1928, pp. 44–5.

[5] Matthew Cullen entered Ballitore School 28 July 1741. Burke had a low opinion of his abilities, as appears in several later letters.

To RICHARD SHACKLETON—12 *July* 1746

Source: MS Dr O. Fisher. Printed *Corr.* (1844) I, 18–20; Samuels, pp. 97–8.
Addressed: To | Mr Richd Shackleton | at Ballitore | Per Killcullen Bridge.
Postmarked: I.Y|12.

Ballitore[1] July 12th 1746

Dear Dick

You may excuse indeed my long Silence if you know the Cause of it, since nothing but the most dangerous illness my Mother ever had could prevent my writing to remove the distrust you seem to have express'd in a late Letter of my friendship—In all my life I never found so heavy a grief—nor really did I well know what it was before, you may well beleive this when I tell you that for 3 days together we expected her death every moment, and really I was so low and weak myself for some time after that I could not sit down to write, but now as the Cause is removed and my Mother (thank God) on the mending hand I shall be no longer Silent. I cant however pretend to say you shall hear often from me till you see me which will be about the end of next week when your namesake whom you will once more take into your protection may answer your questions vivâ voce. Now Im on that subject I am surprizd at[2] what Mr Bayly[3] reported about my fathers quarrell with yours. I always heard him at all times when he had occasion to mention him do it with all the regard, and gratitude that so great Care and merit deserved; and furthermore I can say that he intended to send him back at the expiration of his quarter as my Mother told your aunt and the only cause of his removal for that time was to divert my Mother as she was beginning to relapse into her old disorder[4]—and not for any misunderstanding—I am glad Sisson's Company was agreeable to you and I wish you may every day meet friends as pleasing, for really after all whatever motives it may be founded on Nil ego prætulerim jucundo sanus amico[5] as has been said a thousand times before. I have got a good many new acquaintance and some odd ones too whose Characters may divert us when we meet. Quicquid agunt homines, votum timor, ira, voluptas,

[1] Burke wrote 'Ballitore' by mistake. He was in Dublin, and this letter was addressed to Shackleton in Ballitore.

[2] MS: as

[3] The reference is probably to Burke's friend Jack Bayly or a relative.

[4] Writing his friend Charles O'Hara 30 October [1762] Burke spoke again of a 'very cruel nervous disorder' which afflicted his mother. Mrs Burke herself in a letter to her niece in 1766 (printed in *Corr.* [1844], I, 111–14) spoke of 'the very long time that I was in a very poor way amongst you all, which makes me shudder as often as I think of it, and I believe it has been worse with me than I can recollect'.

[5] When I am sensible, there is nothing I prefer to a cheerful friend; see Horace, *Satires*, I, v, 44.

gaudia discursus, nostræ sunt deliciæ.[1] I spend three hours almost every day in the publick Library where there is a fine Collection of Books[2]—the best way in the world of killing thought—as for other Studies I am deep in Metaphysics and poetry. I have read some history. I am endeavouring to get a little into the accounts of this our own poor Country. I'll hear from you next post—how you spend your Time and whats your present Study—I have done now and am with Complements Yours

To Richard Shackleton *and* Richard Burke, Sr—25, 31 *July* 1746

Source: MS Dr O. Fisher. Printed *Leadbeater Papers*, II, 81–5; Samuels, pp. 99–101.
Addressed: To | Mr Richd Shackleton | at Ballitore | per Castledermot.
Postmarked: MALLOW.
MS torn and repaired with tape. Two words restored.

Caranatta[3] July 25th 1746

Dear Dick,

I am here after a tedious journey and have join'd to that so murder'd Sleep with dancing these 3 nights past that I can hardly hold up my head (which you will doubtless say I never did). Nothing but my inviolable regard for you could prevail on me to write with so bad a pen, and nothing but the great Confidence I place in your Candour and forgiving temper could prevail on me to send you the produce—but so much by way of digression at the beginning to try your patience. Could this tongue the poor representative of my generous Soul, could this pen even faintly express half what I feel, it would assure you how passionately I have Lamented the bitter absence which tore one Soul in two and hinderd that Charming, that transcendently divine and transporting pleasure (transporting to round the period) of Communicating every thought and movement of our Breasts[4]—this is the 31st of the month and I am now at Ballyduff. The preceeding nonsense I was forced to break off where you see the writing Change, by my mothers calling me to go away with

[1] Whatever things move men, longing, fear, anger, pleasure, joys, discourse, these are our delights; see Juvenal, *Satires*, I, 85–6.

[2] Burke probably refers to the Trinity College Library. The sole entry of his name in the Library's list of readers is for a later date: 'Burke (Edmond) Esquire, 1761'.

[3] The *Corke Journal* for 10 February 1756 advertised to be let 'the dwelling house of Caranatta in the Co of Corke...being 2 small miles from Mitchelstown, two from Glanworth and 4 from Kilworth, all market towns. Proposals will be received by Mr Arthur Hyde, Hyde Lodge, near Castle Lyon'. The Hydes were an influential Protestant family, friendly with the Nagles.

[4] Burke apparently wrote to this point on 25 July, and went on (with a different pen) on the 31st.

her since which I had not time to finish it, and really it was a releif to me for I was quite Stupid and at a loss what to say tho you gave me a Subject, but I was then unequal to it, and was oblig'd to write the Nonsense I began with as an essay in the Cullenian Stile,[1] for to tell the truth I was Capable of nothing else. If you remember you proposed me two subjects to write on, what I thought proper for you to read, and my thoughts on the Education of Boys. The second I beleive I must reserve for Winter, as privelege is almost expiring. You have confined your Study to that part of learning they Call humanity, and I beleive very justly for it contains the most essential and most pleasing part of all Sciences, besides the continual pleasure we receive in reading the authors by the happy turn of expression with which they are adorned and as they convey those precepts which will be of most use to us in common life in the easiest manner. Your office of a Schoolmaster throws you amongst the antient authors who are generally reputed the best, but as they are commonly read and taught the only use that seems to be made of em is barely to learn the language they are written in, a very strange inversion of the use of that kind of learning! to read of things to understand words, instead of learning words that we may be the better enabled to profit by the excellent things which are wrapt up in em. I would therefore advise you to be less inquisitive about the grammatical part of the authors than you have been, not only for the above mentiond reason but because you will find it much the easier way of attaining the languages—you will be pleased to consider after what manner we learn our mother tongue we first, by Conversation (to which reading where the language is dead is equivalent) come to know the signification of all words and the manner of placing em. Afterwards we may if we will know the rules and laws by which they are to be placed so and so which will then be quite easy to us as they are only the laws of custom reduced to writing. Poetry and history are the Chief branches which are taught. I would have you read less of one and more of t'other if you have a mind to have your latin pure, and not like me who when I attempt to write prose latin, 'tis prose on Stilts or poetry falln lame.[2] For latin, I would have you read Virgils Georgics, Juvenals Satires, and a Comedy or two of Terence. For prose Salust, Cicero's Orations for Archias the poet, for M. Marcellus. for Pompey, for Milo. and the first Phillippic. In Greek the first six books of homer, the embassy to Achilles, and that part from the Death of hector to the end of the poem. What I shew'd you of Lucian, Tabula Cebetis. and Xenophon, You Should read with abundance of Care,

[1] Doubtless the style of their common acquaintance Matthew Cullen. (See letter of 1 June, p. 66.)

[2] *Dunciad*, I, 190.

I dont mean as to the Grammatical part, the Georgics, Salust's Cataline and Tabula Cebetis.

I have been very tedious in saying very little but you must forgive a defect I cant mend. I think often of our Dispute about murdering Sleep and as I have since read that excellent play of my favourite Shakespear I am rather more in love with the passage observe with what horror it's attended. Macbeth, immediately after murdering his royal Guest and all his attendants and describing the Stings of conscience that afflicted him during that horrid work he speaks thus to his Wife

Macb. Methought I heard a Voice cry, Sleep no more!
Macbeth doth Murther Sleep, the innocent Sleep
Sleep that knits up the ravelld Sleeve of Care
The Death of each days life, sore labours bath
Balm of hurt Minds great natures Second course
Chief Nourisher in lifes feast.
Lady. What do you mean?
Macb. Still it cry'd, Sleep no more! to all the House
Glamis Doth murther Sleep, and therefore Cawdor
Shall Sleep no more, Macbeth Shall Sleep no more.

I was not In Corke so you may judge I had not the pleasure of seeing my friend Sisson. Farewell I write the rest to my Brother.

Dear Brother

We arrived in this Country after a tedious journey of six days in the Worst Weather in the World, but I have the Satisfaction to acquaint you that my mother is greatly recoverd she rides out every day and will I hope soon be perfectly well, as are all your friends here who enquired very kindly for you. I have a piece of news for you your Sister Miss Polly hennassy[1] has been married this fortnight to a Gentleman of Corke. I have not yet seen that family. My Mother desires her Blessing to you and all your friends here their Complements. I am your affectionate Brother

EDMD BURKE

[1] Mary Hennessy, a distant relation of Burke on his mother's side, married John Shea, a merchant of Cork, in 1746.

To RICHARD SHACKLETON—19 *August* 1746

Source: MS Dr O. Fisher. Printed *Leadbeater Papers*, II, 85–6; Samuels, pp. 101–2.
Addressed: To | Mr Richd Shackleton | at Ballitore | per Killcullen Bridge.
Postmarked: A.U|19.

August 19th 1746

Dear Dick

I confess our Correspondence has of late been a little upon the Stand, and I as freely own thro' my fault for it Cant be Denied that you wrote last. I beg however that we may renew it with as much alacrity as before for I am now pretty well got over an indolence which has of late possessd me to that degree that I have been lost to my Seff and to all my friends—a bad excuse I know this, but I had far rather you should think me Lazy than illnaturd—I shall say no more on this head now, because I know too minute an enquiry into it will be but little to my Credit—only like a good Child—I shall do so no more.

Beleive me, dear Dick I could not[1] think my time spent so agreeably and profitably as in your Company but there are so many invincible obstacles in my way that I cannot think of it at least yet awhile, I am now just after examinations and in less than a month others far greater are to succeed than ever I had my time is very short and my business very great yet notwithstanding I would be very willing to forfeit whatever profit might accrue from them, for the sake of spending a week or two with you, did not some disgrace and some anger perhaps from a Certain quarter[2] attend it—your fathers watch shall be sent by dick who will be with you in a few days—he desires to be remembred to you. Greek is a plant that thrives as ill in Dublin as Munster, and the soil is as unpro[pi]tious to Latin.

I hope by this time you have pretty well got over your troubles. As for me I am in Statu quo. I spend most of my idle time with Sisson. He has a great regard for you, and I assure you I like him as well if not better than ever notwithstanding some appearances which a thinking man should never judge from. I have the pleasure too, to inform you that he has of late no despicable share of business. He has now in hands and finishd almost the Speaker,[3] and his family, the Ld and Lady Ikerrin[4] &c and I think it a pity that so good a painter has not better encouragement. Your last was very Laconick, I hope this shall have as Much honour as the famous general (I forget whom) in making you lengthen your Sentences[5] beleive me to be yours

[1] MS: not not

[2] Doubtless Burke's father.

[3] Henry Boyle, (later) 1st Earl of Shannon (*c.* 1686–1764).

[4] Somerset Hamilton Butler, 7th Viscount Ikerrin (1718–74), had married (1745) Juliana (*c.* 1728–1804), daughter of Henry Boyle.

[5] The allusion has not been traced.

To RICHARD SHACKLETON *and* RICHARD BURKE, SR—29 *November* 1746

Source: MS Dr O. Fisher. Printed Samuels, pp. 105–6.

Dublin Nov: 29. 1746.

Dear Richard

Bawn went so suddenly out of Town that I had not Time to send my answer to the Letters I receiv'd by him, you will therefore excuse[1] me for not answering that or the one I received before from you untill now.—The Cyrus[2] I sent you is my own it is the very best edition as I since discover'd—you may use it as long as you please—I beleive one will serve both you and Dick—however I kept your half guinea. to buy you Xenophons Memorables, or any other book you will be pleas'd to send for—You tell me you meet some difficulties in the Cyropedia if I can I will clear 'em up myself if not, I will get somebody else to do it—but you dont tell me how you approve the author. I was with Exshaw[3] about the Books—he has not yet imported them but will very soon—he has not Hubners Geography[4]—but he has another Book wrote by the Same author calld I think a Geographical and historical account of all nations.[5]—Bayle's Dictionary[6] was Sold the evening before your father spoke to[7] me—you have no great Loss in them for they as well as all the Books which were Sold at That auction sold very dear—So much for all business and that being dispatchd I have very Little to say beside—but that as I beleive I shant live in the College this winter I fancy I shall have the pleasure of seeing you at Ballitore this Christmas. I have spoke to Brennan[8] and he says he will come if I go—As for the Character of your dear self perhaps I shall give it you some other Time when you have forgot you desired it and shant know whom it means. I have I know not how got into the Trade of Character drawing[9] and got by it the ill

[1] MS: fexcuse

[2] Xenophon's *Cyropaedia.*

[3] Either Edward Exshaw (d. 1748) bookseller, or John Exshaw (d. 1776) bookseller, printer, and publisher. Though they became partners shortly before Edward's death, they seem to have had separate shops at this time (Plomer, *Dictionary of Printers*, p. 383).

[4] Probably a German work by Johann Hübner, translated into English as *A New and Easy Introduction to the Study of Geography by way of Question and Answers.* A 2nd ed. of the translation is dated 1742 (Library of Congress Catalogue).

[5] Perhaps an otherwise unknown English translation of Johann Hübner [Jr's] *Vollständige Geographie*, or possibly a French translation entitled *Géographie universelle* published in 1746 (Yale University Library Catalogue).

[6] Pierre Bayle's *Dictionnaire historique et critique* had been translated into English in 1710 and again in 1734–41 (*C.B.E.L.* II, 770).

[7] MS: to to

[8] Beaumont Brenan (d. 1761) poet and playwright. There is a brief account of him in *D.N.B.*, to which several facts might be added from Burke's letters.

[9] E. J. Payne comments on Burke's use of 'characters' in his speeches and writings (*Select Works*, Oxford, 1887, I, xliii). A regular section of the *Annual Register* was

will of one of my acquaintance who is not Thoroughly reconcil'd to me Since—The rest of what I write here is for Dick I intend it to save each of you expence 'twill be but [four][1] pence apiece.

Mr Philospher, and Knight of the Woful Countenance, for I think that famous hero whom you personate was like you a great philosopher—tam Marti quam Mercurio[2]—I cant but take notice of the pitiful Case of your Beard which you have mauled so in your passion, indeed it looked humorous enough at first but we have seen it so often that It nauseates—I would therefore recommend to you for the future rather to nourish your Wisdom than beard for if the latter makes so great a progress as it has for some time past it will soon outgrow the other to a Surprizing degree. I am glad to see you are going now into Juvenal, you shall have it when Bawn comes next to town—you have now Learned so much that I fancy you will for the time to come be able to get something from what you read more than bare words. Therefore if Dicky thinks proper I should be Glad you would read Xenophon. I dont know any Book fitter for Boys who are beginning to Comprehend what they read.

When you come next to town you wont find us in the old house for my father has taken another on Lower Ormond Quay to which with Gods help we'll remove before Christmas. Now I talk of houses I had a narrow escape Last great Storm. As I sat in a Shop under Dicks Coffee house the Back house which joind it fell and buried Pue the Coffe hous keeper[3] in its ruins and his wife but by the most wonderful providence they were dug out alive and unhurt—The same day an accident happend me indeed more humorous than the former. For as I was Joking in the Street with a friend my hat and wig were blown off which while he pursued for a long way to the infinite Diversion of the Spectators. My Coat too[4] Was blown off and I left quite bare. I am in haste and can no more but that I am your most affectionate

EDMD BURKE

entitled 'Characters' and contained specimens of this kind of writing from many sources.

[1] MS: your

[2] As much like Mars as like Mercury. Perhaps Burke really wants this the other way round: Don Quixote and Richard are philosophers as well as warriors—and equally deranged in both roles.

[3] Richard Pue (d. 1758), printer, and publisher of *Pue's Occurrences* (Plomer, *Dictionary of Printers*, p. 399). He was the proprietor of Dick's Coffee House in Skinner's Row, a meeting place of Dublin literary people. The *Dublin Journal* for 22–5 November describes his narrow escape from being buried alive.

[4] MS: to

To RICHARD SHACKLETON—5 *December* 1746

Source: MS Dr O. Fisher. Printed *Leadbeater Papers*, II, 87–8; Samuels, pp. 104–5.
Addressed: To | Mr Richd Shackleton | at Ballitore.

Dublin 10br 5th 1746.

The State of mankind and mine in particular is so uncertain that I can hardly depend upon any thing—I flatter'd myself, nay I was certain that I should have the pleasure of spending this Christmas with you which hope I grounded on an assertion of my fathers that I should not live in the College—but he since Changed his mind—and as the foundation begins to fail we must suppose the superstructure will tumble of Course. so that I am under some difficulties on that head—If I come at all I may stay three weeks. Brenan will be so far from hindering it that he may stay as long as he pleases but I cannot.—I beleive you will not have many books from me if you limit them to what new ones come out that I approve—beleive me Dear Dick we are just on the verge of Darkness and one push drives us in—we shall all live If we live long to see the prophesy of the Dunciad[1] fullfilled and the age of ignorance come round once more—redeunt Saturnia regna magnus ab integro seclorum nascitur ordo[2]—is there no one to releive the world from the Curse of obscurity? no not one—I would therefore advise more to your reading the writings of those who have gone before us than our Cotemporaries—I read for my College Course Tully's offices a blameless piece—I got yesterday Waller whom I never read before nor did you I beleive for 'twou'd be needless[3] to tell you if you had that he is one of the most Charming poets of England tis surprizing how so much softness and so much granduer could dwell in one Soul his panegyricks are wonderfully fine—his Chief excellence lies I think In making apparent defects of persons become their greatest praise and that in a manner quite new all his thoughts by the surprize they give us seem to have something epigrammatical in them and in many places he is faulty in that respect but that proceeds from their being exprest in the strongest and most concise manner and so formed that his thoughts are not interwoven so as to form a Continued discourse but is each by itself and strikes you full alone—Take for an example those lines on the kings navy[4]—what shall I say now,—As I put my hand to my pocket to look for the book I found I left it at home (for I am now at the office) but I will make it up in my next. This has struck

[1] The concluding lines of Bk IV.

[2] The Saturnian reign returns, and the great order of the centuries is born anew; see Virgil *Eclogues*, IV, 5–6.

[3] MS: needness

[4] Quoted in Burke's next letter.

me so blank that I can say no more than that I am Dear Shackleton yours affectionately

EDMD BURKE

I cant forbear laughing when I think how you will be baulk'd when you come to the quotation how you'l put your mouth in form and begin in a lofty Theatrical tone to read What shall I say? and how as a Strutting hectoring fellow ⟨that⟩ by Chance treads a Snake you will draw back your foot or mo⟨uth⟩ like him when he finds one confront him with equal looks ⟨or⟩ superior.

To RICHARD SHACKLETON—19 *December* 1746

Source: MS Dr O. Fisher. Printed *Leadbeater Papers*, II, 89–90; Samuels, pp. 106–7.
Addressed: To | Mr Richd Shackleton | at Ballitore | ⟨per⟩ bawn. This to be read Last

Dublin Decbr 19th 1746

Dear Dick

Bawn was with me just now—I shall take care to obey your Commands by him. Your man disappointed me the Last time he was in town for I had not your Letter till near 9 at night. I had the Blackball[1] ready for him at 2 next day—but he was gone—You wont be displeasd that I Laid out some of your money on the books you have per bearer. I found 'em (as I thought) sold Cheap at an auction and as I thought they might be useful to you I bought em, Voitures[2] Character is I beleive known to you for one of the finest genius's france ever produced and a pattern for that way of writing. Price. 1s 7d—The other I bought on the Credit of the great man of whom it treats price 5. 6. I have seen your Dear friend Cullen at the Coffee house pretty often. I knew him perfectly but not as yet condescended to speak to him he is grown a great Count.—I shall let you know the Day I shall meet you which will be I fancy sometime before the holidays my father will go your way in about a week next thursday or friday I think. In my first Letter I did not give you the quotations from W⟨aller⟩ hear them now and think whether I was right—part of the poem to the king on his navy.

Should natures self invade the world again
And oer the Center spread the Liquid main

[1] Samuels suggests that here and in his letter of [5 March 1746/47] (p. 86) Burke may mean by 'Blackball' the blind poet Blacklock. If any reference to poetry is intended, it is more likely that Burke means his own lines on the Blackwater (see below, letter of [*circa* 3 February 1746/47], p. 79). But a blackball was a common object used in shining shoes.

[2] Vincent Voiture (1597–1648).

Thy power were safe, and her destructive hand
Would but enlarge the bounds of thy command
Thy dreadfull fleet would Still the Lord of all
And ride in Triump round the drowned Ball
Those Towers of Oak oer fertile plains might go
And visit mountains where they once did grow.
  The worlds restorer never could endure
That finishd Babel should those men secure
Whose pride design'd that fabrick to have stood
Above the reach of any second flood
To thee his Chosen more indulgent he
Dares trust such power with so much piety.

In his panegyrick on Cromwell preferring to Alexander

He safely might old troops to battle lead
Against th' unwarlike persian or the mede
Whose hasty flight did from a bloodless field
More Spoils than honour to the victor yield
A race unconquerd by their Clime made bold
The Caledonians armd with want and Cold
Have by a fate indulgent to your fame
Been thro' all ages kept for you to tame.

Vale amice Lector—Thine in the Lord
Will: Haine[1]

I am greatly oblig'd to you for the Spyglass. Tis unreasonable you should always be giving and I never returning any thing.

To RICHARD SHACKLETON—27 *December* 1746

Source: MS Dr O. Fisher. Printed *Leadbeater Papers*, II, 91; Samuels, pp. 107–8.
Addressed: To | Mr Richd Shackleton | at Ballitore | Per Killcullen Bridge.
Postmarked: D.E|27.

Dublin Decbr 27th 1746 almost 47

The prospect I have (Dear Dick) of seeing you so soon keeps me from being able to write you much, were I to tell you after this manner my opinion on the points you proposed it would be quite unsatisfactory both to you and myself for while I should be writing my thoughts would be entirely taken up with the pleasure of your approaching presence and

[1] William Hayne (d. *c.* 1631), editor of a popular textbook of Latin grammar, *Lilies Rules Construed*, had concluded his preliminary remarks to the reader: 'Farewell, Thine in the Lord William Haine'.

I should cry out—What the Devil do I write and puzzle me to express myself wretchedly on what I shall have my friend so soon to help me out and mature my imperfect and abortive conceptions. So I shall now only tell you that I shall set out early on monday morning (God willing) towards you. I shall be Glad to meet you that day either at Kill or Killcullen—by no means at Naas—till then God be'w'i you—I heartily long ⟨to⟩ see you if you have an equal desire we shall meet half way—for you know the power of equal forces meeting in the same direction—Brennan cannot come—once more farewell yours assuredly

R S[1]

To RICHARD SHACKLETON—24 *January* 1746/47

Source: MS Dr O. Fisher. Printed *Leadbeater Papers*, II, 92–4; Samuels, pp. 109–10.
A short postscript, not in Burke's hand, is omitted.

Dublin Jan. 24th 1746

My dear Dick

The Silence I have kept so long has been as painfull to myself as it could possibly have been to you and the Cause of it was almost as troublesome as the thing itself, for the Short time I had to read, hurryed me so much as to deprive me of the common Consolation of all the unfortunate, to think over my old pleasures and lament their Loss, the utmost I could do was to steal a sigh now and then from, and immediately to return unto 'de modis mixtis, et pondera erunt velut' &c.[2] So you see I paid the best tribute of Sighs I could to your memory 'for a sigh the absent claims, the dead a tear'[3] if you think that not sufficient, blame my fate, not me, for at that time were I to chuse, I had rather have sat Lamenting myself, and composing sad ditties 'all the Day Long',—however, I have succeeded far beyond my expectations not to say well—the good success I have had from my small reading gives me hope that if I do it more diligently for the future I shall have still more success—The few acquaintances I have here and your absence disposes me very strongly to study and throw aside my old Laziness not that I make any merit of this for had I my old inducements and you in town I doubt not but all my fine resolutions would fall to the ground, for tis I fear with me as (to use a very threadbare comparison for I find no better at present) with those who quit the world not from devotion but because they[4] can no Longer enjoy its pleasures. I wish sincerely that it may be always the

[1] In place of his own signature Burke has written R S and a prolonged flourish. Samuels suggests he may have intended 'R S's E B'.

[2] No source for this quotation has been found. In studying philosophy Burke would be learning *de modis mixtis* (of complex ideas).

[3] Pope, 'Epistle to Robert Earl of Oxford', l. 14.

[4] MS: the

reverse with you, that you may never want all the pleasures it is able to give and at the same time that your desire for Learning may be as great as ever and what is more than all that you may know properly how to value each. I have not had time yet to Correct the flights and prune the wing of your Phaeton.[1] What I think now should be done is to soften the Burlesque at the beginning and Changing it so as to come near the grave severe Satyr, for by that means it will be like the rest which is in that way, for of that Burlesque there are not seven Lines in the whole and these at the very beginning—I really think a poem should be all of a piece, tho' yours I must confess is like the Subject for he kept not the middle path but came so low as to endanger burning the earth and then all at once rose up into the heavens again. You will find the truth of this by comparing

'The trembling boy with dire amaze,
Sees all the world around him blaze' and
'She wipes his eyes and blows his nose'

I shew'd it to Brenan and many others who all greatly Lik'd and found the same fault with it. I will send it to London when I can get an English frank for they dont take 'em in here. I could not get e'er a Second hand Longinus but rather than you should want it I bought a new one—2s 2d. Tis I think a very good translation and has no bad notes.[2] There are no Davidsons Metams.[3] Ekshaw will soon have home your Books. I wish you all happiness and am Dear Dick your affectionate friend

EDMD BURKE

To RICHARD SHACKLETON—[*circa* 3 *February* 1746/47]

Source: MS Dr O. Fisher. Printed *Corr.* (1844) I, 14–16; Samuels, pp. 110–11.
Addressed: To | Mr Richd Shackleton | at Ballito⟨re⟩ | per Killcullen-⟨bridge⟩.
Postmarked: F.E|3. MS cut.

Dear Dick

I receiv'd both your favours—and answer'd in a former Letter your question concerning examinations—be assurd that whatever sensations you had at parting were fully answer'd by mine—however I cant call what I then felt and do in part feel now, directly grief. It was rather A

[1] A poem of Shackleton's which Burke discusses and criticizes in several of the following letters. It was a satirical squib on the Young Pretender. It was published in March. Samuels reprints (pp. 123–4) what he asserts was its final form—though it bears so little resemblance to the lines Burke criticizes that one wonders if it could be an entirely different poem.

[2] Probably the Rev. William Smith's edition of *On the Sublime*, first published 1739, re-published in 1742 and 1743.

[3] Either Burke or Shackleton may have intended to refer to Joseph Davidson's edition of Ovid's *Epistles*, published in 1746; his edition of the *Metamorphoses* was not published until 1748 (*C.B.E.L.* II, 767).

kind of melting tenderness tinged with sorrow, which took me wholly up while I was alone in thinking on the company I had so lately Left a contemplation too delightfull to let me taste anything like grief—and why should we grieve? We had made the best use of the time we were together and omitted nothing in our power to make it entertaining and improving —and now we must break off because the necessity of our affairs require it—and we still live in hope to see and converse with one another again on the same footing—our parting (if I may make such a comparison) is like the sensation a good man feels at the hour of his death, he is conscious that he has us'd his time to the best advantage and now must thro the condition of human nature depart—he feels indeed a little sorrow at quitting his friends, but its very much allay'd by considering he shall see em all again.

You need not fear our friend Faulkner[1] at least yet awhile your mentioning him makes me think what motives men have in general for esteeming indifferent things—not from their real value but from the names that overawe their judgement. Had any one now overlook'd our Letters they should find 500 faults, and think (may be) one part entirely ridiculous, but let us once get a reputation by our writings or otherwise, they shall immediately become most valuable pieces and all the faults be construed into beauties—Pope says all the advantage arising from the reputation of wit is the privilege of saying foolish things unnoticed,[2] and it really is so as to letters or any thing committed to writing—but I dont think it holds good with respect to conversation for I have observed that where a man gets a reputation for being a little witty all shun, fear, and hate him and carp at and canvas his most triffling words or actions—you must forgive me if this Letter be heavy and dull you know the writer is known by his writing many things conspire to make me so—I have been within all day—read—wrote and eat my Dinner which Last generally most effectually damps my Spirits for a while—Now I mention my writing I have done some part of my poem[3] even as far as the invocation which is this how like you it

Ye beauteous Nymphs who haunt the dusky wood
Which hangs recumbent oer the Christal flood

[1] The publisher.

[2] 'The greatest advantage I know of being thought a wit by the world is, that it gives one the greater freedom of playing the fool' ('Thoughts on Various Subjects' in *Works of Alexander Pope*, ed. W. Elwin and W. J. Courthope, London, 1871–86, X, 553).

[3] Burke's poem on the river Blackwater. Burke had spent about five years of his boyhood with his mother's relations in the neighbourhood of the Blackwater in County Cork (see below, letter of [17 April 1759], p. 125). Prior says (2nd ed. I, 28–9) that a poem on the Blackwater 'was, with several letters written by Mr Burke during the early part of his career in London, borrowed by his father from Mr Shackleton, and never returned'. The lines in this letter are the only part of the poem to survive.

Or risn from Water, as the water fair
'Mong the Cleft rocks divide your amber hair
Oft as delighted with my rural Lay
Earnest you Listned all the Summers day
Nor thought it long—with favour hear my bow
And with your kind assistance help me now!
And you whose midnight dance in mystick round
With a green Circle marks the flowery ground
O aid my voice that I may wake once more
The Slumbring Echo on the Mulla's Shore[1]
Thou Chief,—of floods blackwater, hoary Sire
With all thy beauties all my breast inspire
To trace the winding channell of thy course
And find the hidden wonders of thy Scource &c—

Now proceed we to your poem—the corrections you have made are very judicious—I think to leave out or Change all the part that represents him as a blubbering Child as you may seen in the Copy I send you—just as I wrote thus far my father called me and is now sending me out so that I must defer the rest 'till friday[2] good night, my dear Swift in genius and affection Farewell—

EDMD BURKE.

To RICHARD SHACKLETON—[*post* 3 *February* 1746/47]

Source: MS Dr O. Fisher. Printed *Leadbeater Papers*, II, 69–71; Samuels, pp. 122–3.
Endorsed: March 1746.
MS bears no date. Samuels, following the endorsement, placed the letter in March, but it seems to be the criticism of Shackleton's *Phaeton* which Burke was promising at the end of his last.

Young Phaeton as poets tell us
Fell in with some hot-headed Fellows
Where boasting Phœbus was his Sire
The board immediate smoke the Liar
Expel him their society
Until he proved his pedigree
*Stung thus to see his grandeur Sunk,
*And forcd to own his birth to punk

[1] Edmund Spenser had lived at Kilcolman Castle in the neighbourhood of the Blackwater during most of the time he was writing the *Faerie Queene*; he had given the poetic name of Mulla to the Awbeg, one of the river's tributaries. Sylvanus Spenser, the poet's son, married Ellen Nagle, great-aunt of Burke's mother.

[2] MS cut off here, doubtless for the signature; the words that follow and Burke's name have been written in by another hand.

Home to his mother goes the Squire
*With downcast eyes and all on fire†
She asks what means that thoughtful brow
Which he had never worn till now?
*For Study never broke his prime
*With horses hounds and whores he spent his time

I have Changd you see the verses by the Line from the original and indeed not to my Satisfaction submitted.

* The markd Lines I like not I only give 'em to you as hints that you may improve on for the blubbering Child must not stand—

† What if here was a Simile of a bitches joy for the regaining of her long lost puppy she licks it tumbles it over &c applyd to the mothers joy at seeing him.

I assure you my Dear friend I find an infinite deal of difficulty in making verses to supply those of yours which must be left out with any Spirit for where the subject is not our own and we are not warmed with the Chain of thought it is exceeding hard, to make new and as if it were interline verses and I beleive you will find it so when you make lines for those you have here. I know they are extremely bad but they Shew you the connexion that I think should be made dont scruple altering em out of any complement to me for by it you will hurt yourself and disoblige me but you must be speedy and make a last copy which send by all means by sundays post for they must appear before the pretender grows stale or they wont do so well. Let this consideration induce you to pay me no Complement but make your poem as good as you can and as soon for were we to triffle the time away we would be too late.—As for the rest of the poem I think it is extremely good—except this Line

The Car he mounts with glad surprize

Glad surprize seem's a little unintelligible—I wish youd mend it, for I protest after turning it twenty ways I could do nothing I lik'd so well as the Original—The Pun of Skye tho a pun and a false one will do very well for the precise place is not requisite and because among those I have Shewn it to it has met many admirers.

Farewell I expect to hear from you impatiently for the Very post after I receive your's phaeton mounts the chariot. I am Dear Dick your affectionate friend

EDMD BURKE

Did your Aunt get the oranges which I sent per Bawn

To RICHARD SHACKLETON—21 *February* 1746/47

Source: MS Dr O. Fisher. Printed *Leadbeater Papers*, II, 65–9; Samuels, pp. 115–18.
Addressed: To | Mr Richd Shackleton | at Ballitore | per Killcullen-Bridge.
Postmarked: F.E|21.

Feb. 21st 1746

Dear Dick

Your letters gave me abundance of pleasure for besides the ordinary one of hearing from you I had the additional Satisfaction of having a very great uneasiness removed which your long Silence for which I could give no reason caused in me, during that horrid interval you can hardly think how many melancholy suspicions I had one while I thought you sick then dead, then that the same had befallen my brother—at last I knew not what to think—but thank God your letter has at last dissipated all those gloomy clouds—Your poem I think an excellent one and much better since the Last correction—in short it shews ⟨it⟩self to be true gold every time it goes into the fire it ⟨comes⟩ out brighter but not better it had all the intrin⟨sick⟩ value before—the fire but removes the dross and makes it display itself—I send it if I can get a frank to night. As for my own Scheme[1] it is going on (bonis ominibus) but slowly as yet I seldom write half an hour in ten days.

I shall now give you some news but not as news for I fancy you heard it before, I mean the grand Theatrical squabble between Mr Kelly gentleman,[2] and Sheridan the Player[3] which has divided the town into two parties as violent as whig and tory—and because the Scholars of our University have engaged themselves on Sheridans side possibly some reports may have been spread as far as you, to our disadvantage. To prevent them from having any influence on you I shall relate the affair as impartially as I can and with the utmost regard to truth. First then you must know that sometime ago there was a play performed here which greatly pleas'd the town call'd Æsop[4] during the performance Mr Kelly comes in flush'd with Liquor and going into the green room where the players dress begun to entertain the actresses with the most

[1] Probably the lines on the Blackwater.

[2] Although Mr Kelly provoked the riot which Burke describes in this letter, only the initial E. of his first name is known (*Dublin Journal*, 20–24 January). He is identified as a 'young man from Galway'.

[3] Thomas Sheridan (1719–88), father of Richard Brinsley Sheridan, had been manager of the Theatre Royal in Dublin since the autumn of 1745. The riot in his theatre is very fully treated by Samuels (pp. 116–22); other accounts are in *An Apology for the Life of George Anne Bellamy*, 3rd ed. (1785), I, 153–61; in *Gentleman's Magazine*, XVII (1747), 123–4; and—a secondary account—in J. F. Molloy, *Romance of the Irish Stage*, London, 1897, I, 204–20.

[4] By Vanbrugh.

nauseous bawdry and ill Language cal⟨l'd⟩ them bitches and whores put his hands under their petticoats and would have forced some of them (if his ability answerd his inclination). This was represented to Sheridan who is manager of the Theatre upon which he orderd Kelly out of the house—enraged at this he goes into the pit and as soon as Sheridan came on the Stage pelted him with oranges ⟨...⟩ and call'd him a thousand ill names bidding him go off the Stage and quite interrupting the performance at length Sheridan advances to the front of the Stage and tells him that unless some gentleman takes care of him he would be obligd to turn him out of the house—ten times more enraged at this he goes after the act to Sheridans room and insults him again sheridan represented calmly to him his abuse of the female players and of himself—and he persisting in his ill language Sheridan gave him a good flogging which he bore with Christian patience not however without vowing revenge—which he effected the next night by bringing such a party as hinderd sheridan from playing broke open all the Doors and would very probably have killd him had he not escaped, (by the usadge they gave the playhouse taylor). These doings made him shut up the playhouse and indict Kelly who also indicted him during this time thousands of States of cases, answers Replys &c flew about from both parties and a great deal of dispute concerning the word Gentleman for it seem's Sheridan had said he was as good a gentleman as Kelly or (as others will have it) as any in the house. This gaind Kelly a great party who call'd their cause the Gentlemans quarrell taking it extremely ill that a Gentleman should be struck by a Player. And insisted that Sheridan should never play till he had publickly ask'd Kelly's pardon. The Scholars who had till now stood neuter seeing how ill one who had been of their body[1] was treated, and the town deprived of their diversion by a private pique took the affair on themselves and encourag'd Sheridan to open the Theatre again which he did and acted Richd the 3d where a numerous body of the Scholars appear'd to keep peace. At the beginning the party began to be riotous but by proper menaces they were kept quiet and one or two of the principal turnd out. Thus the play went on regularly to the Satisfaction of the Audience. Next night was to be acted the fair pænitent[2] for the Benefit of the hospital of incurables the Scholars were persuaded that common humanity on account of the Charitable design of the play would keep the faction quiet so not above 7 or 8 went there that night—but they were mistaken no ties of honour or Religion could bind em they raisd another tumult calld for Sheridan to wreck their Vengeance on

[1] Sheridan entered Trinity College in 1735, graduated B.A. in 1739.
[2] By Nicholas Rowe.

him and drove the Actors off the Stage not content with this Some of them abus'd the few Scholars that were there pelted them with oranges declared there were no gentlemen among them but that they were all a pack of Scoundrels. The Scholars being informed of this, early next morning searchd the whole town for Mr Martin[1] the principal offender and not finding him returned to the College when about 10 they were informed where he lay (at that time I came to the College and joind the rest) they immediately went for him and found him in bed. They made him rise and brought him to the College where after making him sensible of his crime he kneeld down in a large Circle of us ownd his fault and begg'd pardon then we agreed to seize Captain Fitzgerald[2] and went to the Number of about 100 well arm'd to Cassle Street where he livd and as they opend not the door went in at the window and brought out Mr Fitzgerald whom they put into a Coach with John Brown Esqr of the Neale,[3] and two Scholars well armed and conveyed the Coach under a Strong guard of us to the College where he was oblidged to make his Submission. Kelly then to avoid ill usage came of himself and did the Same. That evening came a Letter from the Lords Justices desiring in a very polite manner we should not go out in Large Bodies, and that they would look into the affair and give us due Satisfaction. In the mean time those above mention Gentlemen notwithstanding their promise of better behaviour threatned the lives of the Scholars when they met any of em alone and hird ruffians to assault them at night the Scholars incensed at this once more were resolved to punish em but the provost to avoid bloodshed orderd that none of the Scholars should be sufferd out and in the mean time sent those whose lives where threatned to my Ld Chief justice[4] who sent a Tipstaff for Martin so that affair ended. Kelly and Sheridans Tryals came on a thursday[5] in which Sheridan was honourably acquitted and Kelly found guilty and fined this day £500—a months close imprisonment and to give security for his behaviour for 7 years so ended that affair in which justice took place[6] farewell yours

EDMD BURKE

your franks dont pass.

[1] Not identified.
[2] Probably George Fitzgerald (d. 1782) of Turlough, County Mayo.
[3] Later Lord Kilmaine (1730–94).
[4] Thomas Marlay (d. 1756), Lord Chief Justice of King's Bench in Ireland.
[5] 19 Feb (*Dublin Journal*, 17–21 February).
[6] The incident closed with Sheridan interceding successfully to get Kelly out of his fine, and ultimately going bail for him (Molloy, *op. cit.* I, 219). Such softness to his opponent may have been a reason why the Trinity students later turned against Sheridan. See below, letters of 2 February 1747/8 and May 1748 (p. 102).

To Richard Shackleton—[*circa* 5 *March* 1746/47]

Source: MS Dr O. Fisher. Printed *Leadbeater Papers*, II, 73–6; Samuels, pp. 125–6.
Addressed: To | Mr Richd Shackleton | at Ballitore | Per Killcullen Bridge. *Endorsed*: March 5th 1746. *Postmarked:* M.R|5.

Dear Dick

I receivd both your Epistles, which tho of very different natures were equally welcome to me, because one reminded me of my faults (a friendly office) and the other heald all my rancour by a seasonable and well timed praise for which to speak the truth I very much longed, tis a great deal for a poet to receive applause for his work when finished but to receive it before is more than he possibly could expect and as unexpected must be the more agreeable, it gives him a kind of foretaste of what he is to receive hereafter and inspires him with courage to proceed. It is (if I may use such a Comparison) as when a Saint to encourage him under his afflictions gets a transient view of heavn slight as it is he sees that all human sufferings are but trivial to attain such an enjoyment. And he cheerfully finishes ⟨his⟩ Course. I confess you had good reason to assure me ⟨you⟩ had not taken glass when you wrote your last ⟨for⟩ upon the first reading of your most sublime and Oriental period I immediately concluded you intended it as a Jest on me, or was the effects of a Certain fluid—from the first opinion you will scarcely batter me. The whole has something of Burlesque on me—but if I am mistaken and must answer seriously what you wrote, Let me assure you my vein (such as it is) will never be esteemed by me so great an honour or happiness as that I had so deserving and so ingenious a friend, one who can perform so well himself and knows so well to judge of the performances of others and my highest ambition that the World should know it—or if any of my writings can conduce to that end, or to one I have more at heart, that is to please you they shall never be wanting—dum cœptis adspirat Apollo.[1] We have early commenc'd our friendship and I am confident will end it Late (very Late I hope)—all I desire is that we may continue as we are. and that you will love me while you live as well as you do now and as I do you—if so I am absolutely contented it should be no greater for then twou'd be violent and you know how likely to last things violent are, nor think me the Less sincere because I scribble, nor beleive what that rogue Pope says—Each bad author is as bad a friend.[2] I continue scribbling that thing the Specimen of which you say pleases you so much —if so, I have some hopes, for in my opinion that is far from being the most shining part of it—and indeed twoul'd be sad if the invocation

[1] While Apollo inspires beginnings. [2] *Essay on Criticism*, II, 319.

should be the best part of the poem—but such as it is when finish'd you shall have it. I am sorry it is of such a nature that it will by no means admit of what you desire and this is what I shall always think a very great defect in it—I had once a thought of printing it, but I have entirely dropt all thoughts of that for even supposing it good there [are] so many discouragements in this Town to a mans turning Author that twould be almost madness to at⟨tempt⟩ it—to mention no more tis ten to one (good or bad the same) whether you shall be read by ten in the City, the people here are the very reverse of the Description St Paul gives of the Athenians, that their whole business is to hear or relate something new[1] —they have no sort of curiosity that way further than party Leads them, and no wonder—for books either in prose or verse seldom enter the Conversations of even people of fortune and those who have leisure enough—so that an Authors first cries cannot be heard but he is stiffled in his birth. And what can be the cause of this? I'll tell you—the only passions which actuate the people high and low are those two—avarice and an abandond love of Sensual pleasure—wherever these entirely take possession, they entirely exclude every thing else great and laudable and bury them in a Lethargy to whatever pleasures are above their own sordid level, I wish your poem may fall into better hands as it deserves to do and indeed it has taken its flight in a happier clime. If so you need not desire to be taken notice of by me you yourself will sufficiently shew your own merit—or will you have it as I have elsewhere expressd it

As merit which can neer be long conceald
By its own Lustre always is reveald.[2]

I inquird concerning McEuen[3] and do beleive as I am informed that the report is false and that he has left the College with a good Character. As to the part of your Poem that was criticized I find no fault int. You soon shall have the Blackball and Longinus. I wish we could read him together.

Write no more to Edmd Burke Esqr but to your humble

Servant and friend
EDMD BURKE
longer letters, as
long as this at least.

[1] *Acts* xvii, 21.

[2] The lines are not found in any of Burke's surviving poems.

[3] James McEuen taught Hebrew in Dublin privately and in Trinity College. Richard Shackleton had taken lessons from him (Ballitore MSS, A. Shackleton to Mary Barnard, April 1745); this seems to be the only basis for considering Shackleton a Trinity student. See below, letter of 10 August 1757 (p. 124).

To RICHARD SHACKLETON—[*circa* 12 *March* 1746/47]

Source: MS Dr O. Fisher. Printed *Leadbeater Papers*, II, 71–3; Samuels, pp. 127–8.
Addressed: To | Mr Richd Shackleton | at Ballitore | per Kill-cullen-Bridge.
Postmarked: M.R|12. *Endorsed:* March 12th 1746.

Shall I never hear from you? or are you resolved that we never shall correspond on equal terms, but one or other must flag? for no sooner had I repented of my Negligence, and began to make some amends for it, by a long letter, than a tedious and painfull Silence on your Side ensued. This Conduct make me imagine our Correspondence, very much resembles a Clublaw, where as long as one party runs, the other most Swiftly and couragious pursues, but no sooner do they face about and begin to make a vigorous defence, but the pursuers in their turn take to their heels, and so on to the end of the Chapter—if it continues as it has hitherto done I think I shall allways fly, and then I shall have the pleasure of receiving all your Letters, without giving you any interruption by mine, for I receive such a pleasure from your letters as I would from the Company of some great man whom I could always hear without desiring to have any part of the Conversation myself—this I grant you is not like myself but you know I always distinguish between a mans talkative and writative Character. Seriously If you knew how much trouble your Silence gives me after a long letter from me, you would never disappoint me—when I write but a little to you then as a punishment you may defer answering me a post or two—but after a great deal tis quite unpardonable in you tis upon my word—make me proper amends in a Sheet close wrote as this—for let me tell you though you generally send me paper enough, you seldom fill it—Can you beleive that your letters can ever be too long? Or that I can ever think anything tedious that comes from you? Say something to me—let me if you have any troubles Lessen 'em by bearing my part, or if any thing is extraordinary agreeable to you, sure you wont be so ungenerous as to deprive me of so much pleasure as I shall have in hearing it—do you study and improve in Learning? it will be a good example to me—do you give your mind and time wholly to your boys? I shall rejoice at their happiness and particularly at my brothers—or if you intirely devote yourself to rural Sports I joy in the Stock of health you are Laying up—tell me every thing so that I may say of you (absens presens ut sus) whether thou Chuse Cervantes serious air—or Laugh and shake in Rab'lais easy Chair,[1] whether you write sonnetts to Armida, or Lash your Enemies in Hudisbrasticks—now I touch on this String (as a Madman when you happen

[1] *Dunciad*, I, 19–20.

to hit the Cause of his distraction can talk of nothing else) tell me have you any work in hand? What it is, and how far it has proceeded—prepare Something to succeed Phaeton which will come into the world more opportunely—Brenan has finishd his Comedy[1]—when printed you shall judge of it—I beleive it will soon come on the Stage—he has lately publishd a Thing calld Fleckno's Ghost.[2] Another of my acquaintance one Dennis[3] has publish'd a paper on this occasion also, calld Brutus's Letter to the town[4]—a good thing I think and on what occasion wrote you shall hear soon. Adieu Dear Dick—remember me—

To RICHARD SHACKLETON—21 *March* 1746/47

Source: MS Dr O. Fisher. Printed *Corr.* (1844) I, 20–3; Samuels, pp. 128–9.

Ormond Quay, March 21st 1746–7

Your Last favour which I receiv'd gave me the greatest pleasure, in which you mentiond your sending me another which I received not; in this you say you answerd my Queries—I beg you will answer them in your next—I think you take no bad method to fix the Substance of your Letter in my memory by making some parts of it so dark as to oblige me to read it over three or four times, and in this too you do me a piece of Service for possibly were it quite clear I might pass over it without due consideration and by that means loose abundance of pleasure and advantage that I might gain from a more attentive perusall—such as (to mention one) I dont yet very well understand 'it was imported hither from the Country of Job alias the Land of uz.' To mention more would be to show my own Stupidity tho' I have now come to the understanding of all the rest—you ask me if I read? I defer'd answering this question 'till I could say I did. Which I can almost do. For this day I have shook

[1] Probably his comedy *The Lawsuit*. See Prior, *Life of Goldsmith*, II, 315–17; also D. E. Baker, *Biographica Dramatica* (1812 ed. I, pt I, 63), and below, Burke's letters of [17 October 1747] (p. 98) and 25 August 1761 (p. 143).

[2] Where published at this time has not been found. Among the Halliday Pamphlets in the Royal Irish Academy (Box 210, no. 2) is what may be a re-publication: *The Stage: or Coronation of King Tom. A Satyr.* By B—t B—n. Dublin: Printed for the Author, in the year 1753. It is a mock panegyric closely modelled on Dryden's *Macflecknoe*. When Dulness is crowning Thomas Sheridan as legitimate heir of 'father Flecknoe' she says:

Not all regard to B—kes pen is due,
Some sparks of love remains, dear child, for you....

[3] William Dennis (*c.* 1730–74), later a close friend of Burke's. *Alumni Dublinenses* lists two William Dennis's in Burke's class, but has almost certainly made a mistake. The Trinity Entrance Book mentions only one, entered 7 July 1743: 'Gulielmus Dennis Penns: Filius Barneby Gen: Annum Agens 14m. Natus Dublinii Educatus sub ferula Ma. Quigg....'

[4] A short prose pamphlet on Sheridan's side of the Kelly controversy. A copy is among the Halliday Pamphlets (vol. 200) in the Royal Irish Academy.

off[1] Idleness and began to buckle to—I wish I could have said this to you with truth a month ago, 'twould have been of great advantage to me, my time was otherwise employ'd,[2] Poetry, Sir, nothing but Poetry could go down with me—tho I have read more than wrote—so you see I am far gone in the poeticall madness, which I can hardly master, as indeed all my Studies have rather proceeded from Sallies of passion than from the preference of sound reason and like the nature of all other natural apetites have been very violent for a Season and very soon cooled and quite absorb'd in the succeeding. I have often thought it a humorous consideration, to observe and sum up all the madnesses of this Kind I have fallen into this two years past—First I was greatly taken with natural philosophy which while I should have given my mind to Logic, employd me incessantly this I call my furor Mathematicus, but this worked off as soon as I begun to read it in the College, as men by repletion cast all off their Stomachs all they have eat then I turned back to logic and Metaphysicks here I remaind a good while and with much pleasure. And this was my furor logicus. A disease very common in the days of ignorance, and very uncomon in these enlightned times. Next succeeded the furor historicus which also had its day but is now no more being entirely absorbed in the furor poeticus, which as skillfull Physicians assure me is as difficultly cured as disease very near[3] akin to it namely[4] the itch (nay the Hippocrates of poets says so expressly 'tenet insanabile multos scribendi cacoethes' Lib I. Aphor. p. 12).[5] But Doctors differ and I dont despair of a Cure.—Now to what you shall read. which shall be non juveni naris obesæ but curvatæ.[6] I must confess I would recommend Salust rather than Tully's Epistles which I think are not so extreamely valuable, besides Salust is indisputably one of the best Historians among the romans, both for the purity of his Language and Elegance of his Stile he has I think a fine easy and diversified narration mixt with reflections moral and political neither very trite and obvious nor out of the way and abstr⟨act⟩ which is I think the true beauty of Historical observation, neither should I pass by his beautiful painting of Characters—in short he is an Author that on all accounts I would recommend to you. As for Terence and Plautus what I fancy you will chiefly get by them (as to the Language) is some insight into the common manner of speech us'd by the Romans, one excells in the Justness of his

[1] MS: of

[2] The Trinity Examination Book under date of 10 April 1747 reports Burke cautioned for neglecting morning lecture.

[3] MS: near nearly

[4] MS: name

[5] An incurable disease of writing takes hold of many; see Juvenal, *Satires*, VII, 51–2.

[6] For a youth not of thick but of curved nostrils; see Horace, *Epodes*, XII, 3.

pieces, the other in the humour. I think a play in each will be sufficient. I would recommend to you Tullys Orations excellent indeed. You will pardon me if I have been too dogmatical but remember that what I say is always with this restriction that it is submitted to your better Judgement. Dunkins Beotia[1] is I think to be reckoned among the Bad pieces and is in my humble opinion the worst thing I ever saw of his—quite ⟨...⟩ There is also another poem Lately publish'd here call'd the Gentleman[2] but of the run—I can not yet send Madden[3] for Brenan cant find it. I will send you that and a Little miscellaneous Book of his poems[4] soon. I did t'other Day a little thing in a merry vein almost extempore you have it enclosed. Your opinion of it. Adieu.

P:S: Send me Some of Dicks Rhimes—

EDMUND BURKE *and* WILLIAM DENNIS *to* RICHARD SHACKLETON—28, 29 *May* 1747

Source: National Magazine (1830), pp. 91–3; Prior, *Life of Goldsmith*, I, 79–85.

Dr French Laurence (1757–1809), Burke's literary executor, in a letter to Mrs Burke of 27 July 1799 told of being approached by a Dr Hales, probably William Hales (1747–1831), who wished to sell him a small collection of early letters of Burke to Shackleton and Dennis. The Dennis letters, Dr Laurence said, extended '...from an early period to the year 1770. In some years not more than one letter, in others none. Several of these letters 2 or 3, hardly more, are of a finished kind, and would [do] excellently well for publication; and all of them would enable me to track him [Burke] from place to place and residence to residence during that period of his life, when I am most in want of such information'. Sir Richard Bourke (1777–1855), editor of *Corr.* (1844), saw three or four of the letters by Burke and many more by Dennis, when they were in the possession of a Mrs Crawford, a daughter or granddaughter of Dennis (see endorsement on a letter of Edward Johnston to Bourke 14 July 1830 (Bk 36) at Sheffield). Four letters which must be from this collection—the two following and those below dated 21 November 1747 (p. 99) and 2 February 1747/48 (p. 101)—were printed in the *National Magazine* in 1830.

Burke and Shackleton had discussed plans for a Society of their friends in Dublin as early as 1744 (letter of 24 November), and some sort of club was in existence the following year (letter of 16 July 1745), but the formal inauguration of a debating club, meeting twice weekly and calling itself an Academy of Belles Lettres, took place in George's Lane, Dublin, 21 April 1747. The business of

[1] The Rev. Dr William Dunkin's *Boeotia! A Poem Humbly Addressed to His Excellency, Philip, Earl of Chesterfield*, Dublin, 1747.

[2] *The Gentleman, An Heroic Poem*, Dublin, 1747, a contribution to the Kelly-Sheridan controversy. A copy is among the Halliday Pamphlets (vol. 200) in the Royal Irish Academy.

[3] Probably a volume published in 1747 entitled *Verses Occasioned by the College Examinations, and the Scheme for Distributing Premiums, First Contrived and Promoted by Samuel Madden.*

[4] Madden had published a poem entitled *Boulter's Monument*, Dublin, 1745. No other 'miscellaneous Book of his poems' or of Brenan's poems—for Burke's phrase is ambiguous—is known to have been published by this date.

the club was described as 'speaching, reading writing and arguing, in morality, History, Criticism, Politics, and all the useful branches of Philosophy'. The seven young men who subscribed to its laws took themselves very seriously indeed. They have been taken seriously by others. Though we have no evidence that their meetings continued for more than three months of 1747, the Trinity College Historical Society when it was founded in 1770 regarded the older Club as its predecessor, as it has done ever since. The Trinity Society is now the oldest university debating society in Great Britain or Ireland. (For an account of its history, see R. P. McDermott, *The College Historical Society*, Dublin, printed at the University Press, 1932; for an account of the Club in Burke's time, with a full printing of the Minute Book of the Club's Proceedings, see Samuels, pp. 203–18, 225–95.)

28th May, 1747.

[Burke begins]

Scene I.—Burke, Dennis—The Club-room—Dennis goes away about some business. Manet Burke solus.

As the committee appointed for the trial of Dennis, has just now broke up, without doing any thing for want of members sufficient, I have time enough on my hands to write what you desire—an account of the proceedings of our society since your departure,[1] in which you have been a perfect prophet, for Mohun[2] was formally expelled last lustrum by the Censor, Mr Dennis. After an examination of his conduct from the first formation of the society, it was found exceeding bad, without one virtue to redeem it, for which he suffered the above sentence; he was tried sometime before, (Burke, Pres.) for his bad behaviour, but behaved still worse at trial, which brought fresh punishments on him, and at length, expulsion. This is not the only revolution in our Club. Mr Buck's[3] conduct much altered for the worse: we seldom see him, for which he has not been spared; Dennis, Hamilton[4] and your humble—ha! ha! attend constantly, Cardegoif,[5] as we expected, middling: you all this while are uneasy to know the cause of Dennis's accusation; it is no less than an attempt to overturn this Society, by an insolent behaviour to the President and Society. I am the accuser, and when you know that, you will tremble for him.[6] I must congratulate you likewise on the Censor's minor thanks which you received with a declaration, that had you entered earlier into the Society, you had been entitled to the grand thanks. The Censor gave

[1] Shackleton had been elected to the Club on 14 May and had attended a meeting on the 15th.

[2] Mathew Mohun was first President of the Club; he is otherwise unidentified.

[3] Andrew Buck (*c.* 1724–1801), later Principal of the Hibernian Academy.

[4] Joseph Hamilton, a founding member; not otherwise identified.

[5] Abraham Ardesoif, a founding member, not otherwise identified.

[6] According to the Minute Book, on 26 May 'Mr Dennis towards the latter end of the night behaved very ill continually contradicting the President declaring he was injur'd, and affronting the members nor could he be quieted but declared he valued not the censure which obliges Mr Pres to censure him'.

himself the grand thanks, and the same to me. We had during your absence the following debates very well handled, on the Stadholder—Burke, an oration,[1] lenity to the rebels, a debate; Dennis for—Burke against—Prince of Orange to harangue his troops—Dennis. The sailors in a ship turning pirates—Dennis for: Burke and Hamilton against. Catiline to the Allobroges—Dennis. General Huske for engaging at Falkirk—Burke: Hawley against Dennis. Brutus the first, to the Romans—Burke: Hamilton is now President, and a very good one. You use me oddly in your letter; you accuse me of laziness and what not, (though I am likely to fill most of this,) I did not expect this from your friendship, that you should think I would in your absence refuse you my company for a few lines, when I attended you in town for many a mile. You behave to me just after the manner that a vile prologue I've read desires the audience to use the actors—'but if you damn, be it discreetly done: flatter us here, and damn us when you're gone.'[2] (You see I have not lost my faculty of quoting Grubstreet,) just so, when here you blarney me: in the country you abuse me; but that shall not hinder me from writing on, for (to shew you my latin,) 'tenet insanabile multos scribendi cacoethes:'[3] Come we now to Shar[4] the beginning is dark indeed, but not quite void of connection, 'for whose good effects', &c. connects with the first line; all the rest is, properly, between parenthesis. Phaeton sells well still; tell me exactly what is said concerning his appearance in print in the country. Miss Cotter[5] is quite charmed with your writings, and more of them would not be disagreeable to them. I have myself almost finished a piece—an odd one;[6] but you shall not see it until it comes out, if ever: write the rest Pantagruel, for I can stay no longer;[7] past nine. I am now returned, and no Pantagruel. Your oration on Poverty is, I think, very good, and has in some parts very handsome touches; you

[1] The speeches mentioned in this letter and those mentioned or briefly digested in the Minute Book are the earliest reported speeches of Burke.

[2] The epilogue to Farquhar's *Constant Couple* ends with the lines:

> Our Business with good Manners may be done,
> Flatter us here and damn us when you're gone.

[3] An incurable disease of writing takes hold of many; see Juvenal, *Satires*, VII, 51–2.

[4] Samuels points out (p. 140) that this must be a misreading for 'Sheer'—the name of the hero of *The Poet's Dream*, a poem published in Dublin this year, perhaps written by Shackleton.

[5] Sarah Cotter (*fl.* 1751–65), who succeeded Joseph Cotter as a printer and bookseller in Dublin (Plomer, *Dictionary of Printers*, p. 379).

[6] What is said of this composition by both Burke and Dennis makes it probable that it is the first form of the essay on the *Sublime and Beautiful* which Burke published in 1757 but much of which was supposed to have been written 'before he was 19 years old' (Prior, 2nd ed. I, 58). Burke told Edmond Malone, 'The subject...had been long rolling in his thoughts before he wrote his book, he having been used from the time he was in college to speculate on the topics which form the subjects of it' (Prior, *Life of Malone*, London, 1860, p. 154).

[7] No source has been found for this.

shall have the Club's opinion next time, which was deferred till we should have a full house. I received your novel,[1] and will read it and peruse it carefully.

[Dennis begins]

Dublin, May the 28th, 1747.

Dear Richard—You may be surprised to see the date in the middle of a letter, but I have heard your resentment at letters not being dated, and I must tell you, tho' I don't read news, or consult proposals for Grubean works, yet I know the day of the month as well as Burke who does both, yet does not give an account of it. Now I have gott so far upon that important matter of time, (for we chronologists are very careful of it,) I'll come to business; and first I have prosecuted Mohun (while a private member,) with the utmost vigour, and when censor expell'd him; and now for my good services, I am threatened with expulsion by Burke, who is a terrible fellow, and is very active (at getting me punish'd,) in the Club, though I have hitherto shewn myself a good member, I'm now accused of a design of destroying the Club, (thus modern patriots urge every thing an introduction to popery and slavery, which they don't like,) when, alas! no one has a greater desire to preserve it; nay, so strong is it, that tho' I find in myself a strong desire to keep the chair when I gett it, yet my regard for four or five members quells it. The approbation I met with in the character of Cato has made me so much the more a stickler for liberty, that not bearing any encroachment on it in our assembly I am deemed a criminal; and what's worse, my accuser a violent one and my judge the person whom I've injured; you see the justice.

Friday morning, May 29th.

Burke is now writing the proceedings of the assembly,[2] and just saying he'll pass over part of the Debates because he is tired, you find he is semper eadem, as lazy as you imagin'd, tho' I must do him the justice to say he design'd writing last night, what prevented it heretofore was our expectation of your first challenge, and likewise Ned thought it preposterous to be threshing his brains for you when he is writing for the public: pray laugh heartily now lest you should split when you see the subject he has chosen and the manner he has treated it; but I will not anticipate your pleasure by acquainting you any more. I wonder Ned did not acquaint you with several important affairs which have

[1] It has not survived.

[2] Most of the Minute Book of the Club—now a possession of the Trinity College Historical Society—is in Burke's hand.

happened in town, but I'll supply his place.... Brennan is well and so is Garret, who gives his service to you. Ned desires me to tell you the caps he will send by the next opportunity. Excuse the shortness of this, but I shall be more prolix in my next, till when believe me your sincere friend and humble servant,

William Dennis or Cato the unfortunate.

Ned gott your letter first and keeps it to join with those he has of yours; he insists I have no right to it though it was directed to me; pray settle that point in your next.—Adieu,

Si Vales Valeo.

Your old friend Garrett desires to be remembered to Blarney.

WILLIAM DENNIS *and* EDMUND BURKE *to* RICHARD SHACKLETON—22 *August* 1747

Source: National Magazine (1830), pp. 95–6.

Dennis's portion of this letter, dated 22 August 1747, begins with a solid piece of philosophical criticism: an explication of several of the main ideas of Aristotle's *Poetics*, of which Shackleton had asked to be sent a copy. This part is omitted here, as of less interest than more personal matters.

[Dennis begins]

...Ned has not been well today and the old pain in his hip[1] which you might have heard him complain of has been very uneasy to him all day. This sickness and the desire of seeing the city I mentioned in my last, put him on going a Pilgrimage to the Lady of Loretto, but I believe the dread of being unable to walk with the pain in his hip, has made him reject that notion, till he grows better and has learned French so as to be able to discourse with the people of France during his journey. I have read over my letter, and begin to dislike it for being too grave, nor do I know how to help it, being in a very serious mood (pray what is the meaning of 'you can take nothing apropos I believe out of my collection.' Burke fancies it alludes to a letter of his about the Epistolary stile,[2] explain it to me) you need not answer what is between the parenthesis, and likewise tell me what faults you see in my stile, I fear it is too stiff,

[1] Burke suffered during his boyhood and much of his youth from a complaint, probably tubercular, which gave him pain and restricted his physical activity. Though he ultimately overcame it and enjoyed extraordinary health for most of his life, it may have left a slight mark upon him in a peculiarity of his walk, which Sir Joshua Reynolds once said 'gave him the idea of his having two left legs' (Prior, 2nd ed. II, 413).

[2] It has not survived.

did Burke mention any thing of it, in the letter I mentioned? I should be glad to know your Judgment that I may endeavour at amending it,—Garrett is very well and desires to be remembered, Mr Parker[1] last night drank your health, all other friends are well and give their service to you.

Yours,
WM DENNIS

[Burke begins]

Dear Shackleton—I am better and will write to you tho' after a solid piece of criticism as the above is I should not intrude my trifling line, but the most light if not the most relishing things are good after a solid feast; if not wine, water, if not fruit, sallad and herbs: you may perhaps too blame me for not writing to you by myself, I say you must not expect always a Letter from each, you bundle us together when you write and it is but justice we should answer you in that manner, however if you mend and write to us separately I may be induced to do so, but not otherwise but I see[2] — point as to your question concerning Sophocles, I believe you may read him in the Latin, all the beauties of the contrivances and thought are in it, but of the expression I must confess myself no proper judge tho' doubtless tis inferior.[3] Concerning what Dennis mentions of the paragraph in your letter you need not trouble yourself, we understand it of the poems of which I like some much better than ever I did. The order they stand in my esteem is thus, pardon if not right, Phaeton, Strangman, I know not which to prefer but I totter to Phaeton, Friendship to Herbert when first souls tremble. Blackwater, friendship forgotten, the Beau, to me and Epistle, the Dream, the acrostic (not the religious): I don't like the Phedris nor the rest much; I was at Cotter's this evening, Sally Cotter would adore you were you not a...but she admires your talents and admires you are so, this caused a controversy between her and Dennis which ended like all other religious disputes; farewell and may no such storm fall on us. These words are from Denham[4] whom read if you have, if not I shall endeavour to send it. Yours for ever,

EDMD BURKE

[1] Not identified.
[2] A blank here in the printed letter.
[3] *National Magazine:* his inferior.
[4] From Sir John Denham's poem 'Cooper's Hill'. Burke quotes this same passage in his *Reflections on the French Revolution* (*Works* [Bohn], II, 388; [Little, Brown], III, 386).

To RICHARD SHACKLETON—[17 *October* 1747]

Source: Prior (5th ed.), pp. 22–4.

The letters of Burke to Shackleton which Dr French Laurence saw in the possession of Dr Hales, he described to Mrs Burke as follows:

'The letters to Shackleton are all of the year 1747, or the beginning of 1748; not more than three or four of the latter year: of the former year apparently a regular series. They did not come at all through Mr Dennis [the son of Burke's friend], nor could they have been originally transmitted by Shackleton to Dennis the father, as he was in Dublin with Mr Burke when they were written. This correspondence is all interspersed with some of those excellent and wise sentiments and principles, which distinguished our dear departed Friend through life; and there are some passages of good literary criticism. There is nothing at all to discredit him; yet if I had them, I should not publish above 2, 3, or 4 of them: and I convinced Dr Hales, I believe, that the rest ought not to be printed. There are however many detached sentiments which I should weave into my narrative as illustrating his character at those early years: and there are very full traces of his first literary labours, and the progress of his education.'

Prior seems to have had access to these letters at the time he was preparing his 5th edition; at least he printed one letter (the following) entire and extracts from two others (those of December 1747 and May 1748 below) which would seem on probabilities to belong to this collection. The date of 17 October 1747 which Prior gives the complete letter does not appear in its printed text—whose last words even sound as if there had never been a date. Prior may however have seen one upon a cover or endorsement.

You have so loaded me with letters and compliments[1] that I find it very difficult to answer either, and they were unmerited as they were extraordinary, for I am neither an extraordinary correspondent nor writer, though if my writing was to be judged by its success in the inverse rule we use, it would be thought excellent. However, I must say I was by no means displeased with it, and you needed not to have desired me not to shew your last, for I should be the vainest fellow in the world if I did. I do really believe you to be my friend if any one is, for I see you can no more forbear praising me than Belinda,[2] or dispraising Tremble.[3] I am not such a master of the expressive part of friendship, but believe me, dear friend, I am by no means behindhand in the affectionate. This is sincere, and the only answer I can make to your (I won't say compliments) expressions of kindness, and I should be better pleased with your approbation of my pieces, bating the profit, than King George's.

I don't know whether I shall congratulate or lament with you on your falling in love, for I see ('tis vain for you to deny it) you are over head

[1] Probably compliments on his verse. Dennis wrote Shackleton in the following month 'Ned has finished the first canto of the Blackwater' (Prior, 5th ed. p. 21).

[2] Shackleton had written a poem 'Julia and Belinda' about the two girls in whom he was most interested. 'Belinda' was Elizabeth Fuller (1726–54) whom he later married; 'Julia' may have been Burke's sister Juliana, as Samuels assumes (p. 45), though in a copy of the poem among the Shackleton MSS in Trinity College she is identified by a marginal note as Jane Ducket. The Duckets were a prominent Quaker family living near Ballitore.

[3] Probably James Trimble, usher at Ballitore School. See letter of 15 February 1745/46 (p. 62).

and ears, and what is more extraordinary, with two. The judgment and sagacity with which you have drawn the character of the ladies shew that you perfectly know them, so that any advice from me on that score were quite needless. Belinda, I am glad, has triumphed; however, you seem to quit Julia with regret. How happy if you could have both to serve different ends of matrimony!

I [rode][1] to the Park before dinner, and after it went to Mr Goddard[2] with the money; he is greatly obliged to you; she looked charmingly, Dick, this evening,[3] but I am insensible to charms, when I tell you I do but perceive and not feel them, particularly when pointed by wit—'Man delights not me, nor woman neither.' I carried her Brennan's Satyr;[4] she is out of patience at it, and vows could she write as well, men should stand marked for more wickedness then e'er the race could redress. I doubt whether I should send you them lest they should cool your desire for matrimony, but by all means let not your mistress see them, unless the one you have a mind to discard. To her, indeed, you may present one, and 'twill affront her, I warrant....

Now we are on love, &c. Do your parents forward this affair? Are they ignorant of it? Or are you purposely together? I believe my friend will soon be a Paterfamilias, and then we shall in some measure lose Dick Shackleton, who will look with contempt on us bachelors. Whenever it happens I pray it may be fortunate, and so pray we all. We were together last night and did not forget you. We were rather mad than merry—but parted sober as to liquor.

When I went to Kearney, Mrs Kearney[5] asked me whether I was come to Levy.[6] I said No! That couple (forgive me, I say it *entre nous*) are very haughty. I examined Michy[7] before them in Horace and Homer; he performed very well, and answered his geographical questions with a facility that surprised me. He did not give very good English, and I did not wade very deep with him in the grammatical part of the Greek, because as the boy was little when taken out of his depth he might be in danger—and not at all for fear that I should slip myself; so I asked only some obvious questions. How were his parents ravished to hear their boy read Greek!

[1] Prior: wrote

[2] Perhaps Thomas Goddard (d. 1763), Dublin lawyer; he entered Trinity College 15 June 1737.

[3] This probably refers to Mrs Goddard, who inspired some romantic admiration among Burke's friends (letter of Dennis to Shackleton 3 January 1757 in Ballitore MSS).

[4] Probably *A Panegyrick on the Fair Sex*, Dublin (R. James), 1747. There is a copy in the British Museum.

[5] Mother of Burke's friend Michael Kearney.

[6] Mrs Kearney probably asked whether Burke had attended levee at Dublin Castle.

[7] Michael Kearney the younger, who entered Trinity College 11 June 1748.

How is Cavenagh![1] Poor Parker is not very ill, yet can't go out. I like prodigiously your proposals; the thing will be improving to the boys, and I will send some materials towards it, but am very little at leisure. The Black ⟨water⟩ runs about a couple of ⟨...⟩ in a fortnight. What you mention about D—[2] seems at first view very practicable, but is not so. As for his mother she says that he is the only tie she has in this kingdom, else she would go and live with her relations in England; but tuition and usherships are harder to be got than you can well imagine without interest, &c. which he very much wants. As for panegyrics on the fellows that would give the *coup de grace* to his fortunes. Sure your verses would do honour to Sappho. Were they all as good as four of them, they would be some of the first in the tongue; but I am surprised that you who every where else are so smooth, are not so here where it is most necessary—such are the fifth, ninth, and tenth lines, and some others. But when I found the above ⟨...⟩ I had not read your similes of David and Goliath;[3] more just or beautifully turned I never saw—I should have said not carefully enough; not but they struck me more strongly at first, but the multiplicity of matter drove them out of my head. Don't think I flatter when I say I think them excellent, as is the conclusion. What punishment will you inflict when I tell you I have constantly forgotten to carry Balbus to Mrs Goddard, but ⟨...⟩ don't say, for before I can write again, T. A.[4] will set that matter right.

The Comedy will be acted before Christmas, when we will expect you, sans excuse. Mrs Kearney said 'tother day we shall all soon see it for nothing, but I thank her for nothing. New plays are not seen for nothing; if they were, the author would get nothing by them, than which nothing can be worse—so there's nothing for nothing.[5]

I forget who he was that told me at the coffee house the other night that Cullen said he and I were very great, and have often lately been merry together—I laugh just now at your penny pot drinker. When I can find Tremble I will, but I wish he may be hanged in the mean time.

[1] John Kavanagh, usher at Ballitore School. [2] Probably Dennis.

[3] Shackleton was writing the verse introduction to a small anonymous volume of *Poems on Several Occasions* published the following year. The volume contained at least two poems of Shackleton's and two of Burke's; its list of subscribers included the names of Abraham Ardesoif, Beaumont Brenan, Andrew Buck, William Dennis, Joseph Hamilton, Juliana Burke and Elizabeth Shackleton. A copy is among the Halliday Pamphlets (Box 202, Tract 15) in the Royal Irish Academy. The simile of David and Goliath is in a passage which Samuels reprints (p. 154).

[4] Not identified.

[5] Burke and his friends were attempting to force Sheridan to produce Beaumont Brenan's *The Lawsuit* (see above, letter of [*circa* 12 March 1746/47], p. 88). They did not succeed before Christmas. Prior quotes (*Life of Goldsmith*, II, 316–17) a letter of Dennis to Shackleton 14 January 1748, saying: 'Ned Burke some time since wrote a paper called Punch's Petition to Mr Sheridan for admission into the theatre...three hundred were sold yesterday.'

Who knows what Providence may have in store for him! What has happened you after quitting Julia and Belinda has happened me in the very same manner often on such occasions. Don't you think a concave better than a spy-glass, as the latter are commonly so bad?[1] Farewell, dear friend, and believe me to be yours most sincerely,

EDM BURKE.

Supply the date.

To RICHARD SHACKLETON—21 *November* 1747

Source: National Magazine (1830), pp. 93–4.

Nov. 21st, 1747.

My dear Friend—You should have received a letter from me before, but I could not settle myself so soon after your departure to write, for after a personal conversation it seems confined and awkward, and beside that at best I do not take very great delight in writing to my best friends: that you will say you have experienced, but not only you but Dennis, he wrote me while I was in the County Corke four letters to which he received no answer, 'tis with shame I own this, yet no one likes the personal conversation of his friend more than I, however nothing is more blameable than such a conduct. I put it in this black light that you may avoid falling into the same error, and chuse to make myself an example to deterr you rather than you should want one, you see I do but chit chat and that the stile answers the sentiment, the corruption of the latter giving the former the gout; the disuse of writing, having but little to say and not caring how I say that little, must needs make this tho' too long deferr'd, not agreeable at last. I was going to say parturiunt montes[2] but I will avoid sticking you with any thing uncommon and choose to be without a quotation rather than give you so new a one. When a man has nothing to say it is good for him to tell it, for by that means he has one sentence out. This is just my case. I fill my letter by telling you I cannot, but dont think my friend that this proceeds from any want of affection for you—but that I am at present, as an author of this age expresses it, in a kind of thoughtful thoughtlessness—and if your friendship could bear with my conversation in such a humour I hope you will shew an equal favour to my letters. How does the country agree with you? do you ever think of us? when we never forget you. If we could be as

[1] The reference is probably to the purchase of an eye-glass or a pair of spectacles. See Burke's letters of 19 December 1746 and 17 July 1764. Mrs Leadbeater describes her mother's first meeting with Burke at nearly this time: 'Both he and his friend were remarkably short-sighted, and they were trying which could read best by twilight' (*Leadbeater Papers*, I, 47).

[2] Mountains are in labour; see Horace, *Ars Poetica*, 139.

united in place as we are in mind we should be happy—but this world, an enemy to every thing good, keeps us asunder. Does Apollo visit your shades? I believe he might be tempted to take up his abode in the valley of Ballitore in exchange for the Hill of Parnassus, did not the fiery face of Rufus, who in confidence of that sets up for another Apollo, deter him, but we won't be frighted or shamed so. We can see through him and find him to be no other than a Midas tho' he has made a shift to gild his ears, which nothing but what is gilded also with a little...can tickle. This same Apollo has been chased from hence by a parcel of Midases and is given out on change as a Bankrupt so that his goods are selling by auction—Brennan one of the Trustees is endeavouring to put off one of his letters, but as he departed with the reputation of a bankrupt, his goods are cried down here as worthless and unfashionable, you heard doubtless that when this same piece of goods was offered to a Trader he refused even giving it a place in his warehouse without payment.[1] At last we have found one James a Bookseller[2] (for I can carry on the allegory no longer) to print it, but he clogs it with this difficulty that we must take off 60 of the copies to lighten the burthen. I fancy you will be able to dispose of some, will you and how many think you? It will make...if this takes and the printer be willing...follow Catius &c.[3] Egad we'll cram the press till it spews out again. I did not see the bearer of your letters or you should have had the books. Write me all the orders that you gave me in Town and I shall carefully execute them or any others you can have for your very sincere friend.

EDM BURKE.

Brenan gives his &c. to you.

To RICHARD SHACKLETON—[24] *December* 1747

Source: Prior (5th ed.), pp. 30, 44.

One of the passages which Prior quotes in his 5th edition—probably from the Burke-Shackleton correspondence once held by Dr Hales—is described as the commencement of a letter of 'December 1747':

There was a young fellow hanged here yesterday for robbing his master of a few guineas. A few days before another was pardoned for the murder of five men. Was not that justice?

[1] The passage is obscure. Burke's 'Rufus' may be William Rufus Chetwood (d. 1766; referred to under the name 'Rufus' in the *Dublin Courant*, 14–18 March 1748/49). An advertisement in Burke's paper the *Reformer* (see next letter) makes it clear that Chetwood was in prison for debt.

[2] Richard James (d. 1757), Dublin printer and bookseller 1746–55 (Plomer, *Dictionary of Printers*, p. 391).

[3] Catius in Pope's *Moral Essays* (Epistle I, 138–9) 'prefers, no doubt, a Rogue with Ven'son to a Saint without'.

A hanging for theft occurred in Dublin 23 December 1747, and excited much public indignation, ending in a riot, since it happened within a few days of the royal pardon of a murderer (*Dublin Journal*, 15–19 and 22–26 December, and 29 December–2 January). This seems to give the passage a fairly certain date of 24 December. Hence it is probably from the same letter as another passage which Prior quotes with an exact date of 'December 24, 1747'. According to Prior the second passage speaks of Burke's friend Dennis:

Don't you think had he money to bear his charges but 'twere his best course to go to London? I am told that a man who writes, can't miss there of getting some bread, and possibly good. I heard the other day of a gentleman who maintained himself in the study of the law by writing pamphlets in favour of the ministry.

To RICHARD SHACKLETON—2 *February* 1747/48

Source: National Magazine (1830), p. 96.

To Mr. Richd. Shackleton in Ballitore per Kilkullen.

Cotter's Shop,[1] Feb. 2d, 1748.

Dear Shackleton.—I should have run out the penalty had I delayed any longer to write to you, but by being so long silent I have contracted such a barrenness that I have little to say. Correspondence is to me what a flow is to water, while it runs it is clear and plentiful but whenever it is stopp'd it stagnates and stinks—I doubt whether I should have wrote now as not yet being at perfect leisure (by means of the Reformer[2] &c.) had not you in a manner forced me by your many expressions of kindness in your letter and the poem on your Mistresses[3] which it was impossible for me to read and forbear telling you how much I am obliged to you for such an excellent entertainment, I confess tho' I had an excellent opinion (founded on experience) of my friend's capacity, I could not believe so much of it, we shall call you the Anacreon of our Society, as you have all his ease and perhaps a strength of thought superior, particularly I like the comparison of the ladies to the shade and house, 'tis highly poetical and with all the warmth of Eastern poetry has a French bienséance and

[1] Joseph Cotter a Dublin printer and bookseller had his shop 'Under Dick's Coffee House, 1747–9' (Plomer, *Dictionary of Printers*, p. 379). This is the coffee house in Skinner's Row whose collapse Burke described in his letter of 29 November 1746 (p. 73).

[2] On 28 January Burke had brought out the first number of a weekly periodical of his own, written after the model of the *Spectator*. Thirteen numbers were produced before the magazine was suspended, 21 April, 'for the ensuing Summer'. Samuels discusses the magazine fully and reprints twelve of its thirteen numbers (pp. 160–79 and 297–329). The only surviving copy is in the Pearse Street Library, Dublin.

[3] Again, Shackleton's 'Julia and Belinda'. The poem is reprinted entire in Samuels (pp. 164–6).

exactness. I shall more in another letter. We have nothing to complain of the sale of the Reformer, few things have sold better, but we will be soon able to judge whether it was not the novelty that sold it by the reception the Town gives our next,[1] we talk in a manner that surprises some and you see by the enclosed that the scribblers do us the honour to take notice of us.[2] We desire nay we command you to send us some Essays on useful subjects or bare hints or whatever you please; I have no news but that Sheridan is to lose his house which we count a judgment on his arrogance and ignorance, but what's that to you? The hurry in the shop prevents me from saying more than that I ever will be one of the sincerest of your friends.

EDMD. BURKE.

I can't say when I can go to you.

To RICHARD SHACKLETON—*May* 1748

Source: Prior (5th ed.), pp. 21, 22.

Prior quotes from a letter of 'May 1748' a brief passage:

Your father mentioned to me the Reformer, and said it had not, he believed, success. I ⟨...⟩ with four or five members being a little surprised at it, as I did not think he knew the author; but I am satisfied he does, and I am sure it is in good hands.

And again from a letter of 'May 1748', not improbably the same letter, a phrase describing Thomas Sheridan:

a pitiful fellow, who was never able to defend himself, and whose defenders are as weak as the cause.

To RICHARD SHACKLETON—5 *January* [1748/49]

Source: Fitzwilliam MSS (Sheffield), Bk 28.

Dr French Laurence made a special remark upon one of the letters of Burke which he saw in the possession of Dr Hales:

> One of the letters ascertains his age. He writes on the 5th of January *1748*, that he was then *twenty*; consequently he was born in *1728*, and in his *seventieth year*, when it pleased Providence to take him from us.

[1] Prior quotes (*Life of Goldsmith*, II, 318) a letter of Dennis to Shackleton 4 February: 'I send you enclosed the second number of the Reformer, with this comfort that the generality of the town likes it I believe, by the sale which was about 500 to-day. The first number the town bought near 1000 of; we have set out *bonis ominibus*...Ned is writting for his degree!'

[2] Samuels calls attention to one reply to the *Reformer*: Paul Hiffernan's *Tickler*. Its first issue is dated 18 February (copy in Halliday Pamphlets [vol. 203] in Royal Irish Academy).

The inference is not inescapable. A tablet to Burke in Beaconsfield Church asserts that he was sixty-eight—that is, in his sixty-ninth year—when he died in 1797. His birth has usually been placed in January 1728/29, which is consistent with that assertion. Dr Laurence appears to be forgetting the complications of Old and New Style when dealing with dates in the first three months of the year. Burke's letters in the 1740's show that he had no fixed practice of always writing his date as in the earlier year, or always in the later. Thus if he described himself as twenty in a letter dated '5th of January 1748', it is at least as likely as not that he was writing in the year which we would cite as 1748/49. If he was, there is no reason to disturb our present beliefs concerning the year of his birth.

To WILLIAM BURKE—*November* 1750

Source: Fitzwilliam MSS (Sheffield) Bk 40.
Printed *A Note-Book of Edmund Burke*, pp. 21–5.

One of several verse epistles and other compositions by Edmund and William Burke to be found in a MS notebook at Sheffield. The date is open to question: '1752' seems to have been written first and then altered to '1750', both on Edmund's lines and on Will Burke's reply to them, suggesting that both may have been copied into the notebook when the date of their writing was no longer clearly remembered.

For the period from January 1749 to the autumn of 1750 no letters of Burke survive. It is probable that he was beginning to apply himself to his father's profession of the law. He had been entered at the Middle Temple, London, 23 April 1747, and he crossed to England to begin his studies three years later; his bond there is dated 2 May 1750. One of the sureties who signed the bond was 'John Burke of Serjeants-inn, Fleet-street, Gent.' John Burke (d. 1764) was the father of William Burke (1728–98), who entered the Temple 26 May 1750 and soon became Edmund's closest friend. Whether there was a blood relationship between them is doubtful, though henceforth they called each other 'cousin'. William was one year older than Edmund, had been educated at Westminster and Christ Church, Oxford, and was eventually called to the Bar. From the beginning of their friendship the two young men lived together on the most intimate terms, shared each other's studies and developed similar ambitions.

The Muse divorced

An Epistle from Mr E. Burke to his friend Mr W Burke.

Croyden Nov. 1750.

His Life who changes has a Deal to do,
To break old habits, and establish new;
His nature rises for the good old cause,
His little Kingdom will assert its Laws,
Custom opposes; pride itself is strong;
We own by Changing that, we once were wrong;
Our Interests sometimes we're induced to part,
Our Vanity grows nearer to the Heart:

This felt a grave Divine as well as we
Who not to Damn his Book, renounc'd his see;[1]
Full half his Laurels Richlieu would resign,
O Envied Corneille, for one Branch of thine.[2]
Who e'er has faults, and chuses not to mend
By great examples may his faults defend.
But I whose Ardor, thinking daily cools,
And time has taught, for time e'en teaches fools,
Galled with the straitness of the Marriage Noose,
Tho late, did thus repudiate my Muse.
'Hence from my Doors! begone! I set thee free!
Take all the portion I receiv'd with thee!
All the vain hopes of Profit and of praise,
The blasted Ivy and the Hungry Bays,
The time ill spent or lost (the Dreamers lot)
The Idle Learning, which I wish forgot,
The high romantick flights, the mad Designs,
Th' unnumbered number of neglected Lines,
The Itch, that first to scribbling turn'd my Quill
The fatal Itch, that makes me scribble still
Take these, and all the relicts of thy store,
The Rich in that, are poorest of the Poor;
Go! and may better fate thy Steps attend[3]
Go! and Learn better how to chuse a friend;
Some Fop whose pride and vast Estate admit,
The Weighty charge of Idleness and Wit.'
Thus whilst I spoke, my better Genius led;
And yet anon I wish'd it all unsaid.
The poets ail no Remedies can ease,
Because we cherish still our own disease;
What e'er the Turn of mind still[4] verse presents,
Here all the Passions have their Proper vents.
Are we Enraged? Revenge presents us soon
The murdering Dagger of a keen Lampoon.
If proud—in Lofty Odes we tread the Sky,
Swell in Heroics, strut in Tragedy—

[1] The author of the Greek romance *Aethiopica* was once supposed to have been Heliodorus, bishop of Tricca in Thessaly; the story was told that confronted with the alternative of disowning the romance or resigning the bishopric he chose to resign.

[2] Protagonists of literary culture have always been pleased that Cardinal Richelieu envied Corneille his success as a playwright.

[3] This line is inserted in pencil and in another hand.

[4] MS: stills

If the soft impulse of Desire we prove
What so ally'd as Poetry and Love?
If wiser grown, we would redeem our time,
'Tis but good manners[1] to take leave in Rhime
If we succeed, success gives cause t'indite,
If we should fail, Despair provokes to write.
The strong and weak consume in the same fire,
The force unequal, equal the Desire.
What Whips! What Stings! what furies drive us on?
Why all this Mighty rage to be undone?
Why still persist when ruin and Disgrace,
When want and Shame present their hideous face?
When scornful Silence loudly cries, Abstain,
Our friends advise, our parents preach in vain.
Well sage Astrologers, I yield at Last,
I own the folly of my Wisdom past.
Your Convert grown with Rev'rence I reflect,
On time, and Quartile. and Malign Aspect.
Whate'er the stars determine at our Birth,
Whether to conquer, or to Plough the Earth;
Whether to wear the Ribband, or the Rope,
Whether to be, or whether burn a Pope,
Whether in gouty Pride on down to loll,
Or Range with Midnight whores the cold patrol,
This Rules our Days; in vain the Wretch would fly
His Stars o'erlook him with a conscious Eye,
Drag back the Rebel to his destined Hate;
The Chain refusing strugling with his fate.
Een I while arming for the wordy war
Neglect the spoils and trophies[2] of the Bar,
Drawn by th'attraction of my natal Ray.
Against my Reason often Quit my way.
Yet preach to others in the same distress,
Dissuade with Words, and then dissuade no less,
By sad Example of my own success.
O what a Shameful Fate does he endure,
Who sees his fault, and seeing cannot cure,

[1] In MS the final s is added in pencil.
[2] MS: Strophies of the Bar. One of Burke's MS notebooks at Lamport (N.R.S., A xxx 6) confirms the truth of the line, as it begins with legal notes and soon turns into drafts of poetry.

When scenes like these afflict the tortured soul,
Say is the Lynx more happy than the mole?
  Yet sure he happy is, or happy none,
Whose choice and Interest in one Channel run,
His greatest toils his greatest pleasures prove,
For how can Labour weary which we love
On all he Acts propitious Venus smiles,
And Graces weave their Dance among his Toils.
  He's happy too, who lets no Care Destroy
The Prosp'rous moment of the present Joy.
The hopeful parson new arriv'd in town,
Who just has got a wife, and just a Gown,
Tho' young, yet rev'rend; warm yet Nice in Love,
Enjoys chast raptures with his Turtle Dove,
What pretty Chat! what soft endearing Arts!
What blending souls! what Sympathy of Hearts!
Mindless the while of Duns impatient calls,
The Grocers hooks, the Vict'lers fouler scrawls.
And Chandlers endless scores that Whiten all the Walls.
*This swain, if Nature to the Test we bring
Tastes more true joy and nearer to the spring
Than we, who vainly wise consume our years,
Ills to prevent, that only mock our Cares,
Or tho' our fortunes our desires should Shape,
Gain all we wish, and all we fear escape;
  In this alone, my friend, true Quiet lies
Wholly to be a fool, or wholly wise.
The space betwixt is but a mangled Scene,
Here the Extreams are Golden not the mean,
Those hapless Lands that warring Realms divide
By turns are wasted by the conquring side,
A like or worse Distraction we shall find,
In minds so mixed in Contraries so join'd;
While follys dreams are still by Wisdom cross'd,
And wisdoms Schemes by Headstrong folly Lost,
With great Designs a fickle mind ill suits
An equal Sky must ripen generous fruits
Under whatever Standard we Inlist,
'Twere better ne'er begin, than not persist.

* These Lines allude to Mr C. a very honest Young Divine very much in Love and more in Debt. Very Orthodox and very poor [Burke's note].

Rous'd with these thoughts I lash my Lazy side,
And all my strength collect and all my Pride
All boyish dreams for ever disavow
Then dream, and Triffle, play, and rhime as now,
This of myself I know, and more amiss
But should Will: Burke presume to tell me this,
'The fool! the Coxcomb! the ill mannered Elf!
Who dares to think me—What I think myself.'
Can we, my friend, with any Conscience bear
To shew our minds sheer naked as they are,
Remove each veil of Custom, pride or Art,
Nor stretch a hand to hide one Shamefull part?
An equal Share of Scorn and Danger find,
A Naked body, and an open mind
Both sights unusual, sights which never fail
To make the Witty laugh, and pious Rail,
The Children fly for fear, the women scream
And Sages cry the World has Lost its Shame.
And ev'n some friends (that sacred Name) we have
Whom so to keep, 'tis proper to deceive—
Who Lofty Notions build on Plato's plan—
And grow quite angry when they find you *man*;
Who can be friends, and yet be Judges too?
Few can be such, then Let me keep those few.

Will Burke's reply to this Epistle, dated from London in the same month (MS at Sheffield, Bk 40; printed in *A Notebook of Edmund Burke*, pp. 26–7), was mostly in conventional vein:

Tho' Claret flow not at thy humble feast
The Muse's voice shall gladden every Guest;
Your heart is hers, in her be all your joy;
But Let the law your Graver thoughts employ....

One couplet has a greater interest, because it suggests more genuine feeling:

Your word, Dear friend, has been my guiding Line,
Your Conduct was, and is, the Rule of mine....

To RICHARD SHACKLETON—26 *February* 1750/51

Source: MS Dr O. Fisher. Printed *Leadbeater Papers*, II, 94–6.
MS repaired with tape. About twenty-five words restored by another hand.

Dear friend

It is so long since we have had any Correspondence that I really forget whether I am indebted to you for a letter, or you to me: perhaps I am in the fault, if I be I can say with a great deal of truth, that it did not proceed from my having in the least forgot you or the obligations I have to you (if any such thing ought to be named among friends,) or if you have omitted to write in your turn, I give you with all my heart the forgiveness I should myself expect in the same case, I shall however be always willing to attribute your Silence to any thing, rather than inconstancy and while there are so many thousand things that may cause such an Omission, I shall chuse any rather than that which would wrong you and make myself uneasy; for my part I am in my writing, in the same Case that I am in my Conversation, if I am in Company with a Silent person I repay his Silence fourfold, but if on the contrary I happen with a man who talks, he incites me to do so too, I could wish with all my heart to hear oftner from you, nor can want of matter whilst[1] you have affairs of your own: to make me by letter as you were so good formerly to do by discourse, acquainted with them would be very agreeable to me as such a confidence would show that your good opinion of me still continues the same; I wish that nothing worse than want of Somewhat to say, that want of health is not the cause of your Silence. I hope my fears are without foundation, but I must beg leave to observe that your great application to Business both in and out of School as well as your so close reading at night may impair both your health and Eyesight neither of the Best, I therefore pray you as a friend and as one that has an Interest in your life and welfare to indulge yourself more in little amusements and cheerfulness if you have a mind your life should last or whilst it lasts be easy.

I have had some trouble for a good while, on account of the almost generall illness of our family of which I suppose you may have heard as well as of their recovery.

I had a letter after a long intermission of writing from Dennis, I beleive him to be the same worthy man I always thought him he tells me that he spent some days lately at your house and seems very sensible of your friendship and Civility to him.

Thus far I wrote before Dinner, and I am now prevented from writing

[1] MS: whillt

more by a Gentlemans coming in upon me, I have only to desire you to remember me very kindly to your Spouse,[1] to your father and all the good family there and still to think you have a very

sincere friend in
EDMD BURKE

London feb. 26th 1750.

A Bill was brought into the house of Lords yesterday by the Earl of Chesterfield for altering the Stile tis thought it will pass.[2]

To RICHARD SHACKLETON—5 *April* 1751

Source: MS Dr O. Fisher. Printed *Leadbeater Papers*, II, 96–8.
Addressed: To | Mr Richard Shackleton | at Ballitore | Per Killcullen Bridge | in Ireland.

Dear friend

I received your letter with more pleasure than you may think from my having delayed so long to answer it but the true Cause of my waiting was that I might have the Satisfaction of seeing your Uncle and Cousins, and by that means make my letter more welcome to you by some Account of them, but I failed in my design for I could hear nothing of[3] your Uncle at the East India House, whither I went according to your directions about O neils affair, I must advise that Gentleman not to appear so sollicitous about his Brother's health, lest he (as all men are not of the most unsuspecting nature) should think he has a greater love for his Effects, than for their owner, nor to promise to persons here half of them to recover the whole for him, for he is too Good a Scholar not to remember the case of the huntsman that sold the Bearskin before he had killed the Bear; I no sooner enquired concerning a Chaplain at Bencoolen than the person I asked (Judge you whether he was a Conjurer) informed me about what business I came and that some others had been there on the same Errand; observing that this Gentleman seemd to long for his Brothers death, at the same time telling me for his comfort that nothing but a constitution of Steel could keep the body and Soul together in that Climate. However, that the Chaplain had a pretty Good one, was a Sober man and had lived with pretty tolerable health in the hundreds

[1] Shackleton had married Elizabeth Fuller (1726–54) 2 April 1749. Burke wrote some lines: 'To Richard Shackleton on his Marriage', dated 1748 (printed in *A Collection of Poems...by Several Hands*, Dublin, 1789, pp. 220–2; later printed by Prior, 2nd ed. I, 29–30; MS copy at Sheffield, Bk 27b).

[2] Lord Chesterfield's bill for reforming the calendar was introduced into the House of Lords 25 February and received the Royal Assent 22 May.

[3] MS: off

of Essex. Our friend is a divine and may take the Good, and bad of this Account together. When they heard last from Bencoolen, he was well and that about next August they shall have a further Account.[1]

I am much obliged to you my good friend for your desire of knowing my affairs, really they are such as nothing but friendship could have any delight in hearing; my health is tolerable, thank God, my Studies too in the same degree, and my Situation not disagreeable. I intend soon to go a good distance from town in hopes of bettering all three, as well as lessening my Expences. If you are desirous of knowing any thing more particularly let me know and you may be assured I shall take pleasure in Satisfying you.

I am glad your family continues in good health you will in return for her kindness give my best respects to Your Spouse. The same to your father and all friends as tho I had named them. I saw Kennedy[2] at a Coffee house a few days since, he has been at the East Indies, in what Station I cannot tell and intends for the same quarter again he is much improved both his appearance and behaviour since I saw him at Ballitore.

Farewell dear Shackleton and believe me with

great sincerity yours

EDMD BURKE.

London April 5th 1751.

To RICHARD SHACKLETON—31 *August* 1751

Source: MS Dr O. Fisher. Printed *Corr.* (1844), I, 24–6.

Dear Shackleton

If having very little to say was a Sufficient excuse for my Silence I fear I should continue it much longer, the truth is I have been so long

[1] The Rev. Arthur O'Neil (b. *c.* 1711) brother of Felix O'Neil (see above, letters of 29 May and 29 June 1744, pp. 11, 23) was suffering a moral if not a physical collapse in Sumatra. The General Letter to the Court of Directors dated 11 December 1753 from Fort Marlborough reported home about him: 'We are concerned to say Mr Arthur O'Neill's Behaviour ever since his Arrival on this Coast being so very bad and unbecoming a Clergyman, the Deputy Governour could not avoid, seeing no hope of his amendment of Life to require the Opinion of the Board, whether he was deserving of the Gratuity your Honours were pleased to allow his Function...' (India Office Library, Factory Records: Sumatra, v. 9 (Misc. letters, etc. 1740–53), doc. 428, par 63). He carried out at least his most rudimentary functions. His signature 'Arthur Neill, Chaplain' is upon a list of burials (ibid. Chaplain's List no. 20, doc. 1118), including the burial of 'John Wilkinson, Bookbinder, 15 December 1752'—perhaps a relation of Shackleton, whose mother's maiden name was Wilkinson. A printed document (ibid. 'The Case of John Cranmer', doc. 1045), unfortunately undated, records that Arthur Neill 'minister at Bencoolen' returned to England.

[2] William Kennedy entered Ballitore School 10 November 1743.

an invalid and a traveller (a sort of people to whom great allowances must be made) that I was always either too weak or too much hurried to Set about any thing. But tho I omitted to write I have not forgot how much on every account I am indebted to your friendship. I dont think it necessary when a man writes to his friend that he should make his letter a Gazette for news or puzzle himself for something deep and philosophical, or is obliged under penalties and pains to be witty, it is enough in my opinion to give our friend some proof that we still keep him in our memory and receive the same from him. And I assure I think in this plain intercourse of honest Sentiments there is more Satisfaction and more merit too, than in any affected complements let them be ever so fine, which none can admire, but those who dont know how they are produced, and on what occasions. I hope your little family is well,[1] I believe you are so good a husband and father as to talk of it with pleasure and that you think me so much your friend as to hear it with satisfaction tho I am no father nor ever was except of some metaphorical Children which were extremely shortlived and whilst they lived (as you know) too scandalous to be ⟨owne⟩d. I hope my present ⟨stu⟩dies may be attended ⟨with more⟩ Success, at least I have this comfort that tho a middling Poet cannot be endured there is some quarter for a middling Lawyer. I read as much as I can (which is however but a little,) and am but just beginning to know something of what I am about, which till very lately I did not; this Study carries no difficulty to those who already understand it and to those who never will understand it, and for all between those extreams, (God knows) they have a hard task of it. So much is certain tho the Success is precarious, but that we must leave to providence. I am now at Monmouth where I live very satisfactorily, am well and know by experience of the Contrary what a blessing that is. I wish you may not labour too much for your constitution which now at least you are obliged to take care of. My most sincere respect to your father mother Spouse aunt and Sister, and believe me your very affectionate friend and Servant

EDMD BURKE.

Monmouth Augst 31st 1751.

Direct to me at Mr Hipkis's Ironmonger in Monmouth my Service to Hobbs[2]—Dennis has acquainted me of his good intentions towards me.

[1] Shackleton's first child, Deborah, was born 6 March 1749/50.

[2] William Gill (d. 1787) steward at Ballitore School, was called Hobbes by Burke and Shackleton, who regarded him as an unlettered philosopher. For accounts of him see Prior, 2nd ed. I, 16–17; *Leadbeater Papers*, I, 41, 165–6, 171.

To Richard Shackleton—28 *September* 1752

Source: MS Dr O. Fisher. Printed *Corr.* (1844), I, 26–31.
Addressed: To | Mr Richd Shackleton | at | Ballitore per | Killcullen Bridge | Ireland.

My Dear friend

I have several letters to write this day, and must begin every one of them with an apology for not having written before. I think I have greater occasion to apologize to you than to any of them, because I love you better, and have used you much worse; but I know that tho my fault should require a great deal to be said your goodnature will dispence with it; you will believe I could not forget you; and if you do, my Business is done; for that in short is all I can say in my defence. I have now before me your letter which I received about this time last year in Monmouth. I now sit down to Answer it at Turlaine in Wilts;[1] you have compared me for my rambling disposition to the Sun as the Simile was about the Sun, it was probably a compliment, if so, I thank you for it; if it was rather a reproof, why I thank you too, it may possibly do me more good. But sincerely I cant help finding a likeness myself, for they say the Sun sends down much the same influences whenever he comes into the same signs, now I am influenced to shake off[2] my laziness and write to you at the same time of the year and the same West country that I wrote my Last in. Tis true I am not directly at the same place, but you know to those who are at a vast distance, things may be a good way asunder and yet seem near. But not to run this allusion quite out of Breath, since I had your letter I have often shifted the Scene, I spent part of the Winter that is the Term time in London,[3] and part in Croydon in Surry; about the beginning of Summer finding myself attacked with my old complaints I went once more to Bristol and found the same benefit. I thank God for it, and wish I had Grace to take in its full extent your very friendly and rational advice. I dont know whether I said much to you, of our adventures at Monmouth they would almost compose a

[1] In his verses in the next letter Burke gives the name of this place as Turley, which is closer to its modern name of Turleigh. R. E. Peach, *Historic Houses in Bath*, London, 1883, says of Burke (I, 28): '*At Turley House*, near Bradford, he visited more than once his friend Mr Atwood, whose family for two centuries had been connected with Bath.' Mrs Leadbeater writing to Jane Burke 10 February 1807 (Sheffield, Bk 28) lists among correspondence of Burke and Shackleton a letter not otherwise known, from 'Turlaine in Wilts May 7 1758'.

[2] MS: of

[3] The Butler's Collections Book of the Middle Temple records a payment: 'Collected on the Roll Hillary Term 1752...Burke, E. Pentions 11/8 Minister 7/ Officers 2/4 Total 1/1/–'. Burke continued eating dinners in the Middle Temple for another three years. The last whole week's board charged to his name is in November 1755, though he continued a member of Middle Temple till his death.

Novel and that of a more curious and entertaining kind than some of those we are entertaind with from the press. I assure you, we formd discourse for that Town and the adjacent Country whilst we staid there, and even when we left it. Whilst we staid, they amused themselves with guessing the Reason that could induce us to come amongst them, and when we left them, they were no less employed to discover why we went away without effecting those purposes they planned for us. The most innocent Scheme they guessd, was that of fortunehunting, and when they saw us quit the Town without wives, then the Lower sort sagaciously judgd us spies to the French King. You will wonder that persons of no great figure should cause so much talk; but in a Town very little frequented by Strangers, with very little business to employ their bodies, and less speculation to take up their minds the least thing sets them in motion and supplies matter for their Chat; what is much more odd, is that here, my Companion and I puzzle them as much as we did at Monmouth, for this is a place of very great Trade in making of fine Cloaths, in which they employ a vast Number of hands; the first conjecture which they made was, that we were Authors; for they could not fancy how any other sort of people could spend so much of their time at Books, but finding that we received from Time to Time a good many letters, they concluded us Merchants and so from inference to inference they at last began to apprehend that we were Spies from Spain on their Trade; our little curiosity perhaps cleard us of that imputation, but still the whole appears very mysterious, and our good old woman, cries 'I believe that you be Gentlemen, but I ask no questions,' and then praises herself for her great Caution and Secrecy; what makes the thing still better; about the same time we came hither arrived a little parson equally a Stranger, but he spent a good part of his hours in shooting and other country amusements, got drunk at Night, got drunk in the morning and became intimate with every body in the Village, he surprised no body, no questions were askd about him because he lived like the rest of the world, but that two men should come into a strange country, and partake none of the Country diversions, seek no Acquaintance and live entirely recluse is something so inexplicable as to puzzle the wisest heads even that of the parish Clerk himself.—We are however as satisfactorily fixed as we can wish, we live in a pretty large house which we have almost to ourselves, our Landlady[1] has been once a rich woman, but happening to go down in the world on the accession of the Hannover family to the Throne, she attributes all her misfortunes to that event, it is the pleasantest thing in the world to hear the Good folks opinion of

[1] Mrs Druce; see Burke's postscript.

State affairs, in short they are hearty Jacobites, that is a sort of people whose politicks consists in wishing that right may take place, and their religion, in heartily hating presbyterians. Our family consists of the old Gentlewoman, an old woman her Sister, and a young fellow her Son who is a great Scholard and knows what is what, and therefore much esteemd by some of the neighbouring Squires. I have troubled you perhaps with too many triffling particulars but they may possibly give you a better Idea of our people than a more labourd description as for this Country tho the Soil is generally poor in our Part of it, it is extremely pleasant, sweetly diversified with hills and Woods, intermixed with Villages, we have one point of View from which we can reckon 6 Steeples. The Country is very populous, and it is the only one, I ever saw where children are really an advantage to their parents for I have seen little Girls of 6 or 7 years old at the wheel and I am told they can earn 3s. 6d. a week each, which is more than their keeping can amount to; tho I hear them say that Trade is decaying amongst them, and that formerly they had greater prices.

I had a letter from Dennis some time since he mentions nothing of his affairs, but seemd angry with me for my long Silence. I wrote him an answer to excuse myself, I wish him very well and would gladly know how the world goes with him. As for you I suppose you have long since been a second time a father,[1] I hope most sincerely all manner of happiness both to the Children and the father and mother, pray remember me in the best manner to her that I have last mentiond. Assure your father and mother that I have the most grateful and affectionate remembrance of them and give my hearty Services to all friends believe me with great sincerity my dear dick

your friend and Servant

EDMD BURKE

Turlaine September 28th 1752.

Direct to me at Mrs Druces at Turlaine near Bradford in Wilts.

[1] Shackleton's second child, Margaret, had been born 18 October 1751.

To DR CHRISTOPHER NUGENT—*September* [1752]

Source: Fitzwilliam MSS (Sheffield), Bk 40.
Printed *A Note-Book of Edmund Burke*, pp. 35–9.

The copy of this letter in the MS notebook at Sheffield is clearly dated 'Turlaine Sepr 1751'. There is, however, a probability that the letter was written in the following year. Burke says of Dr Nugent:

> 'Tis now two Autumns, since he chanc'd to find,
> A youth of Body broke, infirm of mind....'

As Burke (the youth) was not in England before the spring of 1750 this would seem to put the composition, at least of these lines, as late as 1752. We know from the previous letter that Burke was in Turlaine in September 1752; we do not know of his being there in 1751, when he tells us he was at Monmouth. The reason for uncertainty may be again that the lines were transcribed into the notebook long after their composition. See above discussion of the date of Burke's letter of November 1750 (p. 103).

Burke's health was uncertain in his early years in England, which led him at various times to consult Dr Christopher Nugent (1698–1775), an Irish physician practising in Bath. A stay in the Doctor's house for medical treatment is supposed to have nourished his romantic feelings for the Doctor's daughter Jane Mary (1734–1812), whom he married in 1757.

An Epistle to Doctor Nugent by E B.

Turlaine Sepr 1751

A grave Philosopher, whom Fate had thrown
'Midst all the Busy Bustle of the Town,
Could never compass his exalted Views,
While this of stocks enquires, and that of News,
His thoughts are broken with discordant Sounds,
An Almanacks Cry, an Epocha confounds;
Just as he finds, what Long his Labours crosst.
An Idle friend pops in, and all is Lost.
To Courts and Alleys, then in vain he flies,
For Courts and Alleys have their louder Cries.
Such were his days, but were his nights secure?
The Barbarous watchman thunders at the Door.
Tormented thus, he pants for rural Shades,
The thoughtfull Coverts, and the silent glades,
To draw from rivulets that murmur there,
From ancients Books, calm Sleep, and frugal fare,
The sweet oblivion of a Life of Care.
Suppose him now, in a sequestred Grot
Deep, very Deep, into the Country got;
For none can think, 'tis by the Learn'd confess'd,
Unless from Town full fifty Leagues at Least,
First then, Romes Centinels proclaim the Day
An hundred Cocks salute the Morning Gray;

The Rooks a Clamorous Council hold on high;
The oxen low; the fiery Coursers neigh,
A thousand throats awake ten thousand more,
Till Hills, and woods and Vales are all aroar.
What shall our Student do? why Shift the Scene,
Pack up his Books and turn to Town again.
  This Tale, dear friend in his own striking way,
(Murder'd by me) you'll meet in Rabelais,[1]
Some end it serves, if it can mirth produce,
It serves a better, if it turns to use.
For Solitude is neither here nor there,
Turley's no more retired than Westminster,
In vain we fly from place to place to find
What not in place consists, but in the mind.
If I am fearfull, insolent, or proud,
Or torn with Passions, that distract the Croud,
If these I carry to my Country Seat,
Am I in Solitude and in Retreat,
But if I feel my soul confirmed and free,
What is the Town and what the Croud to me?
  As men in pain no posture can abide
But Shift in hope of Ease from side to side.
Thus Kings of Empire sick, of all admired,
From thrones of Care to Convents have retired,
Sick of the Convent too, too late have known
The fault was in themselves, and not the Throne.
In vain we strip the Purple from the Skin
If Deeper purple still remains within.
  Perhaps I drive too fast in this Career,
And you good Sir, may Whisper in my Ear,
That those who willingly run down a Hill,
Are forced to run yet more against their Will,
So men oft hearted with Conceits they Love,
Prove more by half, than does them good to prove.
  I love retreat, I own, no mortal more,
Shall I applaud my Virtue on that Score?
When, were my Soul laid open to your Veiw,
'Tis more to Indolence than Virtue due.
  Heav'n bless those folks, who seeming to be wise
With specious names their faults would canonize—

[1] *Gargantua and Pantagruel*, Bk. III, ch. XIII.

Yet under Planets so perverse are born,
They wish to be the very things they scorn,
That Sage, who calls a fop mankinds disgrace,
Envies that fop, his figure and his face.
That Dame, who rails at whores from morn' till Night
Repines that infamy can buy Delight;
And I, who think it is the times reproach,
To see a Scoundrel Gamester in his Coach,
Think modestly 'twould have a better Air,
To see my humble self exalted there.
  Self Love its End pursues by various ways,
We censure others, but ourselves to praise.
Why should I list on the severer side?
Will my Own Conduct such a Test abide?
Great Faults we ought in Charity to spare,
And if they're small, they not are worth our Care;
Since from the same contracted notions move,
Th'excessive hate of Triffles, and the Love.
I knew a man, who to th'extreme had brought,
The strictest Virtue, and the deepest thought
Who science lov'd, and yet had only trod—
The Path of Science, as a road to God.
The Arts and Virtues join'd, his soul possess'd,
And Taste diffused a Sunshine o'er the rest
But Art and Taste and Learning only stood,
To fill the time, he breath'd from doing good.
This man so grac'd, so little was allie'd,
Or to the Courtly or pedantick pride,
His temper cheerfull, innocent, and free
Could stoop to all things;—he could stoop to me—
His easy virtue never wore a frown,
He mentioned others faults as they their own.
Nor even ingenuous follies did he hate
But left the Proud t'enjoy their sullen State.
  'Tis now two Autumns, since he chanc'd to find,
A youth of Body broke, infirm of mind,
He gave him all that man can ask or give,
Restor'd his Life, and taught him how to Live,
But what, and when and How this youth shall pay,
Must be discuss'd upon a Longer day.

Mean time ten thousand[1] cares distract my Life,
And keep me always with myself at Strife;
Too indolent on flying Wealth to seize,
Of wealth too covetous to be at ease.
I look at Wisdom, wonder, and Adore
I look, I wonder, but I do no more.
Timrous the Heights of every thing I fear,
Perhaps even Wisdom may be bought too Dear,
The Tortoise snatch'd aloft, to highest Air,
Was high 'tis true, but was not happy there.
Shall I then vapour in a stoic strain,
Who, while I boast, must writhe myself for Pain;
Shall I, who grope my way with purblind Eyes,
Shall such as I, pretend to dogmatise?
Better in one low path secure to crawl,
To Doubt of all things, and to Learn from all.
Why should I grieve? in quiet here I dwell,
Our Irish Kings were never Lodged so well,
Blest with a friend, with indolence and peace,
Oh! would kind Heav'n a fortune add to these!
The hopefull end of all my reasning see!
Thus have I been and thus shall alway be.
What now I have, I wish'd a year ago;
I have my Wish, and am I happy? No—
Had I this fortune, that I now require
Is there in Nature nothing to desire?
But Providence has more than made amends
And giv'n what fortune cannot give us—friends.
This pleasing thought yet further to pursue
I want the aid of such a friend as you
And Hers no less, in whom just Heav'n has join'd,
The weakest body, with the firmest mind,
We'll give you such good Humour as we have,
Nay I will laugh, William shall be grave,
Our fair and Absent friend we'll toast the while.
(I will not wrong her in this creeping stile)
What would you more? the Skies, the roads are fine,
The sun preparing for the Vernal Sign.
Stay if you dare, remember that in Spring
An Angry Poet is a dangerous thing.

[1] MS: thousands

To RICHARD BURKE, *his father—11 March* 1755

Source: MS Osborn Collection. Printed Prior, 2nd ed. I, 50–1. Only the last line, date-line and signature are in Burke's hand.

Between September 1752 and August 1757 there is a single surviving letter of Burke. Prior says (5th ed. p. 41 n.) that it was recovered from the lining of an old chair. A large fraction of the MS—a quarter of the folio sheet—has been torn away, but from what remains it appears that Burke had considered applying for a colonial post which was vacant. His father, on hearing of the plan, strongly disapproved. Burke wrote to soothe his anger.

Honoured Sir

I had a Letter by the last post from Mr Nagle[1] in which he tells me that he gave you my Letter and informs me at the same time of the Reception which the proposal it Containd met with from you and the family. I am, I own Surprizd, and very much Concernd that this proposal should prove any Cause either of grief or anger to you, certain I am that nothing ever was further from my Inclination than the least intention of making it so. When I informd you of my design it was not to declare any determind Resolution which I had taken but to desire your opinion on an affair which I believd it adviseable for me to engage in. This affair seemd to me neither to be wrong in itself nor unattended with a reasonable prospect of Success.

I proposed it to you as I must and ought to propose to you everything I think to my advantage, with a View of having your advice upon every material Step I should take in it. This is what in prudence I ought to have done and what every motive of Duty and Gratitude ought to have obliged me to.

I have nothing nearer my heart than to make you easy and I have no Scheme or design, however reasonable it may seem to me that I would not gladly Sacrifice to your Quiet and submit to your Judgment, you have surely had trouble enough with a Severe disorder without any addition from uneasiness at my Conduct ⟨...⟩ing in this business is capable of affecting me so much as the th⟨...⟩ lying heavy on you ⟨...⟩
⟨...⟩ My Brother ⟨...⟩
solely with a view to my Zeal In
and truly thankfull for it, but then
advice as a friend on any design of
may wear, and that I have not only
my Duty so to do and to abide by

[1] David Nagle (1718–1800) of Ballygriffin and Bath is perhaps the 'Mr Nagle' most likely to have acted as an intermediary between Burke in London and his father in Dublin.

Contrary to my own, and sure if I hav
I am not obstinate nor opiniona
mine ought only to intitule it wit
-sideration. I own I was a good de
wrote in that time if I had not wa
to write; During that interval I ha
left this and a very probable prosp
province now vacant a place of C
averse to my design I intend to dec
first Enterd on this affair, I consult
and knowledge of the Circumstances w
they all to a man highly approvd of it
it to you resolved to let the Ballance
you should direct, this is my opini
utmost success of that design or of
much as the thought of having acqu
utmost in my power to please you
Truest Interest and shall therefore follo
but with pleasure and realy nothing has this long time chagrind me so much as to find that the proposal of this matter has been disagreeable to you, I ought to have a Satisfaction in desiring your Judgment on whatever appeard to my Advantage as this strongly did. I shall be Ready to yield to it always and to go to Ireland when you think proper and the End for which you desire I should go can be answerd, I feel to the bottom of my Soul for all you have this long time sufferd from your disorder and it grieves me deeply to think that at such a time your Suffering should be at all encreasd by anything which looks ill judgd in my Conduct. May God make them lighter every moment and Continue to you and my Mother very many very happy Years and every blessing I ought to wish you for your Care, your Tenderness and your indulgence to me. I am in some trouble and Anxiety about this matter but in real truth in all my designs I shall have nothing more at heart than to shew my self to you and my Mother a dutiful affectionate and oblidged Son

EDMD BURKE

London 11 Mar 1755

To JOSEPH EMIN—[*circa* 7] *August* 1757

Source: MS Morgan Library.

A joint letter of Edmund and Will Burke. Will's portion, dated 7 August, is omitted. Edmund's date of 'Augst 1' though clearly written is impossible: reports of the battle of Hastenbeck first appear in the London papers 4 August, and the first full account 6 August (*London Chronicle*, II, 119, 127). Emin wrote

Dr Messenger Monsey (1693–1788) 30 July, enclosing his own account of the battle, to be given to Mrs Montagu and his other 'ladies and Patronesses'. In a postscript (probably written 1 August) he told Dr Monsey: 'Now I would have you ask Mr Burke's advice about this letter before you coppy it for my friends' (Climenson, *Mrs Montagu*, II, 108).

Joseph Emin (1736–1809) in his *Autobiography* (pp. 89–91) describes a meeting with Burke which must have taken place late in 1755 or early in 1756. Emin had come from India to seek his fortune in England and was very much in need of countenance and patronage. He saw Burke walking in St James's Park in company with a Mr Bodly, a lawyer, whom Emin had once seen in Calcutta. He accosted Burke as the more affable-looking of the two, and was soon in conversation with both. '...They took him with them into the small Wilderness where they ate some rusks and drank some milk, and came out of the park' and at nightfall Burke invited Emin to his rooms 'up two pairs of stairs, at the sign of Pope's Head, at a bookseller's near the Temple'. After hearing the young man's story Burke introduced himself: 'Sir, my name is Edmund Burke, at your service. I am a runaway son from a father, as you are.' He offered Emin money, which was refused, but discovering his need of employment he set him to copying two works he then had in manuscript, the *Vindication of Natural Society* and the *Sublime and Beautiful*. He later helped Emin to get a military appointment and assisted him with friendly advice, as appears in this letter written a year or so afterwards.

My Dear Emin,

I take it very kindly, that you remembered me so early. For my part I never cease to think of you, and to wish you with the greatest warmth not only safety, but honour. Your Uncle Will answers for himself; but I think I may say for both of us, that there are none in England, who rejoice so heartily at the reception you had from the Duke[1] and at every other instance of your good fortune, as we do. His Royal Highness has behaved nobly and like himself; he loves the Art military too well and values a man of Spirit too much not to love and encourage you. I am indeed quite happy that you are so well settled; and though I am sensible that you might have great advantages from seeing a variety of Service, yet as you are encouraged where you are and have good opportunities to see and to learn, I think you need trouble yourself with no further views. What I said of the King of Prussia[2] was upon another supposition. We have received the very disagreeable news that his Royal Highnesses' Army has suffered something and been obliged to retreat before the superior numbers of the Enemy.[3] It was however some consolation to us and inspires us with better hopes for the future to hear of the surprising behaviour of your Army. Amidst the public concern for an Event which touches us so deeply, I must own I feel a private concern, lest you should

[1] Emin was serving with the Duke of Cumberland (1721–65), Commander-in-Chief of the British forces in Germany. [2] Frederick the Great.

[3] Cumberland was defeated by the French at Hastenbeck 26 July.

be wounded or made a prisoner; for I am satisfied it was not danger you shunned in the late Engagement if you were in it. But I trust, that, Providence which I believe gave you such a Spirit for some great purpose will preserve you to answer it. I need not I suppose recommend to you to be more observant, than is common for young Soldiers of the Grand operations; at least as much as your Circumstances will admit; I mean of the order, and method, of marching, encamping, chusing proper Situations, Convoys, and the like, in which you will, I imagine, have better opportunities in the defensive part which your Army is to act, than you could have in any other. You will laugh perhaps to hear a man of the Gown presume to advise a Soldier, and a Soldier too, who has now seen real Service. But I am content to make you laugh provided you may derive even the slightest advantage from it. For as you are not to rise by slow Gradations in a regular Service, but to shine out at once by your knowledge and Capacity among your Countrymen, so it is peculiarly necessary for you to aim, and that as soon as possible, not so much at such things as constitute what is called a good officer, but on those which make a good Commander. Your Case is not like that of the other Gentlemen among whom you serve. And you do not want capacity to execute things in a much better spirit than I can advise them. Forgive me, if I presume on one word more of advice—that when you go into your winter Quarters, you perfect your self in Geography and fortification. This advice which I venture to give you, if it does not display much Prudence, it shews at least affection; but you know I am grown, though so near London, a meer country fellow, and borrow all my Notions from the Farm yard; where you may have seen an hen that has hatchd Ducks; when they run into the Water the poor hen is in great Anxiety; she makes a great noise and a vast deal of chiding; but after all her care, she can do nothing for them; they know that element better than she does; whatever I say or do, whether right or wrong may God preserve you, and make you in the Eye of the world as great a man as I know you to be in Spirit and inclination and believe me Dear Emin

your faithful K⟨a⟩ry[1]
friend and Servant
EDM BURKE.

Battersea[2] Augst 1. 1757.

Pray write to me immediately for all your friends are very anxious about you.

[1] Perhaps the Irish word *cára,* friend. In Will Burke's part of the letter the word is spelled 'Kerry'.

[2] Burke's son Richard, born February 1758, is described in the entrance books of Westminster School and of Christ Church, Oxford, as son of Edmund Burke 'of Battersea, Surrey'.

To RICHARD SHACKLETON—10 *August* 1757

Source: MS Dr. O. Fisher. Printed *Corr.* (1844), I, 31–6.
Endorsed: Edmund Burke | Battersea 10 Augt. 1757 | Answered 21/3 mo. 1759.

Dear Shackleton,

If you will not pardon my long Silence without any apology, I am satisfied that no Apology I can make will induce you to pardon it; I have broken all rules, I have neglected all Decorums, every thing except that I have never forgot a friend whose good head and heart have made me esteem and love him and whose Services to me have caused obligations that are never to be broken. What appearance there may have been of neglect arose from my manner of Life, checquerd with various designs, sometimes in London, sometimes in remote parts of the Country, sometimes in France,[1] and shortly please God, to be in America.[2] During that time however of my Silence, my enquiries about you have been warm and frequent; and I had the pleasure (you will I hope believe it a sincere one) of hearing that you are not deficient in success in the world, nor in Domestick Satisfaction. I do not know of any disappointment that vexed me so much as having missed seeing you when you were in London your Letter came to Mr Burkes in Serjeants Inn,[3] while I was in the Country; and they did not forward it to me, expecting me in Town every day. But when I arrived and found your Letter, I found at the same time that you were returned to Ireland. Opportunities of that kind happen so seldom and are of such value, that it is very mortifying to miss them. This letter is accompanied by a little performance of mine, which I will not consider as ineffectual, if it contributes to your amusement.[4] It lay by me for a good while, and I at last ventured it out. It has not

[1] Prior mentions (5th ed. p. 39) Burke speaking of 'three or four journeys he had made in France...previous to the year 1773'. There is no stronger evidence than this phrase for any of the early journeys.

[2] William Dennis wrote of Burke to Shackleton 5 August (Ballitore MSS, A/38): 'He...tells me his purpose for America holds when the present Troubles admit him.' Four years later Burke was still talking of such a purpose. See his letter to Charles O'Hara 10 July 1761 (p. 141).

[3] Will Burke's father. The Register of admissions to the Middle Temple describes him as 'JOHN BURKE, of Serjeant's Inn, City of London, gent.' Will is described in the same Register as 'son and heir of John B., of the Middle Temple, London, gent.', and in the admission Registers of Westminster School and Christ Church, Oxford, as son of John Burke 'of St James's, London'.

[4] The essay on the *Sublime and Beautiful*, published by Dodsley 21 April 1757. Prior records (2nd ed. I, 72) a copy sent by Burke to Shackleton with an inscription:

> Accipe et haec manuum tibi quae monumenta meorum
> Sint—et longum testentur amorem:

It appears from a letter of Dennis to Shackleton of March 1758 (Ballitore MSS, A/40) that Shackleton had made no haste to read the book. Dennis, who is reading it himself for the third time, says 'I wonder at your little curiosity not to read a friends performance before now'.

been ill received, so far as a matter on so abstracted a subject meets with readers. Will you accept it as a sort of offering in Attonement for my former delinquencies? If I would not have you think that I have forgot you, so neither would I have your father, to whom I am under obligations that I neither can nor wish to shake off. I am really concerned for the welfare of you all, and for the Credit of the School where I received the Education, that, if I am any thing, has made me so; I hear with great Satisfaction on this account, of Kearneys being chosen a fellow in our College.[1] My Brother Dick is now with me, and joins me very sincerely in the Sentiments I have for you, your father and your mother, and shall I add for Mrs Shackleton? for I will not suppose myself a Stranger to one who is so nearly related to you.[2] I am now a married man myself,[3] and therefore claim some respect from the married fraternity, at least for your own Sakes you will not pretend to consider me as the worse man. I do not know whether it ever falls in your way to see Doctor Sleigh; he was not at School in my time, but I knew him in London, and I have known few more ingenious, and valuable men.[4] You see, my Dear Shackleton, that I write you a rambling Letter without any connection just as the matters come into my head. But whatever I write, or in whatever way believe me it is Dictated by the sincerest regard to you from him who is your truly affectionate and obliged friend

EDM BURKE

Battersea Augst 10th 1757.

I lately received a letter from Dennis concerning a publication which he has on hands.[5] I answered it in a pretty long letter. But

[1] Michael Kearney became a Fellow of Trinity College, Dublin, in 1757. Shackleton's name is listed in *Alumni Dublinensis* as having entered 'circa 1745'. A note adds: '(Matriculation unrecorded)'.

[2] The death of his first wife in 1754 had left Shackleton, according to his daughter's account, 'at the age of twenty-eight a sorrowful widower with four young children' (*Leadbeater Papers*, I, 38). On 17 October 1755 he married Elizabeth Carleton (1726–1804).

[3] Burke had married Jane Mary Nugent 12 March 1757 (*Notes and Queries*, 6th ser. v, 274–5).

[4] Dr Joseph Fenn Sleigh (1733–70) of Cork. He entered Ballitore School 1 May 1745, later studied medicine at Edinburgh, where he knew Goldsmith. He and Goldsmith renewed their acquaintance in London in 1757 (John Forster, *Life of Goldsmith*, 6th ed. London, 1877, I, 48, 76). Burke also renewed his acquaintance with Goldsmith at about the same time (Prior, 5th ed. p. 80).

[5] Dennis's poem *Man's Redemption* was published in Dublin, 1758. Dennis told Shackleton (letter of [*post* 5 August], Ballitore MSS, A/39) that Burke approved it: 'he extolls greatly from the 14th to the 25th stanza.' In the same letter Dennis spoke of Burke's literary activities: 'Ned I fancy writes Pamphlets for the great ones for he continues to visit Lord Egmont very constantly [John Perceval, 2nd Earl of Egmont, 1711–70], as I hear from one here who was his fellow student. He is well known to Lord Granville [John Carteret, 2nd Earl Granville, 1690–1763]; and I hear farther, is speedily to get £300 for a Book he has in hands whose title is unmention'd' (no doubt Burke's *Abridgment of English History*; see below, note on letter of [March 1763], p. 164).

have heard nothing from him since you will direct to me at the Grecian Coffeehouse London.[1]

To PATRICK NAGLE—[17 *April* 1759]

Source: MS National Library of Ireland. Printed *New Monthly Magazine*, XIV, 380–1.

The MS bears no date, and no cover survives. When the letter was printed in the *New Monthly Magazine* in 1825 it was given a full address and date: 'London, Wimple-street, Cavendish-square, April 17, 1759'. The Dublin MS, though apparently in Burke's hand, is not incontestably the original.

Because of ill health in one period of his boyhood Burke had left his father's house in Dublin, often unwholesomely damp from its closeness to the Liffey, and spent about five years with his mother's relatives in the south of Ireland. One of the warmest attachments of his life was to his maternal uncle Patrick Nagle (d. 1768), of Ballyduff, near Castletownroche, County Cork.

Dear Sir,

Cousin Will Burke left London yesterday.[2] He made our little Sett very happy by his company, and by the account he gave of all our friends on the Blackwater.[3] He said that you were so good to express some desire of hearing from us; I am too much pleased with the intelligence to enquire very closely into it, but gladly lay hold of the first opportunity of assuring you, how heartily I am rejoiced to find I have still some place in your remembrance; I am sure I should entertain a very bad opinion of my own memory, and a much worse of my heart if I was capable of forgetting the many obligations I owe you. There are very few persons in the world for whom I have so great a respect, or whose good opinion I should be more glad to have than yours. When I had resolved to write to you I was at a loss to know how I should make my letters worth the trouble I must give you in sending for them, (for you must know I intend to trouble you in that way very often,) but I recollected that some of our London News papers might prove no disagreeable entertainment to you; and that by this means you would receive some accounts earlier than the Dublin Papers can give them. I therefore enclose with this what I think one of our Best and most entertaining News Letters as it not only contains as much of all foreign transactions as any of the others, but often such remarks upon them, as may serve to explain many publick

[1] In Devereux Court, Strand. Prior says of Burke at about this time (2nd ed. I, 48): 'One of his chief resorts was the Grecian coffee-house, where his habits for a long time were well remembered, and his conversation quoted many years subsequently by the members of the Middle Temple Society.'

[2] Not the usual 'Cousin Will', but an Irish relative otherwise unknown.

[3] Many of Burke's maternal relations of the Nagle family, as well as the Barretts and Hennessys with whom they had intermarried, lived in the neighbourhood of the Blackwater between Mallow and Fermoy.

affairs; as at least shew some thing of the general conversation here concerning them. It contains besides some accounts of the New books which are from time to time published. I should have done this some days ago, but I waited to get in such a stock of Franks as to enable me to continue to send you the Papers without interruption.

In the beginning of my Letter I made mention of Will Burkes having began his journey; but least his family should hear of it, and expecting to see him soon may be uneasy if they find him delayed longer than the Journey requires, it is proper to let you know that he may probably be obliged to wait some days in Chester for the arrival of Hugh Massey.[1] By the little I have seen of that Gentleman he seems to have a great deal of Goodnature. He is to go to Ireland in company with my Lord Carberry,[2] and will labour and I hope with Success to extricate Cousin Garret[3] from the troublesome Situation which I am heartily sorry to find he is in.[4]

I could employ what remains of my Paper and with great Satisfaction to myself in desiring my best remembrance to my friends with you and about you, but they are so many and my good wishes for them all so hearty that I should find it much easier to fill my Paper than to satisfye myself. I must therefore to trust to yours and their goodnature to represent what I must still be defective in if I had said a great deal more. Mrs Burke has not the pleasure of being known to you but she joins me in the sincerest regards for you all; She desires in particular to be remembered to her Sister Peggy,[5] of whom she has heared many things that pleased her Very much, from Mr Burke; My Love to her. My Brother is in the City at a great distance from us[6] or he would gladly join us in the same sentiments to you and to her and to all our friends

I am My dear Uncle
Yours most affectionately
EDM BURKE

[1] Hugh Massy (1700–88), created Baron Massy in 1776; or his son (1733–90).

[2] George Evans, 3rd Baron Carbery (d. 1783), a relation of Hugh Massy.

[3] Garrett Nagle (d. *c.* 1791), Patrick Nagle's son and Burke's first cousin, later a frequent correspondent. Several Burke scholars have referred to him as 'Garrett Nagle, Jr', wrongly assuming that his father's name was also Garrett ('Garrett, Sr').

[4] The Exchequer Bill Book, Public Record Office, Dublin, records under date of 3 February 1758 a lawsuit between Lord Carbery and Garrett Nagle. Garrett Burke appears as his cousin's attorney.

[5] Perhaps Margaret Nagle (d. 1798), who married Daniel Curtin (d. 1786), a merchant at Cork. She was expecting a child; her daughter Catherine was born 28 May.

[6] Prior asserts (2nd ed. I, 90 n.) that 'the first views of Richard Burke were directed to commerce'. In the autumn of this year Richard seems to be receiving assistance from John Bourke (*c.* 1722–1806), a merchant in the City (see below, letter of 11 October, p. 135).

To ROBERT DODSLEY—[*circa* 6 *September* 1759]

Source: MS N. Loftus.
Addressed: To | Mr Robert Dodsley at | Mr Leakes Bookseller in | Bath. *Postmarked:* 6|SE B.

Robert Dodsley (1703–64) and his brother James (1724–97) were the actual, though not the ostensible, publishers of Burke's *Vindication of Natural Society* in 1756, the publishers of his *Sublime and Beautiful* in 1757, and had engaged him to edit their *Annual Register*, of which the first volume appeared in May of 1759. They had also published in 1757 William Burke's *Account of European Settlements in America*, in which Edmund had some share. Robert Dodsley's biographer thinks that the publisher may have met Burke through Arthur Murphy (1727–1805) as early as 1752 (Ralph Straus, *Robert Dodsley*, London, 1910, p. 254).

Dear Sir,

I admit that I am greatly to blame for having so long denied myself the pleasure of corresponding with you. The agreeable places you have been in, and the very agreeable people you have been with, could not have failed through your hands of paying me abundantly for any trouble I should have had in sending you now and then a little false news of the Town, or a few lines of nonsense of my own. It is but an indifferent compliment to myself to say that I find trouble in writing to a friend I value and esteem as much as I do you. But the fact is so; and I have observed it in general of those who are very fond of scribbling other things that they are of all people the least to be depended on for writing Letters. God forbid that any of my friends should judge of my regard for them by the punctuality of my correspondence. This is, I am sensible a bad habit, but along with other bad ones it grows upon me every day. Now Sir, I am to tell you a piece of news which will make you ample amends for all those which I have omitted to send you. If it were not for this I do not know how I should be able to meet your indignation. Know then that Mrs Gataker[1] is at the point of setting out for Bath where you will see her about the End of next week. I congratulate you on this meeting; though, upon my word we suffer not a little by what you gain. You are a lucky man and meet friends wherever you go. You cannot meet anybody who is more your friend than Mrs Gataker is, or whose friendship does you more honour. I claim some of the merit and satisfaction of this meeting by being the first to tell you of it. Other news I have none. The Town, and I suppose the Country too, rings of Lord George Sackville;[2] he meets some friends, and a good many Enemies; but

[1] Mrs Thomas Gataker, *née* Anne Hill (d. 1797).

[2] Later Lord George Germain (1716–85), Lieutenant-General of the Ordnance and Commander-in-Chief of the British forces in Germany. At the battle of Minden, 1 August 1759, he failed to bring up the cavalry as ordered by Prince Ferdinand of

Grubstreet I think is unanimous against him, and Grubstreet is no despicable Enemy in affairs of this Nature. However there does not seem to be the same Violence nor the same artifice against him that was used against Byng.[1] Besides a party in his favour seems to be forming much earlier: The Duke of Richmond, and the aid de Camps Fitzroy and Legonier I am told lean against him.[2] When Politicks are so dead in the middle of Summer which is their Season[3] what can you expect of the Literary world? The Literary campain does not, you know, open until the other is closed. If you have had the happiness of Mr Shenstones[4] company on your Ramble, and that he is now at Bath pray present my best complements to him. I am much obliged to him for the partial Sentiments he is pleased to entertain of me. I know that I am indebted to you for this. If he should at any time come to Town, I should desire you to go a Step further to introduce me to his acquaintance. I do not know whether you have met a Mr Frampton at Bath. He is a Clerg⟨yman⟩ and a very particular friend of Mine. He has a little living somewhere near Lansdown,[5] though I am afraid he does not come to it at this time of the year. If you see him be so good to remind him of me; and be acquainted with him; for he is a very worthy man and very clever. I saw your brother two or three days ago, He is very well. Mrs Burke desires her compliments to you very particularly. So does my Brother. Mr Wm Burke is very much yours. He is not yet set off for his part of the world.[6] Believe me

dear Mr Dodsley

yours very Sincerely

EDM BURKE.

Brunswick, commanding the allied armies. For this he was dismissed 10 September and after a court martial declared incapable of holding any military command.

[1] Admiral John Byng (1704–57) commanded a squadron in the Mediterranean in 1756 and for his failure to engage the French fleet off Port Mahon was court martialled and shot 14 March 1757.

[2] Charles Lennox, 3rd Duke of Richmond (1735–1806), later Burke's friend and correspondent, Charles Fitzroy (1737–97) and Edward Ligonier (1740–82) were Aides de Camp to Prince Ferdinand at the battle of Minden. Fitzroy carried the order to Sackville to advance.

[3] A puzzling observation. Parliament was in recess in the summer, which was surely the least active political season.

[4] William Shenstone (1714–63) the poet. Dodsley had written him concerning Burke the previous year: 'That Mr Burke, who writes so ingeniously, is an Irish Gentleman, bred to the Law, but having the grace not to follow it, will soon I should think make a very great figure in the literary world' (Straus, *Robert Dodsley*, p. 256). On the publication of the second edition of the *Sublime and Beautiful*, Dodsley sent Shenstone a copy (see his letter of 20 February [1759], Add. MS 28959, fol. 120). Shenstone wrote his friend R. Graves 3 October 'Of all books whatever, read Burke (second edit.) "Of the Sublime and Beautiful"...' (*Letters of William Shenstone*, ed. Marjorie Williams, Oxford, 1939, p. 525).

[5] Matthew Frampton (b. *c.* 1719), Rector of Langridge, near Bath, from 1750 to 1769; in a letter to David Garrick, 7 April 1768 (Forster Collection, Victoria and Albert Museum), he sent compliments to 'Mr Burke'.

[6] The West Indies. Will Burke had been appointed Secretary and Register of the Island of Guadaloupe 10 August (*Journal of the Commissioners for Trade and Plantations*,

To ADAM SMITH—10 *September* 1759

Source: MS Osborn Collection.

Adam Smith was Professor of Moral Philosophy at Glasgow when Burke's *Sublime and Beautiful* appeared. A remark of his that the author of that essay would be worthy of a university chair may be the origin of a particularly hardy legend that Burke once applied for the chair of Logic at Glasgow (Prior, 2nd ed. I, 45 n.). When Smith's *Theory of Moral Sentiments* was published in 1759, David Hume made certain that a copy was sent to Burke (*Letters of David Hume*, ed. J. Y. T. Greig, Oxford, 1932, I, 303). Burke wrote an appreciative letter to the author.

Sir

I am quite ashamed that the first Letter I have the honour of writing to you should be an apology for my conduct. It ought to be entirely taken up with my thanks to you for the satisfaction I received from your very agreeable and instructive work, but I cannot do that pleasing act of Justice without apologising at the same time for not having done it much earlier. When I received the Theory of Moral Sentiments from Mr Hume, I ran through it with great eagerness; I was immediately after hurried out of Town, and involved ever since in a Variety of troublesome affairs.[1] My resolution was to defer my acknowlegements until I had read your book with proper care and attention; to do otherwise with so well studied a piece would be to treat it with great injustice. It was indeed an attention extremely well bestowed and abundantly repaid. I am not only pleased with the ingenuity of your Theory; I am convinced of its solidity and Truth; and I do not know that it ever cost me less trouble to admit so many things to which I had been a stranger before.[2] I have ever thought that the old Systems of morality were too contracted and that this Science could never stand well upon any narrower Basis than the whole of Human Nature. All the writers who have treated this Subject before you were like those Gothic Architects

1759–63, London, 1935, p. 56). He was reappointed in 1761 (*ibid.* p. 177), and later appointed Receiver General of Revenues (letter of Frederick Corsar 20, 21 April 1763; MS at Sheffield).

[1] Hume had told Smith 28 July: 'I am very well acquainted with Bourke, who was much taken with your Book. He got your Direction from me with a View of writing to you, and thanking you for your Present: For I made it pass in your Name. I wonder he has not done it: He is now in Ireland' (*Letters of David Hume*, I, 312). There is no other evidence of Burke having been in Ireland; and see below, letter of 11 October, where Burke's phrasing seems to make it improbable.

[2] Burke's review of the book in the *Annual Register* for 1759 praises particularly Smith's originality: 'this author has struck out a new, and at the same time a perfectly natural road of speculation on this subject.... We conceive, that here the theory is in all its essential parts just, and founded on truth and nature. The author seeks for the foundation of the just, the fit, the proper, the decent, in our most common and most allowed passions; and making approbation and disapprobation the tests of virtue and vice, and shewing that those are founded on sympathy, he raises from this simple truth, one of the most beautiful fabrics of moral theory, that has perhaps ever appeared.'

who were fond of turning great Vaults upon a single slender Pillar; There is art in this, and there is a degree of ingenuity without doubt; but it is not sensible, and it cannot long be pleasing. A theory like yours founded on the Nature of man, which is always the same, will last, when those that are founded on his opinions, which are always changing, will and must be forgotten. I own I am particularly pleased with those easy and happy illustrations from common Life and manners in which your work abounds more than any other that I know by far. They are indeed the fittest to explain those natural movements of the mind with which every Science relating to our Nature ought to begin. But one sees, that nothing is less used, than what lies directly in our way. Philosophers therefore very frequently miss a thousand things that might be of infinite advantage, *though the rude Swain treads daily on them with his clouted Shoon.*[1] It seems to require that infantine simplicity which despises nothing, to make a good Philosopher, as well as to make a good Christian. Besides so much powerful reasoning as your Book contains, there is so much elegant Painting of the manners and passions, that it is highly valuable even on that account. The stile is every where lively and elegant, and what is, I think equally important in a work of that kind, it is well varied; it is often sublime too, particularly in that fine Picture of the Stoic Philosophy towards the end of your first part which is dressed out in all the grandeur and Pomp that becomes that magnificent delusion. I have mentioned something of what affected me as Beauties in your work. I will take the Liberty to mention too what appeared to me as a sort of Fault. You are in some few Places, what Mr Locke is in most of his writings, rather a little too diffuse. This is however a fault of the generous kind, and infinitely preferable to the dry sterile manner, which those of[2] dull imaginations are apt to fall into. To another I should apologise for a freedom of this Nature.

My delay on this occasion may I am afraid make it improper for me to ask any favour from you. But there is one, I have too much at heart not to sacrifice any propriety to attain it. It is, that whenever you come to Town, I may have the honour of being made personally known to you. I shall take the Liberty of putting this office on our friend Mr Hume who has already so much obliged me by giving me your Book. I am Sir with the truest esteem for your Work and your Character

your most obliged and
obedient Servant

Wimple Street Cavendish Square EDM BURKE.
Westminster September 10th 1759

[1] *Comus*, ll. 634–5. Burke uses the quotation in a similar way in his Speech on Conciliation with the Colonies (*Works* [Bohn], I, 489; [Little, Brown], II, 154). [2] MS: of of

To MRS ELIZABETH MONTAGU—24 *September* 1759

Source: MS Bristol Archives. Printed Climenson, *Mrs Montagu*, II, 169–71.

Burke's literary works made him friends in society as well as among writers and scholars. Mrs Elizabeth Montagu (1720–1800), 'Queen of the Blue-Stockings' and worth impressing, formed a high opinion of the young author's abilities and a still higher of his moral earnestness. On 24 January 1759, sending a copy of the *Sublime and Beautiful* to her friend Mrs Elizabeth Carter (1717–1806), she filled her letter with praise of 'Mr Burke, a friend of mine...in conversation and writing an ingenious and ingenuous man, modest and delicate, and on great and serious subjects full of that respect and veneration which a good mind and a great one is sure to feel, while fools mock behind the altar...' (Climenson, *Mrs Montagu*, II, 159–60).

Madam

I have now the honour of writing to you for the first time, and the subject of my Letter is an affair that concerns myself. I should stand in need of many more apologies than I know how to make both for the Liberty I take and for the occasion of it, if I had not learned by experience that I give you a pleasure when I put it in your Power to exert your goodnature. I know it is your foible to carry this principle to an extream, and one is almost sure of success in any application, or at least of pardon for having made an improper one, when we know judiciously to take advantage of a persons weak point. I do not know any thing else which could give me confidence enough to take the Liberty I am now going to use. The Consulship of Madrid has been vacant for several Months.[1] I am informed that it is in the Gift of Mr Secretary Pitt,[2] and that it is valuable.[3] I presume however that it is not an object for a person who has any considerable pretensions by its having continued so long vacant, else I should never have thought of it. My Interest is weak. I have not at all the honour of being known to Mr Pitt; nor much to any of his close connections. For which reason I venture to ask your advice whether I can with propriety proceed at all in this affair; and if you think I ought to undertake it, in what manner it would be proper for me to proceed. If my little Suit, either in itself, or in the persons through whose hands it must necessarily pass, should be attended with any Circumstances that may make it disagreeable to you to interfere in it, I shall take it as a favour equal to that I have asked, if you will be so good to tell me you can do nothing in it. I shall think such a declaration a great mark of your

[1] John Burnaby Parker, Consul-General at Madrid, had died 6 July 1758.

[2] William Pitt (1708–78), at this time Secretary of State for the Southern Department.

[3] Its value appears to have been £1000 per annum (Civil List accounts, *Journals of the House of Commons*, 12 January 1770).

confidence. I am sensible that there are in all peoples connections many points that may make a person of delicacy unwilling to ask a favour in some quarters, and yet more unwilling from the same delicacy to tell the person for whom it is to be asked that they have such difficulties. There are undoubtedly many Circumstances of propriety in every persons situation, which none can feel properly but themselves. I am not however, if I know myself, one of those expectants who think every thing ought to be sacrificed to their Interests. It occurred to me that a Letter from you to Miss Pitt might be of great Service to me.[1] I thought too of taking the Liberty of mentioning Mrs Boscawen;[2] The Admiral has such great merit with the Ministry and the Nation that the want of it will be the more readily overlooked in any person for whom he may be induced to apply. But these are crude Notions and require the understanding they are submitted to, to bring them to form and maturity. To say the Truth I am quite ashamed to have dwelt so long upon so indifferent a Subject. Your Patience is almost equal to the rest of your Virtues if you can bear it. I dwell with far more pleasure on my acknowlegements for what you have done for my friend in so obliging and genteel a manner.[3] He has but just now succeeded after a world of delays and no small opposition. He will always retain a very grateful Sense of what you have done in his favour. Mrs Burke desires me to present her respects to you and her best wishes for your health. When last I had the pleasure of seeing Doctor Monsey[4] he told me that the Country still agreed with you, else I should most wickedly wish this fine weather over that you might be the sooner driven to Town. This fine weather suffers nothing good to be in Town but itself. We are much obliged to the doctor for the Satisfaction he gave you in uniting his Care with yours for Mr Montagu's recovery.[5] I congratulate you very sincerely on that event; If I could find some agreeable circumstance in your affairs for congratulation as often as I wish I should be the most troublesome

[1] Prior names Miss Anne Pitt (1712–81) in a list of important persons to whom Burke was introduced by his early writings, adding that Burke thought her 'the most perfectly eloquent person he ever heard speak' (2nd ed. I, 94). She was not at this time on good enough terms with her brother to give much help to Burke's application.

[2] *Née* Frances Glanville (1719–1805), wife of Admiral Edward Boscawen (1711–61). The Admiral had won an important naval victory at Lagos in August.

[3] Probably Will Burke. Mrs Montagu thanked Lady Barbara Montagu (sister of Lord Halifax) in a letter of 3 August for 'the great favour you have done me in behalf of Mr Burke' (Climenson, *Mrs Montagu*, II, 163). Will's appointment in the West Indies was dated 10 August. See above, letter of [*circa* 6 September] (p. 128).

[4] Dr Messenger Monsey.

[5] Edward Montagu (d. 1775), Mrs Montagu's husband, had been ill of a throat infection (Climenson, *Mrs Montagu*, II, 164–5).

Correspondent in England for nobody can be with greater Respect and Gratitude

Madam,
your most obliged and
obedient humble Servant
EDMD BURKE

Wimple Street Cav. Square
Septr 24th 1759.

Burke was certainly in earnest about the application, and was supported through more than one channel. His friend Dr William Markham (1719–1807) recommended him highly to the Duchess of Queensberry: 'his chief application has been to the knowledge of public business, and our commercial interests;...he seems to have a most extensive knowledge, with extraordinary talents for business, and to want nothing but ground to stand upon to do his country very important services' (*Chatham Correspondence*, I, 432). The Duchess wrote a letter to Pitt (Clements Markham, *Memoir of Archbishop Markham*, Oxford, 1906, p. 15). Pitt did not give the post to Burke.

To MRS ELIZABETH MONTAGU—6 *October* 1759

Source: MS Huntington Library.

Madam,

For many publick as well as private reasons I am sorry that you have not an influence on Ministers of State; but the qualities which some persons possess are by no means those which lead to ministerial Influence. The reasons you have been pleased to give me, for not making the applications I took the Liberty to propose, are very convincing and obliging. Before I applied I was well aware of the difficulties that stood in my Way; and there was no necessity of many arguments to prove, that Mrs Montagu is very strongly disposed to serve those, to whom she does the honour to profess a regard. I must however confess that I am not sorry you have taken that trouble, because I am flattered to think you were sollicitous to satisfie me in a point, that I must at least be as anxious about, as the Success of this Negotiation. It is not very easy to have access to Mr Pitt, especially for me who have but very few friends. I mentioned those methods, not that I was satisfied of their propriety but because I would try every method which occurred to me, and these were the only ones that did, occur. I had heared indeed that Alderman Beckford had great Weight with Mr Pitt;[1] but I was utterly at a loss how to get at him. I had never heared that he was known to you. At that time none besides him and those I mentioned occurred to me. I had

[1] William Beckford (1709–70), M.P. for London, was Pitt's leading supporter in the City.

perhaps never thought at all of the thing, if I had not been pretty credibly informed that little competition could be expected as I was very conscious that the slightest competition must have set aside a person with so little Interest as I have. I am ashamed to have now a second time taken up so much of my Paper on such a Subject, and I must Madam, have recourse to your usual Goodness for my Excuse. We have very little News either Political or Literary; the one of these has always some influence on the other; in that light we ought to have had something remarkable, as the misfortune or misconduct of a General[1] affords much ampler matter to writers than their most shining exploits, for Panegyric is comparatively but a cold thing. But in reality in this famous dispute there does not seem to have hitherto appeared any thing that deserves much attention. People begin to turn their thoughts another way and to entertain great apprehensions for General Wolfe;[2] not through a doubt of his Capacity or Spirit but of his force. Let this affair turn out how it will there seems to be something Generous and right in the Sentiments of most of those whom I have heared speak of it. There does not appear the least disposition to reflect on the General for the fortune which may attend the expedition; They have before hand acquitted him in their minds.

Give me leave, Madam, once more to return you my thanks for your Good wishes and endeavours. I should not have deferred them so long if I had not been called out of Town a day or two after I had the honour of your Letter and was obliged to continue in the Country until this morning. Mrs Burke is much obliged to you for your kind remembrance and desires her most respectful compliments

I am Madam
your most obedient
and obliged Servant
EDM BURKE

Wimple Street
October 6th 1759.

To PATRICK NAGLE—11 *October* 1759

Source: New Monthly Magazine, XIV, 381–2.

Dear Sir,—My brother has been beforehand with me in almost every thing I could say. My conduct stands in need of as many apologies as his, but I am afraid our apologies might be almost as troublesome as our

[1] Lord George Sackville.

[2] Wolfe was killed 13 September and Quebec surrendered 17 September, but the news did not reach England until 16 October.

neglects. All I can say is, that I have been, I think it is now eleven years, from the county of Cork, yet my remembrance of my friends there is as fresh as if I had it left yesterday. My gratitude for their favours, and my love for their characters, is rather heightened, as the oftener I think of them they must be, and I think of them very often. This I can say with great truth. Believe me, dear Sir, it would be a great pleasure to me to hear as often from you as it is convenient. Do not give yourself any sort of trouble about franks; I value very little that trifling expence, and I should very little deserve to hear from my friends, if I scrupled to pay a much higher price for that satisfaction. If I had any thing that you could have pleasure in, to send you from hence, I should be a punctual correspondent; there is nothing here, except what the news-papers contain, that can interest you; but nothing can come from the Blackwater which does not interest me very greatly. Poor Dick is on the point of quitting us; however, he has such advantageous prospects where he is going, that I part from him with the less regret. One of the first merchants here has taken him by the hand, and enabled him to go off with a very valuable cargo. He has another advantage and satisfaction in his expedition; one of our best friends here goes at the same time in one of the first places in the island.[1]

Mrs Burke is very sensible of your goodness, and desires that I should make you her acknowledgments. We equally wish it were in our power to accept of your kind invitation; and that no greater obstacle intervened to keep us from seeing Ballyduffe, but the distance. We are too good travellers to be frighted at that. I have made a much longer journey than the land part of it this summer.[2] However, it is not impossible but we may one day have the pleasure of embracing you at your own house. I beg you will salute for us the good houses of Ballydwalter, Ballylegan, and Ballynahaliok,[3] *et nati natorum, et qui nascuntur ab illis*.[4] Our little

[1] Charles Dilke remarked sarcastically on this passage that translated from Burke's Irish eloquence into plain fact it may have meant only that Richard was going out to the West Indies as supercargo (*Papers of a Critic*, London, 1875, II, 319). The merchant in England giving Richard help was probably John Bourke, a 'kinsman' of the Burkes who had important West Indian connexions. The well-placed friend in the island was Will Burke (see above, letter of [*circa* 6 September], p. 128).

[2] According to David Hume, Burke had been in Ireland (see above, note to letter of 10 September, p. 129).

[3] In a book of miscellaneous papers now preserved in the Genealogical Office in Dublin Castle (G.O. MS 295 Rock, p. 85) is a formal statement made by two residents of Castletown Roche, County Cork, dated 26 May 1765 and witnessed by 'the undersigned Gentlemen...

Patt: Nagle of Ballyduffe
Athan. Nagle of Ballilegan
James Nagle of BallyWalter
Gar[ret]t Nagle Ballinhalisk
David Crotty of Straw Hall'.

[4] See Virgil, *Aeneid*, III, 98.

boys are very well,[1] but I should think them still better, if they (or the one that is on his legs) were running about the Bawn at Ballyduffe[2] as his father used to do. Farewell, my dear uncle, and believe me your affectionate kinsman and humble servant,

EDM BURKE

Wimple-street, Cavendish-Square, 11th October, 1759.

I forgot to say any thing of the irregularity which you may have found in the papers for some time passed. The summer has made the town thin of Members of Parliament, so that we were sometimes at a loss; but now we shall be pretty secure on that head, and you shall have your papers more regularly.

To AGMONDESHAM VESEY—10 *September* 1760

Source: New Monthly Magazine, XIV, 382.

Burke's father had not entirely forgiven him for his desertion of the law. Charles M'Cormick (*Memoirs of Edmund Burke*, London, 1797, p. 27) says that the *Sublime and Beautiful* helped the situation: on reading his son's performance the father 'was so enraptured...that he immediately sent him one hundred pounds'. The following letter shows that even in 1760 some diplomacy was still thought useful between father and son. Agmondesham Vesey (d. 1785), 'a man of gentle manners' as Burke later described him when proposing his name for the Literary Club, was an excellent choice for an intermediary.

Dear Sir,—I cannot express how much I am obliged to you for your kind and successful endeavours in my favour: of whatever advantage the remittance was, the assurance you give me of my father's reconciliation was a great deal more pleasing, and both indeed were rendered infinitely more agreeable to me by passing through your hands.[3] I am sensible how very much I am indebted to your goodnature upon this occasion. If one has but little merit, it is some consolation to have partial friends. Lord Lyttelton[4] has been at Hagley for this month past, or near the matter; where for the first time he receives his friends in his new house. He was so obliging to invite me; I need not say that I am much concerned to

[1] Mr I. Moreton Wood (*Notes and Queries*, 6th ser. vol. v, 274) quoted from 'the family Bible, in Edmund Burke's writing' exact dates for the births of the two sons: '...Richard Burke, born at Battersea between 7 and 8 o'clock in the morning, February the 9th, 1758. Christopher Burke born at Wimple Street, Cavendish Square, 40 minutes after 6 in the morning the 14th of December, 1758; died an Infant.' This Bible is now in the possession of Mrs S. E. Pixley, Hill Place, Knaphill, Surrey.

[2] The enclosed area around his uncle's house.

[3] It is possible that this refers to the same remittance as M'Cormick's anecdote. The copy of the *Sublime* which Burke inscribed to his father, now owned by Basil O'Connell of Dublin, is of the second (1759) edition.

[4] George Lyttelton, 1st Baron Lyttelton (1709–73), politician and author.

find I shall not be able to obey his Lordship's commands, and that I must lose, for this year at least, the sight of that agreeable place, and the conversation of its agreeable owner. Mrs. Montagu is, I believe, at Tunbridge, for she told me, on her leaving town, that she intended to make a pretty long stay there. May I flatter myself with the hope of seeing you this winter in London? I cannot so easily forget the evenings I have passed not to be most desirous of renewing them. I wish most heartily that Mrs. Vesey's[1] [health] may be so well established, that she may be able to bear the late sitting up, for I foresee that must be the case whenever she comes to London; it is a fine she must pay for being so agreeable. Mrs. Burke looks upon herself to be very unhappy that she had not the honour of being known to Mrs. Vesey, but is in hopes that she may this winter be so fortunate. Once more I give you thanks for your kind interposition. Believe me, dear Sir, your much obliged humble servant,

EDM BURKE

Sunning Hill, September 10th, 1760.

To Agmondisham Vesey, Esq. at Lucan.[2]

To CHARLES O'HARA—3 *July* 1761

Source: O'Hara MSS. Printed Hoffman, pp. 276–8.

One of Burke's most important correspondences was with Charles O'Hara (*c.* 1715–76) of Annaghmore, County Sligo, a member of the Irish House of Commons well acquainted with the ruling group in Ireland and almost equally interested in leaders and parties in England. Burke wrote him very frankly about English politics, both in the period when he was himself only a spectator and later when he was acquainted with some of the inner secrets. Two letters of O'Hara to Burke dated 'November 20' and 'April 10' seem by their contents to belong to the years 1759 and 1760 respectively. The following, the earliest surviving letter of Burke to O'Hara, is clearly part of a correspondence already well established.

Dear Sir

I did not believe it possible, that a Letter from you could give me uneasiness. But I own, I was sorry, and most heartily ashamed, to see a second Letter from you before I had answerd your first; especially as it was written in a time of so much hurry, and attended with all those obliging circumstances with which you know so well how to grace every thing you do. My excuse is that I waited to get to Town, to discover if

[1] *Née* Elizabeth Vesey (*c.* 1715–91), one of the leading London Blue-Stockings.
[2] Lucan House, Vesey's seat near Dublin.

possible into what posture things had fallen since you left us, in order to fill my paper with something that might entertain you. But my most diligent enquiry was without much Effect; either there is great Secrecy, or there is nothing done; however people speak as confidently of peace as if they knew more; The stocks rise, and we expect in a very short time to hear of a cessation.[1] As to domestic affairs, my Lord Talbots reformations make the greatest Noise, who has made great sweepings of the Kitchen.[2] Most of the officers have either resigned or been turned out; and those that remain abridged of their profits, and obliged to a small certain Salary and known perquisites, lament the bountiful times of an avaricious King. In the mean time I dont find that the reformation is very popular; we are so degenerate that we cannot bear the redress of these Evils we complained of. As to the Irish Politicks, except what I have had from you, I hear very little, and understand still less. I took the Liberty of communicating to our friend[3] what you said of the difficulties which arose concerning the commissions. He desired me to tell you, that he did every thing he could to remove these difficulties, but at the same time begged leave to laugh a little at the fears they occasiond the true spirit and Character of which he enterd into perfectly. I heartily wish that things may go on quietly and that my Ld Lt may find his government as successful as the means I dare say, he intends to employ in it are fair and disinterested.[4] As for the Secretary, every thing, is with him, as you know, manly and honest; he is one of the few men of business, whose honour, I am satisfied is entirely to be relied on, and can neither deceive nor betray; and as to being deceived, you know, that is not over easy. If there be a party in Ireland that goes into opposition because the Country has been misrepresented, I am afraid it is not the right way. It may perhaps be rather a means by which they may be truly represented as much to their disadvantage as by the former misrepresentation. However I exclude the honest men you mention, who I sup-

[1] Peace negotiations between England and France had begun in March.

[2] William Talbot, 1st Earl Talbot (1710–82), appointed Lord Steward in March, was attempting economies in the Royal Household, based rather on parsimony than principle. When years later Burke was involved in his own attempts to reform the Household, he recalled the difficulty Talbot had had *because the King's turnspit was a member of Parliament* ('Speech on Economical Reform', *Works* [Bohn], II, 86, [Little, Brown], II, 309).

[3] William Gerard Hamilton (1729–96); sometimes called 'Single-Speech Hamilton' from having made a great reputation in the House of Commons by a brilliant maiden speech, after which he was abnormally silent. Burke was introduced to him in 1759 and served him as a secretary for six years. Little has ever been known of their relationship, except that it ended in a violent quarrel in the early part of 1765.

[4] George Montagu Dunk, 2nd Earl of Halifax (1716–71), had been appointed Lord Lieutenant of Ireland in March. William Gerard Hamilton was appointed his Chief Secretary.

pose are some of the most respectable persons you have. I own I am somewhat out of humour with patriotism; and can think but meanly of such Publick spirit, as like the fanatical spirit, banishes common Sense; I do not understand that Spirit, which could raise such hackneyed pretences, and such contemptible Talents, as those of Dr Lucas to so great consideration, not only among the mob, but, as I hear on all hands, among very many of rank and figure.[1] If any of them do it through Policy, one may predict without rashness, that he will give them room to repent it. I do not know how it is, but I feel myself hurt at this, and the rather as I shall be obliged from decency and other considerations to hold my Tongue. I find I have run on at a vast rate, but you are kind and will be as indulgent to me as when we met over a little Stirabout at St James street. As to the figure he makes in the medical way I do not at all wonder at it; That Profession is the proper Sphere of Pretenders; and it is not odd that people should be imposed upon in what they do not understand, and indeed well cannot, when they cannot distinguish Nonsense and absurdity in a common advertisem⟨ent.⟩ Willy[2] Left us more to his satisfaction than ours in about a week after you had quitted London. Mr Cleaver[3] tells me, that the place seems well to be liked and that the person most concernd seems to be pleased with his Situation; but the Doctor[4] and I thought, if you approve, that in about a month or so, Mr Cleaver would do well to pay him a visit, and see how all goes on. I am much obliged to you for your very kind visits to my father; You spoke of my going over quite in the proper way, enough to try the Ground and no more. I am obliged both to your friendship and your prudence in this point, as indeed in what am I not? I expect Will every week from

[1] Dr Charles Lucas (1713–71), a Dublin apothecary and pamphleteer, had been an active 'patriot' opposed to the ruling group in Ireland in the late 1740's. He was voted an enemy by the Irish Parliament in 1749 and forced into exile, but in 1761 he was permitted to return to Ireland, where he began at once to take an active part in the agitation for shorter parliaments. Burke's attitude toward him has been a subject of debate. Prior thought it was hostile and contemptuous (2nd ed. I, 34); Samuels argued (pp. 180–202) that it might really have been sympathetic, and suggested Burke as the author of some anonymous pamphlets which favoured Lucas when his activities were exciting violent controversy in Dublin (pp. 331–95). Dr Gaetano Vincitorio of St John's University, Brooklyn, New York, has recently drawn attention to the weakness of Samuels's case ('Edmund Burke and Charles Lucas', *PMLA*, LXVIII, 1047–55).

[2] William Henry King O'Hara (*c.* 1750–80), younger son of Charles O'Hara (see *Commissioned Officers of the Royal Navy*, National Maritime Museum, 1954; also T. O'Rorke, *History, Antiquities, and Present State of the Parishes of Ballysadare and Kilvarnet, in the County of Sligo*, Dublin, n.d., p. 399).

[3] John Cleaver (*c.* 1737–76), tutor of William O'Hara and of his elder brother Charles, Jr (1746–1822).

[4] Dr Nugent, Burke's father-in-law, who by this time had left Bath and settled in London. A diagnosis in his hand, signed by him, is in the Wellcome Historical Medical Library in London; it is dated 15 October 1761 from Panton Square.

the W. Indies.[1] The Doctor is I think better than when you saw him as I must tell you if he does not, and he will forgive me this kind of remark on Looks. Adieu my dear Sir

and believe me your ever obliged
and faithful humble Servant
ED BURKE.

July 3d 1761.

To CHARLES O'HARA—10 *July* 1761

Source: O'Hara MSS. Printed Hoffman, pp. 278–80.

Dear Sir

Every time I hear from you gives me occasion for thanks for some new instance of your friendly attention. I am much better since I came into the Country, though by [no] means free from pain, nor perfectly restored to my natural rest. However I find myself getting forward in strength and spirits; for I ride some miles every day, which does me almost as much service as if I had taken Dr Hills five medicines, or Dr Lucas's one.[2] If the Latter Mountebank should now descend from his Stage, it would be of great service to his Character, which, if he returns to the usual unhealthy soundness of his intellects, will infallibly come to be known by the dullest of his admirers; and thus his medical quackery will cover the Blunders of his political. According to all reports from your side of the water, you will, of all losses, hardly miss a Patriot; we are told, that they abound; and that the mob act the part of those Troops, that are placed in the rear of Soldiers of suspected Courage to push them forward with their Pikes. This I assure you fills me with a real

[1] Henry Fox (later Lord Holland, 1705–74) told Lord Egremont (Charles Wyndham, 2nd Earl of Egremont, 1710–63) 1 March 1763 that Will had been 'a great while' in Guadaloupe (see below, note on Will's letter of 20 November 1762, p. 154). The Governor of the island, Campbell Dalrymple, wrote home 15 April 1761: 'I return you many thanks for your recommendation of Mr Burke, he is one of the few comforts in this dissolving climate' (Public Record Office, C.O. 110/1).

[2] John Hill (*c.* 1716–75) was an ambitious and resourceful quack. Burke wrote a mock Funeral Oration upon him 'to be Pronounced in the Bedford Coffee house by Mr Macklin' (copy in MS notebook (Bk 40) at Sheffield with a date of 1751; printed in *A Note-Book of Edmund Burke*, pp. 42–5). A page of notes on Burke's early compositions (Sheffield, Bk 34) also lists 'A Satire in 1753—general declamation against the Knavery and dupery of the town, Elizabeth Canning, Dr. Hill &c'. Hill's 'five medicines' are named in newspaper advertisements (e.g. in *Lloyd's Evening Post*, January–June 1762). Lucas's one medicine was no doubt water, for which he made great claims. Dr Johnson, who reviewed the *Essay on Waters* in the *Literary Magazine* in 1756, was not convinced that Lucas had proved that cold bathing was conducive to health. 'It is incident to physicians, I am afraid,' he said, 'beyond all other men, to mistake subsequence for consequence' (*Life of Johnson*, I, 91 n.).

and sensible concern; The disposition which you observed so general here with regard to Ireland, still continues, and seems growing into something like a Principle of Government. There is but one voice about these matters; unless we except Mr Pitt's;[1] who will however, not probably consider them of importance enough to put his whole Strength to them, especially as he would probably stand alone in the attempt. As to those most immediately concerned, I am desired to tell you, that they have no notion of dividing in order to govern, they only propose not to be absolutely *governed*, and to Effect that, by whatever means shall be presented. To speak my own opinion, any driness, slowness, or sang froid in the proceedings in that quarter, probably comes from an intention to try new expedients; and if possible to do Business on an independent footing and at any hazard; but this is only my own conjecture; for, as you see, what I have said from authority, is general enough. However, in putting together what you have hinted in your Last, with what I have been able to observe, I am more and more confirmed in my opinion; if this be the plan, you see it puts the whole to a short issue, and on a single point, I apprehend they will be supported in this method of proceeding. If I had answerd your Letter immediately, I should have told you that the report of the delay on account of the coronation had nothing in it; neither had it at that time; But as the Marriage is now settled and declared,[2] I imagine my Ld Lt will wait to assist and to pay his duty to the new Queen. Part of her establishment is already fixed: Lord Harcourt is Master of the Horse,[3] and is to go for her immediately. D. of Manchester[4] is Chamberlain; and Mr Stone Treasurer.[5] This letter will probably find you in your rural amusements at Nymphsfield.[6] When you look at the Atlantick ocean do you think of America? In our old fabulous History I think I have read that the Prophet Moses advised the antient Scots to go as far Westward as possible;[7] is this good advice to their posterity? I have been a day in Town lately and saw the Doctor and

[1] The British Privy Council had been offended in the previous autumn when an Irish money bill was not transmitted to them in the usual manner; Pitt alone refused to sign the letter rebuking the Lords Justices (see Walpole, *Memoirs*, I, 23–4).

[2] George III's intended marriage with Princess Charlotte of Mecklenburg-Strelitz was announced 8 July, and took place 8 September.

[3] Simon, 1st Earl Harcourt (1714–77), was Governor to George III as Prince of Wales 1751–2, Master of the Horse to the Queen 1761–3, and Lord Chamberlain to the Queen 1763–8.

[4] Robert Montagu, 3rd Duke of Manchester (*c.* 1710–62), a Lord of the Bedchamber since 1739.

[5] Andrew Stone (1703–73), formerly the Duke of Newcastle's private secretary. He was sub-Governor to George III as Prince of Wales, 1751–6, and Private Secretary 1756–60.

[6] O'Hara's seat in County Sligo.

[7] No such History has been found.

your friends in Wimple Street[1] who are well and as usual entirely yours a Vertice usque ad talum;[2] from the Doctor down to Dick.

I am dear Sir

your ever obliged and obedient Servant

E BURKE.

July 10th 1761.

I hope you have got my last. Excuse the blots. I can scarce ever write without mistakes and I have as seldom time to copy.

To RICHARD SHACKLETON—25 *August* 1761

Source: MS Dr O. Fisher. Printed *Corr.* (1844) I, 36–7. MS cut.

The Irish Parliament sat in Dublin in alternate years. As 1761–2 was to be a 'Parliament winter', Lord Halifax as Lord Lieutenant and William Gerard Hamilton as his Chief Secretary planned to be in residence. Burke crossed to Ireland in advance of his superiors.

Dublin. Augst 25th 1761.

Dear Shackleton.

I believe you will not be displeased to hear of my being once more in Ireland, of the stay I intend to make here, for the winter, or of my resolution to pay you a Visit as soon as I possibly can. I have been very blameable as a correspondent both to you and to Dennis and indeed to every body. I shall attempt no apology, and only speak for my heart, which has always done justice to your merit, and to our long friendship. I daily expect my Wife and family;[3] and shall be very happy to hear that you, and yours are well. I really long to see you. We have, (and I suppose you have heard it), lost our poor friend Brenan. He died of a very long and painful illness, in which however he was exposed to no want, and which he bore with constancy. Sure he was a man of first rate

[1] Apparently Burke's family was staying with Dr Nugent in town while Burke lived with Hamilton at Hampton. Horace Walpole wrote George Montagu 22 July of a visit he paid Hamilton: 'there were Garrick and a young Mr Burk, who wrote a book in the style of Lord Bolinbroke that was much admired. He is a sensible man, but has not worn off his authorism yet—and thinks there is nothing so charming as writers and to be one—he will know better one of these days. I like Hamilton's little Marly—we walked in the great *allée*, and drank tea in the arbour of *treillage;* they talked of Shakespear and Booth, of Swift and my Lord Bath...'(*Horace Walpole's Correspondence*, ed. W. S. Lewis, New Haven, 1937– , IX, 380).

[2] From head to heel; see Horace, *Epistles*, II, ii, 4.

[3] Burke's second son was still alive at this time. Shackleton's daughter tells of her parents having visited Burke in his apartments at Dublin Castle and found him seated on the floor playing with his two little boys (*Leadbeater Papers*, I, 48–9). When the younger died is not known; he was mentioned by name in Burke's father's will, dated 4 November 1761 (printed Samuels, p. 407).

Genius, thrown away and lost to the world.[1] I have not now much time, further than to pray my respects to[2] Mrs Shackleton, your father and your mother, and believe me most truly your ever affectionate and obliged friend

E B.

To RICHARD SHACKLETON—8 *September* 1761

Source: MS copy National Library of Ireland.

My dear Shackleton,

I thank you for your very kind letter; for your kind invitation; for your sketch of your Wives picture, for every thing. However I am resolved to acquiesce as little as possible in Pictures, but hope to see you originally and face to face next thursday. I mention the day that you may if you have no pressing engagement stay at home. I can stay but a short time and I should be heartily vexed to miss you. My Wife is too a Good sort of Woman enough and would be most heartily glad to see yours, but she cannot now possibly go and this is a disappointment to her.

Adieu my dear friend and believe me yours

very truly
E BURKE

8 Sepr 1761 Dublin

To WILLIAM DENNIS—[1761]

Source: Fitzwilliam MSS (Sheffield) Bk 28.

One of the letters of Burke to Dennis which Dr French Laurence saw in the possession of Dr Hales (see above, p. 90, introductory note to letter of 28, 29 May 1747), Laurence described to Mrs Burke as being

'...highly honourable indeed, as every scrap that ever I have found is highly honourable, to the memory of one of the best as well as greatest men, that ever existed. In the close was a short passage relative to an Union. It was written, when Mr Burke first went in a confidential capacity under Government to Ireland; and is just such as under similar circumstances he would have written

[1] William Dennis had written Shackleton 6 October 1759: 'Brennan has strayed to London, and is lost amid the crowd of new wits and new faces and forgets those who valued him most' (Samuels, p. 213). Burke may at this time have planned to bring out a subscription edition of Brenan's play *The Lawsuit* (see above, note to letter of [*circa* 12 March 1746/47], p. 88). The unfinished 'Hints for an Essay on the Drama' (*Works* [Bohn], VI, 175–83, [Little, Brown], VII, 143–56) contain a passage on this play, and may have been projected as an introduction to it. A MS draft of the 'Hints' at Sheffield (Bk 27e, f) is written on the back of a letter dated 16 January 1761.

[2] The original is cut off at this point. The following words and Burke's initials are supplied from a copy among the Ballitore MSS.

at the last moment of his life. He touches a little gently on the furious clamour raised by the Irish Patriots, before they knew whether an Union would be offered; throws out a little sarcasm at "the *dread* of a beggar (a description applicable enough, as you know to Ireland at that time, but by no means so now) at the prospect of being taken into partnership by a rich Merchant"; but then gravely adds "*that the question of an union was a matter of deep and difficult enquiry*"; and concludes by observing, that all he could say about it was, that he did [not] know it to be in contemplation by the Government either of England or Ireland.'

CHARLES O'HARA *to* EDMUND BURKE—10 *August* 1762

Source: Fitzwilliam MSS (Sheffield). Printed Hoffman, pp. 281–3.

Burke must have remained in Ireland to the end of the parliamentary session, returning to England at some time in the summer of 1762. No letters written *by* him survive from the first seven months of 1762. Only one letter written *to* him survives—from Joseph Wilcocks (1724–91), who in 1759 and 1760 had been working with him upon an unidentified collection of 'illustrious lives' (mentioned in letters of Wilcocks to Ambrose Isted now on deposit with the Northamptonshire Record Society, Sotheby-Ecton, E (S) 1140). Wilcocks wrote from Antwerp 1 May 1762, addressing Burke 'at the Rev'd Dr Markham's Head-Master of Westminster School'. A letter of Charles O'Hara 10 August, though chiefly interesting as a characteristic utterance of O'Hara himself, also throws a little light upon Burke in this period.

Nymphsfield 10 August 1762

Dear Sir

I was as lucky in the receipt of your favour last night, so much sooner than answers generally come from London, as I have been ever since I saw you in uninterupted good health. You may figure to yourself what you please of the happiness of retirement in a place of ones own; but tis by no means such, as not to receive an immense increase from your letters. Tis however pleasant; not perhaps what you think it, who from the relish you have had for places not your own, are left at liberty to suppose that every void you feel, woud be agreably filld up by *Property*. Tis very well when mixd with a good deal of the world: when one brings from thence a stock of materials for reflection and speculation. The disposition and habits acquird in one state are corrected by the other; and Philosophy has fair play. But ones mind relaxes too much in constant retirement: it is at last *made weak with musing*. If one is religious, one falls into meditation, which is the indolence of religion; if one is prudent, the heart contracts, and grows stingy. If one had any natural address, it turns to cunning and one looks out for a contiguity from a neighbour. This all my knowledge of people who live constantly in the Country leads me to think. Then ambition in retirement is the devil: a Bashaw over the poor; an intriguer for injustice and opression on grand Juries, and a false neighbour. Tis a shocking caricature of *manliness*. I must in addition to all this, tell you a discovery that I have made of myself: that too much of the pleasure one has in improving a place of ones own is from vanity. I am never so fond of my walks as when I find strangers in them, that think them worth seeing. Nay it even descended to servants, til they tore all my flowering shrubs, and obligd me to retrench this gratification of my vanity. No, a mixture always does best; I shall go to my solitude on the Curragh[1] the last day of this month, stay there the meeting, spend a fortnight about Dublin, then to Celbridge races; then home for a month to plant, til November ensures me a new gale, and enables me to see you Mrs Burke, the Doctor my boys and some other friends. And here I congratulate my two friends with great sincerity on their success in negotiating their several points.[2] Your brothers arm I suppose almost well, as no fever followd it.[3] But pray my good friend give me leave to ask you how you came to shew my letter to Mr Hamilton? Wives I have heard shoud keep no secrets from their husbands; but I never knew that this was a rule in friendship. What I said of him I dont remember; but I am sure it was of a sort that I woud not say to him. I dont believe he'll ever answer my letter; and I suppose I must pay the Kings plate out of my own pocket.[4] This in addition to the multiplicity of business in the new Department,[5] leaves me no sort of chance. However, if rightly informd, I have the solamen miseris,[6] that nobody on this side the water, has been taken much more notice of than myself. I think his Grace of Bed[ford] will do well at Paris.[7] For a Resident Minister he woud not do. But at this time I think him the properest man in England to bring the French to speak with precision. But if Spain and Portugal be not included, they'll only change ours into a land war; and the scene from Westphalia to the confines of Portugal.

[1] The Curragh of Kildare.

[2] Will and Richard Burke had not been successful in defending their interests in the West Indies, as Edmund tells O'Hara in the reply to this letter.

[3] It is odd that Richard should have had accidents on the two occasions when he was home from the West Indies; his broken leg in 1767 long delayed his return. Goldsmith spoke of Richard in *Retaliation* as 'Now breaking a jest, and now breaking a limb'.

[4] O'Hara was Ranger of the Curragh; there were two King's Plate prizes of 100 guineas each offered yearly at the pleasure of the Lord Lieutenant (Rowley Lascelles, *Liber Munerum Publicorum Hiberniae*, London, 1824–30, vol. I, part III, opp. p. 53). Presumably O'Hara had applied through Hamilton to have the expense of one of them approved.

[5] Halifax had become First Lord of the Admiralty in June (while continuing as Lord Lieutenant of Ireland).

[6] See above, letter of 16 January 1745/46.

[7] On 28 July the Cabinet agreed to send the Duke of Bedford as plenipotentiary to Paris, to conclude peace.

I shall write presently to Mr Jack Burke,[1] who I hope is by this well. He tells me Will's Father has brought over some books for me; I suppose from you. I guess what they are, and am much obligd to you. Whether Jack will come here before I set out, or come back with me, is as yet doubtful. When I get into the world again I'll write to you, without waiting for your answer. This phrase of *going into the world* puts me in mind of an island about six leagues from Sligoe, which I have but lately known anything of; calld Enish Murray.[2] The race of Inhabitants now there are by their tradition of many hundred years standing. If ever they come to our Continent, they call it going into the great world. They are an unmixd people, Their Irish purer than our people speak and many of their stories I am told, have all the natural beauty so well *counterfeited* in Fingal.[3] They have ruins very singular and of great antiquity. But the innocent simplicity of their lives is extraordinary. Extremely hospitable to any stranger that goes among them; and miraculously chaste; whatever disputes may arise, are settled among themselves; they were never known to carry a complaint into *the great world*. Tis a part of our County, and yet few of our Gentlemen had ever heard of it. When I go to London, I shall try to get this Island. I think you'd pay me a visit there; tho' you wont here. I went yesterday to divide a very large mountain farm among its inhabitants, who according to their own tradition have livd under *me* there 500 years; tis their phrase. With great difficulty I divided them into four villages, for twas an innovation; but I told them they must be moderniz'd. They were sufficiently so as to vice, and I have a desire to make them industrious, and to preserve them. You'd hardly expect this from a man you usd to accuse last winter of being as bad as any Cromwelian. I therefore tell it, to retrieve your favour. My eyes wont admit of much longer letters; well for you that some defect obliges me to conclude for I shoud otherwise gratify myself without mercy to you. A conclusion in form, I have no room for, yours most truly, Chs O'Hara.

[1] Perhaps John Bourke (*c.* 1729–92), later (1790) 2nd Earl of Mayo.

[2] Inishmurray is the modern spelling.

[3] Burke had shown his own interest in the controversy over Macpherson's Ossianic forgeries. The *Annual Register* for 1760 had reviewed at length the *Fragments of Ancient Poetry*; the *Register* for 1761 had devoted ten pages to *Fingal*. Boswell quotes Burke as saying in 1787 that when the fragments came out, he could not tell whether they were ancient or not, but when there was a mass of material, he realized the imposture (*Private Papers of James Boswell*, ed. G. Scott and F. A. Pottle, New York, 1928–34, XVII, 51). The *Register's* review of *Fingal* still thinks the poems 'or rather the greater part of their expressions and ideas, the production of Ossian whose name they so often mention'.

To CHARLES O'HARA—[*ante* 23 *August* 1762]

Source: O'Hara MSS. Printed Hoffman, pp. 283–5.
Undated. Burke mentions the marriage of the Duke of Bedford's daughter as an event which has not yet taken place. It took place 23 August.

Dear Sir,

I returned from London yesterday; I there received your obliging Letter from Nymphsfield. I need not say how agreeable it was to two or three people whose satisfactions you have always been kind enough to think worth your attention. I shall say no more in favour of retirement, lest I should hear still stronger arguments against it; but I shall *feel* as much as ever in its favour, notwithstanding the very Philosophical, that is to say, the very solid and very ingenious reasons, you have given on the other side. As I allowed Celsus's Maxim, that a Change from City to Country, and so reciprocally, is best for the health of the body,[1] I must yield as much to you, that a change of the same Nature is most conducive to the health and soundness of the mind. What Pity it is that[2] there should be so much reason and experience against one of the most agreeable delusions with which the human mind has been ever entertained. To settle my thoughts I must enter into a Course of Cowley;[3] I shall appeal from the Philosophers to the Poets, because, (as a servant of Mr Hamiltons said the other day) *I know well enough* they will determine on my side. Thus far you must admit, that while you reasond against this way of Life, you have given a very agreeable Picture of it. You charm me with this account of your Little New world, which you have discoverd so near home. Of what size is this Island, or is it described in the Map? I wish you may get it with all my heart; for I know that you will be no Cortez, Pizarro, Cromwell or Boyle[4] to the Natives. Happy and wise are these poor Natives in avoiding your great World; that they are yet unacquainted with the unfeeling Tyranny of a mungril Irish Landlord, or with the Horrors of a Munster Circuit.[5]

[1] Aulus Cornelius Celsus, *De Medicina*, I, i.

[2] MS: that that

[3] Abraham Cowley (1618–67).

[4] Richard Boyle, 1st Earl of Cork (1566–1643).

[5] Burke was strongly interested in the agrarian disorders which broke out in southern Ireland in the early 1760's, and which were punished by a number of hangings, partly from a belief of the government that they were an organized Jacobite rebellion. (See an unfinished paper printed in *Corr.* [1844], I, 41–5.) Among Burke MSS at Sheffield (Bk 8a) is a letter of William Fant to the Lord Lieutenant of Ireland (a document one is surprised to find among Burke's private papers), dated 18 October 1761 and endorsed in Burke's hand 'First information of the forged Plot. from Fant who himself first r⟨ai⟩sed the White Boys'. Fant describes a meeting in June 1760 at which he thought he had seen the Pretender disguised as a woman. Burke's concern over the contents of this letter is not hard to explain. Fant's charges touched some of his maternal relatives: 'Hugh Massy Ingoldsby who is since that dead the Nagles and Hennesys were the

I have avoided this subject whenever I wrote to you; and I shall now say no more of it; because it is impossible to preserve ones Temper on the view of so detestable a scene. God save me from the power, (I shall take care to keep myself from the society) of such monsters of Inhumanity. An old acquaintance of mine at the Temple, a man formerly of integrity and good nature, had by living some years in Corke, contracted such horrible habits, that I think, whilst he talked on these late Disturbances, none but hang men could have had any pleasure in his company. Can you get drawings of any of the ruins on Inis Moray?

We expect hourly an account of the conclusion of a peace.[1] This will entirely destroy the hopes of our two friends, upon which, you founded your last kind congratulations. They have certainly agreed to give up all their Conquests in the W. Indies; with them go down a great part of the Views both of Will and Dick, who are in a great Measure at sea again.[2] Will had got almost ready before this determination of our Ministry, a piece, not to prove, but to demonstrate the superior Value of one of those Islands only to every thing else we should have acquired by the last Treaty, or by the present, which is on the plan of that which we read together in Dublin. It is mortifying, that he suffers so deeply by this, and yet dares not tell the publick that they suffer too.[3]

The D. of Bedford continues in his resolution of going to Paris; it is thought he will set out in a fortnight. Before he goes the marriage

Promoters of the Meeting'. The *Corke Journal* of 5 April 1762 and the *Dublin Journal* of 6–10 April 1762 report the imprisonment of a 'Garret Nagle' one of a group of men arrested 'on suspicion of their aiding and assisting of the clan called White Boys'.

[1] The news awaited at this time was only whether Spain would agree to the preliminaries.

[2] Will had already, before the cession of the islands, lost some of the support he might have expected from the Governor of Guadaloupe. Dalrymple wrote home to Pitt 14 September 1761 concerning him and the Receiver General: 'their pretensions to enter into the Council of the Island were not well founded; as their Influence was not necessary there to support the affairs of Government, And as they could not with propriety propose themselves for Judges, in a French Court of Justice' (Public Record Office, C.O. 110/2). Dalrymple disapproved of officials engaging in trade (see his letter to Pitt, 15 July 1761, C.O. 110/1). When the island was finally surrendered to the French, a list of debts owed to British merchants was drawn up, of which one entry read: 'a Wm. Burke & Co par son bilan du 2 Avril 1763 193065 Livres 2 S 4 D' (C.O. 101/9).

[3] The pamphlet entitled *An Examination of the Commercial Principles of the late Negotiation between Great Britain and France in 1761* published by Dodsley, September 1762 (Straus, *Robert Dodsley*, p. 378) was anonymous, but has usually been attributed to Will Burke. An earlier pamphlet in the same controversy, *Remarks on the Letter address'd to Two Great Men*, published by Dodsley 20 January 1760 (Straus, p. 370), was attributed to him by Dr Hunt in *D.N.B.* and by Lecky, but his authorship is more questionable. See a review of the whole controversy over the treaty: W. L. Grant, 'Canada versus Guadaloupe, an Episode of the Seven Year's War', *American Historical Review*, XVII, 1911–12, 735–43. A passage in the later pamphlet (p. 50) '...it has happened exactly as I at first foresaw...' seems to refer to a passage on the same topic in the earlier (p. 35—concerning trade between Canada and the Islands); this perhaps strengthens the case for Will Burke's authorship of both pamphlets.

between his Daughter and the D. of Marlborough will be concluded.[1] This alliance is you see a vast accession of Strength to Lord Bute.[2]

Nothing done about Irish affairs in general—but the Curragh Business[3] Mr Ham. tells me has been settled long ago.

Mrs Burke and my Brother are both come to Town. They met with Charles and Mr Cleaver on the Road to Luton; both well. I do not hold it right, very much otherwise, mutually to communicate to each other the secrets of ones friends. But there was nothing I knew, ill meant, ill wrote, or ill taken in your Letter. Mr H. if I do not mistake is as much as any man almost in your Interests. I am a little heavy and I take the Liberty of scribbling something to you in all humours, as in all humours I am most truly,

my Dear Sir,

Your most affectionate and obliged humble Servant

E. BURKE

Hampton

To CHARLES O'HARA—9 [*October*] 1762

Source: O'Hara MSS. Printed Hoffman, pp. 286–9.
A joint letter of Edmund and Will Burke, with a postscript by Dr Nugent. Will's portion and the postscript are omitted. Burke's date of 'Sept. 9th 1762' is a mistake: the duel described took place 6 October.

Will has taken all the friendly part, and has only left me that of a newsmonger. However I submit to the condition, and am ready to assume any Shape in which it may be in my power to divert you. You remember where the correspondence between Ld Talbot, and Wilkes ended in my last Letter.[4] Every thing then wore, as you must have observed, a very pacific appearance. After a proper time for recollection, My Lord renewed the Negotiation, by sending Wilkes a challenge to meet him the next day about five miles from Town. Wilkes said he was engaged on a very jolly good humourd party for that day, whom he would be very sorry to disappoint; especially as Sr Francis Dashwood[5] made one

[1] Bedford set out for Paris 6 September. His daughter, Lady Caroline Russell, married George Spencer, 4th Duke of Marlborough, 23 August.

[2] Hardly vast. Marlborough had three representatives in the Commons: his brother, Lord Charles Spencer (1740–1820), Lord Bateman (1721–1802) and Anthony Tracy Keck (d. 1767), who sat for Marlborough's pocket borough of Woodstock.

[3] See O'Hara's letter of 10 August.

[4] Missing. The quarrel of John Wilkes (1727–97) and Lord Talbot began when Wilkes in the *North Briton* for 21 August satirized Talbot's economies in the Royal Household and made fun of his horsemanship when he officiated as Lord High Steward at the Coronation.

[5] 2nd Baronet (1708–81); later (1763) 11th Baron le Despenser; he was a friend of Talbot's, as well as a fellow member with Wilkes of the Hell Fire Club.

of the company; and if he missed him, would not fail to guess the occasion, and probably might disappoint his Lps. Intentions; At the same time he agreed with my Lords friend for another day at Bagshot Heath. My Ld consented to the delay, and to the other appointment; and had not been long at the Inn at Bagshot before Mr Wilkes arrived. Norbonne Berkley,[1] was my Ld Talbots second; It was late in the Evening and Wilkes proposed with an air of levity that they might pass the Evening together and do their Business coolly and at leisure in the morning, adding that their parti quarrée[2] that night would not spoil the Duet which was to be the entertainment of the following day. The proposal was rejected with great disdain and much abuse; Mr Berkely was commissioned to tell Mr W. that he was a great Scoundrel; and that my Ld looked upon him as the most impious and profligate of all men who could think of jesting upon an Affair of that Nature. This Message was Literally and with a true Homerian fidelity deliverd by the serene and Gentle Norbonne; a Situation which I think must make you laugh. Wilkes observed that the abuse in their Circumstances was a matter of no consideration; that if my Lord considered the Business they came upon as any way criminal, he was himself alone to blame who brought him from London to engage in it. That he Valued his Life as much as my Ld and thought it as valuable as his Lps and though he expressd himself with Levity; he really would be glad of time to write a Letter or two; his affairs being in the utmost confusion (which is but too true). The decision, on these reasons was put off to the next morning. They came to the ground; ten paces were measured; and while this ceremony was performed my Ld vented a Torrent of Billingsgate against Wilkes of which he took no sort of notice. But when they had taken their Ground he addressed himself to my Ld and told him that if his Lp should happen to fall he must expect to be prosecuted with all the rancour backed with all the power which an enraged administration could employ against him, he therefore desired that before the Gentlemen who were present he would declare that it was at his Lps desire he came to that meeting. My Ld could not refuse this acknowlegement. Their Pistols were mutually discharged without any execution; the seconds interposed to prevent a recharging and thought enough had been done. Wilkes took the Word again. 'My Ld I have given you one of the Kinds of Satisfaction you desired; I will now give you the other; I *am* the author of the Paper which you thought reflected upon you. I am likewise the Author of such and such offensive paragraphs in other papers, which may be thought

[1] Norborne Berkeley, later (1764) 4th Baron Botetourt (*c.* 1717–70).
[2] Or carré: a party of four.

to reflect upon your friends. I give this explanation once for all and cannot be expected to be ready to answer every call, whenever your Lordship shall think fit. I desire that we may finish every thing here, with a perfect reconciliation, or a perfect satisfaction.' The former part of the alternative was accepted; I suppose by the interposition of the seconds. The publick always malevolent to great men; think this Business ended to the advantage of Wilkes, who they think behaved more firmly consistently, and coolly than Ld T. from the beginning to the End. I have not seen H.[1] since I saw your Letter to the Dr. I think I shall speak to him about the affair of Charles's Commission. The Negotiation for Peace is at a dead stand. No Council has been lately held. Coalitions among the great are talked of; but nothing done.[2] In short so far as can be discoverd all things are in an entire confusion. Compare Ld Butes situation with yours on the ocean Shore.[3] Adieu and believe me Dear Sir

ever yours

E BURKE

Sepbr 9th 1762 I rejoice that we shall soon talk over these things together. Dr Crane is made Bishop of Exeter by our all powerful Lord Lieutenant. Keppel had the promise.[4]

To CHARLES O'HARA—30 *October* [1762]

Source: O'Hara MSS. Printed Hoffman, pp. 289–91.

My dear Sir

I suppose you found large pacquet's at Nymphsfield from the Doctor, from Will Burke, and from me. Some of them will entertain, and others at least occupy, a good part of your time; and prevent something of that *Ennui* which other wise might prey upon you a little, in spite of Farming, Hunting, and Country Squires. I assure you I am not the only person who is pleased with the approach of November, and the hopes of seeing you shortly in London. The Gentleman from whose house I write[5] has

[1] Hamilton.

[2] The Cabinet was to have met 4 October to consider the terms of peace. But the Secretaries of State, Lord Egremont and George Grenville (1712–70), were standing out for better terms; Bute decided to postpone the Cabinet meeting to enable him to make changes in the Administration.

[3] Bute, anxious to share the responsibility for the peace treaty, had sounded Newcastle about returning to office, and had even made overtures to Pitt and the Duke of Cumberland.

[4] Burke is mistaken. The Rev. Frederick Keppel (1729–77), Canon of Windsor, was nominated for election to the See of Exeter 16 October. 'Dr Crane' is probably Dr Edward Crane (*c.* 1696–1777), Prebendary of Westminster. He had been Halifax's Chaplain.

[5] Hamilton.

very many good wishes for you. We shall go to Town tomorrow for the Winter. I have at last got an house, pretty dear, very good, and extremely remote. I know you play Cards some times near Cavendish Square, and we may expect to see you (when you happen to break up early) about twelve; and whenever you have ill luck, you need not fear a Robbery. If you had not the management to bear that ill luck tolerably, we should have the misfortune of never seeing you, but in an ill humour: for when you were winner you could not be rash enought to attempt Queen anne street so it will be called—*nunc sunt sine nomine Terrae.*[1] As the Session approaches things come nearer to a decision. The D. of Devonshire resigned or was rather turned out last Thursday. Lord Bessborough resigned yesterday.[2] This may make pretty sport in Ireland and may provide matter for a very *manly* opposition.[3] I am heartily sorry for the Primate.[4] All the accounts of him which I have seen correspond with yours. I think, take him all in all, he would be a real loss to that Country. You have by this read Wills Pamphlet; which with regard to the publick approbation has the success it deserves; with regard to its ultimate object it will I fear have none. Our virtuous ministry intend to make a clear evacuation of all the French Islands. His hand cannot save his Pergamus. Nothing has however been omitted. My Brother went to Liverpool and excited those sluggish Traders to a sense of the danger they were in of losing so vast a Trade. They addressed; and their address has been presented by their Member.[5] *Atlas*[6] was 'surprised at the greatness of the Trade'—'knew it not before'; 'obliged by the information'—'But it was now too late'. This was his answer. I own I think it hard to form an Idea of a shameful peace, if this is not the most shameful that ever was made; and with the least possibility of an excuse. Our friends in London are well. I am sure you will be concerned to hear that my Poor

[1] Now the lands are without a name; see *Aeneid*, VI, 776.

[2] William Cavendish, 4th Duke of Devonshire (1720–64), Lord Chamberlain, was dismissed 28 October. William Ponsonby, 2nd Earl of Bessborough (1704–93), joint Postmaster General, was Devonshire's brother-in-law and resigned his own post in protest.

[3] Since the Hon. John Ponsonby (1713–87), Speaker of the Irish House of Commons, and one of the Lords Justices, was Bessborough's brother and had also married one of Devonshire's sisters, the dismissal of Devonshire and the resignation of Bessborough were expected to affect Irish politics. Will Burke wrote to O'Hara 20 November 1762 (printed Hoffman, pp. 292–6): 'Lord Bessborough resigns to serve his friend, and for fear it should serve him, he writes, as possibly you know, to the Speaker, that he does it, not from resentment or dislike, but simply to avoid the unfitness of voting in the same house on a different side from the Duke of Devonshire....'

[4] George Stone, Archbishop of Armagh (*c.* 1708–64).

[5] It is among the Liverpool MSS in the British Museum (Add. MS 38200, fols. 47–50), docketed 'In Sr Wm Meredith's of 1762'. Sir William Meredith, 3rd Baronet (*c.* 1725–90), was later a friend and correspondent of Burke and a leading member of the Rockingham group.

[6] Presumably Lord Bute.

Mother is in a very declining way under a very cruel nervous disorder.[1] There will I fear one of my strongest links to Ireland be snapped off. I think I have told you every thing. I need not tell you with what truth I am

Dear Sir

your ever affectionate
humble Servant
ED BURKE

Hampton Octr 30th

WILLIAM BURKE *to* CHARLES O'HARA—20 *November* 1762

Source: O'Hara MSS. Printed Hoffman, pp. 292–6.

Will Burke himself had been ironical about the pamphlet he had written against the peace, which was an obvious attempt to defend interests of his own in Guadaloupe. 'I inclose you my last effort to *save my Country*' he told O'Hara 9 [October], adding that O'Hara would readily guess 'my country' to be Guadaloupe. In its first purpose the pamphlet failed. Will had, however, still some hope of advantage from it, as appears from a passage in a long letter he wrote O'Hara in November.

...You very elegantly bid me employ another hand in telling you the success of my pamphlet, after what you are so kind to say, I will not say that my Vanity is unconcerned for your approbation is not an indifferent thing to me. It was in vain to deny it. It was laid at my door, some said it was like me, and that whore the publick swore I had an Interest in it, it was therefore time to see what was thought of it, where I hoped to be well thought of; I waited upon Fox,[2] who began with saying he was much displeased with my having wrote it, why did it not come out sooner, why did I not send the copy &c &c &c. I have always observed that a justification is of more weight than an Excuse; in short you give your money sooner to a robber who demands it, to a beggar who sues for it. As to sending it, I said that he must know that it would have been thrown under the table—not to trouble you with all I said, the most material was, that when I wrote, he was not in the Ministry, that my dependence was on him and him alone, and consequently I was to consult the pleasure of none other, but to pursue the likeliest measure to me, for my own Interest. And I had conceived that if I could draw the publick Attention, I hoped that, of the Minister would follow. He did not he said suppose I meant to hurt my friends; owned that he was not

[1] See above, letter of 12 July 1746 (p. 67). David Murphy wrote Burke 16 August 1764: 'I saw your mother at Mr Ridges, and she looks but ghostly....' Mrs Burke died in 1770 (*Leinster Journal*, 19–22 September 1770).

[2] Henry Fox, Paymaster General and Leader of the House of Commons.

then the Minister, (I thank God he now is) a day or two after, I went to him to let him know that I hoped I had some weight with L. Verney, who had more than one voice,[1] it happened to be the very man he knew not how to come round, and from whom he had received no answer to a Letter he had wrote,[2] I had before applied for the Government of the Granades;[3] he now renewed his promises of services; and I left town that moment, found my friend had wrote to him, but pretty much as I could have wished, not warm, and no offer of Service, I got his leave to write to fox that he and his friends would be with him; upon my return I waited on F he said he had already mentioned me as one who might and would serve them, was answered that so I ought, for that I had hurt them damnably—I smiled and said that if I had meant to hurt them, it was the *present* not the late treaty which I should have examined[4]—at which he grinned and said it was all one. He is however a Man to be depended upon,[5] and I have good hopes that something will be done. If I get the Granades (and I hope nobody is yet applying) tho I lose the bett, I have made a good hedge. We are all, even to little dick if he is father or mothers child all yours

Most affectionately

W B.

London. Nov 20 1762.
I am seriously almost ashamed
of the length

[1] Ralph Verney, 2nd Earl Verney (*c.* 1712–91) was M.P. for Carmarthen borough, and he also controlled one seat for Wendover, Bucks, which was held at this time by his first cousin Verney Lovett (*c.* 1705–71), later held by Edmund Burke. Will had some reason to speak confidently of his influence over Lord Verney. Fox wrote to Lord Sandwich a year later, concerning Will: 'He is a very clever fellow, and I believe a very honest one. He has as great a sway with Lord Verney, as I ever knew one man to have with another. Lord Verney has another vote besides his own. I owed them both to Mr Burke last sessions, and they were never absent' (letter of 12 November 1763, quoted in L. B. Namier, *England in the Age of the American Revolution*, London, 1930, p. 214 n.).

[2] Doubtless the circular letter Fox had written to those members of the House of Commons he hoped would support the Peace Preliminaries, due to be laid before Parliament in the coming session.

[3] Fox wrote to Lord Egremont 1 March 1763 supporting this application. He said of Will: 'He is an ingenious and knowing Man and has been a great while in Guadaloupe. He desires to be Governor of the Granades, an Employment which I earnestly beg for Him.' Nothing having come of the application before 18 April, he wrote again suggesting Will for the government of Carolina, then vacant (Public Record Office, Egremont Papers, 30/47/29/3).

[4] Will's pamphlet was written before the peace treaty took its final form. See above (p. 148), Burke's remark in his letter of [*ante* 23 August]: 'Will had got almost ready before this determination of our Ministry, a piece...'.

[5] Will told his friend George Macartney (1737–1806) 21 December 1765 that he made Fox 'my Great North Star to direct my political opinions' (MS Osborn Collection).

To CHARLES O'HARA—23 *November* [1762]

Source: O'Hara MSS. Printed Hoffman, pp. 296–8.

Dear Sir,

If you are in Dublin you can have no loss in missing this Letter; if you are still at Nymphsfield to which I direct, you may possibly not receive the intelligence it conveys so early by another way. The Campain is at the point of opening and is likely to be fought with more acrimony and with a more ballanced strength than any one has for a good while past imagined.[1] Some time ago Mr Walpole, the great remitter in the City,[2] was sent by the D. of Newcastle[3] to Mr Pitt to renew the proposals of accommodation he had formerly made to him; which Pitt rejected as before with disdain; though he had, about that time, made very express declarations, which were carefully Spread about the City by his Friends, that he would take a warm part against the peace, which he called a *felonious* one; inglorious, and inadequate to our Successes.[4] Last Wednesday the Duke of Cumberland went to him, and by pledging himself and Lord Hardwicke[5] for the Duke of N's fidelity, prevailed upon him to enter into the coalition; which is now so perfect in all its parts, and of such strength, that it threatens to all appearance a more powerful and determined opposition, than has perhaps ever been known before in the commencement of any combination of that kind, and in the outset of the administration they would oppose.[6] It was expected we should have no less than 25 resignations yesterday; but as this has not happend, I suppose they chuse rather to wait to be turned out. Lord Mansfield I believe now suffers inwardly for the part he has taken.[7]

[1] Parliament was due to meet 25 November, and the chief business of the first weeks was the consideration of the Peace Preliminaries. Opposition was expected from Newcastle, Pitt, and the Duke of Cumberland; and Fox had been working to secure a majority for the Preliminaries. This and the three following letters deal with the preparations for the debate and the debate itself. Burke had no contacts with the opposition at this time and greatly exaggerated their strength and unity.

[2] Thomas Walpole (*c.* 1728–1803), M.P. for Ashburton, a banker who had held a Government contract for remitting money to Germany.

[3] Thomas Pelham Holles, 1st Duke of Newcastle (1693–1768).

[4] This approach from Newcastle to Pitt via Walpole, who was on good terms with both, took place 13 November. Pitt did not reject the proposal 'with disdain', nor does he seem to have inveighed so strongly against the Peace Preliminaries (see Namier, *op. cit.* pp. 451–2).

[5] Philip Yorke, 1st Earl of Hardwicke (1690–1764).

[6] The meeting between Pitt and Cumberland took place on Wednesday 17 November. Pitt, wrote Newcastle, 'disclaimed, at least at first, any connection, or open correspondence with us'. Though he later proved more amenable, this meeting did not result in the formation of the strong coalition which Burke describes.

[7] William Murray, 1st Baron Mansfield (1705–93), Lord Chief Justice of the King's Bench. He hated Pitt, but was too timid to come out in full support of Bute. 'He is but half a man', wrote the King to Bute 4 November, 'timidity and refinement make him unfit for the present turbulent scene, he I am certain feels that, and therefore cries out against everything but *moderation*' (*Letters from George III to Lord Bute, 1756–1766*, ed. Romney Sedgwick, London, 1939, p. 157).

Ld Halifax is to take the Lead in the house of Lords.[1] His character is, without any jest, as high as ever, almost any mans was in this Country, for ability for unspotted honour, and for the equal Love and confidence of all Parties. This is the fact. Let the learned reason on the cause. This combustion is supposed will be very fortunate to Lord G. Sackville and may very probably terminate in something to his advantage. You know, that he is said to have refused to take a part if he is not restored to his rank in the Army; This is however not yet done.[2] Ch. Townshend is thought not yet to be quite fixed.[3] There is no more News. We are all well thank God. Will has wrote by the last post. His object is the Government of the Grenades. What will become of my Brother I know not. Adieu Dear Sir and believe me most truly and faithfully yours

E BURKE

23d Novr

We expect daily to see you.

To CHARLES O'HARA—25 *November* 1762

Source: O'Hara MSS. Printed Hoffman, pp. 298–300.

Dear Sir. I wrote to you by last post, and directed to Nymphsfield. A body of opposition was then regularly formed; and great expectations were entertained of their proceedings today. But if their army is not in disguise, their operations are. This day of so much expectation, has ended in nothing but a very fine Coach, a very long speech, and a very unanimous Dutiful and loyal address from both houses of Parliament.[4] The administration had so contrived the Speech and the address, that the one did not State the preliminaries as finished, nor the particulars to which they related, but kept aloof in pompous and general (though

[1] Halifax could hardly take the lead in the House of Lords while Bute remained First Lord of the Treasury.

[2] Lord George Sackville, disgraced while Newcastle and Pitt were Ministers, naturally looked to Bute for rehabilitation. Bute in a letter to Sir Henry Erskine (8 April 1763) explained that the King thought Sackville's rehabilitation would be 'attended with too many untoward circumstances' and 'would revolt numbers about him' (Hist. MSS Comm. *Stopford-Sackville MSS*, I, 58–9; see also *Letters from George III to Lord Bute*, p. 179 n.).

[3] The famous Charles Townshend (1725–67), 'the delight and ornament of this House, and the charm of every private society which he honoured with his presence' (see Burke's character of him in 'Speech on American Taxation', *Works* [Bohn], I, 426, [Little, Brown], II, 64). He was Secretary at War and hoped for something better.

[4] Burke is writing on the day of the opening of Parliament. The King's speech had been in such general terms as to be difficult to oppose; the King's coach—the ornate vehicle still in use at the coronation of Elizabeth II—was a more satisfactory feature of the occasion.

very ill conceived) terms and the other did not of Course contain any particular approbation, but many general expressions of satisfaction and confidence. This it seems satisfied the Gentlemen of the opposition. You will I think conceive no great Idea of the opposition by their falling into so common and poor a *piege*; and not contriving one of the many very obvious methods, for bringing on a debate, which would have given the people an Idea of their activity, if not of their strength; and spread about an early discontent. All the plans which I hear they intend to pursue seem to me incomprehensible; It is said Mr Pitt in his agreement with the D. of New[castle] made some reserves; what they are I do not hear.[1] He was not in the house today; He has the Gout in both his hands; and is besides ill of a fever.[2] Fox was also absent on account of the Reversion of the Clerkship of the Pells which is fallen to him.[3] Lord Carysfort[4] opend the address and Ld Charles Spencer seconded. Lord Carysfort began his Speech—'In the Splendour of Athens &c' you may judge how it was from the outset. Calvert, a mad member,[5] after saying some rambling things about the peace promised the house that he would make them Laugh before he had done; and notwithstanding the boldness of this declaration, he succeeded very happily. He observed that his reading had taken the same turn of the noble Lord's who made the motion; and that he found, all he had said, in the Preface to the Bishop of St Asaphs sermon upon the peace of Utrecht[6] which he repeated; and which was very near word for word the same with my Lords Speech. He observed that my Ld had stopped short and not gone so far as the Bishop; for that the part of the Preface which my Ld had borrowed only mentiond the *hopes* of the nation, when a treaty was carried on by a virtuous Whig ministry; and then repeated from the same Preface an invective against that which was afterward made by the Tories. It was every way well, and applicable; the house was pleased, and my Ld infinitely disconcerted. I think one must have sufferd for him. This, with a little grumbling by Beckford, and a little defence by Townsend, who took the lead in Foxes absence, formed the whole of this days work

[1] Pitt had no agreement with Newcastle (see Namier, *op. cit.* pp. 452–5).

[2] Pitt told the Duke of Cumberland 17 November that he did not intend to be present the first day of the session, and was against any opposition to the Address.

[3] Fox's accepting an office of profit under the Crown would automatically vacate his seat; he was re-elected 30 November.

[4] John Proby, 1st Baron Carysfort (1720–72).

[5] Nicolson Calvert (*c.* 1725–93). Horace Walpole describes him as 'a mad volunteer, who always spoke what he thought, and sometimes thought justly' (*Memoirs*, I, 131).

[6] William Fleetwood (1656–1723), Bishop of St Asaph (1708–14). The reference is to his sermon against the treaty of Utrecht, intended to be preached before the House of Lords on 16 January 1712.

among the commons. Ld Egmont moved the address in the house of Lords. He spoke a good while; and ill enough as I thought. The general drift of his discourse was to shew we were a reduced, beggard, depopulated, undone Nation, who were notwithstanding very Victorious glorious &c. &c. in the stile which you will find the bon ton among us at present. Lord Weymouth[1] seconded. There were but 240 at the Cockpit last night,[2] though most of the members were in Town of these five were not friends, and one of the five a capital Enemy, Wilkes. It was rather impudent of him to appear there. Ld Temple[3] it is said will not be in Town till Christmas. Do you know what to make of all this? Pray come hither as soon as you can, and try to decypher us; if you can, you will deserve Bath and Wells at the next vacancy.[4] I saw Charles today. He is grown a very fine fellow; he is certainly much handsomer than when you saw him. The fireside here, for which you are so kind to entertain much good wishes, are your very humble Servants and believe me dear Sir

your most affectionate and obliged
friend and Servant
E BURKE

Nov. 25. 1762

To CHARLES O'HARA—9 *December* [1762]

Source: O'Hara MSS. Printed Hoffman, pp. 300–2.

Dear Sir, At this instant both houses are sitting on the Preliminaries; they are on a work in which they do not require a great number of Spectators, and have accordingly, to my great mortification, issued such orders as have excluded me and the rest of the mob from hearing their debate;[5] before this goes off I shall tell you some particulars; the Issue in general we know beforehand. It was a long times doubt among many Gent of the discontented party whether they should oppose the address of thanks intended on this happy occasion; but they began at last to perceive that if they concurred universally in applauding the administration for a transaction of this importance their opposition afterwards

[1] Thomas Thynne, 3rd Viscount Weymouth (1734–96).

[2] The eve-of-session meeting of Government supporters, held at the Cockpit in Whitehall.

[3] Richard Grenville Temple, 2nd Earl Temple (1711–79).

[4] Edward Willes, Bishop of Bath and Wells (1694–1773), was employed by the Post Office to decipher intercepted despatches.

[5] On 26 November the House issued orders forbidding the entry of strangers. Strangers were theoretically always excluded, but were not invariably challenged.

would not prove so graceful, nor perhaps quite so effectual. They have therefore resolved to draw out their forces on this day, and reckon that they may divide, the moderate people say 110, the sanguine, 170. Not that they imagine this contains their whole strength; but many who will infallibly join in the general opposition, will not concur in opposing this measure; as some of them before their party was regularly formed, had pledged themselves to support the peace; and many others had been the avowed abettors or makers of Terms as bad, or if, possible, of worse. They threaten to commence their great Game after Christmas. They certainly have derived no small strength from the desertion of Ch. Townshend. He resigned last Tuesday.* He wanted the Board of Trade with all the Plantation Patronage which it possessed in Ld Halifaxes time and the Cabinet which in the same office had been formerly refused to Ld Halifax. The Administration never Loved him; and they trusted him no more than he is commonly trusted; and it was thought too hard a measure to strip Ld Egremont, who had just set his hand to the peace, of so material an appendage of His office, as the plantation patronage.[1] I think the opposite party want him more than the administration and that they ought to receive him with open Arms. They will this day chiefly oppose on the articles of the Fishery[2] and the East Indies;[3] the parties are all concerned one way or another in overlooking the West India concerns. Would you believe that the french Ministry is charmed with the Duke of Bedford; so reasonable, so moderate, so polite; whenever any difficulty arose, they always left it to himself, and he always put it on the most conciliatory footing imaginable. The Air of Paris makes people practicable. You could not learn this secret in Ireland. The Merchants have taken great Offence at the Article which surrenders the conquerd Islands in 3 months from the definitive Treaty.[4] They Petitiond Ld Egremont; it is said he orderd himself to be denied they gave the address to Beckford, and I hear he was to lay it before the house of Commons this day.[5] I have staid until the post is ready to go out (I mean the Bellmans). The debate still continues. However the address of thanks will pass; which from a very extravagant, has been lowerd to

* not on this day I am now told [Burke's note].[6]

[1] Which he held as Secretary of State for the Southern Department.

[2] Article 5 of the definitive treaty confirmed the French right to fish off Newfoundland. Pitt condemned this article in his speech of 9 December.

[3] Article 11 of the definitive treaty restored France to the position she had occupied in India in 1749.

[4] Guadaloupe, Martinique, and some smaller West Indian islands were restored to France.

[5] No such petition appears in the Journals of the House of Commons for 9 or 10 December, but see *Letters from George III to Lord Bute*, p. 171.

[6] He resigned on Wednesday 8 December.

a very modest approbation in order to fit it to the narrow swallow of some squeamish people.[1] I am told you are in Love with the peace in Ireland.

Adieu Dear Sir and believe me
Your very affectionate and obliged humble Servant
E BURKE.

9th Decr Thursday.
Q. Anne Street Cav. Square.

To CHARLES O'HARA—12 *December* 1762

Source: O'Hara MSS. Printed Hoffman, pp. 302–3.

Dear Sir

I wrote to you directed at Frederick Street last post. I mentiond the debate and expectation of that day. You know the blustering of the opposition. The Court divided 319 against 65.[2] In the House of Lords there was no division. Lord Hardwicke spoke very nonsensically, and in every respect, both of manner and matter, wretchedly; confounded as he was between his attachments to the Duke of Newcastle, his attentions to his family interest, and the natural Love he has for a bad peace, and every thing low and pusillanimous. Ld Mansfield with his usual dexterity; Lord Bute for two hours; The ministerial people, say admirably. Ld Halifax above par.—In the house of Commons Pitt spoke three hours and twenty five minutes; an apology for himself rather than attack on the peace; very tedious, unconvincing, heavy, and immethodical. He only spoke some paltry things about St Pierre and Miquelon.[3] They would not hear Beckford. Ch. Townshend said little.[4] Hamilton, Elliot[5] &c nothing. They did something towards resuming the Debate next day but it went very little further than a matter of order, though they sat long on it. In short all parties are involved in the wrong System, and while they stick to that, they will bungle for ever. The D. of Newcastle was quite ridiculous. Pray when shall we see you at our New fire side, which is as cheerful as the old one? I really long for your coming and am with great Truth your very affectionate and obligd friend and Servant

EDM BURKE.

Q. Anne Street 12th Decr 1762.

[1] It described the preliminaries as 'no less honourable than profitable, by which will be ceded to Great Britain such an addition of territory, attended with so great an extension of our commerce'.

[2] 9 December, on the motion to approve the address of thanks for the Peace Preliminaries. On 10 December, when the address was reported, the figures were 227 to 63.

[3] Returned by Great Britain to France. Pitt did not stay for the division.

[4] He voted for the Preliminaries.

[5] Gilbert Elliot (1722–77), later (1766) 3rd Baronet.

I forgot to tell you that though Ld Hardwicke opposed, his two Sons voted in the house of commons for the address. Will tells me that I am wrong and that they went out of the house before the division.[1]

To CHARLES O'HARA—30 *December* 1762

Source: O'Hara MSS. Printed Hoffman, pp. 304–6.

My dear Sir we receivd your last letter with less satisfaction than usual because we expected your own arrival; and your letter was a sort of disappointment; it would indeed be a very heavy one, if the winter should pass over without our seeing you here. Indeed the world here is dull enough; even faction is languid; but still you may find more entertainment, than in one of the intermediate winters in Dublin.[2] Your next will be sufficiently animated if I am not mistaken. Though you love peace in Ireland, it seems you have no objections to an army. A scheme for maintaining 18000 effective men on the Irish Establishment has been lately sent over here, warmly supported and recommended by my Ld Lt. Last tuesday it was agreed to in Council and that Number for Ireland will be in the next mutiny Bill.[3] Here it will certainly meet little or no opposition; and we are assured that no measure can be more universally agreeable to, or more ardently desired by, the whole People of Ireland. For my part this same people of Ireland, their notions and their inclinations have always been a riddle to me. Why they should love heavy Taxation; why they should abhor a civil and covet a military establishment I cannot, I confess, in the least conceive. As to the latter point, I believe it is really true. I observed that the least Pension, or raised employment was far more odious and unpopular than ten times that military expence. The Truth is this military servitude is what they have grown up under; and like all licentious, and wild, but corrupt people, they love a Jobb better than a Salary; It looks more like plunder. After all I cannot, from any State of the revenue which I could collect last

[1] Philip Yorke, Lord Royston (1720–90), later 2nd Earl of Hardwicke, voted for the address; his brothers Charles (1722–70) and John (1728–1801) abstained.

[2] Winters in which the Irish Parliament did not sit.

[3] The scheme was ultimately dropped. The question was submitted to the Attorney-General whether the Act 10 William III c. 1, which limited the number of troops on the Irish Establishment to 12,000, was still in force. The Attorney-General gave his opinion that it was, and that the number could not be increased in time of peace without an Act of Parliament (*Calendar of Home Office Papers, 1760–65*, pp. 210–11). In 1768 the number was increased to 15,235, and Burke claimed that he was the only member of the House of Commons who directly opposed it (letter of 20 February [1768], p. 343).

winter among you, conceive where you can discover funds for this amazing augmentation. A Land Tax would not displease me who have no Land; if I did not see, that this Tax would terminate in some measure on the wretched poor whose Burthens are already so lamentably heavy. It may look whimsical but I really am of opinion that this last Stroke, (if something is not done towards enlarging your Trading advantages in some little proportion to your new Expences) is given to Ireland. You had none but a landed interest which had any strength or body in Ireland; and if this is broke and crumbled to pieces, you are gone without redemption. Good God what can these men mean who carried through this serious measure in meer *gayeté de coeur*; and did not take half the time to think of it, that a man of sense would, who was going to add a single footman to his family? But I hate to think of Ireland, though my thoughts involuntarily take that turn, and whenever they do meet only with objects of grief or indignation. They speak of Ld Hertford[1] or Ld Waldgrave[2] for you; Lord Gore[3] has declined it; Ld Waldgrave, if it were not for the General,[4] would not be very fond of it; and as it is, I believe will not pursue it with great earnestness. Lord Hertford inclines that way strongly, but it is not so certain that they will give him what he desires. Our ministry is thought to have some internal uneasiness. All the Friends of Ld Bute are to the last degree jealous of the progress of Fox. On the other hand their common Enemies charge upon Fox all the late violent measures[5] and he is far enough from disavowing them. He seems growing fast into a minister; and in a short time we shall see [whether][6] Caesar and Pompey can divide power between them. The D. of Devonshire was not turned out in the last disposition of Lieutenancies;[7] I believe they chuse to leave a door open for him—with a little stooping he may enter into it, and I imagine he will stoop. He is thought to be narrow and proud, and that character is to be wrought

[1] Francis Seymour Conway, 1st Earl of Hertford (1719–94), Lord of the Bedchamber. He was Lord Lieutenant of Ireland 1765–6.

[2] James Waldegrave, 2nd Earl Waldegrave (1715–63).

[3] Granville Leveson-Gower, 2nd Earl Gower (1721–1803), brother-in-law of the Duke of Bedford.

[4] General John Waldegrave (1718–84) M.P. for Newcastle-under-Lyme, Lord Waldegrave's brother.

[5] The proscription of Newcastle's followers, carried out by Fox after the Preliminaries of Peace had been approved.

[6] MS: who

[7] On 23 December Newcastle, Grafton and Rockingham (Charles Watson Wentworth, 2nd Marquess of Rockingham, 1730–82) were dismissed from their Lord Lieutenancies because of their opposition to the Preliminaries of Peace. Fox, who had formerly been on close terms with Devonshire 'affected to make a point of saving him' (Walpole, *Memoirs*, I, 185) but Devonshire resigned the Lord Lieutenancy of Derbyshire 29 December.

upon by being treated with the proper contempt. You can send us no news so agreeable as that of your speedy arrival. Adieu my Dear Sir

most affectionately yours

E BURKE.

Thursday Decr 30th 1762.

They have got into a New Scrape about the great Fishery.[1] It may delay the definitive Treaty for some time.

To MRS ELIZABETH MONTAGU—[3 *March* 1763]

Source: Blunt, *Mrs Montagu*, I, 41.

Permit me Madam, to condole with you on the very melancholy account which for the first time I heard in the evening paper of last night.[2] What a heart like yours must feel from such a blow to such a friend I can easily conceive from what you suffer on much lighter occasions. However you have occasion for all your spirits in order to lighten to my Lord[3] the sense of his great misfortune; and if in these circumstances anything can be called happiness, it is such to his Lordship to have a friend so capable of sympathizing with his sorrows and of relieving them. Be so good to let me know whether I may with propriety send or wait on his Lordship, and how soon. I am really very much concerned; I would not be deficient in an attention which is so much my duty; on the other hand a violation of propriety on these occasions is of all others the greatest error.

To WILLIAM GERARD HAMILTON—[*March* 1763]

Source: Copy in Fitzwilliam MSS (N.R.S.). Printed *Corr.* (1844), I, 46–51. Two copies of this letter survive: one in the Bodleian Library (MS Malone 38), one in possession of the Northamptonshire Record Society. The latter has been followed, as far closer to Burke's normal principles of spelling and punctuation. It is endorsed '1762', which is probably too early a date. Burke was granted his pension 19 April 1763 (*Calendar of Home Office Papers, 1760–65*, p. 374). The date of March 1763 assigned by the editors of *Corr.* (1844) is thus probable, and a date in April quite possible. The Bodleian copy is dated 'Thursday'.

At the end of two years' service as Chief Secretary to the Lord Lieutenant of Ireland, Hamilton secured an important sinecure post for himself, and secured for Burke as his protégé a pension of £300 a year on the Irish Establishment.

[1] See above p. 159, note on letter of 9 December [1762].

[2] The death of William Pulteney, styled Viscount Pulteney, son of William Pulteney, 1st Earl of Bath (1684–1764), took place in Madrid 12 February; news of it appeared in the London papers 2 March (*London Chronicle*, XIII, 217, 3–5 March 1763).

[3] Lord Bath.

Burke, full of gratitude, wrote a formal letter of thanks, in which, however, he marked out one important reservation he wished to make in his further devotion of himself to his patron's affairs.

Dear Sir,

I am now on the point of acquiring through your friendship an establishment which I am sensible is as much above my merits, as in any other channel it may be above my reasonable expectations.—I should think myself inexcusable in receiving this pension, and loading your interest with so heavy a charge, without apprizing you of those conditions on which alone I am able to take it; because, when I have taken it, I ought no longer to consider myself as possessed of my former freedom and independence.

I have often wished to explain myself fully to you on this point. It is against my general notions to trust to writing, where it is in one's power to confer otherwise. But neither do you hear, nor do I speak, on this subject, with the same ease with which we converse on others. This is but natural; and I have therefore chosen this method as less liable to misunderstanding and dispute; and hope you will be so indulgent to hear me with coolness and attention.

You may recollect when you did me the honour to take me as a companion in your studies, you found me with the little work we spoke of last Tuesday, as a sort of rent charge on my thoughts.[1] I informed you of this, and you acquiesced in it. You are now so generous, and it is but strict justice to allow that upon all occasions you have been so, to offer

[1] The editors of *Corr.* (1844) were doubtless right in assuming this to be the *Essay towards an Abridgment of English History* (*Works* [Bohn], VI, 184–422, [Little, Brown], VII, 157–488), which Burke never finished. Dodsley printed at least six sheets of it. The copy of these in the British Museum contains a MS inscription by Dr Charles Burney: 'This Essay, which was never finished, was begun by Mr Burke, for Mr Dodsley; among whose Books in quires it was found by Mr Nicol...and by whom it was given to me.' A similar note, by an unknown hand, is in a copy in the Yale Library: 'This fragment given to me by Mr Nichol the Kings book seller was written by Edmund Burke and discontinued on the publication of Hume's History—.' A letter of Isaac Reed which is among the Boswell Papers at Yale sets forth the conditions of Burke's agreement with the Dodsleys, entered into 25 February 1757; Burke agreed to finish the work by 25 December 1758 and was to be paid £300 by instalments. Reed copied into his own letter an earlier letter of John Hughs (1703–71), Dodsley's printer, who gave Dodsley 11 March 1769 a brief account of the printing of the *Abridgment*. 'I find', Hughs had written, 'that in the beginning of the year 1760, 6 sheets of it were worked off, and 9 sheets composed....' Thomas Gray reported to Horace Walpole 28 February 1762 that Burke was engaged upon the work, which was still expected to appear (*Horace Walpole's Correspondence*, XIV, 122). There have been wide differences of opinion as to the value of the *Abridgment*. G. M. Young thinks it nearly valueless, and asserts without offering any evidence that it is 'demonstrably a translation from the French' ('Burke', in *Proceedings of the British Academy*, XXIX, London, 1943, p. 6). Lord Acton, commenting on the story that Burke discontinued his History of England because Hume published his, said 'it is ever to be regretted that the reverse did not occur' (quoted in Herbert Butterfield, *Man on his Past*, Cambridge, 1955, p. 69).

to free me from this burthen. But in fact though I am extremely desirous of deferring the accomplishment, I have no notion of entirely suppressing that work; and this upon two principles, not solely confined to that Work, but which extends much further, and indeed to the plan of my whole life.

Whatever advantages I have acquired, and even that advantage which I must reckon as the greatest and most pleasing of them, have been owing to some small degree of literary reputation. It will be hard to persuade me that any further services which your kindness may propose for me, or any in which my friends may wish to co-operate with you, will not be greatly facilitated by doing something to cultivate and keep alive the same reputation. I am fully sensible that this reputation may be at least as much hazarded as forwarded by new publications. But because a certain oblivion is the consequence, to writers of my inferior class, of an entire neglect of publication; I consider it as such a risk as some times must be run. For this purpose some short time at convenient intervals and especially at the dead time of the year, will be requisite, to study and consult proper books. These times, as you know very well, cannot be easily difined nor indeed, is it necessary they should. The matter may be very easily settled by a good understanding between ourselves, and by a discreet liberty, which I think you would not wish to restrain nor I to abuse. I am not so unreasonable and absurd enough to think I have any title to so considerable a share in your interest, as I have had, and hope still to have, without any or but an insignificant return on my side; especially as I am conscious that my best and most continued endeavours are of no very great value. I know that your business ought on all occasions to have the preference, to be the first and the last, and indeed in all respects the main concern. All I contend for is, that I may not be considered as absolutely excluded from all other thoughts in their proper time, and due subordination:—the fixing the times for them to be left entirely to yourself.

I do not remember that hitherto any pursuit has been stopped, or any plan left defective through my inattention, or through my attention to other matters; and I protest to God I have applied to whatever you have thought proper to set me, with a vigour and alacrity and even an eagerness that I never felt in any affair of my own whatsoever. If you have not observed this, you have not I think observd with your usual sagacity. But if you have observed it and attributed it to an interested design, which will cease when its end is in any degree answered, my mind bears me witness that you do not do me justice. I act almost always from my present impulse, and with little scheme or design, and perhaps generally with too little.—If you think what I have proposed unreasonable, my request is, that you will, which you may very easily do, get my Lord Halifax to postpone the Pension, and afterwards to drop it, we shall go on as before until some other more satisfactory matter occurs. For I should ill brook an accusation either direct or implied, that I had through[1] your friendship acquired a considerable establishment and afterwards neglected to make any fair return in my power. The thought of this has given me great pain, and I could not be easy without coming to some explanation upon it. In the light I consider things, it can create no great difficulty: but it may possibly to you appear otherwise. Let this be how it will I can never forget the obligations, the very many and great obligations which I have already had to you, and which in any situation will always give you a right to call on me for any thing within my compass. If I do not often acknowledge my sense of them, it is because I know you are not very fond of professions, nor am I very clever at making them, you will take in good part this liberty which sincerely is not made for the purpose of exercizing my pen impertinently. Two words from you would settle the point one way or other.

I am with the utmost truth
Ever yours,
E Burke

To Richard Shackleton—[*post* 19] *April* 1763

Source: MS Dr O. Fisher. Printed *Corr.* (1844), I, 51–3.
MS repaired with tape; parts of five words restored by another hand. Burke dates this letter 'April 1763' but as he refers to his pension as already granted, it is at least *post* the 19th.

Dear Shackleton. I am very unfeignedly glad to hear from you; and much obliged to you and your Wife for your kind remembrance. As to your Cloak I do not care how much of you it covers, provided I can see as much of the face of my old friend as his lank testimonial hair, which needs the Vanity of a Velvet cap to keep it out of his Eyes, will permit.[2] You rejoice me very much with the prospect of your coming to London this Summer; but I should be as well satisfied you staid at home, if you will not spend an hour with me at our Court End of the Town, where you will find as much honesty, and almost as much sincerity as any where

[1] MS: thought [apparently altered to through]

[2] Burke seems to be giving directions for the execution of a portrait. The only known portrait of Shackleton, that reproduced (facing p. 103) in Samuels, was painted for Burke by Richard Sisson. See below p. 271, letter of [19 October 1766].

in the City, except in Gracechurch Street.[1] Be assured I should think myself mad, if I took offence at your religious discourses. They are full of real piety; sometimes of good sense and sometimes they contain a phrase or two which I *certainly*, and yourself *perhaps*, do not understand. I love you should speak that of which your mind is full; if I cannot agree with you in a point or two, we agree perfectly in twenty others, and a difference in opinion and a quarrel, between you and me, have never been the same thing. I congratulate you sincerely on the addition to your family;[2] and heartily thank you for the friendly concern you take about the Welfare of mine. I have had no addition to it; but I have had a small one to my fortune, which you, though a steady Irish Patriot, will not I suppose be sorry for; I have just had a pension of 300 l. a year on your Establishment. You are so much our friend that I believe you will take a part in another Circumstance of my present Satisfaction. My Brother Dick has got a good place, that of Collector of the Grenadoes;[3] an employment lucrative enough, though in a remote and an unhealthy Climate, this is some Drawback. Lord Northumberland is I believe fixed for your Ld Lieut. If Mr Hamilton should go his Secretary as I imagine he will, I shall try whether my going to Ireland next Winter can answer any End to me.[4] I am indebted to him and to my Ld Primate for what I have already got.[5] My Wife insists that you let us know as near the time as possible on what day you imagine you may be in London and desires her affectionate regards to you and Mrs Shackleton. Adieu Dear Shackleton remember me to your father and mother and believe me to you and yours a most real and sincere friend

E BURKE.

Q. Anne Street. Cavendish Square
April 1763.

I am heartily glad of the good account you give me of my friend Dennis and of my still holding a place in his affections. Dick desires to be rememberd to his friends at Ballitore.

[1] The Yearly Meeting of the Friends, which Shackleton often attended, was held in White Hart Yard, Gracechurch Street.

[2] Shackleton's son George Rooke had been born 17 June 1762.

[3] See letter of Burke to Wedderburn 29 July 1763.

[4] Hugh Smithson Percy, 2nd Earl of Northumberland (1715–86), was appointed Lord Lieutenant 27 April with Hamilton as his Chief Secretary; Burke did accompany Hamilton to Ireland the following winter.

[5] The application for Burke's pension had been submitted on the 'Primate's list'. See letter of Hamilton to Sir Robert Wilmot 14 April, quoted by Prior (2nd ed. I, 113–14): 'There is a mistake in one of the pensions which I desire may be rectified at any hazard, as I was the occasion of it.—It is not William Birt who is to have a pension of 300 l. per annum upon the Primate's list, but Edmund Burke.'

To JOHN RIDGE—23 *April* [1763]

Source: Fitzwilliam MSS (Sheffield). Printed Hoffman, pp. 307–8.
Addressed: To | John Ridge Esqr Counsellor at Law | Jervis Street | Dublin.
Franked: Free | W: G: Hamilton. *Postmarked:* 23|⟨A⟩P. *Endorsed:* EB | to Joh | Ridge | April 23d 1763.

John Ridge (*c.* 1728–76) was Burke's lawyer and one of his most trusted friends in Ireland. He had entered Trinity College Dublin in 1743 and the Middle Temple in 1753.

Dear Ridge, I hope though you have not answerd you have receivd my Last; It gave a short account of our change of ministers;[1] every thing still remains in a state of the utmost uncertainty. The Duke of Rutland is disgusted,[2] and Ld Granby[3] of Course, not well pleased; Charles Townshend is in the great⟨est⟩ and most merited disgrace for his unsteady Behaviour; he was offerd the admiralty; deliberated on it; accepted it; and on the very day and at the very moment, when his fellow Commissioners were kissing hands, refused it, because two of his friends (who never had any promise) were not brought in with him. The King orderd Ld Halifax, to send him word early the next morning, that he had no occasion for his Service in any capacity.[4] What is not a little extraordinary Ld G. Sackville who has long been in favour is now coming into place some speak of Treasurer of the Houshold, others of the Navy but that he is coming in is not doubted.[5] He will not be a Ballance for the loss of Townshend; and he seems to me to bring only an additional reinforcement of unpopularity to the administration, without a full, though with some, proportion of ability. The Irish arrangement is at length fixed. Ld N. and H. Lieutenant and Secretary.[6] This will be I dare say a thing advantageous to the Country, and it is to me particularly agreeable, as I may hope to see you this Winter. Be so good to give me a very full account of all the Speculation on this Subject, which you have on your

[1] Bute resigned 8 April; on 16 April George Grenville was appointed First Lord of the Treasury and Chancellor of the Exchequer.

[2] John Manners, 3rd Duke of Rutland (1696–1779), had agreed to exchange his office of Master of the Horse for that of Lord Chamberlain, but the Duke of Bedford insisted that Lord Gower should become Lord Chamberlain. Rutland refused other offers and remained Master of the Horse.

[3] John Manners, styled Marquess of Granby (1721–70), son of the Duke of Rutland.

[4] See letter following. Townshend was offered the Admiralty in exchange for the Board of Trade; he first refused, then accepted, but on 15 April insisted that Peter Burrell (1723–75) should be one of the junior Lords, and when this was refused, declined the Admiralty. He was dismissed 16 April. Nothing has been discovered concerning a second friend who had Townshend's promise; Burke may be mistaken in speaking of two.

[5] Sackville was at Court 20 April and had 'particular notice taken of him by the King' (letter of Thomas Birch to Lord Royston, 23 April, quoted in *Letters from George III to Lord Bute*, p. 228 n.) but nothing was done for him.

[6] Lord Northumberland and Hamilton.

side of the water. I see by Williamsons last Paper that they are reviving the Rebellion Stories; and have produced a second song, indeed more plausible as to the manner than the former; they assert it was proved on the Trial of Dweyr at Clonmel;[1] for Gods sake let me know a little of this matter, and of the history of these new levellers. I see that you have but one way of relieving the poor in Ireland. They call for bread, and you give them 'not a Stone,' but the Gallows. Adieu my dear Ridge; we have no news, we are all thank God well and wish to hear as soon as possible that you are so. God bless you Kitty[2] and your Little ones and beleive me with great Truth yours

E BURKE

April 23d

Though Ld B. is out it is universally believd that he govens every thing and indeed appearances are favourable to that supposition.[3]

To MRS ELIZABETH MONTAGU—[25] *April* 1763

Source: Blunt, *Mrs Montagu*, I, 42. Dated by Lord Sandwich's appointment. See note 4.

Monday night April 1763.

It is certain Lord Sandwich has kiss'd hands for the Admiralty;[4] Mr Townshend had given a promise to Mr Burrell to bring him into the Admiralty with him; the Ministers offerd Mr Burrell to put him into some good place when there was a vacancy, but not into the Admiralty; he insisted on his bond upon Townshend with as much pertinaciousness as Shylock the Jew in the play, and Mr Townshend therefore thought himself obliged to decline being first Lord of the Admiralty; perhaps if Bassano's advocate had found a clause by which creditor Burrell was forbidden *to draw blood* the bond had been set at

[1] John Dwyer was found guilty of high treason, sentenced to death 22 March, and executed 31 March 1763 (*Dublin Journal*, 29 March–2 April; *Dublin Gazette*, 5–9 April). No copy seems to have survived of the issue of Matthew Williamson's *Universal Advertiser* which reported the trial.

[2] Mrs Ridge.

[3] The belief that Lord Bute was the real influence behind the Throne continued to confuse politics for the next five years. In August 1763 he attempted to replace the Administration by one including Pitt; this failed, and the King promised Grenville he would not allow Bute to interfere. Yet Grenville remained suspicious of Bute's influence. When the Rockingham Administration was formed in July 1765 the King repeated this promise, but did not convince Rockingham of his sincerity. In August 1766 the King and Bute broke off all correspondence, yet the Rockingham group continued to believe that Bute was the power behind the Throne. Only after he retired to the Continent in 1769 did these suspicions die.

[4] John Montagu, 4th Earl of Sandwich (1718–92), was appointed First Lord of the Admiralty on Saturday 23 April.

naught. Mr Fox has his Peerage and his place.[1] It is said Count Vivi's son is to have a pension of a thousand pound a year for twenty years upon Ireland.[2] A certain great man is not going to Harrogate,[3] is avowedly by his friends in as much power as ever. They affect to say it is no matter by whom the places are fill'd, it is sufficient to shew that the K— can fill them with whom he pleases and change them as often as he pleases. There is something of truth in this, but at the same time one trembles to think of the consequences of this maxim push'd too far on one side, or too violently resisted on another....

Ld Ligonier is made an english Peer to soften the affront of not having informed him his place was destined to Ld Granby till he saw his Lordship kiss hands for it.[4] Mr John Pitt[5] was surprized at the drawing room to see Sr Edmund Thomas[6] kiss hands, asked for what? and was told it was for his own place, that he had not given the least offence. Mr Montagu saw Ld Sandwich this morning in the hurry and embarassment of changing his intended embassy to his present home station.[7]

To Mrs Elizabeth Montagu—29 *July* [1763]

Source: Blunt, *Mrs Montagu*, I, 50–3.

July 29th

I have foreborn writing all this time in hopes of some news which might entertain you. But I am resolved to wait for it no longer. I have been for these two months past an insufferable companion to others, in order to qualify myself to be an agreable correspondent to you. My whole conversation turned upon nothing but what might lead to intelligence; However I have succeeded so ill, that I fear my eagerness may have frustrated my pursuit, and I fancy people began at length to take me for a spy; a character in which (as I receive none of the secret

[1] Fox was created Baron Holland 17 April. Bute expected him to resign the Pay Office on leaving the House of Commons, but Fox refused.

[2] According to Walpole (*Memoirs*, I, 211, 268) it was Francesco, Comte de Viri (d. 1766), himself, and not his son Francesco (1736–1813), who received the pension, 'in the name of one Charles'. In the *Calendar of Home Office Papers 1760-65*, p. 375, is the entry 'Charles, George, of Leicester Fields, Esq., his executors etc., £1000 per annum pension in Ireland for 31 years'.

[3] Bute set out for Harrogate 2 May.

[4] John Ligonier, 1st Viscount Ligonier in the Irish peerage (1680–1770), was created Baron of Ripley in the peerage of Great Britain 27 April. According to Walpole (*Memoirs*, I, 204) he was 'by force removed' from his place as Master-General of the Ordnance, 'but softened with a pension, which he refused to accept till accompanied with an English peerage'.

[5] (*c.* 1706–87), M.P. for Wareham.

[6] 3rd Baronet (1712–67), M.P. for Glamorgan, formerly Groom of the Bedchamber to the Prince of Wales. The place he obtained was Surveyor General of Woods and Forests south of Trent.

[7] Sandwich had accepted the post of Ambassador to Spain at the end of the previous year.

service money), I do not yet chuse to appear. I confess that until this moment I could not call up confidence enough to address a letter to you without the passport of some sort of news; but as I see the Court forsaken, Westminster Hall shut, the dinners adjourned, the chiefs of the opposition hanging their trophies o'er their garden gates, the Ministers employed only in scraping together reversions, and Mr Wilkes only scraping together a guinea subscription,[1] the whole political campain reduced to a *petite guerre* of printers, Devils, and Diablotins, and that the very best of our paltry but furious animosities afforded nothing that was worthy of Mrs Montagu, I have at length sat down to write because in duty bound, without the least hope of diverting you or of satisfying myself, for if I were to speak from what I feel of my opinion of Mrs Montagu's genius, of her virtues, and of my innumerable obligations to her friendship, I should say indeed what would be very sincere and very true, but then I should say, what to her would be the most unentertaining thing in the world. So that the only subject upon which I can speak is the only one which it is improper for me to mention. Besides Madam I observe that Panegyric, even when applied to those who deserve it most or like it best is sure never to please above one, and will certainly offend fifty. To say the truth Satyr is now so much the safer and (what is now the only rule of right) the more popular way, that I am resolved to stick to that, especially if I can have the good fortune to get elected for Aylesbury.[2] The old rule was pictoribus atque poetis, quid libet audendi semper fuit æqua potestas,[3] this shall for the present at least be limited by a little Scholiast's remark in the margin 'provided they have privilege of parliament,' which is a privilege as extensive as ever the wildest poet in his wildest reveries could ever figure to himself. In the next session it is reported that they will extend this privilege to us all, or take it away from themselves; otherwise there will be no fair play; the report of the former part is however predominant.[4] All our law de libellis famosis is to be changed, and the Pillory is only to be reserved for unsuccessful flatterers. Having therefore much regard to the law, more to the fashion, and most of all to my ears, I think to try my hand at invective, and to sketch out a North Briton which shall equal the

[1] John Wilkes had been arrested 30 April for an alleged seditious libel against the King in no. 45 of the *North Briton*. He pleaded privilege as an M.P. and was discharged 6 May. Soon after his release he set up a printing press in his own house and 'advertised the proceedings of the administration, with all the original papers, at the price of a guinea' (*Annual Register* for 1763, pp. 142–3).

[2] Wilkes was M.P. for Aylesbury.

[3] 'Painters and poets have always had an equal right in hazarding anything'; see Horace, *Ars Poetica*, 9–10.

[4] On 24 November 1763 the House of Commons resolved 'that privilege of Parliament does not extend to the case of writing and publishing seditious libels'.

spirit of the celebrated and indeed *golden number*, *45*. The subject of it shall be, for we scorn blanks and dashes,—Mrs Montagu herself. After a few preceding touches upon Scotchmen and Excise, I intend to observe on the scandalous neglect of our Board of Treasury, who have suffered the most valuable staple products of the kingdom to be carried out with [out] the least opposition. I shall show that France has of late discovered that she wants our wisdom as much in her manufactories of policy in War, as she does our wool in her clothes and stuffs; and yet that I could prove our Ministry suffered to be shipped for Calais in one vessel and in one day more genius, more learning, more wit, more Eloquence, more Policy, more Mathematics, more Poetry, more Philosophy and Theology than France could produce in a century. I shall point out that Mrs Montagu who has long been a clandestine dealer in goods of this sort, and who had several of them about her own person at the very time, was the capital smuggler on this occasion and carried off all the rest.

Whilst I was preparing this wonderful piece my Lawyer whose opinion I take on all my libels and who points out exactly how far the breach of the law may be separated from its penalties, informed me that this time my satire was quite stingless. That no exeat regno lay for wit and genius. That we might freely export the whole sense of the Kingdom. (I don't mean the sense of the Nation, for that's quite another thing.) He thought this freedom founded upon a very proper principle that it operated like the Bounty upon the exportation of corn which only made it cheaper and more plentiful at home. This theory I confess had something specious in it, but as I have been a sort of dabbler in theories myself, I was no way surprised to find that on experiment it did not prove worth a farthing; for I cannot discover that anything extraordinary has started up to supply the great loss we have had; we do not grow as bodies do sometimes a bit the fatter for all this bleeding. As the Nation had so great a loss I wanted to know whether the Revenue had any great benefit by this extraordinary Trade, on examining the Custom House books I found you may imagine to my astonishment a small but heavy parcel, marked with a capital M was charged but at one penny three farthings duty. The officer told me that on the entry he claimed more, and would have had twice as much had the point been tried by the Excise Laws, but that he was obliged to try it by a jury *misportico*[1] or as our lawyers would express it *de medietate Linguae*[2] of six ladies from this end of the town, and six of Wapping, and so unanimously brought a verdict by their

[1] This Latin word seems to be of Burke's invention. The Oxford Dictionary lists one use, by John Donne, of 'misport', meaning to 'import unlawfully'.

[2] Composed half of Englishmen and half of foreigners.

Forewoman that no higher rate than 25 per cent ad valorem should be laid on such goods, so that they valued the whole parcel just at sevenpence and no more. I'm informed if they had summoned four fifths of the Ladies of the Kingdom they would not have rated it a penny higher. I had a curiosity to look at the import of this hand and the state of the Revenue on this Branch was flourishing, it consisted for that day of three parcels of the French academy manufacture, the 1st a scheme for opening living sculls in order to discover the seat and nature of the soul, the second was a proposal to dig to the centre of the earth by a confederacy of Princes in order to settle effectually the balance of Power; the third was to promote the happiness of Mankind and the prosperity of states by extirpating religion and virtue, and substituting self interest in their place. Thus stood the trade, and I was obliged to suppress my libels.

Might I presume to flatter myself with an idea of hearing how the Spaw has agreed with you. I inquired as long as I could find anybody to inform me. Can you think of London, surrounded by Princes and Heroes whilst the terrors of Europe are prancing about on poneys, and whilst you grow familiar with everything we admire. Be so good to thank Mr. Montagu for his kind remembrance of me before his departure, and present mine and my brother's humble and grateful respects to Lord Bath;[1] we are infinitely obliged to him for his generous endeavours, though they remain just as they were. Be so good as to make my compliments to Miss Carter, and to Dr or Colonel Douglass,[2] be so kind as to forgive me for having wrote so tiresome a letter. It is the longest I ever wrote in my life. Believe me Madam with the truest respect, and sincerest gratitude, your most obedient and obliged humble servant

E. BURKE

To ALEXANDER WEDDERBURN—29 *July* 1763

Source: Sotheby Catalogue, 15 April 1899, no. 108.
Only an extract of this letter has been preserved.

Burke's acquaintance with Alexander Wedderburn (1733–1805) probably began in the late 1750's when Wedderburn left Edinburgh for London to pursue his fortunes at the English Bar. Burke is supposed to have advised him to take lessons with Charles Macklin the actor to rid himself of his Scottish accent. (Prior, 2nd ed. I, 48; see also *Boswell Papers*, x, 190, for Burke's caustic com-

[1] Richard Burke's suit to Lord Bath is discussed in the next letter.

[2] Mrs Montagu and her friend Mrs Elizabeth Carter were accompanying Lord Bath on a trip to the Continent. Dr John Douglas (1721–1807), later Bishop of Salisbury, was at this time Lord Bath's private secretary; his account of the trip in his *Autobiography* (MS in British Museum, Egerton 2181) makes no mention of a 'Colonel Douglass'.

ments on the plan.) Wedderburn was able, extremely ambitious, influential with Lord Bute, and on his way to the judicial posts he was to attain: Solicitor General (1771–8), Attorney General (1778–80), Chief Justice of Common Pleas (1780–93), and Lord Chancellor (1793–1801).

My Brother, who has the honour to be known and to be obliged to you, was recommended by Lord Bath to Lord Bute for the Joint Office of Collector and Receiver-general of the Grenadoes. His Lordship was pleased to make a promise to Lord Bath of the office for my Brother on the extent of the request. But a few days before his resignation he appointed him to the Collectors only, on a presumption (as his Lordship himself explained it), that no Inland Revenue existed in the Grenadoes.[1]...

Wedderburn wrote from Paris 6 August to George Grenville in support of Richard's application: 'A friend of mine for whom I have the warmest regard, has done me the honour to imagine that my recommendation of a person to your Protection, might possibly be in some degree serviceable to him. Mr Edmund Burke, who writes on his brother's behalf, is a gentleman whose least merit is his being one of the most ingenious Men as well as one of the best writers of the age, and whose greatest fault is his desire of concealing that merit. His Candour is such that he would not be partial even in the case of a brother, and in the present instance I am sure he is not, because I know his Brother, Mr Richard Burke, to be a very sensible young man' (Sotheby Catalogue, 15 April 1899, no. 108).

To [JAMES] DODSLEY—9 *February* 1764

Source: MS British Museum (Add. MS 22130, fol. 10). Printed Wecter, p. 18 n.

Addressed: To | Mr Dodsley | Pall Mall. The 'Mr Dodsley' of the address is almost certainly James Dodsley. Robert Dodsley had retired in 1759, leaving his brother to carry on their publishing business (Straus, *Robert Dodsley*, p. 253).

Dear Sir,

I suppose, that By this, our Work is in the press, and advances prosperously.[2] The part immediately in my hands is in considerable forwardness, so that next week, please God I propose to send over a good part of it, executed rather more to my satisfaction than I could have

[1] *Gentleman's Magazine*, XXXIII, 519 (October 1763) lists among promotions: 'Rich. Burke, Esq; collector of the customs at the Grenades,—receiver general of all the revenues there'.

[2] The *Annual Register*, of which the volume for 1763 was published 17 May 1764. In his original contract for editing the magazine, Burke had agreed that each year's issue was to be 'corrected from the press and published by the Lady day following'; the editor was to receive his salary in two £50 payments per year, the second due on the date of publication (Straus, *Robert Dodsley*, pp. 257–8). It is probable that until 1764, or even till Burke entered Parliament in 1766, the terms of the original contract were not altered. See T. W. Copeland, *Our Eminent Friend Edmund Burke*, New Haven, 1949, pp. 94–8.

flatterd myself was practicable, considering what we had to go upon. I have occasion to pay some money in London pretty speedily, I beg therefore you will pay Dr Nugent fifty pounds on my receipt, which you have along with this. Be so good to remember me affectionately to your Brother and believe me

Dear Sir
your most obedient Servant and friend
E BURKE.

Dublin Feb. 9th 1764.

To RICHARD SHACKLETON—[29 *March* 1764]

Source: MS Dr O. Fisher. Printed *Leadbeater Papers*, II, 98.
Endorsed: E Burke Esqr | Dublin 29 | 3 mo. 1764.
Part of the original of this letter has been cut away; what remains bears no date. A copy among the Ballitore MSS is complete and is dated 'Dublin: 29 March 1764'.

My dear Shackleton,

Though I have been long silent, I dont think it necessary to say a great deal now; as I hope to be with you in a few hours after you receive this. I could hardly flatter myself some time ago, that it would be in my power to spend a day or two with you, and it is not easy to say how much pleasure I have in the Idea that I may now meet Dick in our old Head quarters and talk over old times. Mrs Burke is of the same Sentiment with me and is to accompany me. Adieu. Give our Love to Mrs Shackleton and believe[1] me Dear Shackleton affectionately yours.

E BURKE

To RICHARD SHACKLETON—17 *July* 1764

Source: MS Dr O. Fisher. Printed *Corr.* (1844), I, 53–4.

William Gerard Hamilton was dismissed from his post of Chief Secretary to the Lord Lieutenant of Ireland in May 1764. He returned to England, where, as O'Hara told Burke (letter of 24 July) 'Hampton shoud be his abode, and silence his policy for some time'. Burke also returned, with better cause than his patron to fear a period of enforced unemployment.

My dear Shackleton Many thanks to you for your kind Letter, and pray give as many in our Name to your father for his friendly Visits;

[1] The following words and the signature have been cut off the original but pencilled back in by another hand. The Ballitore copy contains the words but ends with the initials E B rather than a signature.

which though not near so frequent as we wished, were yet more so than we could have expected, considering the distance of his situation and the shortness of the time he had to spend amongst us; In this act of kindness he did not follow your example; Pray do you follow his; and remember, that if you come to this side of the water we have a fair claim to some part of your time; You will find every one in this house extremely glad to see you. Poor Dick indeed is probably not for some years to expect that satisfaction; he sets off at the beginning of next week for the Grenadoes, thank God, in good health and Spirits; which are all but little enough to Battle with a bad climate in a bad Season; But it must be submitted to; Providence never intended, to much the greater part, an entire Life of ease and quiet; a peaceable, honourable and affluent decline of Life must be purchased by a Laborious or hazardous youth; and every day, I think more and more, that it is well worth the purchase; Poverty and age sort very ill together; and a course of struggling is miserable indeed when strength is decayed and hope gone, Turpe senex Miles.[1] These thoughts are our comfort on a separation, which, you will easily believe, is affecting enough to us. Dick desires to know how your Spectacles answer; If they are too deep, or not concave enough; return them with your observation on the defect, and you shall have others. The grand Test of their fitting you, is your power of reading with them at a distance.

Jenny and all here (for all this house knows you, personally or by Character) are sincerely yours; and desire to be rememberd to Mrs Shackleton to whose friendship we have many obligations and for whose Character we have a real Esteem. Adieu believe me

most affectionately yours

E BURKE

Q. Anne Street 17th July 1764.

To [WILLIAM] YOUNG—31 *December* 1764

Source: MS F. W. Hilles.

O'Hara had spoken in his letter of 24 July of Burke's being in search of a new engagement, either to replace or to supplement his engagement with Hamilton. 'I learnd from Will Burke', he wrote, 'that the employment offerd to you, woud have taken upon your whole time. This was certainly one reason, and I can immagine some others against your accepting of it. I shoud fancy it however of use, to have the sort of thing you woud like known to people.' Burke was casting about for a change, as appears in the following letter. When the letter was

[1] Shame when an old man is a soldier; see Ovid, *Amores*, I, IX, 4.

advertised for sale in 1939 (*The Ingatherer* [Colbeck Radford and Co.] Catalogue 78) it was described as addressed to 'Sir Jo Young'. It is more likely to have been addressed to William Young (1725–88), later (1769) a baronet and Lieutenant-Governor of Dominica.

Dear Sir

Your kindness and partiality to me on an acquaintance much slighter and much shorter than I wished, will I hope, excuse the Liberty I take in my present application to you.

The conquerd Islands which compose Genl Mellvilles Government, in all likelihood must soon think of appointing an Agent for managing their affairs here, upon the footing of the other Colonies.[1] As the Government is now constituted, I apprehend that this appointment is in the Governour and Council; Under any constitution they cannot fail of having a considerable share in it.

I am desirous of serving them as their Agent; If I obtain that honour I shall endeavour to act for them with Care and Fidelity.

Being scarcely known to Genl Melville, I have made my Application to him through my friends. To you I apply directly and flatter myself that I shall not only have your own Vote, but your friendship and assistance with the other Gentlemen, who are concerned in that appointment.

My determination to look for this employment has been so very recent, and the ships are just now in such readiness to sail that I have not time to look about for any news which might entertain you. I fear indeed that if my time had been much longer that my attempts might be equally unsuccessful. Every thing here stagnates like a pool; and though Parliament is on the point of meeting, one sees none of that eagerness and movement, which usually precedes a Session in which much has been expected. I shall be happy to hear that you have all imaginable satisfaction and success in your present employment. Believe me

Dear Sir
your most obedient and
obliged humble Servant
EDM BURKE.

London Decr 31st 1764.

Burke did not obtain the post. Richard Maitland was appointed in 1767 and remained agent until 1775 (Lillian M. Penson, *The Colonial Agents of the British West Indies*, London, 1924, p. 254).

[1] The conquered islands were Grenada, the Grenadines, Dominica, St Vincent, and Tobago. Lieut.-Col. Robert Melville (1723–1809), appointed Governor in October 1763, held the rank of Brigadier-General in the West Indies. An appointment as London agent for these islands, besides any financial advantages, would have given Burke some foothold in an area where Richard and Will already had interests.

WILLIAM GERARD HAMILTON *to* EDMUND BURKE—[*ante* 12 *February* 1765]

Source: Fitzwilliam MSS (Sheffield). Printed *Corr.* (1844), I, 55–6.

This and the three following undated letters were certainly written before Burke's letter to Robert Jephson of 26 February [1765]; very likely they were written before 12 February when Hamilton requested Dr Joseph Warton (1722–1800) to suggest someone to replace Burke as his secretary (John Wooll, *Biographical Memoirs of Joseph Warton*, London, 1806, pp. 299–300).

Hamilton had still a seat in the British House of Commons and could look forward to resuming his political career there. He was naturally eager to know whether Burke would continue to serve as his secretary. Perhaps he was too eager. In a bitter quarrel which broke out between them Burke's chief complaint was that Hamilton was asking him to promise to remain a secretary permanently. A dozen letters and drafts of letters bear witness to the importance the quarrel had for both parties, before it ended in a complete rupture of their friendship.

Dear Sir,

My Servant has this Moment inform'd me of your Kindness in calling upon me, for which I consider myself as extremely oblig'd to you. I am perswaded you will do me the Justice to believe me, when I assure you most sincerely, and upon my Honour, that my wishing, (independent of very particular Business) to decline the pleasure of seeing you this Morning, is founded upon reasons, which tho extremely mortifying to myself, are in no way dis-resspectfull to you. The lively Sense I entertain of your Unkindness, and the very humble one which I entertain of my own Command of Temper, make me unwilling to hazard ev'n a Possibility that any thing may pass between us, which would endanger a Friendship, I have for many reasons look'd upon as so very valuable, and particularly, because I concluded it would be so very lasting. I am apt to believe that the Disagreement between us is already sufficiently difficult, and I should be sorry to make it impossible, to be reconcil'd. Whenever any thing occurs on which I may wish to have the pleasure of conversing with you, I shall so far presume upon the Indulgence you are pleas'd to allow me, as to take the Liberty of troubling you.

I am, Dear Sir Your Most Obedient
and
Faithfull Humble Servant
W G H.

Sunday 1/2 past Twelve.

A draft of this letter, considerably longer than the version sent, is among the papers of Edmond Malone (Hamilton's literary executor) in the Bodleian Library. One passage of the portion omitted suggests that Hamilton already regarded his quarrel with Burke as nearly irreconcilable: 'But of this, My dear Sir, I am determin'd beyond the Possibility of Change, that no Consideration whatsoever upon Earth, that no Prospect of Honour or Advantage shall ever induce me again to expose myself to that degree of Misery and of Wretchedness which I have felt from the want of Friendship of those whom I lov'd, and had oblig'd in Ireland; and from your Unkindness in England. All I can propose to myself is the Friendship of some Man of Letters who can never give me half the Uneasiness, because He can never afford me Half the Pleasure which I have experienc'd from your Acquaintance; And who may perhaps make up what He wants in Talents, by his Friendship, Fidelity, and Affection—' (MS Malone 38, fol. 126). The person who succeeded Burke as Hamilton's assistant—though his duties were of a rather different character—was apparently Samuel Johnson (*Life of Johnson*, I, 489–90; 519–20). He was to the end of his life a faithful and affectionate friend to Hamilton, and not wanting in talents.

To WILLIAM GERARD HAMILTON—[*ante* 12 *February* 1765]

Source: Copy in Fitzwilliam MSS (Sheffield). Printed *Corr.* (1844), I, 56–61.

Dear Sir

Your Letter which I received about 4 o Clock yesterday seemed not to have been written with an intention of being answered. However on considering the matter this morning, I thought it respectful to you, and in a manner necessary to myself, to say something to those heavy charges which you have made against me in our last conversations, and which, with a polite acrimony in the expression you have thought proper to repeat in your Letter.

I should indeed be extremely unhappy if I felt any consciousness at all of that unkindness of which you say you have so lively a sense. In the six years during which I have had the honour of being connected with you I do not know that I have given you one just occasion of complaint: and if all things have not succeded every way to your wishes, I may appeal to your own equity and candour, whether the failure was owing to any thing wrong in my advice or inattention in my conduct. I can honestly affirm, and your heart will not contradict me, that in all cases I preferred your interest to my own. I made you and not myself the first object in every deliberation, I studied your advancement your fortune, and your reputation in every thing with zeal and earnestness, and sometimes with an anxiety which has made many of my hours miserable. No body could be more ready than I was, to acknowledge the obligations I had to you; and if I thought, as in some instances I did and do still think, I had cause of dissatisfaction I never exposed to others, or made yourself uneasy about them. I acted in every respect with a fidelity which, I trust, cannot be impeached. If there be any part of my conduct in life upon which I can look with entire satisfaction it is my behaviour with regard to you.

So far as to the past. With regard to the present, what is that unkindness and misbehaviour, of which you complain? My heart is full of friendship to you: and is there a single point which the best and most intelligent men have fixed as a proof of friendship and gratitude in which I have been dificient or in which I threaten a failure? What you blame is only this: That I will not consent to bind myself to you for no less a term than my whole life: in a sort of domestick situation, for a consideration to be taken out of your private fortune, that is, to circumscribe my hopes, to give up even the possibility of liberty, and absolutely to annihilate myself for ever. I beseech you, is the demand, or the refusal the act of unkindness. If ever such a test of friendship was proposed in any instance to any man living, I admit that my conduct has been unkind and if you please ungrateful.

If I had accepted your kind offers, and afterwards refused to abide by the condition you annex to them, you then would have had a good right to tax me with unkindness. But what have I done, but at the end of very long, however I confess unprofitable service, but to prefer my own liberty to the offers of advantage you are pleased to make me? and at the same time to tender you the continuance of those services (upon which partiality only induces you to set any value) in the most disinterested manner, as far as I can do it consistent with that freedom, to which for a long time I have determined to sacrifice every consideration; and which I never gave you the slightest assurance that I [had] any intention to surrender, whatever my private resolves may have been, in case an event had happened which, (so far as concerns myself) I rejoice never to have taken place. You are kind enough to say, that you look'd upon my friendship as valuable, but hint that it has not been lasting. I really do not know, when and by what act I broke it off. I should be wicked and mad to do it; unless you call that a lasting friendship which all mankind would call a settled servitude and which no ingenuity can distinguish from it. Once more put yourself in my situation and judge for me. If I have spoken too strongly, you will be so good to pardon a man on his defence, in one of the nicest questions to a mind that has any feeling. I meant to speak fully not to offend. I am not used to defend my conduct, nor do I intend for the future to fall into so bad a habit. I have been warmed to it by the imputation you threw on me, as if I deserted you on account solely of your want of success. On this however I shall say nothing, because perhaps I should grow still warmer, and I would not drop one loose word which might mark the least disrespect, and hurt a friendship which has been and I flatter myself will be a satisfaction and an honour to me. I beseech you, that you will judge of me with a little impartiality and temper. I hope I have said nothing in our last interview, which could urge you to the passion you speak of. If any thing fell which was strong in the expression, I beleive it was from you, and not from me; and it is right that I should bear more than I then heard.

I said nothing but what I took the liberty of mentioning to you a year ago in Dublin. I gave you no reason to think I had made any change in my resolution. We, notwithstanding, have ever since until within these few days proceeded as usual.

Permit me to do so again. No man living can have an higher veneration than I have for your abilities, or can set an higher value on your friendship, as a great private satisfaction, and a very honourable distinction.

I am much obliged to you for the favour you intend me in sending to me in three or four days, (if you do not send sooner) when you have had time to consider this matter coolly. I will again call at your door, and hope to be admitted. I beg it and intreat it. At the same time do justice to the single motive which I have for desiring this favour, and desiring it in this manner.

I have not wrote all this tiresome matter, in hopes of bringing on an altercation in writing, which you are so good to me as to decline personally, and which in either way I am most sollicitous to shun. What I say is, on reviewing it, little more than I have laid before you in another manner, it certainly requires no answer. I ask pardon for my prolixity, which my anxiety to stand well in your opinion has caused. I am with great truth,

Your most affectionate
and most obliged humble Servant
E. BURKE.

To the Right Honourable
William Gerard Hamilton.

WILLIAM GERARD HAMILTON *to* EDMUND BURKE—[*ante* 12 *February* 1765]

Source: Copy in Fitzwilliam MSS (Sheffield). Printed *Corr.* (1844), I, 61.

Monday Night

Dear Sir,

As you thought it polite to answer my Letter, I conclude you would think it unpolite, if I did not at least acknowledge your's—I have only to say, that I have thought as cooly as I can, and what is more, as I wish to think, upon a Subject on which I am so much hurt. I aprove entirely of your Idea that we should not write, in order to avoid Altercation; and for the same reason I am of opinion we should not converse.

Yours & &
W G H.

To WILLIAM GERARD HAMILTON—[*ante* 12 *February* 1765]

Source: Bodleian Library (MS Malone 38, fol. 124).

Dear Sir,

I wrote yesterday, in order to do every thing in my power towards reconciling a difference, to which I did not think, any voluntary fault of mine had given occasion. But the Sense of my Situation with regard to you, and that alone, induced me to it. I intreated most earnestly to see you at a proper time. You have refused me. I shall, though with concern and reluctance, obey your orders. When you are so good to change your mind, I shall also obey you, but with a very different kind of feeling. I shall always be with the most real Esteem Dear Sir,

your most Obedient
and most obligd humble Servant
E BURKE.

Tuesday.

BURKE'S *statement concerning* HAMILTON'S *conduct*

Source: Fitzwilliam MSS (Sheffield) Bk 25c.

At some stage in the development of their quarrel Hamilton had the very natural idea of citing Burke as a witness against himself. Burke was saying in 1765 that it was ridiculous and unthinkable for him to bind himself to his patron for life. But had that been his language when the pension was procured for him two years before? No, he had then talked of his tie to Hamilton as if it could be permanent—indeed as if it had become so by the receipt of the pension. Hamilton was so unwise as to treat Burke's letter of [March 1763] as if it had, or ought to have, the validity of a legal document. Burke on his side drew up a formal refutation of any such contention.

Mr Hamilton asserts that the Pension of 300 pounds a year Irish during the Kings pleasure which he procured for me, by his mediation with the Late Primate of Ireland and Lord Halifax,[1] was on condition of my personal Domestick attendance on him during the continuance of my Life.

This condition I deny to have been meant on my part, or, so far I am capable of judging, to be understood on his.

To confirm his assertion he produces a Letter written by me in which I have used the words, 'that I no longer think myself possessed of my former independence' that in the Winter his Business shall always be my principal, if not my sole concern—and that in some other part I have used the words; This extends to the plan of my whole Life.

To this I answer, that in the whole Tenor of my conversation, I never gave him the slightest reason to think I had any intention of entering, for such a consideration into such a species of Servitude. But as this is as easily denied as asserted, I shall not dwell on it. This being for Mr H.'s own interior satisfaction. I doubt he never recollects any conversation to this purpose, and conversations are more light and unguarded than writings. To this therefore I expect neither admission or denial.

I am therefore to apply myself solely to that Letter, and to endeavour to shew why Mr H's construction on it is neither natural nor equitable.

And first I will observe, that any construction ought rather to be put on a writing, than such as necessarily Supposes the writer to proceed in the absurdest manner; and without the least attention to the Nature and quality of the Contract into which he Enters. This I say is Mr H's construction on E.B's Letter. For is it possible, that he could agree to a positive engagement during his whole Life for a consideration during pleasure and that not even during the pleasure of the party with whom ⟨he⟩ contracts. Such is the Pension Mr B. has received; of which the caprice of a minister the illtemper of the house of Commons, or the deficiency of the Revenue might totally deprive him and of which a Tax on Pensions (an event not impossible because it has before happend and is hourly threatned) would be sure to deprive him of a considerable part. For this Pension originally not great and doubly incertain in value and in duration E B.[2] was obliged to measures with the Primate (in whose

[1] As Lord Lieutenant, Halifax would have had to approve the application.
[2] MS: E B. he

name alone the recommendation stands) he was obliged to keep well in with Lord H. who is the direct Patron from whence the request went to the Crown and with both of whom Mr H. has quarrelled and to have his name put to the Credit side on the General Patronage of Government to Literary people which has been already urged to him; and urged (Mr H. knows) as an obligation which required a return on his part. To all these various tyes and obligations Some of them *almost* contradictory Mr H. supposes Mr B. to have superradded the further obligation of the personal domestick service of his whole Life. This I say is a construction not possible to be put whilst any other is possible; Secondly Mr H's construction supposes Mr B. to have given up all Idea of retiring in quiet at any age or period of his Life to enjoy freedom and obscurity; or to be employd at any time with dignity and consideration; The two circumstances are the only things which carry a man through his Labours especially the first; the known End of any mans Life and Labours viz to acquire some time or other a state of some Sort of independence. This great End of Life and Labour E.B. is supposed to have renounced for the above consideration ⟨clogged⟩ as it was with all the other abovementioned additional Charges on it. Thirdly Mr H. is begged to consider that no obligations which include the whole Life and existence of a man are valid; in any Country from which actual Servitude is excluded. For this reason men therefore in their Speech or writings, when they speak of Continuance of connection during their Lives even in the Strongest Terms, never yet were in any single instance to mean but with a condition necessarily annexed that is than whilst they agreed; or it did not materially affect their interest or peace to continue it. I insist, no such words were ever meant to convey more; or that any man Ever has been accused for doing what E.B. has done and which shall be stated presently. There was no mutual Contract.

Now I shall come to what I say is the fair construction on my Letter to be deduced from the intent and meaning of it. The purpose of that Letter was this. When E.B. perceived that Mr H. had by degrees engrossed his whole time; he observed that it would in the End prove extremely detrimental to the improvement of his mind, destructive of any ⟨...⟩ of Literary reputation which he possessd; and inconsistent with all his family satisfactions. He therefore determined before he receivd the Pension from Mr H. to know whether he proposed to engage his whole time as he had hitherto done; being resolved if he did, let what would happen not to receive the Pension. He therefore marked out to Mr H. that he required a good part of his time especially in the Summer to himself; he strongly expressed his desire of devoting the winter to his Commands; and being to receive a favour was not sparing in his expressions of obligation and gratitude, without due care of the wording, Expressions which he has since more than fulfilled; and of which he would have given more and very disinterested proofs if Mr H. would have sufferd him. This account of the occasion of it naturally explains the expressions in the Letter. Mr B. meant to distinguish the times of his attendance not to fix an eternal Duration to it. He wished indeed and meant to continue it; with every kind of office and of acknowledgement but he neither did, nor will any Candid person think he meant to preclude himself for ever from fortune and independence if such should offer or from a tranquil obscurity if he failed in all his Views in the World. No man was ever absurd enough to offer or unreasonable enough to expect such conditions of Servitude.

There is a turn of expression in this Letter which being more submissive and professing than is common with E. B. to any man, and as it may surprise his acquaintance will need some explanation and will serve to throw more light on the genuine intention of the writing in Question—Mr H. was in the habit of frequently expressing to E. B. his regard to him; The pleasure he received from his company and The Sense with infinite exaggeration, of the Services he did him. E.B. was always fearful Lest H. should imagine he took advantage of his strong frequent expressions to impose difficult Terms on him. His delicacy in this respect has betrayed him into a mode of expression very unusual with him and of the consequences of which he was not at all aware. Let Mr H. consider with himself the generosity of this procedure.

I know Mr H. affects to attribute Mr B.'s Letter[1] and mode of expression &c. to the abjectness of his then condition; and the smallness of his hopes either from any Abilities of his own, or any protection he possessed or could reasonably procure. And attributes the firmness of E.B.'s resolution not to admit that he had engaged in absolute Servitude to a scheme of his Enemies to draw a friend from him who was of so near a Connection. And that for this purpose they have made him considerable offers. It is true, that extreme distress may at some times compell men to submit to many things for the present which are ruinous upon the Sum total of Life. That this was not my resolution will appear by the Letter itself. I was so far from meaning to submit to every condition that I absolutely refused to receive the Pension (though sufficiently due to me for passed service) if he understood that I[2] should be with him in the Summer. It is odd that I should be so careful of a distribution of my time and so prodigal of my whole Life. But does

[1] MS: Mr B. Letter   [2] MS: I I

Mr H. really think the condition of my mind and fortune such as to make me at that time desperate? He knows I had friends of disposition and ability to serve me. That they encreased every day, and that I should have had many more, if unfortunately following him for two years to Ireland I had not broken the Chain of my connections and pursuits—Those friends he knew meant to serve me; and to impose no Servitude on me in return. Mr H. has valued himself to me on his Patronage and friendship. Let him look about him and see whether any man in any degree of power has done less where he has professed a regard; or where any man who has done the greatest service ever exacted so severe an acknowledgement.

It is true Mr H. offers to give more, even to a very considerable amount; but this he contends[1] to be of his own mere favour as he still persists to hold me bound for Life, by what I have already ⟨agreed to,⟩ declaring that he might have ⟨...⟩ action against me for breach of contract on the Letter in question and offered to submit it putting it as the Case of two mercantile people, to the opinion of a Lawyer. I cannot help smiling at this assertion and offer. Sure Mr H. knows full well (for he is himself not quite unconversant in Law Learning) that Such an agreement allowing it to be what he supposes, and to be executed in every form would be altogether void; and that the imposer of it would run the risque of being committed by the Court for an act of oppression.

So far as to the Letter. Few I believe will agree, that it is possible such a Letter on such an occasion should ever bind a man in that manner he contends for. Mr H. has shewn it to two of his friends. They think it does. He referd it originally to two others of my own nomination. I would not accept the arbitration; though I knew they were prejudiced in my favour, and would most certainly declare for me. First because I never would even suffer a question to be put whether I was a slave or free. Next because I will not call any persons to sit in judgment on my Character even though I were certain they would decide favourably for me.

The Course I therefore took was this; to put an End to all dispute by surrendering the Pension.

To Robert Jephson—26 *February* [1765]

Source: Draft in Fitzwilliam MSS (Sheffield). Printed *Corr.* (1844), I, 62–3.

The agreement Burke made regarding his pension was not to having it cancelled, but to having its income reassigned to another person chosen by Hamilton. Burke remained the nominal holder. The person chosen by Hamilton was

[1] MS: this he contends this

Robert Jephson (1736–1803), a wit and playwright later well known in the literary society of London and Dublin; at the time of the reassignment he had been living for two or three years in Hamilton's household.

Dear Jephson, I waited at home Friday and saturday last until Dinner time, in hopes that Mr Colthurst[1] (agreeably to what you mentiond from Mr H.) would call on me to settle the affair of the Pension so as to assure it to Mr H. in the most satisfactory manner. Mr Burke has told me you intended to call yesterday; and I waited for you. As I had not seen Mr Colthurst or you, I enquired concerning the method usual in such transactions; and I am informed that it is very easy, and expeditious; that upon being properly authorized, the people of the Treasury in Ireland have a short instrument by which they transfer the Pensions at a Triffling charge. Mr H. will mention this to Mr Colthurst. And I shall be ready to call on him (Colthurst) or to see him here, whenever he thinks it convenient, to send over the proper powers for making this Transfer. If Mr Colthurst thinks any other way more eligible, on seeing him, I shall be very glad to come into it, having no Choice in the mode of the Conveyance. I am dear Jephson yours &c

E B.

Tuesday. 26. Feb.

ABBÉ LOUIS-ANTOINE DESFRANÇOIS *to* EDMUND BURKE—6 *March* 1765

Source: Fitzwilliam MSS (Sheffield).

Burke's *Sublime and Beautiful* had reached its fourth English edition in 1764. A French edition was thought worth attempting. Mrs Montagu's friend Sir James Macdonald, 8th Baronet (1742–66), wrote her from Paris, in June: 'A translation of Mr Bourks Book will very soon appear in this country. I have seen the Manuscript and have rendered him the service of correcting some egregious blunders of the translator, though I do not pretend to have rectified all his mistakes' (Blunt, *Mrs Montagu*, I, 105). Apparently the translator was himself worried about his deficiencies, for which he sent apologies to Burke along with the completed work. He signed himself only 'L'abbé Desfrançois' but can be fairly certainly identified as Louis-Antoine Desfrançois, who was tried and acquitted before the revolutionary tribunal in 1794. *Le Moniteur* 19 February 1794 described him as 'né et demeurant à Paris, rue des Boucheries, faubourg Saint-Germain, âgé de soixante-six ans, ex-abbé et interprète du ci-devant roi, maître de langue'. See also H. Wallon, *Histoire du Tribunal Révolutionnaire de Paris*, Paris, 1880, II, 426 and n. An Abbé Desfrançois is listed in the *Almanach Royale* for the years from 1769 to 1788 as interpreter of English and Italian to the King.

[1] Matthew Coulthurst (1720–70), Hamilton's lawyer.

Monsieur,

Je desirerois fort que la Version que j'ai l'honneur de vous envoyer[1] vous donnât autant de Satisfaction; que j'ai eu de plaisir à la faire. Mais je crains que malgré tous les soins que j'y ai apportés, et toute l attention que j'y ai donnée, elle ne soit imparfaite dans quelques passages; du moins on me le reproche; vous verrez mieux que personne Si l'on a raison, ou non. Quoiqu'il en soit la pluspart de nos journaux en ont dit beaucoup de bien. Ils n'ont fait que rendre justice au mérite de votre ouvrage. Quelqu'excellent qu'il soit, je doute que nous soyons dans le cas d'en faire une seconde édition. Cependant comme la chose n'est point impossible, je vous prierois, Monsieur, de me communiquer vos remarques Sur ma version. Vous pouriez addresser votre lettre *au caffé de toutes les nations ruë dauphine au coin de la ruë christine.* Je Suis avec tous les Sentimens qui vous sont dus, Monsieur, Votre trés humble,

et très obeissant Serviteur L'abbé Desfrançois.

a paris ce 6 mars 1765.

To William Gerard Hamilton—10 *April* 1765

Source: Copy in Fitzwilliam MSS (Sheffield). Printed *Corr.* (1844), I, 64.

Burke was very willing that his pension should be transferred to Robert Jephson, with whom he was friendly; but since the surrender was meant to be a public gesture of defiance to Hamilton, it occurred to him that a direct transfer to Jephson might be open to misunderstanding. Jephson was a friend; some might think Burke was making the transfer out of friendship, or even that Jephson had secretly agreed to pay all or part of the money back to him. Burke therefore asked to be allowed to make his transfer to Matthew Coulthurst, Hamilton's lawyer. Hamilton agreed to this (letter of 8 April at Sheffield, printed in *Corr.* [1844], I, 63). Burke explained his motives in a final letter.

Sir

In compliance with your directions I have executed an assignment of my pension to Mr Coulthurst. I chose him rather than Mr Jephson because I would have it appear on the face of the transaction that this conveyance was no act of friendship, nor an assignment in trust for any uses of mine, but that it was made solely to you, as a compliment to my own feeling, in consequence of the demand which you persisted in

[1] Published under the title *Recherches philosophiques sur l'origine des idées que nous avons du beau et du sublime, précédées d'une dissertation sur le goût*, 2 vols. Paris, 1765. The translation is dedicated to Lord Hertford, British ambassador in Paris, who the preface says had suggested its being undertaken. David Hume, his Lordship's secretary and Burke's friend, very likely took some part in the enterprise.

making upon me, and that no man should have even a colour to assert that I received a compensation where I refused to perform the service which was expected in return for it. Permit me just to remind you, that not Capn Jepson but Mr Coulthurst was your first nomination, and that in chusing him I have only adopted your own original Idea.

I am Sir
your most obedient and
most humble Servant

I shall in half an hour send all your Books which I can just now find in print or manuscript except the loose Pamphlets. The latter shall be sent as soon as possible, and if any should remain of the former, I shall faithfully return as I find them.

April 10. 1765—

HAMILTON'S *notes on* BURKE'S *conduct*

Source: Bodleian Library (MS Malone 38, fol. 125).

Hamilton's feelings about the quarrel with Burke are partly revealed in a page of rough notes in his hand found among Malone's papers in the Bodleian. Whether the notes were jotted down as preliminary to some more formal statement, or whether they record what was said or felt at an interview, one cannot be sure from their form. They must have been written shortly after the transfer of the pension was completed.

Took Mr: B: up, unknown £2000.

Pension got not by the Primate—Primate would not answer his Letter.—Ireld: turn'd out Ill—offer'd in Ireld: to give up for Him—offer'd here to go to Mr: Grenve:[1]—

Said He had a Family—offer'd him £5000—would be gratefull for Ten Years—

If to engage with any other, beg'd He would keep the Pension but never come near me—Resigning it an additional Affront[2]—Propos'd to Jeph:—He promis'd it, and afterwards went off. Jeph: has it—

Agreed to refer it to any one. Lawyer's Opinion—Give him the Money if I did not speak—Consult Mr: Wn:[3] through the whole. But denied He had spoke to any one—Copy of a Conveyance for Years—Told Mr: Smith[4] the Letter was directly contrary—Wanted to prejudice Jeph—

[1] George Grenville, First Lord of the Treasury 1763–5.
[2] In MS the words 'message by Jeph:' written above this phrase.
[3] Probably Dr Joseph Warton; see above (p. 178), first letter of [*ante* 12 February].
[4] Hamilton's letter to Burke, 8 April, mentions a message Hamilton had been sent by Burke through 'Mr Smith and Mr Jephson'. 'Mr Smith' is probably William Smith, M.P. for Athy, who was Second Secretary to Lord Northumberland when Hamilton was Chief Secretary.

Gone to my Rivals, and my Opponents—A thousand Opportunities He sought of quarrelling with me.

Speech against R: Cath: B[1]—

Said a 1000 times to Jeph: the Man of all others to live with.

Offer'd to join with any Friend.

Primate. Obligations to ⟨L.lt⟩[2]—Offer'd to go in to Opposition; if He would not desert me—I brought it on myself, He was to direct me in Politics or leave me—Mr: B: justifies it by saying the Letter is not a Promise. Not that He ought not to keep to it, if it is a Promise—No objection to the Mode of Conveyance—Never produc'd the Letter 'till He defied me—Mr: B: says we were to go on in Politicks[3] Had got £15 from booksellers[4]—Two Children—The time at which He made these Professions—Jew, and a Jesuit—All He wanted was his Wife, and Child—Footing of mere Friendship, but denies Gratitude—Worst Judgment upon Earth—A Will—I brought on the Conversation in Ireld:, not that you should forsake me—Living with me Slavery—The End of resigning the Pension—Presum'd upon my Carlesness that it was destroy'd, and asserted it was directly the Contrary—He did not forsake me—Legal Idea of Slavery valuable Consideration.

Would not a Man have said instead of I can't be with you any part, I will the whole as you are disstress'd. He would have been in jail—Liberty then—Keep a Man in your Confidence who says He will forsake you—I deny the Demand ever was made—Wish you Joy of one

[1] Perhaps a bill brought into the Irish Parliament in 1762 to allow Roman Catholic nobles in Ireland to enter the military service of Portugal. According to Francis Hardy's *Memoirs of the Earl of Charlemont*, 2nd ed. London, 1812, I, 130 the bill was moved by Hamilton and 'supported by a torrent of eloquence which bore down all before it', but being strongly opposed by the Irish Protestants, '...this measure, which undoubtedly might have been carried, was finally given up by government' (*ibid.* I, 132). Burke's feelings on such a bill, and especially on its abandonment would be a likely cause of disagreement with Hamilton.

[2] Hamilton uses an abbreviation which is not clearly legible. It appears to be 'L.lt', and in the context 'Obligations to Lord Lieutenant' is plausible.

[3] In MS the words 'tho I fail'd, He prosper'd—' written above this phrase.

[4] The basis for this figure is not known. Burke was very modestly rewarded for the *Vindication of Natural Society*, his first published work of any length. A memorandum signed by Will Burke and Robert Dodsley (Berg Collection, New York Public Library) describes the conditions of payment: 'Memorandum that Mr Doddesly has on this 10th of May paid Mr Wm Burke the summ of six pounds six Shillings for the Use of the Author of a Pamphlet intitled Natural Society Vindicated and if the said Pamphlet comes to a second Edition he the said Mr Doddesly does hereby agree to give the said Author six Gs more, and to print of but 500 in this first Edition—

R Dodsley
W: Burke.'

A receipt for the *Sublime and Beautiful* is recorded (Hist. MSS Comm., 9th Report, App. (*Morrison MSS*), p. 478): '16 February 1757. Edmund Burke's receipt for twenty guineas paid him by Messrs R. and J. Dodsley "for a copy of a work on the Sublime and Beautiful, it being understood that if the said Messrs Dodsley shall print a third edition of the sd work they shall pay the author the further sum of ten guineas in consideration of the entire property of the said copy".'

another—To say He wasn't under Engagements; every Dinner that He eat—[1]

Chandler's Shop—Slavery, give up his Freedom—dung Hill—Did I ever refuse him Money—Provok'd to be generous that a Man of Talents should be hurt by his Attachment to *me* Jew—Jesuit

HENRY FLOOD *to* EDMUND BURKE—9 *May* 1765

Source: Fitzwilliam MSS (Sheffield).
Addressed: To | Edmund Bourke Esqr | Queen Anne Street, Cavendish | Square | London. *Postmarked:* ⟨...⟩|MA

Henry Flood (1732–91) might have begun his acquaintance with Burke when an undergraduate at Trinity College in the late 1740's, when studying law at the Inner Temple in the 1750's, or after he returned to Ireland and entered the Irish Parliament in 1759. He was the most active spirit of a rising popular party in Ireland.

My dear Bourke

I hoped to have had the pleasure of seeing you in London again, but that being over I must endeavour to make myself some amends by engaging you if I can to let me hear from you now and then. I hear many things have been said and some done with respect to this wretched Country in a certain assembly since I left you. But these accounts are so loose and in some parts so improbable that I can make nothing of them. If anything has past I beg you will let me know it. If any new book of merit comes out, or any old one comes to your memory that will be of use to my Hibernian labours pray hint it to me, but above all let me know what you are doing yourself about which I feel myself sincerely interested. Will my being so, prevent my being impertinent in asking whether you and Hamilton have so quarrelld as it is said you have? If it be so, and this or any other circumstance shoud further incline you to look at all towards this Country, and anything which I and my friends can do coud be fashiond into a further inducement, I beg you will let me know it, and that you will consider this as a *serious* not a *civil* speech. I hope Mrs Burke is well and that your young Julus[2] goes on to promise every satisfaction to you. I am my dear Bourke

Your faithfully affectionate friend and obedient
Servant
HENRY FLOOD

Comps to the Doctor
and to Will: Bourke

Thursday May 9: 1765

[1] MS ends here. The following words Hamilton jotted into the margin, not attaching them to any specific passage.

[2] Ascanius, Aeneas's son, was sometimes called Julus by Latin authors; the gens Iulia claimed descent from him.

To HENRY FLOOD—18 *May* [1765]

Source: Fitzwilliam MSS (Sheffield). Printed *Original Letters to Henry Flood*, pp. 1–4; *Corr.* (1844), I, 76–81.
Endorsed: Edm. Burke | 18. May. 1765.

My dear Flood, I thank you for your kind and most obliging Letter. You are a person whose good offices are not snares, and to whom one may venture to be obliged, without danger to his honour. As I depend upon your sincerity, so I shall most certainly call upon your friendship, if I should have any thing to do in Ireland; This however is not the Case at present, at least in any way in which your interposition may be employed with a proper attention to yourself; a point which I shall always very tenderly consider in any applications I make to my friends.

It is very true, that there is an eternal rupture between me and Hamilton, which was, on my side, neither sought nor provoked. For though his conduct in publick affairs has been for a Long time directly contrary to my opinion, very reproachful to himself, and extremely disgustful to me, and though in private, he has not justly fullfilled one of his engagements to me, yet I was so uneasy and awkard at coming to a Breach where I had once a close and intimate friendship, that I continued with a kind of desperate fidelity to adhere to his Cause and person; and when I found him greatly disposed to quarrel with me I used such submissive measures as I never before could prevail on myself to use to any man; The occasion of our difference was not any act whatsoever on my part; It was entirely upon his, by a voluntary but most insolent and intolerable demand amounting to no less than a Claim of Servitude during the whole Course of my Life, without leaving to me at any time a power either of getting forward with honour, or of retiring with tranquility. This was really and truly the substance of his demand upon me, to which, I need not tell you, that I refused, with some degree of indignation, to submit. On this, we ceased to see each other, or to correspond, a good while before you Left London. He then commenced through the intervention of others a Negotiation with me; in which he shewed as much of meenness in his proposals, as he had done of arrogance in his demands; but as all those proposals were vitiated by the taint of that Servitude with which they were all mixed, his Negotiation came to nothing. He grounded those monstrous claims, (such as never were before heard of in this Country) on that Pension, which he had procured for me through Col. Cunninghame[1] the Late Primate, and

[1] Colonel Robert Cunninghame, later Baron Rossmore (d. 1801). He was A.D.C. to Lord Halifax when Halifax was Lord Lieutenant.

Lord Halifax; for through all that Series of Persons this Paltry business was contrived to pass. Now, tho' I was sensible that I owed this Pension to the goodwill of the Primate in a great degree, and though, if it had come from Hamiltons Pocket instead of being derived from the Irish Treasury, I had earned it by a Long and Laborious attendance, and might, in any other than that unfortunate connection, have got a much better thing, yet to get rid of him completely and not to carry even a memorial of such a person about me, I offerd to transfer it to his Attorney in Trust for him. This offer he thought proper to accept. I beg pardon, my dear Flood, for troubling you So long on a Subject which ought not to employ a moment of your thoughts, and never shall again employ a moment of mine.

To your Enquiry, concerning some Propositions in a Certain assembly of a nature injurious to Ireland, since your departure, I know none of that kind, except one attempt made by a Mr Shiffner[1] to lessen the Number of[2] the Ports of Entry in Britain and Ireland allowed for the Trade of Wool and woollen Yarn of the growth of the Latter Country. This attempt was grounded on the decrease of the Import of those commodities from Ireland; which they rashly attributed to the greater facility of the illicit Transport of Wool from Ireland to France by the indulgence of a Number of Ports. This Idea founded in an Ignorance of the Nature of the Irish Trade had weight with some persons; but the decreased import of Irish Wool and Yarn being accounted for, upon true and rational principles, in a Short memorial deliverd to Mr Townshend;[3] he saw at once into it with his usual Sagacity; and he has silenced this complaint at least for this Session. Nothing else was done or meant, that I could discover, though I have not been inattentive; and I am not without good hopes, that the menaces in the beginning of the Session will end as they began, only in idle and imprudent words. At least there is a strong probebility that New men will come in, and not improbably with New Ideas.[4] At this very instant the Causes productive of such

[1] Henry Shiffner (1721–95), M.P. for Minehead. On 22 March the House of Commons agreed that a bill should be prepared limiting the number of ports in Ireland from which wool could be exported and limiting the number in England into which it could be imported. Shiffner was one of those ordered to prepare the bill. He presented it to the House 27 March, but it never completed the committee stage. It was revived the next session. Lord Charlemont reported to Flood on the debate of 12 March 1766 '...Burke supported the cause of Ireland in the most masterly manner, and the bill was rejected' (*Original Letters to Henry Flood*, p. 40).

[2] MS: of of

[3] Not improbably by Burke himself. See below, letters of [*post* 29 May] to Mason and 25 June to Townshend (p. 204), for Burke's connexion with Townshend at this time.

[4] On 13 May the King commissioned the Duke of Cumberland to sound the opposition about taking office.

a Change are strongly at Work. The regency Bill[1] has shewn such want of concert and want of Capacity in the ministers such an inattention to the honour of the Crown, if not such a design *against* it, such imposition and surprise upon the King, and such a misrepresentation of the disposition of Parliament to the Sovereign;[2] that there is no doubt that there is a fixed resolution to get rid of them all (unless perhaps of Grenville) but principally of the Duke of Bedford.[3] So that you will have much more reason to be surprised to find the ministry standing by the End of next week than to hear of their entire removal. Nothing but an intractable Temper in your friend Pitt can prevent a most admirable and Lasting System from being put together; and this Crisis will shew whether Pride or Patriotism be predominant in his Character; for you may be assured, that he has it now in his power to come into the Service of his Country upon any plan of politicks he may chuse to dictate; with great and honourable Terms to himself and to every friend he has in the world; and with such a stretch of power as will be equal to every thing but absolute despotism over the King and Kingdom.[4] A Few days will shew whether he will take this part or that of continuing on his back at Hayes[5] talking Fustian, excluded from all ministerial and incapable of all Parliamentary Service. For his Gout is worse than ever; but his Pride may disable him[6] more than his Gout. These matters so fill our imaginations here, that with our mob of 6 or 7000 Weavers who pursue the ministry and do not leave them quiet or Safety in their houses, we have little to think of other things.[7] However I will send you the new Edition of Swifts Posthumous Works.[8] I doubt you can hardly read this hand; but it is very late. Mrs Burke has been ill and recovers but

[1] In February and March 1765 the King had been ill, and on his recovery he ordered a regency bill to be prepared. On 24 April the bill was recommended to both Houses of Parliament in a speech from the throne. The Regent was not named in the bill, but was to be left to the King's nomination.

[2] On 3 May Halifax and Sandwich, Secretaries of State, had persuaded the King to agree to the omission of his mother, the Princess Dowager, from the list of those who could be Regent. They had argued that 'it would make the whole easier, and particularly in the House of Commons, where some gentlemen might otherwise have difficulties about the meaning of the general words' (Grenville's diary, *Grenville Papers*, III, 150). This was agreed to by the House of Lords, but on 9 May the bill was amended in the Commons to include the Princess Dowager.

[3] Burke, like most of his contemporaries, did not realize that the King's aversion was to Grenville, not Bedford.

[4] The King's dislike of Grenville was such that he was prepared to agree to almost any terms that Pitt could ask.

[5] Pitt's house in Kent.

[6] MS: him him

[7] Burke is referring to a series of mass meetings, ending in some rioting, on the part of the Spitalfields weavers. See William Hunt, *History of England, 1760–1801*, London, 1905, p. 66.

[8] Vols. 15 and 16 of Hawkesworth's edition of Swift's *Works* were reviewed in the *Annual Register* for 1765.

slowly, she desires her respects to you and Lady Frances;[1] Julus is much obliged to you. Will Burke always remembers you with affection and so does My dear Flood your most affectionate humble Servant

E BURKE

18th May.

Pray remember me to Langrishe[2] and to Leland[3] and Bowden.[4] Dr Nugent desires his compliments to you in the strongest manner. He has conceived a very high esteem for you.

Burke wrote Flood another letter, which has not survived, before receiving his reply of 30 May. The reply is rather cool as to the Hamilton quarrel, in which Flood does not take sides; otherwise it is full and friendly. One reference to Charles Townshend suggests that the lost letter may have spoken of the connexion Burke had formed with him. After speaking of 'the eloquent and informd Townshend' Flood adds, 'If I coud envy a man I love, I shoud envy you your intercourse with this latter bright genius'.

To JOHN MONCK MASON—[*post* 29 *May* 1765]

Source: Draft in Fitzwilliam MSS (Sheffield). Printed *Corr.* (1844), I, 70–75. This draft is undated, but its reference to 'Lord Weymouth's government' places it after 29 May 1765, when Weymouth was appointed Lord Lieutenant of Ireland.

John Monck Mason (1726–1809) had been three years ahead of Burke at Trinity College, had studied law at the Middle Temple, been called to the Irish Bar in 1752, and entered the Irish House of Commons in 1761. He was an active correspondent of Burke at this time, though the letter of his which approved Burke's conduct in the Hamilton quarrel has not survived.

My dear Mason, I am hardly able to tell you how much satisfaction I had in your Letter. Your approbation of my Conduct makes me believe[5] much the better both of you and of myself;[6] and I assure you that that approbation came to me very seasonably. Such proofs of a warm, sincere, and disinterested friendship were not wholly unnecessary to my support, at a time when I experienced such bitter Effects of the perfidy, and ingratitude, of other, much longer, and much closer, connections. The way in which you take up my affairs binds me to you in a manner I cannot express: For to tell you the Truth, I never can, (knowing, as I do, the principles upon which I always endeavour to act) submit to any sort of compromise on my Character; and I shall never therefore

[1] Flood's wife, *née* Lady Frances Maria Beresford (1731–1815).
[2] Hercules Langrishe (1731–1811), later a correspondent of Burke.
[3] Dr Thomas Leland (see above letter of [*circa* 24] May 1746, p. 65); a friend and correspondent.
[4] Probably the Rev. John Bowden (d. 1776).
[5] In MS 'believe' is crossed through. [6] MS: of both of you and of mysef

look upon those, who after hearing the whole story, do not think me *perfectly* in the right, and do not consider Hamilton as an infamous Scoundrel, to be in the smallest degree my friends, or even to be persons for whom I am bound to have the slightest Esteem, as fair or just estimaters of the Characters and Conduct of men. Situated as I am and feeling as I do, I should be just as well pleased that they totally condemned me, as that they should say that there were faults on both sides, or that it was a disputable Case, as I hear is I cannot forbear saying, the affected Language of some Persons. Having let you into this perhaps weak part of my Character, I must let you into another which is I confess full as weak and rather more blameable, that is some degree of mortification which I cannot avoid feeling on the Letters I receive almost daily and from several hands from Dublin, giving me an account of a violent outcry of ingratitude which is there raised against me. If the absurdity of an accusation were a sufficient antidote against the poison of it this would I suppose be the most innocent charge in the world: But if its absurdity weakens the force of it to the conviction of others it adds to my feeling of it, when I reflect that there is one person who has ever seen my face that can listen to such a Calumny. H's Emissaries do more for him than he has ever attempted to do for himself. He charges me with receiving that Pension during the Kings pleasure (in getting me which he had the least share of four who were engaged in it) not at all a favour, but as the consideration of a Bargain and sale of my Liberty and existence. It cannot be, at once a voluntary Benefit claiming gratitude, and a mercenary consideration exacting service. They may (if they are contented to Speak a consistent falshood) accuse me of breach of faith but they can never, without nonsense as well as injustice say I am ungrateful, until they can prove that some favour was intended to me. In regard to their own understanding they will be so gracious as to drop one or the other of the Charges. In modesty they ought to drop both of them unless serving their friend with six of the best years of my Life whilst he acquired at their expence a ministerial fortune and then after giving him my[1] Labour, giving him also a Pension of 300 a year be not unless these be thought as great faults towards him, as perhaps they were towards the publick, and unless those delicate friends[2] do not think their late grateful, sincere disinterested Secretary has not yet enough on their Establishment. You cannot avoid remarking my dear Mason, and I hope not without some indignation at the unparallel'd Singularity of my Situation. Was ever a man before me expected to enter into formal, direct, undisguised Slavery? Did ever a man before him confess an

[1] MS: by

[2] MS: friends of

attempt to decoy a man into such an illegal Contract, not to say any thing of the impudence of regularly pleading it? If such an attempt, be wicked and unlawful (and I am sure no one ever doubted it), I have only to confess his Charge, and to admit myself his Dupe to[1] make him pass on his own Shewing for the most consummate Villian that ever lived. The only difference between us is not whether he is not a rogue; for he not only admits but pleads the facts that demonstrate him to be so, but only whether I was such a fool as to sell myself absolutely for a consideration which so far from being adequate, (if any such could be adequate) [is] not even so much as certain. Not to value myself (as a gentleman a freeman a man of Education; and one pretending to Literature) is there any situation in Life so low or even so criminal, that can subject a man to the possibility of such an engagement? Would you dare attempt to bind your footman to such Terms? Will the Law suffer a felon sent to the Plantation to bind himself for his Life and to renounce all possibility either of elevation or quiet? And I am to defend myself for not doing, what no man is Sufferd to do and what it would be criminal in any man to Submit to. You will excuse me for this heat, which will in spite of me attend and[2] injure a just cause whilst Common judgments look upon coolness, as a proof of innocence though it never fails to go along with guilt and ability. But this is the real State of the Affair. H. indeed I hear has the impudence sometimes [to] pretend that my going to Mr T.[3] is the Cause of our Rupture. This is I assure you an abominable falshood. I never had more than a very slight acquaintance with Mr T. till long after our rupture. O'Hara through whom a part of the Negotiation passed will let you see that our rupture had no sort of relation to him ⟨...⟩ But Ridge[4] will explain the point to you at large. You will Shew this much as you like to any you think fit of our common friends, meaning that H. should know in what a manner I speak of him on all occasions.

You are my dear Mason by your Bedford connection involved in the support of Ld W's government and I could heartily wish, that your Task were less difficult, with an unsupported and beggard Lord Lt attended with officers to do business at a doubtful time, the best of them with middling ability and no experience. My Ld Lt himself is a genteel man and of excellent Natural Sense is as univerally said.[5] I wish it may turn

[1] MS: to to

[2] MS: and to

[3] Charles Townshend. In MS 'my leaving him' is written above 'My going to Mr T', which has not been deleted.

[4] John Ridge (see above, letter of 23 April [1763], p. 168).

[5] Burke is charitable. Horace Walpole (*Memoirs*, II, 126–7) described Weymouth as 'an inconsiderable, debauched young man, attached to the Bedfords, but so ruined by

out for your advantage, and that the barrack board[1] may be not the seat of Bench but a Step of the Stairs. You know I suppose that H. endeavourd by his connection with the Thynne to intrude into that Family and wanted to stipulate[2] for a month or six Weeks service to get for a Cousin of his a Deenery,[3] but I imagine they hear on all hands.

If Mason was more willing than Flood to take Burke's side against Hamilton, he was a good deal less disposed to congratulate him on his new patron Charles Townshend. 'I have no great reliance', he wrote 28 June, 'on the faith, or affection of men so entirely devoted to Ambition as your late Master, or your new friend; but I hope I wrong the latter; the other I have no doubts about, he has proved himself a thorough rascal.'

To JOHN HELY HUTCHINSON—[*May* 1765]

Source: Fitzwilliam MSS (Sheffield). Printed *Corr.* (1844), I, 65–70.
The MS of this letter at Sheffield is incomplete and bears no date. As Irish interest in the Burke-Hamilton quarrel was at its height in May, that is a plausible guess as to the time of composition. It is obviously a possibility (as it also is for the previous draft to Mason) that no letter much resembling what we have was ever sent. None is mentioned in the Hist. MSS Comm. Report on the Donoughmore MSS (12th Report, App. Part IX).

John Hely Hutchinson (1724–94) had begun his career in the Irish House of Commons as a strong 'patriot', but had soon become a leading supporter of government, a Privy Councillor and Prime Serjeant-at-Law. He was Hamilton's chief friend in Ireland, where Burke had also known him. There is a story transmitted by Hamilton and ultimately written down by James Boswell, Jr, of a literary contest in which Hutchinson, Hamilton, and Burke tried 'who could write the best sermon the best psalm and the best song: and Burke (said Hamilton) beat us in all three!!' (letter of James Boswell, Jr, to Dr Walker King 28 October 1818 (Bk 34) at Sheffield). Burke had of course no hope that Hutchinson would take his side against Hamilton. But neither was it prudent to neglect him altogether, as his opinion was always of some importance in Ireland.

Dear Sir,

It is so necessary for me to apologize for my long Silence, and I am so unable to satisfye, even my own Ideas, with any apology I can make, that I have twenty times begun to write, and as often desisted from my undertaking. The truth is, a certain awkardness arising from some late

gaming, that the moment before his exaltation he was setting out for France, to avoid his creditors'. Having been appointed Lord Lieutenant at the end of May, Weymouth was removed in July, without ever having crossed to Ireland.

[1] Mason became Commissioner and Overseer of the Barracks 23 April 1765 (*Liber Munerum Publicorum Hiberniae*, I, pt ii, 115).

[2] MS: stipulated

[3] No connexion of Hamilton with Lord Weymouth's family has been traced. His cousin in orders was probably the Rev. Anthony Hamilton (1739–1812).

Events, has added a good deal of my difficulties on this occasion. To write upon mere matters of indifference, when the very turning of my thoughts towards you filled my mind with those that were very interesting, would have given my Letter an air of coldness and constraint, very foreign from my natural manner, and very unlike the Style in which I should always wish to converse with you. On the other hand, if my Letter were to go, impressed with the genuine feeling of my heart, when it was full of resentment, and of resentment which had for its most just object one with whom I suppose you live in confidence and friendship, it might have had an appearance of disrespect: an appearance as contrary to the real sense I have of the honour you do me by your friendship, as any air of reserve would be to that oppenness and candour, which I suppose first recommended me to your regard, and which I am sure can alone make me worthy the continuance of it. On some deliberation, I think the safer course is to speak my mind freely; for as Mr Hamiltons calumnies, (circulated by Agents worthy of him) made it necessary for me to open myself to others, it might seem some sort of distrust of your equity or my own innocence, if I held back from you who know both the Parties, and do not want sagacity to look into their true Characters. I do not expect that you should honour me with an answer to this part of my Letter; because a Neutrality is all I can in reason expect; and on this Subject I am perhaps less reasonable than I wish to be thought upon others; Nothing less than whole approbation being sufficient to content me; and I can construe Silence into what I please.

You are already apprised by what Mr H. has himself caused to be reported that he has attempted to make a property, a piece of Houshold goods of me. An attempt, in my poor opinion, as contrary to discretion as it is to justice. For he would fain have had a *Slave*, which, as it is a being of no dignity, so it can be of very little real utility to its owner; and he refused to have a faithful *friend*, which is a creature of some rank, and (in whatever subject) no trivial or useless acquisition. But in this he is to be excused, for with as sharp and apprehensive parts in many respects as any man living, he never in reality did comprehend even in Theory, what Friendship or affection was; being, as far as I was capable of observing, totally destitute of either friendship or enmity; but rather inclined to *respect* those who treat him ill. In spite of some knowlege and feeling of this part of his Character, but actuated by a sense of what is owing to close connection, (upon whatsoever principles it may have been enterd into) how faithful, how attached, and how Zealous I have been to him, you were yourself in part a Witness; and though you could be so only in part, yet this was enough I flatter myself to let you see that, I deserved to be considerd in another manner than as one of Mr H's Cattle, or as a piece of his Houshold stuff.

Six of the best years of my Life he took me from every pursuit of Literary reputation or of improvement of my fortune. In that time he made his own fortune (a very great one), and he has also taken to *himself* the very little one, which *I* had made. In all this time you may easily conceive, how much I felt at seeing myself left behind by almost all my cotemporaries. There never was a Season more favourable for any man who chose to enter into the Carrier of publick Life; and I think I am not guilty of Ostentation, in supposing my own moral Character and my industry, my friends and connections, when Mr H. first sought my acquaintance were not at all inferior to those of several, whose fortune is at this day upon a very different footing from mine.

I suppose that by this, my friend Mr Ridge has informed you of the nature of the agreement which originally subsisted between that Gentleman and me; He has I suppose let you into the manner in which it was fulfilled upon Mr Hamiltons side; how that Gentleman shifted and shuffled with me in order to keep me in a state of perpetual dependance, never made me an offer of indemnity for all his Breaches of Promise, nor even an apology, until he imagined it was probable that others were inclined to shew me more attention than he did; and then having presumed to put a Test to me, which no man not born in Africa ever thought of taking, on my refusal broke off all connection with me in the most insolent manner. He indeed enterd into two several Negotiations afterwards; but both poisoned in their first principles by the same spirit of Injustice with which he set out in his dealing towards me; I therefore could never give way to his proposals; The whole ended by his possessing himself of that small reward for my services, which I since find he had a very small share in procuring for me. After, or indeed rather during, his Negotiations he endeavourd to stain my Character, and injure my future fortune by every Calumny his Malice could suggest. This is the sum of my connection with Mr Hamilton. However I am much obliged to him for having forcibly driven me from that imprisonment with him, from which otherwise I might never have had Spirit enough to have deliverd myself. This I thought it necessary to say to you on the Subject of a man with whom you still Live in friendship, and with whom I have had unfortunately so close a connection. You cannot think that in using this freedom I mean to deviate in the slightest degree from the real respect I ever entertaind for your Character or from the gratitude I ought to feel for your obliging Behaviour to me whilst I was in Ireland.

Nobody has spoken at all times and in all Companies with more justice to the importance you may be of to any Government from your Talents and your Experience in Business; and though from my situation in Life, my opinion must be of very little consequence to your Interest, it will Speak for the fairness of my Intentions with regard to you. Though I

DR JOHN CURRY *to* EDMUND BURKE—8 *June* 1765

Source: Fitzwilliam MSS (Sheffield).
Addressed: To | Edd Burke Esqr | Queen Ann's Street

Dr John Curry (*c.* 1702–80), one of Burke's friends in Dublin, was the author of a controversial work on the Irish Rebellion of 1641, which he felt had usually been described in a way unjust to the native Irish Catholics. Burke agreed with him as to the injustice; he shocked friends in England such as David Hume and William Markham by the vehemence with which he argued against their British and Protestant interpretations of the Rebellion (Bisset, 2nd ed. II, 426, and letter of [*post* 9 November 1771], printed *Corr.* [1844], I, 336–8). Burke had called Curry's attention to a line of argument helpful to the Irish side of the question, and agreed to take some part in bringing out a London edition of his work. Curry wrote to prompt him to action, as well as to express confidence in his good intentions in the Hamilton quarrel.

Dear Sir

I should have Answered Your kind Letter Much Sooner, but that I waited for a Confirmation of an Account Sent hither from England, that a New Edition of the Memoirs was Almost printed off by One Balf a Printer in London.[1] But having heard Nothing more of that Matter I Conclude, Either that the Account was groundless (tho' it Came from Mr Cuningham the Publisher of the Law dictionary)[2] or, if it be true, that as they Undertook that Affair without having first Consulted the proper persons, and of their own head, they have none but themselves to blame for Any loss they May Suffer by a much better, more Enlarged and Correct Edition: which, as Soon as you Give Orders to a Printer to begin the Work, Shall, from time to time, be Punctually Sent You. The Inserting the Note You Mention into the text, is Extremely Proper, and Easily done. From the hint You Gave me, when here Concerning the Massacre in the Island of Magee, I have made a further Search, and Sent You in a Long Letter the Result of it.[3] I Ardently Wish to have

[1] Probably Richard Balfe, who printed the *North Briton* for Wilkes. London editions of Curry's *Historical Memoirs of the Irish Rebellion* were printed in 1765 and 1767, but neither has the name of Balfe on its title-page.

[2] Timothy Cunningham (d. 1789) published a *New and Complete Law Dictionary* in 1764–5.

[3] Curry's letter of 15 December 1764, at Sheffield.

your Opinion of it. I am Clearly of opinion, for many Reasons, which it would be too Tedious to Mention here, that it is better, on Every Account that the New Edition Should Come out in London. In My Life I never Saw So much Nonsensical Malice Vented in News-papers, on any Occasion, as I Constantly Meet with in All the English Prints that Come here, most Unchristianly, and Inhumanly Levelled at P—[1] which never fail to be Reprinted here; and are as Surely believed as Printed. Since you are So Good as to take part in these Memoirs; and in the Republication of them, I shall, upon Notice of its being begun, Submit to your Judgement, Whatever Alterations, or Additions I have Since Made: for, without Complement, I believe and know you to be a more Competent Judge of these Matters than I am;[2] and that you will Steal a few hours from Your more Interesting Concerns to Contribute to the Cause of truth, and Justice, in favour of your much Slandered, and Injured Country. Which, I think You know, and which God knows, was my Only Motive for first Undertaking So troublesome, dangerous, and Expensive a task; and which Surely Ought to have fallen to the Lot of Some Man of a different Caracter, and more Abilitys—Your difference with Mr Hamilton is Generally, and variously talked of here, but mostly in your favour. As to the Sin of Ingratitude I make no Sort of Scruple to Pronounce You *Impeccable*; and In so doing, I Really Pronounce, what I think a Conscious truth. But, it would Give me the highest Satisfaction to have; from Yourself a little Glimpse of Light into this Affair: You know I had the best Opinion of Mr Hamilton's head, and heart, when he was here; and I am one of those, who part with Such an Opinion of Any Man, not without violence, and with a Sort of Agony. This I Shall not Require, if you think it Improper; but the Matter of difference between you is So publickly talked of here, that I thought I Might Venture to Mention it to you. I am delighted with the hint You have Given me of the Large Work You are Engaged in, and the Progress You have Made in it;[3] I long for Nothing So much as to See it finished,

[1] Papists [?]

[2] Burke told William Markham in 1771 that he had studied Irish history 'with more care than is common' (*Corr.* [1844], I, 337). He gave assistance to several Irish historians of his time: Dr Curry, Dr Thomas Leland, Dr Thomas Campbell (1733–95) being the chief (*ibid.* I, 223–4; III, 441–2). He made his own explorations among the unpublished papers of Strafford, of which transcriptions in his hand are among the MSS at Sheffield (Bk 27d).

[3] This may be Burke's *Abridgment of English History*, undertaken for Dodsley seven years before (see above, letter of [March 1763], p. 164). More probably it is the work begun at about this time on the *Laws against Popery in Ireland*, of which fragments are published in *Works* [Bohn], VI, 5–48; [Little, Brown], VI, 299–360. A MS copy of ch. 2 of this piece, considerably fuller than the version published, is among the Rockingham MSS at Sheffield (R 103). In the previous year Burke had composed a statement of the grievances of the Irish Catholics. When in 1778 a bill for their relief was passed by the Irish Parliament, Curry wrote Burke (letter of 18 August, printed in

and In the hands of the Public, for I am persuaded, that as your Intention was the Public Service, and Advantage, the Execution, and Event will be Every way Answerable. Mr Charles O Connor[1] is Extremely Obliged to You for the Kind Letter you lately Sent him. He Loves You Almost as much as I do; But, you must know, I will Allow Nobody but Mress Burke, and my Worthy and dear freind Dr Nugent, to Love You Quite as much. Pray Present my best Respects, and Affection to them; and in order to Tempt You to throw away a few minutes in Writing to me Soon, I beg you to believe most Assuredly, that no One Can have more Pleasure in hearing from You, than

Dear Sir,
Your most Obedient
And Affectionate
Humble Servant
JOHN CURRY

Dublin.
June 8th
1765

DR JOSEPH FENN SLEIGH *to* EDMUND BURKE—17 *June* 1765

Source: Fitzwilliam MSS (Sheffield).

In the latter part of 1763 Burke's friend Dr Joseph Fenn Sleigh had introduced to him a young painter, James Barry (1741–1806), who was attempting to make his way in Dublin. Sleigh hoped that Burke would help a countryman of talent. Burke welcomed the opportunity. He encouraged Barry to cross to England, and there found him work with James Stuart (1713–88), the classical artist. He also introduced him to the leading painters of the capital, and later, with the assistance of Will Burke, sent him to Italy to study.

Corke June 17. 1765

Dear Burke,

It gives me much pleasure to find by your encouragement of Mr Barry that you partly approve of the judgement I formed of him and it would

Corr. (1844), II, 237–8): 'That address and petition which you may remember you drew up and left with me, in the year 1764, was found by us here so excellent a performance in every respect, and that it set forth our grievances in so affecting a manner, that we happily resolved to begin our humble suit, by laying it before our viceroy in due form, and requesting he would transmit it to be laid before his majesty; which we are assured was done, and made such an impression as was, in a great measure, productive of what has since followed, far beyond expectation.'

[1] Charles O'Conor (1710–91), Irish antiquary. He had written Burke 25 April a long letter dealing with revolts among the Catholic peasants of Munster in the early 1760's.

give me still more to hear from yourself what chance you think he has of improving those marks of genius he seems to have, and whether you think Italy would not forward him.—He acknowledges in every letter to me the numberless obligations he lies under to you.

I have been astonished at the number of discoveries in antiquities in Stuart's Athens.[1]—What sagacity does he display in the investigating of truth among what seemed before insuperable difficulties?—It is surprising how easy every thing is to him—Spence's accounting for the insignia of Eurus seems to be more just than Stuarts.[2]

You will excuse my breaking in upon your serious hours of employment, when I tell you the principal end is to assure you I shall always retain the sincerest wishes for your welfare and happiness—

JOSEPH FENN SLEIGH

To CHARLES TOWNSHEND—25 *June* 1765

Source: MS The Duke of Buccleuch. *Endorsed:* Mr Burke | Recd June 26th 1765 | Ansd—June 27th.

Burke told Mason that he had never had more than a slight acquaintance with Charles Townshend until 'long after' the break with Hamilton (see above, letter of [*post* 29 May 1765], p. 197). For a time it seemed possible that Townshend was to be the patron to take Hamilton's place. He was appointed Paymaster-General 8 June in Grenville's government, but was not involved in its fall. He wrote Burke 23 June concerning his political hopes: 'my only wish is that some means may be found of forming an Administration...led by men of Talents, acting under the countenance and Superintendency of Mr Pitt.... I had rather remain as I am, than pass to any station of power, until things have taken some settlement, and the traces of the late unwise and Sudden changes have been effaced...by a series of more temperate and conciliatory measures.'

Dear Sir

I was not so fortunate as to receive your very obliging Letter until this morning. I wrote a word or two to you from Grosvenor Square[3] whither I went yesterday in hopes of meeting you. Independent of the consideration of your health and of another motive more selfish, I am no wise concerned, that you are not in Town at present. The Scene so far as I can judge of it would not please you a whit the better for your

[1] *Antiquities of Athens Measured and Delineated* by J[ames] S[tuart] and N[icholas] R[evett]. 4 vols. London, 1762–1816. Burke was a subscriber to the work, and reviewed the first volume enthusiastically in the *Annual Register* for 1763.

[2] Joseph Spence (1699–1768) in the thirteenth dialogue of his *Polymetis: or, an enquiry concerning the agreement between the works of the Roman Poets and the remains of the Antient Artists*, London, 1747, comments upon a bas-relief of Eurus; Stuart and Revett's remarks on the same bas-relief are in their third chapter.

[3] Where Townshend lived.

seeing it in a nearer point of View.[1] Mr Pitts stile of acting may be very noble, but it certainly has not been very pleasing. I found, for the few hours I was in Town this morning, most people who used to be tolerably well informed, entirely at a Loss, and not very well satisfied that they were so. Mr P. has very little consulted the leading men in opposition; and both the D. of Newcastle and the Devonshire Set are grievously offended, not only at the real want of confidence, but at the want of respect, in not preserving in the Eyes of the world, the least appearances of it. They have been very little, if at all consulted, with regard to any part of the arrangement; and if one may prognosticate their future Conduct from their present Temper, this new administration may be, (still supposing it should ever rise beyond a project), falls short of that Stability, which the material and the Architect seem to promise; and the king may, after having sacrificed some of his Dignity in order to purchase quiet and firmness to his Government, find it necessary to make new sacrifices of himself and of others. You know that P. would not go beyond his *outline* without Lord Temple. This day they were to fill it up;[2] and I understood that Ld Bristol[3] went to St James's with them. Every one expected, that this mornings work would have been a final Settlement; but by what I hear, Lord Temple and Pitt differed; and their difference has left every thing still in uncertainty.[4] The D. of Grafton[5] was offerd to be secretary of State or Chamberlain, but I hear he has refused both. I have seen so few people this day, that I hardly know how to risque this sort of triffling news. You have undoubtedly much better; but yet as I have known myself sometimes mistaken in such an imagination, I venture it; especially as I know that if you have not a great deal of Patience, you have a sufficient stock of good nature; and that you can forgive even those who tire you; and that, I confess, the last Effort of Human Virtue. The Weather continuing fine, I have good hopes, that your Cough will not hold. Be so good, to let my anxiety about you give me so much importance, as to intitle me to ask

[1] Pitt had had audiences with the King on 19 and 22 June. After the second he wrote to Lord Temple: 'things have advanced considerably....Upon the whole, I augur much good, as far as intentions go...' (*Grenville Papers*, III, 61). The King was to see Lord Temple and offer him the Treasury.

[2] Temple saw the King on 25 June and refused to take office.

[3] George William Hervey, 2nd Earl of Bristol (1721–75). He was a follower of Pitt. He was not present at the audience of 25 June.

[4] Pitt saw the King on 26 June and declined to come into office, giving as his reason Temple's refusal to serve.

[5] Augustus Henry Fitzroy, 3rd Duke of Grafton (1735–1811). When Cumberland was first entrusted with the task of forming a new administration he offered Grafton the post of Secretary of State or First Lord of Trade 'with the Cabinet Council' (Cumberland's memorandum; Albemarle, *Memoirs of Rockingham*, I, 194). Grafton replied: 'no inducement could lead me to take a Court employment' (Grafton, *Autobiography*, p. 43).

for a line, as soon as you can, to Let me know something of your health. I am sincerely concerned about it and with the utmost Esteem and Gratitude

Dear Sir
your most obedient
and affectionate humble
Servant
E BURKE

Chiswick 25th June 1765.

EDMUND *and* WILLIAM BURKE *to* CHARLES O'HARA—4 [*July* 1765]

Source: O'Hara MSS. Printed Hoffman, pp. 315–17.
Burke dated this letter 'Thursday 4th June', but nothing like the political situation it describes existed 4 June (a Tuesday) or before the end of the month. The date of 4 July (a Thursday) is clearly established by a letter of Charles Townshend to his brother, printed in *Grenville Papers*, III, 67–9.

[Edmund begins]

My dear Sir, I never received a Letter from you which gave me more joy than your last; for having calculated, that I ought to have heard from you a good deal earlier, I began to apprehend something for your health; and my fears were confirmed by your appearing not [to] be quite so well as usual when you left us. I do declare, I do not think there is a man living for whose welfare I should be more heartily sollicitous than yours. We were making a sort of Scale of our affections yesterday, and we were unanimous in that opinion. For Gods sake attend a little to yourself, and remember, that though fifty is a good age for business, it will not bear the kind of riotous Life that you lead. Things here are still in confusion. You know, that by the defection of Lord Temple to his Brother George,[1] the minority is divided; Pitt will not part from his family;[2] but declares much obligation and gratitude to the King; and a resolution in consequence not to oppose. Mr Pitt having declined all share in the Negotiation, the Whigs are resolved to try whether they cannot make up an administration by themselves.[3] The King has left the Terms and the men entirely to themselves and protests himself

[1] George Grenville and Temple had quarrelled in October 1761, when Temple had resigned with Pitt but Grenville had remained in office with Newcastle and Bute. They were reconciled on 22 May 1765, and remained politically connected until Grenville's death.

[2] From his brothers-in-law, Temple and Grenville.

[3] On 30 June the Opposition leaders met at Claremont, Newcastle's seat in Surrey, to consider whether they could undertake to form an Administration. Opinions were divided, but on 1 July Newcastle, Rockingham and Conway saw Cumberland and agreed to accept office.

willing to acquiesce in any thing, but the present administration. They proposed last Night, that the King should send for Townshend, who is in the Country, and not in the best state of health to desire him immediately to come to Town. They intend to offer him the Chancellorship of the Exchequer with an addition of Salary, and a proper measure, of power, suitable to the place.[1] This scheme was yesterday sent to Richmond to the K. and I suppose a messenger went that Night to Atterbury.[2] So that unless it met some remora at the first suggestion at Court, Townshend will be up to night. You will hear that Lord Temple flew off on account of Lord Bute; but do not believe a Syllable of it.

[Will begins]

Your Letter was indeed equally grateful to us all. Ned could not on your own account wish more to see you just now that I do. But I, with whom our interest weighs more than with him, for their sakes, can wish more ardently than he, that some chance had detained you here till now, if that had been the case, I verily believe some good would have turned up to us both, but for want of such a friend as you to forward, to ripen the little budding hopes that arrive, get birth today and dye tomorrow, nothing will be. Lord John Cavendish,[3] possibly from some things dropt by yourself, has mentioned us both as fit men to be employed to Lord Rockingham, who received it well, but what then? We have not a friend in the world to keep the impression alive. Something will I hope however turn up. A Dieu you shall have your act and the customs.[4]

[Edmund begins] We ought not to forget how much we are obliged to Fitzherbert[5] for his most friendly and zealous, and indeed well managed and elegant recommendations of us, to all this Batch of people. I cannot express to you, how much and how well he has done. Lord Rockingham went down to Townshend; but as neither are yet returned, though it is now near ten at Night, we know not the effect of that

[1] Before 1766 the Chancellor of the Exchequer, unless he was also First Lord of the Treasury, was not a member of the Cabinet.

[2] Adderbury, Townshend's seat in Oxfordshire.

[3] (1732–96), M.P. for Knaresborough.

[4] Will is promising to send O'Hara printed copies of Acts of Parliament. O'Hara reminded him of his promise in his letter of 30 July (printed Hoffman, pp. 322–3).

[5] William Fitzherbert (*c.* 1712–72), connected politically with Rockingham and the Cavendishes. Dr Johnson once drew his character: 'There was (said he) no sparkle, no brilliancy in Fitzherbert; but I never knew a man who was so generally acceptable. He made every body quite easy, overpowered nobody by the superiority of his talents, made no man think worse of himself by being his rival, seemed always to listen, did not oblige you to hear much from him, and did not oppose what you said' (*Life of Johnson*, III, 148–9).

Negotiation.[1] It is certain, that if they act wisely, they cannot fail to make up a lasting administration. I call taking in Lord Bute, or at least not quarrelling with him, and enlarging their Bottom by taking in the Tories, and all the men of Business of the house of commons not listed against them, acting wisely. As to the Ld Lieut, that totally depends on the other arrangements; this only I can say for certain; that Let the arrangement be what it will, Lord Weymouth may go if he thinks proper by means of the D. of Portland.[2] I am much hurried and it is late; Next Saturday I shall enlarge on all the points you mention in your Letter. My humble respects to the Primate.[3] You see I am little affected by Hamilton. However I should not have been sorry had you called on the parties we first mentiond. Adieu my dear Sir

your ever affectionate friend
E B.

Thursday. 4th June.

To CHARLES O'HARA—9 *July* 1765

Source: O'Hara MSS. Printed Hoffman, pp. 317–20.

My dear Sir,

In this immense stir and uncertainty of affairs, I know you cannot be unconcerned even at Nymphsfield; though you, whose mind, gaming and politicks cannot disturb in Almacks and Arthurs,[4] will hardly be driven out of your Course on the Shore of the atlantick ocean. But if politicks do not find the way to you, to disturb your domestick and rural happiness, your friendships will still engage you to think a little of those, whose ambition, or necessities oblige them to live in the Storm: you have friends high enough to be actuated by the one, and low enough to be impelled by the other; and if the latter are the least considerable, they are the most innocent, and, I am sure, as much therefore, in your thoughts and wishes as the former.

[1] Townshend refused to be either Chancellor of the Exchequer or Secretary of State.

[2] William Henry Cavendish Bentinck, 3rd Duke of Portland (1738–1809), later a friend and correspondent of Burke. Weymouth had married his sister.

[3] Richard Robinson (*c.* 1708–94) became Archbishop of Armagh after the death of Archbishop George Stone in December 1764.

[4] London clubs. O'Hara had some reputation as a gambler and sportsman. A local historian speaks of the many stories of 'his wonderful horses Arpinus and Sejanus, with their silver shoes; his Irish servant Johnny Cuffe, who was more than a match for all the English turfites and jockeys; his fabulous feats of horsemanship, such as the jump from the precipice of Knocknashee, and his successes, but, still more, his losses by gambling...' (T. O'Rourke, *History...of the Parishes of Ballysadare and Kilvarnet*, p. 399).

After several Consultations and much irresolution, the principal people who are to compose the new administration kiss hands tomorrow. The delay was chiefly owing to Charles Townshend; who, in this affair, acts a part which time, and circumstances concealed at present may shew to have been a proper one;[1] but which as far as I can look into the motives, conduct, and consequences of it, gives me no satisfaction. His actions, which seem never to have been influenced by his most wonderful abilities, are grown of a much worse complexion, (because they are less his own,) since his reconciliation and close connexion with Lord Townshend.[2] This connection, which ought in the order of Nature and common justice, to be for the advantage of the younger Brother, has been totally carried on for the interest, and been governed by the Spirit of the elder.[3] It has drawn tears of indignation and grief from me, to see the manner in which they proceed. The party coming in who would have derived from, and given dignity to Charles Townshend, by his management, has been hurt very considerably; and they in return have put him backward in the estimation, of a great part at least, of the world. His situation and abilities gave him great importance; he might have, and was sollicited to chuse, his place; and he might have had it with much importance, and much honour; and *there*, (but not where he is,) might be in a capacity of correcting the Errors, which certainly exist in this System. But his Brother, hating and hated by, the Duke of Cumberland;[4] and probably held down besides, by some concealed engagements with Mr Greenville, and wishing, as I know he did, for the Lieutenancy of Ireland, (which it is not clear that he could get) has kept Charles from taking the Seals or the Chancellorship of the Exchequer, or standing forward in this new administration. He proposes indeed, and engages to support, but, *I am told*, will not come forward into any of the active Situations. I say I am told; because I saw the two brothers this morning, just as they were going to Court; they talked in a dissatisfyed manner, but I imagined, knowing Lord T.'s object, and the necessity of pleasing Charles at this time, that they would have settled every thing at the Queens House.[5] I proposed to see them on the return but missed them;

[1] Because of the weakness of the Rockingham Administration.

[2] George Townshend (1724–1807), 4th Viscount Townshend, an Army officer and Lieutenant-General of the Ordnance. He was Charles Townshend's elder brother.

[3] Charles wrote to Lord Townshend on 4 July that he had told Rockingham he could not enter the new Cabinet without consulting his brother (*Grenville Papers*, III, 68).

[4] The real head of the Rockingham administration. It is said that Townshend had displeased Cumberland by outspoken criticisms on the campaigns in Flanders during the War of the Austrian Succession (C. V. F. Townshend, *The Military Life of George, first Marquess Townshend*, 1901, pp. 128–9). Walpole speaks of their mutual hatred (*Memoirs*, I, 18).

[5] On the site of what is now Buckingham Palace.

I tell you what I heard. However, the arrangement proposed on his declining, is Lord Rockingham the Treasury D. of Grafton and Conway[1] Secretaries of State. Dowdswell[2] Chancellor of the Exhequer. The other Lines are not, at present, worth knowing; These are principal. Conway had engaged to be Chancellor of the Exchequer, but is got off of it, at his own desire. I am not clear whether he will even stick to the seals.[3] But next Gazette will settle all. So much for the ambitious. Now for the honest Necessitous. Will and I are down on their Lists. And I hope and believe will be attended to. Words cannot paint to you the indefatigable, unconquerable Zeal and friendship of FitzHerbert to serve us; I shall give you an history of his good or ill success by the next post. In the mean time thank God appearances are tolerable. The young Gentlemen[4] will Learn Classical Elegance and honest agriculture with you; in both which I envy them; whilst we are tagging at the heels of factions. But they too will be so engaged; but with better abilities, and in more honourable Stations, with better success; but not with more honest intentions. Pray continue to love us, who value you as much as any man ought to be valued. Oh! What a loss to us, that you are not here for a few hours! I never felt the loss of you more than now; no not the day you left me. Your Ld Lieutenant not fixed. I fancy Lord Hertford.[5]

Tuesday 9th July 1765.

You go to Rich hill.[6] Pray present my most affectionate Duty to my Lord Primate. You will tell Sr Septimus[7] that I am most sensible of his kind partiality to me. My Respects to Mr Robinson.[8] I remember a saying of my Lord Primates that we had not in Ireland the materials of a Nation. Assure his Grace that we are not in a Condition to supply that deficiency from England. Shall we never see men? You are narrow in Ireland; but you know what you would be at. If you find my friend Dean Barrington[9] say I am a sad Dog for to him, I am so, and he will be goodnatured enough to contradict you.

[1] Henry Seymour Conway (1719–95).

[2] William Dowdeswell (1721–75), later Burke's friend and correspondent.

[3] He became Secretary of State for the Southern Department and Minister in the House of Commons.

[4] Charles and William O'Hara.

[5] Francis Seymour Conway, 1st Earl of Hertford (1719–94), Conway's elder brother. He was Lord Lieutenant of Ireland July 1765 to August 1766.

[6] Where the Primate was living (James Stuart, *Historical Memoirs of the City of Armagh*, Newry, 1819, p. 445).

[7] Sir Septimus Robinson (1710–65), brother of the Primate.

[8] Probably William Robinson (1705–85), brother of the Primate.

[9] Benjamin Barrington (*c.* 1710–*c.* 1774), Dean of Armagh 1764–8.

To CHARLES O'HARA—11 *July* 1765

Source: O'Hara MSS. Printed Hoffman, p. 320.

My dear Sir, My Letter by last post was a long one. This will be very short. The Papers shew you the ministerial Changes, in which you will be pleased to see your friend Conway in possession of the Seals. I have got an employment of a kind humble enough; but which may be worked into some sort of consideration, or at least advantage; Private Secretary to Lord Rockingham,[1] who has the reputation of a man of honour and integrity; and with whom, they say, it is not difficult to live.[2] Will is strongly talked of for a better thing.[3] All my Speculations are in my last Letter. Adieu my dear Sir, Affectionately yours

E BURKE.

July 11th 1765

To DAVID GARRICK—16 *July* 1765

Source: MS Victoria and Albert Museum. Printed Garrick, *Corr.* I, 189–90.

This is the earliest surviving letter of Burke to David Garrick, though there is evidence of the two men being acquainted as early as 1758. (See Straus, *Robert Dodsley*, p. 144; Donald C. Bryant, *Edmund Burke and his Literary Friends* [Washington University Studies, new series, 9], St Louis, 1939, pp. 136–53.)

My dear Garrick, You have made me perfectly happy by the friendly and obliging satisfaction you are so good to express on this little gleam of prosperity which has at length fallen on my fortune. My situation is, for the present, very agreeable; and I do not at all despair, of its becoming in time solidly advantageous. So far at least, I thank God, the designs of my Enemies, who not long since made a desperate Stroke at my Fortune, my Liberty, and my reputation, (*all! Hell kite! all at a Swoop*,) have failed of their Effect; and their implacable and unprovoked malice has been disappointed.

[1] The post of private secretary to the First Lord of the Treasury was an unofficial one, and its status depended on the characters of the men concerned and their relationship to each other: the private secretary might be a mere amanuensis or a confidential man of business to his principal. The post was unpaid, but it was customary to reward the holder with a sinecure. Rockingham neglected to do this for Burke, though some money was certainly paid to him. Among the Rockingham MSS at Sheffield are several notebooks (R 15) recording secret service payments. In one is entered under date of 25 November 1765 'Mr. Burke on Acct. £150', to which is added an explanatory note in Rockingham's hand: 'for obtaining various Informations and Materials relative to the Trades and Manufactures.' Another entry, under date of 19 April 1766, names 'Mr. Burke on acct for obtaining various informations and materials relative to Trade &c. £100'.

[2] Burke entered upon his secretarial duties at once. Professor Ross Hoffman has called my attention to a copy in Burke's hand of a letter of Rockingham to Lord Shelburne, dated 11 July 1765 (Rockingham MSS, R1–245).

[3] William Burke was appointed under-Secretary of State to General Conway. It was an official position and formally ranked higher than Edmund's office. But Edmund was nearer the centre of power and had more possibilities of influence.

Your attention to my Brothers affair is in the Strain of your usual good nature. There too the impotence of the attack was equal to the Baseness of it. The Commissioners of the Customs, who will not readily believe him to be a guilty, because they know him to be a very meritorious, officer, have written some days ago in the strongest terms, assuring him of their perfect satisfaction in his Conduct, and promising him a most effectual support in the continuance of it.[1] So that if the wickedness of those Rascals has not made too deep an impression on a mind, whose only fault is its oversensibility, he has nothing to fear from them, whatever some of them may have to apprehend from the Natural consequences of their own Villainy; and he will have hereafter no occasion I hope for the interposition of good Offices from either of us; though with yours he shall Certainly be made acquainted; and I am convinced he will have a proper sense of them, for I assure you (I will speak though he is my Brother) that he is a very honest young man, and a person every way worthy of your friendship.

Will Burke is much obliged to you, for your good opinion of his readiness to serve you on every occasion. He tells me that the best book he ever met with on the subject of the English Islands, and indeed in general on the Trade of our Plantations, is a little French work called *L'Histoire des Antilles Angloises*.[2] With regard to the Queries we might, so far as it is prudent for you or us to go, satisfye you much better, if we had the pleasure of a little previous discourse together. What day will you eat a morsel with us, in Town; or spend together a few cheerful hours in an Evening? Pray tell us, for we long for it I assure you. You have heard of Wills Promotion, and I make no doubt you are glad of it. He is sincerely desirous of your good opinion. You little Horace, you *Lepidissime Homuncio*[3] when will you call to see your Mecenas atavis,[4] and praise this administration of Cavendishes and Rockinghams in Ode, and abuse their Enemies in Epigram? Though your performances may be short surely they will not make your salary so.

[1] Neither Richard Burke's affair nor Garrick's part in it has been traced. Customs records for the plantations in the period before 1767 were kept in the Custom House, London, which was burned in 1814 (C. M. Andrews, *Guide to the Materials for American History to 1783 in the Public Record Office of Great Britain*, Washington, 1914, II, 113). A phrase in a letter of O'Hara to Richard of 25 March [1766] suggests that part of the opposition he met may have been from General Melville, Governor of the island: 'A Scotch Governor is a damnd thing to deal with.' But a letter Melville wrote home 28 May 1766 sounds as if he were at least neutral, and perhaps disposed to protect his Receiver General against a hostile Assembly. The Governor asked: '. . . when a New Assembly is called, whether I am to insist on the Taxes raised being payed into the Hands of the Receiver General as His Commission is thought to Import, and which has been already very strongly and Unanimously Objected to. . .' (Public Record Office, C.O. 101/1).

[2] [G. M. Butel-Dumont], *Histoire et Commerce des Antilles Angloises*, 1758.

[3] See Suetonius, *Vita Horatii*.

[4] Horace, *Odes*, I, i, I.

I should grieve to send our excellent Fitzherbert to the Ape and Monkey Climes upon any Terms.[1] You know and love him; but I assure you, untill we can talk some late matters over, you even you, can have no adequate Idea, of the worth of that man. It is no small satisfaction to find, that, if some men are capable of making the basest return to affectionate faithful, and long, long service, and if they can endeavour to asperse you whose *conscience* bears the most faithful witness to your integrity, yet that there are others who without any previous services whatsoever, generously, disinterestedly and nobly forward and aid their friends upon every occasion. When we meet you shall hear more of what you have an heart that can relish. Adieu my Dear Garrick, and believe me ever

your most affectionate and obliged
humble Servant
E BURKE.

Q. Anne Street
July 16. 1765.

I did not get your Letter until 1 o'Clock this morning. Mrs Burke and I join in our affectionate Compliments to Mrs Garrick.[2]

To DAVID GARRICK—⟨25⟩ *July* [1765]

Source: MS Harvard Library.

A joint letter of Edmund and Will Burke. Edmund's portion is dated only 'Thursday'; Will's (here omitted) has a date probably intended to be 'July 25' though it looks as much like 'July 22'. As a reply of Garrick's intervened between this and Burke's to Garrick of 16 July, this could easily be as late as the 25th, which was a Thursday.

My dear Garrick Many thanks for your kind Letter and your sensible admonitions. Nothing shall intrude to spoil a party in which you are engaged. Will you and Mrs Garrick favour Mrs Burke and me to dine here at half an hour after four? (if you come half an hour sooner the better) next Monday. You will meet FitzHerbert and you will make us happy.[3] Most affectionately Dear Garrick

your friend
and humble Servant
E BURKE

Thursday.

[1] Garrick in his reply says: 'I am told for certain that he goes to Barbadoes.' Fitzherbert was, however, appointed to the Board of Trade, and stayed in England. The phrase 'Ape and Monkey Climes' is from *Dunciad*, I, 233.

[2] *Née* Eva Maria Veigel (1724–1822).

[3] Garrick's letter had asked Burke to 'make me as rich a Holly day as you can and desire Mr Fitzherbert to Emerge from Politicking for a few hours only to make me happy' (MS undated, Forster Collection, Victoria and Albert Museum).

CHARLES O'HARA *to* EDMUND *and* WILLIAM BURKE—30 *July* [1765]

Source: Fitzwilliam MSS (Sheffield). Printed Hoffman, pp. 322-23.
Addressed: To Edd Burke Esqr | Queen Anne Street | Cavendish Square | London. *Postmarked:* Country | Boyle 7|AV

O'Hara had congratulated Burke 19 July (printed Hoffman, pp. 320–2) on his appointment as Rockingham's private secretary: 'Ld Rockingham is the properest man for you in the world. Extreme good sense, of very gentle manners, and what pride there may be is of a sort never to offend.' He referred to the difficulty Burke might have from his existing arrangement with Townshend: 'I understand from Yours, that you stil go on with him, tho you belong to Ld Rockingham. This may grow a nice card to play....' On 30 July, having had the news of Will Burke's appointment as under-Secretary to Henry Seymour Conway, he wrote again to both Burkes.

Nymphsfield 30 July

I greet you both with sincere congratulation; Will, with all thy noise, etourderie and abuse, thou art now connected with the gentlest manners, and the best heart that ever approachd the Ministerial rank. I hope you'll neither of you catch from the other. Your noise woud make a strange riot in Conways character, and you dont want either his honesty or his good nature. Edmund you are little less lucky than Will. You have pride to deal with, but much softend by manner: and exceeding good sense, but you must feed it, for it cant feed itself. I dare say Conway has long since talkd you over to him. I shall always join with you in most sincere regard and esteem for Mr Fitz Herbert, I feel a share in the obligation, and in the gratitude which shoud accompany that feel....

To CHARLES LLOYD—1 *October* 1765

Source: Grenville Papers, III, 86–7.

Charles Lloyd (1735–73), George Grenville's private secretary, had been appointed by Grenville Receiver of the Revenues of Gibraltar. Lord Rockingham on taking office had dismissed several Grenville appointees, usually in order to restore their predecessors. Lloyd, dismissed from his office as Receiver of Revenues, had protested, pointing out that this could not favour his immediate predecessor, who was dead. The dismissal convinced him of Rockingham's hostility to himself, and he tried through Burke to make sure he would not be dismissed from a second office, that of Paymaster General of the Band of Gentlemen Pensioners (letter of [*ante* 1 October] at Sheffield). Burke wrote to reassure him.

Queen Ann Street, October 1, 1765.

Dear Sir, I hope you will do me the justice to believe that my long delay in answering your letter did in no respect arise from a disregard to your character, or an indifference to the success of your desires. A good deal of business, together with some returns of the same complaint I suffered under when you saw me, were the real and only causes of a delay, which I confess I cannot entirely excuse, but which you will have the goodness to forgive.

On communicating the contents of your letter to Lord Rockingham, his Lordship seemed much surprised to find that you think you have *already* received some marks of his displeasure, as you have used the expression of a fear of *further* marks of it. His Lordship thought you had been sufficiently apprised of the true cause of your removal from the office of Receiver of Gibraltar; this change having been made in consequence of a general arrangement which his Lordship and his friends apprehended to be required from them by the rules of strict justice in favour of former sufferers; and by no means from any particular dislike or resentment to you. Many persons suffered from the same disposition whose persons Lord Rockingham valued, and whose situations he sincerely pitied.

As to the expression in my letter to which you have excepted,[1] I must beg leave to explain myself, and to assure you that it related to the substance of the question, and not at all to your motives in asking it.

It was meant to express the impropriety of giving any answer to it, from the obvious consequences which must have resulted from an answer, and not from the smallest intention of reflecting upon you, for your having desired satisfaction upon a matter concerning which you must naturally be very anxious.[2]

I am with great esteem, and very real good wishes, &c., E. BURKE.

To PATRICK NAGLE—14 *October* 1765

Source: MS Osborn Collection. Printed *New Monthly Magazine*, XIV, 383–4.

My dear Sir, Since I heard from you, our little party at Queen Ann Street has been reinforced by a person who loves you as well as I do, poor Richard of Grenada. He left that Island in no very good state of health, and after a great deal of vexation from, but also after a great and perfect Triumph over his Enemies, a set of the greatest Villians that ever existed. He has a leave of absence for six Months; and is I think already as completely reestablished in health, strength and spirits as we

[1] Lloyd's letter, to which Burke was replying, says: 'I cannot conceal from you that the word *Insidious* which was the Epithet given to my Representation has given me the greatest uneasyness...'.

[2] Lloyd did actually lose both his posts.

could wish. We all join in giving you joy on the occasion of our friend Kattys match;[1] and only wish her that she may be as happy in an husband as her mother was;[2] and much as we regard her we cannot wish her better. Pray remember our hearty congratulations to the young Couple.

I am sincerely concerned for the match that Garret Atty was so unfortunate as to make;[3] and did from the beginning expect no better Issue of it, in a Country circumstanced as ours is; Assure my Uncle, that there is no one Step on earth in my power that I would not gladly take to give ease to his mind, which must be cruelly agitated; I most sincerely pity him; but I believe, when he reflects, how newly, and almost as a stranger I am come about these people, and knows the many industrious endeavours, which malice and envy, (very unprovoked indeed) have used to ruin me,[4] he will see, that so early a request to suspend the operation of the Laws, upon my bare word, against the finding of a jury of the greatest County of the Kingdom, and that upon the most unpopular point in the world, could have no other effect, than to do me infinite prejudice, without the least possibility of succeeding in the object I aimed at. This I am sure, your own good sense will point out to both of you, and will satisfye My Uncle, that no vain and timorous delicacy, but the real conviction I have of the inefficacy of the application with regard to him, prevents my taking a warm and active part in this affair. My Brother tells me, that poor Barret[5] is likely to do well in Grenada; He is industrious and active; He must indeed struggle with some difficulty and much Labour at first; but it is the road and the only road to an establishment. It is now time for me to make some enquiry about my young friend your Grandson Ned.[6] I have really been so hurried with the many changes which have happend in my affairs and those of my friends for some time past, that I have not had leisure to enquire much about him. My Brother and I will consult some proper

[1] Catherine Nagle, daughter of Uncle Patrick, married (1765) Michael Courtenay (d. 1772) of Mallow.

[2] Patrick Nagle married (1715) Ellen O'Donovan.

[3] Burke's phrasing is discreet. Garrett Nagle (b. *c.* 1728), eldest son of Edmund's uncle Athanasius Nagle, had abducted the Protestant heiress Elizabeth Forward (*c.* 1744–1817), niece of John Hely Hutchinson. He was fortunate not to be hanged for the offence. He conformed to the Established Church 2 June 1765, and again 19 January 1766 (Egerton MS 77).

[4] One attempt of the kind has often been described. According to Lord Charlemont (James Caulfeild, 1st Earl of Charlemont, 1728–99), soon after Burke had been appointed Rockingham's secretary, the Duke of Newcastle chanced to hear that the new man was connected with Roman Catholics and might himself be dangerous. He told Rockingham of his fears. Rockingham summoned Burke, who was able to convince his patron of his absolute loyalty (Hardy, *Memoirs of Charlemont*, II, 281–3).

[5] Not identified.

[6] Edmund Nagle (1757–1830) was the son of Patrick Nagle's son Edmund (d. 1763). He entered the Navy in 1770 and ultimately rose to the rank of Admiral.

method of having him sent to Sea under honest and goodnatured management; give me some account of him, and whether you still continue of opinion that this way of Life will be advisable for him. If your Sentiments are the same they formerly were upon this Article, I hope you had an eye to the Sea in the Education he has since had; we may in a short time compleat it here. You cannot think how happy you would make us by writing often, and being as particular as you can about any thing that concerns you. Thank my Cousin Garrett for his kind concern in my affairs; whenever he has any account to make up he will settle it with you; By this you have my Letter of Attorney empowering you to act for me.[1] If you should see Counsellor Murphy[2] and the Colonel,[3] make my hearty compliments to them. Once more I beg to hear speedily from you. Jane and Dick are truly yours so is, My dear Uncle, your afectionate friend

E BURKE

Octr 14th 1765.

I saw Dick Hennessy here some time ago. His family is well,[4]—his Wife ready to fall to pieces.[5] I recollect that Garrett in his Life time used to allow to a poor Neighbour of yours, some Mault or some such small present at Christmas, let it be continued to him, and charge it to my Account. Jenny intended as much more; Let him have it either in that way or any other which he may like better. And if poor Thelpot[6] be alive You will direct that he should have a dozen of Port or some good

[1] Burke seems to be referring to a rather complicated property arrangement which has offered one of the stock puzzles to his biographers. Garrett Burke, Edmund's elder brother, had died in April 1765. His chief bequest to Edmund was an estate at Clogher, formerly the property of a branch of the Nagle family. The Nagles as Roman Catholics were legally incompetent to buy land or to hold a lease for a longer period than 31 years, and had undoubtedly requested Garrett Burke as a friendly Protestant to help them mitigate the consequences of these disabilities. By a complex legal procedure involving a 'Protestant discoverer', Garrett had obtained a long lease from the Nagles' landlord and had himself given his relatives new leases for 31 years or less. Garrett's death left Edmund with the responsibilities which his brother had assumed. These may have been complicated by private family arrangements, the nature of which is not known. In any event, until 1790 when he disposed of his interest in the estate to another friendly Protestant, Edmund Nagle ('grandson Ned' of this letter), Burke was landlord to his relatives. He appointed as his agent to run the Clogher estate his cousin Garrett Nagle, Uncle Patrick's son.

[2] Probably David Murphy (d. 1775) of Killarney, a lawyer who had written Burke from Dublin 16 August 1764.

[3] Probably Colonel Richard Murphy, apparently a relation of Counsellor Murphy. Both are mentioned in Mrs Morgan John O'Connell's *Last Colonel of the Irish Brigade*, London, 1892.

[4] Richard Hennessy (1720–1800) had married in 1763 Ellen, widow of James Hennessy of Brussels, who was a daughter of Margaret Nagle and James Barrett. He later settled in Cognac and founded the famous distillery which still bears his name.

[5] To give birth to a child. Her son James (1765–1843) was born in Brussels 11 October (Richard Hayes, *Biographical Dictionary of Irishmen in France*, Dublin, 1949, pp. 121–2).

[6] Not identified.

strong wine at Christmas, and now and then a bottle or two before that time. You will advance the money to Cousin Garret and place it to my account. Until they can be had to Dublin be so good to be very careful of the Papers in your hands.

CHARLES O'HARA *to* EDMUND BURKE—22 *November* [1765]

Source: Fitzwilliam MSS (Sheffield).

Earl Verney had long had a plan of bringing Will Burke into Parliament. As the time approached for carrying out the plan, Will himself felt that Edmund's abilities better deserved the seat, and he asked the Earl to tranfer his promise of support. Edmund with some misgivings accepted Will's sacrifice, and began preparing to enter Parliament. One essential step was to make sure that the record was clear as to the resignation of the Irish pension. O'Hara consulted the records and reported to Burke on the situation.

Dublin 22d Novr

My Dear Sir

I write to you from Lady Brandons[1] with the worst pen paper and ink that ever man was plagud with. I had got a return brought to the table of the assignments of pensions from last Session of Parliament. The dates the assignees and the considerations. In which is Edmund Burke Esqr during pleasure to Mathew Couthurst of Chancery Lane in the County of Middlesex Gent for the sum of 31 sterling during the continuance of said pension &c and by him assignd to Robt Jephson of Paulin Street &c for like sum. Soon after I got this I had yours, wherein you told me that you grew daily more and more indifferent about it. Last night I met Jephson for the first time at the Castle, with whom I had some conversation about it, for he became uneasy about the use which I meant to make of it.[2] I told him my aim was to let every body see that you had no pension and had not got any consideration for it. Immediately after I went home, and found your last, in consequence of which, I shall now shew the Office return to Ld Hertford and say some civil things from You. And I must I think be decided by what he says. And then I shall write to you again....

O'Hara, though he continued to be friendly with Hamilton, took pains to make Burke's position in the quarrel clear to persons in power. He had earlier, in a

[1] The Countess of Brandon, *née* Ellis Agar (*c.* 1709–89).

[2] Jephson's feelings about the pension are partly described in a letter he wrote Hely Hutchinson 26 September (Hist. MSS Comm. 12th Report, App., pt IX [*Donoughmore MSS*], pp. 257–8). He insists: 'It was not once, but fifty times; it was not by one person, but by ten; that Mr. Hamilton desired Mr. Burke should retain the pension...Mr Burke indeed has done me the justice to mention the earnestness and sincerity with which I laboured for an accommodation....'

letter of 19 July (printed Hoffman pp. 320–2), told Burke of his efforts to explain things to Henry Seymour Conway. He now saw Lord Hertford, transmitted to him a letter of Burke's, and said the 'civil things' Burke wanted said. Hertford was himself very civil, wrote of Burke in the most flattering terms (see his letter to O'Hara dated 14 December, enclosed in O'Hara's letter to Burke of 17 December, now at Sheffield), but did not grant the favour Burke especially wished of striking the pension from the list.

To [GREY COOPER]—10 *December* 1765

Source: MS Public Record Office (S.P. 37/4/351–2).
Since this letter concerns Treasury business, it was probably addressed to Grey Cooper (*c.* 1726–1801), Secretary to the Treasury.

Dear Sir

I have laid Martinots Case before Lord Rockingham;[1] He wishes, that as the application was originally made at General Conways office, and that you can be better supplied there with every necessary Document, General Conway would himself Determine what shall be given to this unfortunate man, as of the Kings Bounty, by way of indemnification for his Losses; Lord Rockingham will be perfectly satisfied with whatever General Conway does in it, the General when he has made the Enquiries which he may think proper will himself speak to the King. The money for the Subsistance of the French Prisoners is to be paid to Lord Barrington;[2] Lord How[3] has been spoken to on the subject and is quite satisfied.

I am Dear Sir
yours sincerely
E BURKE

10th Decr 1765.

Please to look for the Precedent of the Letter which used to be written to the Lords.

[1] Jean François Martinot was captain of the *Marianne*, of Marseilles, 'which ship being stranded on the coast of Cornwall...the inhabitants seized the whole cargo, and stripped to their shirts the people on board, using them with great barbarity'. Martinot petitioned for redress. See *Calendar of Home Office Papers, 1760–65*, pp. 328, 447, 448; *ibid. 1766–69*, p. 4. A packet of papers relating to the case is among the Rockingham MSS (R 71) at Sheffield.

[2] William Wildman Barrington Shute, 2nd Viscount Barrington (1717–93). As Secretary at War he would receive payment from the French government for the subsistence of French prisoners the British had held during the war.

[3] Richard Howe, 4th Viscount Howe (1726–99). As Treasurer of the Navy he would be concerned with payments for French naval prisoners.

JAMES BARRY *to* EDMUND *and* WILLIAM BURKE
[*circa* 20 *December* 1765]

Source: Barry, *Works*, I, 34–6.

The editor of Barry's *Works* heads this letter 'Paris, without date'. It was certainly written after Barry's letter of 5 December 1765 (Barry, *Works*, I, 30–4; MS at Sheffield clearly dated): on 5 December Barry sent his greetings to Burke's brother Richard in London; here he says that Richard is with him in Paris. Barry here also sends his greetings to Lauchlin Macleane (*c.* 1728–78), who left Paris for London in mid-December (letter of Macleane to John Wilkes 13 December [Add. MS 30868, fol. 210]).

Edmund and Will in their new prosperity had carried out a plan long discussed of sending James Barry to France and Italy to train himself as a painter. Barry set forth from England in the latter part of October, and letters from both sides in the following weeks tell us of his enjoyment, and the Burkes' vicarious enjoyment, of his travels through France. He made his first long stop in Paris.

My dear Sirs,

I have since had but little time to myself to answer either of the kind letters I received from you by Mr Morison,[1] and now that I have sat down to it I could wish myself some excuse to defer it still longer. I am confounded to think what I shall say to so much and so unmerited kindness. Love and gratitude urge me on to expressions which I must lay aside to avoid the awkward situation of being detected in the language that is so common in the world, and which may be found in a person who has very little of what I think is in my bosom, when I remember what I owe you and the family whose friendship is alone what has counterpoised and sweetened the other circumstances of my life, which God knows have been disagreeable enough. Mr Richard Burke's arrival has, you may conceive, given me no small pleasure and advantage. Every day lays me under new obligations to him and to you; all that union which is so visible in the family is as manifest in your carriage towards me as it is in every thing else, insomuch, that when I mention kindness and generosity, I am at a loss to know on which of you I shall first lay my finger. What you say of me in your letter to Mr Richard is very flattering; yours and Mr Reynold's[2] good opinions must be no small argument to me of my own importance, which you will have no difficulty of believing, as you know but too well how ready my vanity is to catch

[1] Will Burke sent a letter to Barry 26 October, by way of 'Mr Morrison, secretary to the Duke of Richmond' (Barry, *Works*, I, 27); Richmond was at this time Ambassador at Paris.

[2] Joshua Reynolds (1723–92), to whom Burke had introduced Barry in London. According to Boswell (*Life of Johnson*, I, 477) Reynolds had been the first proposer of the Club founded in 1764, of which Johnson, Burke and Dr Nugent were among the original members. Malone said of Reynolds that at his death (in 1792) his friendship with Burke had lasted unbroken for thirty-four years (Prior, *Life of Malone*, p. 434). This would put their first meeting in 1758.

at any thing that may do me credit, and you must allow that it can no where meet with what is more grateful to it than in the present instance: to be at all thought of by such people is a stimulus that must oblige one to stretch every nerve to endeavour to merit it.

As soon as I can obtain permission I shall set about copying the Alexander I mentioned to you.[1] It will be more profitable to me to be about it than any thing else, and though you may not be inclined to keep it, you may give it to somebody or other. The academies are open at night only, so that copying that or any other picture will not interfere with my attendance there.

The varnished paper which Mr Richard Burke wrote to you of is to be had here, we did not know it then, and you will excuse the mentioning it to you. My most sincere love and respects to the Doctor, to Mrs Burke and the family, and to Mr Macleane.[2] Mr Drumgold[3] would be obliged to the Doctor to let him know the title of Malcolm's book on the Scotch and British antiquities.[4]

I am, dear Sir,

Yours with great respect and sincerity,

J. B.

I would have wrote to Mr Barrett,[5] to Mr Creagh,[6] and others of my friends, but that I have the greatest aversion to letter writing, though nobody wishes his friends better than I do. I find in myself at times a strong disposition to saunter and idle about here; one may do it with profit: the leisure I have from visits is employed in remarks upon and

[1] A picture of Alexander the Great by Eustache Le Sueur; Barry had seen it in the Palais Royal and described it to Burke in his letter of 5 December as 'incomparably the first picture I ever saw in my life'.

[2] Lauchlin Macleane was a friend of Edmund and Will Burke. He was admitted to Trinity College Dublin 29 May 1746. Barry had known him in Paris, and received financial aid while on his travels from him as well as from the Burkes (Barry, *Works*, I, 159–60).

[3] Probably Colonel John Drumgold (1720–81), four of whose letters to Burke are among the Fitzwilliam MSS. See Hayes, *Biographical Dictionary*, pp. 73–4; also *Life of Johnson*, II, 526–7. Dr Johnson met him during his stay in Paris in 1775 and told Boswell of his social usefulness: 'I was just beginning to creep into acquaintance by means of Colonel Drumgould, a very high man, Sir, head of *L'Ecole Militaire*, a most complete character, for he had first been a professor of rhetorick, and then became a soldier' (*Life of Johnson*, II, 401–2).

[4] Presumably David Malcolm's *Letters, essays, and other tracts illustrating the Antiquities of Great Britain and Ireland*, London, 1744.

[5] George Barret (*c.* 1728–84) a landscape painter. Burke had assisted him in Ireland by introducing him to Lord Powerscourt (Edward Wingfield, 4th Viscount Powerscourt, 1729–64) who became his first patron. In 1762 Barret crossed to England, where his paintings sold well and he made a considerable reputation. Burke later helped secure him a post as Master Painter at Chelsea Hospital—a post he held for life and which his son held after him.

[6] Not identified. Will Burke's letter of 26 October had remembered all members of the Burke household to Barry, concluding: 'I should not omit that poor Creagh, who is here, loves and esteems you; if there are little particularities, they are by no means of a bad mind, he loves you, and the regard of a good man is always valuable' (Barry, *Works*, I, 28).

sketching of what I see, so that I hope my friends will be indulgent enough to accept of my good wishes, which, whether I write or not, is always sure to attend them.

To SIR GEORGE MACARTNEY—[*post* 23] *December* 1765

Source: MS Osborn Collection.

A joint letter of William and Edmund Burke. Will's portion, omitted here, is dated 'Dec. 21. 1765'—a Saturday—and mentions the coming-on of the election in which Lord Verney had promised Edmund his influence: 'the writ is gone to Wendover and next Monday We hope Ned will be a Member'. Edmund's portion of the letter seems to have been written after the election was over; he refers to the 'place where I am chosen' and the 'person by whose means I came in'. It was not impossible, of course, for him to have used such expressions before the election; no other candidate was nominated.

Sir George Macartney, a brilliant young Irishman, protégé of Henry Fox, was at this time Envoy Extraordinary to Russia. He was a friend of both William and Edmund Burke; Edmund wrote him concerning the election at Wendover and the generosity of Will which had made it possible.

My dear Sir George, For the present permit me to add a word to our Friend Williams Letter; another time I may have more leisure, more matter, and more power of entertaining you, though it is impossible I should at any time have more true value and affection for you or a more sincere satisfaction in hearing that you are well, and that you keep your old friendships. I hope you will have no reason to repent of them, if having chosen honest and sincere men can secure you from a Change in your opinion. In all the rest, for my part, I confess, I tremble for the partiality of my friends, and in particular for yours, who by your warm and friendly engagements for me have made yourselves responsible at the peril of your Judgement, for my Success in a New Walk of Life, for which I am little prepared, and about which I entertain so many anxious apprehensions, as greatly to abate the satisfaction I should otherwise find on making so considerable a Step in the World. You see by the particular place where I am chosen, the person by whose means I am come in, and you can thereby form some Judgment of the Nature of that friendship, which could not only desire but press me to get upon his own ground. What should become of me, if I should be a means of putting back that friend without getting forward myself? but I will say no more of this. As to Politicks I have at present little room for them. With regard to the Literary world it has produced little except one most able piece in the Polemical Way between Louth and Warburton,[1] in which the Latter is

[1] *A Letter to the Right Reverend Author* [William Warburton, Bishop of Gloucester] *of 'The Divine Legation of Moses demonstrated'...By a late Professor in the University of Oxford* [Robert Lowth, Prebendary of Durham], 1765.

handled with an asperity equal to his own, but I think with more ability and sense (not with more ingenuity for that is not easy) than his own. The Next Messenger will take it to you. As to Dennis your kind remembrance of him must gladden the poor mans heart; I shall let him know it. I have already interested some friends in Ireland in his favour who have put him I hope well with the Primate. I think so, as he has lately given him a small living in addition to the little ⟨Benefit⟩ he had before.[1] Adieu for this time and believe me with the truest affection yours

E BURKE.

Macartney's reply to Edmund has not survived. His letter to Will, dated 10/21 February 1766 from St Petersburg, shows an affectionate interest in both friends. He enquires particularly about Edmund's *début* in the House of Commons: 'I have no Idea of abilities greater or more parliamentary than his and I shall be very impatient till I know whether the rest of the World does him as much Justice as I do. Tell me at the same time, whether you are likely soon to get in to Parliament yourself: I am sure I know of no man more worthy of a Seat there than him who made so generous a Sacrifice of his own Pretensions to the Advantage of his friend....'

To CHARLES O'HARA—24 *December* [1765]

Source: O'Hara MSS. Printed Hoffman, pp. 324–5.

My dear Sir, I am to thank you though I have neither time nor Spirits to do it as I ought for your most affectionate Letter, and for that very gracious and polite one from my Lord Lieut, that attended it.[2] I shall say more to it next post, please God. This is only to tell you, in a few words that yesterday I was elected for Wendover, got very drunk, and this day have an heavy cold.[3] This News would all together give you pleasure so I have not delayed it one post. George Grenville debated every day about America, taking care to call whore first. On the rebellion

Macartney had been a pupil of Dennis (letter of Dennis to Shackleton 15 August 1767 in Ballitore MSS [A/43]). 'Throughout life', says his biographer, 'he retained a grateful memory of Mr Dennis, and in later years, when it was in his power to do so, rewarded his tutor's care and instruction by the gift of the benefices of Clane and Dunmore' (Helen Robbins, *Our First Ambassador to China*, London, 1908, p. 7; see also Burke's letter of 19 February 1772). A William Dennis became Vicar of Carnalway in 1764.

[2] O'Hara's letter to Burke of 17 December enclosing the letter of Lord Hertford (see above, letter of 22 November).

[3] Lauchlin Macleane who was at Wendover for the electoral celebrations described their character in a letter to Wilkes in Paris. He had created some of the excitement himself by proposing a toast to Wilkes with the company on their knees: '...all the Dishes were broken in the same Instant; in a few minutes the Room was cleared of Smoke and full of—Liberty. Wilkes and Liberty, Burke and Wilkes, Freedom and Wendover; Empty Bottles, broken Glasses, Rivers of Wine, Brooks of Brandy, Chairs overturned, with the Men that sat upon them, while others in rising from their Knees fell under the Table...' (letter of 24 December, Add. MS 30868, fol. 221).

there he moved for amendment to the address the first day;[1] seconded the motion for papers the second day,[2] and opposed the adjournment the third.[3] These two last days he divided the house. His best 35 to 70, the Last day the same Number to 78. He was kind to shew his personal insufficiency and his party weaknesş at the very opening of the Campain; his uncandid and ungentlemanly opposition, contrary to his publick declarations to men who were not present to answer him has done infinite Service.[4] He shews I think no Talents of a Leader; he wanted the stage of administration to give him figure. He is eager, petulant, inaccurate, without dignity, and quite the Reverse of that Character, which might be expected from a man just descended from such great Situations. Charles Townshend who handled him very roughly described him admirably in two words of his Speech Quantity without force. They tell a mighty good humourd thing of Rigby; when somebody said to him, Rigby you made but a poor figure on the Division; but you had the advantage of being in the right in point of Argument. 'In the right; No! Dammé a minority never was in the right from the beginning of the world to this day; a minority is always absurd.' I never saw opposition carried to such a length as in Rigby Laughing aloud in the house at George Grenvilles dull Jokes. Calcraft is routed at Rochester.[5] All their maneuvres have been unsuccessful, and this administration, that could not live for an hour, seems to have pretty strong stamina. I wish you would be as good as your word and see our fireside here this Winter; but you talk of Christmas just on the Eve of the day. Wherever you are may you pass it to your hearts wish. God bless you. The Doctor, Will, Jenny, all are sincerely yours.

Decr 24.

[1] The Stamp Act had been received in America with riots and disturbances. Parliament met on 17 December and the King's Speech referred to these riots as 'matters of importance...which will demand the most serious attention of Parliament'. Grenville moved an amendment 'to express our just resentment and indignation at the outrageous tumults and insurrections...in North America', and to 'support his Majesty in all such measures as shall be necessary for preserving and securing the legal dependance of the colonies'. After some debate the amendment was withdrawn.

[2] On 18 December Richard Rigby (1722–88) moved an address for papers relating to the American disturbances. Grenville seconded, and they divided the house.

[3] On 20 December Administration moved to adjourn to 14 January, Grenville to 7 January. Grenville divided the house on his own motion, 35 to 77.

[4] Twenty-three Members who had accepted office under Rockingham were absent because of their re-elections. These included Conway, leader of the House, Dowdeswell, Chancellor of the Exchequer, and most of the principal Government speakers.

[5] John Calcraft (1726–72), formerly Henry Fox's man of business'. He was defeated at Rochester 23 December by the Government candidate, Grey Cooper.

To JOHN RIDGE—24 *December* [1765]

Source: Fitzwilliam MSS (Sheffield). Printed Hoffman, p. 326.
Endorsed: E—B to John | Ridge | Decbr 24 1765 | Postscript by Dr Nugent.
The postscript, here omitted, is dated 'Christmas Eve'.

My dear Ridge, I know you are too much interested in every thing which relates to us, not to be very angry with me, if I should omit for a single post giving you an account of any thing advantageous that happend in our affairs. The Cover, before you read this, will let you know, that I am returned for Wendover.[1] I was elected yesterday. Lord Verney whose kindness was without bounds, went down with us. I feel the effects of the drinking and exposure to a very nipping Air this Day. Will was with us, and has a sufficient headach also. I shall when I am better and a little clearer tell you some of our News; But in one word, hitherto the unstable administration stands firm; and never did an adversary shew more fury and impotence together than G. Grenville and his set did in their three days opposition. Their best division, when they thought they had surprised Government, and so in Truth they had by a stolen march, was but 35 to 70; the Grand Financier[2] behaved like a rash hot headed boy. Remember me most affectionately to Leland Reddy[3] and all my friends—adieu Jenny desires her love to Kate and the little ones—we all embrace you. Pray let us hear from you soon; in the mean time we wish you a merry Christmas. Pray give my most sincere Regards to Mr Lyster.[4] I have been so hurried that I have not yet been able to attend to his Business, but as it is his, I cannot easily forget it. Pray my affectionate Compliments to Mr Harward.[5] Let my mother and Julia know this piece of News.

DR WILLIAM MARKHAM *to* WILLIAM BURKE—29 *December* 1765

Source: Fitzwilliam MSS (Sheffield). Printed *Corr.* (1844), I, 92–4.

Dr William Markham, Dean of Rochester, later Bishop of Chester and Archbishop of York, had been a friend and frequent counsellor of Burke since they first met through Will Burke in 1753. He had corrected and revised the *Sublime and Beautiful*, had given advice on the plan of the *Annual Register*, and stood godfather to Burke's son Richard (Clements Markham, *Memoir of Archbishop*

[1] As a Member of Parliament Burke now had the right to frank letters.
[2] Grenville's reputation hitherto had rested mainly on his financial ability.
[3] Probably Richard Reddy (b. *c.* 1718), named as a physician in Wilson's *Dublin Directory* for 1766. Ridge's letter to Burke 8 April speaks of a 'Dr Reddy'. See also Hist. MSS Comm. 8th Report, App. (*O'Conor MSS*), pp. 465–6.
[4] Probably William Lyster (d. 1789), an attorney practising in the Exchequer Court.
[5] William Harward (*c.* 1709–70), Ridge's law partner.

Markham, pp. 12–13). Like other of Burke's friends he saw the crucial nature of the coming *début* in the House of Commons—as to which he wrote frankly to Will.

My dear Sir

I thank you most heartily for your affectionate letter, and am ashamed of my inattention in suffering those who take so warm a part in our happiness to be so long in suspence about it. Our house has been Full of people till yesterday when Mr Cooper[1] and his family left us. During that time I wrote many letters, and thought that one of them had been to you. We are all perfectly well. The measles have run through all the children. The youngest who gave us most apprehension had them more slightly than any of the rest.

I was informed of Ned's cold by a letter from Skynner,[2] I am very glad to hear it is so much better. I shou'd be grieved to hear he was ill, at any time, and particularly at so critical a time as this. I think much will depend on his outset, I wish him to appear at once in some important question. If he has but that confidence in his strength which I have always had, he cannot fail of appearing with lustre.

I am very glad to hear from you that he feels his own consequence, as well as the crisis of his situation. He is now on the ground, on which I have been so many years wishing to see him. One splendid day will crush the malevolence of enemies as well as the envy of some who often praise him; when his reputation is once established, the common voice will either silence malignity or destroy it's effect.

As to my good wishes towards him and you God knows you have always had them, though it has not been in my power to give you much proof of them.

What is done about the Irish pension? I hear it is taken from Hamilton, and that Ned is to have it in a more agreeable shape.[3] I think the session has open'd with as many circumstances of disgrace to your

[1] Presumably Grey Cooper, in Rochester to contest an election (see above, letter of 24 December, p. 224).

[2] John Skynner (*c*. 1724–1805); he was a peacemaker between Markham and the Burkes in a famous quarrel they had in 1771 (see letter of [*post* 8 December 1771]).

[3] Until 16 December the pension had continued on the books in Burke's name although the proceeds of it were paid to Robert Jephson. But Burke had finally decided that even this arrangement compromised his record. He had therefore requested Lord Hertford to cancel the pension. Hertford, knowing the situation, had refused, doubtless because he knew he would be disobliging Jephson and Hamilton without giving Burke any financial benefit. But Burke persisted (probably directing his appeal this time to Lord Rockingham) and the pension was terminated completely as of 16 December. A fresh pension for the same amount was later secured for Jephson, with, according to Charles O'Hara, 'the arrears paid up from the time of its being recalld' (letter to Burke 22 October [1767]).

opponents as you cou'd possibly wish, and that your prospects brighten every day.

We propose being in Town, in about a fortnight, though we do not yet know where; We shall probably have a furnishd house in Pallmall.

Adieu my dear Burke, and make our best compliments to the house in Queen Anne Street. I am

most affectionately yours
W. MARKHAM

Rochester
Dec. 29. 1765.

To PATRICK NAGLE—[*post* 30 *December* 1765]

Source: MS Pennsylvania Historical Society. Printed *New Monthly Magazine*, XVI, 161.

Undated. Burke speaks of his election as having taken place 'Monday sennight', so the letter is presumably at least a week after 23 December.

My dear Sir,

I am not a little ashamed to find myself so long in your Debt, especially as your health seemed in so uncertain a situation at the time when you wrote. Believe me I was not indifferent to you, though a most excessive hurry of various sorts of Business scarce left me a moments leisure to tell you so. In reality I am even now far from idle. Be so good to Let me hear from you soon, and gratifye me with an account of your amendment. There are few things could give me a more sincere uneasiness than any suffering of yours. You mention some particulars relative to my accounts;[1] you know I am not very knowing in the particulars of them, and may easily be guilty of mistakes. I leave all to your discretion and friendship. I could wish that the little commissions, I spoke of in my last Letter should be performed; and as you have probably nothing of mine in your hands you may draw on me for the Charge, as well as for what other matters you may think fit to do for the poor of your Village and parish at this rigorous Season.

To be sure the Trees ought to be replaced; and too many of them cannot be planted; as allowance must be made for those that naturally will be stolen and destroyed in a Country so ill supplied with Wood as yours.

If I remember right, you said something about poor Garretts[2] Horses; I dont now remember what. Do as you think best; always remembering,

[1] Again Burke is referring to the administration of the Clogher estate (see above, letter of 14 October, p. 217).

[2] Garrett Burke.

What he said at his Death, that those of them he was fond of, should be put into such hands as would use them tenderly. His steward at Clohir I think was a sort of favourite of Garretts; if so he will in all things be treated accordingly. If the poor on that Farm be in distress you will relieve them a little, and you may depend on it, your Bills for the whole will be punctually answerd; Else it would not be reasonable to desire that you should be in advance for me.

Dick has been for some time past at Paris. It is true he has not wrote; but no man living loves and values you more; not even myself. He will make up for his Neglects.

By your saying Nothing of Ned,[1] though I have been very particular about him two or three times, I conclude you have changed your mind in relation to our former plan for him. In whatever way you think best to put him You shall always find me equally ready to assist him; for I loved his father,[2] and I think very well of the Boys own dispositions. Jenny and little Dick desire me to wish you all many happy years. Pray remember us affectionately to our dear friends at Ballywalter, to all the Garrets,[3] to my friend and Agent,[4] to Ballylegan, and to all those with whom I hope you passed a Christmas in the old manner; Cheerful and happy. May you have many of them.

I am myself well, other than a Cold I got on Monday sennight at my Election at Wendover. The event of that Election I am sure will give you pleasure; and at your next meeting you will Drink Lord Verney and my old friend (and indeed yours) Will Burke. It was on Lord Verneys Interest I was Chosen at that Borough. I am with unalterable affection my dear Uncle

your affectionate

E Burke

To Charles O'Hara—31 *December* [1765]

Source: O'Hara MSS. Printed Hoffman, pp. 327–8.

My dear Sir, I do not know how to thank you sufficiently for having rememberd me so often and so kindly in the midst of that hurry of Business you must have been in. It is but a poor return I can make you.

[1] Edmund Nagle (see above, letter of 14 October 1765, p. 216).

[2] Edmund Nagle, Patrick Nagle's son, hence Burke's first cousin. He had died in 1763 (*Dublin Journal*, 20–23 August 1763).

[3] Six Garrett Nagles are known among Burke's fairly close relations: (1) the son of Uncle Patrick of Ballyduff; (2) the son of Uncle Athanasius of Ballylegan; (3) the son of Uncle James of Ballynahalisk, Ballywalter; (4) Garrett Nagle of Clogher; (5) Garrett Nagle of Rinny; (6) Garrett Nagle of Bloomfield. There were undoubtedly others, and some Garretts who were not Nagles.

[4] Garrett Nagle, Patrick's son.

I am myself as much occupied as you have been; and, I am sure, I am far less able to fill up the vacant moments, by furnishing entertaining accounts of any publick *occurrences* (if I may venture to use a word which our great Statesman G. Grenville has proscribed).[1] At present there is a sort of Cessation from the exterior operations of Politicks; and it will continue during the recess. However, in this narrow but dreadful interval, preparations are making upon all hands. There are wonderful materials of combustion at hand; and surely, since this monarchy, a more material point never came under the consideration of Parliament. I mean the Conduct which is to be held with regard to America. And there are difficulties in plenty interior and exterior. Administration has not yet conclusively (I imagine) fixed upon their plan in this respect, as every days information from abroad may necessitate some alteration. In the mean time the Grenvillians rejoice and Triumph as if they had obtained some capital advantage, by the confusions into which they have thrown every thing. With regard to myself and my private opinion, my resolution is taken; and if the Point is put in any way[2] in which the affirmative or Negative become the Test of my Voting I shall certainly vote according to them; though some of my very best friends should determine to the Contrary. You will think me ridiculous; but I do not look upon this as a common question. One thing however is fortunate to you, though without any merits of your own, that the Liberties, (or what shadows of Liberty there are) of Ireland have been saved in America. I do not know how I come to concern myself about Ireland, where sure, I have been latterly treated in a most unhandsome manner.[3]

I received your Letter yesterday; and I waited on General Conway about it this day; As soon as he was apprised of the present state of your Bill, for he had formerly had an account of its progress at Large from My Lord Lieut., He wrote to Mr Yorke,[4] that it might pass without alteration.[5] And I believe it will pass accordingly. At every instant you feel the want of an Agent; I heard that my friend FitzGerald[6] was to be

[1] Will Burke wrote his friend Macartney 21 December 1765 (MS Osborn Collection) that Grenville, protesting against the discreet language in which the Speech from the Throne treated events in North America, 'harrangued upon the impropriety of terming the disturbances in N. A. *occurences*; he called them a rebellion...'.

[2] Burke has deleted the words 'favourable to my Notions', writing the twelve words which follow here above his deletion.

[3] Burke is probably referring to Lord Hertford's refusal to strike off his pension (see above letters of 22 November and 29 December).

[4] Charles Yorke, the Attorney General.

[5] O'Hara had written Burke 24 December: 'We are sending over heads of a bill to ascertain the duties to be paid on imported spirits under the act of excise. Pray give your aid to its coming back unalterd.'

[6] Probably Robert Fitzgerald (*c*. 1717–81), who wrote to Burke 20 March 1766 about another post.

appointed. I hope nothing has defeated his pretensions. I shall be glad to give him every little assistance in my power.

I have not the most astonishing good opinion of the firmness of the house of *Commons*. Will the *Lords* shew a little attention to their personal honour, and to their dignity as a body? Here has Joe Hickey[1] become security in a sum of more than 3000 pounds for that shabby rascal Lord Lisle.[2] His Lordship last year ran away from his security, and Hickey has been obliged within these few days to pay the money. Can you get a Peer to present his Petition, desiring that Lord Lisles privilege may be withdrawn, and that he may have Liberty to sue him? A more infamous affair was never heard of. If you have any friend who regards Justice and the honour of the Peerage and of our Country, sure he cannot refuse this most reasonable request. I heard Lately from *Paris*. Dick was very well. Will you entreat Charles[3] sometime or other to come to Town, and to Let me have a moments conversation with him. Indeed I may do this myself. Adieu my dear friend. What Has the archbishop done?[4]

31st December.

To RICHARD BURKE, SR—[*ante* 14 *January* 1766]

Source: Fitzwilliam MSS (N.R.S.).
Endorsed: To my Brother at | Paris abt Wilkes.

This letter is undated, but must have been written shortly before 14 January 1766 when Parliament re-convened after the Christmas recess. A brief postscript by Jane Burke is omitted.

My dear Dick, I am ashamed to say, that this must be as short, almost as my last. A thousand things croud into the narrow interval between this and the meeting on the adjournment,[5] which is the 14th And I have really scarce a moment to spare between making cursed necessary Visits, attendance at Lord Rockinghams, and tumbling over acts of Parliament at home. The last is indeed unfortunately the Least of my occupations. FitzHerbert is still in the Country. To my surprise even after what you have said, I find it reported that Wilkes is arrived, or on the point of arriving in Town.[6] Macleane told us he would submit to whatever Fitz

[1] Joseph Hickey (*c.* 1714–94), the Burkes' lawyer.

[2] John Lysaght, 1st Baron Lisle (*c.* 1702–81). As a peer he could not be sued for debt unless his privilege was withdrawn by an act of the House.

[3] Charles O'Hara, Jr, had entered Christ Church, Oxford, 26 November 1763.

[4] William Carmichael (1702–65), Archbishop of Dublin, O'Hara's brother-in-law, had died 15 December.

[5] Burke means the meeting on the day to which Parliament had been adjourned.

[6] Burke had heard a false rumour; Wilkes did not come to London at this time. Boswell dined with him and Richard Burke in Paris 19 January (*Boswell on the Grand Tour*, ed. F. A. Pottle and F. Brady, London, 1953–5, II, 284).

and I should think right for him.[1] He has not, it seems, waited our decision or even our consultation. He ought to be sensible that though the true *motives* for all his prosecutions were political, the prosecution he actually Labours most under, is not at all political, but for an offence against the ordinary Laws; for Blasphemy, for which it would be rather awkard to desire his pardon. Even if the pardon was granted any single Peer moving the house to have him committed for breach of Privelege could carry it;[2] no opposition being ever made in such Cases. It is true he is capable, as an incendiary of doing some Mischief; but it would fall ten fold on his own head whilst it would not conciliate the affection of his former Enemies and would be sure to exasperate his former friends. Between ourselves; Lord R. is extremely averse from asking any thing for him from the K. at the same time that he is willing to do almost any thing for him from his private Pocket, and to avow it to the K. or to any person.[3] If Wilkes has the least Knowlege of the Nature of popularity and the smallest degree of attention to his own Interest he will wait the convenience of his friends who do not forget him. But this to be insinuated more or less, or not at all according to your discretion. I am called off adieu.

To CHARLES O'HARA—18 [*January* 1766]

Source: O'Hara MSS. Printed Hoffman, pp. 329–31.

My dear Sir,

Last Tuesday we drew up the Curtain,[4] and discoverd the Great Commoner, attended by his Train, *solus*. From better correspondents you have heard of that most extraordinary day; of Mr Pitts disclaimer of the Late ministry and all their Works; his good opinion and his doubts of the present; and his strong reiterated declaration of our having no

[1] Lauchlin Macleane had returned to England in December, and pleaded Wilkes's cause with the Rockingham administration.

[2] Because the House of Lords had already resolved that Wilkes's *Essay on Woman* was a breach of privilege: Wilkes's notes were an impudent burlesque of Bishop Warburton's notes on Pope.

[3] Wilkes was not to be softened by such private proposals. He had written George Onslow 12 December: 'Mr Fitzherbert has offer'd me, in the name of some of the present Ministry, the annual sum of £1000, to be paid out of the income of their respective places. I have rejected this proposal as clandestine, eleemosinary, and precarious. I demand from the justice of my friends a full pardon under the great seal for having successfully serv'd my country. I will wait here till the first day of the New Year. If I shou'd not then have receiv'd it, I shall have the strongest proof that the present Ministry are neither the friends of Mr Wilkes, nor of justice...' (copy in Wilkes's hand, Add. MS 30868, fol. 209).

[4] Parliament met 14 January, and Conway presented to the House papers on the American disturbances.

right to impose an interior Tax on the Colonies. This proposition and some others similar to it, brought on an altercation of several hours between him and G. Grenville. They were both heated to a great degree; Pitt as much, as contempt, very strongly marked, would suffer him. The ministers Messrs Conway and Dowdeswell did just what was necessary and no more; leaving Pitt to do Grenvilles Business. Conway went perhaps too far in his compliments to Pitt; and his declared resolution to yield his place to him. The day ended a little awkardly; for the address being carried without any Dissent, The friends of Government went off, and Rigby finding a thin house carried a motion for printing the Papers. This had been the same day refused by the Lords on a motion of the D. of Bedford. You see this was getting into a scrape, and the worse scrape, as the Lives of some in America would be endangerd by such a publication. Yesterday it was set to rights; in the intervening time between that and the first day it had been carried to refer the dangerous Papers to the Speaker, that he might cut out the parts which might expose those who communicated intelligence to Government, to the resentment of the populace in America; Yesterday the Speaker was of opinion that no precaution of that kind would be sufficient for the purpose. And Mr Dowdeswell moved, on the Speakers report, to discharge the order for printing. This brought on a Debate which lasted till near ten. Mr Conway never shone so much; He was attacked on every side and supported himself with so much spirit, energy, Modesty, and good humour, as drew more and sincerer applause from the house than ever I knew a man to receive. He made an apology on being attacked for adulation to Pitt. He made his apology with so much dignity as not only fully to bring back what he might have lost by his first declarations on the Subject, but to get him new Credit. Rigby said some Good things; that he had heard of a Doctor malgré lui, but never before of a Minister malgrè lui, and that on such compulsion he never could expect a good Physician or a good statesman. That day I took my first trial. Sr Wm Meredith desired me to present the Manchester Petition;[1] I know not what struck me, but I took a sudden resolution to say something about it, though I had got it but that moment, and had scarcely time to read it, short as it was; I did say something; what it was, I know not upon my honour; I felt like a man drunk. Lord Frederick Campbell[2] made me some answer to which I replied; ill enough too; but I was by this time pretty well on my Legs; Mr Grenville answerd; and

[1] A petition from the merchants of Manchester complaining of the decay in the trade to the North American colonies, owing to the restrictions laid on it by government. It was one of ten similar petitions presented the same day.

[2] (1729–1816).

I was now heated, and could have been much better, but Sr G. Saville[1] caught the Speakers eye before me; and it was then thought better not to proceed further, as it would keep off[2] the business of the day. However I had now grown a little stouter, though still giddy, and affected with a swimming in my head; So that I ventured up again on the motion, and spoke some minutes, poorly, but not quite so ill as before. All I hoped was to plunge in, and get off the first horrors; I had no hopes of making a figure. I find my Voice not strong enough to fill the house; but I shall endeavour to raise it as high as it will bear.[3] This is prattling like a Child to a father. Whenever I enter into these minutiae about myself I beg you throw my Letter into the fire. All here are yours. The last bell rings. We are in an odd posture. Adieu.

18.

O'Hara did not agree to the suppression of all personal *minutiae*. They are a part of friendship, he told Burke in his letter of 25 January, and 'that severity of restraint which may guard against them, is no more to my taste, than platonic love was formerly'. He both encouraged and warned Burke about his speaking: 'your voice will form from practice, your manner will improve, the great point you are to attend to is temper. Was it not Jephson that usd to tell you that in some circumstances you had an air of anger. Get rid of this air.'

DAVID GARRICK *to* EDMUND BURKE—18 *January* [1766]

Source: Fitzwilliam MSS (Sheffield). Printed *Philological Quarterly*, XVIII (1939), 369–70.

Janu the 18
Saturday

My dear Sir

In the first place—I am very sorry that I can't dine with you—I had forgot an Engagement of a fortnight's standing that I had made, and was reminded of it by a Card at my return last Night from the house of Commons—where, I had the honour and Pleasure of Enjoying Your Virgin Eloquence! I most sincerely congratulate you upon it—I am very Nice and very hard to please and where my friends are concern'd most Hyper-critical—I pronounce that you will answer the warmest Wishes of your Warmest friend—I was much pleas'd—I have much to say, which you will politely listen to, and forget the next moment, however you shall have it—

I have sent you a whimsical letter of Madame Riccoboni by which you

[1] Sir George Savile, 8th Baronet (1726–84), M.P. for Yorkshire and a leading member of the Rockingham party.

[2] MS: of

[3] MS: will, bear.

will know, how your Brother is treated by the Dames françoises.[1] I fear that he has put my Nose out of joint—You see likewise by the Same letter, that I am somewhat under a Cloud with my Friend the Baron D'Holback[2]—will you disperse it for me and let me wait upon you at your own time to morrow Morning 8, 9 or 10 o'Clock? Sooner or later as you please. Pray do if you can, and I'll pray for you all my life after—What a Mistake our blundering housekeeper made about your Sweet Boy! He put him into the front insted of my Box that was kept for him—I hope you have got him again—pray ask his pardon for the Mistake in the Name of Me and the Boxkeeper, and to pacify him, assure him that the wild beast will attend him at any time that he may inspect his foot[3]—My best respects to your Lady

Yours Ever
and most Truly
D G—

To the Marquess of Rockingham—[*January* 1766]

Source: Fitzwilliam MSS (Sheffield).

Undated but possibly written about 27 January when the Glasgow merchants presented to the House a petition against the decay of trade following the Stamp Act disturbances.

My Lord,

I dont know whether your Lordship has been informed, that when Mr Grenville went out of the house of Commons last Night, it was to have a meeting with Mr Mackenzie,[4] Cadogan,[5] Eglington,[6] and Jenkin-

[1] Marie Jeanne Riccoboni (1714–92) the novelist, one of Garrick's admirers in Paris, was either much impressed by Richard Burke or eager to convince Garrick that she was. Her letter of 16 January had a great deal to say of 'a very pretty, a very charming creature: des grâces de l'esprit comme un ange, une noble aisance, deux grands yeux à bruler le monde, une bouche si belle, un si joli sourire, et tout cela vient étudier le François au coin de mon feu' (Garrick, *Corr.* II, 461). She wondered whether the French ladies would run after him as much as they had after David Hume. She herself continued to drop bouquets for him into her letters to Garrick for fully a year's time. Richard's response was probably less eager than she expected. After six months he sent her a courteous letter, 'des excuses de sa longue négligence, mille politesses, un badinage léger, de l'esprit...' with a copy of *The Vicar of Wakefield* (*ibid.* II, 493).

[2] Paul Heinrich Dietrich, Baron d'Holbach (1723–89).

[3] Young Richard, aged seven, had apparently had a seat at Drury Lane—not quite high enough for him to see all of the spectacle. The Christmas play this year was one of Garrick's perennials: 'Harlequin's Invasion'.

[4] James Stuart Mackenzie (*c.* 1718–1800), Lord Bute's brother.

[5] Charles Sloane Cadogan (1728–1807), Treasurer to the Duke of York. The Duke of York was opposed to the repeal of the Stamp Act, and Cadogan helped to bring about the meeting of 12 February between Grenville, Bedford, and Bute, with a view to a coalition against the Rockingham Administration.

[6] Alexander Montgomerie, 10th Earl of Eglinton (1723–69), a close friend of Bute. For his part in bringing about the meeting of 12 February see *Grenville Papers*, III, 361–3, and *Correspondence of John, 4th Duke of Bedford*, London, 1842–6, III, 326–9.

son,[1] who had been before an hour together in close conference.[2] The Subject of this consultation may easily be guessed. I give it to your Lordship now, as it is just possible, you may not have heard of it, and as, It will, I fear be difficult for me to wait on your Lordship until I go to the house; for Sr Al. Gilmour[3] and the Glasgow Merchants are to breakfast with me upon Business. I am with the utmost truth

My Lord
your Lordships
most obedient
and most obliged humble Servant
E BURKE

JANE AND EDMUND BURKE *to* MRS JULIANA FRENCH—6 *February* 1766

Source: Prior (2nd ed.), II, 54–6.

Juliana Burke, Edmund's sister, had been married in January to Patrick William French of Loughrea, County Galway. Jane Burke wrote a letter of congratulation, to which Edmund added a postscript.

[Jane begins]

I most truly and affectionately wish you, my dear sister, joy on the change you have made in life. It is a change that I make not the least doubt will insure happiness to you, and to all your friends the pleasure and satisfaction that an union made by you must give them; we are all very happy in being connected with a man of Mr French's character, which Mr Ridge has very fully and very satisfactorily given us. I wish you many years to enjoy the satisfaction and happiness that lies before you; and many years I hope you will live to enjoy it; I can only add my prayers and hearty wishes that you should, which I do from the bottom of my heart. I leave it to you, and surely I cannot leave it in better hands, to make my love to Mr French. I wish I had it in my power to wish you both joy myself by word of mouth, but I hope before the summer is over I shall do so, as we think, if possible, to take a turn to Ireland about that time.

[1] Charles Jenkinson (1727–1808), formerly Bute's private secretary and Grenville's Secretary to the Treasury.

[2] Grenville's diary, printed in *Grenville Papers*, makes no mention of this meeting with Grenville, and Burke was probably passing on nothing more than a rumour. If a meeting took place it was very likely that its purpose was to form a combined opposition against the Rockingham Administration.

[3] Sir Alexander Gilmour, 3rd Baronet (*c.* 1736–92), Clerk Comptroller of the Board of Green Cloth, and at this time a follower of Rockingham.

I had wrote thus far when I got your letter, and it makes us all very happy to hear you are well, and so much pleased with your present situation. Ned is so taken up that he has scarce time to eat, drink, or sleep; he has not been in bed this week until three or four o'clock in the morning, and his hurry will not be over, I am afraid, the whole winter. If he can he will add to this, but if he should not be able so to do, I am sure you will not doubt of his love and affection for you both. Dick is not yet come home, but we expect him every day, nay he may be here before I seal this, and if he is, you shall hear of him.

Your nephew is grown very stout, strong, and tall; he is at school about four miles from town, at present learning Latin, and very eager he is at it; he does not forget his aunt Julia, nor her goodness to him. He is to be home on Saturday for a week, which he has got on account of his birth-day, so that you see what consequence a birth-day is to us now.[1]

Mr William Burke desires I would assure you from him how happy he is at every thing that gives you pleasure, and that he sincerely wishes you joy on the present occasion. My father joins in the same wish, and in love and compliments to Mr French and you: believe me, my dear sister, no one more truly and affectionately loves you, or wishes for every happiness to attend you more than your affectionate sister and humble servant.

JANE BURKE

Queen Anne Street,
Feb. 6, 1766.

[Edmund begins]

My dear Julian.

Upon my word I have only time to say I most heartily wish you and Mr French much joy; and to you both the good sense and good nature to make it your endeavour to contribute all you can to one another's happiness: I wish you both many years enjoyment of it, and am, with my regards to my brother, my dear Julia,

Your most affectionate,
E BURKE

[1] Richard's birthday was 9 February. The Burkes made a great deal of it as a family festival. William Hickey says (*Memoirs*, ed. Alfred Spencer, London, 1913–25, III, 311) that Will Burke always celebrated it. He describes one occasion in India in the year 1786: 'we sat down to a splendid dinner, consisting of turtle, venison, and every rarity that was procurable. The party consisted of one hundred and twenty persons, accommodated in a suite of three rooms. Lord Cornwallis, who with the rest of the great people was invited, pleaded indisposition, and sent an excuse, but the whole of the staff attended; it turned out as usual a drunken business....'

To [WILLIAM PITT]—[7 *February* 1766]

Source: MS Sir Edward Hoare, Bart.

Undated, and Burke does not name his correspondent. On Friday 7 February 1766, in the committee on American papers, Charles Yorke's motion for the Chairman to leave the chair was carried by 274 to 134. This is news which Rockingham would have wished to convey to Pitt, who took part in the debate but left before the division. At this time Rockingham still hoped that Pitt would join his Administration.

Sir

I have the honour to inform you that the Committee divided on the Question for voting the Chairman out of the Chair. The Majority of the Ayes was 274; the Noes 134. I take the Liberty of congratulating you on this Event; Nothing could add so much to the satisfaction, I dare say, of all who divided in that Majority, as to find that their Conduct had your approbation, and that their Success gave you pleasure. I have the honour to be with the highest respect and esteem

Sir
Your most obedient
and most humble Servant
Ed Burke

Friday night
near eleven.

RICHARD BURKE, SR *to* JAMES BARRY—11 *February* 1766

Source: Barry, *Works*, I, 45–6.

Dr Johnson said at the time of Burke's parliamentary *début* that he had 'gained more reputation than perhaps any man at his [first] appearance ever gained before. He made two speeches in the House for repealing the Stamp-act, which were publickly commended by Mr Pitt, and have filled the town with wonder' (*Life of Johnson*, II, 16). Records of parliamentary speeches at this time are few and inadequate, but there is no lack of evidence that Burke's success had delighted his friends and quite exhilarated his family. Brother Richard, returning from Paris, reversed the habits of a lifetime by sending off a letter promptly, to tell Barry of the general happiness.

London, 11th February 1766.

My dear Barry.

Partly to keep my promise, but more to gratify a very worthy fellow, I sit down to write you a few lines. As I am of the most importance (to myself I mean) I shall begin by telling you that I arrived here safe and sound this morning at (I am an Irishman) midnight. I must tell you also, that this pleasure was seasoned by a delay of five days at Calais, from whence I wrote to you. You begin now to be impatient to know what the gratification is which I propose to give you; why, sir, I flatter myself that you will have some little pleasure in knowing that I am well, and I will increase it by telling you that I found all here perfectly well, and perfectly your friends.—There are two courses for you without either cray fish or oysters, and you shall have an excellent desert.

Your friend has not only spoke, but he has spoke almost every day;[1] as to how, I shall leave you to guess, only saying, that to a reputation not mean before, he has added more than the most sanguine of his friends could have imagined. He has gained prodigious applause from the public, and compliments of the most flattering kind from particulars; it will add to what I know you already feel on this occasion to be told, that amongst the latter was one from Mr Pitt,[2] who paid it to him in the house in the most obliging manner and in the strongest terms. It is fit that I should tell you the little, very little, which I know of the question which has been the subject of the late debates. The ministry assert the right of taxing the colonies, but propose to repeal the stamp act as inconvenient, impolitic, and detrimental to this kingdom, as well as oppressive to the colonies. This you will say is a very imperfect and unsatisfactory account—so it is, but I make you as wise as myself, and what more can you expect? the affair is not yet decided, nor is it very certain how it will be decided. Though unsatisfactory the account, yet you must allow me some merit in telling you even this little so immediately after my arrival.—Ned is at the house—Will at the opera—the Doctor, Jane, Jack Nugent,[3] and I at home—but wherever we are, be assured that we are very much yours. Farewell, dear Barry, take care of yourself, but not too much; dispute, but not too much; be a free-thinker, but not too much; drink, but not too little. Whilst I am yet writing, Macleane is come in, and desires to be cordially remembered to you.—Adieu, again, and believe me, Yours sincerely,

RICHARD BURKE

Compliments to Colonel Drumgold.

[1] Four speeches by Burke are recorded between the day of his maiden effort and the day of Richard's letter:

(1) 27 January—mentioned in Fortescue, *Correspondence of George III*, I, 247 (see also Walpole, *Memoirs*, II, 193);

(2) 3 February—Fortescue, I, 255 (see also Walpole, *Memoirs*, II, 199, and below, letter of [*ante* 8 March], p. 242);

(3) 5 February—Albemarle, *Memoirs of Rockingham*, I, 309–10 (see also Fortescue, I, 262–4);

(4) 7 February—*ibid.* I, 267.

[2] See below, letter of John Ridge to Will Burke [*ante* 8 March], p. 243. None of the recorded speeches of Pitt contains his praise of Burke, though it is mentioned in a number of contemporary letters and memoirs.

[3] John Nugent (1737–1813), Mrs Burke's brother. He was at this time a Surveyor of Customs in London.

To CHARLES O'HARA—1, 4 *March* 1766

Source: O'Hara MSS. Printed Hoffman, pp. 331–4.
Addressed: To | Charles o'Hara Esqr. M.P. | Merrion Square | Dublin.
Postmarked: 4|M⟨ ⟩ FREE.

Burke did not achieve his blaze of parliamentary fame without extraordinary efforts. In a famous passage of his *Letter to a Noble Lord*, written thirty years later, he recalled the strains to which he had subjected himself: 'The first session I sat in Parliament, I found it necessary to analyze the whole commercial, financial, constitutional, and foreign interests of Great Britain and its empire. A great deal was then done; and more, far more, would have been done, if more had been permitted by events.' Not very surprisingly he suffered a physical breakdown. 'Then, in the vigor of my manhood, my constitution sunk under my labor.' The illness mentioned at the beginning of this letter he thought had brought him 'very near death'.

My dear Sir, I catch a moment of very interrupted leisure and of very precarious health to write to you. I have been extremely ill of a flux, which was relieved by violent sweats; both these Causes, together with the heavy cold with which the Session began, and which this Session was ill calculated to relieve, have so reduced me, that I am scarcely the shadow of what I was when you saw me. However, weak as I am, I thank God, my Spirits have not wholly deserted me; and I am now once more able to apply a little to Business. We have just got the resolutions,[1] (I mean those which were intended for Laws), reduced in the Committee into acts, (Repeal and all,) and we shall have the third reading please God on Monday,[2] so that they may go without delay to the Lords. There an opposition will certainly be raised; but I am convinced their Courage will never carry them to those Lengths, which their Strength might enable them to go. The repeal will be carried there.[3] Lord Chesterfield went down to the House of Peers a day or two ago to qualifye; He said he could not die in peace if he did not send his Proxy to be used for the repeal; nothing can be more sanguine than he is for the present measures. They are honest ones. We now prepare for a compleat revision of all the Commercial Laws, which regard our own or the foreign Plantations,

[1] On 24 February the Committee of the whole House which had been considering the American papers reported, and the House adopted seven resolutions. The first resolution was the substance of the Declaratory Act; the seventh, the repeal of the Stamp Act. On this the opposition moved to recommit the resolution, but were beaten by 240 to 133.

[2] The bill to repeal the Stamp Act received its first reading on Wednesday, 26 February, was read a second time on the 27th, committed on the 28th, and reported on Monday 3 March. There was a division on the third reading, on Tuesday 4 March of 250 to 122.

[3] But not so easily as Burke seems to assume. On 11 March the opposition divided against committing the bill, and were beaten by only 73 votes to 61; thirty-three peers signed a protest against the repeal. There was another protest, signed by twenty-eight peers, on the third reading (17 March), but no division.

from the act of Navigation downwards; It is an extensive plan. The N. Americans and West Indians are now in Treaty upon it;[1] and as soon as they have settled some preliminaries; (and they are better disposed, than any one could think, to practicability and concord) the whole arrangement will be orderd, between them and some of the Board people[2] and detached Members,[3] and will be brought into the house, a regular and digested Scheme.[4] This you see will find me at least as much Business as the Evidence on the Stamp act; but it is a Business I like; and the Spirit of those I act with is just what I could wish it, in things of this Kind. Could not Ireland be somehow *hooked* into this System? Send me some Arguments from those who are most intelligent relative to the direct import of English W. India Sugars into Ireland; and that as soon as you possibly can. The late regulations here were to shut out in a Civil way the Portuguese;[5] but I think they have hurt the whole Trade. Cannot the good be kept and the bad part be rejected? The principles I remember, the details have passed away from my memory. If good men were as practicable for the sake of their good purposes, as the people of the world are for theirs, this administration would be on a rock. What it *will* be I know not; I indeed scarcely ask; I mind my Business to the best of my power, and leave the rest to providence; so little have I profited by my long connections with the arch politician, *your friend*.[6] This same *friend* of *yours*, and *man* of *Pitts*, (and whose will he be in Heaven!) to manifest his thorough consistency of *Character* by a thorough inconsistency of *Conduct*, voted on the Question of the repeal against this very Pitt, notwithstanding his contrary professions these three months past.[7] All parties, as far as they descend to think of him, think of him just alike—As to myself I work on, and I thank God, not

[1] They reached agreement 10 March (Public Record Office, T.I. 452, fol. 211).

[2] The members of the Boards of Treasury and of Trade.

[3] Independent Members, not holding office, but supporting Government.

[4] This ambitious project was never brought into the House. Burke seems to have worked on it himself and had assistance. Joseph Harrison wrote John Temple 15 April of this year (*Massachusetts Historical Society Collections*, 6th ser. IX, 72): 'Ever since the beginning of this session of Parliament I have liv'd at the Marquis of Rockingham's, employ'd as an assistant to his private secretary Mr Burke...and my intimate acquaintance with American affairs has at this time enabled me to be particularly usefull....' One of the Secret Service payments made to Burke for his researches on trade and manufacturing (see above, letter of 11 July 1765, p. 211 n.) was dated 19 April 1766.

[5] Burke is probably referring to the act 5 George III, c. 45 (1765), which, among other things, tried to prevent frauds in relation to the drawbacks payable on refined sugar.

[6] Hamilton.

[7] Hamilton gave John Calcraft his opinions concerning the right of Parliament to tax the Americans: 'For my own part, I think you have no right to tax them, and that every measure built upon this supposed right stands upon a rotten foundation, and must consequently tumble down, perhaps, upon the heads of the workmen' (*Chatham Correspondence*, III, 203 n.). Nevertheless he voted against the repeal of the act. He seems at this time to have been attached to Temple rather than Pitt.

without some encouragement. Mr Pitt has been very kind and generous in protecting me by very strong and favourable expressions, twice or thrice in publick, and often in private conversations. Those who dont wish me well, say I am abstracted and subtile; perhaps it is true; I myself dont know it; but think, if I had not been known to be the Author of a Book somewhat metaphysical, the objections against my mode of Argument would be of another nature, and possibly more just. However until I know better, I intend to follow my own way. Observe when I say so much of myself it is for your private ear. You would perhaps think me full as affected, if I did not speak to you of whatever touches myself nearly. Adieu. Pray let us hear often from you. You have many thanks from us all for your Last Letter.[1] Adieu. God bless you.

March 1 1766— You dont wholly forget Dennis and Sisson—pray give my most humble respects to my Lord Primate, whose excellent Conduct in his high station is not unknown here as I hope it is not unfelt in Ireland.[2] I wrote this last Saturday and foolishly forgot to send it. No alteration since. I am only to tell you that Rigby made an able stand for Ireland; (foolishly brought into the Debate on the Bill for ascertaining the Right of Taxing the Colonies), with Spirit and sense. I spoke too on the same subject to the purpose I think in some degree; but my Weakness of body made me long and diffused. Rigby really spoke like a man of Business and of Spirit. This Night the Repeal will be got through; but the previous Debate will make it long and tedious. We shall Sit I fear till morning. I now write in one of the Committee Rooms. The Commissionership you mention in your Last was intended for Milbanke and I think he will still get it.[3] We are in an odd way, too much so for this Letter to explain; in the Road of being the strongest ministry ever known in England are our Superiors now; In the probability of being none at all. My disease is (thank God) gone but a weakness remains.—I tell you every thing. My argument to night has I think hurt me. Not for the matter but the propriety. The house was teezed to Death and heard nobody willingly.

[1] O'Hara's letter of 20 February; MS at Sheffield.

[2] The rest of the letter was clearly written 4 March. The debate that evening, not yet over when Burke was writing, ended about 11 p.m.

[3] John Milbanke (d. *c.* 1806), brother-in-law of Lord Rockingham. His appointment as Commissioner of Revenue in Ireland is dated 5 March.

JOHN RIDGE *to* EDMUND *and* WILLIAM BURKE—[*ante* 8 *March* 1766]

Source: Fitzwilliam MSS (N.R.S.).

In the latter portion of this letter, here omitted, Ridge begins an account of happenings in the Irish Parliament 3 and 4 March 1766, promising to complete it 'by the next post'. His letter of 8 March at Sheffield, contains the completion.

My Dear friends

If the Dirty uninterrupted course of drudgery in which my unpropitious stars have involved me, had left me leisure to indulge my inclinations; you shoud have found me a very voluminous letter writer for two months past. But as our Courts were shut this day, The Remainder of this evening, shall be devoted to crowd as much matter into this sheet of paper, as it will contain. And first, my good William, Let me thank you most heartily, for considering, for gratifying the longings of your friend, who really yearned for the intelligence you sent him. There were many other Accounts of Ned's speech on the general Question of 'binding the colonies by Acts of the British Legislature' before your letter brought me intire satisfaction.[1] For surely his principle was as just and judicious as coud be, and I think I may add (whether it was so intended or not,) it was in a ministerial light extreamly artfull, as it left him open to choose what part he afterwards woud take in that business; Indeed it was a part which one might rather expect him to

[1] A MS report preserved in Treasury Bundles (Public Record Office, T. 1. 446, fols. 139–40) summarizes Burke's speech on the Declaratory Act: 'Some of Charters declare the Right others suppose it none deny it. The Courts to which they apply determine against them. There is a real Distinction in every Country between the speculative and practical Constitution of that Country arising from the Circumstance proper for securing the first Principles of its Constitution. The Kings Negative The Rights of the Clergy in Convocation to tax themselves Let them evaporate do not expunge them. The British Empire must be governed on a Plan of Freedom for it will be governed by no other. They were mere Corporations Fishermen and Furriers they are now Commonwealths. Give them an interest in his Allegiance give them some Resemblance of the British Constitution some Idea of popular Representation. Draw the line where you please between perfect and no Repres. but draw the Line somewhere between the two Extreams and I shall vote for this Motion because I know not how to fix Bounds to the coercive Power of the British Legislature.' Burke's position as to the taxing of the colonies was summarized by the Rev. R. Palmer in two letters to R. Cust. In the debate of 3 February Burke argued 'that it was right in Theory, but not at all expedient in *Practise*' (Lionel Cust, *Records of the Cust Family, ser. iii, Sir John Cust 3rd Bart*, London, 1927, p. 95). In the debate of 21 February, according to Palmer, Burke attempted, 'without entering on the *right* of Taxation—to shew from constant *Usage*, that Internal Taxation was never once thought of since the first emigration of the Americans from this Country, and that England never thought of any other power over them or Interest in them, but that of regulating their Commerce to the advantage of their Mother Country' (*ibid.* p. 97). Mrs Montagu wrote her friend Mrs Vesey concerning this debate, 'Mr. Burke spoke divinely, yes divinely, dont misunderstand me, and report he spoke as well as mortal man could do, I tell you he spoke better' (Blunt, *Mrs Montagu*, I, 139).

take when he had grown old in parliamentary arts, than at his first setting out in the house; and was the only Medium which coud reconcile or ought, Power Subordination and liberty with each other. This Explained to me, What was meant by some previous Accounts of Ned, which said he was too 'refined and Metaphysical'. I easily perceived, the Writers of such intelligence had no great pleasure in advancing Ned's reputation; and comforted myself at first, that he coud not be refined without being ingenious, and that when the Sun shines brightest it breeds most Maggots. One called his speech 'an Essay on Government'; Another said in a letter to Lord Beauchamps[1] 'that it was in short "The sublime and beautifull".' But this last was an admirer and not a Malignant. But immediately after these, came Letters, which repeated Pit's compliments to Ned—'His congratulating the house on so valuable an acquisition', 'That he was proud to walk in the line which that ingenious gentleman had chalked out'. And on the Question of repeal; 'That his speech woud be much shortened by what Mr B. had offered, and that he had delivered his sentiments thr'o the Medium of a Much better understanding than he (Pit) was ever endowed with, and with a Degree of precision which he believed was never before heard in that house'. Charles Townsend either wrote, or declared to somebody who did write, That tho he had all along formed the highest Idea of Ned's abilities, he owned that on that occasion he went beyond his utmost conception'. Hutchinson was kind enough to shew me a letter from the provost,[2] which mentions Burke in the highest terms. And Leland sent me a letter without a name, (but which I take to be Lord Charlemounts,)[3] on the late Debate, which does Ned's Merrit great justice; it mentioned that last compliment of Pit's. I think Will, I have now repaid you, (especially as you tried my patience for a post or two before you wrote). 'The Echo is often more pleasing than the sound which created it'. I know, all together afforded me the only pleasure I ever felt without the least allay. My Dear Ned don't let it make you mad, even tho' Pit shoud harness himself to your chariot, and draw you with his foundered hoofs to Cavendish square....

[1] Francis Seymour Conway (1743–1822), styled Viscount Beauchamp, later (1794) 2nd Marquess of Hertford. He was at this time Chief Secretary to his father.

[2] Dr Francis Andrews (*c.* 1718–74), Provost of Trinity College Dublin.

[3] Charlemont wrote Flood (13 March 1766): 'I some time ago sent to Leland a short account of our friend Burke's unparallelled success, which I suppose he has communicated to you. His character daily rises, and Barrè [Isaac Barré, 1726–1802] is totally eclipsed by him; his praise is universal, and even the Opposition, who own his superior talents, can find nothing to say against him, but that he is an impudent fellow' (*Original Letters to Henry Flood*, p. 40).

To CHARLES O'HARA—11 *March* [1766]

Source: O'Hara MSS. Printed Hoffman, pp. 338–9.

The house of Lords has not yet come to a division on the Committment of the repeal Bill. But it will be carried, and by a sufficient Majority reckoning the Proxies.[1] Lord Chancellor,[2] though in most things adverse, spoke for the repeal; and spoke extremely well. The ground he took was the inconveniency of putting the King into that difficult and distressing Situation, that he should have a Law upon his hands which by his oath he was to execute, disavowed by that part of the constitution from which alone he could derive support and supply. Lord Mansfield took the ground of the consequences which must arise from yielding, by raising the presumption of the Americans to the attack of other Laws. He was in some parts very ingenious, but in general unequal to his usual performances. Lord Cambden[3] replied and I never heard him or any man more able. It was a long speech supported with much spirit and much argument quite through. The Duke of Grafton spoke in a manner extremely Beautiful, and had a vast deal of matter. The Duke of Richmond shewed much shrewdness; I think he will become a considerable man. I thought Lord Lyttelton well on the other side. Last Friday[4] the motion for the repeal of the Cyder act was carried without difficulty or division; The Enemy breaks fast. I spoke about half an hour on that subject. Dowdswell made the motion Pitt seconded. I wrote in low spirits on what I said about Ireland.[5] I have had since some compliment on it, through another, from Lord Hardwicke[6] and others. Oh! What are you doing? The reins are thrown over the Neck of your house of Commons. Sure the expunging was most shameful to Government.[7] How comes all this?—You love a bon mot; on that accidental mention of Ireland,[8]

[1] The commitment was carried by 73 votes to 61; the proxy votes were 32 to 10.

[2] Robert Henley, 1st Earl of Northington (*c.* 1708–72). According to Grafton's report Northington was the eleventh speaker, and had been preceded by Grafton and Richmond.

[3] Charles Pratt, 1st Baron Camden (1714–94).

[4] 7 March.

[5] In his letter of 1, 4 March.

[6] Philip Yorke, 2nd Earl of Hardwick; formerly Lord Royston (see above, letter of 12 December 1762, p. 161 n.).

[7] In a debate 28 February in the Irish House of Commons, the Attorney-General had asked that an entry in the Journals of the House of 16 April 1615 be read out. On 3 March it was moved somewhat unexpectedly that this entry be expunged from the Journals 'as a disgrace to Parliament'. This motion was passed *nem. con.*, but the next day the Government forces, having decided on consideration that its tendency was hostile to them, took advantage of a technicality to bring it to another vote and defeated it. Burke received accounts of the affair in O'Hara's letter of 4 March and Ridge's of 8 March.

[8] In the debate of 4 March on the Declaratory Bill.

most of those who had been secretaries of Ireland[1] spoke, somebody asked Sr Charles Bunbury[2] why he did not? He said he waited for *your* friend to speak first;[3] it is late, and I snatch this from Business at Sr A. Gilmours. How good you are to write—continue your goodness.

11th March.

WILLIAM BURKE *to* JAMES BARRY—23 *March* 1766

Source: Barry, *Works*, I, 42–3.

Will Burke was not to wait very long for his own seat in Parliament, which he obtained 16 June. But meanwhile he could enjoy Edmund's successes and the consciousness of his own part in them. Dr Thomas Leland, sending him the good wishes of his Irish friends in a letter of 4 March, added: 'They say that in particular your Attachment to Ned is very noble and aimable. But they are fools; it only shews that you have sense.'

London, March 23, 1766.

...As for ourselves, Richard eats, drinks, sleeps, and laughs his fill—Ned is full of real business, intent upon doing real good to his country, as much as if he was to receive twenty per cent. from the commerce of the whole empire, which he labours to improve and extend. As for me, I am as you left me, with much to do in what is called business, which is mostly attendance, with this satisfaction in it still, that the modest nature and real worth of the man I do attend, makes every thing pleasing. The Doctor goes his rounds, and is in pretty good health, as I should say we all were, had not poor Mrs Burke been visited by a most severe cold; the delicacy of her frame, and that infinity of intrinsic worth that makes her dear to us, raised some anxious apprehensions, but, thank God! she is so much better that our fears are no more: the little boy who was at home a few days ago, is perfectly well. Our friend, Mr Macleane, is Lieutenant Governor of St Vincent,[4] the profit small, but, as he must go there, it is a satisfaction to be the first man. I hope too, by the mediation of Lord Cardigan,[5] he will be made a commissioner for the sale of lands, which will gild the plume the other gives. Remember us all very heartily to Mr Drumgold. I don't trouble him with a letter, but in this tell him

[1] Who had held the office of Chief Secretary to the Lord Lieutenant of Ireland. Three former Chief Secretaries (Rigby, Conway, and Sackville) spoke in this debate.

[2] Sir Thomas Charles Bunbury, 6th Baronet (1740–1821), was to have gone to Ireland as Chief Secretary to Lord Weymouth in May 1765.

[3] Hamilton's silence was proverbial. He had, despite his nickname, made more than a single speech in the British House, and he had spoken several times very effectively in Ireland. But after the break with Burke in 1765 he sat for over thirty years in the British House without ever speaking again.

[4] He was appointed, but actually remained in England as under-Secretary of State.

[5] George Brudenell, 4th Earl of Cardigan (1712–90).

from us all, that if in spite of *you* he does not obtain the immediate permission of your admittance to make the copy, we shall be sincerely disappointed.[1] It is impossible but he can do it, and if he knew how much we interest ourselves in it, it is impossible we flatter ourselves, but he would do it. Adieu, my dear friend, all prosperity be with you.—I as secretary in the name of all, declare our earnest regards.

WILLIAM BURKE

To CHARLES O'HARA—[27 *March* 1766]

Source: O'Hara MSS. Printed Hoffman, p. 341.
Undated. Burke says in his next that he wrote 'by the last post...a short and hurrying Letter'. He also mentions the fact that the House 'sat to ten on Thursday'. Thursday 27 March is the probable date.

My dear Sir, I write this late in the house, whilst[2] one of our Witnesses is examining. Many thanks for your Letters. Your proposition about Camblets and Cotton will not do. They cross British manufactures, at least in prejudice and things are not ripe for it. As to the Sugar it shall be tried.[3] So shall soap. But none of your hints obviated my difficulty upon foreign Sugars. The revision to be made of the Trade laws was not proposed to be total; but only so far as they regarded America. Adieu my dear Sir; I have not a minute. How can many of the particulars you mention be squeezed into the American Act? We have no Evidence here that I know of to examine to a single point.

To CHARLES O'HARA—29 *March* [1766]

Source: O'Hara MSS. Printed Hoffman, pp. 341–2.
Addressed: To | Charles o'Hara Eqsr M.P. | Merrion Square. | Dublin.
Postmarked: 29|MR FREE FREE.

My dear Sir, By the last post I wrote you a short and hurrying Letter; This I fear will scarcely be more long or more leisurely. I have considerd all the proposals you have made concerning Trade, and am sorry, (I think you may believe me) to say, that they seem, at this time, every one of them impracticable; because they all stand directly in the way of some predominant prejudice, and some real interest or supposed, of this Country; and therefore they require time and leisure to make their way by the slow progression of reason into the minds of people here, who

[1] Barry had complained in his previous letter: 'The academies are all shut up on account of the extreme cold, and probably I shall be shut out for some time from copying at the palais-royal' (Barry, *Works*, I, 46–7).

[2] MS: whllst

[3] For O'Hara's proposals about sugar, see his letter to Burke of 10 March, printed Hoffman, pp. 335–7; the remarks on camblets and cotton may have been in the lost enclosures in the letter of 13 March (Hoffman, p. 337 n.).

just now seem shut against them. Sure you dont think Camblets will not be thought to interfere with the British manufactures? And will they be fond of encouraging any thing like a Fabrick of Cottons in Ireland—you remember Cotton is the Basis of one of the most extensive and most favourite manufacture of England, that of Manchester. Are not printed Linnens directly in the same predicament? And as to Sugars, you have not said a word to my difficulty with regard to the foreign. But this however, I do not think of so much weight as another, which I found on conferring with Mr Benson[1] on this subject. The great Quantity of Sugars both raw and refined sent hence to Ireland this very Year will make the difficulties in giving some indulgence to Ireland at this time peculiarly great. Indeed our hands are so full of America, that I do not see how it is possible to attend with effect to any thing else this Session. The Irish affairs are a System by themselves, and will I hope one day or another undergo a thorough scrutiny, but in my opinion it would only hurt them to attempt crowding them into the train of an act relating wholly to America. Do you know that we sat to ten on thursday?[2] yet we did not get through half our Evidence; nor shall we be able to propose our first resolution until Thursday fortnight.[3] The only thing I have any Chance for is the Sope. You see I hope these difficulties or rather impossibilities in a right point of view. As to the other matters I shall call on Yorke[4] about them. Oh how I long for an hour with you to give you the whole of the private History of this family since I saw you. Your friend Mrs Burke is just now slowly recovering from a Complaint in Her Bowels. Dick is far from well, and the Doctor has got the Gout. You see we are an infirmary. Yet we can all, from the bottom of our hearts, rejoice on the pleasing prospect of an establishment to your satisfaction for Your young Ladies.[5] Let us hear something further. You say nothing of the parties. Cleaver is by me and desires his respects to you. Adieu.

29th March.

[1] Probably John Benson (1744–1827), later Clerk of the Journals and Papers of the House of Commons; he assisted in the preparation of private bills. See O. C. Williams, *Clerical Organization of the House of Commons 1661–1850*, Oxford, 1954, pp. 78, 183.

[2] 27 March. The House had been hearing evidence by the London merchants about trade with America.

[3] On 27 March the House adjourned until 7 April for the Easter recess, but the resolutions on American trade were not reported until 9 May.

[4] Charles Yorke, Attorney-General.

[5] O'Hara had written Burke 10 March (printed Hoffman, pp. 334–8): 'I am about marrying both my Niece and my daughter. Forms are verbally settled, and I think the conclusion will soon happen.' Burke refers again to the daughter's marriage in his letter of [21 April]. The niece, Charlotte O'Hara, married Eyre Trench in 1768 (*Dublin Journal*, 5–8 March 1768).

To CHARLES O'HARA—8 *April* [1766]

Source: O'Hara MSS. Printed Hoffman, pp. 342–4.
Endorsed: 8th April 1766.

My dear Sir,

I am ashamed of talking any longer of Business as an apology for the small number and the small value of my Letters. No Business I believe could employ my time better, and I am very sure, none could employ it half so pleasantly, although, in general, I find the things which I have most at heart going on very much as I could wish them; I mean the Transactions in Parliament, which find my thoughts Some employment both in and out of the house, and which I stick to exclusively of every thing else, not only as a satisfaction, but as a refuge. There I go on, in my own imprudent way, speaking my mind without fear or Wit, as the old Proverb says; and doing my party what service I can, without asking in what light they will consider or attend to it. Last Night we closed the examination of our Witnesses to the propriety of opening Dominica as a Free port,[1] which concludes the enquiry previous to the resolutions, that are to be the foundations of the New American Trade act. These Resolutions will be proposed in the Committee for America, next Monday.[2] I do not now look for much opposition; The Spirit of the adverse faction begins to evaporate; Even Mr Grenville begins to slacken in his attendance; His Language is, I am told, that of despair of the Commonwealth, Prophecies, Omens, ruin, &c. &c. In short if some foolish measure of those at the head does not precipitate them from their situation, or if some Court earthquake, (the thing most to be dreaded in this Climate) does not shake the ground under them, I see nothing in the union, the ability, or the spirit, of opposition, which is able to move them. So much popularity never was possessed by any set of people who possessed great offices. Yet all is in an odd way, which nothing less than a long conversation can explain; if even that were capable of explaining so odd a situation of things.[3] General Conways illness redoubles the perplexity; He went to the Country in a tolerable state of convalescency, but making too free with himself, he was again struck down; He is said

[1] A bill 'for opening and establishing certain ports in the islands of Jamaica and Dominica, for the more free importation and exportation of certain goods and merchandises' was introduced into the House 15 May.

[2] The House was to have debated the American resolutions in committee on Monday, 14 April, but owing to Conway's illness this was postponed.

[3] The weakness of the Rockingham Administration was due not to the opposition but to its own divisions. Egmont and Northington wished Rockingham to become reconciled with Bute's friends; Conway and Grafton wished to see Pitt at the head of Administration; while Rockingham was equally unwilling to admit Bute's friends or to yield his place to Pitt.

to be quite out of danger; I wish he may; but he gets on slowly. His loss would be inexpressible. I do believe he is a most virtuous man in every particular publick and private, and he has ability for any thing. If he could Stick a little more steadily to his points he would be, by far the best Leader of an house of Commons, I ever saw.[1]

I find you go on in Ireland plotting; alarming; informing; seizing; and imprisoning as usual; What surprises me is to find by one or two of your Letters, that you are a little giving way to the ingenious Bon ton of our Country. I see it is impossible totally to avoid it. You seem to think, that if they do not discover the cause of their distemper by the dissaction of Sheehy,[2] they will leave off Their villainous Theories of Rebellions and Massacres. Sic notus Ulysses?[3] I hear they intend to poke in the Bowels of a few more for further discoveries.[4] Why had I a connection of feeling or even of knowlege with such a Country! I am not sorry that our Schemes for it; for the present at least, will not do. On this we will talk more in the Summer. I tried last Night the free exportation of Soap from — to the West Indies. The Evidence turned out as well as we could wish. I had some little weight with some of the Merchants of the out-Ports; and they will not oppose. It will be indeed no great matter; but a beginning is somewhat. Adieu. We are all well. Are all yours so. God bless you.

8th April.

[1] Horace Walpole, Conway's intimate friend, and with a longer experience of the House of Commons than Burke, did not think so. He wrote about Conway: 'His heart was so cold that it wanted all the beams of popular applause to kindle it into action' (*Memoirs*, II, 150); he 'could not be induced to traffic with Members' (*ibid.* II, 297–8), and 'paid too much deference to what men would say of him' (*ibid.* III, 56). He was an unsuccessful leader of the House of Commons, and was never happy in the post.

[2] Nicholas Sheehy (1728–66), a Roman Catholic priest, had been tried in Dublin 10 February on a charge of inciting to riot and rebellion. He was acquitted, but then tried in Clonmel on a further charge of instigating to murder. Lecky called his second trial 'one of the most scandalous ever known in Ireland' (*History of Ireland in the Eighteenth Century*, London, 1896, II, 42–3). Sheehy was hanged, drawn and quartered 15 March.

[3] Thus have you known Ulysses? See *Aeneid*, II, 44.

[4] Burke's papers at Sheffield prove his interest in Sheehy and in the persons arraigned and executed shortly after him on similar charges. In one packet (Bk 8a) are a printed letter of Sheehy, dated the day before his execution, and MS copies of: a petition of Edmund Sheehy (executed 3 May); the substance of another petition of Edmund Sheehy; Edmund Sheehy's last speech declaring his innocence; the last declaration of James Farrell (executed 3 May); the last declaration of James Buxton (executed 3 May); a letter written by James Buxton while in Kilkenny Gaol, asserting that he had been urged to give evidence against certain Roman Catholic gentlemen (including Burke's relative James Nagle), for which evidence he might have had his pardon.

To CHARLES O'HARA—[21 *April* 1766]

Source: O'Hara MSS. Printed Hoffman, pp. 348–9. *Endorsed:* Subsequent to 8 Apl. but | without date.

Burke is writing on the day Dowdeswell's bill for the regulation of the Window Tax is to be reported to the House; he writes before the division has taken place, but twice says it is to be 'this day'; it was voted upon 21 April.

My dear Sir, I thank you for your Letters, enclosures &c &c. They give me light into your affairs, and into the spirit and Temper of your time and Country. I see, that weak unsystematick Government will be more odious, as well as more contemptible, than wicked Government. As to us here, with such real abilities as perhaps few men at the head of affairs have had in our time, by looking for a support exterior to themselves, and leaning on it, they have weakend themselves, renderd themselves triffling, and at length have had drawn away from them that prop upon which they leaned.[1] Pitt, because administration (at least a part of it) would not submit to such terms, as no man with a drop of blood in his Veins would hearken to,[2] came down to the house some days ago, when Conway and Dowdeswell were both of them ill, and absent, and abused administration in the grossest and most unprovoked manner.[3] This will, I hope, open their Eyes; and bring them to themselves, to union, self-dependence, consistency and firmness. They opposed[4] Dowdeswells regulation of the Window Tax for the supply of the year, in the Committee, and oppose it with great rancour.[5] They oppose it this day on the report; we divided, but 162 to 112. I suppose this day will be no better.[6] Conways long illness is a dreadful loss to us. I am in haste. I rejoice in the happy establishment of my friend your Daughter.[7] We all rejoice in every instance of your felicity. Adieu. We live in a strange time.

[1] Burke exaggerates the unity, strength, and abilities of the Rockingham Administration. Without Pitt's support it is doubtful if they could have repealed the Stamp Act; now that Pitt was drawing away from them their remaining in office became very difficult.

[2] Pitt laid down no terms, but refused to discuss taking office with anyone but the King. But his taking office would have meant the exclusion of Newcastle and Rockingham.

[3] Walpole writes (*Memoirs*, II, 224) about Pitt's speech in the debate of 14 April on the militia regulations: 'He went to the House, and made a vociferous declamation against the Ministry, who, he said, aimed at destroying the militia; he would go to the farthest corner of the island to overturn any Ministers that were enemies to the militia.'

[4] The followers of Grenville and Bedford.

[5] On 18 April, when Dowdeswell introduced his Budget. The division, as Burke mentions below, was 162 to 112. The window tax was unpopular, and some who normally supported Administration voted against it.

[6] The window tax was reported from the Committee of Ways and Means on 21 April, and was carried by 169 to 85.

[7] O'Hara's daughter Mary (b. 1748) had married James Carrique Ponsonby of Crotto in County Kerry.

To CHARLES O'HARA—23, 24 [*April* 1766]

Source: O'Hara MSS. Printed Hoffman, pp. 347–8. *Endorsed:* 23d. April.

My dear friend,

I fly to your correspondence as a refuge from Solitude, at a time when I do not find it pleasant to be alone. On my return from a City feast, where the Majority (on the Stamp act) of Both houses dined with the North American Merchants,[1] I found the Doctor gone to Hampton. Jenny has been there for some time for the recovery of her health. Dick is with her; and Will remains with Genl Conway in the Country. I was driven home, almost immediately after Dinner, by the accident of a fish bone sticking in my throat. It gives me some pain, but much more uneasiness. It will look as if I slunk from Duty at a time of danger. God knows that kind of fear and managment is far from my heart, and the appearance or suspicion of it would make me half distracted—Since I wrote the above, Gataker[2] has been with me; he gives me great comfort; he thinks the bone is got down, and sees no sign of inflammation. And assures me that please God, I shall be able to go out without danger tomorrow. Tomorrow our American resolutions come on.[3] In how oversanguine a light friendship sees things! Of twenty good projects, it is well if two can be brought to bear; and it is well too, if one at least of these two, be not maimed mutilated, and deprived of its vital Spirit and efficacy. When the Freeport came to be debated in a full Cabinet, the old Stagers fritterd it down to an address to the King for the opinion of the boards on the matter &c.—so we come hopping into the house with half a measure; the most odious thing, I am sure to my Temper and opinions that can be conceived.[4] However, even this miserable remnant is better than nothing. The great Commoner sets his face against it. I went down to Hayes with a very respectable Merchant of Lancaster, to talk him, if possible, out of his peevish and perverse opposition to so salutary and unexceptionable a measure. But on this point, I found so

[1] The *Annual Register* described the occasion (1766, p. 87): 'The company last Wednesday [23 April] at Draper's-hall was very numerous, and the most brilliant almost ever seen in the city of London. It is said there were about 240 who dined, amongst whom were nine Dukes, and a very considerable number more of the nobility, and the members of the house of Commons, who honoured the American merchants with their company.'

[2] Dr Thomas Gataker (*c.* 1718–68).

[3] In the Committee of the whole House on the American papers.

[4] On 9 May the Committee on the American papers reported 'that it is the opinion of this committee, that it will be for the advantage of the trade, navigation, and manufactures, of this Kingdom, to establish one or more port or ports in his Majesty's dominions in America, for the more free importation and exportation of certain goods and merchandizes, under proper regulations and restrictions'. The Free Port bill was introduced into the House on 15 May (see above, letter of 8 April, p. 248).

great a man utterly unprovided with any better arms than a few rusty prejudices. So we returned as we went, after some hours fruitless conference. But the truth is, he determined to be out of humour; and this was the first object he had to display it upon; for he had in a better Temper approved of all the previous regulations.[1] We are, it is true, demolishing the whole Grenvillian Fabrick. Rigby is right.[2] But we must clear the Ground. After all but too much I fear will remain in spite of all our Labours. Dont be surprised if you should hear of some strange alteration in a week.[3] Adieu. We are in a most unaccountable way.

23d

This day 24th Pitt came down, and made a fine flaming patriotick Speech, chiefly against any sort of personal connections; he means with any besides himself.[4] It was a Speech too virtuous to be honest. I am quite well. The Enemys Plan seems to be to start object after object to keep off our doing any thing on the American affairs. And they have hitherto been but too successful. This day nothing is done. God knows when any thing will.

[1] There is in the Newcastle Papers (Add. MS 32974, fols. 417–23) a document, dated 18 April 1766, and headed 'An Account of Mr Thomas Walpole's Conversation with Mr Pitt; and, afterwards, with the Duke of Newcastle'. Walpole thus reported Pitt: 'That he knew nothing of the intention to make Dominica a Free Port 'till the Friday before the Monday that it was to be proposed in Parliament [i.e. Friday, 11 April], when Mr Burke was sent by my Lord Rockingham to acquaint him with it. That he (Mr Pitt) entirely disapproved it; and made some observations also upon some of the resolutions which were intended to be proposed relating to the trade of America and the West Indies. That this conduct towards him by the Administration shew'd a great slight, and was not consistent with the professions which had been made to him. That Mr Burke when he was with him also expressed my Lord Rockingham's great desire to have things brought to a happy conclusion between them; and particularly that his Lordship wished that Mr Pitt would explain himself to the King's Ministers upon what conditions he would come into the King's service. Mr Pitt took that up warmly and said: Mr Burke, I wonder you should make that proposition when I have given it under my hand in a letter to my Lord Rockingham that I will open myself upon that point to nobody but *to the King himself*.'

[2] O'Hara's letter of 15 April (printed Hoffman, pp. 344–6) had said: 'Rigby writes us word that the present Ministers are solely employd in undoing what their Predecessors had done.'

[3] On 21 April Grafton had a conversation with Rockingham, in which Rockingham said 'that he would never advise his Majesty to call Mr Pitt into his closet, that this was a fixed resolution to which he would adhere'. Grafton, considering this as 'an absolute opposition to Mr P. coming into the Ministry at all', told Conway on 22 April that he would resign (Grafton, *Autobiography*, p. 71).

[4] Pitt's speech was made on a petition of the sugar refiners of London complaining of the high duties on imported foreign sugar. Dowdeswell was against referring the petition to the Committee on American papers, but Pitt was for it, and the House agreed without a division to refer it to the Committee.

To JAMES BARRY—[*circa* 13 *May* 1766]

Source: MS F.W. Hilles. Printed Barry, *Works*, I, 53–5.
Addressed: A Monsieur | Monsr. Barry, chez | Monsr. le Colonel Drumgold | a l'Abbayé de St Germains | a Paris. *Postmarked:* 13|MA.
A brief postscript by Dr Nugent is omitted.

My dear Barry, I hope your kindness and partiality to me, will induce you to give the most favourable construction to my long Silence. I assure you, that disregard and inattention to you had not the smallest share in it. I love you and esteem you, as I always did ever since I knew you; and I wish your welfare, and your Credit, (which is the best gift of providence in the way of fortune) as much as any man; and am much pleased with the steps which I hear you are taking to advance them. Mr Macleane, your very good friend, tells me, that you are preparing to set out shortly for Italy. As to what regards you personally I have only to advise, that you would not live in a poor or an unequal manner; but plentifully, upon the best things, and, as nearly as you can, in the ordinary method of other people. Singularity in Diet, is in General, I believe, unwholesome; your friend the doctor, is, in that way of thinking. I mention this, as Macleane tells me you have been ill, by ordering your diet on a plan of your own. I shall be happy in hearing that you are thoroughly recoverd, and ready to proceed on your Journey with alacrity and spirit.

With regard to your studies, you know, my dear Barry, my opinion. I do not choose to lecture you to death. But to say all I can in a few Words. It will not do for a man qualified like you to be a connoisseur, and a sketcher. You must be an Artist; and this you cannot be but by drawing with the last degree of noble correctness. Until you can draw beauty with the last degree of Truth and precision, you will not consider yourself possessd of that faculty. This power will not hinder you from passing to the great Style when you please, if your Character should, as I imagine it will, lead you to that Style in preference to the other. But no man can draw perfectly that cannot draw Beauty. My dear Barry, I repeat it again, leave off sketching. Whatever you do; finish it. Your Letters are very kind in remembering us; and surely as to the Criticisms of every kind, admirable. Reynolds likes them exceedingly. He conceives extraordinary hopes of you; and recommends above all things to you the continual Study of the *Capella Systina*, in which are the greatest Works of Michael Angelo. He says, he will be mistaken if that Painter does not become your great favourite. Let me entreat, that you will overcome that unfortunate delicacy that attends you, and that you will go through a full Course of Anatomy, with the knife in your hand; you will never be able thoroughly to supply the omission of this by any other method. The p⟨resent⟩ exhibition is, I think much the best that we have had. West has two pieces which would give you very great hopes of him; I confess some time ago, I had not any that were very sanguine; but in these he has really done considerable things.[1] Barret enquires very kindly for you. He makes a very good figure in this exhibition.[2]

To Charles O'Hara—24 [*May* 1766]

Source: O'Hara MSS. Printed Hoffman, pp. 349–51.
Endorsed: 24 May.

My dear Sir,

I am sure I receive nothing agreeable to my mind from Ireland, but your Letters; I am truly obliged to you for remembering me so often. I am rejoiced at the account you give me of the settlement of my fair friend;[3] and that there is such a prospect of the mutual happiness of the young people, from the good Character I hear of one of them, and from the good dispositions I know of the other. To them I cordially wish many happy years; and as to you, who are almost an old Beau, I wish you the humiliating satisfaction of being speedily a Grandfather; and I have my reasons for this wish; For in order to fly from that respectable and mortifying Character, you will come over to us; and then I shall have one tie the Less to Ireland, and its concerns. Indeed while you stay there, I shall be glad to hear even of their politicks; for in passing through your mind, they will lose something of their original Nature; and will soften from Faction into Philosophy. The last thing I did in the house was to make a Battle, and I made a strenous, though an unsuccessfull one, for the Irish Sope Bill.[4] The season was far advanced, the house thin, the proposition (as they said) new and serious. The Treasury Bench gave way under me; I debated *alone* for near an hour, with some sharp antagonists; I grew warm; and had a mind to divide the house on it; but as I saw myself unsupported, and that a Negative might affect the pro-

[1] Benjamin West (1738–1820) exhibited five paintings at the Society of Artists this year: (1) 'The Continence of Scipio'; (2) 'Pylades and Orestes', its companion; (3) Cymon and Iphigenia'; (4) 'Diana and Endymion', its companion; (5) 'Two young ladies at play'. Algernon Graves, *Society of Artists of Great Britain, 1760–1791*, London, 1907, p. 275.

[2] George Barret exhibited at the Society of Artists: (1) 'A View of Welbeck Park, the seat of the Duke of Portland'; (2) 'A View of the great tree in Welbeck Park'; (3) 'A Landscape, study from nature'. *Ibid.* p. 22.

[3] O'Hara's daughter (see above, letter of [21 April], p. 250).

[4] In the debate of 15 May 'A motion was made, that leave be given to bring in a bill, for permitting soap manufactured in Ireland, to be imported from thence to any of his Majesty's Colonies and Plantations' (*Journals of the House of Commons*, XXX, 825).

position essentially, I escaped over a Bridge which Oswald[1] laid for me; who pressed me, in very flattering Terms to withdraw my Motion, and to make it early in the Next Session. This I pledged myself to do. I was mortified to the last degree, having had all the reason in the world to be certain that the motion would not meet with the slightest opposition. You see all the trading arrangements, and the Freeport are carried.[2] They talk of some opposition to them in the Committee, and on the report; but I believe it will be trivial; at least in the House of Commons.[3] I attended your Corn Bill with assiduity and warmth.[4] I think it a right Bill; and it has so far had fair play, that the Council have not rejected it; they resume the consideration of that Bill next Tuesday. General Conway is for it; at least for the principle; but the truth is, the corn system of Ireland is so ill contrived, that its greatest embarrassments arise from its own confusion. For instance, they began with a Bounty Bill, in the Duke of Bedfords time, so low, that it did no sort of service.[5] In 1762 They passed a Corn Bill allowing *half* the English Bounties; which was rejected, I suppose, as too high;[6] and now they send over one, near *four fifths* of ours. It makes that Bounty cease at 1 L.6 s.* The quarter, which seems to infer, (if this be thought an *high* price and equivalent to the 2 L.8 s. at which our Bounty stops here) that the *ordinary* price of Corn is excessively low in Ireland and that they want no Bounty at all. However no endeavour shall be wanting to get it through. As to the grand constitutional Bills I leave them to those who understand them; I am sure the people ought to eat whether they have Septennial Parliaments or not.[7] We are all in a Blaze here with your plots, assassinations, massacres, Rebellions, moonlight armies, French Officers and French money. Are you not ashamed? You who told me, that if they could get no discovery from

* I dont know when it has been at that price [Burke's note].

[1] James Oswald (1715–69), M.P. for Dysart burghs.

[2] The Free Port bill was read a second time 16 May, and the bill to defray the expenses of opening the ports, 23 May.

[3] The bills passed without a division.

[4] The Corn Bill (5 Geo. III, *c.* 19 of the Irish Statutes) which the Irish Parliament had given to the Lord Lieutenant for transmission to England 19 March. After approval it was returned to Ireland, passed 6 June, and received the royal assent 8 June.

[5] 29 Geo. II, *c.* 9.

[6] See *Journals of the Irish House of Commons*, XIII, 211, 222, 233, 241–2.

[7] Until 1768 Irish parliaments were dissolved only by the death of the Sovereign. The Irish were very eager for legislation which would limit them to seven, or at least to eight years. Burke had long since become sceptical of the efficacy of such measures. Dr French Laurence, writing to Earl Fitzwilliam concerning Burke's papers (Fitzwilliam MSS (N.R.S.), letter of 11 August 1797), spoke of an 'important document in regard to the history of his principles;—a fragment of the year *1755*. It is in favour of long, rather than short Parliaments'. Laurence must be referring to a discussion of the relative merits of long and short parliaments which is in one of the early notebooks (Bk 41) at Sheffield; a marginal note in Burke's later hand identifies it as his, and dates it 1755. But it is not strongly on the side of long parliaments.

Sheehy, they would cool and leave off their detestable plot monging?[1] You think well of Ireland; but I think rightly of it; and know, that their unmeaning Senseless malice is insatiable; *cedamus patria*! I am told, that these miserable wretches whom they have hanged, died with one Voice declaring their innocence: but truly for my part, I want no man dying, or risen from the dead, to tell me, that lies are lies, and nonsense is nonsense. I wish your absurdity was less mischievous, and less bloody. Are there not a thousand other ways in which fools may make themselves important? I assure you, I look on these things with horror; and cannot talk of such proceedings as the effects of an innocent credulity. If there be an army paid, and armed, and disciplined, and sworn to foreign powers in your country, cannot Government know it by some better means than the Evidence of whores and Horse Stealers. If these things be so, why is not the publick security provided for by a good body of Troops and a stronger military establishment? If not, why is the publick alarmed by such senseless Tales? But I know not why I reiterate such stuff to you; every company here is tormented with it—adieu! it is late; and I am vexed and ashamed, that the Government we live in, should not know those who endanger it, or who disturb it by false alarms; to punish the one with knowlege and vigour; or to silence the other with firmness. Adieu.

Yours ever
E BURKE

Saturday. 24.

JOHN WILKES *to* EDMUND BURKE—12 *June* 1766

Source: Fitzwilliam MSS (Milton).
Addressed: To | Edmund Burke Esqr. | Member of Parliament | in Queen Anne Street | near Cavendish Square | London | Angleterre. *Postmarked:* 16|IV | ⟨IDCX⟩ | 7 | W.

Wilkes had finally grown tired of waiting in Paris for his friends in England to improve his situation for him. Early in May he crossed the channel himself and attempted a direct negotiation with the Ministry. According to Prior's account (2nd ed. I, 153) Rockingham refused to see him: 'Mr Burke, accompanied by Mr Fitzherbert, was sent as his deputy, when, after five different interviews, his modest demands to compensate for his sufferings,—viz. a free pardon, a sum of money, a pension of 1500 l. per annum on the Irish establishment, or equivalents —were peremptorily rejected, with a recommendation to leave the country. The negotiation, however, was conducted with such address and temper by the

[1] O'Hara had tried to reassure Burke in his letter of 15 April (printed Hoffman, pp. 344–6) that the persecuting mania which had shown itself in the Sheehy trials could not be long-lived—unless it were inflamed by injudicious opposition: 'When left to its own pursuits, it wastes itself, and dies. Til at last, no foundation for it being discoverd, it turns upon the people who first raisd it. The turn of the tide is now not far off.'

secretary, that, after a douceur of three or four hundred pounds, collected from the private purses of Ministry, this pattern of morality and suffering patriotism retraced his steps to the French capital.' Burke still professed to think reasonably well of Wilkes's prospects after his departure. Lauchlin Macleane wrote Wilkes 6 June (Add. MS 30869, fol. 42): 'I have seen our common, I mean our uncommon Friend Burke. He says the handsomest things possible of you, and bids me assure you of his intire regard, he thinks your matters will be made very easy in a few Days.'

Paris, Rue des Saints Peres.
June 12. 1766.

Dear Sir,

I have so very particular obligations to you that I cannot content myself with having only desir'd Mr Fitzherbert to tell you the gratefull sentiments of my heart. I beg'd that favour of him as soon as I arriv'd at Calais, and you must now give me leave to repeat that I feel as I ought your generous endeavours to serve me, and the warmth of your friendship. It shall be the study of my life to make you the most gratefull returns, and yet I must own that you have done such handsome things with respect to me in the very setting out, that I am likely ever to remain in a long arrear to you.

The great object of my hopes is a pardon, which I wish to owe to his Majesty's goodness, and to the favour of our friends. I shou'd endeavour to merit it from my Sovereign, and my friends wou'd not find me ungratefull. I am very thankfull to you all for what you have done in the cause of liberty, and I persuade myself justice will be done to the greatest sufferer in it. I go farther. I am desirous of becoming your fellow labourer, and shou'd be pleas'd even to bring you the bricks and mortar, when I know what beautifull edifices you construct. I hope cement will not be wanting, and then a rotten stone or two tumbling out can do no harm.

I am here feeding among the lilies, in a state of trifling amusement, but casting my longing eyes towards England, and wishing to be usefull to my country, there, or any where. I am ready to any good word or work, of which I may be thought capable, and I live in the impatient hope of returning soon, and perhaps aiding to keep the boars out of the garden.

May I trouble you to assure Lord Rockingham of my regard and attachment?

I am ever, dear Sir,
your most affectionate, and
oblig'd, humble Servant,
JOHN WILKES.

To Sir George Savile—16 *June* [1766]

Source: Foljambe MSS. Abstract and Extract printed Hist. MSS Comm. (*Foljambe MSS*), p. 145. *Endorsed:* Mr Burke June 16th. 1766 | No. 98.

This letter deals with a punishment inflicted upon Edward Burrows, Collector of Customs at Hull. Inspectors from the Surveyor-General's Office, London, had reported irregularities in the conduct of the Customs House of Hull (Customs letter-book, Hull, Board to Collector, 28 May 1766). No charges were at first made against Burrows, and he was specifically cleared of some other charges brought against him at nearly the same time (see minute in Public Record Office, T. 11/28, p. 71); but further investigation resulted in a decision to reprimand him 'in the most publick and severe manner in the Custom House in the presence of every officer at the port who shall be able to attend' (Customs letter-book, Hull, 28 May (*bis*) and 6 June). Perhaps Sir George Savile thought the public humiliation too severe a punishment and protested to Rockingham on Burrows's behalf.

Dear Sir

Mr Hammond[1] gave me your Letter from Leeds. You may be assured, that I shall attend very carefully to any business in which you have an interest. However I fear, that in spite of all that can be done, the affair of the Collector of Hull cannot be brought to a speedy conclusion. The Commissioners you know examined into his Conduct, decided upon it, sentenced him to such a Penalty as they thought proper, and this sentence is submitted to and actually executed. You know my Lord Rockinghams delicacy in a Business circumstanced as this is. He is therefore of opinion that the whole proceeding should be revised by the Treasury, in a publick and solemn manner; and this, you are sensible must take up a good deal of time. The papers are already Large enough to make a very decent figure in a Chancery suit. But the tedious mode of proceeding will not be renderd additionally dilatory by any kind of delay not necessarily connected with the very nature of the Enquiry. My Lord R. is well, and begins to breathe a little. I am with the truest respect and regard Dear Sir

Your most obedient
and humble Servant
E Burke

16th June.

Burrows's appointment at Hull was revoked on 9 July; he was, however, later appointed Collector of Greenock. I am indebted to R. C. Jarvis, Esq. of King's Beam House, London, for details concerning this affair.

[1] William Hammond (d. 1793) of Kirk Ella, Warden of Trinity House, Hull, a Rockingham supporter.

To JOHN WILKES—4 *July* 1766

Source: British Museum (Add. MS 30877, fol. 56).
Endorsed: Receiv'd at Paris July 9. 1766.

Dear Sir,

Will you have the goodness to excuse my delay in answering your very polite and obliging Letter; the Date of which I am ashamed to look at? I am sure it deservd the best and speediest return I could make to it; Your thinking of me at a time so critical to your interest, and in a place so favourable to your pleasures, was very kind of you, both as a man and as Mr Wilkes; and I assure you, I am far from being insensible to your Civility. Whether your late excursion hither was within the frigid rules of sedate and measured prudence, I will not undertake to determine; but I know, I consider myself as served by that step; as it gave me the opportunity of your conversation, which supported the opinion I always entertained of your abilities, and improved that which I had conceived of your heart and Temper.

I am sorry that I must direct to you at Paris. But since it is yet decreed, that you must be *a little longer* from home, I am pleased that you are not confined to an inhospitable Tomos, like your Roman predecessor[1] in Wit, gallantry and misfortunes. Since you are in a foreign pasture, I am glad (to use your own expression) that you feed among the Lillies. We would all choose the home field for you, though our English Roses bear thorns not a few, and though the down of the Scotch Thistle is coverd with a sufficiency of Prickles, which you have turned and sharpend against yourself.

Your offers of service are most obliging; and they are understood as they ought to be. But hitherto the System of the next Winter is not so clear as to point out any regular dijested plan of measures either in the offensive or the defensive. Whenever they are, for me, I wish you restored to those friends who are as they ever have been, unwearied in their desires to serve you, and whose services you are so capable of rewarding by your Society. FitzHerbert is well and I believe will shortly write to you. I am going to Ireland in a few days on my own little affairs. I am Dear Sir with great Truth and regard, and the most sincere wishes for your speedy[2] return to your Country—

your most obedient
and most humble Servant
ED BURKE

London
Q. Anne Street
4th July 1766.

[1] MS: prodecessor; Ovid was exiled from Rome to Tomi (Constanta) on the Black Sea.

[2] MS: spedy

Wilkes's chances weakened with the Ministry. Lauchlin Macleane wrote him 15 July: 'All is Mystery and confusion; the Sky is clouded in such a manner that Nobody can judge of the Horizon till the Sun breaks out' (Add. MS 30869, fol. 56). He wrote again 22 July: 'Lord Rockingham I fear will lose his Office, General Conway continues in his...If Lord Rockingham does nothing spirited for you before he goes out I shall think it very odd' (Add. MS 30869, fol. 62). Neither Rockingham nor his successors met Wilkes's demands.

To the DUKE OF PORTLAND—[17 *July* 1766]

Source: Portland MSS (Nottingham). *Endorsed:* July. 17. 1766 | Mr Edmd Burke | R/.

On 7 July the King had asked Pitt to form a new Administration. Pitt intended to take the existing Rockingham Administration as a basis for his own, but wished the post of First Lord of the Treasury to be offered to his brother-in-law Lord Temple. Temple saw the King, but on 17 July declared that he could not accept. This revived the spirits of the Rockingham group, as it made it likely that more of them could remain in office.

My Lord

It is certainly with no very great reluctance that I obey Lord Rockinghams commands, in informing your Grace, that Lord Temple, with a Spirit and resolution truly worthy of him, has differd with Mr Pitt, and just Left town in Anger, with a resolution to have nothing to do in the administration. I give your Grace Joy of this at least. It may lead to something better. I am with the truest respect and esteem

My Lord
your Graces
most obedient
and most humble Servant
EDM BURKE

Thursday Night.

To the EARL OF DARTMOUTH—[18 *July* 1766]

Source: Dartmouth MSS. Printed Hist. MSS Comm. (*Dartmouth MSS*) p. 183. *Endorsed:* Marq. of Rockingham | July 1766.

William Legge, 2nd Earl of Dartmouth (1731–1801), was First Lord of Trade in the Rockingham Administration.

My Lord

The Marquess being just now extremely hurried has orderd me to give your Lordship a short sketch of the present situation of things. I think it looks rather better than it has done for some time. About ten last Night Lord Temple set out for Stow: much chagrined, and with a determined resolution to take no part in the arrangement of Mr Pitts System of administration. They differd in opinion exceedingly, and I hear with much heat, at least upon one Side. It is probable both from rational conjecture, and tolerably good information, that their difference was upon the two capital points of G. Grenvi⟨lle⟩ whom Lord T. desired to be brought in, together with Lord Lyttelton but in what rank I do not hear.[1] This proposition Mr Pitt strenuously resisted. The other Point of my Lord T. was the exclusion of Lord Northumberland and Mackenzie on which he found Mr P. equally untractable.[2] The first, I take to have been the real cause of difference; The second, the ostensible cause of Quarrell. Whatever the motives to this Step were, the Step itself is certainly an happy one; as it narrows the ground of disagreement between Pitt and this party very considerably, both with regard to the quantity, and the quality of the objection.[3] I take it for granted that this will not find your Lordship in Town, or I should have taken the Liberty of waiting on you with the News. I am with the greatest truth and respect

My Lord
your Lorships
most obedient humble Servant
E BURKE

Friday morn

To CHARLES O'HARA—29 *July* [1766]

Source: O'Hara MSS. Printed Hoffman, pp. 353–5. *Endorsed:* 29 July 1766.

My dear Sir, I take the Chance that my Letter shall find you in Dublin. At the same hazard I directed a little article of intelligence to you at Plymouth. All that I was then able to communicate, went no farther,

[1] Burke's view that Temple refused the Treasury because Pitt would not give office to Grenville was generally held but was incorrect. Temple asked office for neither Grenville nor Lyttelton: he demanded, however, to be 'at *least* equal to any man' in the King's service, and suggested Lord Gower for Secretary of State as a test of Pitt's willingness to share power. (The King to Northington, 17 July 1766; Fortescue, I, 377.) Temple declined office when he realized Pitt would not allow him co-authority with himself.

[2] Mackenzie was Bute's brother and Northumberland was connected with Bute by marriage; Temple was alleged to have demanded their exclusion as a sign that Bute was to have no share in the new Administration. But in fact the discussion between Temple and Pitt seems not to have gone as far as particular appointments.

[3] Pitt's followers also believed that Temple's refusal would allow the Rockinghams to take office under Pitt. On 24 July 1766 Lord Camden, appointed Lord Chancellor in the new Administration, wrote to Thomas Walpole: 'Lord T[emple]'s wild conduct, tho Mr P[itt] is grievously wounded by it, may, for aught I know, turn out to be a favorable circumstance, to reconcile him more to the present Ministry, out of which corps he must form, as he always intended, this our Administration' (Grafton, *Autobiography*, p. 94).

than to let you know the Event of Lord Temples interview with Pitt, which broke off in great ill humour between them. Lord Temples demands at first included the bringing in of G. Grenville, but he soon gave up that point. Those at which he stuck were, Lord Gower for Secretary of State, and Lord Lyttelton for President of the Council. These were his demands; his objections, which were kept in reserve, and only to be produced in Case the demands were not complied with, went to Lord North[umberlan]d and Mackenzie. On the whole, it appeard very clearly, that his madness took the turn, to which it has been long inclining; that he ought to have the lead of Pitt. Whatever may [be] the ill Effect of his Phrenzy on his own affairs, on those of our party, it has produced none that are good for much. It is divided; and with Circumstances that will alienate I fear the minds of people as much from one another, as their Situations are seperated. The Plan was originally, that all should be wished to keep their places, who were sufferd to remain in them; and that those who were put out should smother their resentments, and concur in the support of a System, which if they could destroy, they could not replace with a better.[1] But in such a plan, temper must have its share as well as policy. When it was once seen, that so great removes were effected, when Ld Rockingham, Newcastle, Richmond, Winchelsea,[2] and Dowdeswell were swept off at a Stroke, and without any softening Circumstance to them,[3] or any sort of declaration how far the proscription was to proceed with regard to the party, an ill humour, very contrary to the Spirit of support, and yet not vigorous enough for the Spirit of opposition, got up, and grows every day.[4] The Southern department with the American Patronage is for Ld Shelburne.[5] Dartmouth who has firmness and feeling enough, will never endure the cutting off his American pretensions by the New People, when He contended for that point with his old friends.[6] It was indeed by them conceded to

[1] Rockingham and Newcastle wished their friends to remain in office under Pitt, and expected Conway and Grafton to look after them. Burke was one of those who had to 'smother their resentments'.

[2] Daniel Finch, 8th Earl of Winchilsea (1689–1769).

[3] Burke overstates the Rockingham grievances. Dowdeswell was offered a place by Pitt but refused it (*Chatham Correspondence*, III, 22–3); Pitt was willing to employ Richmond (Walpole, *Memoirs*, II, 241); while Newcastle, aged 73, and Winchilsea, aged 77, could hardly expect to retain office much longer. Still, Pitt tried to soften Newcastle's fall with the offer of a pension, which was refused. Pitt could not be expected to offer Rockingham that share of power he had refused to Temple, and nothing less would have suited Rockingham. Pitt told Conway that he was 'sorry to displace' Rockingham (Walpole, *Memoirs*, II, 241), and when the Ministry was formed paid a courtesy call upon him and was rudely treated by Rockingham.

[4] Rockingham wrote Conway 26 July: 'Mr Pitt's intentions and conduct are and will be the most hostile to our friends' (Rockingham MSS, R 1–411).

[5] William Petty, 2nd Earl of Shelburne (1737–1805).

[6] Lord Dartmouth wished the colonies to become the department of a third Secretary of State, and resigned when this was refused him.

him without difficulty. Lord John Cavendish has sent word to the D. of Grafton, that he will not be in the New Commission.[1] Can the D. of Portland stand after this.[2] What with the removes, and the resignations, which will be the inevitable consequence of them, The party has none, who may properly be called theirs (except perhaps Conway) that remains in any situation of importance.[3] What Can they do? Join in opposition with G. Grenville? It can never be. Oppose without that party, and not with a third of your own forces? ridiculous and ineffective. Well! Events must be trusted to. C. Townshend took twenty turns and play'd twenty tricks before he was finally kicked up into Chancellor of the Exchequer.[4] How like you Pitts new Title? Earl of Chatham and Viscount Pitt of Pynsent Burton.[5] As to the Step itself, I think it not a good one. He ought to have kept the power of superintendency, if not of direct management of the H. of Commons, in his own hands, for some time at least. But imprudent as it is, I do not see any thing so fatal in it, as is commonly imagined. His popularity may suffer something; but he stands on the Closet Ground,[6] I mean the Bute Ground, which is better;[7] he will indeed become rather the more dependent on that interest, which will be attended with some unpleasant Circumstances. He omitted the great Line of Policy so plain before him, of joining the present People, and running, jointly with them, the Cabal to the Wall. Perhaps he thought this not so honourable, knowing upon what principles he was sent for. Terms I am told were made for three of those who are

[1] Lord John Cavendish resigned his office of Lord of the Treasury. 'I was much surprized', wrote Rockingham to Newcastle 26 July, 'as I did think that our friends would have waited and been more temperate' (Add. MS 32976, fols. 253–4).

[2] The Duke of Portland was treating for a marriage with Lady Dorothy Cavendish, Lord John's niece. 'He knows my opinion,' wrote Newcastle to Lord John, 26 July, 'which is that in our present circumstances our friends should not resign' (Add. MS 32976, fol. 271).

[3] The Rockinghams hoped that Conway and Grafton would be 'two friends in the first departments of government able and willing to protect them' (Lord John Cavendish to Newcastle, [26 July 1766]; Add. MS 32976, fol. 269). Newcastle told Conway 29 July that 'we think ourselves perfectly safe in your hands and the Duke of Grafton's' (ibid. fol. 315).

[4] Townshend told the King 'that what he held [Paymaster General] was more honorable and worth £7000 whilst the other [Chancellor of the Exchequer] was but £2500' (The King to Pitt, 25 July 1766; Fortescue, I, 380).

[5] Pitt was created Earl of Chatham and Viscount Pitt of Burton Pynsent 4 August. He was much criticized for taking a peerage, but his health was hardly good enough for him to lead the House of Commons.

[6] He had the support of the King.

[7] Rockingham was soon convinced that Chatham and Bute were allies. 'I understand', he wrote to Newcastle 29 August 1766, 'that the Administration profess being *totally* unconnected with Lord Bute. I believe it of many of them but not at all of Lord Chatham' (Add. MS 32976, fol. 489). In fact Bute was annoyed because Chatham had appointed his friends to office without consulting him. 'I have for ever done with this bad public', he wrote to the King about this time, 'my heart is half broke and my health ruined, with the unmerited barbarous treatment I have received' (*Letters from George III to Lord Bute*, p. 256).

in, and three only; Talbot; Litchfield;[1] and Egmont.[2] I believe among those who are to be brought in, Lord Despenser is thought of.[3] As to myself, I hear nothing. I consider myself as rather ill with Pitts whole party. The situation and conduct of my own friends is most unfavourable to me. But my way, though unpleasant, is thank God, plain. And nothing is truly miserable but a puzzle. I prepare God willing to set out for you in a very few days. Adieu my dear friend. E B.

29. July.

They kiss hands tomorrow.

To CHARLES O'HARA—19 *August* [1766]

Source: O'Hara MSS. Printed Hoffman, pp. 356–8.

Burke had told Wilkes 4 July that he was going to Ireland shortly on his own affairs. He crossed to Dublin in August with his wife and his brother Richard, and went to O'Hara's new house in Merrion Square, only to find that O'Hara had just left it for his seat in County Sligo.

My dear Sir, I was exceedingly mortified, at my arrival in Dublin, to find you just gone. The quick turn by which we missed you aggravated our vexation. But here however we are, thank God, well after our Voyage, situated by your kindness in an admirable house and in a fine Air. By the way, being well lodged is a mighty convenient thing, and I think you did wisely, even with some little difficulties, to get into so good an house. There is none better; I wish indeed your Ink was as good as your Study. If you find the writing white, pray accuse yourself. I had no civility from any of the New people, except a fine Speech Lord Shelburne made to Will about me. He wished of all things to embrace me before I left town. I told Lord R. of it, and said I would call on him. I did call on him. He was not at home, and I had no message to wish me a good Journey or any thing. As to Conway I called twice on him, to inform him of my going. I received, from him, no civil Message, even by Will; As to the others it is natural and I dont mind it. But in Mr Conway it was not over kind. As to the Policy of this Conduct, with regard to me it signifies little or nothing; but it has done great hurt in

[1] George Henry Lee, 3rd Earl of Lichfield (1718–72).

[2] Lord Egmont; see above, note to letter of 10 August 1757 (p. 124). No terms were made with any of the three whom Burke names. Talbot, as Lord Steward, and Lichfield, as Captain of the Band of Gentlemen Pensioners, retained their offices until they died. Egmont, who hated Pitt, resigned his post of First Lord of the Admiralty in August and never held office again.

[3] Lord le Despenser, who as Sir Francis Dashwood had been Bute's Chancellor of the Exchequer, was made joint Postmaster-General by Chatham.

regard to others. I know the whole of our Party that has staid in has taken great Offence at it. Not a word has been said to one of them. If an house had changed its master, more attention would have been paid to the footmen of the former family.[1] I say this with regard to the placemen. I just hear, that there is a great resignation in the Board of Admiralty. Ld Egmont, I am told, chooses to go out. His dispositions towards Pitt are well known; but his Devotion to Lord Bute is known too.[2] If it be true, that S. Mackenzie declines the Privy Seal of Scotland, which, I know was offerd to him,[3] it will, combined with the affair of Ld Egmont, demonstrate, that Ld Bute is not satisfied with the proceedings of his new Earl. Much of Egmonts conduct is to be always attributed to his feelings and his humours. Perhaps Pitt treated him with the same high hand he has done others.[4] That would be sufficient. But I fancy the Truth is, Ld Bute requires much more to be done than the restitution of Mackenzie. I know it was hinted to our people from very sufficient Authority, that a good deal more would be expected of *them* if they hoped to continue; and less will not satisfie him from Pitt. News we have no more; direct to me Dr Lelands, who will forward my Letters to me wherever I am. You have given us no Idea of your Route. But I beg you will be so good to let us know exactly how and where we may contrive to meet. I should wish the County of Kerry. Jane, whom you have lodged so pleasantly is much yours, and desires to be most affectionately rememberd to you and to those with you. Dick is truly yours. Adieu my dear friend.

19 Augst

[1] Rockingham made a similar complaint at the treatment of those of his friends who had stayed in office. He wrote Newcastle 26 July: 'There seems to be much anger among many at the total silence of Mr Pitt, and that neither directly nor indirectly thro' either Conway or the Duke of Grafton any mark of attention or civility, of even desiring or wishing for their concurrence has as yet been made' (Add. MS 32976, fol. 253). Burke's dislike of Pitt was growing rapidly. In some notes he later made on his own *Thoughts on the Cause of Present Discontents* (Sheffield, Bk 31, a copy; another copy Bk 6) he remarked upon Pitt's arrogance: 'He was angry as his Sister told me and as the fact undoubtedly was if any one but hinted that there was such a thing as an honest Man. He even hated or seemed to hate all those that were thought so, as far as he loved or hated any body, for he was free from those human infirmities not having one friend in the World.'

[2] Egmont was not devoted to Bute, who he felt had supplanted him at Leicester House after the death of Frederick, Prince of Wales.

[3] Burke is mistaken about the fact. Stuart Mackenzie was restored by Chatham to his office of Privy Seal of Scotland (taken from him by Grenville in May 1765), but without the disposal of Scottish patronage.

[4] Egmont, in addition to his personal dislike of Chatham, opposed Chatham's proposal for an alliance with Prussia and Russia.

To the Marquess of Rockingham—21 *August* 1766

Source: Fitzwilliam MSS (Sheffield). Printed *Corr.* (1844), I, 105–9.

My dear Lord,

I have let slip a post since my arrival in Dublin without paying my respects to you on your arrival at Wentworth. I am ashamed of the appearance of a Neglect, so contrary to my Duty, and, (I hope you will believe), to my Sentiments. The truth is, I wished to learn a little of the *Bon ton* of this place relative to the late and present administration before I troubled you with a letter. This great Town is indeed at present only a great desart; but amongst those who remain, there is but one opinion with regard to your Lordship; They are loud in declaring that no minister ever went through employment, or retired out of it with so much true honour and reputation. About the new System there is much doubt and uneasiness. There is still a little Twilight of popularity remaining round the great Peer; but it fades away every moment; and the people here who, in general, only reflect back the impressions of London, are growing quite out of humour with him. We have odd accounts from thence of which it is not very easy to find the Solution. I begin almost to fear, that your Lordship left Town a little too early. I think your friends must since then have wanted your advice on more than one occasion. Am I to attribute the resignation of Saunders to his having receivd some new instance of disregard from the great disposer?[1] I thought it was a settled point that none should go out without the concurrence of the party.[2] But gentlemen, who are really such, do not easily submit their feelings to their Politicks. After this can Keppell[3] or any of the rest stay in? And is Lord Egmonts resignation the Effect also of Temper. That Event I own surprised me. It looks as if Mr Pitt would find, that the Offer of Privy Seal of Scotland was by no means sufficient for Lord Bute; Nothing but weakness appears in the whole Fabrick of his ministry; yet I do not see what strength the party is likely to derive from thence; His necessities and his anger may drive him into the arms of the Bedfords;[4] for I confess I think he is gone too far to think of

[1] Sir Charles Saunders (*c.* 1713–75), one of Rockingham's followers, succeeded Lord Egmont as First Lord of the Admiralty. He had not resigned; Burke, in Ireland, may have relied upon a mistaken newspaper report.

[2] There was no such 'settled point'; Rockingham had expressed a wish that his friends should remain in office, but he could not prevent those who wished to, from resigning. Similarly in December 1766 when he wished his friends to resign, he could not compel them to do so.

[3] Admiral Augustus Keppel (1725–86), a Lord of the Admiralty and a follower of Rockingham.

[4] On 15 August Chatham offered the Admiralty, vacant by Egmont's resignation, to Lord Gower, brother-in-law of the Duke of Bedford. Gower, however, refused to

returning to the good ground which he originally declined to stand upon. I saw in the Chronicle an account of the address;[1] and I confess I have seldom in my Life been more thoroughly mortified. It was not very long, it was really simple, Neat, and elegant. The abstracting, (which by the way was not very well done), did great mischief to it. I do not like your Lordships method of putting your popularity into your Cabinet like a curious medal; It is current coin, or it is nothing. I am really vexed, as I think properly managed, it would have led the other Towns. May I flatter myself that whenever your Lordship has a leisure moment I may be favourd with your remembrance, and your directions. You would not do me justice, if you thought, any person attached to your interest, your honour, or your satisfaction with a warmer Zeal, than

My Lord
your most obedient
and ever obligd humble Servant

Dublin 21. Augst 1766. E BURKE

I beg your Lordship will present my humble respects with those of Mrs Burke to Lady Rockingham.[2] I hope The air of Wentworth has reestablishd her health. I just hear that they are negotiating with York.[3] I fear for him. Permit me to remind your Lordship, if you should honour me with your Commands, to enclose your Letter to the Revd Dr Leland. Trinity College. This is a safe Channell.

To RICHARD SHACKLETON—[*August* 1766]

Source: MS Dr O. Fisher. Printed *Corr.* (1844), I, 109–10.
Endorsed: Edmund Burke Esqr. | Dublin—8th mo: 1766.

My dear Shackleton, I am much obliged to you for your kind and early remembrance of me. But why should you dash this obligation by telling me of Bishops and Horse Races, and meeting my Brother? As to Bishops you know they may be had for two a penny in Parliament winter in Dublin; Horse Races I neither understand nor like; and as to my Brother a days difference in seeing him, whom I had so very lately seen before

take office without his friends. In October and November Chatham tried to secure the Bedford party as a whole, but failed.

[1] An address of thanks to Lord Rockingham 'from the Merchants of London, trading to the West-Indies and North America'. See *London Chronicle*, XX, 142 (7–9 August 1766).

[2] *Née* Mary Bright (1735–1804).

[3] Charles Yorke had resigned his post as Attorney-General when Chatham took office: he was offered the post of Chief Justice of the Common Pleas but would not take it without a peerage.

could hardly take me a Journey of thirty miles. Therefore, my friend, do not be civil and peevish at once; But attribute my Visit then, as I would have you attribute that which, please God, we shall shortly make you, to their true and only cause, the sincere affection which we have for you and yours. We propose to spend a very happy day in Ballitore; but circumstances are such that I cannot just now settle the exact time, so that I fear I must not promise myself the pleasure of meeting you at Dennis's.[1] I am vexed at this as I am sure I wish your Company as long as we can have it. Mrs Burke gives her Love to Mrs Shackleton and will wear a Cap at this time at Ballitore in compliment to her and it will be as large as she can desire,[2] and yet will leave her something to observe upon too; For next to finery in a Lady herself, the Criticism of it in anothers Case, is the highest satisfaction that can be; and this is one way of indemnifying ones self for the plainness of their habits. So much for you Mrs Shackleton. I owe it to you.[3] Pray remember us at the other side of the River[4] and believe me with very hearty affection dear Shackleton

ever yours

E BURKE

The elder Richd (but not the younger) is with us, and would not be forgot at Ballitore.

WILLIAM BURKE *to* CHARLES O'HARA—4 *October* 1766

Source: O'Hara MSS. Printed Hoffman, pp. 360–4.

While the other Burkes made visits in Ireland, Will was examining the situation in London, and reporting to O'Hara on a wonderful turn of fortune.

...The meeting of P so soon will make it proper for Ned to be here by the End of this Month at farthest.[5] For, tho there is not to appearance any resolution of applying to him, I think still possible that before the Campain opens, it may be thought necessary to make the force as strong

[1] William Dennis was at this time a schoolmaster at Naas, County Kildare.

[2] Mrs Leadbeater describes an earlier visit of the Burkes to Ballitore, to which Burke is here referring. It was her first view of her father's old friend, 'leading in his wife, a pretty little woman, with no covering on her head but her beautiful unadorned auburn tresses. On Elizabeth Shackleton expressing surprise that she wore no cap, in which respect she was singular at that time, she said that she dressed conformably to her husband's taste; however, she promised to put on one, and next morning appeared in the first French night-cap that was ever seen in Ballitore' (*Leadbeater Papers*, I, 47).

[3] Mrs Shackleton was of course a Friend. Her daughter says that 'In her youth she indulged in dress as far as she could...' but 'Before the season of youth was past she renounced all those delights' (*ibid.* I, 38).

[4] To Shackleton's parents, who lived on the other side of the Greese from his own house.

[5] Parliament was opened 11 November.

as possible,[1] whether it may or may not be proper for Ned to join them, I think is not without its doubt, but that, as indeed our whole conduct, upon either supposition of his being, or not being engaged, must depend on circumstance and the resolution taken â re nata, only one thing to be resolved upon, to act upon principle, unbiassed by any view of personal advantage; it is the only road of comfort and satisfaction, and, when it is understood to be the walk a Man has chosen, the world is not so bad as not to smooth the way.

If Ned gets to you, which I doubt whether he will be able to do, he will tell you that our fortunes are in a condition to second our views of Independency, and our resolution of acting in our publick Capacity with the same correctness as we have had the good fortune to observe in private Life.[2] You will be glad to know that in this we have no division of our Obligations, all this, Like as the all before we owe to Lord Verneys wonderful goodness and friendship; in one word the necessary rise of value of East India stock was foreseen, before the price rose or an increased dividend was talked of, but as that increase might possibly not be determined on in 3, or 6, or 9 or even 12 Months those who bought on what they call speculation, that is, who agreed to pay such a price for such a quantity at a particular day, ran the risk of loosing if the price at that particular day happened not to answer his Speculation; so that no one could with safety venture on buying with safety but those who could actually pay down their money, and keep their Stock in their possession quietly till the dividend was increased, This Lord Verny could you know easily do and [if] he had chosen to lay out a Million that way no one could have objected to his taking the consequential Benefit of all the money he employed that way, but he considered this as an oportunity of making us independent, and actually paid down of his own above £9000 and engaged for above forty more for me. The dividend is come

[1] Grafton wrote to Chatham 17 October that in his own and Conway's opinion Burke was 'the readiest man upon all points perhaps in the whole House', adding, 'If I mistake not, he was offered the board of trade during the last year and declined it, aiming at a higher board, or some equivalent. I cannot help saying, that I look upon it, that he is a most material man to gain, and one on whom the thoroughest dependence may be given, where an obligation is owned' (*Chatham Correspondence*, III, 110–11). Chatham replied that he thought Burke a man of parts and an ingenious speaker: 'As to his notions and maxims of trade, they can never be mine. Nothing can be more unsound and more repugnant to every true principle of manufacture and commerce, than rendering so noble a branch as the Cottons, dependant for the first material upon the produce of French and Danish Islands, instead of British.' He spoke of an engagement to Lord Lisburne for the next opening at the Board of Trade, 'nor is it a thing possible to wave for Mr Burke' (Grafton, *Autobiography*, p. 108).

[2] Will had written his friend Macartney 29 September (Osborn Collection): 'The death of His [Edmund's] Brother, and of my father and a little prudent management of our own, has arranged our little affairs, and we cannot be driven to any compliance not altogether agreable to us.'

sooner than I expected, and though the accounts are not yet settled, I may within compass say that I have made £12000 at least. It would be idle to use words to express what we owe to this Mans disinterested unaffected worth and goodness to us. The season too is so critical, that surely we may think it providential, and without any superstitious vanity too, if the thought of it, reminds us to endeavour to grow better Men as we grow richer. It is our good fortune you see to have this advantage without even the Imputation of Stock jobbing, or the term of Bull or Bear being applicable to us[1]....

To RICHARD SHACKLETON—[19 *October* 1766]

Source: MS Dr O. Fisher. Printed *Leadbeater Papers*, II, 99–100.
Addressed: To | Mr Richd Shackleton. *Endorsed:* Edmd Burke Esqr | Ballitore 19 | 10 mo. 1766.

My dear Shackleton, I am sorry to be obliged to correspond with you from your own house. But we cannot help it. Had we been able to fix a time for being here, this very mortifying accident would not have happend; however it was not in our power.[2] This day we proposed having the happiness to spend with you, and came tolerably early. But another day is absolutely out of our disposal; as we have already outstaid our time very considerably. Since It is so determined, that I must go to England without seeing you, to my no small vexation, Let me at least have the pleasure of hearing from you whilst I stay in Dublin, which will be, but whilst I wait for a ship. My horse, (not mine indeed, but borrowd from a friend) has fallen ill upon the road. I must, and I think I freely may, commit him to your Care until I can send for him. Adieu my dearest Shackleton. Think how vexatious this accident is to us, but do not add to it by yours or Mrs Shackletons vexation. We are all most truly and ever affectionately yours, E B.

Sunday. From some Wild Chat of Brocklebys[3] with Will Burke I am given to understand that you had received at some time a Letter

[1] Will's operations were certainly stock speculations though Lord Verney, who was generous even if he was unwise, appeared able to meet his own and Will's losses if the market collapsed—as it ultimately did. Lauchlin Macleane seems to have been directing these speculative ventures. At some time in 1766 Will and Edmund borrowed £500 at 5 per cent from Henry Fox. Fox's executor was still struggling, unsuccessfully, in 1780 to get either principal or interest repaid (L. S. Sutherland and J. Binney, 'Henry Fox as Paymaster General of the Forces', *English Historical Review*, LXX [1955], 241–2).

[2] The Burkes had been visiting their sister Juliana—now Mrs Patrick French—in Loughrea, County Galway. They had set off for Dublin the evening of 17 October, after the birth of Juliana's daughter Mary (letter of Burke's mother to Mrs Nelly Hennessy 25 October printed in *Corr.* [1844], I, 111).

[3] Richard Brocklesby (1722–97), later Burke's physician. He entered Ballitore School 29 May 1734.

from England, some way relating to me. Have you ever receivd such a Letter?[1]

Now I must say one word at conclusion which must be peremptory. You desired that Sisson should not come hither to meet us. I did not appoint him, (not because you desired it) but because I couldn't fix the time. But I must insist upon it, as a favour, which I would be very uneasy to be refused, that he may come hither and finish that (Deed without a name) which he has begun.[2] It neither is nor can be wrong; nay it must be right in itself—and as it is at best but decorum to avoid it, sacrifice Decorum to friendship, I am sure it is the lesser to the greater Virtue—adieu.

To CHARLES O'HARA—[21] *October* 1766

Source: O'Hara MSS. Printed Hoffman, pp. 365–6.
Endorsed: October 21st. 1766.
Burke dates this 'Tuesday Octr. 20. 1766'; 21 October was a Tuesday.

My dear Sir, I thought to have found your house properly occupied but I am sorry to feel, that we have but too much room in it. Vexed as I am on this occasion the Cause of your absence is certainly right, I must confess it. Arrange yourself well at home, and then you will come abroad, and stay abroad with more satisfaction to yourself, and because to yourself, to us too, than ever. I do indeed most heartily feel your not being here; an hours Chat would be a great deal in this Crisis; yet the Business of Nymphsfield is more important; and I should be grieved yet more,

[1] Among the Ballitore MSS (A/98) is a portion of a letter, apparently to Shackleton and endorsed 'Dublin 15/5 mo 1766'. Shackleton's correspondent wrote: 'After Closing this Letter I opened it at the Request of my Kinsman E. Strettle who had a Letter from a particular friend in England Requesting to be advised of the family Connections Religion (if any) and General Character of Edwd Bourk Secretary to the Marquis of Rockinham, this enquiry is not made with any Design to prejudice E. Bourk but as he apprehends quite the Contrary therefore I request thou wilt give me Such an Answer as thou thinks proper and Post per return.' Having no suspicion whatever that the facts he had to relate might be used maliciously, Shackleton wrote a most complimentary short sketch of his friend. More than three years later it was printed in the *London Evening Post*, 14–17 April 1770, and was the occasion of a brief quarrel between Burke and Shackleton. See letters of 19 and 28 April and 6 May 1770; the sketch and the correspondence relating to it is reprinted in Samuels, pp. 398–404.

[2] Burke had commissioned Sisson to paint a portrait of Shackleton, which may have been started a great deal earlier than this (see above, letter of [*post* 19] April 1763, p. 166). As a strict Quaker, Shackleton had qualms about his part in such vanity. Richard Burke wrote him 25 October (Ballitore MSS, C/48): 'Why do you torment yourself about that deed without name, which is already done? The only question now is whether it shall be well done; and if your conscience be made uneasy, do not for that reason make our eyes uneasy by placing before them an unfinished Dick Shackleton. Sisson will have the happiness of spending another day with you, the credit of a good performance, and your friends the resemblance of a man whom they sincerely love.'

to snatch a premature hour of Satisfaction, which would debar me of, I hope, so much longer and so much greater. Wills news[1] is indeed marvellous in the success, marvellous in the Conduct, marvellous in the motives of action. It is really a Joint stroke of Providence and friendship which is not easily equalled. His manner of telling it is quite (as the painters say) in his own manner, as indeed the action itself is in all its parts. This certainly leaves one with some freedom of Conduct, but the time holds out Nothing to guide that freedom. For my part, I see nothing on either side of the Water but thick darkness and utter confusion. What Light and what order may be brought out of them, is hardly, I believe, known to the great *Anarchs* themselves who rule in the midst of these discordant Elements. The offers you mention were unquestionably made, or at least something like them was made, to the Bedford Clan. They as certainly declined for that time to accept; But I hear today, that the Duke and Dutchess are, both of them, in a very bad state of health, and gone to Bath:[2] This will drive the Corps to accept any thing, as they are buying by Inch of Candle;[3] and that they will be bid for, there is no Doubt. I hear that Ld Chatham says it is very possible he may, from his ill state of health, never more be able to take a part in any public assembly, or even in the Kings Councils; but that he will leave an administration so nobly composed, and on so broad a bottom as has never been before seen in England. In such an administration must not Rigby, Sandwich, and Vernon[4] have places?[5] The Contempt and odium of your Late Lord Lieutenant[6] is not easily to be expressed. Never did I hear from a single person, a single good word of him. Great apprehensions are entertaind of the New.[7] He promises to head very nearly in the Steps of his predecessor, as far as I can judge, though in a more affected and effeminate pace, something between an Effeminate foppery and a stiff spanish Stateliness; a good portion of hypocritical Cant, for the

[1] See above, Will's letter of 4 October (pp. 269–70).

[2] The Duke and Duchess of Bedford went to Bath in the middle of October. Chatham, Northington, and Camden had gone at the beginning of the month.

[3] Buying as at an auction where bids are received only so long as a small piece of candle continues burning.

[4] Richard Vernon (1726–1800), M.P. for Bedford borough.

[5] Bedford, at his meeting with Chatham 31 October, asked places for Weymouth, Gower, and Rigby, the Garter for Marlborough, a peerage for Thomas Brand, and told Chatham his other followers would also have to be provided for. Chatham offered places only to Gower and Weymouth, and on this the negotiation broke down.

[6] Lord Hertford.

[7] The Earl of Bristol. He had been Ambassador to Madrid, 1758–61. Walpole described him as 'a very Spaniard...in formality and pride' (*Memoirs*, I, 101), and about his resignation wrote to Horace Mann 18 August 1767: 'Lord Bristol has given up Ireland, content with fourteen or fifteen thousand pounds, with having made his brother a bishop, and his brother-in-law, Phipps, an Irish baron, and not willing to expose himself to the torrents of abuse that were prepared for him'. *Letters of Horace Walpole*, ed. Mrs Paget Toynbee, Oxford, 1903–5, VII, 127.

publick, and numerous family to be made snug and warm. Well! Well!—I dont look on the affair of the Resident Ld Lt as a question of right or wrong; but of practicable or impracticable.[1] It never can hold five years. Adieu my dear friend. Please God when we get on the other side of the water, you shall hear more from us.

Tuesday Octr 20. 1766.

Jane and Richd are most sincerely yours. Remember us all to Charles. I hear Pomeroy has got a regiment I wish you joy of it.[2]

EDMUND *and* RICHARD BURKE, SR *to* RICHARD SHACKLETON—28 *October* 1766

Source: MS Dr O. Fisher. Printed *Leadbeater Papers*, II, 100–3; Samuels, pp. 396–7.

[Edmund begins]

My dear friend. I am sorry, that you should think me capable of being offended with any Letter which you could think proper to write about me.[3] That which you did write, replete with the feelings of the most sincere friendship, and a partiality which arose from them, can displease me in nothing but in setting me up so high as to make it very difficult for me to give it any sort of Credit by my Conduct. However I am glad to find you think of me in such a manner; and for this piece of knowlege at least, I am indebted to the malice of my Enemies. Their purpose was, since they were not able to find wherewithal to except to my Character for the series of years since I appeard in England, to pursue me into the Closest recesses of my Life, and to hunt even to my Cradle in hope of finding some blot against me. It was on this principle they set on foot this Enquiry. I have traced it as far as Mr Strettel,[4] who refuses to let me know from whom in England he received his Commission. The want of suspicion of their ill designs, and want of an exact

[1] It had hitherto been the practice for the Lord Lieutenant of Ireland to reside only in alternate years. Bristol was appointed on the understanding that he would reside constantly; he resigned without having set foot in Ireland.

[2] John Pomeroy (d. 1790), a neighbour of O'Hara (O'Hara to Burke, 18 September). O'Hara had written Burke 10 March (printed Hoffman, pp. 334–8), disturbed at the delay in his getting a regiment. He became Colonel of the 64th Foot, in 1766.

[3] Distressed by Burke's anxiety over the personal sketch he had written (see above, letter of [19 October], p. 271), Shackleton had written 21 October to say that he had had no reason to suspect treachery, but if Burke found evidence of any, '...I insist upon knowing it, that I may search to the bottom of this affair'.

[4] The request sent to Shackleton had been prompted by 'E. Strettle'. See above, note to letter of [19 October].

knowlege of what affects a man in the world, made you enter into a more minute detail about my father, Mother, and Wife, than was strictly necessary, or than I believe those who wrote to make the enquiry expected, or could flatter themselves they would receive, especially in the affair of religion, which being a leading part in your account, though not in the general thoughts of men of publick business, they will therefore think could not have taken up so much Room but for special reasons; and these they will take care to construe into such as are not the most favourable. I think too, that your manner of stating the Condition of my father is, by the mode of expression, made to convey, to the Ears in which it will sound, impressions, different from what you intended, and from the reality—You say he was an Attorney of the Province of *Munster* in *moderate* Circumstances; and this (from the Evident Partiality which reigns in the whole account, and which seems to *soften* every thing) will be saying, he was an hedge Country Attorney of little practice.[1] Now you know, that the upper part of this profession is very reputable, as any can be; the Lower absolutely otherwise. The fact is, that my father never did practice in the Country, but always in the superior Courts; that he was for many years not only in the first *Rank*, but the very first *man* of his profession in point of practice and Credit; until by giving way to a retired and splenetic humour he did, in a manner, voluntary contract his practice; and yet, after some heavy losses by the banks, and living creditably for near 40 years, (one time pretty expensively), laying out something on Dicks establishment, and on my Education in the Temple, (a thousand pound or thereabouts for me) he died worth very near 6000 pounds. This I mention, as poverty is the greatest Imputation (very unjustly I think) that is ever laid on that profession. One or two other mistakes of fact there are, of little consequence. But in general, the rule is certainly right; when enquiries of this kind are made to confine ones Self to the person as much as may be on every account; for as accounts of connections are multiplied so are occasions of Cavil too, on the part of the hearer, and of mistake on that of the relater.

I have read over what I wrote, and am surprised to find how long I have talked on this nothing. But I am alone, which I seldom am, and my pen runs on. Be assured whatever little mistake there may be, it evidently can do me no kind of prejudice; whereas strong declarations of esteem

[1] Surprisingly little is known about Burke's father. He seems to have been born near Bruff, County Limerick, and to have conformed to the established church 13 March 1722, about the time he began to practice law in Dublin. See Basil O'Connell, 'Edmund Burke, a Basis for a Pedigree' in *Journal of the Cork Historical and Archaeological Society*, LX (July–December 1955), 69–74.

from an early friend, who knows you entirely is the fullest presumption in your favour. The rest is ones own Conduct, on which nine tenths of every thing depends. Be assured my dear Richard the account on the whole will much disappoint the enquirers. The only anxiety I have is to discover these enquirers, that I may not in my mind lay the charge on those who may possibly be innocent of it. So much for that;—but returning on my Steps, I again and again caution you not to give yourself a moments uneasiness for a most trifling inadvertance which came up amidst the effusions of affection, and which nothing but great affection could have caused. Let me add too that no piece of writing can be more Spirited and elegant.

I propose going immediately. We are all, Jenny, Dick, and I most sincerely and with the truest regard yours. Salute your wife for us whom we value on her own account as well as yours. Your father, I hope, believes we love him with a great mixture of reverence to his truly venerable Character. Adieu. God Almighty bless you. Yours ever

E BURKE

28. Octr 1766.

After all, on thinking and talking over this matter with Dick I am far from clear that the Enquiry may not have been from a friend.[1]

[Richard begins]

Dick said no more than that it is just *possible* that it may be from a friend. My Mother is very well. God keep yours so and all of you.

To PATRICK NAGLE—6 *November* 1766

Source: MS Hyde Collection. Printed *New Monthly Magazine*, XIV, 384–5; *Adam Catalogue*, I (Letters of Edmund Burke), 3.

My dear Sir,

I know you are too much concerned about us to suffer any little Event of our Lives to be altogether without importance to you. I sit down therefore to let you know, that we are at last got, safe and well, to our own house in London; and had the satisfaction of meeting all those we love, at least, as well as we left them. Our Passage was extremely rough. We never had been in any Storm like it. All of us very ill. But thank

[1] Richard had not thought so three days earlier, when he wrote Shackleton: 'The world is not yet good enough, to make enquiries about men, merely to serve them, nor nice enough, if resolved to serve them to enquire into their merit to justify that service' (Ballitore MSS, C/48).

God, we were not very long at Sea; and very fine Weather, and tolerable Roads from Holyhead hither, made us ample amends for the tossing we sufferd at Sea. I received your Letter in favour of Mr James Nagle.[1] His Case is undoubtedly a very severe one. But the Plot is laid deep; and the persons concerned in it are very determined and very wicked, as far as I can judge, by the enquiries I have been capable of making into this affair. To attempt even in the slightest manner to take it out of the Course of Law would be very idle; it would aggravate instead of alleviating the mischief, and would furnish a new handle to those, who are already willing to use every method to oppress the innocence of their Neighbours. All I can do is by my advice. The Counsell which these Gentlemen have had are certainly men of Ability and Character, whom by all means they ought still to retain. But they ought to add to them some man of longer Standing in the Profession, and who by being a member of Parliament will have weight, both in the Court, and in representing the affair above, for very obvious reasons. Mr Harward[2] is a man of great honour and spirit, perfectly well acquainted with every thing which relates to Criminal Law, and in every respect the fittest man they can possibly choose. It is the Course I would advise you to take if you were in the same Circumstances. I am thoroughly convinced of the innocence of these Gentlemen, but far from sure, that their lives are not in the greatest danger. They ought to Neglect no means, nor grudge any Expence they can go to. I did hear indeed with an astonishment, which I can scarcely express, that this measure had been originally proposed to them, and that they rejected it on account of the Charge. If that consideration, in such a Case, has any weight with them, I have nothing to say, but to lament their fate, as that of men whose avarice has betrayd their lives, Characters, and fortunes too, into the hands of their most bitter Enemies; and whose weakness will make it impossible to take a single step in their favour. You will (without sending him my Letter)[3]

[1] James Nagle of Garnavilla (d. *c.* 1782), a distant relative of Burke, was one of a group of Roman Catholic gentlemen charged with treason and participating in White Boy activities. Burke's friend Dr John Curry says that in July of 1766 evidence against them was being solicited by notices in the newspapers (Curry's pamphlet 'A Candid Enquiry', quoted in R. R. Madden, *Life of the Countess of Blessington*, London, 1855, I, 426). Those accused were tried at Clonmel March 1767 and acquitted. James Nagle conformed to the Established Church 22 December 1766 (Egerton MS 77).

[2] See above, letter of 24 December [1765] (p. 225). There is no record of Harward's having been engaged, but the prisoners at the trial should have been ably enough defended: their counsel included Sir Lucius O'Brien, 3rd Baronet (d. 1795); John Fitzgibbon, later Earl of Clare (1749–1802); John Scott, later Earl of Clonmel (1739–98); and Barry Yelverton, later Viscount Avonmore (1736–1805). See *Leinster Journal* for 28 March 1767 for an account of the trial.

[3] Burke is conscious of the dangers to himself should this letter fall into unfriendly hands.

take some method of conveying these sentiments from me to that Gentleman, whose Condition, I sincerely pity. Jenny and Dick, and so do the Doctor and Will, join me in our most sincere and affectionate Regards to Roches Country. I shall soon write to my friend at Bloomfield.[1] I am my dear Uncle, most affectionately yours

E BURKE

Thursday Nov. 6. 1766.

To CHARLES O'HARA—[*post* 11 *November* 1766]

Source: O'Hara MSS. Printed Hoffman, pp. 367–70.
Undated. Burke writes after the opening of Parliament, which took place 11 November.

My dear Sir, It pleased God that we got safe through the Storm to Holyhead; and by easy and pleasant Journeys arrived hither time enough to see how the Land lay and to consult with our friends about the Spirit and tendency of our future operations. In this consultation resentment (as it was right it should) had but little share. The consideration that a large Majority of our friends were in place,[2] and none but our worst Enemies in opposition, that every thing would go to pieces if we fell out with the one, or joind with the other, and that Lord Butes game could not be more effectually played than by distressing even the administration which he made,[3] These considerations altogether determined Lord Rockingham to go himself to the meeting of the Peers at the D. of Graftons and to wish all his friends in the H. of C. to go to the Cockpit,[4] and such as were asked to the previous private meeting at Conways to attend there.[5] I was at both.[6] However this support is entirely voluntary, and neither expresses nor implies any contract. but will I suppose be more or less vigorous, as my Ld Chatham shews himself better or worse

[1] A Garrett Nagle was living at Bloomfield in 1768 (*Corke Chronicle*, 22 August 1768).

[2] When the Rockinghams broke with Chatham at the end of November only seven of the party resigned—four peers (Portland, Bessborough, Monson, and Scarbrough), and three commoners (Saunders, Keppel and Meredith).

[3] Rockingham wrote to Newcastle 29 August: 'I believe we should answer Lord Chatham's and Lord Bute's views very effectually if we grow angry and disunite' (Add. MS 32976, fol. 489).

[4] The meeting of Government supporters, held on the eve of the opening of Parliament to hear the King's Speech read.

[5] Before the Cockpit meeting the Minister in the House of Commons held a meeting of Government speakers and men of business. Rockingham wrote to Newcastle 7 November: 'When I saw Mr Dowdeswell he seemed to think it would be right for him to attend Mr Conway the evening of the meeting when at Conway's house, and doubted about going to the Cockpit' (Add. MS 32977, fols. 340–1).

[6] It is a sign of Burke's standing in the House that he was invited to the meeting of the men of business.

inclined to the Party. If I could lay open to you fully the solid grounds upon which this plan of moderation and at the same time of freedom, is built, I am sure you would highly approve it. At first I thought otherwise;[1] but every day convinces me of the rectitude of the measure. The first day of the Session was as curious to a man of Speculation as any that ever parliament met upon. There was a kind of Torpor in the house of Commons almost without example. No joy, no Grief, no love, no hatred; no hope or fear, no anxiety or desire whatsoever; opposition was without Spirit, and support without firmness. G. Grenville indeed stood out with his usual stubborn resolution. He inveighed against the Illegality of the Embargo;[2] agreed that had he been in the Council he would have advised it; but laid a heavy hand on the supineness and neglect, which had renderd that illegal remedy a necessary one. He fell, as usual with him, into some contradictions; but in the main pushed his points with force and dexterity enough; and in short shewed that he was willing to lead any opposition if he could find followers. But he scarcely found any. The Bedford people held off; their Bargain, though not concluded, is I believe, in Treaty.[3] G. Grenville did not divide on the amendment which his former Secretary made,[4] and which he supported whilst he could. In the House of Commons, the Proclamation was not defended on the Legality, (If it had, I, for one, would have opposed the address) but on the Necessity, which has been made very evident, and is a plea sufficient. Grenville tried another amendment, (by way of a little, and indeed a very little bait for popularity) containing a proposal for supplying the poor out of the sinking fund.[5] I found the Treasury Bench, though resolved to put a Negative on his amendment, so little, sui Juris, that they did not venture to decide directly on his proposal, not knowing how it may have chimed with the opinion of the great director; and only spoke to the impropriety of mixing it with the address. Conway was very well for a man in such a Situation; but Good God! what a situation for him! I had not any such reasons for caution, and therefore went roundly to work with the proposition itself, and I am told

[1] See letter to O'Hara 29 July (p. 262).

[2] Shortage of grain had led to riots in the southern and eastern counties, and a committee of the Privy Council had advised imposing an embargo on the export of corn. Grenville argued that this embargo, without consent of Parliament, was illegal.

[3] The Bedfords did not attend the Cockpit meeting, but lay by waiting for another offer from Chatham.

[4] This amendment (regretting that Parliament had not been summoned earlier) was moved not by Thomas Whately (d. 1772), formerly Grenville's Secretary of the Treasury, but by Grenville himself.

[5] Grenville's motion, for giving a sum of money towards the relief of the poor, was rejected without a division.

made some impression.[1] It was a lucky point for my situation; I was not unwilling to shew early, that I had not changed my opinion of the Grenville knot; that where the interests of the administration *as a body*, were not concerned, I was willing to go with them, and that I had particular regards for Conway—but would go no further. I think I made a shift to mark out this; and our friends thought it was as it should be. The house of Peers was the great Scene. Ld Chatham played all his house of Commons pranks there with as good success as ever in the former Scene. He has taken formal possession of his new Freehold, and I think will be at least as despotic there as ever he was with us. Lord Temple opposed, but did not dare to strike home. Lord Mansfield all for Liberty, Lord Cambden for prerogative—publick necessity made Law—That this Embargo was a power Junius Brutus would have given to Nero. That at worst, it was but 40 days slavery[2] &c, &c—It was a most curious Scene. You will have more satisfactory accounts of it.

As to my own peculiar. Conway sent to me, and soon after my coming to Town, and with many obliging expressions of his own opinion of me and of that of his Collegues; spoke of my supporting, and their intentions and hopes of making me offers that would be pleasing to me. The conversation was long; The substance of my resolution was, and I explaind it to him in Terms strong and precise; That I had begun with this party, That it was now divided in situation, though I hoped not in opinions or inclinations; that the point of honour lay with that division which was out of power; and that if the place which should be offerd, should prove in itself never so acceptable, I could take it only on condition that, in accepting it, and in holding it, I must be understood to belong not to the administration, but to those who were out; and that therefore if ever they should set up a standard, though spread for direct and personal opposition, I must be revocable into their party, and join it. But would act fairly and give due notice. He told me, he feard that this condition might frustrate the whole—The last Bell rings. Adieu. You lose nothing for nothing is yet done—But I have acted right and will tell you the rest next Post. Choice Augustus![3] Nil oriturum alias[4]—He moved the address and took occasion to commend the peace and abuse the repeal of

[1] Walpole is slightly misleading as to Burke's position in this debate. He says that after Grenville had 'held forth on the illegality' of the embargo Burke 'spoke finely on the same side' (*Memoirs*, II, 264–5).

[2] Chatham, in answer to the complaint that Parliament should have been summoned earlier, argued that by usage Parliament could not meet until forty days had elapsed from the time of the last prorogation. Hence Camden's description of the embargo as but forty days' slavery.

[3] Augustus John Hervey, later 3rd Earl of Bristol (1724–79); 'choice' as an example of inconsistency.

[4] Nothing of that kind will ever arise; see Horace, *Epistles*, II, i, 17.

the Stamp act.[1] Happy effect of coalition and broad bottom.[2] Will has taken his Seat.[3]

To CHARLES O'HARA—27 [*November* 1766]

Source: O'Hara MSS. Printed Hoffman, p. 374. *Endorsed:* Novbr. 27th.

On 17 November 1766 Lord Edgcumbe, appointed Treasurer of the Household by Rockingham in 1765, was dismissed to make way for a friend of Chatham, and Rockingham made his dismissal the occasion for a break with Chatham. Burke had already decided to adhere to Rockingham whether in or out of office, and was much happier at the prospect of opposition than he had been at supporting Administration without office.

My dear Sir,

I have only time, just to tell you, that affairs are come to a Crisis.[4] The D. of Portland, Lord Bessborough, Lord Scarborough,[5] and Lord Monson[6] resigned this morning.[7] Their resignation was most graciously recievd; and nothing could be more kind than the expressions of the King on the occasion. Nothing like the least displeasure or resentment.

[1] Hervey's speech on moving the Address is described in Grenville's diary as 'a direct *opposition* speech' (*Grenville Papers*, III, 383). Burke later thought he had seen signs at this time that Chatham was altering his stand on the repeal of the Stamp Act. In a note on his own *Thoughts on the Cause of Present Discontents* (MS at Sheffield, Bk 31, a copy; another copy Bk 6) he wrote: 'When I returned from Ireland I was satisfied that a return to the Principles of the Stamp Act was intended, the language of all those who adhered to Lord Chatham was totally changed. Lord Chatham indeed told Lord Rockingham that he could not resist the Arguments which the King urged drawn from the Declaratory Act. Lord R. answered that he who made that act had been able to resist those Arguments. He told Lord R. also that he was brought in expressly for the purpose of destroying his Party, in fact Ld C. was as ready for the measure at least as any of the Set and thereby as much the Author of all the Calamities which followed. But this confession of his being only in private conversation it would not have been either prudent or proper to mention it. Townsend was very willing to take the whole on himself. Lord Camden and others resorted to the old distinction of internal and external Taxes and contended that those were external.'

[2] Hervey, though a Groom of the Bedchamber and newly appointed Chief Secretary to the Lord Lieutenant of Ireland, professed himself a follower of Grenville.

[3] Will Burke, through Lord Verney's influence, had been elected M.P. for Great Bedwyn.

[4] On 21 November Portland presented Rockingham's ultimatum to Conway: Edgcumbe must be reinstated immediately, Rockingham's followers must be treated with 'regard, respect and countenance' and 'must stand as forward to be provided for as any other persons whatever', and Chatham must share his power with Conway as security for his good behaviour (Portland to Newcastle, 21 November, Add. MS 32978, fols. 11–13). On 26 November Portland wrote to Newcastle: 'All hopes of accommodation are over. Ld Chatham has absolutely refused to treat...' (ibid. fol. 78).

[5] Richard Lumley Saunderson, 4th Earl of Scarbrough (1725–82).

[6] John, 2nd Baron Monson (1727–74).

[7] At a meeting of Rockingham's friends on 19 November (at which Burke was present) it was decided 'that the persons of the first quality and consideration should shew their high disapprobation of these proceedings by an immediate resignation of their employments' (Newcastle's 'Short Narrative of what passed at my Lord Rockingham's', ibid. fols. 1–5).

More resignations will follow.[1] The ill humour is incredible. The E. India company is a great rescource; but requires great management to make it subservient to the national advantage.[2] Lord Chatham chose to act on this occasion, not by his nominal ministry, but by Beckford.[3] They supported the general motion for a Committee of the whole house to examine into the affairs of that Company; but they gave up all his Grounds, amended his motion, and rejected that part of it which required the laying their Charters, accounts, &c &c, before the houses.[4] The motion was made in direct contradiction to the opinion of the second rate ministers, on the express Order of the Supreme director.[5] Never ministry made a more shameful figure. They were beat about like footballs. We divided 76 to 129 on the main question;[6] we should have had about 10 more had we put the previous. We got into odd Company, Bedfords, Grenvilles &c. but we did not go in their Train. To avoid an appearance of this, I jumped up instantly on Beckfords making his motion and took my own Ground,[7] I think very cautiously, lest they should give us a ground on which we should not be able to act. When you shall have heard distinctly what has been doing, you will approve it, and I flatter myself see that we do not act on the principles of factious opposition. Lord Hertford is Chamberlain. Oh Conway! Conway! My heart bleeds for thee.[8] Adieu. Adieu.

27. Thursday.

[1] At the meeting of 19 November Newcastle warned Rockingham that their followers in the Commons were unwilling to resign, but Rockingham would not believe him. 'I am afraid,' wrote Newcastle to Bessborough 22 November, 'our good friend the Marquess is too much set upon *resignations* and flatters himself with such immediate success as I own I can have no notion of. He supposes Lord Chatham will resign in *two days*; he does not know my Lord Chatham...Lord John [Cavendish]'s *honest warmth*, and Mr Dowdeswell's and Mr Burk's impatience too much influence our good friend' (ibid. fols. 35–6). Only three of Rockingham's followers in the Commons resigned.

[2] The main business of the session was to be an enquiry into the East India Company, with a view to acquiring for the state part of the increased wealth which had come to the Company through the Seven Years War.

[3] The motion for a committee of inquiry was made on 25 November by Beckford, Chatham's chief liaison with the City and a known enemy of the Company, not by Conway, the Government spokesman in the Commons.

[4] The motion was for a committee 'to inquire into the state and condition of the East India Company', the phrase 'together with the conduct of all or any persons concerned in the direction or administration of the said Company', being deleted. This did not prevent the House from ordering the Company's charters and papers to be laid before them.

[5] Conway and Townshend agreed with Chatham that the State was entitled to draw a revenue from the Company, but disagreed with his method of a committee of enquiry and wished to establish the Company's right to its Indian territories.

[6] The question for a committee of enquiry.

[7] 'Our friend Burke rose first in opposition', wrote Henry Flood to Lord Charlemont, 'and acquitted himself very honourably' (*Chatham Correspondence*, III, 144n.).

[8] 'Mr Conway', Lord Hardwicke wrote to Charles Yorke 2 December, 'has declared to his Friends that He will not remain in Office much *longer*, Ld Rockingham will *endeavour* to *accelerate* this Resolution' (Add. MS 35362, fol. 53).

To CHARLES O'HARA—[29] *November* [1766]

Source: O'Hara MSS. Printed Hoffman, pp. 374–6. *Endorsed:* Novr. 9th 1766. Burke's date of 'Saturday, Nov. 9' is an error. Contents show the letter was written 29 November, a Saturday.

My dear Sir,

Our confusions still continue; but they are drawing to an End. A Settlement is coming on; but differing only from the present state of things, as Tyranny differs from Anarchy. Yesterday the Admiralty tumbled down. Sr C. Saunders, Keppell, and Sr W. Meredith resigned their places. Lord Gower was immediately sent for;[1] and that day he and Rigby went together to Woburn.[2] They are not yet returned, that I can hear. But nobody doubts the result of that Consultation. They must be mad to refuse the offers that are now made them. Lord Chatham has in a manner surrenderd prisoner at discretion to that party; by which he has purchased a momentary support, at the expence of a little more remote, but a certain ruin. You may depend upon it, that he is not cordially supported by Lord Bute. Speculate on that disposition, and this negotiation. The Grand difficulty made by the Bedfords is about G. Grenville;[3] but they will abandon him, at least for a time; not that they will wholly do it; for they have nobody to lead the house of Commons who is so near their party, or their principles, at least as far as their bad principles, are any motives to their bad conduct. You had, I take it for granted, my Letter of Thursdays post. But I am not sure, that I gave you an account of the steps that Led to this grand Change. Take them in a few Words. Lord Edgcumbe, Treasurer of the household, was orderd to walk into the Bedchamber, to make room for Jack Shelley.[4] His Lordship had, to oblige the Late administration, and Genl Conway in particular, brought Lord Beauchamp into Parliament last year;[5] though he did not take his Seat until this Session. He demurred a little at the arbitrary order which proposed the exchange to him; and he was instantly turned out. The party took fire, and General Conway seemd to be mortally offended. Several meetings were held,[6] in which, upon full consideration of all Circumstances, it appeard to everybody that

[1] On 27 November by Chatham.

[2] The Duke of Bedford's seat in Bedfordshire. Gower and Rigby went on 28 November.

[3] Bedford had indicated to both Chatham and Grenville that he was prepared to take office without Grenville. But for the next year the Rockinghams believed that Bedford and Grenville were united.

[4] John Shelley (*c.* 1730–83), M.P. for East Retford.

[5] Lord Beauchamp was Conway's nephew. He was returned by Edgcumbe for Lostwithiel 4 April 1766.

[6] Rockingham's friends held two meetings, one on 19 and one on 27 November. Burke was present at both.

Ld Chatham had resolved the ruin of the Party, and that staying in Office exposed to such ill designs and shameful indignities, would break every part of the yet remaining strength of the Body and could be attended with no sort of good consequence to the publick. Yet such is the pacific disposition of our party, that Lord Bessborough, if possible to accommodate Lord Chatham, offerd to give up his Post Office to Lord Edgcumbe and take the Bedchamber.[1] Judge of the humility of that offer! Judge of the Insolence that refused it! Judge of the Patience that bears that refusal. Lord Hertford has every thing!!!!!![2]

As to me, I hope you will always find my little skiff, out in the fair open Sea—far away from the rocks, shelves, and quicksands of politicks. I jumped in first; and plumped over head and Ears. You cannot think with what spirit and system our little Corps went on last Tuesday without the least previous consultation or concert between ourselves, or any of the casual auxiliaries.[3] I have broke off all Negotiations with the powers that be. So leave off flattering yourself with reading any thing about me in the red book, for some years. I suspect you will soon see W. Burkes name also effaced from that book of Life.[4] Adieu. Adieu. Prepare to congratulate Rigby—perhaps even your *friend*.[5] *Fortunam ex aliis*.[6]

Saturday Nov. 9.

To CHARLES O'HARA—2 *December* [1766]

Source: O'Hara MSS. Printed Hoffman, pp. 376–7.
Endorsed: 2d December 1766.

My dear Sir, I mean just to give you a minute, *de die in diem*, of what is going on. Lord Chatham is in for it; and he plunges deeper and deeper, with a glorious alacrity in sinking, every day. On Keppels *resignation* of the admiralty, without waiting until he gave a vote in opposition, he was *turned out* of the Bedchamber.[7] Sr Edw. Hawke[8] has got to the head of the Board of admiralty; Sr Piercy Bret[9] has got one of

[1] Bessborough's offer was made to Conway 21 November. It disconcerted Rockingham and his friends because it would have satisfied Edgcumbe and enabled the dispute to have been patched up.

[2] Hertford had succeeded the Duke of Portland as Lord Chamberlain.

[3] On 25 November, on Beckford's motion for an enquiry into the East India Company.

[4] Will Burke did not resign until February 1767. In Rockingham's list of the House of Commons (compiled about this time) he is classed as a Whig in one column, but as 'Swiss' (i.e. one who would follow any administration) in another.

[5] Hamilton. If he had a connexion with the Thynne family (see above, letter of [*post* 29 May 1765], p. 198), he might profit by their connexions with the Bedfords.

[6] From me, boy, learn virtue and honourable labour; fortune learn from others; see *Aeneid*, xii, 435–6.

[7] Keppel was dismissed from his post of Groom of the Bedchamber.

[8] Sir Edward Hawke (1705–81).

[9] Sir Peircy Brett (1709–81).

the vacant places at it. The final determination of the Bedfords is yet uncertain.[1] I believe they have agreed to the gross of the proposition; but there are some difficulties as to the Detail. Some people more conversant, than I am, about their particular dispositions, and general Situation, still affect to think they will not come in but I stand firm, that they will; that they ought, upon every one of *their* principles; and that they must. As to our set, we must fairly content ourselves with cooling our heels on the Lobby of power for a couple of years longer.[2] Lord Chatham sent for Ch. Townshend a day or two ago, as I am told, and read him a severe Lecture on his Conduct and told him he expected, not an official, but a determined, manly and earnest support. Oswald and Elliot, have had Likewise, I am informed, a rap over the knuckles. To say the truth the whole Bute party have been playing fast and loose. I know not what will be the End of it. Adieu dear Sir all here are yours. Salute for me those who are with you.

Tuesday Decr 2.

To CHARLES O'HARA—23 *December* [1766]

Source: O'Hara MSS. Printed Hoffman, pp. 378–81.

My dear Sir, We receivd last Night your Letters of the 6th and 12th.[3] We are not surprised to find you take an interest in our affairs. I know not how, but our own little concerns grow important in our Eyes, when we find others anxious about them and our conduct grows more firm and assured, when judicious friends go along with us in our Notions. I think we are very, very far from port; but we keep the open Sea; far likewise from rocks and sands and shelves, and all the mischiefs of an unfaithful Coast. I see, that an union of the Corps in opposition (I mean the Grenvilles, the Bedfords, and ourselves) is an affair of infinite difficulty; and without such an union, our opposition may be respectable; but never can be effective.[4] In the mean time, I should conceive, that Lord Chatham gathers strength; not only from our total disunion, but from the immense services he has done the Bute party. Lord Bute, to be sure,

[1] Bedford and Chatham met on the evening of 1 December, and Chatham rejected Bedford's terms for joining the Administration.

[2] It was the general opinion among Rockingham's friends that Chatham's administration could not last long.

[3] O'Hara's letters of 6 December to Burke (MS at Sheffield; printed Hoffman pp. 377–8), and of 12 December to Richard Burke (MS at Sheffield).

[4] Rockingham, Newcastle, and Bessborough met 17 December, and agreed to sound the Bedfords about a union of opposition. Bessborough was eager for it; Rockingham lukewarm, because he did not believe the Bedfords would join without the Grenvilles and Grenville would insist on the Treasury in any future Administration; and others of the Rockinghams (e.g. Lord John Cavendish) were hostile (see Newcastle's report of this meeting, Add. MS 32978, fols. 404–7).

is uncertain and unquiet in his Nature; but who *will* do more, who *can* do more to satisfie him, than the present Minister? I therefore take it for granted, that he will continue his year at least. But if he should fall then, or even before that time, I cannot conceive that *we* shall rise by his fall. The Bedfords and Grenvilles, as a set of people at once more bold and more tractable than our party will be preferred to us, and will run their Course as others have done theirs. It may possibly, in the revolution of this Political Platonick year, come again to our turn. But I see this Event, (if I see it at all) at the End of a very long Visto. The View is dim and remote; and we do nothing in the world to bring it nearer, or to make it more certain. This disposition, which is become the principle of our party, I confess, from constitution and opinion, I like:[1] Not that I am enamourd of adversity, or that I love opposition. On the contrary it would be convenient enough to get into office; and opposition never was to me a desirable thing; because I like to see some effect of what I am doing, and this method however pleasant is barren and unproductive, and at best, but preventive of mischief; but then the walk is certain; there are no contradictions to reconcile; no cross points of honour or interest to adjust; all is clear and open; and the wear and tear of mind, which is saved by keeping aloof from crooked politicks, is a consideration absolutely inestimable. Believe me, I who lived with *your friend*[2] so many years feel it so; and bless Providence every day and every hour to find myself deliverd from thoughts and from Characters of that kind. Will feels so exactly as I do, that if ———[3] does not go out in a very short time indeed, he will get away from a situation of Nicety, and fix himself upon more decided Ground. He has staid so long in Babylon, merely in compliance with the desires of his friends.[4] We have not been inactive in Parliament. The indemnity has been carried to the house of Lords with a preamble stoutly declaratory of the illegality. There we had a curious Debate in which North[ingto]n and Cambden fought, the one stoutly, the other insidiously for the dispensing power in Cases of Necessity.

[1] Burke told his friends at the Literary Club in 1778: 'I believe in any body of men in England I should have been in the Minority; I have always been in the Minority' (*Life of Johnson*, III, 235).

[2] Hamilton.

[3] Conway.

[4] Will Burke had been feeling the discomfort of his situation ever since the Rockingham group had lost power in July. Conway, his superior, remained in office; Edmund, a much closer friend, was deeply committed to Rockingham and opposition. Will wrote his friend Macartney 5 August (Osborn Collection): 'As to my personal connection with G. C. [General Conway] I have every reason on earth to be satisfied, I esteem and love the man. I have no where seen more worthiness of nature, nor more real Capacity and Understanding; But I can forsee a Case possible enough, that may oblige me to leave this situation, without being disgusted and without finding my Interest in leaving it, for from my own nature it is utterly impossible for me to continue with a divided Mind, holding an office under one set, and wishing success to another, so that if Ned does not come to me, it is most probable I shall go to him....'

Ld Chatham trimmed between the Legality and illegality with more skill than Success or applause. Lord Mansfield stood for the Constitution with his usual ability, and with an intrepidity that surprised friends and foes. They all felt his superiority. We fought the best battle we could, on a question of adjournment upon Beckfords motion (Friday sennight) for the E.I. papers. We however divided but 56 for the question.[1] Our friends were out of Town. But the fight was as spirited as you could wish. We held it until near twelve. You desire to know something in particular of my conduct. I spoke a long time, upwards of an hour I believe. I was well heard; and have had some Credit out of Doors on the occasion. But I had not the good fortune to please your Secretary Aug. Harvey, who called me to order while I was pouring out some humble and warm supplications to Ld Chatham, to implore him not to destroy that National Credit to which he owed the glories of the late War.[2] The marine Secretary had however no reason to pride himself on the reception his point of order met with from the house; and he did not in the least embarrass me. It rather gave me an opportunity for some explanations, that I was not sorry to bring out. Conway seemd hurt at what I had said of the situation of the ministers. I got up a second time, and satisfied him as to his own particular. It was on the whole a good day for me. Adieu my dear Sir. I am ever yours. On reading this Nonsense over, I suspect you had a good deal, if not most of it except the Fridays Debate before. You know that Lord Lornes[3] Peerage was in the D. of Bedfords Budget.[4] He had his Graces and G. Grenvilles leave to

[1] Beckford's motion for the East India papers was made on Tuesday 9 December.

[2] Sir Matthew Fetherstonhaugh, in a letter to Clive of 30 December 1766, described Burke's speech in this debate: 'After pointing out the ill effects which so violent a measure might have on the public credit,—"But perhaps", said he, "this house is not the place where our reasons can be of any avail: the *great person* who is to determine on this question may be a being far above our view; one so immeasurably high, that the greatest abilities (pointing to Mr Townshend), or the most amiable dispositions that are to be found in this house (pointing to Mr Conway), may not gain access to him; a being before whom 'thrones, dominations, princedoms, virtues, powers (waving his hand all this time over the treasury bench, which he sat behind), all veil their faces with their wings:' but though our arguments may not reach him, probably our prayers may!" He then apostrophised into a solemn prayer to the Great Minister above, that rules and governs over all, to have mercy upon us, and not to destroy the work of his own hands; to have mercy on the public credit, of which he had made so free and large a use. "Doom not to perdition that vast public debt, a mass seventy millions of which thou hast employed in rearing a pedestal for thy own statue". Here Augustus Hervey called him to order, to the regret of many' (*Chatham Correspondence*, III, 145–6n.). Walpole writes that Burke replied to Hervey: 'I have often suffered under persecution of order, but did not expect its lash while at my prayers. I venerate the great man, and speak of him accordingly' (*Memoirs*, II, 289).

[3] John Campbell, styled Marquess of Lorne, later 5th Duke of Argyll (1723–1806); created Baron Sundridge, in the British peerage, 22 December.

[4] One of Bedford's conditions for entering Administration had been a British peerage for Lord Lorne. This was refused, but a few days later Lorne applied directly to Chatham who agreed to recommend him to the King.

make a seperate request of it.[1] But it was neither their consent nor his request that I think carried it.[2] A New Link to Conways chain. Ld Beauchamp has not given us a Note yet. But as soon as his father got the Chamberlainship, he went to Sr T Molyneux[3] Usher of the Black Rod, and frightend him out of his Wits, by enquiring of him *whether he held his Office by Patent for Life*. Does he degenerate?

23d Decr

RICHARD BURKE, SR *to* CHARLES O'HARA—27 *December* 1766

Source: O'Hara MSS. Printed Hoffman, pp. 381–2.
Addressed: To | Charles OHara Esqr at | Nymphsfield | Boyle | Ireland.
Postmarked: 27|DE 27|DE.
A joint letter of Richard Burke, Sr, and Dr Nugent. Only a passage from Richard's portion is printed here.

My Dear Sir

You must certainly think that I begin to imagine my letters to be of no small importance to you, when I venture to force one of them on you without a frank. Ned is gone out of town to spend the recess at the D. of Portlands with Ld Rock[ingha]m Will and Jenny are gone for a few days to a friends at Plaistow;[4] little Dick is gone to domineer at his nurses, and I am left at home to quiet the violence of the Doctors temper by the mildness and quietism[5] of my disposition. If you learn nothing else by my letter, you will at least know how your friends of this house are disposed of, and that people out of place can amuse themselves in the Country as well as Ministers. Every thing is dead in town, all the Ministers being out of town; this is a bad stile, I should not be sorry to

[1] Lorne asked if Bedford had any objection to his applying for a peerage; he did not ask Grenville.

[2] Lorne was Conway's brother-in-law, and Burke implies that the peerage was granted at Conway's request: 'Mr Conway would not oppose the request', writes Walpole, 'though circumstanced as he was, he would not ask it' (*Memoirs*, II, 292).

[3] Sir Thomas Molyneux (*c.* 1724–76).

[4] Will Burke owned property in Plaistow, Essex (deed among Burke MSS at Sheffield). Prior, describing events around 1760, says (2nd ed. I, 99–100): 'About this time Mr [Edmund] Burke occasionally resided at Plaistow in Essex. A lady, then about fourteen years old, and residing in that neighbourhood, informs the writer that she perfectly remembers him there; that his brother Richard lived chiefly with him; and that they were much noticed in the neighbourhood for talents and sociable qualities, and particularly for having a variety of visitors who were understood to be authors soliciting a private opinion of their works, and not unfrequently men of rank.' Henry Percy Thompson in the second volume of his *West Ham Gleanings*, says that '"*Brunstock Cottage*" (now no. 83) on the west side of Balaam Street, Plaistow, where Edmund Burke resided with his brother Richard from 1759 to 1761, is now the South West Ham Labour Club. The original cottage, described as being a large oldfashioned house, is said to have been partly pulled down and the rest refronted, so that probably little of Burke's house now remains.'

[5] MS: queitism

have been able to mend it by leaving out the last *of town* and ending with *out*; but good Lord how long? Well patience must be the comfort. We are not I think here of a nature easily dejected, or at least not apt to lye very long under any dejection, and we are by no means without our satisfactions. To know that Ned is acting a free manly and honourable part is an happiness that none of us would part with, and tho it brings no profit, yet we ought not to complain whilst it brings a just reputation....

To GARRETT NAGLE—[1766]

Source: MS Hyde Collection. Printed *New Monthly Magazine*, XVI, 157–8; *Adam Catalogue*, I (Letters of Edmund Burke), I. This letter is undated, and nothing fixes even the year in which it was written. 'Nephew Ned' (Edmund Nagle, nephew of Garrett Nagle of Ballyduff, to whom Burke is writing) has not yet left Ireland, and 'Betty' (probably Elizabeth Nagle [*c.*1732–1802; m. 1754]) has a young son in school. These, the best hints, suggest a date around 1766—probably in the summer or early autumn when Burke was in Dublin.

My dear Garret I have only time to say a very few words—You have two Books of Husbandry, Lisles[1] and Duhamels[2]—the last is the most regular and methodical; The first has more matter in it, but it is worse digested; but I think it may be of considerable use to a Practical farmer, (though wrote a good while ago) as it contains a vast variety of observations, which his own thoughts may improve. I know you will be glad to lend them to any of our friends about you, that they may be as extensively useful as possible—Many odd words occur in Lisle's Husbandry, but they are explained at the End of the Book. The other Books are to be deliverd to Dr Patrick Nagle,[3] for the young part of the families, so as to accommodate them as well as can be done by so few Books. The Book called the *art of Thinking*,[4] is a Book that the Doctor will I dare say think very fit to be put into the hands of the Boys who have got through their Classicks, in the School he patronises, as a good introduction to any thing else they may read. There are some Books of Arithmetick in a common way—these too may have their use—I shall direct something on surveying and Mensuration—though on recollection if you buy as many of these books, as shall be wanting, I will pay for them. Pray give your

[1] Edward Lisle's *Observations in Husbandry*, ed. Thomas Lisle, London, 1757.

[2] Henri Louis Duhamel du Monceau's *Elements d'agriculture*, 2 vols. Paris, 1762; the English version is entitled *Elements of Agriculture*, transl. and rev. by P. Miller, 2 vols. London, 1764.

[3] Son of Burke's uncle Patrick of Ballyduff; hence Garrett Nagle's brother. He is mentioned in the will of Richard Burke, Edmund's father. He was born *c.* 1729, became a Doctor of Theology and a Roman Catholic priest.

[4] A book with this title was among the assigned texts at Trinity College in Burke's time (Trinity College Examination Book). Dodsley published, 31 March 1761, a book entitled *An Introduction to the Art of Thinking* (Straus, *Robert Dodsley*, p. 373).

Children Education—It wont cost much. Whether farmers, or what else, they cannot be the worse for it. I am really sollicitous for the welfare of all the people about the Blackwater, and most grateful for their friendship in this I speak to all our friends, for I consider you all as one, and hope (as I am sure you do, if you are wise) that you consider yourselves in the same way. Remember me to your Nephew Ned, whom I hope, when he is fit for it, to see in London. Betty has a Son here,[1] a pretty Boy with good parts, who is making an exceeding quick progress. She, I am told, intends to remove him; surely this is not well considerd, until the Boy has done something more. If she does, he will lose what he has got; tell her I beg she would not think of it; and that some way may be found of having him here in careful hands during the Vacation.

To WILLIAM DOWDESWELL—[*circa* 8] *January* 1767

Source: Sotheby Catalogue 18 July 1933, lot 414;
Anderson Galleries Catalogue 4289 (1937), lot 82.

Lord Rockingham wrote Dowdeswell 8 January 1767 (Rockingham MSS, R1–479): 'I have been a tour to Welbeck and to Wentworth and to Sir George Savile's and returned to town last night. This expedition as I took Mr Burcke along with me, has retarded his sending you back the papers you had entrusted him with.' The letter of Burke to Dowdeswell of January 1767, known to us only by a brief passage in a catalogue, perhaps was sent by Burke when he returned these papers. It should be studied in relation to other records of Burke-Dowdeswell correspondence at about this time. (1) J. E. Dowdeswell wrote the 5th Earl Fitzwilliam 19 September 1846 (MS at Sheffield, Bk38), mentioning a 'letter of Mr Burke's... in my possession...without date but written I believe in Dec 1765. It relates solely to a pamphlet of my father which he then intended to publish....' In December 1765 when he was Chancellor of the Exchequer, William Dowdeswell was far less likely to write a pamphlet or to seek advice from Burke—then a very obscure person—than he would have been in December 1766 or January 1767 when the Rockinghams were in opposition and Burke an important political figure. (2) There is a letter of Dowdeswell in the Clements Library in which he applies to an unidentified correspondent for criticism of a pamphlet which he intends to publish. The letter is dated 'Jan 4th 1766' but bears another endorsement '1767'—which has been crossed out. From its contents the letter is almost certainly to Burke.

As to the question of the Stamp Act, and the merits of its repeal, I fear it will swell the book too much if you enter at large with that very wide field...Will it not be sufficient to damn the stamp act as a scheme of Revenue, that it would require an army to enforce obedience to it.

In replying to Rockingham's letter of 8 January, Dowdeswell said of Burke's views on the Stamp Act: 'I will adopt Burkes ideas as strong as I can upon the inexpediency of that act as well from perpetual as from temporary considerations,

[1] Edward Nagle (1758–1826).

not only from the present condition of the Colonies but from their constant state under a true system of Colonisation' (Dowdeswell MSS, Clements Library, letter of 10 January 1767). So far as we know, Dowdeswell did not publish any pamphlet in the early part of 1767.

To CHARLES O'HARA—15 *January* [1767]

Source: O'Hara MSS. Printed Hoffman, pp. 385–7. *Endorsed:* 18 Jany 1767.

My dear Sir. I give you up for this Winter; but I am glad you are occupied as you seem to be. As to the rest, your correspondents may, among them, give you as good an account of publick matters, as if you were in the midst of the Bustle. I think you are a little mistaken in the Situation and plan of politicks of my friend.[1] The Entrée was asked last summer, to supply an omission, at a former time, of claiming a right he had, as being of the Bedchamber.[2] It went no further; nor do I think it has been used ever since. You are undoubtedly right, that the *weak* party with the fair Character would be chosen on a new Change. But if you are right in your principle, are you not mistaken in the application? The party you allude to is by a good deal the strongest, of any, seperated from Government, and their connection the closest. They certainly stand fairest in point of Character; but that fairness which they have kept, and are determined still to keep, goes against their practicability; which is a quality you know and feel to be indispensible with, upon such an occasion; and the person now at the head of them, neither would, nor I am sure could, take a lead upon such Terms as the Earl holds it on. He is not desirous to lead that way; and if he did, most assuredly, he never would be followed; and indeed how could he. Is not the present Court System built on the ruins of his, and where would you lay the foundation of his, but on the ruins of theirs. All these considerations satisfye me, that their turn never can be the next, whilst any party, of not more strength, and more practicability, may be found; and it may very easily. I look therefore upon our Cause, viewed on the side of power, to be, for some years at least, quite desperate; from the difficulty, not to say impossibility, of its coaliting with any body in or out of possession. As to Conway, if you hear, that he stays in with the approbation of his *Family* connexions, your intelligence is certainly good. If

[1] Rockingham.

[2] Rockingham had been a Lord of the Bedchamber from 1751 to 1762, and through his appointment had acquired the right of entrée to the King's Closet. In August 1766 he wrote to Lord Pomfret, a Lord of the Bedchamber, to ask if he still had this right or if he should apply again; Pomfret, on the King's orders, replied that no fresh application was necessary (Pomfret's letter is in the Rockingham MSS, R 1–421).

with that of his old friendships, and political *connexions* (if he will own the latter Idea) you are extremely misinformed. He holds his present office, to their great grief, and inexpressible detriment; and contrary to their unanimous Sense. He has given them a dangerous blow indeed. Whether he will indemnifye the publick for the mischief he has done the party, I know not; but I greatly doubt it. The great Guide,[1] as he advanced in his project of contesting the right of the E. I. company, (instead of bargaining with them for a part of it) grew sick, I fancy, of his Success.[2] I imagine he found, that Votes and Majorities cannot always get money in every way, at every time, and in every quantity. The thing, on examination, however considerable, fell short of his magnificent Ideas. He grew discontented. He changed his plan; went off to the Country; and left powers with *his* administration to *treat* with the Company.[3] This intention was signified to the general Court; and they empowerd the directors to treat, a fortnight ago.[4] Yesterday the Court met by adjournment; the Directors reported, that they had obeyd the order of the General Court; had offerd to treat with the ministry; but that nothing whatsoever was done.[5] The truth is, the people in Office, when they came to act, did not know what to propose; They had no settled Scheme; or if they had any thing like one, they did not dare to propose it for fear it should not receive the sanction of the real minister. He was as unfurnished as they; less open to information and at a distance of 100 miles;[6] So nothing was done. And Thus they carry on Business. What they will do in the committee, or how they can at once carry on an adverse inquiry, and an amicable Agreement I do not very well understand. However, thus things are at present. Little as I like opposition, I relish it much more than the support of such an administration; Indeed I never could have brought myself to the support of so monstrous a plan of Government from any principle of connection. At least, I deceive myself much, if I could. We meet tomorrow,

[1] Chatham, who in 1761 had explained that he was resigning from office 'in order not to remain responsible for measures, which I was no longer allowed to guide' (*Annual Register* for 1761, p. 300).

[2] Chatham's plan was to obtain a declaration from Parliament that the right to the East India Company's territories lay in the Crown, and then to yield the administration of the territories to the Company in return for a revenue. Conway and Townshend believed that the Company had the right to their territories, but that the Crown should share their revenue.

[3] Chatham did not authorize Administration to treat with the Company, but Townshend stimulated the Company into making overtures to Administration in the hope of being able to cut the ground from under Chatham's feet.

[4] 31 December.

[5] The Directors sent their proposals to Grafton 6 January. Grafton sent them to Chatham, who rejected them and insisted that the Company's right must first be determined (Chatham to Grafton, 10 January; Grafton, *Autobiography*, pp. 111–12).

[6] Chatham was then at Bath.

and the Guide not yet in Town. Will is still in but how long so?[1] the only difficulty is to seperate without a quarrel; and that will be if possible. Adieu my Dear friend. God prosper your plantations, and protect your enclosures, and make every thing about you full of growing! All the fireside salute you. I take it for Granted we shall see Charles as soon as he can let us have that pleasure.

15th Jany. Thursday.

EDMUND *and* WILLIAM BURKE *to* JAMES BARRY—[*ante* 19 *February* 1767]

Source: MS F. W. Hilles. Printed Barry, *Works*, I, 86–90.
Addressed: A Monsieur | Monsieur Barry, | Gentilhomme Anglois | au Caffee Anglois | A *Rome*.

Undated but written after Will Burke resigned office in February and certainly before Richard broke his leg—an event Edmund would not have failed to tell Barry. Lord Charlemont mentioned the broken leg to Flood in a letter dated 19 February (*Original Letters to Henry Flood*, p. 32).

[Edmund begins]

My dear Barry,

I am greatly in arrear to you on account of correspondence; but not, I assure you, on account of regard, Esteem, and most sincere good Wishes. My mind followed you to Paris, through your Alpine Journey, and to Rome; You are an admirable Painter with your Pen, as well as with your Pencil; and Every one to whom I shewd your Letters, felt an interest in your little adventures, as well as a satisfaction in your descriptions; because there is not only a Taste, but a feeling in what you observe; something that shews you have an heart; and I would have you by all means keep it. I thank you for Alexander;[2] Reynolds sets an high esteem on it, and thinks it admirably drawn, and with great Spirit. He had it at his house for some time, and returned it in a very fine frame; and it at present makes a capital ornament of our little Dining Room between the two Doors. At Rome, you are, I suppose, even still so much agitated by the Profusion of fine things on every side of you, that you have hardly had time to sit down to methodical and regular study; When you do, you will certainly select the best parts of the best things, and attach yourself to them wholly. You whose Letter would be the best

[1] See above, letter of 23 December [1766] (p. 285).

[2] The copy Barry had made for the Burkes of a painting by Le Sueur; see above, letter of [*circa* 20 December 1765] (p. 221). In the catalogue of Burke's pictures and statues sold after his death (a copy is in the British Museum, annotated with names of the buyers) the painting appears as by 'N. Poussin...Alexander and his Physician, circular'.

direction in the world to any young Painter, want none yourself from me, who know little of the matter. But as you were always indulgent enough to bear my humour under the Name of advice, you will permit me now, my dear Barry, once more to wish you, in the beginning at least, to contract the circle of your Studies; The extent and rapidity of your mind carries you to too great a diversity of things; and to the completion of a whole, before you are quite master of the parts in a degree equal to the Dignity of your Ideas. This disposition arises from a generous impatience, which is a fault almost Characteristic of great Genius. But it is a fault nevertheless; and one which I am sure you will correct, when you consider, that there is a great deal of *mechanic* in your Profession, in which however the distinctive part of the Art consists, and without which the finest Ideas can only make a good Critic, not a painter. I confess I am not much desirous of your composing many pieces, for some time at least. Composition (though by some people placed formost in the list of the ingredients of an Artist,) I do not value near so highly. I know none, who attempts, that does not succeed tolerably in that part. But that exquisite masterly drawing, which is the glory of the great school where you are, has fallen to the lot of very few; Perhaps to none of the present age in its highest perfection. If I were to indulge a conjecture, I should attribute all that is called greatness of stile and manner in drawing, to this exact knowlege of the parts of the human body, of Anatomy, and perspective. For by knowing exactly and habitually, without the Labour of particular and occasional thinking, what was to be done in every figure they designed, they naturally attained a freedom and spirit of outline; because they could be daring without being absurd. Whereas ignorance, if it be cautious, is poor and timid. If bold, it is only blindly presumptuous. This minute and thorough knowlege of Anatomy and Practical as well as theoretical perspective, by which I mean to include foreshortening, is all the Effect of Labour and *use* in *particular* Studies, and not in general compositions. Notwithstanding your natural repugnance to handling of Carcasses, you ought to make the knife go with the pencil, and study Anatomy in real, and, if you can, in frequent dissections. You know that a man, who despises as you do, the minutiæ of the Art, is bound to be quite perfect in the noblest part of all; or he is nothing. Mediocrity is tolerable in middling things; not at all in the great. In the Course of the studies I speak of, it would be not amiss to paint pourtraits often and diligently; This I do not say, as wishing you to turn your Studies to Pourtrait Painting. Quite otherwise; but because many things in the human face will certainly escape you without some intermixture of that kind of Study. Well! I think I have said enough, to try your humility on this Subject. But I am thus troublesome, from a sincere anxiety for your success. I think you a man of honour, and of Genius; and I would not have your Talents lost to yourself, your friends, or your Country, by any means. You will then attribute my freedom to my sollicitude about you; and my sollicitude to my friendship. Be so good to continue your Letters and observations as usual. They are exceedingly grateful to us all, and we keep them by us. Since I saw you, I spent three months in Ireland. I had the pleasure of seeing Sleigh but for a day or two. We talked a deal about you, and he loves and esteems you extremely. I saw nothing, in the way of your Art, there, which promised much. Those who seemed most forward in Dublin, when we were there, are not at all advanced, and seem to have little ambition. Here they are as you left them; Reynolds, every now and then striking out some wonder. Barrett is fallen into the painting of Views; It is the most called for and the most lucrative part of his Business. He is a wonderful observer of the accidents of Nature, and produces every day something new from that Scource—and indeed is on the whole a delightful Painter, and possessed of great rescources. But I do not think he gets forward as much as his Genius would entitle him to; as he is so far from studying, that he does not even look at the Pictures of any of the great masters, either Italians or Dutch. A man never can have any point of pride that is not pernicious to him. He loves you and always enquires for you. He is now on a Night Piece, which is indeed noble in the conception and in the execution of the very first merit.[1] When I say he does not improve, I do not mean to say that he is not the first we have in that way; but that his Capacity ought to have carried him to equal any that ever painted Landscape.

I have given you some account of your friends among the Painters here. Now I will say a word of ourselves. The Change of the ministry you know was pleasing to none of our houshold. Their measures since pursued both with regard to men and things have been so additionally disagreeable, that I did not think myself free to accept any thing under this administration nor did your friend Will think it proper to hold even the place he had. He has therefore, with the Spirit you know to belong to him, resigned his Employment. But I thank God, we want, in our New situation, neither friends, nor a reasonable Share of Credit. It will be a pleasure to you to hear, that, if we are out of play, others of your friends are in. Macleane is under Secretary in Lord Shelburnes Office; and there is no Doubt but he will be, as he deserves, well patronised there.

[1] See below, letter of 26 April (p. 308).

[Will begins]

I have my dear Barry little to add, I am willing enough to subscribe to Ned at most times, I never can do it more to my Hearts content than in his regards for you. I know your regards for him will prevent your being offended at the Liberty he has taken of advising you in your own art. His sanguine wishes for your excelling have drove him to it, and there is to a man totally unskilled such apparent good Sense that I cannot persuade myself that the man of real knowledge can be offended with them. As to our private affairs Ned has told you that I am no longer in Office, it so happened, that consistent with proprieties I could not continue, and I thank God that my affairs are in that situation that I had no temptation from fear, to be backward in doing what I ought, I just mention this lest your friendship might induce you to be alarmed unneccessarily. Mrs B the Dicks and the doctor are all well. Let us hear from you soon. Adieu.

To the LORD MAYOR OF DUBLIN—25 *February* 1767

Source: Copy in Fitzwilliam MSS (Sheffield). Printed *Corr.* (1844), I, 114–15.

Burke's friend John Ridge had written him 17 January from Dublin: 'the Freedom of this city was unanimously voted to you Yesterday. And by the next packet You will have a letter from Sankey the Lord Mayor to inform you of it.' Burke seems to have given some offense by not sending a prompt acknowledgement and thanks. Ridge writing to Will Burke (letter of [February]) sent Edmund an urgent message: 'for God's sake do it immediately, and Excuse yourself for not having done it before.'

My Lord,[1]

The honour which I have lately received from my Native City has been much heightend by the polite and obliging manner in which your Lordship has been pleased to convey it to me. I have no small Satisfaction in finding, that there is any thing in my Character or conduct capable of recommending me to the attention of so worthy a Man and so excellent a Magistrate as your Lordship. The City of Dublin; in rating my endeavours upon the partial representations of my friends, has set them much above any thing they could deserve. But they cannot overrate, I am sure, my intentions for the welfare of Ireland; for the total of which, if I were not very sollicitous, I should ill discharge my Duty as a Member of this Parliament.

I have much to regret that my short stay in Dublin did not permit me to pay my respects to your Lordship. Your permission and a more favour-

[1] The Hon. Edward Sankey (d. 1786); he was elected Lord Mayor 18 October 1766.

able opportunity will I hope indemnifye me for that loss. I shall be extremely happy in knowing more perfectly a Gentleman who has engaged my esteem and Gratitude, by his General Character and by the private obligations he has done me the honour to confer upon me.

I am with the truest sentiments of esteem and regard
My Lord
your Lordships
most obedient
and most humble Servant
E: BURKE

Queen Anne Street Febr 25th 1767

To CHARLES O'HARA—28 [*February* 1767]

Source: O'Hara MSS. Printed Hoffman, pp. 388–90. *Endorsed:* 28 Feby 1767. A joint letter of Burke and Dr Nugent. The Doctor's part is omitted.

My dear Sir, I have been a poor correspondent for some time past. I wish I had the excuse of being usefully employd to others or to myself in excuse for my Neglects. But there is nothing unfriendly in my Laziness. It is rather Laxity, than perverseness of disposition; at least *I* think so; and I trust *you* will think so. Why have I heard nothing of Charles? I suppose when he plans an expedition to London he will announce himself. I take it, after all your partial accounts of me, that we must soon be well acquainted; and I fancy, our intimacy will not break off suddenly. I confess, as to his Politicks, I should not be sorry that he was initiated in the School of our Party; His age will make him relish such Doctrines, and will enable him to wait their Effect; for if they have any it will not be sudden. Is not this odd Language, and sounding like an unnatural despondency in us, who gained yesterday one of the compleatest Victories, for the substance, for the manner, and for the time, that ever was known? Yesterday then the Chancellour of the Exchequer moved the Land Tax at 4s in the pound. Dowdeswell, (as had been preconcerted)[1] got up after him; and shewing from the general State of the revenue, that the Landed Interest might be relieved, and yet leave a large sum for the discharge of Debt, moved to amend the question, by substituting 3s in the place of 4. A long debate ensued. On the division it was carried for the amendment by 206 against 188. The ministry had called down all their forces. On our part, The Majority of

[1] At a meeting of Rockingham's followers 11 February. Burke attended this meeting, 'gave no opinion, and went away early' (Lord Hardwicke to Charles Yorke, 11 February, Add. MS 35362, fol. 66).

the Rockinghams, The whole Bedfords, and Grenvilles, reinforced by the almost compleat Corps of the Tories, came united into the field.[1] Such a victory, on such a question, shews plainly enough into what a contemptible state administration is fallen. At another time twenty four hours after the division, another set of people would have been in possession of the Closet—Certainly nothing like it, has been known in this Century. But as things stand at present; it is matter rather of Laughter and surprise, than any ground to reason or act upon.[2] It discovers indeed the weakness of all administration; especially of this most foolish and contemptible System; but that is all. It is easy to overturn the ministry; far from easy to find one to succeed. Observe, that in this Division, the Bute party stood firm, and voted to a man with the administration. Will Burke is out. Conway has got David Hume for his Secretary. Will feels easy in the freedom he has purchased at so good a price. But it is freedom. You are out, I believe in the Date of Ld J. C's Letter.[3] There was a time when it was true: afterwards it was much otherwise.

I know you will feel with us, for the unfortunate accident which has befallen poor Richard. He broke his Leg about eight days ago. Ever since he has been upon his Back; but the Symptoms are as good as they can be in so unhappy an affair. He bears it in general with his usual Spirit and resolution. Adieu my dear Sir. God bless you.

Saturday 28th

To CHARLES O'HARA—7 *March* [1767]

Source: O'Hara MSS. Printed Hoffman, pp. 390–1.
Endorsed: 7th March 1767.

My Last Letter left things in an odd Situation. They continue so. Lord Chatham, the day of his coming to Town,[4] saw nobody, but Lord Bristol; who, I suppose, is his go between at the Closet. There were two Cabinet

[1] Burke absented himself from this debate. Lord George Sackville wrote of him to General Irwin 2 March '...his opinion was with the ministry, and he did not care to separate himself from his friends in a point of this importance' (Hist. MSS Comm. 9th Report, App. III [*Stopford-Sackville MSS*] p. 26).

[2] Newcastle called it a 'great and surprizing success' (to Rockingham, 28 February, Add. MS 32980, fol. 187), and Rockingham thought the Ministry should take it as 'not quite a serious defeat, yet...a very unpleasant event' (to Newcastle, 1 March, *ibid.* fols. 194–5).

[3] O'Hara was inclined to approve of Conway's policy of staying in office instead of joining the Rockinghams in opposition. In his letter of 7 February to Burke (printed Hoffman, pp. 387–8) he had defended his judgment by quoting a letter of Lord John Cavendish, 'pretty good authority one would have thought'. He does not give the date of the letter or make it entirely clear whether it was written to him or to someone else.

[4] Chatham reached London 2 March, after an absence of more than two months.

Councils on Indian affairs; one the day before the guide[1] came to Town, the other the day after; in both which C. Townshend and Genl Conway differd from all the rest of the Cabinet. They held that the propositions made by the directors were a good Basis of a Treaty;[2] the rest were of opinion (as they were directed) that they ought wholly to be rejected. Beckford moved yesterday, that they should be laid before the house. The Chancellor and Secretary wished nothing more; but they fought shy; They said, that the Terms were not sufficiently clear; Lord Granby declared them totally inadmissible; Sir E. Hawke, (out of the Gallery) informed the House, that the ministry were divided on the Subject. Then Ch. Townshend got up; he said his situation had put him under difficulties before, but that now he thought himself at Liberty; he began with great Spirit, reserved himself on the Question of right and jurisdiction; but asserted strongly the preference of Treaty to force. He agreed to the bringing in the papers. However he grew a little more shy and dubious towards the Latter End. The day ended with nothing more than the Conversation. Lord Chatham, before that day exerted every Nerve to get a New Chancellor of the Exchequer; or at least somebody who would make or support his adverse measures to the Company.[3] But every body declined. His plan is dictated solely by the miserable situation of his private affairs, which makes employment Necessary to him. He took it at first, subservient to my Lord Bute as to *persons*; and since it must be so, he will hold it (if he can) subservient to Townshend and Conway, as to *Measures*; For I hear his *Ton* now is, that since he differs from such able and knowing persons on the India point, he grows doubtful of his own opinion and submits the whole to the wisdom of Parliament:[4] He puts the same face, and holds the same Language on the loss of the India Question; but this was not, until he despaired of getting any one to take the places of those two rebellious officers. Their plan is, not to resign. As to Ld Chatham, he must make some Capital Change in his System, or it wont do. Ld Bute seems serious at last in supporting him; but is at a loss for means. As to himself (as usual with him at such times)

[1] Chatham.

[2] The East India Company had submitted new proposals as early as 6 February. They were considered by the Cabinet 14 February and referred back to the Company for further explanation. The Company replied 21 February, and their consideration by the Cabinet was postponed until Chatham returned to London. Chatham did not attend the Cabinet meetings of 1 and 3 March.

[3] On 4 March Lord North was offered Townshend's place; he refused, and the offer was not repeated to anyone else.

[4] There is no evidence that Chatham ever grew 'doubtful of his own opinion', but he wrote to Grafton about the Company's proposals of 6 February: 'Parliament is *the only place* where I will declare my final judgement upon the whole matter, if ever I have an opportunity to do it' (Grafton, *Autobiography*, pp. 116–17).

he is gone out of Town. All the opposition Parties are still asunder. Nothing but confusion. God send order out of it. Adieu. I am in some haste.

Saturday. 7th March

To CHARLES O'HARA—14 *March* [1767]

Source: O'Hara MSS. Printed Hoffman, pp. 393–4.
Endorsed: 14 March 1767.

My dear Sir, I am obliged to you for thinking of us in your retirement. I shall hardly believe, that it will destroy your social Qualities, or social affections. I heartily wish it may answer all the other good family purposes to which you have devoted it. I do not believe it will contradict those very Ends, which have caused it. Would to God any thing from this bustle would tend to relieve its Languor, or find matter to enrich its speculations! I wrote a couple of posts ago, and directed to Dublin. Your Letter had no Date of place;[1] and from what you said, I suspected you wrote from Dublin. The Ponsonby you mentiond, I took to be the Speaker; I am very sorry to find he has so much nearer a connection with you.[2] If he comes this way he will call to see us. You will make us acquainted. We proceed in Parliament, *victoriously*, yet not *successfully*. Last Monday[3] we divided on a mere question of adjournment. We were 147. they an 180. The Friday before the printing of the East India papers was carried on a motion of Beckfords, with but a little grumbling; for the house was so impatient and tumultuous, that no sort of argument could be heard. You know the impatience into which they sometimes fall. This acquiescence was represented as very ill of us. We moved on Monday to rescind the Motion—Conway moved only to adjourn the debate until Wednesday. On this we divided. We were willing to shew how many would act against the *System* of the administration, totally independent of the Question. This was futile; but futile as these merits were, I think they were rather with us. On Wednesday[4] we came to the body of the Question on the expunging the resolution of Friday. The ministry feard, (what our best Numberers thought might be the Case) that we should beat them and gave us the substance of the Dispute; nothing but the Charters and Treaties being to be printed. Conway and

[1] O'Hara's letter of 20 February (MS at Sheffield) does not name the place from which it is written.

[2] O'Hara had referred to 'Mr Ponsonby's illness'; he did not mean John Ponsonby, Speaker of the Irish House of Commons, but James Carrique Ponsonby, his own son-in-law.

[3] 9 March.

[4] 11 March.

Townshend have declared in favour of Negotiation with the Company, and against all Violence. Ld Chatham seems resolved to ruin the Latter but can get nobody to fill his place. Ld Bute is steady to him; their connection is more declared than ever. The King has given Ld Chatham the fullest powers. He has thrown off his Blankets, laid aside his Crutches, quitted his Litter, and is abroad, and as well looking as ever I saw him.[1] We are still divided. Things are in as odd a way as you can conceive; but we are steady in our principle and in our Conduct; if we succeed, well! If not, we are no ways disgraced. It will be now seen what the Crown can do. And yet it is by yielding, they have held hitherto. Ld Chatham will find some way of quitting his ground of a Claim of right on the Company, and will at length negotiate a Treaty; and Having thus got out of the immediate difficulty, will prorogue the Parliament, and trust to Events in the Summer. Adieu my dear Sir. We are all truly yours.

14th March.

To Charles O'Hara—17 *March* [1767]

Source: O'Hara MSS. Printed Hoffman, pp. 394–6.
Endorsed: 17th March 1767.

My dear Sir, I hope the pacquets you expected brought you my two last. The time is a little critical; and you will naturally expect to hear from us pretty punctually. Things still remain in suspense. Lord Chatham saw the King last Thursday; and he says got the fullest assurances of support; and in consequence, the fullest power over things and persons.[2] However, as to the first, it is not always Royal power itself that can govern them; and as to the seccond, it is easier to destroy than to create; he could turn out Townshend who is grown more and more rebellious, but he cannot readily get one bold enough and able enough to assume his seat in such times as these. In the Indian affair he will I am satisfied get off his high ground, and take that method to which reason ought at first to have directed, but which Necessity at length compells[3] him to pursue, that of fair Treaty and Negotiation upon terms of mutual advantage. He has rejected the Directors proposal even as

[1] However well Chatham looked there is no question but that he was seriously ill. Henceforth he played no part in the affairs of his Administration, and ceased to correspond with the King or the Ministers.

[2] Rockingham wrote to Newcastle 15 March: 'The present news is that Lord Chatham was with the King on Thursday—great assurances of support and unlimited powers for turning *in* or turning *out*' (Add. MS 32980, fol. 297).

[3] MS: Necessity had at length compells

a *basis*. Sullivan[1] made one in the general Court Yesterday. It is believed that he countenances this proposition.[2] That of the directors was to give Government 500,000, advance. Sullivans gives eight—to be raised by a power of enlarging their Capital stock by borrowing that sum, at 250 per Cent.[3] The rest of the 2 Millions acquired by that method, to go in discharge of the simple Contract Debts of the Company. In other respects, The directors proposal seems at least as good, and far less complex than Sullivans. But Sullivan is Ld Shelburnes friend, and His making a proposal acceptable to Government is to lead the way for him into the Direction. All Negotiation with the Bedford party is suspended by the dreadful accident which happend to Lord Tavistock.[4] He was thrown from his Horse, and received a Kick by which his Scull was fractured. The first operation took out a piece of Bone 2 inches Long and about one broad. On this operation he recoverd his speech and senses. This was then thought sufficient; and indeed all that in his condition they could venture to explore. He grew a little more easy and light; but ill Symptoms have appeard again which made new openings Necessary. They have taken out two pieces more of the Scull. There are no great hopes of him. My friend Gataker with great Credit to his Skill and care attends him—The whole Town takes a share in the concern at Bedford House—Your poor friend Richard goes on as well as can be. They are to raise him tomorrow.

17th March St Paddy and sober.

To CHARLES O'HARA—28 *March* [1767]

Source: O'Hara MSS. Printed Hoffman, pp. 396–7.
Endorsed: 28 March 1767.

We Live in expectation of seeing Mr and Mrs Ponsonby.[5] They will be your precursors; but I hope '*Monseigneur vient*.'[6] will not be often reiterated before we see him. Poor Dick gets on apace. He is out of Bed; and the Leg promises well, even as to its future looks; and that to a young unmarried man is a consideration. Thank God, we have now no

[1] Laurence Sulivan (*c.* 1713–86), a friend of Shelburne and a prominent figure in the East India Company.

[2] By 'he' Burke presumably means Chatham. If so he is incorrect: Sulivan's proposals were made without Chatham's knowledge, and ignored Chatham's demand for a decision on the right.

[3] The proposal was that the Company should increase their capital by £800,000 at 250 per cent, i.e. that they would raise a sum of £2,000,000.

[4] Francis Russell, styled Marquess of Tavistock (1739–67), son and heir of the Duke of Bedford.

[5] O'Hara's son-in-law and daughter.

[6] The source of this quotation has not been found.

other anxiety. As to our Politicks nothing is yet decided. Ld Chatham has not seen Conway or Townshend; yet they stay in. The Latter *speaks* very loud Hostilities—and certainly his coming out at this time would be most advantageous. But an advantage depending upon his Firmness is precarious indeed. The Bedfords seem to come a little nearer to us. It is some thing that black blood is over between us; and that our people and they meet and talk amicably. Something may come of it. But you easily see, from the pretensions of Grenville, the Nature of the House of Commons, and the consequence of the Lead there, that our party cannot easily arrange with them, whilst they hold Grenville high; and we have no leader but Dowdeswell, who though by far the best man of business in the Kingdom, and ready and efficient in debate, is not perhaps quite strenuous and pugnacious enough for that purpose; the best in the world to aid and support such an one as Conway or Townshend. Your mind will carry you to the rest. Never was any grief more general than that for Ld Tavistock.[1] The whole family almost ruined in their health by it. I congratulate you heartily on Will, who is beginning to be most active in the house.[2] His speech some days since was far the best in the Debate; well marked, forcible, ingenious, with a decent, (and no more than decent) acrimony to those he answerd. He will be an immense accession to the Party; and you will, without regard to the party, rejoice in his Success. We go on with the E. I. Enquiry. We are now examining vivâ você Evidence. Adieu and believe us all as much yours as any people in the world.

28th March.

To CHARLES O'HARA—30, 31 *March* [1767]

Source: O'Hara MSS. Printed Hoffman, 397–8.
Endorsed: April 1st 1767.

My dear Sir, I have just come in from a long insignificant day in the house of Commons.[3] Your Letter[4] met me at my return, and paid me for the *Ennui* of our Evidence. It is not post Night; but our friends are at Cards; and I cannot employ half an hour better than in writing to you. The first thing I must do is to expostulate with you on some of your Notions.[5] Good God! how do you think it possible, that I could take

[1] Lord Tavistock died 22 March.

[2] Will Burke had taken his seat at the opening of the session. Conway named him to the King as having taken part in the debate of 9 March (Fortescue, I, 465).

[3] The House had been hearing evidence on the East India enquiry.

[4] Of 20 March; MS at Sheffield.

[5] O'Hara had written Burke: 'They want you indeed; you should not be left to opposition at this time.'

on with such an administration, in the conduct of such measures, as the present? If a little rectitude did not prevent it, surely the least particle of pride and spirit would never suffer one to engage under a person,[1] who is incapable of forming any rational plan, and is above communicating even his reveries to those who are to realize and put them in execution. He does not appear even at the Cabinet Councils of his own Creating; His Secretary of State and Chancellour of the Exchequer never see his face. In this great matter of the East India company, not one in the house knows what the plan or design of administration is.[2] Most people believe, that they have never conceived any thing like one. All they do is to run a blind muck at the Companys right to their acquisitions, without knowing the practicability or regarding the Justice of the measure. Beckford, and Lord Clare,[3] (the first confidential, the last a desperate instrument), conduct, (if it can be called conducting) the whole. I do assure you from my heart, that I look with as much horror at the Spirit, as I do with contempt at the manner of this proceeding. We are to set ourselves up as Judges upon a point of Law, to decide between the Subject and the Crown a matter of property of the greatest concern and magnitude without the least colour of right; at once Judge and party![4] I cannot now enter into this Subject but be assured, from the best consideration I can give it, it is one of the blindest and one of the most wicked designs which ever yet enterd into the heart of man. Do you know, that they rejected all Treaty with the company; declared their first Scheme of propositions *inadmissible*, without explanation or discussion; although it will be utterly impossible for the whole strength of Parliament to get any thing from that Country,[5] not only without the *acquiescence*, but without the *concurrence* of the Company. I wrote thus far last Night, and it looks as if I were very angry with the Ministry. At times I am; but I am not so furious as you may think me. I am not so angry as not sometimes to laugh a little. For some days indeed I have been somewhat ill;[6] But it has not made me too peevish. With regard to the popularity you apprehend their System will gain by lowering Taxes;[7] depend upon it they have no such thought; The party they mean to

[1] Chatham.

[2] Grafton wrote in his *Autobiography* (p. 110) about the East India enquiry: 'Lord Chatham did never open to us, or to the Cabinet in general, what was his real and fixed plan.'

[3] Robert Nugent, 1st Viscount Clare (*c.* 1702–88).

[4] It was Grenville's contention that if the right of the Company had to be decided it should be done in the law courts.

[5] India.

[6] Rockingham wrote Lady Rockingham 3 April: 'Burck is not very well. He is at Parsons' Green' (Rockingham MSS, R 156–10).

[7] As a result of the revenue gained from the Company.

relieve is of another kind, and in another Situation;[1] and it is not popularity they seek to acquire by the use they propose to make of this money. You know there are other Necessities besides those of the Subject. Townshend and Conway complaining and complaind of, proscribed by the invisible minister, and called out by every Motive of spirit and resentment, still hold their places. This is not of any great advantage to the Character of Conway, (the other had none to lose) but is very disadvantageous to us in our present Treaty.[2] But our Leader is steady, and nothing will remove him from the clear walk he has taken. Poor Richard sits by me. He has got down to us. The Leg promises to be strait and shapely. Adieu my dear Sir. God bless you. If your retreat dont sink your spirits what have you to Lament in it? Our Bustle I am sure is not worthy of your regret. We have indeed reason to be sorry that you are so long kept away from us.

31st March.

To the MARCHIONESS OF ROCKINGHAM—[16 *April* 1767]

Source: Fitzwilliam MSS (Sheffield).
MS undated; Rockingham's letter (see footnote 3) makes 16 April, a Thursday, the certain date.

Madam, My Lord Rockingham has ordered me to confine the account I am to give of our late transactions to a single side of Paper.[3] I am obliged to his Lordship for precluding me from an apology which I could not make in a manner at all satisfactory to myself and my own Sense of my Late Neglects; But your Ladyship will have the goodness to imagine that *something*, however triffling might have been said, if strict orders had not confined me within strict limits, and that my *excuses* to my Lady Rockingham would have been something more satisfactory if it had not been for my *obedience* to my Lords commands. I would lay the burthen where it may be best supported. It was the opinion of the Leaders of the several Parties, that it would be greatly for the common service to have some Division before the holidays to send down our friends to the

[1] Burke presumably means that the money is to be used for paying the Civil List debts.

[2] Rockingham hoped for the resignation of Conway and Townshend, which he believed would force Chatham to resign. If called upon to form an Administration he intended to include Conway and Townshend.

[3] Rockingham wrote to Lady Rockingham (who was at Bath) 16 April: 'Mr Burcke has undertaken to give you some account of Tuesday night's question and debate, but it is so late, that I have insisted upon confining him to a half page, least the post should call before he has finished' (Rockingham MSS, R 156–14).

Country with a *bonne bouche*, and to collect them again with the greater willingness and spirit. The administration indeed was so irresolute and indetermined, that they seemd resolved to entrench themselves in their inertness, and to draw a sort of strength even from their imbecillity, and fairly declared that, at the end of five months enquiry, they had nothing to propose. It was therefore agreed, from the Necessity of the thing, that we should lead. Accordingly Sr W. Meredith gave notice, about ten days ago,[1] that he should (as last Tuesday)[2] move the dissolution of the Committee. I will not trouble your Ladyship with the Parliamentary forms. This was the substance. The matter was Debated until two in the morning. We divided 157 to 113.[3] Those who chose to be squeamish (not conscientious) were of opinion that the committee ought to be sufferd to sit in hopes that some proposition might be made;[4] this lost us some paltry people: but it lost the Grenvilles many more.[5] We thought, a Committee sitting, by their own Confession, either to exercise powers which we always held to be neither just nor wise, ought to come to as speedy an End as possible. I hope we shall have your Ladyships approbation, though we had not that of a Majority in the house of Commons. It will be altogether comfortless to be beat by the Court and censured by our friends. Such Conduct indeed is not unusual; after being defeated by the Enemy abroad, to be tried by a Court martial at home. I have exceeded my Orders; I have attempted to bully a little; but I submit at last; I have only to end, by assuring your Ladyship that my pride is not owing to my presumption, but to my having lately had the honour of kissing her Grace, the dutchess of Newcastle.[6] This is true; but How it happend shall be a Mystery. The Bellman is impatient[7] and hardly permits me to assure your Ladyship that I am with the truest respect

your Ladyships
most obedient
and most humble Servant
E BURKE

Thursday.

[1] 7 April. [2] 14 April.
[3] The correct figures were 157 to 213; see next letter.
[4] Rockingham told Lady Rockingham: 'Some of our friends thought the motion rather precipitate and divided against us.'
[5] Lady Rockingham disliked Grenville, and was opposed to joining with him in a combined opposition.
[6] *Née* Henrietta Godolphin (d. 1776). [7] MS: impatent

To CHARLES O'HARA—[18 *April* 1767]

Source: O'Hara MSS. Printed Hoffman, pp. 399–400.
Undated. The debate Burke mentions as of 'last Tuesday' had taken place 14 April.

My dear Sir. We have now a little recess; and I assure you I enjoy it very perfectly. Not that we have had business to take up the whole mind of a person of any activity, but there has been always something or other which drew me into a number of small vortices of affairs in which I have been in a sort of whirl for some weeks past. I do not know whether you understand me or not. I am perhaps not very clear in my own meaning. But be the cause what it will, I am pleased to find myself Master of a weeks dissipation. All agreement between the Parties seems further off than ever. Events have happend of late, which though not productive of ill blood amongst us, yet have helpd to shove us a little further asunder. The D. of Bedfords friends, with what discretion I will not affirm, got him to plunge into Politicks as a diversion from the Grief occasiond by his Late great Loss.[1] Accordingly it was announced that he should make a motion in the house of Lords of the greatest consequence. The purport of this motion was kept a profound secret, not only from the administration, but from the Lords of our Party. At length out it came. It was to address the Crown to take into consideration the act of indemnity and Compensation lately passed in the Colony of Masachuset Bay as highly derogating from his prerogative[2] &c. &c. and to act in support of his just rights and those of this country, in such a manner as should appear most fitting to his Wisdom with the advice of his Council. The address was cautiously worded, (I have only given you the Substance) and they flatterd themselves our people would come into it.[3] Conway was reflected upon, by some Lords, in the Debate, as having encouraged the Colonists to this improper act, by some expressions in his Letter transmitting an account of the repeal of the Stamp Duty. There was some difference of Sentiments among the Rockinghams on this Subject. The D. of Newcastle went away.[4] Lord Rockingham and

[1] Lord Tavistock's death.

[2] The Act was intended to pardon those who had been concerned in the Stamp Act disturbances, and was an infringement of the Crown's prerogative of mercy.

[3] Rockingham wrote to Lady Rockingham 11 April: 'Yesterday the Duke of Bedford made a motion in the House of Lords—the matter proper and what *we* might have concurr'd in, but upon the whole it rather appeared to me somewhat *unfair* or *uncandid to the Administration.* Many of our friends were desirous of joining in the question against Administration, and yet I felt as if our joining in it might have the appearance of peevishness and want of candour' (Rockingham MSS, R156–13).

[4] Newcastle wrote to Mansfield 11 April: 'I never was more *in opinion* for a question in my life....I endeavour'd thro' the whole course of the day to prevent *our friend* [Rockingham] from voting with the majority, by all the reasons I could suggest,

the rest (with one or two exceptions)[1] voted with the Ministry.[2] They carried it 63 to 36. Ld R. is of opinion, that if the parties had carried on this measure in concert they would have had a Majority of one. But the Bedfords and Temples chose to be Politick, and did not communicate. A motion in which they would agree, might have easily been settled. For want of *simplicity* in the contrivance the Effect was defeated.[3] The Bedfords were vexed. Ld R. did right unquestionably; but an impression was given which weakend the whole body. I make no doubt that it hurt our division, when we endeavourd again Last Tuesday to hustle this Villainous E. India Enquiry out of the house. Administration divided 213 to our 157. They triumph intolerably on this advantage. It is certainly a point gained to them. We sat to it until two o'Clock. Adieu dear Sir. The Bellman warns.

Saturday.

To JAMES BARRY—26 *April* 1767

Source: MS F. W. Hilles. Printed Barry, *Works*, I, 91–3.

My dear Barry, I am rather late in thanking you for your last Letter, which was like all your others, friendly sensible, and satisfactory. We have had a pretty stirring Session hitherto; and late as it is, I dont think we have got through three parts of it. The opposition to the present Ministry has been carried on with great Vigour; and with more success than has of late years usually attended an opposition to Court Measures; you know too much of our situation and temper, not to see, that we must have taken a pretty active and sanguine Part. You will rejoice to hear, that our friend William has exerted himself two or three times in publick with the highest Credit. This hurry of Business will account in some measure for the Languor of our Correspondence. There was another Event which engaged us very unfortunately for some time; but thank God the Effects of it are now in a great measure over. My Brother about nine weeks ago had the misfortune to break his Leg by a fall

publick and private; but when I found at last that he was determined to vote for the *previous question*, I told him I could not agree with him but I would not *vote* against him; and so I went *openly* away, making that declaration to Bourke and others' (Add. MS 32981, fol. 127). Of Rockingham's other followers, Portland, Albemarle, Bessborough, and Scarbrough also abstained.

[1] Two of Rockingham's followers, Hardwicke and Grantham, voted with the Bedfords.

[2] Rockingham and three of his followers (Dartmouth, Monson and Edgcumbe) voted with the Ministry.

[3] Rockingham wrote to Lady Rockingham: 'There was no tye upon us to vote with the Duke of Bedford &c—for in fact they did not communicate with *us* on the matter. If they had and the question in all parts had been made suitable to our opinions *we* and *they* should have joined and I believe the consequence would have been a majority against the Administration' (Rockingham MSS, R 156–13).

in the street. Both bones were broken, and in two places; but they were speedily and well set. After a long confinement, born with a very good humourd patience, he is now on his Legs again, upon Crutches indeed. But there is an prospect that all will be as well as ever, in appearance, as well as in Effect. You feel so much for your friends, that I am glad to be able to give you the account of his accident and recovery together. All others are as you Left them. The Exhibition will be opend tomorrow. Reynolds, though he has, I think, some better Pourtraits than he ever before painted, does not think meer heads sufficient; and having no piece of Fancy finished, sends in nothing this time. Barret will be better off than ever. He puts in a Night piece in a very noble Style, and another very beautiful Landscape with a part of a Rainbow on a Waterfall.[1] They seem both to be excellent Pictures. Jones[2] who used to be Poet Laureat to the exhibition, is prepared to be a severe and almost General Satirist upon the exhibitors. His ill behaviour has driven him from all their houses; and he resolves to take revenge in this manner. He has endeavourd to find out what Pictures they will exhibit, and upon such information as he has got, has before hand given a poetic description of those pictures which he has not seen. I am told he has gone so far as to abuse Reynolds at guess as an exhibitor of several pictures, though he does not put in one. This is a very moral poet. You are, my Dear Barry, very kind in your offers to copy some Capital Pictures for me; and you may be sure that a Picture which united yours to Raphaels Efforts would be particularly agreeable to us all.[3] I may one time or other lay this Tax upon your friendship. But at present I must defer putting you to the trouble of any such Laborious Copies. Because, until we have got another house it will be impossible for me to let you know what size will suit me. Indeed in our present house, The best picture, (of any tolerable size) would embarrass me. Pray Let us hear from you as often as you can; your Letters are most acceptable to us; All your friends here continue to Love and constantly to enquire after you. Adieu Dear Barry and believe me most sincerely yours

E BURKE.

April 26th 1767.

[1] Two of Barret's pieces exhibited at the Society of Artists this year were 'A moonlight, with the effect of a mist; a study from nature' and 'A view of Creswell Craggs, Nottinghamshire, with a waterfall' (Algernon Graves, *The Society of Artists of Great Britain*, London, 1907, p. 23). Horace Walpole allowed the former piece 'some merit' (MS note in his copy of *A Catalogue of the Pictures Exhibited by the Society of Artists, 1767*, p. 1; this copy is now owned by Mr W. S. Lewis of Farmington, Connecticut).

[2] Probably Henry Jones (1721–70).

[3] In his letter of 13 February (printed Barry, *Works*, I, 77–82) Barry had offered to copy for Burke one of Raphael's paintings, adding however that the one he favoured was 'exceedingly large, and if you would chuse a copy of it, in your next letter send me an account of the size you would have it, the larger the better...'.

A few days before my receipt of your last Letter I wrote you a very long one.[1] I spoke of the Course of your studys, I fear with more freedom and copiousness, than Judgment. But your friendship, I dare say, will induce you to bear with my presumption in a Matter I understand so little. Poor Dick Sisson is dead;[2] I have lost a very dear and deserving friend.

To the MARCHIONESS OF ROCKINGHAM—[28 *April* 1767]

Source: Fitzwilliam MSS (Sheffield).
Parliament reconvened after the Easter recess on 28 April. Burke describes events of the first day's sitting.

Madam, I have not a *place*, I assure you; But for that very reason, and upon the very best precedents, I have a full right to be illhumourd, insolent, and capricious; These are the Liberties and Franchises of opposition. And, I take it, they will account for breach of promise altogether as well, as the falshood and insincerity that are attachd to a Court situation. Of this I am certain, that there is no way of accounting for the least Negligence with regard to your Ladyships orders, but upon some principle as absurd and as faulty as possible; whether it arose from the dispositions belonging to place, or to opposition.

I wish your Ladyship joy of (Not Bay Maltons success) but of the Victory of *Steady* over *Pancake*.[3] I dont much love the Dishes that are *turned* in the Pan. Quietness upon one bottom is better; even though, by the fire, it should be *blackend* upon *one side*. My Lord is quite in the Latter Stile of Cookery; and though it should be the old Kitchen, I must still persevere in thinking it the wholesomer Diet.[4] I begin to think he will bring every one, at length, to a similarity of Palate. As to the old Duke—Well! my Lord R's temper is the first of *his* Virtues; I really believe, the first of *Political* Virtues. For to *bear* with such persons, yet not to *yield* to them; and against their will to make them in the End subservient to your great Ends, is a matter of some praise. Every Engine has been used to bring the Grenvillian System into Vogue among the

[1] Burke's letter of [*ante* 19 February] would have been written before he had received Barry's of 13 February from Rome.

[2] He died 3 April (letter of 4 April, Dr Thomas Leland to Burke). Strickland (*Dictionary of Irish Artists*, II, 356) reports that his widow was in straitened circumstances and 'Edmund Burke afterwards provided for his son'.

[3] Lord Rockingham's horse *Bay Malton* had won heavily for him at Newmarket 21 April. His horse *Steady* had beaten the Duke of Grafton's *Pancake* on the 20th.

[4] Burke's metaphor some might think too elaborate a confection. Lady Rockingham may have relished it, as it was wholly a tribute to her husband.

Rockinghams; but it is as far from being the Fashion as ever.[1] I think it would be as easy to persuade Lord Villiers to wear Georges white Tye wig;[2] as to make any sober man of our people embrace their scheme of Politicks. On the meeting of the House, I went down to look for News. I saw the Chancellor of the Exchequer who was wonderfully in good humour with Lord R. very full of censure on the Conduct of the Butes; and very confident that the present System cannot hold. He told me that Lord Chatham is decaying apace; Lord Northington was taken extremely ill at their meeting last Night.[3] He fell into a sort of Epileptick Fit; and for some time appeard as quite Dead; He was taken home in the worst condition imaginable; a Blister was applied to his head this morning; but my accounts represent it, as over with him. If he should die, it will hasten decision;[4] Not, I confess, that I greatly Wish it until I see the prospect of a proper arrangement more distinctly than I do at present. On Thursday, they go into the Consideration of the American papers.[5] I do not find that the ministry have formed any plan upon them; at least General C. knows of none; Beckford (nearer to a Minister) says the same.[6] If so Grenville will take the lead and probably make some proposition, in which it will be impossible for us to follow him. Friday we resume the East India affairs. Beckford told me he has eight resolutions to propose, which he will serve up in two Courses; four and four; If he should persevere in this design, as I apprehend he will, it will be necessary to make a Call of all friends to the Cause.[7] My Lord is just gone to the opera where he hopes to hear something besides Musick, He has orderd me to put your Ladyship in mind to speak to Mr Finch,[8] and to assure him that my Lord will take care to have his excuses made at the Call of the House.[9] That he would have answerd his Letter, if he had not taken care of the Contents of it. He is extremely desirous that Mr Finch should be here, if possible, at the division on Friday; and let me add, that I hope your Ladyship will be earnest in

[1] Some of the most prominent of Rockingham's followers, such as Dowdeswell, Meredith, and the Yorkes, favoured joining in a combined opposition with Grenville and Bedford.

[2] George Bussy Villiers, styled Viscount Villiers, later 4th Earl of Jersey (1735–1805) was known as a dandy.

[3] The Cabinet meeting.

[4] Northington did not die until 1772.

[5] The House went into committee on the American papers on Thursday, 30 April.

[6] Beckford's importance had been considerably diminished since Chatham's retirement from business.

[7] On 1 May Beckford was to have proposed his resolutions; but 'Crabb Boulton [d. 1773], an India director, informing the House that there was now a prospect of accommodation with the Ministry...Beckford consented to postpone his motions' (Walpole, *Memoirs*, III, 11–12).

[8] Savile Finch (*c.* 1736–88), M.P. for Rockingham's borough of Malton.

[9] The House was called over on 29 April.

pressing his attendance. I shall give your Ladyship an account of our proceedings, as I am encouraged by your bearing the miserable ones I give. I have been with my family for a Week at Parsons Green;[1] We Left it but yesterday. You will find every thing very pleasing, and (except the fruit) very promising on your return. Permit me to thank your Ladyship for the honour of your most obliging Letter, and to assure your Ladyship that I am with the truest Sentiments of respect and Obligation

Madam your Ladyships
most obedient
and most humble Servant
E BURKE

Grosvenor Square
Tuesday Night.

To CHARLES O'HARA—5 *May* [1767]

Source: O'Hara MSS. Printed Hoffman, pp. 400–1.
Endorsed: 6th May 1767.

My dear Sir; It is long since I wrote to you, or, I think, heard from you. In that time some curious Events have happend which affected me at the time, and which, at the time might have entertaind you. But a mighty Tide rushes on; and washes away, and brings forward such things, with such rapidity that yesterdays thoughts and Politicks are as if they had never been. At present, I consider things not absolutely at, but certainly very near a Crisis. Lord Chathams health, understanding, and power are undermined.[2] He cannot possibly stand long. But the ——[3] is resolved to keep up the shew of an administration until the End of a Session; and then to attempt another Administration (for its year) on the old Bute Basis.[4] Lord Egmont, some think will be the undertaker. But if he cannot get, at least some two of the great Corps with him, his undertaking will be ridiculous; if not all, it will be difficult. They have come to a temporary agreement with the E. India directors. The General Court meets tomorrow to confirm it upon their part. There will be some warm work in that body. This day we were to have had the grand

[1] At Peterborough House, a residence of Lord Rockingham. Burke had been staying there earlier in this spring; see above, note to letter of 30, 31 March (p. 303).

[2] Chatham's health and understanding may have been undermined, but both the King and Grafton were waiting patiently until he could resume his power.

[3] The King.

[4] The King had no intention of changing his Administration if it could be avoided, and only agreed to reconstruct it when it was clear that Chatham could not for a long time return to active life.

American Budget of resolutions, regulations, and Duties. The Chancellor of the Exchequer who had raised much expectation on this subject, had a fall last Night by which he was cut over the Eye. Lord North[1] was to move them in his place. But Rigby got up and moved to postpone the Committee on account of his health; The house readily gave way to it. I Doubt whether Charles was much obliged to him for his kindness and candour. Whenever the day comes on it will be as Singular an one as ever was seen. Are we to entertain hopes of seeing you; and when? You have heard of Lord Rockms astonishing success. He brought off 6000 clear; and got as much more or near the matter for his friends.[2] Adieu my dear friend—we are all well.

5th May.

To CHARLES O'HARA—4 *June* [1767]

Source: O'Hara MSS. Printed Hoffman, pp. 403–5.
Endorsed: 4th June 1767.

My dear Sir, This Pacquet will carry you so many more and so much better accounts of those, for whose Welfare you must be at this time particularly anxious, than I can possibly give, that I shall say little of them except what regards my own feelings and opinions of them. Mr Ponsonby, my new acquaintance, seems to be a man of good understanding and good Temper; and seems, I think, to know the value of the possession you have given him. I am really pleased with him, and must thank you for his acquaintance. As to the young Lady, she is every thing which the daughter of such a mother[3] could have promised; I will say nothing of the father—She has something of both of you; but most of Lady Mary. She is quick and observing; and I am sure, a very few years will put her exactly on the platform of her mother. No one could wish her higher. I think Ponsonby looks well. I know not whether he has yet stated his Case to the Doctor.

I thank you for your Letters;[4] and am likewise very thankful, though I confess not a little surprised, that you are at all satisfied with mine. If you understand any thing at all of what is doing here, it must arise from your own correct knowlege of the Carte du pais, than from any informa-

[1] Frederick, Lord North (1732–92), M.P. for Banbury, later First Lord of the Treasury.

[2] The *London Chronicle* (XXI, 416, 28–30 April) reported that 'a certain Nobleman won £15,000 and another Nobleman lost upwards of £12,000'.

[3] O'Hara's wife, *née* Lady Mary Carmichael, had died 17 March 1759. This passage is our only evidence that Burke may have known her personally.

[4] One letter of O'Hara to Burke, 15 May (printed Hoffman, pp. 402–3) is at Sheffield; no others are known to survive from April or May of this year.

tion of mine. We begun the Session early; we have continued it long; and we have done nothing. Never so much Labour, never so little product. The Ministry broken, divided, Weak, and fluctuating; without mutual confidence, united interest, or common consultation, still holds. The Secretary of State and Chancellor of the Exchequer Vote, (on Questions of State and of Finance) in a Minority.[1] No one placeman follows them; and yet they hold their places. Sometimes an inferior Member of an inferiour board;[2] sometimes a person belonging to no board at all,[3] conducts what used to be considered as the Business of Government. The great Officers of the Crown amuse themselves and the house, with jests on their own insignificance. This is our State in the house of Commons, where the Crown is allpowerful, and yet does nothing. The Complexion of the H. of Lords is more adverse to administration. A stubborn Body of sixty one holds together and cannot be beat down one lower in several conflicts.[4] One question was just carried by the Princes of the blood.[5] Two days ago on the Quebeck question, accidents gave the Court a Majority of eleven.[6] But the Minority lost none.[7] In the mean time I am satisfied, the Butes will defend their last redoubt. They are pushed to it. The D. of Grafton seems to have gone over to that set, body and soul; and to maintain his Ground with firmness, not to say obstinacy. Such is the general Situation. We have a weeks recess.[8] I see no speedy End to the Session. If you come, come quickly. Will is in the Country. Dick hobbles about. Adieu my dear Sir.

4th June

[1] Conway voted against Administration 13 May on Townshend's American regulations, and both Conway and Townshend voted against the Dividend Bill 26 May.

[2] Probably Jeremiah Dyson (*c.* 1722–76) a Lord of Trade, who was mainly responsible for the Dividend Bill.

[3] A reference to Beckford, who moved the East India enquiry in the House.

[4] The opposition began their attack in the Lords 22 May, when, over a motion about Massachusetts Bay, they were beaten by only four votes—62 to 58. In the next divisions, 26 May, 65 voted with Administration and 62 with opposition. But on 2 June Richmond's motion on Canada was defeated by a majority of 12—73 to 61.

[5] On 26 May, when the Court's majority was three. The King's brothers, the Dukes of Gloucester and Cumberland, voted with the Court.

[6] Of twelve; the figures were 73 to 61.

[7] Burke is too optimistic. The division of 2 June marked the turn of the tide for the Court: they had gained eight votes since 26 May, while the opposition had lost one.

[8] The House rose on 3 June until 10 June.

To GARRETT NAGLE—[*June* 1767]

Source: New Monthly Magazine, XVI, 160–1.

This letter is undated. The plan it mentions of a trip to Italy suggests 1767 when we know Burke had this plan (see below, letter of 24 August, p. 322). Burke writes as if the parliamentary session were over or nearly over; in 1767 there was a recess from 3 to 10 June and the session ended 2 July.

My dear Garret,

It is true we have been a long time silent, and I fear very blameably so; but the truth is, that, whether importantly or no, we have been as much engaged as possible. The Session has been long and busy; and we have been obliged to appear for some time inattentive to our friends, though I think it impossible we should forget them. We begin now to breath a little, and our consultation must be how we are to dispose of ourselves in the summer. My idea is to go to Italy. It would be pleasing to me, and not without some use; but I am not sure, that something may not happen to disconcert my scheme. Your talking of taking a trip to Parkgate, gives us pleasure; because, perhaps, you may be tempted to come further. London is but two days in the machine from Chester; and I need not say how happy we should all be to see you. If you come at all, I could wish it were soon; that we may not be dispersed before your arrival. James Hennessy's[1] letter I got some time ago; but I do not recollect, and I think I could hardly forget, his mentioning my Uncle Atty's accident. I doubt the letter which spoke of that accident might have miscarried. I know not of what nature it was, but most sincerely rejoice at his being in a way of recovery, as I am at your father's continuing in a good way; I hope he believes there are few things in the world which could give me a more sincere pleasure than good news of him. As to the improvements at Clohir, I must leave them altogether to your discretion. You know pretty nearly what I would wish to have done, and I am sure you know the time and manner of doing it much better than I do. Though my hurry here prevented me from giving any thing like directions about the principal parts, I take it for granted, that so much as regarded Roche's[2] little garden, from the road downward, &c. was done of course, and that he had his usual little relief at Christmas. The planting part you will settle with Mr Crotty.[3] The glins and rocks, I think might be sown to advantage with ash keys and the like. But of

[1] Brother of Richard Hennessy (see above, letter of 14 October 1765, p. 217); he married Ellen Nagle, daughter of Burke's uncle Athanasius of Ballylegan.

[2] Not identified.

[3] See above, letter of 11 October 1759 (p. 135). David Crotty, Garrett Nagle's brother-in-law, did some business in the selling of trees (see advertisement in the *Dublin Journal*, 17–21 November 1744).

that you will judge. I send you inclosed a sensible book on some of the topics which have been bandied about here for this year past. I think you will like it.

Poor unfortunate James[1] came to us, as you guessed he would. I am sorry he behaved as he did on leaving the country. He was in a miserable condition; but severity would not have mended it, or improved the weak understanding that brought him into it. He told us he intended to go to Quebec. Dick gave him some little assistance, and got him sea clothing and necessaries. After this we saw nothing of him for some time, and concluded him on his voyage. But he called here lately; his reception was not quite so good as it had been; and we have not seen him these ten days; but I believe he is still in town. Somebody persuaded him to ask me to get him a place in the Customs. I had two letters from Atty Nagle[2] containing a request of the same kind; a desire that he might be made surveyor of the coast of Cork. I have not yet answered him; but I neither will or can do it. You will be so good as to settle some gossip accounts for me. I think Mrs Burke stood for Betty's daughter,[3] I for Nelly Hennessy's;[4] and Dick for Mrs Garret Nagle's of Rinny.[5] I think the nurses fee on these occasions is three guineas; and you will be so good as to give three guineas to each of the ladies, with our most affectionate compliments and thanks for choosing us. Adieu, my dear Garret, and believe me most truly yours,

EDM BURKE

To the MARQUESS OF ROCKINGHAM—[16 *July* 1767]

Source: Fitzwilliam MSS (Sheffield). Printed Brooke, *Chatham Administration 1766–1768*, p. 194.

Undated. Burke refers to 'two letters which passed this morning'. These were (1) a letter of Grafton to Rockingham, dated 15 July, received the morning of the 16th (Grafton, *Autobiography*, p. 144); and (2) the reply, dated 16 July. Rockingham sent copies of both to Bedford the night of the 16th (*Bedford Correspondence*, III, 368–9).

The month of July 1767 was taken up with negotiations for a new Administration. Conway and Grafton had invited Rockingham to take office. Rockingham had insisted that the Chatham Administration should be regarded as ended, that he should be empowered to form a new one; without direct authority from the King, he opened negotiations with the Bedfords and Grenvilles.

I just saw the D. of Grafton go into Horry Walpoles.[6] I dare say it is to try to work upon Conway to stay in. If your Lordship should not have

[1] Son of Patrick Nagle; he was an epileptic.

[2] Probably the son of Burke's Uncle Athanasius, rather than the uncle himself.

[3] Elizabeth Nagle (see above, letter of [1766], p. 288) had five daughters of whom we have record: Ellen, Catherine, Jane, Eliza and Mary.

[4] One daughter, Eleanor, is known to have been born to Ellen [Nagle] Hennessy.

[5] Rinny was a Nagle property.

[6] Horace Walpole (1717–97).

a very speedy answer from his Grace of Grafton would it be amiss to send the D. of Bedford the copies of the two Letters which passed this morning.

When these negotiations broke down, Conway again invited Rockingham to take office with his own followers only, but Rockingham refused.

To the MARQUESS OF ROCKINGHAM—1 *August* 1767

Source: Fitzwilliam MSS (Sheffield). Printed *Corr.* (1844), I, 132–7.

My dear Lord, I hope you have, by this time, got over a little of your Yorkshire Bustle, after escaping, so much to your Credit, from the Bustle of Westminster. Your Lordships Conduct has certainly been very honourable to yourself, and very pleasing to your friends. If we may judge from appearances, the Consequences which have attended it, are not very displeasing to your Enemies. His M. never was in better spirits; He has got a ministry weak and dependent; and what is better willing to continue so. They all think they have very handsomely discharged any Engagements of honour they might have had to your Lordship; and to say the truth seem not very miserable at being rid of you. They are certainly determined to hold out with the present Garrison, and to make the best agreement they can amongst themselves; for this purpose they are Negotiating something with Ch. Townshend.[1] Ld Bute is seldom a day out of Town; I cannot find whether he confers directly and personally with the Ministry; but am told he does.[2] I saw Genl Conway a day or two after you left us. I never knew him talk in a more alert, firm and decided tone. There was not the slightest Trace of his usual diffidence and hesitation. He lamented your Lordships mistake in not coming into administration at this juncture. But, I declare, his conversation did, to me, more thoroughly justifye your nonacceptance, than any thing I had heard either from yourself or from others on that Subject; as it laid open more clearly the Ideas upon which they went in treating with you. Their plan, in short, was, that your Lordship, with a few only of the chief of your friends should take Offices, and that the rest should wait those vacancies, which Death, and occasional arrangements might make in a Course of time. He dwelt much upon the advantages which had attended this method of proceeding when Mr Pitt acceded to the old administration in 1757. Though I felt indignation enough at this comparison of times and persons, I could hardly help laughing at the Notion of providing for a party, upon a System which supposed the long

[1] This seems to have been a false rumour. Townshend had played no part in the negotiations, and was by now thoroughly distrusted by Grafton.

[2] There is no evidence that Bute took any part in politics after July 1766.

and steady continuance of the same administration. I told him that your Lordships Opinion of the duty of a Leader of party was, to take more care of his friends than of himself; and that the world greatly mistook you, if they imagind, that you would come in otherwise than in Corps; and that after you had thought your own whole bottom too narrow, you would condescend to build your administration on a foundation still narrower, and give up (for that it would be) many of your own people, in order to establish your irreconcileable Enemies in those situations, which had formerly enabled, and would again enable them to distress, probably to destroy you.[1] That beyond this, he was not less fond of a System of extermination than you were. I said a great deal, and with as much freedom, as consisted with carrying on the discourse in good humour, of the power and dispositions of the Bute party; the use they had made of their power in your time; and the formidable encrease and full establishment of that power, which must be the Necessary consequence of the part which our former friends in Office seemd just now inclined to take. This discourse had no sort of Effect. The Bute influence had lost all its Terrours. An apprehension of Grenvilles coming in was the ostensible objection to every thing.[2] Much moderation towards the K's friends, and many Apologies for every part of their Conduct. In the End, he said (I think directly, but I am sure in Effect) that as long as the D. of Grafton thought it for his honour to stay in, he could not resign. I have troubled you with this conversation, as it seemd to me very fully to indicate the true spirit of the ministry. I am quite satisfied that if ever the Court had any real intention that your Lordship should come in, it was, merely to office, and not to administration,[3] to lower your Character, and entirely to disunite the party. This you have escaped. All of the party who are capable of judging, and supplied with the materials for it, will rejoice in your escape; but there are some, who feel anxious and uneasy, as if an opportunity of getting into power had been missed upon mere points of delicacy.[4] Ld Edgcumbe[5]

[1] Burke's meaning is that Rockingham would only come into office as the acknowledged head of Administration, with full power to turn out Bute's friends.

[2] Rockingham attributed the failure of the negotiations to Grenville, while Burke himself, in his letter to Rockingham of 18 August, objected to Richmond's 'dislike of the Grenvilles'.

[3] This was true; the King would have welcomed Rockingham as an ally, but, in the absence of Chatham, wished to retain Grafton as head of Administration.

[4] The division in the Rockingham party was more serious than Burke allows. Newcastle and Hardwicke criticized Rockingham's handling of the negotiations, Richmond believed Rockingham should have accepted office, and the Cavendishes objected to Rockingham's proposed alliance with Bedford and Grenville.

[5] Edgcumbe, over whose dismissal some of the Rockinghams had resigned in November 1766, was anxious to resume office and acknowledged little allegiance to Rockingham.

wrote Lately to Ld Bessborough; The Princess Amely[1] is down with him. He is frightend out of his Wits; all his information comes from that Quarter. Does not your Lordship think that a word from you to set the matter to rights as to the rupture of both Negotiations might be useful with regard to him? He is wofully impatient.[2] You see, my Lord, that, by giving you so free an account of my conversation with Conway this Letter is only for yourself. Ld John Cavendish might indeed have given you the whole of it, as well as of his own; but I apprehend that he will have an opportunity of conveying this to your Lordship before he can see you. Be so good as to present my humble respects to my Lady Rockingham and believe me with the truest esteem and attachment

My dear Lord
ever yours
E BURKE

Parsons Green Augst 1st 1767.

Hopkins has the green Cloth;[3] Lowndes's Brother the Excise;[4] and Bradshaw[5] is Secretary to the Treasury. Wedderburn is gone the Northern Circuit. He told me he would wait on your Lordship at Wentworth.

To JOHN HELY HUTCHINSON—3 *August* 1767

Source: Hist. MSS Comm. (*Donoughmore MSS*), pp. 260–1.
The Hist. MSS Comm. editor describes this letter as: '*Imperfect. Beginning lost*'.

The Lord Chancellor of Ireland, John, 1st Baron Bowes (1690–1767), died 22 July. On 28 July Hely Hutchinson, hoping that some Rockingham influence might help him to get the place, wrote a letter to Burke beginning: 'Are you yet able to make an irish Chancellor?'

1767, August 3. Parsons Green.

I assure you, I have a very sincere desire, in my present humble situation, to do anything that may be pleasing to you. I should have the same if I had as much power, as your partiality could wish me. But I cannot move the machine, or even grease the wheels. My friends are out of power, and likely to continue so. Lord Rockingham is gone to the

[1] Princess Amelia (1711–86), daughter of George II and aunt of George III.

[2] When Edgcumbe was offered a place in October 1767, Bessborough wrote to Newcastle that 'there was a pretty strong inclination in our friend to accept' (Add. MS 32986, fol. 83).

[3] Richard Hopkins (*c.* 1728–99), M.P. for Dartmouth, Grafton's friend, was appointed Clerk of the Board of Green Cloth, an office in the King's Household.

[4] Burke is mistaken. William Lowndes (*c.* 1707–75), brother of Charles Lowndes (*c.* 1700–84) who had been Rockingham's Secretary of the Treasury, was not appointed a Commissioner of Excise until 1772.

[5] Grafton's friend Thomas Bradshaw (1733–74), formerly a clerk at the Treasury.

Country without office and with dignity. Lord Bristol I could not even know.[1] Lord Townshend[2] I do know too well. His brother has no regard for me and I have no confidence in him. Just so matters stand, and I will not make any parade of my willingness to run your errands, because it would look like that cheap and commonplace way of shewing one's good inclinations, when no service is desired, because no service can be done. I think it very likely that the Chancellor will be appointed from hence.[3] In the conversations which I hear, it is talked of as a sort of maxim of Government. But in the end the accommodation of their own arrangement is the principle they will proceed upon. It was this principle that made Lord Townshend Lord Lieutenant, at least I cannot conceive any other, and have but a moderate opinion of their policy even in that. On Lord Chatham's decline in health and capacity, Lord Rockingham was wished with his friends, to accede to the remains of that administration. He tried to form a plan of strength; but in this attempt he failed, and he was unwilling to form the project of a weak one, or to make a part in such a system. The Duke of Grafton and Mr Conway who seemed at first very sensible of the deficiencies of their own system, took courage from the failure of their negotiations, and resolve to all appearance, to hold on that Bute bottom upon which Lord Chatham had left them. As their garrison is very small, it became absolutely necessary that there should be more harmony amongst them than appeared in the last Session. Townshend is become of more consequence; and, if possible to fix his levity, they have made his brother Lord Lieutenant, which I know to have been long his object. Lord Townshend is thought to have a great ascendant over Charles. I imagine this has been their motive; they have wanted agreement within themselves, for I am sure this has given them no strength from without. If they should attempt to enlarge themselves, and to extend their line of debate, they will probably attempt to get Sir Fletcher Norton.[4] If they can compass this the Master of the Rolls[5] will be thrown upon you; and Oh! Earth lay light on him! for sure no man ever burthened it so much. I think their attempt on Sir Fletcher very likely; because I know they had a negotiation with him last winter.[6] If this should fail, and they

[1] Bristol had just resigned his office of Lord Lieutenant of Ireland.

[2] The newly-appointed Lord Lieutenant.

[3] Townshend wished an Irishman to be appointed; but the Cabinet favoured an Englishman. James Hewitt (*c.* 1709–89), later (1768) 1st Baron Lifford, was ultimately appointed; see below, letter of 27 November (p. 337).

[4] (1716–89), later Speaker of the House of Commons.

[5] Sir Thomas Sewell (*c.* 1712–84), M.P. for Winchelsea.

[6] Grafton had written to Chatham 13 March 1767 (*Chatham Correspondence*, III, 232): 'If your Lordship could see Sir Fletcher Norton for a few minutes, I have great reason to think you might quite fix him'; but nothing came of this suggestion.

think of your side, the consideration of the offices which you have to resign,[1] would, I should think, weigh a great deal with Lord Townshend provided he has any man whom he loves enough for the moment to wish a provision for.

To the MARQUESS OF ROCKINGHAM—18 *August* 1767

Source: Fitzwilliam MSS (Sheffield). Printed *Corr.* (1844), I, 138–44.

My dear Lord,

I was just on the point of writing when I received your Letter by Lord Albemarle.[2] I am glad he was with you at Wentworth, and that you had an opportunity of confirming him in the Sentiments which so handsomely arose in his own breast on the first representation of the late Business.[3] Upon my word, every thing I see of that family encreases my opinion (originally no small one) of their honour, spirit, and steadiness. I found the Admiral at Goodwood,[4] and came to town with him. He is very right; and the more laudably so, as he is not without a strong feeling of the inconveniencies attending a protracted opposition from the craving demands of friends and dependents; who will very little enter into the motives to a conduct, which stands between them and all their wants and expectations. He had a good deal of talk with the Duke of Richmond; and I had some. I saw in him many signs of uneasiness, but none of wavering. His Grace cannot be persuaded of the propriety of not accepting the late Offers;[5] or, at least, of not having gone further than you did; so as to put the ministers in the wrong, by driving them to avow more of a Closet System, than they would willingly profess to the world. There was great good opinion, (amounting to veneration) of your Lordship; much satisfaction in the principles of the party; but still a leaning to Conway, and a dislike of the Grenvilles, which operate powerfully towards the Doctrine of acceptance. He fears, that the Corps, which will neither unite with the other Squadrons in opposition, nor accept the offers made by administration must in the

[1] Hutchinson was a Privy Councillor and Prime Serjeant of Ireland.

[2] George Keppel, 3rd Earl of Albemarle (1724–72).

[3] Albemarle, although he was the strongest advocate of the alliance with the Bedfords, had not openly criticized Rockingham's handling of the negotiations.

[4] Augustus Keppel, brother of Lord Albemarle and cousin of the Duke of Richmond. On 5 July Richmond had invited Burke to stay a few days at Goodwood; presumably Burke's visit had been postponed when Grafton began the negotiations with Rockingham.

[5] Richmond wrote to Burke 15 November 1772: 'Had my opinion of taking administration by ourselves, when our negotiation with Bedford House broke of in 1766 (or 1767 I forget which year) been followd, Things would have been very different from what they are at present!'

nature of things be dissolved very speedily, and perhaps not very reputably; as being, to appearance, destitute of any thing like a certain object.[1] I combated this opinion in the best manner I could. The Duke said nothing to me of the part he should take in the next Session. I did not indeed at all lead the conversation that way; thinking the ground delicate; and that in matters of this sort, men are more safely trusted to the Natural operation of things as they strike their own minds, than to any engagements. Keppel went further; and to him he was more explicit. He seemed greatly at a loss for what you meant to pursue; but was extremely willing to take a warm and vigorous part with your Lordship, in case you could come to settle some distinct plan of political and parliamentary Conduct. Keppel has no doubt of him; I have as little hesitation about his honour; but he has an anxious, busy mind. Work must be cut out for him, or he will not be satisfied easily. If this be done, I am persuaded, he will be faithful and resolute; and I am sure he is an essential part of the Strength of your body. The admiral joins in my opinion, of the Necessity of your Lordships writing to him once or twice during the recess.[2] Some attentions of this sort will be expedient, to continue him in affection to the Cause; and to counterballance the influence of Lord Holland, always the Kings friend,[3] and of Genl Conway,[4] newly adopted into that Corps, and probably with all the Zeal of a new convert. It is no reflexion on his Grace to suppose, that in some way or other, these influences, so natural, and in some respects so little blamable, should have their weight.

I beg pardon for having run on so long upon this Topic. When I know Mr Dowdeswells time, I will obey your Lordships commands without delay.[5] Of the Grenvilles I hear nothing. In spite of themselves, they are compelled for a while to be quiet, and to play no tricks. Conway is gone fairly to the devil. Ld Frederick Campbell is Secretary to the Lord Lieutenant.[6] This is Conways Jobb. Conway is also to have Ld Townshends Ordnance; but for the present, I hear, declines the Salary.[7] I hear

[1] On 4 October Richmond wrote to Rockingham and, in a series of rhetorical questions, criticized every aspect of his policy (Albemarle, *Memoirs of Rockingham*, II, 59–63).

[2] Rockingham apparently did not write, but visited Richmond at Goodwood in October. 'His mind is not quite at ease', Rockingham wrote to Dowdeswell 9 November, 'but I have no fears about him, tho' I think he will have some difficulties now and then' (Rockingham MSS, R 1–558).

[3] Lord Holland was Richmond's brother-in-law. Burke exaggerates his influence over Richmond.

[4] Richmond had married Lady Mary Bruce (d. 1796), daughter of Conway's wife by her first husband, Charles 3rd Earl of Ailesbury (1682–1747).

[5] Rockingham was hoping to assemble a council of his closest advisers at Wentworth in the autumn.

[6] Of Ireland. Lord Frederick Campbell was Conway's brother-in-law.

[7] On the appointment of Lord Townshend to be Lord Lieutenant of Ireland, Conway accepted the office of Lieutenant-General of the Ordnance, which he held

too that Pynsent is to be sold,[1] but I dont know who the purchaser is. The D. of N. grumbles as usual. There is one point in which I incline to join with him; That of Elections.[2] Surely, if there be, as there are, monied men in the party, they ought not to let the venal Boroughs to get engaged in the manner they are likely to be. Adieu my dear Lord you will be so good as to forgive this tedious Letter, to present my humble respects to my Lady Rockingham and to believe me with the greatest Esteem and affection ever

your Lordship's
most obedient and
most oblig'd humble Servant
E BURKE

Parsons Green Augst 18th 1767.

Lord Chesterfield has been ill and dangerously so; But I am told is recovering. If he should die this turn, the County of Buckingham would become suddenly vacant.[3] Lord Verney on this Idea desires to know what your Wishes on this subject would be, and in what way his interest (always at the service of the Cause) may be useful.

To JAMES BARRY—24 *August* [1767]

Source: MS F. W. Hilles. Printed Barry, *Works*, I, 93–5.
A joint letter of Edmund and Will Burke. Will's part is here omitted.

My dear Barry, It is with shame I find myself so late in answering a Letter which gave me such sincere pleasure as your Last.[4] Whatever you may think of my delay, be persuaded that no want of regard for you had the least share in it. We all remember you with much esteem and affection; and I hope we are not, any of us, of a Character to forget our friends, because they are fifteen hundred miles distance from us, and away a year or two. I did indeed strongly flatter myself, that Will and I might possibly have taken a trip to Rome in this Recess; But the Session ran to a very unusual and mortifying length; and as soon as it closed, a political Negotiation for bringing in my Lord Rockingham to

along with that of Secretary of State, but without the salary. 'Such noble disinterestedness shut the mouths of Opposition', wrote Walpole (*Memoirs*, III, 78); but it was a fresh cause of resentment against him.

[1] Chatham's estate of Burton Pynsent, in Somerset. Parts of it were sold at this time.

[2] A General Election had to take place by March 1768.

[3] Sir William Stanhope (1702–72), M.P. for Buckinghamshire, was Lord Chesterfield's brother and heir; his seat would be vacant if he became a peer.

[4] Either Barry's letter of 23 May (MS at Sheffield; printed *Corr.* [1844], I, 116–29) or a letter of [June] (printed Barry, *Works*, I, 97–101).

the administration was opend; and thus our Summer insensibly slid away; and it became impossible for me, either in his Company, or alone, to begin an Enterprise that would demand four good months at least. The mention I have made of this Negotiation has, I dare say, put you a little in a flutter. It came to nothing; because it was found not practicable with honour to undertake a Task like that, until people understand one another a little better; and can be got to a little cooler temper and a little more fair dealing. At present there is no prospect of a sudden Change; therefore we remain as we are; but with all the content, which consciences at rest, and circumstances in no distress, can give us. We are now in the Country in a pretty retired spot about three miles from Town. Richard is at Southampton for the Benefit of sea Bathing which has already been useful to his Leg; and he gathers strength in that Limb every day. This is our situation. As to your other friends, Barret has got himself also, a little Country house; His Business still holds on; and indeed he deserves encouragement for independent of his being a very ingenious artist; he is a worthy, and a most perfectly good humourd fellow. However he has had the ill luck to quarrell with almost all his acquaintance among the Artists; with Stubbs,[1] Wright,[2] and Hamilton;[3] They are at mortal war; and I fancy he does not Stand very well even with West. As to Mr Reynolds he is perfectly well; and still keeps that superiority over the rest which he always had from his Genius, sense, and morals. You never told me whether you received a long, I am afraid, not very wise letter from me, in which I took the Liberty of talking a great deal upon matters which you understand far better than I do. Have you the Patience to bear it? You have given a strong, and I fancy a very faithful Picture of the dealers in Taste with you. It is very right that you should know and remark their little arts; but as fraud will intermeddle in every transaction of life, where we cannot oppose ourselves to it with Effect, it is by no means our Duty or our Interest to make ourselves uneasy or multiply Enemies on account of it. In particular you may be assured, that the Traffick in Antiquity and all the Enthusiasm, folly or fraud which may be in it, never did nor never can hurt the merit of living Artists. Quite the contrary in my opinion; for I have ever observed that whatever it be that turns the minds of men to any thing relative to the arts, even the most remotely so, brings artists more and more into Credit and repute; and though now and then the meer broker, and dealer in such things runs away with a great deal of Profit, yet in the End ingenious men will find themselves gainers, by the

[1] George Stubbs (1724–1806).
[2] Probably Joseph Wright (1734–97).
[3] Probably Hugh Douglas Hamilton (*c.* 1734–1806).

dispositions which are nourished and diffused in the world by such Pursuits. I praise exceedingly your resolution of going on well with those whose practices you cannot altogether approve. There is no living in the world upon any other terms. Neither Will nor I were much pleased with your seeming to feel uneasy at a little necessary encrease of expence on your settling yourself. You ought to know us too well, not to be sensible that we think right upon these points. We wishd you at Rome, that you may cultivate your Genius, by every advantage which the place affords; and to stop at a little expence might defeat the Ends for which the rest was incurred. You know we desired you at parting never to scruple to draw for a few pounds extraordinary; and directions will be given to take your drafts in such occasions. You will judge yourself of the propriety; But by no means starve the Cause. Your father[1] wrote to me some time ago. The old Gentleman seems to be uneasy at not hearing from you. I was at some distance in the Country; but Mr Burke opend the Letter and gave him such an account as he could. You ought from time to time to write to him. And pray let us hear from you. How goes on your Adam and Eve.[2] Have you yet got your Chest. Adieu! Let us hear from you and believe us all most truly and heartily yours.

24th Augst

To the DUKE OF NEWCASTLE—30 [*August*] 1767

Source: British Museum (Add. MS 32985, fol. 284). *Endorsed:* R⁄ Sepr 1st. Burke wrote the wrong month in his date line; the letter was certainly written 30 August, a Sunday.

Parsons Green Septr 30. 1767.
Sunday Evening.

My dear Lord,

I have a just sense of the Candour and condescension with which you were pleased to receive a very free explanation of my poor thoughts upon a subject, on which, to say the Truth, my sincerity only, and not my Judgement could entitle me to the slightest degree of your Graces attention.[3] I have, from inclination and principle, a strong attachment

[1] John Barry, described in Barry, *Works* (I, I) as 'in the better part of his life, a coasting trader between the two countries of England and Ireland'.

[2] The only major painting Barry brought with him on his return from Italy in 1771. Charles Brandon's drawing of the exhibition gallery of the Royal Academy at Pall Mall in 1771 shows it hanging in a place of honour. It was given in 1915 by the Royal Society of Arts to the National Gallery of Ireland. See T. Bodkin, 'James Barry', *Apollo*, XXXIII (1940), 145.

[3] Newcastle wrote to Albemarle 29 August: 'I long...to acquaint you with a very long conversation, that I have had this morning with Mr Bourke....He thinks my

to that System of which your Grace forms so eminent a part; And, from my Temper, am disposed to take my little share in it, with earnestness and warmth. I shall most faithfully obey your Commands; and will represent to my Lord Rockingham, as distinctly as I am able to do, your Graces opinion of the conduct to be held at this juncture, as well as your own particular inclinations towards him.

I shall consider myself very fortunate, if I am able to enjoy the continuance of that indulgent opinion with which your Grace is so good to honour me. I am satisfied I shall never forfeit it by my Neglect of any opportunity of expressing the high and sincere Respect, with which I am

My Lord,
your Graces
most obedient
and most obligd humble Servant
EDM BURKE

I believe that a Box sent by the Sheffield Fly will be the safest publick conveyance to Lord Rockingham.

WILLIAM BURKE *to* EDMUND BURKE—[*post* 4 *September* 1767]

Source: Fitzwilliam MSS (N.R.S.).
Undated, but written after the death of Charles Townshend 4 September; the mention of Lord Mansfield becoming Chancellor of the Exchequer suggests a date after 9 September.

We remain in some perplexity about the Box, you continue to mention as sent by the Marquess to you; a Letter there was; which, Mrs B forwarded to you immediately; and which you must have got long since; if the Box however, was directed to you, it may be worth Ld R's while to enquire how any one else came to open it.

Tho I am writing, I am far from clear where or when this may reach you. You are certainly in the right to take your tour, while you are sure of time; and when you are upon it, do not hurry yourself; whether your return to Wentworth is, or not, a day or two later, cannot be material;

Lord Rockingham's honor concerned in not dropping Mr Conway, as he calls it, or suffering him to go out to the Army. He thinks also my Lord Rockingham in the right in all the objections he makes to Mr Grenville, and the part he took upon it' (Add. MS 32984, fol. 358). And from Claremont to Rockingham 11 September: 'Mr Burke was so good as to come here on Saturday, the 29th of last month; we had a very full and free conversation; and I hope he thinks a very friendly one not only to each other but to those concerned in it. Tho' I am sorry that we differ'd so much in opinion; yet as it is a real difference we both lament it, but don't blame each other' (Add. MS 32985, fol. 75).

but hurrying through a place, where your curiosity or Business asks a little stay, may afterwards be inconvenient and vex you; I have some notion that this however may catch you at Wentworth, for Lord Fred Cav[1] whom I met yesterday, told me his Brother Lord John had been sent for by the M, and if He is coming, it is probable to me, you may chuse to see him before you set out; if you do, I could wish you would get him to be explicit in regard to Lancaster[2]—and make him understand that if they personally decline, you personally mean to stand, for I apprehend that they understand it, as if your standing must be on their Shoulders, and, as that requires an Exertion, which I think few of our friends are much fitted for, they will through the mere vis inertia loose it for themselves, and for you; to say the truth I think it clear from Rawlinson that He wishes you personally to be the Man,[3] at the same time for every reason I think you right not to look for it, but with the entire desire of the Cavendishes, for they are right Men, and good Men; and I am persuaded too, they are your friends, but dont let their Idleness and your Delicacy cooperate to hurt you all.

I mentioned in a former Letter my feel upon Ch T's death, I find you, and I beleive most people of feeling experienced the like; but a little recollection must have told every individual that there could be no loss of a Man who having no Sense of his own honour, was incapable of a friendship to be relied upon; and in a publick Light, most certainly a Man whose want of all principle, kept him always unfixt, and therefore altogether incapable of doing great and national Good, and yet whose great abilities put it in his power always to do mischief, such a Man surely can not be regretted as a publick Loss. To speak my own mind truely, I think, nothing threatened so much real harm to the national Character, as that Man's strange Nature in possession of those great Abilities, I mean the public Character as acting in the Course of business in the Parliament; from Constitutional Habit He seemed unable to form an opinion; He has a thousand times reminded me of a Sentiment that I heard early from you, which I think was, that it would be dangerous to a Man's principles, to accustom himself to a display of parts in saying the best things He could on both sides of a question; this unfortunate

[1] Lord Frederick Cavendish (1729–1803).

[2] In a letter of 10 May, Abraham Rawlinson (1709–80), a merchant of Lancaster, had sounded Burke about standing as a candidate for the borough at the next general election, and had suggested that he discuss the idea with Lord George Cavendish (1727–94), whose family had a strong interest at Lancaster; 'if on consideration', Rawlinson said, '...you should Incline to make us an offer, I very much wish it might come recommended by my Ld Rockingham and the Cavendish Family'.

[3] In his letter of May, Rawlinson had told Burke: 'I may own I have always had you and Sir W. M. [William Meredith] in my Eye; he I presume cannot leave Liverpool....'

Man surely verified your saying, and through a vanity of shewing his parts, acquired an incapacity of examining a subject in the view of forming his judgment upon it, and consequently could never argue from a real sense of right or wrong, I will add to your sentiment, that I think He has proved that this practice is a detriment to the very Abilities that are displayed by it, for if Ch T had been able to form real opinions of his own, He would probably have adhered to them, and certainly they would have had a weight which nothing that came from him ever had, and in one word He would have obtained to be, what He would then have deserved to have been, the leading Man and Minister in this vast Empire. But as He stood, able always to do ill, and incapable of Good, He was surely dangerous,—in short from his constitutional Character and a poverty of Spirit, wonderful as his parts were, they displayed themselves most in the pleasing and agreable, and having the tendency of keeping people in good humour, this prevented that Seriousness in Business which bad men and bad times are only afraid of, and alarmed at; and now that He is gone if G G[1] was to take the lead, and that you had no existence I do think that things would fall into a dead Gloomy stupidity, which Ignorant inattention might call Calmness and tranquility, but which might prove one of those calms which the mariner[2] considers as ominous of bad weather, I my Edmund expect that your animation will keep things alive, and confident as I am that you will at least play your own part honestly, and having ended my political reading on poor Townshend, I do seriously profess a greater Indifference in regard to political or more properly ministerial Affairs than those who do not know me to the bottom would easily believe.

I called on G. C[3] yesterday, to offer him a turtle but He said He was so intirely a Country Gentleman coming to town but two or three days in the week, that He did not know what to do with a turtle, He told me that poor Ch. T was for three days fully aware of his Situation, but was altogether composed and easy under it, which G. C expressed some surprize at, from the poor Mans Character and nature; and indeed I should not have been surprised had it been otherwise, but somehow a Mans life is no Standard to conjecture his death by; one thing However more, I cannot help saying, that since He is dead I am glad He was not supposed to have been, at the time, of the Marquess's party, for tho there would not have been the same apparent Reason as the Administration has to lament, who loose their real and efficient leader, yet the party that lost him would have suffered in opinion, and opinion is every

[1] George Grenville. [2] MS: mariness
[3] 'General Conway' written above this in MS.

thing.[1] G. C was in perfect good Humour, we talked much of this death, but not a word that had a tendency to the succession,[2] or to any political matter—Ld Fred who went to him after may perhaps have had some discourse —Ld Fred seemed apprehensive of a dissolution, which I cannot give the least credit to[3]—I hear Ld Mansfield is the pro tempore Ch. of the Exchequer, it is true this is a matter of form,[4] but if it at all carries Him to the closet, He will not omit the opportunity of infusing his Grenvillian venom, and which at this critical moment may be of ill consequence. As to the Ministers they will go on perhaps shilly shally, and perhaps the closet may decide for itself, without that attention lately held in delicacy to the Duke of Grafton, so that I may send you, or you bring me word who is to be minister—I am half ashamed of this long scroll—we are all well. Adieu—

To PATRICK NAGLE—21 *October* 1767

Source: New Monthly Magazine, XIV, 385–6.

My dear Sir,—I am almost apprehensive that my long silence has put even your goodnature and forgiveness to a trial, and that you begin to suspect me of some neglect of you. I assure you that there are but very few things which could make me more uneasy than your entertaining such a notion. However, to avoid all risque of it, though I have very little to say, I will trouble you with a line or two, if it were only to tell you, that we always keep a very strong and very affectionate memory of our friends in Roche's country. Katty and our friend Courtney, I believe, can tell you that we never passed a day without a bumper to your health, which, if it did you no good, was a real pleasure to ourselves.[5] I take it for granted that the party was not much worse for their ramble, nor totally grown foppish by their travels—I mean to except Garrett, who certainly will be undone by his jaunt; he will be like those ingenious farmers in Gulliver who carry on their husbandry in the most knowing

[1] As late as July 1767 Rockingham, if asked to form a new Administration, intended to offer Townshend office, and, if Conway refused, the leadership of the House of Commons (Dowdeswell's memorandum of 23 and 24 July is in the Rockingham MSS, R 1–538).

[2] Lord North accepted the office of Chancellor of the Exchequer 10 September (Grafton, *Autobiography*, p. 167), but the appointment was not immediately announced.

[3] Parliament was not due to be dissolved until March 1768. The rumours of an earlier dissolution seem to have been started by the Duke of Newcastle.

[4] Mansfield held the seals of Chancellor of the Exchequer in his capacity of Lord Chief Justice of the King's Bench. He received them 9 September (see *Grenville Papers*, IV, 162–3).

[5] Mr and Mrs Courtenay (see above letter of 14 October 1765, p. 216) and Garrett Nagle seem to have accepted Burke's invitation (letter of [June]) to pay him a visit in London.

manner in the world, but never have any crop.[1] To complete his ruin, you will tell him, I have not forgot the young bull which I mentioned to him; but I find I antedated my promise a little; for he was not calved when Garrett was here. However, my Lord Rockingham has had one of the finest bull calves that can be; he is of an immense size, though, when I left Yorkshire, he was not more than seven weeks old. His sire is one of the largest I have ever seen, and before he was bought by his present owner, was let to cover at half-a-guinea a time. He is of the short-horned Holderness breed; and undoubtedly his kind would not do for your pastures; but he will serve to cross the stem and mend your breed. I take the calf to be too young to travel; but by the time he is a year old, I fancy the best method of sending him will be to get some careful fellow who comes from your county to harvest in England, to take charge of him on his return. Let this man, if such can be found, call upon me, and he shall have further directions.[2] You see I encourage Garrett in his *idle schemes*; my use of this phrase puts me in mind of my uncle James,[3] (indeed I wanted nothing to put me in mind of him;) I heard lately from Ned Barret[4] of his illness, which gives me a most sincere concern; I hope to hear shortly that he is better. I am told too, that poor James Hennessy, of Cork,[5] is in a bad way. He was as sensible and gentlemanlike a man as any in our part of the county—and I feel heartily for him and for his wife.

Be so good to remember us all most affectionately to John,[6] to Mr Courtney and Mrs Courtney—thank them for the pleasure we had in their company last summer. Give Garrett the enclosed memorandum; if you should find it inconvenient to give us a line yourself, he will be so good as to let us hear from him soon; not but that we are much obliged to him for the letters he has written to us, and to our friend English[7]—assure him that when we have any good news, he will be the first to hear it. Farewell, my dear Sir—all here are very truly yours; and believe me your ever affectionate nephew,

EDM BURKE

Oct. 21st. 1767.

[1] *Gulliver's Travels*, book III, chapt. 4.

[2] See Burke's letter to Lord Rockingham, 18 July 1768, in which arrangements are completed.

[3] (d. 1775), Patrick Nagle's brother.

[4] A wine merchant; probably son of James Barrett and Margaret Nagle.

[5] See above, letter of [June] (p. 314).

[6] John Nagle (d. 1837), son of Garrett, grandson of Patrick Nagle.

[7] Thomas English (*c.* 1725–98), a friend of Burke. He was engaged by James Dodsley in 1765 to carry on some or all of the editorial labour formerly done by Burke on the *Annual Register*. Accounts of him and of his relation to the magazine are in T. W. Copeland, *Our Eminent Friend Edmund Burke*, pp. 102–7; and Bertram Sarason, 'Burke and the two *Annual Registers*', *PMLA*, LXVIII, no. 3 (June 1953), 496–508.

Pat Nagle[1] behaves very well, is exceedingly attentive to his business; and upon my word, from what I see of him, I think him a decent and intelligent young fellow. He has repaid me the twenty guineas he had from me.

To CHARLES O'HARA—27 *October* 1767

Source: O'Hara MSS. Printed Hoffman, pp. 414–15.

My dear Sir,

I was not more pleased with your kind and seasonable Letter,[2] than ashamed of myself, when I recollected, how ill I have acted my part in the Correspondence for some time past. But the truth is, I have been tossed a good deal up and down the world. I spent some time at Wentworth.[3] From thence I went Westward to Manchester, Liverpoole, and Lancaster. At the Last of these places, I got great encouragement to offer myself a Candidate at the general Election. I am satisfied, I might carry a Seat there; but some reasons induced me for that time to decline it.[4] In short, in these excursions, (something of Business, something of compliment, something of pleasure) I spent the Summer; and found on my return other people employd to as little purpose as myself. I am obliged to you most heartily for your Short, but faithful and lively Sketch of your political History. Supported, or even appointed, by all or any of the ostensible ministers Ld T—[5] certainly is not. Instructed by them he is not—according to the Common opinion. I should think, that very possibly, various parts of his System came from various quarters detached, and without any communication; and that he has patched and pieced them together himself. If I were to guess, I would give his Judges to Ld Camden; and his Army to Genl Conway: I have heard that the Latter had from time to time spoken of this project as desirable and feasible.[6] But all this is conjecture; for from whence should I have intelligence?—We get, every day to greater and greater distance from

[1] Patrick Nagle, son of Burke's uncle Athanasius.

[2] Probably the letter printed by Hoffman (pp. 412–13) with a conjectural date of 20 October; MS at Sheffield bears no date.

[3] Burke was at Wentworth early in September (Rockingham to Dowdeswell, 9 September, Rockingham MSS, R 1–551).

[4] Lord Rockingham wrote Burke 6 October: 'your Visit at Lancaster has alarmed a Friend of ours, who has great weight there, as he has got into an Engagement with the old Representative, from thinking that there would be no Stir there.' Lord John Cavendish wrote Burke 12 October: 'my Brother had better not be against Reynolds [Sir Francis Reynolds (d. 1773), the Member for Lancaster borough] warmly, as there is not only a very old intimacy between them, but he was a particular friend of Sir Wm Lowthers [1727–56], through whom alone George has any business to interfere there.'

[5] Lord Townshend.

[6] A plan to augment the Irish Army.

the Ministry. Genl Conway has acted as the knowing ones foretold he would, and as I was very loth to believe he would; His family get every thing. Price I heard sometime ago was the Commissioner. I believe it is very truly reported.[1] In giving you the judges for Life, government loses, I think, but little; and you do not get a great deal.[2] The encrease of the Number will or will not be much desired; as the Seats are, are not given to Interests on your side of the Water. Septennial Parliament is your Idol;[3] how is the Castle as to that? As to what you mention of Cambricks[4] I do not remember any restraint, laid upon the import hither of Irish Cambrick, which might, upon the condition you mention, be taken off.[5] I did not indeed attend the manufacturing of that Law; but I did attend, and diligently the resolutions in the Committee—I remember I opposed, (not the principle) but the quantum of Duty laid on several articles of foreign manufacture, which I thought intemperately and rashly laid on. The Irish Agent for the Linnen Board[6] attended the whole, and did not think the regulations then made detrimental to Ireland—on the contrary he strenuously sollicited them, and seemd not wonderfully pleased with me for not going his lengths on the Subject—and was rather, I think impertinent. I will however cast my Eye on the Act. You will laugh at the publick advertiser of today; who, upon a presumption of my being the author of a very lively Libel on their Council for instructing the Ld Lt—or not instructing him—has abused me in a fine strain.[7] Let us hear from you as soon as you can; and may I beg of you to enclose me your publick accounts whenever they are deliverd. I mean particularly the accounts of the Hers[8] and other

[1] Francis Price (d. 1794), M.P. for Lisburn in the Irish Parliament, a nephew of Lord Hertford. He was not appointed to the vacant Commissionership of Irish Revenue.

[2] Lord Townshend, in his speech from the Throne to the Irish Parliament, announced that provision would be made for giving the judges tenure during good behaviour.

[3] See above, letter of 24 [May 1766] (p. 255).

[4] O'Hara's letter had spoken of 'an act of Parliament passd last Session in England prohibiting the importation of cambricks, in which an option of free trade with England for this commodity, upon condition that we prohibit the importation alsoe'.

[5] Burke refers to the Act 7 George III, c. 43, 'for the more effectually preventing the fraudulent importation and wearing of cambricks and French lawns'. Section 6 forbade the importation of cambrics from Ireland to Great Britain until the importation of cambrics into Ireland had been prohibited.

[6] Not identified.

[7] An anonymous satirical piece in the *Public Advertiser* for 22 October had been answered 27 October by another anonymous piece in which an orator named Brazen, 'a tall, ill-looking Fellow in a shabby black Coat' bored and bullied a meeting of the Council with a 'Scheme and Plan of Opp——n' described as 'the most *beautiful* as well as the *sublimest* System of Politics, that ever sprung from the Brain of Man' until he was thrown out by two footmen. The first piece has been attributed to Junius, on no very strong grounds. See G. Woodfall, *Junius*, London, 1812, II, 482–98.

[8] Probably 'hereditaries'—revenues fixed by usage, as distinguished from those granted by the parliament.

revenue and the general Abstract of the Establishments &c. I wish however the whole—adieu my dearest Sir and believe me

ever yours
E BURKE

27. Octr 1767.

What will be said here to your augmenting your Army without asking any Questions of Parliament here—but go on—and prosper.

To the EARL OF HARDWICKE—[*post* 30 *October* 1767]

Source: British Museum (Add. MS 35350, fol. 36).

Undated. Burke refers to Lord Chatham's repurchase of Hayes, his house in Kent. Thomas Walpole who had earlier bought the house from Chatham agreed in a letter of 30 October (*Chatham Correspondence*, III, 289) to sell it back.

Mr Burke presents his Compliments to Ld Hardwicke, and is much obliged to his Lordship, for the information he has been so good to communicate to him.

Mr Burke thinks he has receivd accounts of Ld Chathams health upon which he can entirely depend. His Lp is, without Doubt, greatly recoverd; enough probably to come to Town; though not, without extreme hazard, to venture to do Business, or to take a share in Debate; For he has still frequent and heavy returns of the Dejection, and flutter, and other Nervous Symptoms, which have so long disabled him from attending to Business. Your Lordship knows that he has repurchased *Hayes*, that he flatters himself, that the air of that place will restore him; and that he certainly intends to be there this Winter.

Monday Even.

To the EARL OF BESSBOROUGH—11 *November* 1767

Source: MS Osborn Collection.

Clearly written to Lord Bessborough, whose reply is at Sheffield.

Burke had decided not to offer himself for a seat at Lancaster (see above, letters of [*post* 4 September] (p. 326) and 27 October (p. 330). He wrote the Earl of Bessborough the news of Lord John Cavendish's being nominated.

My dear Lord,

I just received the enclosed Letter from Ld G. Cavendish.[1] Possibly your Lordship may have had no account of the success of the meeting; so I send you the papers. Lord John you see, is put in nomination, and

[1] Lord George Cavendish's letter of 8 November, at Sheffield.

there is no doubt of the event.[1] So far Mr Hoskins's[2] news is right. In the other particulars He was mistaken. I wish your Lordship Joy of this;

and am with great respect
your Lordships
most obedient humble Servant
EDM BURKE

Q. Ann Street.
Nov. 11. 1767

To CHARLES O'HARA—12 *November* 1767

Source: O'Hara MSS. Printed Hoffman, pp. 415–17.

Q. Ann Street Nov. 12. 1767

My dear Sir,

I am not more obliged to you for your last most friendly Letters,[3] than for that truly indulgent excuse you have made for one of my worst frailties; one indeed so bad, that it merits to rank even with my faults; But be it frailty or be it fault, I will try whether I can shew that I am not the worse on account of forbearance. The Situation of your L. L. is, to be sure critical enough.[4] But on the whole not worse, I should think, on comparing your account with my own former observations, than that of all his Predecessors at this time of the Year. This is the Equinox of your Political Climate, and these are the *Rigs*[5] (as the Sailors call them) that happen, especially in the Irish Channel, at that Season. There is generally a flush of good humour to welcome your Lord Lieutenant; Then some ill humour to bring him into his Trammells; and at last a wonderful deal of kindness and flattery to send him away in a proper Temper for a kind representation in the closet, and for the obtaining all the Jobbs, of which, we all, mutually on both sides of the water, stand so much in need. The account you give me of —[6] is just what I expected in every respect. But what Tricks of the Newcastle folks are those that you allude to? I remember none, except telling lies of all kinds, and hurting me to the best of their power with my principal.[7] In other respects, I had very few transactions with them.

[1] Burke's optimism was not justified. Lord John was defeated.

[2] Charles Hoskins (1728–68) of Oxted, a relation by marriage of Bessborough.

[3] A letter of O'Hara dated 22 October is at Sheffield; no others written between that date and 12 November are known to survive.

[4] O'Hara's letter of 22 October spoke of Lord Townshend's difficulties.

[5] Tempests, strong winds.

[6] Not identified by O'Hara's letter of 22 October.

[7] Again Burke may be referring to the charges Newcastle is supposed to have brought against him before Lord Rockingham: that he was a Roman Catholic or had dangerous relations with Catholics; see above, letter of 14 October 1765 (p. 216).

You express a wish almost like an expectation, that some union may take place between us and Conway. If we liked to get into the shabby situation in which he stands, I think we might tomorrow; But we are not at present in that disposition. As to him, I am at present far from thinking *him*, or what is the same thing, those who guide him, favourable to us. I hear and I am satisfied it is true, that he offerd the vacant half of the pay office to Ld Edgcumbe, who has refused it.[1] What shall we say to the friendly disposition of that man, who would not stir an hand to save a place of 1200 a year to Ld Edgcumbe, when saving him would save the Party;[2] and yet would offer him 3000 when his acceptance must be a stroke of the utmost ill consequence to them, and even lead to their Ruin?[3] I cannot explain all this into any thing that is right. He has given up the Emolluments of Secretary of State, and confined himself to those of Genl of the Ordnance. This is certain; and it looks like a preliminary to the resignation of the Office itself, whenever it shall suit the convenience of our Enemies that he should resign it. In the mean time it looks like a confession, that his staying there is not overhandsome. How all will end I know not. All my reasonings, and all my Auguries lead to ill; to exclude our Party from the least present or future success; And this view does not arise from ill spirits, for I am in the best, nor can it make any change, I think in Wills Conduct or in mine, for it was not the prospect of success that made us adopt it. I fear much that your Ld Lt. will play you a trick in the End; however attend him and ply him. Do you ever see Dennis? A friend of mine got him the Secretarys[4] protection; who has made him a Chaplain and promised to provide for him. Since then Dennis has not written a single word to me, though I wrote twice to him. I begin to fear he has not got my Letters; and may neglect to pay his Court. You are kind about the accounts. Pray send them as soon as you can. You remember you promised me a Copy of the state of your Trade for two years which was laid before Parliament. May I also put you in mind of this—

[1] Early in October, Conway offered to make Lord Edgcumbe joint Paymaster-General, as compensation for his dismissal from the Treasurership of the Household in November 1766. Edgcumbe wished to accept, but was told by Bessborough that Rockingham and his friends considered themselves in opposition to the Administration and would take it ill if he accepted (see letters of Bessborough to Newcastle, [20] and 22 October, Add. MS 32986, fols. 76 and 82–3).

[2] Conway, though he had not resigned, had done what else he could in November 1766 to save Lord Edgcumbe's place.

[3] Newcastle wrote to Princess Amelia 4 November 1767: 'I found Mr Burke, my Lord Rockingham's chief friend, was outrageous with Mr Conway for the means he had used to draw in poor Lord Edgecombe...' (Add. MS 32986, fol. 244). Edgcumbe became joint Vice-Treasurer of Ireland in 1770 and held office throughout the American war.

[4] Lord Frederick Campbell, Secretary to the Lord Lieutenant of Ireland.

Rigbys going over at this time, gives me matter of speculation for this side of the Water as well as for yours. What can be his motive for absenting himself at the beginning of the Session, and does this look like the furious attack which he threatens.[1]

You dont tell me what part Flood takes and how he goes on.[2] Here we have nothing but the certainty, (as they say) of Prices being your commissioner, and Jenkinson our Half-paymaster.[3] Adieu my dearest Sir—all of us jointly and severally most cordially yours.

We quit this house in a few days and remove to Charles Street St James Square. The Doctor continues in this house.[4]

To CHARLES O'HARA—27 *November* 1767

Source: O'Hara MSS. Printed Hoffman, pp. 417–20.

My dear Sir, We have opend our Session,[5] and with more extraordinary circumstances, than perhaps ever happend in so short a space of time. During the summer the Bedfords had frequently complaind that our managements with regard to the ministry at large, and the friendly intercourse we kept up with some of them,[6] made it very difficult to judge of our intentions, and of course very unsafe to go into any close connections with us. We never (except in one instance)[7] courted such connections. However, as the Party had been abandond by Genl Conway, it was necessary to give such a proof of our Spirit and firmness as might induce in all other parties a confidence in our Temper. It might indeed, from the Violence of the Bedfords in all their Conversations, have been expected, that they would have taken a lead in the attack. But in reality Dowdeswell led it, and took a very proper and decisive part, by proposing an amendment to the address of no other importance, than that it obliquely attacked the ministry for their Neglect of some National Concerns, and that it was an amendment.[8] I supported

[1] 'Rigby had passed over to Ireland in hopes of obtaining to have his place of Master of the Rolls there confirmed in the Act for establishing the Judges for life, but had not succeeded' (Walpole, *Memoirs*, III, 85). Rigby was back in England by the time Parliament met.

[2] MS: one.

[3] Thomas Townshend, Jr (1733–1800), not Charles Jenkinson, was appointed joint Paymaster-General.

[4] Dr Nugent told O'Hara the same news in his own way 26 November (O'Hara MSS): 'Our friends live now in Charles Street St James Square where they have a good deal more elbow room, and are much more convenient to St. Stephen's Chapel where they attend every day, very devoutly. I, an old cat, stick by the old tenement in Queen Ann Street.'

[5] Parliament met 24 November.

[6] Particularly Conway and Townshend.

[7] Presumably Burke refers to Rockingham's attempt in July 1767 to form an administration including the Bedfords.

[8] Dowdeswell's amendment was: 'to assure his Majesty that...we will immediately apply ourselves to the further consideration of the most proper methods for assisting

him, was equally decisive, and managed very little either measures or persons.[1] Wedderburn (an individuum vagum)[2] spoke on the same side with great spirit and ingenuity; From the Bedfords, not a word—From Grenville not a Syllable. We did not divide. When this Question was disposed of, Grenville made a general Attack (pretty much, on our Grounds,) upon the Speech; and at the Latter End he stepped out of his Way to fall on us, and on the Idea of our holding Heterodox opinions relative to America, excommunicated our whole party.[3] The Bedfords lookd glum; held their Tongues; and so the day passed over. I wishd to answer on the Spot; but a friend of mine restraind me; He thought it best first to consult the heads of the party; and he thought right. The next day a resolution was taken to demand an explicit answer from the Bedfords concerning the Conduct of G. Gr. and on their declining to explain themselves properly, to seperate ourselves from them entirely.[4] We found, that the Cause of this attack, was a report of Ld Rockinghams having at Newmarket expressed great hostility to the house of Grenville;[5] and notwithstanding the intreaties of Rigby G. Grenville could not be prevented from this method of shewing his resentment. We went down to the house, and in our Turn, in the strongest Terms, renounced him and all his Works.[6] We are since to the great Triumph of the Ministry quite loose.

You may possibly hear of my Speech on the second day, and as possibly may hear some things in it misrepresented. If you should you

and encouraging the manufactures of his Majesty's kingdom, and for preserving, extending, and improving its foreign trade.' Conway described it as 'a very insignificant Amendment' (Conway to the King, 24 November, Fortescue, I, 509). It was rejected without a division.

[1] Walpole says (*Memoirs*, III, 81) that Burke spoke 'with great and deserved applause'. This is the first of his speeches to be fully reported (*Parliamentary History*, XVI, 386–92).

[2] Wedderburn, although he acted with Grenville, was also connected with Rockingham.

[3] There is a document in Newcastle's papers (Add. MS 32987, fol. 113), dated 25 November, about this speech. It reads: 'The substance, tho' not the words, of what it is supposed Mr G. Grenville said yesterday, after declaring his sentiments about America, and of the necessity of enforcing (supposed to mean by some new Act) the superiority of this country over the colonies; that there were persons of contrary sentiments (turning his eyes towards Mr. Dowdeswell) whom he never would support in power or cooperate with; and that he would hold the same distance from them that he would from those who opposed the principles of the Revolution'.

[4] Rockingham's followers met 25 November and drew up a paper complaining of Grenville's behaviour; Newcastle presented the paper to Bedford the next day.

[5] Lyttelton wrote to Temple 25 November, that Rockingham had told the Duke of Bridgwater at Newmarket: '...*he would hear of nothing in which there was a Grenville*' (R. J. Phillimore, *Memoirs and Correspondence of Lord Lyttelton*, London, 1845, p. 740). Rockingham did not deny that he had said this. He wrote to Newcastle 26 November: 'In regard to the particular *words*...supposed *mine* I think it very immaterial in point of the great object whether they are *precisely* exact or not' (Add. MS 32987, fol. 120).

[6] 'On the report of the address [25 November], Grenville engaged in a hot altercation with Dowdeswell and Burke on their different ideas of what ought to be done with respect to America' (Walpole, *Memoirs*, III, 84).

will set the matter right, if not you will be silent about it. Rigby took occasion to speak of Ireland, and of an attempt to augment the Army there, and aimd at raising some apprehension in the house upon that Subject. Conway replied, that there *was* such an intention; that an Army was so far from a matter of uneasiness to the Gentlemen of Ireland, that they liked it; that the augmentation probably would not be opposed there and that he thought it desirable and necessary; because the Country was, in a great degree R. Catholick, and therefore a rotten part of the British Dominions. After I had spoken my mind about N. America; I spoke to the subject of an Army *in general*; expressed my own particular liking of it; considerd it as interwoven with the Irish constitution; and admitted the truth of Mr C.'s observation on the Temper of Gentlemen of that Country with regard to that object; but that this general liking had no relation to the *quantum* of the Army. That liking an Army, and liking new Taxes were different things; and that I did apprehend many would dissent from the augmentation. As to the rottenness of the Country; if it was rotten, I attributed it, to the ill policy of Government towards the body of the Subjects there. That it would well become them, to look into the State of that Kingdom; especially on account of a late Black and detestable proceeding there,[1] which reflected infinitely either on the justice or the policy of English Government in ruining and putting to death many for carrying on a rebellion at the instigation of France, whilst the throne assured us we were in the most profound peace with that Nation. I laid this heavy on the ministries (without regard to any) at these periods; I was not answerd; and the thing dropped. This I thought right to tell you, lest some lies should be circulated, as it is likely there may on so proper a Subject for Slander.

How will your Bar relish Hewet.[2] He never practised in a Court of Equity. Tommy Townshend is joint paymaster. Jenkinson a Lord of the Treasury; and either Ld Beauchamp or Rider[3] will go into the vacant admiralty.[4] Adieu when more happens you shall hear from us.

Charles Street St James's Square.

27. Nov. 1767.

[1] Doubtless Burke was referring again to the hanging of Father Sheehy and the others accused on similar charges. See above, letter of 8 April [1766] (p. 249).

[2] James Hewitt, appointed Lord Chancellor of Ireland 24 November. See above, letter of 3 August (p. 319).

[3] Nathaniel Ryder (1735–1803), M.P. for Tiverton.

[4] The place at the Admiralty Board vacated by Jenkinson's appointment to the Treasury Board was filled in March 1768 by the appointment of Lord Charles Spencer.

CHARLES O'HARA *to* EDMUND BURKE—5 *December* [1767]

Source: Fitzwilliam MSS (Sheffield).

Burke naturally gave some offence when he spoke out about Irish grievances. Hugh Wentworth, Lord Rockingham's estate agent, writing the Marquess from Ireland 31 January had mentioned a report that 'Mr Flood is to be brought into the English Parliament to answer Mr Burke' (Rockingham MSS, R74–10). O'Hara, commenting on Burke's speech of 25 November, urged his friend not to be too imprudent.

December 5th

I have only heard of your speech a general good account; no particulars, no abuse. Yet in general, I think the ground you chose, so far as related to Mr Conways reason for the expediency of an augmentation of the army in Ireland, was tender. The subject is dead amongst us. What little existance it has, is in Corke. But old prejudices may be easily revivd. When you come to have influence with a prevailing Ministerial power, you may do real good. But at present I shoud think the welfare of this Kingdome, too much committed by making it the subject of an attack upon Administration. There are besides, so many others, even our present circumstance one of the first magnitude, that one cant want ammunition. You tell me You managed Persons and measures but little. I wish you woud manage Persons wherever measures do not make a personal attack necessary. It is not possible but you must hurt yourself. And this same object *yourself* weighs more with me than any other political consideration. I congratulate you upon being clear of G Gr.[1] I love the Bedfords, and wish their interest were compatable with *yourself*. But from the day of the breaking off of the last negotiation, I concluded that the introduction of the whole party was impracticable: nothing but death can make it otherwise. I think your present plan too extensive for your circumstances; a divided opposition, and the minds of the people at peace. This added to the approach of new elections, in which Administration must triumph in the main. Besides we are all mortal, the question then is, in what situation may you wait with most advantage for the death of others. I shoud not dare to say this to you in a tete a tete; but you'll forgive me before you write again. And since I am upon the subject, I will say that from the day Mr Conway was proscribd, He coud not resign while you remaind in connexion with the Bedfords.[2] I have never had a word with him, or from him about it: but

[1] Grenville.

[2] In the negotiations of the summer Rockingham had proposed Conway for his Minister in the House of Commons; Bedford had refused to consider his appointment (Brooke, *Chatham Administration 1766–1768*, pp. 209–10).

I will allow that tis a pity He shoud have Ld Hertford for his Brother. Take care that you and Ld R become not the Dupes of your own vertue....

To CHARLES O'HARA—11 *December* [1767]

Source: O'Hara MSS. Printed Hoffman, pp. 420–2.
Endorsed: 14 Decbr 1767.

My dear Sir, As first in importance, I will speak to you first on your Newmarket Business;[1] I am sure it is first in importance to me, as it will prove a means of bringing you over. I am then to tell you from Ld R. That if you do him the favour of sending your horse to his Stable, the best care will be taken of him. If you choose to have him tried with Ld R's young Horses, to know whether he be good for any thing, he will be tried—but if you are previously satisfied of his performance, and do not choose any further experiment, Ld R. assures you, that Singleton[2] will never steal a trial. So you will send, whenever it is convenient to you.

How you were deceived in the Spirit of Conway and the Spirit of the Bedfords? or rather how soon have you forgot all you must have known of both! A Negotiation has been going on between Bedford house and the administration, now for a week passed;[3] and, as I was told yesterday, was just brought to a conclusion; However I hear today, there is some Hitch in it. Conway stays in, as a Scotch warming Pan, to keep the Bed in a comfortable State for those who hate and despise him;[4] He wants but the completion of this Business to finish and round his Character. If it comes to any thing or to nothing, I will take the first opportunity of acquainting you with the Event. This Day all your Supply Bills pass'd the Council, as they passed your house, Nem. Con. The Septennial has not yet come before them;[5] I suppose they wait for Ld Northington, who I am told is ill.

I forgot to mention to you, that the Bedfords and Grenvilles are on this occasion all to pieces. Ld Temple is gone to the Country despairing

[1] In his letter to Burke of 2 December O'Hara had sent a request to Lord Rockingham through Burke: 'I have a horse to run in a sweepstake at Newmarket next October. I wish Ld Rockingham woud let me send him to his Stable, a stable of honour is of immense consequence on such occasions. A fine commission this, in the height of Parliamentary business.' [2] John Singleton, Rockingham's trainer at Newmarket.

[3] Rockingham had finally broken with the Bedfords 27 November, and almost immediately afterwards Bedford began negotiating with the Court.

[4] Conway was succeeded as Secretary of State by Lord Weymouth and as Minister in the House of Commons by Lord North, but agreed to remain in these offices until January 1768.

[5] The Septennial Bill was introduced into the Irish Parliament 16 November. In order to avoid simultaneous General Elections in Great Britain and Ireland the proposed duration of Parliaments was changed from seven to eight years; it was henceforth called the Octennial Bill (see below, letter of 20 February [1768], p. 342).

of the Commonwealth. Grenville has not been in the house for some days; but I hear his *ton* is to take the matter quietly, and to wait Events; and in this, I apprehend, he is right. As to our Corps, which are the *Enfans perdus* of Politicks; we stay just where we were; keeping a distance from all others, shunning, and shunned by them. If we must be dupes, thank God, it is to our rectitude, and not to our politicks, or if you like it better, to our roguery; and I assure you both Will and I feel inexpressible comfort in finding ourselves among a set of men willing to go on all together on a plan of clear consistent conduct. For myself I really have no hopes. Every body congratulated me on coming into the House of Commons, as being in the certain Road of a great and speedy fortune; and when I began to be heard with some little attention, every one of my friends was sanguine. But in truth I never was so myself. I came into Parliament not at all as a place of preferment, but of refuge; I was pushed into it; and I must have been a Member, and that too with some Eclat, or be a little worse than nothing; Such were the attempts, made to ruin me when I first began to meddle in Business. But I considerd my situation on the side of fortune as very precarious. I lookd on myself, with this New Duty on me, as on a man devoted; and Thinking in this manner, nothing has happend that I did not expect, and was not well prepared for. Therefore my dear Sir, cheer up; nothing very much amiss can happen us, whilst it pleases God that we keep our health, our good humour, and our inward peace; None of which is, as yet gone from us. I write, and blot in some sort of confusion—being just risen from an heavy dinner—and in some hurry—Adieu and believe me most sincerely and affectionately yours.

E BURKE

Charles Street S. J. Square

11. Decr

Conway and I were like to fall into some heat in the house a few days ago; but it came to nothing.

I do not know what Share administration had in your Tea project—[1] None at all, I suspect. They had given notice of an intention here to limit the company's dividend for some further Term.[2] They have leave to bring in a Bill for explaining and amending the act of the 10th of K. William, in order to encrease the Army on the Irish Establishment.[3] So you may soon hear of that matter—I dont much like, and think I shall oppose, it.

[1] The duty on tea had been reduced; see Irish Statutes, 7 Geo. III, c. 2.

[2] The Act of 1767 which limited the East India Company's dividend to 10 per cent was for one year only. On 9 December North gave notice he would introduce a bill to extend the limitation for a further year.

[3] This was proposed by Conway 9 December.

To the Duke of Portland—13 *January* 1768

Source: Portland MSS (Nottingham). *Endorsed:* Charles Street St Jas s Janry 13. 1768 | Mr Edmd Burke | Ry. 15.

My Lord

Permit me to remind your Grace of the application I took the Liberty some time since of making for Ld Verney, who is Candidate for the County of Buckingham. I spoke to your Steward Mr Isaac[1] today who told me that he would write to your Graces Tenants to reserve themselves for your Interest; but he would go no further without your own immediate directions; I thought him very right in his Caution, although I thought myself quite sure of your Graces inclinations in this affair. I must now entreat, that it may be signified as soon as is convenient to your Grace, that you wish to support Ld Verney at the General Election. I take this opportunity of congratulating your Grace on the distinguished honour of being selected as the first Victim by this unconstitutional administration,[2] I only hope, that they may excite that Spirit which they mean to suppress; and that however they may think of destroying every thing excellent in the Kingdom, there may still be left, when they come to stand at the Altar, enough of generous Liquor to be poured between their horns.

Do me the favour to present my humble respects to the Dutchess[3] and believe me with the truest respect

My Lord
your Graces
most obedient
and humble Servant
Edm Burke

Charles Street S. James' Square
Jany 13. 1768

[1] Estate agent of the Dowager Duchess of Portland's properties. The Duke, replying to Burke 16 January, corrected him as to the agent's name: 'I have already written to *Mr. Thos: Slaughter* my Steward in Bucks to exert himself in support of Lord Verney....'

[2] Portland and Sir James Lowther (1736–1802), M.P. for Cumberland, were election rivals in Cumberland and Carlisle. Lowther, to strengthen his interest in the county, petitioned the Crown for a lease of part of Portland's Cumberland estate. This property had been granted to Portland's family by William III, but Lowther claimed that the property for which he petitioned, though held by Portland, was not included in the grant. The Treasury Board recommended allowing Lowther's claim, on condition that he determine the title in the courts.

[3] *Née* Lady Dorothy Cavendish (1750–94).

To CHARLES O'HARA—[*circa* 1 *February* 1768]

Source: O'Hara MSS. Printed Hoffman, p. 423. *Endorsed:* Feby 1st.

My dear Sir,

I hope you are by this safe and snug in Merrion Square. God Give you peace and happiness there and every where. Your Act for Limitation of Parliaments has passed as I just now hear;[1] only made *Octennial* instead of *Septennial.* Sr R. Rich is dead. A Good Regiment and an excellent Government to be disposed of.[2] We have got rid of the E. I. question in our house.[3] We battled it for about six hours on our own Numbers and debaters. We divided but 41.[4] Wedderburn, (but I look on him as a seperate person) was with us and did good Service, but almost every man of the Bedfords and Grenvilles sneaked off. However, no man ever got such a drubbing as Lord North. He was ill defended by the Butes who had brought, or rather forced him into the Scrape. God bless you. Ever yours

E B.

To CHARLES O'HARA—20 *February* [1768]

Source: O'Hara MSS. Printed Hoffman, pp. 425–9.

My dear Sir,

I thank you for your accounts of Octennial,[5] my friend Dennis,[6] and the other curious publick and private matters which made the Subject of your two last Letters. The madness of the Government here which passed the Octennial Act is to be equalld only by the Phrensy of your Country which desired it, and the tameness of this Country which bore it. I consider that act as a virtual repeal of one of the most essential parts of Poyning's Law; and I think it will necessarily draw on a change in other parts; and indeed many material alterations in the State of your

[1] MS: here. See next letter for Burke's fuller comment on the passing of this Act.

[2] Field Marshal Sir Robert Rich, 4th Baronet (1685–1768) died 1 February. He was Colonel of the 4th Regiment of Dragoons and Governor of Chelsea Hospital.

[3] The Dividend Bill was read a third time in the Commons 25 January.

[4] 41 against the bill, 131 for it.

[5] The Octennial Bill (earlier Septennial; see above, letters of 24 [May 1766], p. 255, 11 December [1767], p. 339) received the Royal Assent 16 February. It aroused great enthusiasm in Ireland. Lecky says that when it was voted: 'The Parliament house was surrounded by many thousands of men who compelled the members as they entered to promise that they would vote for the Bill, and all over the country the excitement was such that it would have been madness to have resisted' (*History of Ireland in the Eighteenth Century*, II, 91).

[6] O'Hara's letters of 9 and 11 February show him taking an interest in Dennis. In the latter he has seen him and promised him aid: 'He is to bring me a list of his debts next saturday.'

Country, as it stands by itself, and as it is related to England. However, you have your day of Joy, and your drunken Bout for the present.

The Explanation of the Act of K. William is passed;[1] no one directly opposed it in the house of Commons but myself. The temper of the house was this; that they would cheerfully have voted the King a power of keeping forty thousand men more, provided any other than themselves was to find the supply. They opend it on two Grounds. Its necessity towards reforming the arrangement of the Army for the purpose of a more convenient Rotation; and then the propriety of providing a defence for Ireland; which from all Circumstances internal and external they stated to be in great danger. Here we had, slightly from Conway, but much at large from Lord Beauchamp, the Whiteboys, the Foreign Regimentals, the French money and all that miserable Stuff. This was on the second reading.[2] It had been agreed, on account of Grenvilles absence, (who sent word that he had some objections to the preamble of the act), to defer all debate on the principle of the Bill until the third reading. However these two Gentlemen took the line, I mentiond above, though they knew they could not be answerd. When the Bill came to the third reading,[3] I spoke to it very fully and I believe for an hour together. My Chief Grounds were, the danger and impropriety of Leaving the execution of an arrangement, which took in the military establishment throughout the whole British Empire, and which was argued as of absolute Necessity, to the discretion of the Parliament of Ireland; the false representation which had been made of the State of the Irish army; (for it was very false, glaringly so). The absurdity of the stories on which the danger of that Country had been presumed; and the ill policy of encouraging administration to make it a government measure for Ireland to augment its Debt in time of peace. Lord Beauchamp, and Genl Conway answered me. The former was pleasant in his Voice, Language, and manner; In argument as you might expect. He was mightily cried up by all the ministerial people as a prodigy of Genius. Thus Ended the Irish army so far as related to us. It was but just attended, and very little regarded, people seeming to be indifferent enough about the good or ill success of the measure.[4]

You refined rather too much in your Speculations upon what I told you of the complexion of Parties on the last East India day. It was in truth no more than what is the natural consequence of the imbecillity,

[1] By 10 William III, c. 1 the number of troops on the Irish Establishment was limited to 12,000 men (see above, letter of 30 December 1762, p. 161). The Act to which Burke refers, 8 George III, c. 13, increased the number to 15,235.

[2] 3 February.

[3] 12 February.

[4] Parliament was within a month of being dissolved.

disunion, and want of mutal confidence and concord, which prevail in the ministry. However they go on; and I think are sufficiently supported. Last Wednesday[1] Sr Geo. Saville made a motion of which he had given Notice some days before. It was to amend &c. The act of the 21. of K. James the first, and to extend the principles of prescription and Limitation of Claims, which prevail between Subject and Subject, to the Crown.[2] It was agreed to open and to debate the matter upon General Grounds, unless the adversary forced us to an application of particular Grievances.[3] Sr G. Saville, in one of the most elegant performances I ever heard, entirely confined himself to this plan; so did Sr Anth. Abdy[4] who seconded. The Ministers were imprudent enough to urge the nonexistence of such Grievances, as a reason for rejecting the Bill; and this was done in so insolent a manner that out it came at last, (I mean Sr James Lowthers Grant.) It was managed with great address by Yorke, who stated it rather as an example, than as an accusation, at the End of a train of vexatious proceedings, which have arisen for want of some Limitation to the claims of the Crown. The Ministerial people attempted some sort of defence, but so weak, trivial, inconsistent, and indeed childish and absurd, that they sunk far below what either friends or enemies expected from them. Paint as you please to your imagination the figure that they made, either for the merits of their Conduct, or their address and dexterity in defending it, Lower yourself to it as much as you please, you will never sink to the true pitch. Upon my serious Word, it passed all conception. In a state suitable to such a defence, against a most strenuous attack they continued from about half an hour after three to half an hour after eleven. So long the debate Lasted. The Numbers on the Division were, for the Motion 114—against it 134. About six of our people had fallen ill, or rambled for want of whipping in, or, you see, we should have run them very hard. Conway had the decency to absent himself. The temper of the house was such, that I have not the least doubt of our carrying our point next Parliament; they will scarcely venture, I think, to contest it.[5]

[1] 17 February.

[2] The Nullum Tempus Bill was sponsored by Rockingham chiefly on the grounds that an injury had been done the Duke of Portland by the Treasury's decision in favour of Sir James Lowther (see above, letter of 13 January, p. 341). Hitherto no time limit had been set to the claims of the Crown to property held by the subject. The bill placed the Crown on a level with the subject, and made sixty years possession a bar against all claims.

[3] A reference to the Portland case. The Nullum Tempus Bill was not retrospective, hence did not affect Lowther's claim.

[4] Sir Anthony Thomas Abdy, 5th Baronet (*c.* 1720–75).

[5] The Nullum Tempus Bill was introduced again in November 1768 and became law in 1769.

I rejoice to find that your seat is secure.[1] Let us hear from you as often as you can. I look upon our Business as pretty much over for the year. Adieu, and God bless you.

20th February.

As well as I can recollect, the Speakers in the debate[2] were

For the motion	Against the motion
Sr G. Saville	Ld North.
Sr Anth. Abdy.	Ld Clare.
Sr W. Meredith.	Ld Barrington.
Mr Dowdeswell.	Mr Jenkinson.
Mr Grenville.	Mr Beckford.
Mr Yorke.	Mr Price Campbell.[7]
Ld J. Cavendish.	Mr Rigby.
Mr E. Burke.	Mr Stanley.[8]
Mr T. Pitt.[3]	Mr Dyson.
Mr Fred. Montagu.[4]	
(Sr Fletcher Norton, spoke for the Bill though he defended the Legality of the Grant.) He went away without voting—	X Conway absent. X Attorney Genl absent.[9]
Mr Seymour.[5]	
Ld Palmerston.[6]	

For the Motion—114
Against 134

The division was on the Question '*that the order of the day be read*'—They did not choose to Let it appear in the world that they had given a flat Negative to the Bill. They were in much confusion; and seemd to have changed their plan of defence more than once in the Debate.

[1] O'Hara had said in his letter of 11 February: 'I come in for Ardmagh but am orderd not to say so'.

[2] There is a division-list for the voting on this bill among the Burke MSS at Sheffield.

[3] Thomas Pitt, later 1st Baron Camelford (1737–93).

[4] (1733–1800), M.P. for Northampton borough.

[5] Henry Seymour (*c.* 1729–1807), M.P. for Totnes.

[6] Henry Temple, 2nd Viscount Palmerston (1739–1802).

[7] (*c.* 1727–68), M.P. for Nairnshire.

[8] Hans Stanley (*c.* 1720–80), M.P. for Southampton borough.

[9] John Dunning, later 1st Baron Ashburton (1731–83).

To GARRETT NAGLE—6 *March* 1768

Source: MS Dr A. J. A. Alexander. Printed *New Monthly Magazine*, XIV, 386.

My dear Garrett

I received your last from Ballyduff with the most sincere sorrow. Indeed on the return of My Uncles complaints I gave up all hope, considering the Nature of his disorder, and the time of his Life. I did not Neglect to apply to Doctor Nugent, but at this distance, and with no full detail of Circumstances and Symptoms before him, he would not venture to prescribe. I make no doubt that he has skilful assistance in his own Neighbourhood; and Dr Nugent would cheerfully have added to it, but from fear of attempting any thing in a Case which he cannot fully be master of. I suppose this Letter will hardly find my dear friend alive.[1] We shall all lose, I believe, one of the very best men that ever lived; of the clearest integrity, the most genuine principles of religion and virtue, the most cordial Goodnature and benevolence, that I ever knew, or I think, ever shall know. However it is a comfort, that he lived a long, healthy, unblemished Life, loved and esteemd by all that knew him, and has left Children behind him who will cultivate his memory, and, I trust follow his example; For of all the men I have seen in any Situation, I really think, he is the person I should wish myself, or any one I greatly loved, the most to resemble. This I do not say from the impression of my immediate feeling, but from my best Judgment; having seen him at various times of my Life, from my Infancy to the last years, having known him very well, and knowing a little, (by too long habits) of mankind at large. In truth my dear Garret, I fear I have said this or something to the same purpose to you before; but I repeat it again; for my Mind is full of it.

I wish you would let our friends at Ballylegan know, that poor Patrick Nagle[2] is out of all danger, and recovering fast. He had a sharp struggle for it. They will rejoice in his recovery. I take him to be a very worthy and valuable young man in all respects. Here we have nothing New. Politicks have taken no turn that is favourable to us, but, just now, I dont[3] feel the more unpleasantly, for being and for my friends being out of all Office. You are I suppose full of Bustle about your new Elections;[4] I am convinced all my friends will have the good sense to keep themselves from taking any part in struggles, in the Event of which

[1] Patrick Nagle died 21 March (*Corke Journal*, 24 March 1768).

[2] See above, letter of 21 October 1767 (p. 330). [3] MS: dont not

[4] The General Election took place in Ireland as well as England this year. Garrett Nagle as a Roman Catholic would not have a vote.

they have no share and no concern. Adieu my dear Garret and believe me to you and to all with you at Ballyduff and Bloomfield a most sincere and affectionate friend and Kinsman

EDM BURKE

March. 6. 1768

How does Ned Nagle go on. It is time now to think of sending him to Sea and we are considering of the best means for doing it. I suppose you have got Mr W. Burkes Letter.

To the MARQUESS OF ROCKINGHAM—9 *March* 1768

Source: Fitzwilliam MSS (Sheffield). Printed *Corr.* (1844), I, 149–51.

Parliament was to be dissolved on 11 March for the General Election. Burke's own seat for Wendover was again secured him by Lord Verney's influence, but he sent Lord Rockingham a few rumours and speculations as to the chances of their friends.

My dear Lord, I have seen the Duke of Newcastle this morning. I told him that I proposed to write to your Lordship. After asking whether the conveyance was very safe, and binding me to the strictest secrecy; His Grace told me, that he has had lately a very satisfactory conversation with Lord Mansfield; in which he spoke very warmly of your Lordship, and in his expressions came up very near his Graces own Ideas, with regard to you. He further gave the fullest assurances, that he had no sort of connection with the present administration. I know not why I should trouble your Lordship with this important information. That Lord Mansfield is not connected with the present Ministry we all know; That he should speak favourably of your Lordship, is no Miracle. If indeed he spoke of the Necessity of giving your System and your Party the Lead in affairs, then indeed he would say something to the purpose, and what I should think well worth sending an express an hundred and sixty miles to acquaint you with. I must however do his Grace the Justice to say, that he spoke of your Lordship with great affection; told me that he had acquitted himself, and with good prospects of success, of all the commissions you had given him; and that he wished to devolve upon your Lordship all the consequence, Credit, and influence that he had in the world. Rigby and I had joind in a request for bringing a friend in Ireland into Parliament with which he very obligingly complied[1]—

[1] On 9 March, Newcastle wrote to John Garnett, Bishop of Clogher (1709–82): 'As you have always been so good as to take my recommendation I shall be most particularly obliged if your Lordship will do it at this time, and therefore take the liberty to recommend to you the continuance of my Lord Bessborough's nephew, Mr. Moore, for one, and Mr. John Monk Mason for the other of your Members for Clogher, the latter of

but, as they got to complimenting each other on the wonderful good that must have arisen, if their Ideas had been followed in the Negotiation of last Summer, I am afraid I said somewhat a little *Brusque*, for which I am sorry. However it was not a great deal; and I am to see him tomorrow, and will smooth down the feathers. Besides, the first Letter from your Lordship will set all to rights again. I wish it may be early and kind; for to say the Truth he is exerting himself, and told me he had attended to Maidstone.[1] I think him rather lower than when I saw him before. Lady Rockingham tells me the Dutchess is very ill.

Of Gregory I have heard not much. Lord Winchelsea says that things look promising. I have nothing further to trouble you with. We wait with impatience to hear about York[2] I am with the truest affection and attachment

My dear Lord

Your ever obliged

and obedient Servant

EDM BURKE

Wednesday 9 March 1768.

My Lady Rockingham desires that I may not smooth down the feathers; because it was but a very gentle Breeze that could hardly discompose them. Her Ladyship thinks too, that by the Dukes mentioning nothing about the Dutchess's health it can hardly be so bad as she suspected. Mr Frankland,[3] Mrs Pelhams father is dead.

To CHARLES O'HARA—[11 *April* 1768]

Source: O'Hara MSS. Printed Hoffman, pp. 430–1.

Undated. Burke mentions Rockingham's return from Newmarket; Rockingham returned 10 April 'late at night' (see his letter of 12 April to Newcastle, Add. MS 32989, fol. 321). Probably Burke saw him the following day.

I think it is a good while since I heard from you; and perhaps it is still longer since I wrote; but I believe there has been a stagnation of such matter as would prove interesting to either of us; I mean, the real inside

whom is recommended by my two friends Mr. Rigby and Mr. Bourke, who belongs to my Lord Rockingham' (Add. MS 32989, fol. 91). At the General Election of 1769 in Ireland, Moore was returned for Clogher, but not Mason.

[1] Robert Gregory (*c.* 1729–1810) was contesting Maidstone at the General Election. Rockingham thought him 'a gentleman of good fortune acquired really in a very honourable manner in the East Indies', and had asked Newcastle to use his influence with the dissenters at Maidstone in his favour (letter of Rockingham to Newcastle, 4 March, Add. MS 32989, fols. 29–31).

[2] Rockingham was perplexed to find a suitable candidate to stand on his interest at York. See Brooke, *Chatham Administration 1766–1768*, pp. 347–50.

[3] Frederick Meinhardt Frankland (*c.* 1694–1768), father-in-law of Thomas Pelham, M.P. for Sussex, died 8 March.

of Business. That Wilkes has been chosen for Middlesex[1] is an Event which, from the dull state of the publick, and the oblivion into which he had fallen, I confess, I did not at all expect. But at a time, when the people are unfastend from all their usual moorings, as they are at a general Election, nothing ought to occur as matter of surprise. The hatred of Ld Bute never was stronger among the people; and this was a time to signalize it. Besides the crowd allways want to draw themselves, from abstract principles to personal attachments; and since the fall of Ld Chatham, there has been no hero of the Mob but Wilkes. The surprise aided him; Government had not time to take measures; and they are indeed too disunited to take any that can be effectual. There must be a Change, I think, before winter; but I still persist, in the opinion I have long had, that no probable change will be advantageous to us.

Lord Rockingham is just come from Newmarket; he has himself been upon the whole successful there. He had no Room in his Stable just at the time when *Hirpinus* arrived but he has had full as good Care taken of him.[2] It happend that he was not in order to be enterd for any thing; for your Servant, instead of being deficient, was rather over careful of him. So that Ld R. says, he is just now as fat as a Stallion, and as wild as a Colt; and of Course it will be some time before he is in running order. In other respects he will be properly treated.

I am just going off for Italy; I mean in eight or ten days. Write to me as usual; and I shall be rather more than less happy. Adieu my dear Sir, most truly yours

Ed B.

To JAMES BARRY—15 *April* 1768

Source: Barry, *Works*, I, 158.

While the plan of a trip to Italy was being entertained, Burke wrote to James Barry to fix him in Rome.

April 15, 1768.

Dear Barry,

I am heartily ashamed for myself and all your friends, that we have so long neglected to write to you. By and bye we may make up for our neglect; at the present I have only to say, that I thank God we are all

[1] He was elected 28 March.

[2] O'Hara was somewhat disturbed at hearing nothing concerning the horse which he had sent to Lord Rockingham's stable (see above, letter of 11 December [1767], p. 339). He wrote to Rockingham 10 April: 'My Friend Mr. Burke is an excellent Correspondent upon matters of small importance, but the worst in the world about running horses. I trusted imprudently to him, to tell your Lordship that I had made use of the liberty you did me the honour to allow me, of sending my Horse to your Stables. If He has not done so, my presumption will appear greater, even than it was at first, when I desird that permission. Your Lordship will be so just as to impute the fault to him in either case...' (Rockingham MSS, R 75–28).

well, that we shall endeavour to make amends for this neglect, and that you will be so good to continue in Rome until you hear again from some of us.

My dear Barry,
Most affectionately yours,
EDMUND BURKE

To RICHARD SHACKLETON—1 *May* 1768

Source: MS Dr O. Fisher. Printed *Corr.* (1844), I, 151–5.

My dear Shackleton, I thank you heartily for your Letter, and even for the reproaches which it contains. They are, when of that kind, very sure, and not the most unpleasing indications of a real affection. Indeed my Neglect of writing is by no means justifiable, and does not stand well in my own opinion; but I am sorry to say it, I have never been quite correct and finished in my Style of Life; and I fear I never shall. However, if I keep the principal parts tolerably right, I shall, I hope, meet pardon, if not something more, from such friends, as it is the great Blessing of my Life to have had in every stage of it. As to the Neglects of one who is but too much my Brother, I have nothing to say for him. He may write himself if he pleases; and he has nothing to prevent him but too much idleness, which I have observed fills up a mans time much more completely, and leaves him less his own master, than any sort of employment whatsoever.

I am much obliged to Mr Beauchamp[1] for his kind opinion of me, and to your partial representations as the Cause of it. I am willing to do my best to forward Doctor Dunkins subscription.[2] You may easily believe, that your wishing well to it would be sufficient to engage my endeavours (as far as they can go) without any further inducement. But Dunkin deserved some rank among the poets of our Time and Country;[3] and I agree with you in thinking his Son[4] an ingenuous and worthy man. I cannot I fear do a great deal. I am always ready to subscribe myself; and perhaps in general too ready to put forward subscriptions; which weakens my Interest when I want to use it on some extraordinary occasion. I dont say this, as in the least declining the Business you recommend; for I will certainly do all I can.

I know your kindness makes you wish now and then to hear of my

[1] The Rev. Richard Beauchamp (*c.* 1699–1775), Rector of Narraghmore, County Kildare.

[2] Probably a subscription for the publication of William Dunkin's *Selected Poetical Works*, which were brought out in Dublin 1769–70.

[3] See above, letter of 21 March 1746/47 (p. 90), for Burke's low opinion of one of Dunkin's poems.

[4] James Dunkin, William's son, entered Trinity College 3 July 1755.

Situation. It is, politically, just what is was; There is nothing to alter the position of our party; which is, (or rather keeps itself,) at some distance from the Court. I think we act on a right principle; as far as any thing can approach to what is exactly right, in so strange a time as this; It is a pleasure to act with men who mean fairly, and who carry on publick business with, at least, a considerable mixture of publick principle, and with attention to honest fame. I shewed to some of them and among others to Ld Rockingham part of a Letter which you wrote to me some time ago;[1] and they were much pleased, both with the manner and the Substance of it; Ld Rockm desired me to give him a Copy. We have attempted things last Session which have got us Credit with the weighty and sober part of the Nation; I imagine we shall pursue them further, and even against ministerial power, may possibly succeed, from the weight of the measures, and the diligence of the pursuit. You have not enough of the detail to render this perfectly intelligible; I only mention it to you just to point out, that our political Body is not unprofitably or unreputably employd. As to myself, I am by the Kindness of some very singular friends in a way very agreeable to me. I am again elected on the same interest. I have made a push with all I could collect of my own, and the aid of my friends to cast a little root in this Country. I have purchased an house, with an Estate of about 600 acres of Land in Buckinghamshire 24 Miles from London; where I now am;[2] It is a place exceedingly pleasant; and I propose, God willing, to become a farmer in good earnest. You who are classical will not be displeased to hear, that it was formerly the Seat of Waller the Poet, whose house, or part of it, makes at present the Farmhouse within an hundred yards of me. When you take a Journey to England you are obliged by Tenure, to come and pay due homage to the Capital Seat of your once favourite Poet.

[1] Burke is probably referring to a letter Shackleton wrote to Richard Burke 22 November 1767, containing a passage very complimentary to both Burke and his party: 'Ned is tied (I trust) by the noblest bonds to the Good of his Country and the Cause of Religion and Virtue....From my heart I believe that great are the purposes for which he was sent into life, and endowed with such talents as he is possessed of....' After describing the truly Moral Man, conducted by a higher power 'thro' the intricate, treacherous Road of life', Shackleton concluded: 'Happy is he. May this be the happiness of my Friend and of all his Friends.'

[2] The financing of this purchase has been much discussed. Wecter (pp. 27–8) summarizes such evidence as he can find bearing on the problem, and speaks of this account Burke gives to Shackleton as 'a little disingenuous'. One of the friends who assisted Burke was certainly Will Burke, who must have put at least as much money into the estate as Edmund did. He had inherited something at his father's death in 1764, and was speculating, still successfully, in East India stock, with Lord Verney's backing (see above, letter of 4 October 1766, p. 269). The assertion has been made that Lord Rockingham assisted the purchase. There is no authority for supposing it, and Burke told Shackleton (letter of 19 April 1770) that he had had no advantage 'except my Seat in Parliament from the Patronage of any man; Whatever advantages I have had, have been from friends on my own Level'.

I am glad to find my Venerable old friend your father still preserves his health and the even Tenour of his mind. At her age, no friend could have hoped for your mother any thing but the Euthanasia: and In such circumstances it must have been a great comfort to you, that she had it so perfectly.[1] Mrs Burke preserves an affectionate and grateful memory of Mrs Shackletons kindness to her when she was in Ireland, and joins us all in the heartiest Salutations to you both. Adieu my dear friend, and believe me most sincerely yours

EDM BURKE

Gregories near Beconsfield[2]
May 1. 1768

To CHARLES O'HARA—9 *June* 1768

Source: O'Hara MSS. Printed Hoffman, pp. 434–5.

I have that abominable Custom of running up a long arrear, not so much from hatred of paying, as from the general Spirit of procrastination, which very unluckily attends me in at least a good half of all my Business. I am really ashamed to find that I cannot very precisely remember when I wrote to you; but I am very sure, (for I have good tokens to remember your Letters by) that in that interval of my Silence, I have heard several times from you.[3] However dont be very angry with me; I had never less to say. If the world seemd to be very Busy with Wilkes and Liberty and many fine things, one part of these matters, at least, was not your Business nor mine. The plan of our party was, I think, wise and proper; not to provoke Administration into any Violent measure upon this Subject; nor be the means of stirring questions, which we have not strength to support, and which could not be lost, without leaving the Constitution worse than we found it. It could be no service to Wilkes to take him out of the hands of the *Law*, and to drive him under the Talons of *power*; besides we had not the least desire of taking up that Gentlemans Cause as personally favourable to him; he is not ours; and if he were, is little to be trusted: He is a lively agreeable man, but of no prudence and no principles. Had they attempted to attack him, as, I do not think, they could have done it without great Oppression, we must

[1] Shackleton's mother had died 4 March.

[2] Burke called his estate 'Gregories', Gregory being the name of a family who had owned it for many years. He later sometimes called it 'Butler's Court'—again for a previous owner. Most letters written in the country he addressed from 'Beconsfield' or (later) 'Beaconsfield'.

[3] Since Burke's letter to O'Hara [11 April], O'Hara had written to him 19 April (printed Hoffman, pp. 431–2) and 21 April, and to Will Burke 10 May (printed Hoffman, pp. 432–3); MSS of all three letters are at Sheffield.

have defended him, and were resolved to do it; but still as the Cause not the Person. They did not omit to make this attack, from any want of ill will, but from the disunion which prevails among them; and which is greater, than any one, who did not know of what discordant materials they are made up, and how discordantly those materials are put together, could believe. But in my opinion, they are strong from this weakness; no man adheres to another, but every man cleaves to his place; and so they all look to the common Center, none to the circumference; and this centripetal force is as great in Politicks as in Nature. I confess I think they may and will hold; if one may risque any prediction at such a time. Our people are almost all gone into the Country; but we keep our Union and our Spirits, and are encreased in Numbers very considerably. They have managed their affairs in Ireland gloriously. Here Government is only disgraced; with you it is disgraced and defeated.[1] My Sollicitude for Ireland is growing rather less anxious than it was. I endeavour to remove it from my mind as much as I can. My strongest remaining wish is about you; and I shall not be easy until I hear in what manner you have secured your Seat. When that Business is over we may hope to see you. We are in the direct Road between Oxford and London. We have purchased an house, rather superb for us, and about 600 acres of Land just by Beconsfield where we now are, and where we shall be most happy to see you. The Doctor is come to see us, and to spend a day or two, and is yours as usual. So we are all. And this is my only News at the Close of a Session from whose activity you had so much expectation. But as it was difficult to get or keep our people in Town so deep in the Summer, the defensive was thought the better Scheme. Adieu. My dear friend, make us happy by informing us that all is right as to the Election; next by telling us so in person. Adieu.

Gregories near Beconsfield
June 9. 1768

EDMUND *and* RICHARD BURKE SR *to* DAVID GARRICK—13 *June* [1768]

Source: MS Victoria and Albert Museum. Printed Garrick, *Corr.* I, 188.

[Edmund begins]

My dear David, We have now got a little settled in our New habitation. When will you and Mrs Garrick come and make it complete to us

[1] The government's bill for the augmentation of the Irish Army had been defeated in the Irish House of Commons 10 May.

by your Company for a day or two? you have promised us; and we are a sort of persevering Folks, and will not easily let you off. You shall have fowls from our own Poultry Yard; and such Beef and Mutton as our next market Town yields; and to make it complete, we will assure you it is our own feeding; and then you will find it very good. In all sadness we wish, Madam Burke, all with us, and myself, long most hugeously to see you; and will take it ill, if you go and see the new Paymaster,[1] before us starving proscribed folks; You know the unfortunate are always proud and touchy. We only wish you would give us a days notice that we may not ramble. Adieu My dear Garrick and believe me most sincerely and affectionately

yours

EDM BURKE

Gregories Monday June 13.

Mrs Burke desires her Compliments to Mrs Garrick. If you bring your Neighbour the *Thames*[2] with you it will be quite agreeable.

[Richard begins]

Did not Edmund wisely, to add the name, and not trust to the word *Neighbour*; had this been the case, perhaps we should have seen your other neighbour[3] marching after you, snuffing up the air and smelling the carrion; but for that he had better follow you to Rigbys, and he can hardly go anywhere to be more despised. When will you come; I wish I could write such Invitations as some folks do; but tho I cannot say it with much wit, I can with great truth say, that you will make all here very happy, and none more than your humble Slave.

R B.

Gregorys Monday 13th June.

DAVID GARRICK *to* EDMUND BURKE—17 *June* 1768

Source: Fitzwilliam MSS (Sheffield). Printed *Corr.* (1844), I, 155–7.

Hampton June
17th 1768

My dear Friend

If you had a house in the Fens of Lincolnshire, or on the Swamps of Essex, where you were oblig'd to drink brandy, by way of small beer,

[1] Richard Rigby, whom Garrick had promised to visit; see the following letter.
[2] Garrick's villa at Hampton fronted on the Thames.
[3] Hamilton's seat was at Hampton.

to keep the ague out of your bones, I should long to be with you; but hearing what a Sweet place you have, with everything right about you, I am with twins, till I am well deliver'd at Gregories. But I reserve you for a bonne bouche my good Friend, and will certainly not touch your Mutton and Poultry, till I have revel'd at Mistley[1]—I have not a day to Spare till I set out for the Paymaster's; I propose going to Town on Monday, not to return till that annual visit is paid—I am told my righteous Neighbor[2] is very much disturb'd in Mind at Rigby's promotion—Gregories and the Pay office are too much for his digestion, and it is hard to say, Which of the two Masters of these two places he hates the most.

You may depend upon Seeing my Mahogony Countanance at my return, Madam will rejoice with me to pay her Respects to Mrs Burke and we will be as happy as the day is long. and then, some small Art shall be exercis'd to draw You and Yours to our sweet little (I am mad about it) inchanting place. Thank our dear Brother Richard for his writing a few lines to me in your letter—I don't know so sweet a Youth nor one to whom I have more cordial attachment, in spite of his Infidelity—

Pray give me a line directed to my house Covt Garden, in a post or two and let me know, when you go into Yorkshire, or rather when I shall be sure to find you all at Gregories—

I endeavour'd to get Clear of Mistley this Year, but I have sent you the Answer[3]—return it to me in the note You'll send by Saturday's post. Most affectionately Yours

my dear Burke

D. GARRICK

pray give me a full
direction to you.

Mr Tommy Townshend your friend I hear, is woefully angry at Rigby's preferment[4]—I din'd lately with Ld H—x[5] we had great talk about Your quondam Friend, and mine—He knows him to the marrow of him—how will the Malignant Spirit (I can't read the name you give him in

[1] In Essex, the seat of Richard Rigby.

[2] Hamilton.

[3] Rigby's letter to Garrick, dated 13 June (Garrick, *Corr.* I, 304).

[4] On the death of George Cooke (*c.* 1709–68), joint Paymaster-General, Thomas Townshend, the other joint Paymaster-General, was offered Rigby's place of joint Vice-Treasurer of Ireland so that Rigby could become sole Paymaster-General in accordance with the promise Grafton had made when the Bedfords took office. Townshend refused and resigned.

[5] Lord Halifax.

your Letter) determine to do with himself in the Northampton Election?[1] —poor Lady Hinchinbroke will be soon dead—she is in a deep Consumption.[2] Adieu.

To DAVID GARRICK—[17 *June* 1768]

Source: MS Victoria and Albert Museum. Printed Garrick, *Corr.* I, 208–9. Undated but probably written immediately on receipt of Garrick's of 17 June; 17 June was a Friday.

Well, since we are to see you, I am satisfied. I think on the whole you have disposed your matters with judgment. You first sate yourself with Wit, jollity, and Luxury; and afterwards retire hither to repose your person and understanding on early hours, boild Mutton, drowsy conversation, and a little Clabber Milk. As to my Journey to Yorkshire, If I should go at all thither this Summer, it will not be until late; I say if I go at all; because if I get the farm I propose into my hands, it will I believe keep me pretty well employed. The Neighbour, whose Name you could not read is no other than your Silver Thames, whose Company would vastly improve this place, I had no nonsense in my head of your other Neighbour though Dick gave it that Turn. I would not pollute him with the mixture of such a muddy Ditch. Richard is gone pleasuring to Oxford, and Blenheim, but will meet you. Will is here and to continue. So we shall make things as agreeable to you as we can. Madam Burke is very happy to hear that she is to see you and Mrs Garrick in some reasonable time. About when may it be? Adieu Dear Garrick

and believe me most affectionately
Yours
EDM BURKE

Gregories Friday.

Be so good to give my Service and congratulations to the Paymaster.

[1] The General Election of 1768 at Northampton was fiercely contested by candidates on the interests of Lord Halifax, Lord Northampton, and Lord Spencer. Halifax's candidate, Sir George Osborn, was elected, but a petition was presented against him, and Halifax was already trying to get support from Members of Parliament. Hamilton had been Halifax's Secretary in Ireland.

[2] Viscountess Hinchinbroke, *née* Lady Elizabeth Montagu, daughter of Lord Halifax, died 1 July.

APPENDIX

THE LETTER TO MICHAEL SMITH

Burke's biographers have frequently quoted or printed at length a letter they agree he must have written shortly after his arrival in England in 1750. The letter was first published by Charles Henry Wilson in his *Beauties of Burke* (London, 1798), where it was described as addressed to Michael Smith, an early acquaintance of Burke who became a country schoolmaster. 'Several letters passed between them', Wilson said by way of introduction: 'the following is a copy of one which Mr Burke addressed to him, soon after his arrival in London. Mr Smith, it appears, taught the Greek and Roman classics at this time in the parish of Fenagh, in the county of Leitrim.' Wilson omitted a concluding portion of the letter, because it touched upon 'some of Mr Smith's family affairs, which would not be proper to publish'. He printed in full Smith's reply.

The biographers have run into a difficulty in their identifications of Michael Smith. Bisset, who reprinted both the letter and the reply (2nd ed. I, 201–18), asserted that Smith was Burke's 'class-fellow under Mr Shackleton'. The fact is questionable; no Michael Smith appears in the Ballitore School List. Prior guessed at a solution of the problem. When he printed considerable passages from the first letter (2nd ed. I, 36–40), he said they were written to 'Matthew Smith'—a name which does appear in the List. Samuels followed Prior. He reprinted both the letter and reply (pp. 219–24) from the original source in *Beauties of Burke*, as an interchange between Burke and 'Matthew Smith, a school-fellow'. Indeed he went further, for he altered his text, making the salutation read not 'My dear Michael' but 'My dear Matthew'.

There is a greater difficulty, however, which the biographers do not seem to have noticed. If Burke wrote the first letter in the form we have it, he must have done so fairly soon after he reached London in the first half of 1750. But some parts of the letter were clearly not written in 1750. One passage, for an example, describes a visit to Westminster Abbey and comments on the effectiveness of the famous monument to Lady Elizabeth Nightingale. That monument, one of the best-known works of Roubiliac, was not placed in the Abbey until 1761.[1] There is a similar discrepancy in a passage about Peg Woffington. The writer says she is 'rising rapidly into theatric fame'. By 1750 she had been famous, or notorious, for nearly ten years; by the time the Nightingale

[1] Apparently it was not carved until shortly before its erection. See Katherine Esdaile, *Life and Works of Louis François Roubiliac*, Oxford, 1928.

monument was erected, she was dead. The writer asks his friend for details concerning her recantation, which he says has already taken place, 'in a little country church, somewhere in the county of Cavan'. Peg Woffington was in London in 1750,[1] and renounced her Roman Catholic faith in Ireland in 1753.[2]

If the first letter, then, is not what it pretends to be, it may be a pure instance of forgery. There are some reasons to think so. Wilson was little known when he brought out the *Beauties of Burke*, the year after Burke's death; it certainly gave some authority to his preface to be able to quote an important letter from the early life of his subject. The letter, too, is full of 'points' which would impress anyone who had an interest in Burke. The writer is very fond of making judgments: Plutarch is his favourite author; *Il Penseroso* is 'the finest poem in the English language'; agriculture is his favourite pursuit; gothic architecture moves him strongly. One of his aesthetic ideas—in 1750—anticipates a famous essay of Lessing,[3] first published in 1769. His knowledge of electricity seems to be in advance of Franklin.[4] If in one letter it was possible to give proof of such a variety of Burke's interests, perhaps it was worth a forger's while!

Yet an argument can also be made the other way. Some parts of the letter do not strike us as at all likely to have been fabricated. Of the persons named very few would have had exceptional interest for a reader of 1798. Mr Balf and his uncle the General, Dr Sheridan, Smith's brother-in-law Tom—would any of them be known to him at all? Mr Peyton would hardly be known, and yet he sounds like a real person. A Peyton family was living at Driney House in County Leitrim in the mid-eighteenth century. Then too, what are we to think about Michael Smith's letter? Was that also a forgery? It would have very little point as one. And last, does not the supposed letter of Burke really sound like him? '...I would rather sleep in the southern corner of a little country church yard, than in the tomb of the Capulets. I should like, however, that my dust should mingle with kindred dust. The good old expression, "Family burying-ground", has something pleasing in it, at least to me.' Whoever forged that for Edmund Burke was at least no common forger! We can understand why the letter passed muster with lovers of Burke for 160 years.

[1] Janet Camden Lucey, *Lovely Peggy*, London, 1952, p. 187.

[2] Egerton MS 77.

[3] 'I always thought', the writer tells Michael Smith, 'that the image of death would be much better represented with an extinguished torch, inverted, than with a dart.' Lessing has a similar thought in his *Wie die Alten den Tod gebildet*.

[4] The comment upon London's charitable institutions whose turrets pierce the skies and 'like electrical conductors, avert the very wrath of Heaven' implies an understanding of the operation of lightning rods.

There is of course another possibility, that the letter, or a considerable part of it, really is genuine, and we have only been deceived as to its date or its unity. If either Wilson or someone in touch with him had 'several letters' which passed between Burke and Michael Smith, he might do what has been done fairly often by ingenious and irresponsible editors: weave together the most interesting passages from several letters into one. If this were done, there would be no great mystery in the discrepancies we have noticed: a correspondence which began in the 1740's and extended into the 1760's could supply notable passages from any part of the period. It would be natural enough too, if one went that far *toward* forging, to choose the most effective moment as well as the most interesting contents for one's composition. Or perhaps one letter really did give Burke's first impressions of England, and it seemed the best plan to fill that letter out with details borrowed from others.

It is a hypothesis, at least, to explain the letter we have.

To MICHAEL SMITH

Source: Beauties of Burke, I, vi–x.
This letter and Smith's reply are both described by Wilson as taken from copies.

My dear Michael,

Mr Balf[1] was so very kind as to deliver me your friendly epistle about half an hour ago. I read it over, blest the first inventor of letters, and as I have plenty of ink, pens, and paper, and as this is one of my holidays, I intend to dedicate it to friendship.—Balzac[2] having once escaped from a company, where he found it necessary to weigh every word that he uttered, chanced to meet a friend, 'Come,' said he to him, 'let us retire to some place where we can converse freely together, and commit as many solecisms as we please.' I need not tell you the application. You'll expect some short account of my journey to this great city; to tell you the truth, I made very few remarks as I rolled along, for my mind was occupied with many thoughts, and my eyes often filled with tears when I reflected on all the dear friends I left behind; yet the prospects could not fail to attract the attention of the most indifferent; country seats sprinkled round on every side, some in the modern taste, others in the stile of old de Coverley Hall, all smiling on the neat, but humble cottage. Every village as gay and compact as a beehive, resounding with the

[1] See above, in letter of 8 June 1765 (p. 201) reference to 'One Balf a Printer in London'.

[2] Jean-Louis Guez, Sieur de Balzac (1597–1654). The source of this anecdote about him has not been found.

busy hum of industry, and inns like palaces. What a contrast between our poor country, where you'll scarce find a cottage ornamented with a chimney. But what pleased me most of all was the progress of agriculture, my favourite study, and my favourite pursuit, if Providence had blessed me with a few paternal acres. A description of London and its nations would fill a volume. The buildings are very fine; it may be called the sink of vice, but her hospitals and charitable institutions, whose turrets pierce the skies, like so many electrical conductors, avert the very wrath of Heaven. The inhabitants may be divided into two classes, the *undoers* and the *undone*, generally so, I say, for I am persuaded there are many men of honesty and women of virtue in every street. An Englishman is cold and distant at first; he is very cautious even in forming an acquaintance, he must know you well before he enters into friendship with you, but if he does, he is not the first to dissolve that sacred band; in short, a real Englishman is one that performs more than he promises; in company he is rather silent, extremely prudent in his expressions, even in politics, his favourite topic. The women are not quite so reserved; they consult their glasses to the greatest advantage, and as nature is very liberal in her gifts to their persons, and even mind, it is not easy for a young man to escape their glances, or to shut his ears to their softly flowing accents. As to the state of learning in this city, you know I have not been long enough in it to form a proper judgment of that subject. I don't think, however, there is as much respect paid to a man of letters on this side of the water as you imagine. I don't find that genius, the 'rath primrose, which forsaken, dies,'[1] is patronized by any of the nobility, so that writers of the first talents are left to the capricious patronage of the public. Notwithstanding this discouragement, literature is cultivated in a high degree. Poetry raises her enchanting voice to Heaven. History arrests the wings of time in his flight to the gulph of oblivion. Philosophy, the queen of arts, and the daughter of heaven, is daily extending her intellectual empire. Fancy sports on airy wing like a meteor on the bosom of a summer cloud, and even Metaphysics spins her cobwebs and catches some flies. The House of Commons not unfrequently exhibits explosions of eloquence, that rise superior to those of Greece and Rome, even in their proudest days. Yet after all a man will make more by the figures of arithmetic than by the figures of rhetoric, unless he can get into the trade wind, and then he may sail secure over Pactolean sands.[2] As to the stage, it is sunk, in my

[1] *Lycidas*, l. 142.

[2] Midas is supposed to have washed himself in the river Pactolus and by his touch turned its sands to gold.

opinion, into the lowest degree; I mean with regard to the trash that is exhibited on it, but I don't attribute this to the taste of the audience, for when Shakespeare warbles his 'native wood notes,' the boxes, pit, and gallery, are crowded—and the Gods are true to every word, if properly winged to the heart.

Soon after my arrival in town, I visited Westminster Abbey; the moment I entered I felt a kind of awe pervade my mind, which I cannot describe; the very silence seemed sacred. Henry the Seventh's chapel is a very fine piece of Gothic architecture, particularly the roof, but I am told that it is exceeded by a chapel in the University of Cambridge. Mrs Nightingale's monument has not been praised beyond its merit. The attitude and expression of the husband, in endeavouring to shield his wife from the dart of death, is natural and affecting.[1] But I always thought that the image of death would be much better represented with an extinguished torch, inverted, than with a dart. Some would imagine that all these monuments were so many monuments of folly—I don't think so; what useful lessons of mortality and sound philosophy do they not exhibit. When the high-born beauty surveys her face in the polished parian, though dumb the marble, yet it tells her that it was placed to guard the remains of as fine form, and as fair a face as her own. They shew besides how anxious we are to extend our loves and friendship beyond the grave, and to snatch as much as we can from oblivion—such is our natural love of immortality; but it is here that letters obtain the noblest triumphs; it is here that the swarthy daughters of Cadmus[2] may hang their trophies on high, for when all the pride of the chissel, and the pomp of heraldry yield to the silent touches of time, a single line, a half worn-out inscription, remain faithful to their trust. Blest be the man, that first introduced these strangers into our islands, and may they never want protection or merit. I have not the least doubt, that the finest poem in the English language, I mean Milton's Il Penseroso, was composed in the long resounding isle of a mouldering cloister or ivy'd abbey. Yet after all, do you know that I would rather sleep in the southern corner of a little country church-yard, than in the tomb of the Capulets. I should like, however, that my dust should mingle with kindred dust.

[1] The monument of Lady Elizabeth Nightingale (1704–31) was still described in a nineteenth-century work as 'the gem of the Abbey' (*Registers of the Abbey of St Peter, Westminster* (*Publications of the Harleian Society*, x) London, 1876, p. 333 n.). A modern Blue Guide (*London and its Environs*, 5th ed. London, 1947, p. 26) describes it as 'a skilful but theatrical sculpture by Roubiliac, which attracts much attention'.

[2] Cadmus is supposed to have introduced letters into Greece; hence *Cadmi filiolae atricolores* (Ausonius, *Epistles*, 15) as a phrase to describe letters. Burke—if it is Burke—rather loses sight of the meaning of *atricolores* when he refers to 'half worn-out inscriptions', which suggests letters carved in stone rather than written in ink.

The good old expression, 'Family burying-ground,' has something pleasing in it, at least to me. I am glad that Dr Sheridan[1] is returned, and determined to spend the rest of his days in your quarter. I should send him some Botanic writings, which I have in view, if I were not certain that the Irish Hippocrates would rather read nature in her own works; with what pleasure I have seen him trace the delicate texture of a lily, and exclaim with the God in humanity, that 'Solomon, in all his glory, was not arrayed like one of those,' and you know that our lilies are fairer than new fallen snow. I am extremely sorry that any dispute should arise betwixt you and your brother-in-law; he is, I know, a little hot-headed, especially when he takes a glass, and I am afraid he leans a little too much to the social can.[2] Mr Peyton,[3] however, is a peace-maker, and I am sure, if the whole was laid before him, that he would settle it to your satisfaction, and the sooner the better. You are quite mistaken when you think I don't admire Plutarch, I prefer his writings to those of any other.—*Sacra semper excipio, quæ in summâ arce locare fas est et æquum nunquam non in manibus habenda.*[4]

Mr Balfe sets out for Germany in the spring, on a visit to his uncle,[5] who is now in Vienna. The General is very rich, and advancing in years, so that it is probable when he is called to repose on his laurels, that his nephew will be his heir, and I need not tell you that he is worthy of it. I expect, in a day or two, to be introduced to Miss Woffington, our country-woman. She is rapidly rising into theatric fame; I could wish to publish a few anecdotes of her.[6] She is of low origin, it is true, but talents and nature often avenge themselves on fortune in this respect. The roses of Florida spring out of the finest soil, they are the fairest in the universe, but they emit no fragrance. I recollect that she read her recantation in a little country church, somewhere in the county of Cavan. Mr Fleming of Stahalmuck, wrote some verses on that occasion.[7] I wish

[1] Not identified.

[2] Smith replied to this: '...Tom and I are on good terms.—You are right, he drinks whiskey as often as he can get it—*Ore rotundo,* and sometimes

Warm from the still, and faithful to its fires

too, which is worst of all' (*Beauties of Burke*, p. xiii).

[3] For the Peyton family see *Landed Gentry of Ireland* (1912 ed.), p. 561.

[4] I except always the sacred [writings], which ought to be placed in the highest shrine and should never be out of our hands.

[5] Not identified.

[6] Margaret Woffington (*c.* 1714–60). Prior records a highly improbable legend that there was later an 'intimate connexion' between her and Burke (2nd ed. I, 49).

[7] Smith's reply gave a few details: 'She was born in Dublin, read her recantation in the parish church of Lurgan, near Virginy, in the county of Cavan, before the Reverend Mr [James] Sterling, who was a great musician. Mr Fleming did write some verses on that occasion, but it is not easy to procure them, for you know he's a great man—a Justice of the Peace, and one of the Grand Jury' (*Beauties of Burke*, p. xiv). He then quoted his recollection of the opening lines of the poem by Fleming.

you could procure a copy of them for me as soon as possible. I also wish that you could procure some anecdotes of Mr Brooke, author of the justly celebrated tragedy of Gustavus Vasa.[1]

[1] Henry Brooke (*c.* 1703–83). His tragedy *Gustavus Vasa, the Deliverer of his Country*, thought to reflect upon Sir Robert Walpole, attracted attention when it was banned in London in 1739 and again when it was played in Dublin in 1741 under the name of 'The Patriot'. Johnson wrote an ironical 'Vindication of the Licensers of the Stage from the malicious and scandalous aspersions of Mr Brooke' in 1739. Prior asserts (2nd ed. I, 33) that Burke wrote against Brooke in Dublin in 1749, ridiculing him under the name of Diabetes.

you could procure a copy of them for me as soon as possible. I also wish that you could procure some anecdotes of Mr Brooke, author of the justly celebrated tragedy of Gustavus Vasa.[1]

[1] Henry Brooke (1703?–83). His tragedy Gustavus Vasa, the Deliverer of his Country, thought to reflect upon Sir Robert Walpole, attracted attention when it was banned in London in 1739 and again when it was played in Dublin in 1744 under the name of The Patriot. Johnson wrote an ironical 'Vindication of the Licensers of the Stage from the malicious and scandalous aspersions of Mr Brooke' in 1739. Pelet inserts [illegible] Rolt wrote against Brooke in Dublin [illegible] him under the name of Dickinson.

INDEX

Indented sub-headings refer to letters